The Reading and Preaching
of the Scriptures
in the
Worship of the Christian Church

Volume 2

THE PATRISTIC AGE

The Reading and Preaching
of the Scriptures
in the
Worship of the Christian Church

Volume 2

THE PATRISTIC AGE

Hughes Oliphant Old

WILLIAM B. EERDMANS PUBLISHING COMPANY
GRAND RAPIDS, MICHIGAN / CAMBRIDGE, U.K.

© 1998 Wm. B. Eerdmans Publishing Co.
255 Jefferson Ave. S.E., Grand Rapids, Michigan 49503 /
P.O. Box 163, Cambridge CB3 9PU U.K.

Printed in the United States of America

03 02 01 00 99 98   7 6 5 4 3 2 1

Library of Congress Cataloging-in-Publication Data

Old, Hughes Oliphant.
The reading and preaching of the Scriptures in the worship of the Christian church /
Hughes Oliphant Old.
p.   cm.
Includes bibliographical references and index.
Contents: v. 2. The patristic age.
ISBN 0-8028-4357-3 (alk. paper)
1. Preaching — History.   2. Public worship — History.
3. Bible — Homiletical use.   4. Bible — Liturgical use.
I. Title.
BV4207.O43   1998
264'.34 — dc21   97-30624
                                                       CIP

Contents

The Flourishing of Greek Preaching in the Christian Empire — the School of Alexandria

With the coming of the Christian empire, Christian preaching was bound to change. During the years of persecution the preacher had to gather and nourish the congregation to protect it from the world. Now the Christian preacher had become a bishop responsible for the spiritual welfare of the empire. The disciples had indeed gone out to make disciples of all nations, and at least for a major part of the world as they knew it they had succeeded, and now they were responsible for a Christian society. It was the Christian preacher who must now give that world vision and purpose.

The world of classical antiquity had expected the leaders of society to be orators. One awaited from great men a public expression of the ideals that bound society together. A man in high public office had to be able to say at crucial moments in the life of the community what it all meant, where it was all going, and how much it was all worth. Just as Abraham Lincoln was able to sum up in his Gettysburg Address the vision which brought the nation through the Civil War or just as during the Battle of Britain Winston Churchill was able through his magnificent word to keep a battered Britain on its feet, so in classical antiquity the great leader was expected to lead the minds and hearts of the people with the right word,

1

the prophetic word. It was not enough that a public official be a man of power; he had to be a man of the word. He could of course be a man of wealth, of public charm or charisma, of military power, but if he could not lead the people's hearts and minds with his word, he was a mere tyrant.

Classical antiquity had cultivated public oratory as art, and if Christian preachers were to take the public responsibility that had by divine providence come their way, then they too would have to learn that art. And learn it they did. They learned it magnificently. The fourth century saw a flowering of oratory. It was Christian oratory, a true renaissance of the classical art in the service of the Christian faith.

In this chapter we will look at what is surely one of the golden ages of Christian preaching. It was a rather short age, lasting less than a hundred years, beginning toward the end of the fourth century and ending about the middle of the fifth. Even at that it produced a phenomenal number of very fine preachers. One often distinguishes between the School of Alexandria and the School of Antioch when speaking of the patristic age. Sometimes this is done a bit too neatly. Nevertheless, it is a helpful distinction, and so for the most part we will honor it and divide the preachers up into these two schools. With the Alexandrians, of course, we are dealing with a second phase of the school, the first phase having taken place in the time of Origen and Gregory Thaumaturgos. The three Cappadocian Fathers, although devoted to Origen and Gregory Thaumaturgos, began to see the value of the more literal approach to the interpretation of Scripture. The Cappadocians clearly form a second phase of the Alexandrian school.

First, we want to look at several preachers from the Greek-speaking world who, standing in the Alexandrian tradition of exegesis, availed themselves of the classical tradition of high rhetoric and produced masterpieces of Christian oratory in the best Greek tradition. We begin with Cyril of Jerusalem, one of the anchor men of Nicene orthodoxy who presided over the church of Jerusalem during the period in which it took a leading part in shaping the worship of the Christian Church. Then we will look at the three Cappadocian Fathers who established Christian pulpit oratory as the legitimate heir of the rhetoric of classical antiquity. Finally we will look at two preachers from the following generation, Hesychius of Jerusalem and Cyril of Alexandria, who form a third phase of the Alexandrian School. Cyril brought the antithesis of the Schools of Antioch and Alexandria to its climax, and yet he was no friend of Origen. With Cyril the issues shifted from exegesis to theology and yet, as we shall discover, Cyril was a very good expository preacher. It was Cyril of Alexandria, whose ministry stretched into the fifth century, who brought to its brilliant conclusion the final statement of Nicene orthodoxy. It was Hesychius, the consummate preacher of Jerusalem, who brought the school to its close.

I. Cyril of Jerusalem

For the century which followed Origen we know little about the preaching of the Church. This was a period of transition, and we have no significant collection of sermons that shows us how this transition was expressed in preaching.[1] The catechetical sermons of Cyril of Jerusalem (ca. 315-86) which some stenographer took down about the year 350 are the first collection of sermons from the Christian Empire which has survived.[2] How different they are from the sermons of Origen! To some extent this is due to the fact that this series is made up of catechetical sermons. While Origen presided over the catechetical school of Alexandria, we have no record of his having preached a series of catechetical sermons. Cyril, on the other hand, has left us none of his regular Sunday sermons, or even his feast-day sermons, which undoubtedly he must have preached. We hear nothing of the daily preaching he may or may not have done. There is this obvious difference of genre, about which we will have more to say, but even more we find a difference between the role Origen played as the teacher of a congregation of Christians who were a minority in the world in which they lived and the role Cyril played as bishop of a Christian Jerusalem. Origen was a pilgrim moving from a pagan Egypt

1. Two well-known preachers from early in the fourth century were Athanasius and Eusebius of Caesarea. The genuineness of the sermons ascribed to them is under serious question. On the sermons of Athanasius, cf. Johannes Quasten, *Patrology*, 4 vols. (Utrecht and Antwerp: Spectrum Publishers; Westminster, Md.: Newman Press and Christian Classics, 1966-94), 3:50-52. On the sermons of Eusebius of Caesarea, cf. Quasten, *Patrology*, 3:342ff.

2. The classic English translation remains that of R. W. Church as edited and annotated by E. H. Gifford in Nicene and Post-Nicene Fathers, 2nd ser., vol. 7 (Grand Rapids: Wm. B. Eerdmans Publishing Co., 1975), pp. 1-157. For the Greek text, see Migne, *Patrologia Graeca*, vol. 33 (Paris: Migne, 1957-66), pp. 331-1180. There is a more modern translation of selections from lectures 1 to 18 in W. Telfer, trans., *Cyril of Jerusalem and Nemesius of Emesa*, Library of Christian Classics, vol. 4 (Philadelphia: Westminster Press, 1955), pp. 64-192. Citations from Cyril, as from other ancient literature, will be from the traditional divisions of the text (in this case *Catechetical Lectures*), followed by the number of the sermon, a period, and then the number of the section. Quotations will be from the translation in the Nicene and Post-Nicene Fathers series.

to a transcendent Holy Land. Cyril sat upon the episcopal throne of a church built and endowed by Constantine and his successors. It was still a precarious throne for some time — as with other public officials, he was at one time or another either in or out of favor at court — but he did his best to give a solid Christian witness in public life. Even at that Cyril was not a great light, as Origen had been, or as Basil or John Chrysostom would come to be. He was just a bit too much the product of his age and just a bit too short in his grasp of the deepest truths of the gospel. Cyril had some very definite talents, but he was never the theologian Cyril of Alexandria was or the mystical philosopher Gregory of Nyssa was.

Cyril was born about the time Constantine established the Christian Church as the spiritual foundation of the Empire[3] and was brought up in the imperial Church. While we know very little about Cyril's early life, it seems quite possible that he was brought up in Caesarea, the very city where Origen had spent his final years.[4] While Cyril has left us no expository sermons, we do find that his interpretations of Scripture assume Origen's approach to biblical interpretation; therefore, he has traditionally been counted among the Alexandrian School. Cyril was apparently brought up in a prosperous Christian family and was given a good education, the sort which prepared a young man for a role in public life. Consequently Cyril understood politics very well. Classical education, the sort Cyril would surely have received, provided sound training in the art of public oratory.

We have almost no biographical information about Cyril, yet we do know that he was one of the pillars of Nicene orthodoxy. From 357 to 359 he was exiled because of his outspoken opposition to Arianism. Unlike the staunchest supporters of Athanasius, he did not endorse the use of the term

---

3. On Cyril and his catechetical lectures in general, see G. Bardy, "Cyrille de Jerusalem," *Dictionnaire d'histoire et géographie ecclésiastique*, 13:1181-85; Gregory Dix, *The Shape of the Liturgy* (London: Dacre Press, 1945), pp. 187-209 and 349-54; Edwin Hamilton Gifford, *Cyril of Jerusalem* (London, 1893); A. Paulin, *Saint Cyrille de Jérusalem catéchète*, Lex Orandi, vol. 29 (Paris: Les Éditions du Cerf, 1959); A. A. Stephenson, "St. Cyril of Jerusalem and the Alexandrian Heritage," *Theological Studies* 15 (1954): 573-93; A. A. Stephenson, "The Lenten Catechetical Syllabus in Fourth Century Jerusalem," *Theological Studies* 15 (1954): 103-16; A. A. Stephenson, "St. Cyril of Jerusalem and the Alexandrian Christian Gnosis," *Texte und Untersuchungen* 63 (1957): 147-56; and Telfer, *Cyril of Jerusalem*.

4. On the birthplace of Cyril and his connections with Jerusalem and Caesarea, cf. Telfer, *Cyril of Jerusalem*, pp. 19ff.

homoousius because it was not a biblical term. On the other hand he was able to convince Gregory of Nyssa that his Christology was quite sound even if he did express it somewhat differently. All told he was sent into exile three times because of his insistence on the divinity of Christ. It is for his solid theological statement of this that he is today most widely remembered.

A. Catechetical Sermons

Cyril was a man of his time with a sensitivity to the ways of society. He was realistic about the needs of the Church and the problems the Church faced, and in taking up his series of catechetical sermons it is well to keep this in mind. He was fully aware that among the men and women he was preparing for baptism were those who had been moved to join the Church for very practical and worldly reasons. He says this quite explicitly in the preface to his *Catechetical Lectures*;[5] nevertheless, he hopes to move them toward a sounder faith. "I accept this bait for the hook, and welcome thee, though thou comest with an evil purpose, yet as one to be saved by a good hope. Perhaps thou knewest not whither thou wert coming, nor in what kind of net thou art taken. Thou art come within the Church's nets: be taken alive, flee not: for Jesus is angling for thee."[6] Even if the wrong motives may have prompted them to become Christians, that does not prevent them from a sincere repentance and true faith. The whole series is addressed to such people in an honest attempt to win over his hearers. He makes every effort to meet people where they are and to speak to them in their language. This, no doubt, is the reason Cyril presents baptism as a Christian mystery. The Hellenistic world loved drama and was greatly impressed by the dramatic initiation rites of the mystery religions. So Cyril approached these lectures as though he were preparing a group of neophytes for the rites of some mystery. He imposed upon them the *disciplina arcana*. What they learned was not to be told to the uninitiated.[7] Cyril wanted to make it clear that to be initiated into the Church by baptism is a sacred rite, too. In fact, it is a rite far more sacred than any rite they experienced in paganism.

5. The preface, or Procatechesis, is found in the Nicene and Post-Nicene Fathers, 2nd ser., 7:1-5.
6. Cyril of Jerusalem, *Catechetical Lectures* preface 5.
7. Cyril of Jerusalem, *Catechetical Lectures* preface 12.

The twenty-four sermons divide naturally into six introductory sermons, thirteen sermons on the baptismal creed, and five sermons given after baptism. The first six sermons are essentially a call for repentance, an admonition to faith and an offer of baptism. Two sermons are devoted to making clear the call to repentance. For the first of these sermons Cyril takes as his text a verse from Isaiah:

> "Wash yourselves; make yourselves clean;
>   remove the evil of your doings
>   from before my eyes;
> cease to do evil,
>   learn to do good." (Isa. 1:16-17)

Our preacher explains to his catechumens that they are entering into a period of repentance. At that time, the church of Jerusalem observed Lent as forty days of penitential preparation of the candidates for baptism, during which time the candidates were to come to the daily catechetical sessions, hear the Scripture lessons, listen to the sermons, and be exorcised. But this they must do with sincerity. If they have anything against a neighbor they must set it in order. Sincerity is of the greatest importance. For Cyril repentance is obviously something that is done. It is a rite, to be sure, but a rite which must penetrate the soul.

In the next sermon, our preacher begins to come much more to the heart of the matter. He begins to speak of God's love for the human race, his faithfulness and long-suffering. The main body of the sermon gives one example after another of God's patience with sinners. Adam, Noah, Rahab, David, Manasseh, Hezekiah, and Nebuchadnezzar all sinned against God, and yet when they turned to God in repentance he received them. The preacher presents each of these paradigms of repentance in a fresh and vivid manner. Cyril's point was, if God could forgive these sinners, certainly you can be forgiven.

The two sermons on repentance are followed by a sermon on baptism. The Scripture reading which preceded the sermon was a portion of the sixth chapter of Romans, but the sermon itself, as with the other sermons in this series, is not an exposition of the passage but rather a more systematic explanation of baptism dealing with the sacrament as sacred marriage, as enrollment in the army of the Lord, and as consecration on the sacred altar. Cyril is trying to explain baptism in terms that his pagan hearers will understand. They have experienced marriage, they have done military service, they have participated in pagan sacrificial rites. This last example is curious; he tells his congregation, "Regard not the Laver as simple water, but rather regard the spiritual grace that is given with the water. For just as the offerings brought to the heathen altars, though simple in their nature, become defiled by the invocation of the idols, so contrary-wise the simple water having received the invocation of the Holy Ghost, and of Christ, and of the Father, acquires a new power of holiness."[8] Cyril is doing what a good teacher always does. He is starting out with what people understand in order to explain what they do not understand. He is trying to explain Christian worship in terms of pagan worship. There is, to be sure, much traditional material in this sermon, but there is also this disturbing tendency to make the Christian sacrament too understandable to the usual pagan of the day. That is, of course, one of the pitfalls of illustrative material. Sometimes it confuses more than it illustrates. One cannot help but wonder how far Cyril's rhetoric got the average men and women of his day beyond their paganism.

Cyril now dedicates two sermons to the subject of faith. The first is a summary outline of Christian doctrine presented as a Christian decalogue. In the introduction to this sermon Cyril tells us, "For the method of godliness consists of these two things, pious doctrines, and virtuous practice: and neither are the doctrines acceptable to God apart from good works, nor does God accept the works which are not perfected with pious doctrines."[9] The second sermon explains what faith is in terms of the experience of Abraham, Peter, and Lazarus. There is, it would seem, a tension in Cyril's mind between faith as an inclination of the heart and faith as an affirmation of the mind. Nevertheless, for Cyril the business at hand is to teach the faith.

> But in learning the Faith and in professing it, acquire and keep that only, which is now delivered to thee by the Church, and which has been built up strongly out of all the Scriptures. For since all can not read the Scriptures, . . . we comprise the whole doctrine of the Faith in a few lines. This summary I wish you both to commit to memory when I recite it, and to rehearse it with all diligence among yourselves, not writing it out on paper, but engraving it by the memory on your heart. . . . So for the present listen while I simply say the Creed, and

8. Cyril of Jerusalem, *Catechetical Lectures* 3.3.
9. Cyril of Jerusalem, *Catechetical Lectures* 4.2.

commit it to memory; but at the proper season expect the confirmation out of the Holy Scripture of each part of the contents. For the articles of the Faith were not composed as seemed good to men; but the most important points collected out of all the Scripture make up one complete teaching of the Faith.[10]

With this Cyril turns to a phrase-by-phrase explanation of the baptismal creed as it was recited in the church of Jerusalem at the midpoint between the Council of Nicaea in 325 and the Council of Constantinople in 381. We find sermons on the following:

1. One God
2. The Father
3. Almighty
4. Maker of Heaven and Earth and all things visible and invisible
5. And in one Lord Jesus Christ
6. The Only-begotten Son of God, Begotten of the Father, Very God before all Ages, by whom all things were made
7. Incarnate and made man
8. Crucified and buried
9. And Rose again from the Dead on the third day, and ascended into the Heavens, and Sat on the Right Hand of the Father
10. And Shall Come in Glory to Judge the Quick and the Dead; of whose Kingdom there shall be no end
11. And in One Holy Ghost, the Comforter, which spoke in the Prophets
12. And in One Holy Ghost (again)
13. And in One Holy Catholic Church, and in the Resurrection of the Flesh and the Life Everlasting

Just as Cyril promised, in each sermon he expounds this doctrine from Scripture. The Scripture lessons are key passages on the doctrine he presents in each sermon, but the sermons are not formal expositions of the passages but rather expositions of the doctrine as it has been taught by the Church. The preacher treats those passages of Scripture from which the Church has drawn these doctrines. The purpose of these sermons is clearly to teach the catechumens the meaning of the creed they are to recite as their confession of faith at baptism.

10. Cyril of Jerusalem, *Catechetical Lectures* 5.12.

We cannot take the time here to discuss each of these sermons in turn, so we will look at only three to see how Cyril got across such serious Christian teaching. He knew he was presenting complicated doctrine to a group of people who did not have much background in these matters. He directed these doctrinal sermons to beginners, and yet he wanted to make clear the fundamental Christian teaching about the person of Jesus Christ. These sermons have been regarded as classics through the centuries because they present the orthodox faith so straightforwardly and so power-fully. Let us look a bit more closely at the three sermons in which he presents his teaching on Christology, Sermons 10, 11, and 12.

The tenth sermon takes up the affirmation of the creed, "and in one Lord Jesus Christ." The Greek text is as follows: Καὶ εἰς ἕνα Κύριον Ἰησοῦν Χριστόν. Cyril begins immediately with his subject:

> They who have been taught to believe "in one God the Father Almighty," ought also to believe in His Only-begotten Son. For he that denieth the Son, the same hath not the Father. I am the Door, saith Jesus; no one cometh unto the Father but through Me. For if thou deny the Door, the knowledge concerning the Father is shut off from thee. No man knoweth the Father, save the Son, and he to whomsoever the Son shall reveal Him. For if thou deny Him who reveals, thou remainest in ignorance.[11]

Nicene orthodoxy has always been very clear that true faith in God the Father implied faith in God the Son. Jesus is not merely one of the spiritual leaders of bygone centuries or one of the prophets who pointed to God, but rather is God in himself, to be worshiped and adored by the faithful. "If, therefore, any one wishes to shew piety towards God, let him worship the Son, since otherwise the Father accepts not his service."[12]

Cyril had taken for his Scripture lesson I Corinthians 8:5-6, "For though there be that are called gods, whether in heaven or on earth; yet to us there is One God, the Father, of whom are all things, and we in Him; and One Lord Jesus Christ, through whom are all things, and we through Him."[13] Here in this text we have the complete phrase as it is

11. Cyril of Jerusalem, *Catechetical Lectures* 10.1.
12. Cyril of Jerusalem, *Catechetical Lectures* 10.2.
13. Cyril of Jerusalem, *Catechetical Lectures* 10. This text as it appears at the heading of the sermon found in the Nicene and Post-Nicene Fathers sounds a bit awkward. Besides that, Cyril omits part of the text. Scripture quotations throughout this volume reflect the

found in the creed, "One Lord Jesus Christ." This phrase tells us that Jesus is both Lord and Christ. These two titles, "Lord" and "Christ," are the fundamental biblical affirmations about Jesus. Cyril develops this text with the words which came from heaven at the time of Christ's baptism, " 'This is my beloved Son, with whom I am well pleased' " (Matt. 3:17). At the time of Christ's baptism he was identified as the long-awaited Messiah. He was anointed by the Holy Spirit to demonstrate that he was the anointed one whom the Jews had awaited. Visibly the Holy Spirit descended upon him in the form of a dove. The words from heaven heralded Jesus as God's Son. This should have made clear Christ's divinity at the time, as it should even now. Cyril warns his converts not to be turned aside by crafty Jews who insist that belief in the unity of God is compromised by accepting Jesus as the Son of God.[14] Had not the psalmist confessed that the Messiah was to be the Son of God? "The Lord hath said unto me, 'Thou art my Son' " (Ps. 2:7).

With this our preacher takes up a consideration of the different names by which we speak of Jesus. This makes for some most effective pedagogical rhetoric, if we might coin a phrase. What could be a more effective way of unfolding the insights of Christology in a series of catechetical sermons? To explain who Jesus is by explaining his names and titles has been a pedagogical device used for centuries. Karl Barth used it in his catechetical lectures delivered in the ruins of the University of Bonn in 1946.[15] Cyril takes up the titles found in the Gospel of John. Jesus is called the Good Shepherd, the Lamb of God, and the Way, but he is also called the Door.[16] Having gone over these briefly, he then concentrates on the three names found in the creed. He is called Jesus, he is called Christ, and he is called Lord:

> He is called LORD, not improperly as those who are so called among men, but as having a natural and eternal Lordship. He is called JESUS by a fitting name, as having the appellation from His salutary healing.

---

original authors as they are presented in the edition used in the study. In this case the translator has conformed the text to the King James Version. No attempt will be made to identify the translation used by the preacher. As interesting as this might be, we will have to leave such problems to others.

14. Cyril of Jerusalem, *Catechetical Lectures* 10.2.

15. Karl Barth, *Dogmatics in Outline*, trans. G. T. Thomson (London: SCM Press, 1952).

16. Cyril of Jerusalem, *Catechetical Lectures* 10.3.

He is called SON, not as advanced by adoption, but as naturally begotten.[17]

This very neatly summarizes quite a bit of fundamental Christology as it was understood by the orthodox of the fourth century.

An important point Cyril tries to get across to his converts is that in Jesus Christ, the one God who is God from all eternity accommodates himself to our human understanding. God as he is in himself is beyond our understanding, but as a good physician or a good teacher he accommodates himself to our weakness so that he might bring us to salvation. "He is 'made all things to all men' (I Corinthians 9:22), remaining in His own nature what He is. . . . He adapts Himself to our infirmities."[18] That God accommodates himself to our understanding is made clear even in the Old Testament by the story of God's revelation of himself to Moses on Mount Sinai. God hid Moses in a cleft in the rock and then passed by, pronouncing his name (Exod. 33:17–34:8). To have seen the divine essence as he is, would have destroyed Moses; therefore, God came to him in a hidden way.[19] So it is in Christ; God reveals himself to us by coming to us hidden in human form.

In the New Testament this is clear from the very beginning. The nativity narratives tell us that the newborn Messiah is the Lord. "The Son of God then is Lord: He is Lord, who was born in Bethlehem of Judaea according to the Angel who said to the shepherds, 'I bring you good tidings of great joy, that unto you is born this day in the city of David Christ the Lord' (Luke 2:10-11)." An angel also revealed this to Joseph in a dream in which he was told to take the child into Egypt. Then again in the story of the temptations in the wilderness we are told how the angels ministered to Jesus. This surely is a clear indication that even they recognized that he was their Lord, just as they did again at his resurrection. If the angels who dwell in heaven recognize Jesus as their Lord, the creator of the very heavens, then surely we should receive him as none other than God himself. Jesus, then, is indeed the one Lord Jesus Christ as the apostle Paul put it in the Scripture lesson that had just been read.[20]

Cyril then takes up the name "Jesus," explaining its meaning as the one who will save his people. Our preacher develops this in terms of the

17. Cyril of Jerusalem, *Catechetical Lectures* 10.4.
18. Cyril of Jerusalem, *Catechetical Lectures* 10.5.
19. Cyril of Jerusalem, *Catechetical Lectures* 10.7-8.
20. Cyril of Jerusalem, *Catechetical Lectures* 10.10.

priestly ministry of the Savior. Calling on the Epistle to the Hebrews, he makes the point that Jesus has an eternal priesthood.[21] In Hebrew, Cyril tells us, the name Jesus means "savior," but in Greek it means "healer." In the Gospels we read repeatedly of the healing ministry of Jesus. The faithful should look to Jesus in time of physical illness just as in time of spiritual need. It is, however, the eternal salvation of our souls to which Jesus' ministry of bodily healing was intended to point. The priesthood of Christ is an eternal priesthood, not based on genealogy or on some ceremony of anointing, but on the appointment of God, and is therefore effective for our eternal salvation.[22]

This sermon concludes with a beautiful piece of rhetoric which Cyril had obviously learned from the Greek rhetoricians. He calls on a whole list of witnesses to the divine lordship of Christ: the Father and the Holy Spirit, angels and archangels, the virgin mother of God, John the Baptist; the winds on the Sea of Galilee, the five loaves, the wood of the cross, the palm branches carried by the children; Gethsemane, Golgotha, and the Holy Sepulchre in whose shadow even then both the preacher and his congregation stood. The witness of the apostles that Jesus is the one Lord, the Christ of God, has been taken up by a whole army of martyrs and now is being received by the Goths and Persians in most distant lands.

The eleventh sermon takes up the meaning of Jesus' being the only-begotten Son of God. That Jesus is the Μονογενής, the only-begotten Son of God, is a major theological affirmation of orthodox Christianity. In the previous sermon Cyril had spoken of the belief in "One Lord Jesus Christ," making clear the full divinity of the Savior; now he turns to the affirmation that Jesus is "the Only-begotten Son of God, begotten of the Father, very God before all ages, by whom all things were made."[23] With this Cyril teaches us the uniqueness of Christ's divinity:

> And again on hearing of a "Son," think not of an adopted son but a Son by nature, an Only-begotten Son, having no brother. For this is the reason why He is called "Only-begotten," because in the dignity of

---

21. Cyril of Jerusalem, *Catechetical Lectures* 10.11.

22. Cyril of Jerusalem, *Catechetical Lectures* 10.14.

23. This is the text of the baptismal creed as it was recited in Jerusalem between the Council of Nicaea in 325 and the Council of Constantinople in 381. What we recite as the Nicene Creed is in fact the Nicaean Creed as it was revised by the Council of Constantinople in 381. Cf. J. N. D. Kelly, *Early Christian Creeds*, 3rd ed. (New York: D. McKay, 1972).

the Godhead, and His generation from the Father, He has no brother. But we call Him the Son of God, not of ourselves, but because the Father Himself named Christ His Son: and a true name is that which is set by fathers upon their children.[24]

It is by divine authority that Jesus is called the Son of God. This, our preacher shows us, is made clear in the Gospel of Matthew where Peter confesses Jesus to be the Christ, the Son of God, and Jesus responds that Peter knew this only because the Father had revealed it to him (Matt. 16:17).[25] It was not that Jesus had demonstrated to Peter that he was the Son of God. Surely Jesus had done that, but flesh and blood by its own reasoning would never have come to that conclusion if it had not been the will of the Father to make it clear.

There is a distinction between being the only-begotten in relation to the Father and being the firstborn in relation to Christians. Cyril affirms that Jesus is the firstborn in relation to other Christians.[26] We read also that Jesus was the firstborn of many brethren (Rom. 8:29; Heb. 1:6). For Cyril it is important to make it clear that Jesus is the Μονογενὴς in relation to the Father. In this relationship he emphasizes that Jesus has no brother. He is uniquely the Son of the Father.

But if Jesus has a unique relation to the Father, it is also true that he is begotten in a unique way:

> Again, I say, on hearing of a Son, understand it not merely in an improper sense, but as a Son in truth, a Son by nature, without beginning; not as having come out of bondage into a higher state of adoption, but a Son eternally begotten by an inscrutable and incomprehensible generation.[27]

When the Church teaches that the Son was of the Father, it is not to be imagined that the Son became something he was not before. The Son is the Son from all eternity. He is

> above all beginning and all ages, Son of the Father, in all things like to Him who begat Him, eternal of a Father eternal, Life of Life begotten,

---

24. Cyril of Jerusalem, *Catechetical Lectures* 11.2.
25. Cyril of Jerusalem, *Catechetical Lectures* 11.3.
26. Cyril of Jerusalem, *Catechetical Lectures* 11.4.
27. Cyril of Jerusalem, *Catechetical Lectures* 11.4.

and Light of Light, and Truth of Truth, and Wisdom of the Wise, and King of King, and God of God, and Power of Power.[28]

God is not God from something else but from himself. He is not the result of some higher cause or reason nor the product of some necessity. The reason of his being is in himself. He is God of God, very God of very God. It is this which makes God unique, but this does not mean that God is static. What Cyril seems to be saying is that within the one eternal God there are eternal relationships. God is not an eternal loneliness. The eternal God always relates as a father to a son and a son to a father. God is from all time the perfection of paternity. God is the perfection of creativity, the perfection of justice, the perfection of patience, the perfection of mercy. God is love in a way that is beyond our understanding, in a way that is eternal.

Cyril distinguishes the generation of the Son by the Father from the human generation of Isaac by Abraham. Abraham begat Isaac because it was granted to him; of himself he could have no son because Sarah his wife was barren. In spite of Abraham's loss of faith, his confusion and ignorance of the fullness and power of God's promise, God granted him a son. That Abraham became a father shows a certain finitude in his paternity; Abraham was a father in a finite way. Only with the granting of the promise did he become a father and Isaac become a son. It is quite different with God. God was not previously without a Son and then only in time became a Father, but he had a Son from all eternity. The Father begot the Son not as men beget men, but as he himself only knows.[29] We know how Isaac was begotten, but how the only-begotten was begotten is beyond our understanding.[30]

Cyril returns to the first chapter of Hebrews, which had been chosen as the Scripture lesson for this sermon. This chapter makes a strong use of the messianic psalms, Psalms 2, 45, and 110, in developing a Davidic Christology. The Christ is the promised royal son of David, as portrayed in these psalms, begotten from all eternity. The messianic throne is an eternal throne. God himself has anointed his son with the oil of gladness above his fellows.[31] Just as the paternity of God and the virtues, character,

28. Cyril of Jerusalem, *Catechetical Lectures* 11.4.
29. Cyril of Jerusalem, *Catechetical Lectures* 11.8.
30. Cyril of Jerusalem, *Catechetical Lectures* 11.11.
31. Cyril of Jerusalem, *Catechetical Lectures* 11.15.

14

and relationships of paternity are not finite but eternal, so the Son and all the virtues and qualities and relationships of being a son are eternal. The filial wisdom which obeys the Father, the filial power which waits upon the Father, and the filial love which reflects the love of the Father are all eternal, just as the Father and the perfections of paternity are eternal.

Another important passage of Scripture on which Cyril comments is the prophecy of Micah which speaks of the Messiah's being born in Bethlehem (Mic. 5:2). The prophet is very clear that the ruler God will give his people is an eternal ruler, " 'and His goings forth are from the beginning, and from days of eternity.' "[32] Our preacher comments:

> Think not then of Him who is now come forth out of Bethlehem, but worship Him who was eternally begotten of the Father. Suffer none to speak of a beginning of the Son in time, but as a timeless Beginning acknowledge the Father. For the Father is the Beginning of the Son, timeless, incomprehensible, without beginning. The fountain of the river of righteousness, even of the Only-begotten, is the Father, who begat Him as Himself only knoweth.[33]

The whole point here is that God is "the fountain of the river of righteousness." God is the source of all virtues, and in God are all virtues to be found in their fullness — not simply in embryo form or as a foreshadow or even as a desire or design, but in all fullness. God is the fountain of righteousness, not a static pool of virtue, but an ever-flowing source. This we only know, however, because our Lord Jesus Christ is the Μονογενής, the only-begotten of the Father. Cyril quotes Jesus' words to Philip and expounds: " 'He who hath seen the Son, hath seen the Father' (John 14:9): for in all things the Son is like to Him who begat Him; begotten Life of Life, and Light of Light, Power of Power, God of God; and the characteristics of the Godhead are unchangeable in the Son; and he who is counted worthy to behold Godhead in the Son, attains to the fruition of the Father."[34]

With the twelfth sermon in this catechetical series Cyril turns to the humanity of Jesus. He takes up the words of the creed, "incarnate and made man," σαρκωθέντα καὶ ἐνανθρωπήσαντα. This is the title of the sermon. The more traditional wording of the creed is a bit longer, explicitly

32. Cyril of Jerusalem, *Catechetical Lectures* 11.20.
33. Cyril of Jerusalem, *Catechetical Lectures* 11.20.
34. Cyril of Jerusalem, *Catechetical Lectures* 11.18.

stating that Jesus was incarnate from the Virgin and the Holy Spirit. It is not clear whether the phrase ἐκ παρθένου καὶ Πνεύματος Ἁγίου, "from the Virgin and the Holy Spirit," was part of the Jerusalem Creed at the time or whether Cyril borrowed it from a version of the creed used elsewhere.[35] Whatever may have been the case, the sermon puts a strong emphasis on the doctrine of the virgin birth. For Cyril, at least, there was nothing optional or expendable about this doctrine. It was an essential component of Christian faith.

For Cyril the doctrine of the virgin birth is a very carefully thought out formulation of the fundamental Christian belief that Jesus Christ is both true God and true man. Jesus is uniquely the Son of God because God is indeed his Father. God is the Father of Jesus in a way that he is not the father of any of the rest of us. The rest of us are children by adoption, sons or daughters of God through faith, but Jesus is literally the Son of God. He is Μονογενής, uniquely the Son of God. At the same time the doctrine affirms that Jesus was true man because he was born of a woman.

What our preacher has to say is summed up in his opening paragraph:

> Nurslings of purity and disciples of chastity, raise we our hymn to the Virgin-born God with lips full of purity. . . . Hearers of the Holy Gospels, let us listen to John the Divine. For he who said, "In the beginning was the Word, and the Word was with God, and the Word was God," went on to say, "and the Word was made flesh" (John 1:1, 14). For neither is it holy to worship the mere man, nor religious to say that He is God only without the Manhood. For if Christ is God, as indeed He is, but took not human nature upon Him, we are strangers to salvation. Let us then worship Him as God, but believe that He also was made Man. For neither is there any profit in calling Him man without Godhead, nor any salvation in refusing to confess the Manhood together with the Godhead. Let us confess the presence of Him who is both King and Physician. For Jesus the King when about to become our Physician, "girded Himself with the linen" of humanity (John 13:4), and healed that which was sick. The perfect Teacher of babes became a babe among babes, that He might give wisdom to the foolish. The Bread of heaven came down on earth that He might feed the hungry.[36]

---

35. The phrase is in fact found elsewhere in the *Catechetical Lectures*, namely, in 4.9, suggesting that the phrase was part of the Jerusalem version of the Nicene Creed. See Nicene and Post-Nicene Fathers, 2nd ser., 7:72 n. 5.

36. Cyril of Jerusalem, *Catechetical Lectures* 12.1.

The first point that the sermon makes is that the reason for the incarnation is God's concern to save us from our sin. If anyone should ask either Jew or Greek why God should become incarnate, this is the answer: God's loving concern for us. For the piety of the Hellenistic world nothing could be more scandalous than for God to become incarnate in human flesh.[37] For a divine being to do such a thing was surely shameful. When, on the other hand, it becomes clear that God has done this for the love of his fallen creation, then it is truly noble.[38]

Most of the rest of the sermon is a long, closely argued defense of the doctrine of the virgin birth. One is surprised to discover that the arguments advanced by the Jews and those advanced by the Greeks are not very much different from the objections advanced by certain theologians of our own day. Apparently even in the fourth century the fact that the text of Isaiah 7:14 in the original Hebrew could simply mean that a young woman would conceive had already been noticed. Even at that Cyril was able to cite several texts from the Old Testament where that same Hebrew word does mean a young woman who had not had sexual intercourse.[39] Also, quite apparently, there were some in those prescientific times who insisted that a virgin birth was impossible. Skepticism about the miraculous was not unique to the Enlightenment; even classical antiquity had plenty of skeptics when it came to anything that sounded miraculous.[40] As Cyril understood it, such skepticism would have to end up denying any kind of belief in a divine creation, let alone any sort of doctrine of redemption. From the beginning our preacher made it clear that for the wise such questions are not decided by philosophical argument but by the plain teaching of the Holy Scriptures.[41]

The conclusion of the sermon comes down very strongly on the moral application of the doctrine of the virgin birth. That Jesus our Savior was born of the Virgin is a strong argument for a life of chastity. Here Cyril is quite explicit that by chastity he means both sexual abstinence before marriage and sexual fidelity in marriage. The sexual relationships of the faithful married couple are sacred. They only lose their purity through fornication or adultery. The doctrine of the virgin birth makes it

---

37. Cyril of Jerusalem, *Catechetical Lectures* 12.4.
38. Cyril of Jerusalem, *Catechetical Lectures* 12.14.
39. Cyril of Jerusalem, *Catechetical Lectures* 12.21-26.
40. Cyril of Jerusalem, *Catechetical Lectures* 12.27-30.
41. Cyril of Jerusalem, *Catechetical Lectures* 12.5.

clear that chastity has a spiritual power about it. That salvation should come to the human race because of the chastity of the virgin Mary is indeed a strong argument for Christians to maintain a life of innocence and purity.

The conclusion of Cyril's sermon is as prophetic today as it was at the close of the Hellenistic age:

> But let us all by God's grace run the race of chastity, "young men and maidens, old men and children" (Ps. 148:12); not going after wantonness, but praising the name of Christ. Let us not be ignorant of the glory of chastity: for its crown is angelic, and its excellence above man. Let us be chary of our bodies which are to shine as the sun: let us not for short pleasure defile so great, so noble a body: for short and momentary is the sin, but the shame for many years and for ever. Angels walking upon earth are they who practise chastity: the Virgins have their portion with Mary the Virgin. Let all vain ornament be banished, and every hurtful glance, and all wanton gait, and every flowing robe, and perfume enticing to pleasure. But in all for perfume let there be the prayer of sweet odour, and the practice of good works, and the sanctification of our bodies: that the Virgin-born Lord may say even of us, both men who live in chastity and women who wear the crown, "I will dwell in them; and walk in them, and I will be their God, and they shall be My people" (2 Cor. 6:16). To whom be the glory for ever and ever. Amen.[42]

One can well understand why these sermons have been treasured by the Church century after century. They present in a crisp and brief fashion the essential doctrines of the Christian faith. There is something classical about them which speaks to us generation after generation.

B. Preaching as Mystagogy

The last five sermons in the series were preached by Cyril after the baptism of his converts and are significantly called mystagogical catechisms.[43] They

---

42. Cyril of Jerusalem, *Catechetical Lectures* 12.34.

43. On the title of these five lectures, cf. Cyril of Jerusalem, *Catéchèses mystagogiques*, ed. Auguste Piédagnel, Sources chrétiennes, vol. 126 (Paris: Les Éditions du Cerf, 1966), pp. 15ff. and 82ff.

explain the rites of initiation which the newly baptized had just experienced. Here we see with particular clarity how Cyril explains these rites in terms of the mystery religions. While the term "mystagogical catechism" is strange to us, it was very familiar to Cyril's converts. It was the term used to explain to those who had gone through the cultic mysteries what had happened to them. Cyril explains each of the rites in turn: the renunciation of the devil, the confession of faith, the anointing with exorcised oil, the baptism itself, the chrism, and finally the various parts of the eucharistic service. What interests us here is that, for Cyril, the explaining of the sacraments occupies an important, if not the climactic, part of catechetical preaching. Under Cyril this catechetical teaching on the sacraments has become mystagogy. For the Christian Church this is the beginning of a totally new approach to teaching and preaching.

These last five of Cyril's catechetical sermons constitute an important innovation, one of the most important innovations in the history of Christian worship.[44] It is not surprising that a good number of patristic scholars have raised questions as to whether the mystagogical catechisms come from Cyril or from his successor John of Jerusalem (387-414).[45] Some, particularly Protestant scholars, find it hard to imagine that one so orthodox in his Christology could have been so heterodox in matters of worship. Still, Cyril of Jerusalem is one of our fathers in the faith, and as such we respect him nevertheless.

Such charges against a champion of orthodoxy notwithstanding, it seems likely that the creative mind behind this innovation was that of Cyril. It was he who had the insight to recognize the role Jerusalem could play in the life of the Christian empire. Cyril was a very gifted church leader who had a talent for filling up his church, but he was also a man of integrity. He had several times paid the price of exile for his opposition to Arianism and had therefore won enough respect from many of the foremost Christian thinkers of the day to be regarded as a leader whose liturgical practice could be safely followed. To be sure, no one followed it in every point, but that is the way it usually is. Cyril's leadership in the church of Jerusalem lasted a

---

44. This study is based on the *Sources chrétiennes* edition of August Piédagnel. English quotations are from the edition found in the Nicene and Post-Nicene Fathers.

45. For a well-balanced discussion of the problem, see Quasten, *Patrology*, 3:363-66. See as well Piédagnel, ed., *Catéchèses mystagogiques*, pp. 18-40; and Enrico Mazza, *Mystagogy: A Theology of Liturgy in the Patristic Age*, trans. Matthew J. O'Connell (New York: Pueblo Publishing Co., 1989), pp. 150ff.

long time. Thousands of pilgrims came to the Holy City, participated in its dramatic worship so splendidly performed in the holy sites, and went home and tried to do something similar. The Spanish nun Etheria, whose pilgrimage journal was apparently written some five years after Cyril's death, shows how influential Jerusalem's worship could be on the pilgrims who experienced it. It was Cyril who gave Jerusalem and its worship that kind of exemplary form.[46] However one may account for some of the discrepancies between the last five sermons and the earlier eighteen, it seems more likely that it was Cyril who came up with the idea of preaching mystagogical sermons to those who had been initiated by the Christian mysteries of baptism, chrismation, and Eucharist.[47]

This was a very new concept for Christian catechetical preaching, and it inspired at least to some extent Theodore of Mopsuestia, John Chrysostom, Ambrose of Milan, and indirectly, Augustine of Hippo — each of whom developed the concept quite differently. For example, it has often been speculated that Ambrose of Milan was dependent on Cyril. Ambrose was well known for being inspired by the example of Greek theologians; his sermons on Luke were inspired by those of Origen and his treatise on the Holy Spirit by the treatise of Basil. Even his work on the ministry, *De officiis,* took as its model Cicero's famous Latin treatise bearing the same title. We should hardly be surprised if Ambrose took Cyril of Jerusalem's five sermons on the rites of initiation as his model even if he says very different things about these rites and what they mean. Augustine, whom Ambrose himself had baptized, took this postbaptismal catechetical preaching in yet another direction. We will look at these various adaptations of Cyril's mystagogical preaching as we proceed through this volume.[48] The point we want to make here is that Cyril is

46. On the subject of Cyril as the genius behind the liturgical creations of the Holy City, cf. Dix, *The Shaping of the Liturgy,* p. 350; and Telfers, *Cyril of Jerusalem,* pp. 29-30.

47. In all probability the five mystagogical sermons, whether from Cyril or another, are a later addition. The prebaptismal catechism may go back to the earlier years of Cyril's ministry in Jerusalem, even if it did not achieve literary form right away. That sort of thing tends to happen when one goes over the same material year after year. The material evolves and the manuscript is revised. The postbaptismal sermons may have been developed later in his ministry and achieved their literary form still later. If this be the case, then some of the discrepancies could easily be explained.

48. Enrico Mazza's thought-provoking volume *Mystagogy* arranges his examples of mystagogy so that Ambrose comes first and "Cyril" last. In fact, he figures they are the work of John of Jerusalem, not Cyril. He does not include a study of Augustine's postbaptismal sermons.

the innovator of this practice, a practice which was to have a long and complex development.[49]

Let us now study these five mystagogical sermons and try to put our finger on just exactly how Cyril understands their function in worship. First we need to make clear what takes place in these mysteries, and then, how preaching relates to it.

We begin by looking at what Cyril has to say about baptism. The key to Cyril's understanding of baptism is his interpretation of the sixth chapter of Romans, which he chose for the Scripture reading for the second of these mystagogical catechisms. This has been a key passage for baptism down through the centuries,[50] although interpretations of it have diverged widely. The way Cyril interprets Romans 6 is that by our participation in the ceremonial imitation of the death and resurrection of Christ we receive the benefits of these mighty acts of salvation accomplished by the Son of God. What we have here is a Christian application of the Greek concept of μίμησις.

We cannot go into a long discussion of the term μίμησις here, but it was a fundamental concept in the development of the Hellenistic mystery religions. Basically the idea was that by dramatizing a cosmic creative or redemptive act one could reactualize it for the benefit of those who participated in it.[51] While the subject of the influence of the mystery religions on the sacrament must remain outside our field of inquiry, it cannot help but have strong implications for how preaching relates to worship. Once worship was understood in terms of the mystery religions, the Christian approach to preaching changed radically.

This does not mean that the older covenantal understanding of baptism had completely disappeared. The making of the vows of faith, which

49. On the development of the allegorical explanation of the liturgy as a form of literature, see Adolf Franz, *Die Messe im deutschen Mittelalter* (Darmstadt: Wissenschaftliche Buchgesellschaft, 1963), especially pp. 333-740.

50. See my study of baptism, *The Shaping of the Reformed Baptismal Rite in the Sixteenth Century* (Grand Rapids: Wm. B. Eerdmans Publishing Co., 1992), pp. 2ff., 18, 31, 176, 272, and 286.

51. There is a wide literature on this subject. Most important would surely be the work of Odo Casel, *Das Christliche Kultmysterium*, 4th ed. (Regensburg: Fr. Pustet, 1960). A most significant refutation would be André Benoît, *Le baptême chrétien au second siècle* (Paris: Presses Universitaires de France, 1953); Rudolf Schnackenburg, *Baptism in the Thought of St. Paul*, trans. G. R. Beasley-Murray (Oxford: Blackwell, 1964); and Günter Wagner, *Das religionsgeschichtliche Problem von Römer 6,1-11* (Zurich: Zwingli Verlag, 1962).

has strong covenantal implications, is the subject of the first eighteen sermons. When Cyril first preached his catechetical sermons the making of the vows was for him, obviously, the center of attention, but as he began to think of the sacraments as mysteries and catechetical preaching as mystagogy, and as his converts had already been baptized, another understanding of baptism and therefore catechetical preaching came into play. Sermon 19, the first of the mystagogical catechisms, is devoted to the renunciation of Satan. Cyril says the meaning of this rite is the breaking of the covenant with Satan.[52] One might say that this has negative covenantal implications, the main point of the sermon being that in the baptismal rites of renunciation one is separated from Satan. Even the typological interpretation of the exodus is reshaped so that the point is escaping the power of Pharaoh. Pharaoh is a figure of Satan whom the newly baptized have renounced. This traditional type of baptism has become a type not only of baptismal washing but also of the renunciation of Satan. A bit of ceremonial is discussed here. The renunciation is made facing the west, the land of darkness, after which the convert is turned toward the east, the land of light. Facing the east, the convert recites the creed. When explained this way, the reciting of the creed has positive covenantal implications.

Much of the new ceremonial which baptism picked up during the early centuries had to do with escaping the power of Satan. As baptism more and more took on the nature of a mystery, various forms of exorcism came to dominate the rite. This made sense in a world pervaded with sorcery and magic. In the second mystagogical sermon our preacher first takes up the removal of the clothing. What had originally been a practical necessity before bathing is thoroughly allegorized. If the School of Alexandria had taught preachers to allegorize the Scriptures, then what was more logical than allegorizing the sacraments as well? The removal of the clothing is an allegory of the putting away of the old man with his practices. Having taken off one's clothes, one is naked in imitation of Christ on the cross. On the cross, Cyril tells us, Jesus disarmed the forces of evil by his nakedness. This also symbolizes the innocence of Adam.[53] Cyril discusses the anointing of the converts with exorcised oil before they enter the baptismal font.[54] Here again what had originally been the normal procedure of one wishing to take a bath has been given an artificial religious significance. Through this anointing the new

---

52. The word Cyril uses is διαθήκη, that is, covenant. *Catechetical Lectures* 19.9.
53. Cyril of Jerusalem, *Catechetical Lectures* 20.2.
54. Cyril of Jerusalem, *Catechetical Lectures* 20.3.

Christian becomes a participant in the true and genuine root stock of the olive tree. Cyril goes on, following the metaphor of the apostle Paul (Rom. 11:18-24), to explain that when we are separated from the wild olive tree, we are then grafted into the true and genuine root stock and thereby become participants in the abundance of the true olive tree. The exorcised oil, Cyril says, symbolizes participation in the abundance of Christ, which puts to flight all traces of demonic power. This is a fascinating example of the way a biblical metaphor, which originally was purely literary, has been made into a liturgical rite. It is a bit far-fetched, actually. Cyril makes it even more obtuse when he tells us that this exorcised oil, through the invocation of God's name, receives power to purify from demonic influences.[55] For some of us this sounds like the sort of magic of which the Hellenistic mystery religions were full.

There is, however, another way of looking at this. No doubt, it has to be admitted, Cyril was effectively communicating with his audience. The wisdom of Cyril may have been to recognize that he could only take his converts so far. If the typical pagan in the Hellenized culture of the late fourth century had come only part of the way Cyril had led them, it was surely an impressive accomplishment! If one takes this approach, however, one has to ask whether Cyril's converts were really converted. If they believed in this kind of cultic magic, were they not still part pagan? Cyril communicated but he also confused.

These auxiliary rites of baptism multiplied greatly under the influence of the Hellenistic mystery religions, and it is through these same auxiliary rites that a good number of alien attitudes developed around the sacraments. They all fed on the basic idea that religious ceremonial which was seen with the eyes and experienced with the senses communicated better than the reading and preaching of Scripture. Cyril made clear in his first mystagogical catechism that this was the way he felt about it. He waited until one had experienced the mysteries to explain them because he well knew, as he put it, that seeing is more persuasive than hearing.[56] That was the whole philosophy behind his developing the splendid ceremonial of the church of Jerusalem. Cyril, all quite innocently, was preparing the way for making ceremonial the principle way of communicating the gospel. More and more the Church gave its attention not to the proclamation of the gospel but to its ceremonial dramatization. It was as

55. Cyril of Jerusalem, *Catechetical Lectures* 20.3.
56. Cyril of Jerusalem, *Catechetical Lectures* 19.1.

though the dictum of the apostle Paul (Rom. 10:17) had been reversed; faith comes not so much by hearing as by seeing.

When we get to Cyril's explanation of baptism proper, we discover that our preacher bases his strong emphasis on ritual on the apostle Paul's words in the sixth chapter of Romans, "For if we have been united with him in a death like his, we shall certainly be united with him in a resurrection like his" (Rom. 6:5). Cyril, as many others before and after him, understood this to mean that the rite of baptism is primarily a dramatization of the death, burial, and resurrection of Christ. The rite of immersion particularly was thought of as a reenactment, in a grave of water, of the saving burial and resurrection of Christ. The key word here in the Greek text is ὁμοιώματι, likeness or imitation. The idea was that by participating in this dramatic likeness of the saving action of Christ, one was saved. The act of immersion was a likeness, a replica, a reenactment of Christ's saving death and resurrection:

> O strange and inconceivable thing! We did not really die, we were not really buried, we were not really crucified and raised again; but our imitation was in a figure, and our salvation in reality. Christ was actually crucified, and actually buried, and truly rose again; and all these things He freely bestowed upon us, that we, sharing His sufferings by imitation, might gain salvation in reality.[57]

It is hard to escape the conclusion that Cyril understands the apostle Paul in terms of the Hellenistic mystery religions which were so popular at the time. Cyril sees the ceremony as an imitation, μίμησις, of Christ's saving death and resurrection, and those who go through it are saved thereby. Whether Cyril correctly understood Paul or not is another matter.[58]

One of the problems those who adopt this interpretation of the apostle Paul have is explaining why, if immersion is a dramatization of the burial and resurrection of Christ, the immersion is repeated three times. Trine immersion more naturally signifies the washing away of sin. Cyril senses this difficulty and devotes an allegorical explanation to the trine immersion so widely practiced in the fourth century.[59] The three immersions represent the three days in the tomb.

Whatever problems Cyril may have sensed there were to his explana-

---

57. Cyril of Jerusalem, *Catechetical Lectures* 20.5.
58. Schnackenburg, *Baptism*, pp. 184-87.
59. Cyril of Jerusalem, *Catechetical Lectures* 20.4.

tion, there is no question as to what he meant. He firmly believed in salvation by ceremony, just as the adherents of the Greek mystery religions did. Cyril quotes the apostle Paul, "For if we have been planted together with the likeness of His death, we shall be also with the likeness of His resurrection."[60] Then he comments:

> Well has he said, *planted together.* For since the true Vine was planted in this place, we also by partaking in the Baptism of death have been *planted together* with Him. And fix thy mind with much attention on the words of the Apostle. He said not, "For if we have been planted together with His death," but, *with the likeness of His death.* For in Christ's case there was death in reality, for His soul was really separated from His body, and real burial, for His holy body was wrapt in pure linen; and everything happened really to Him; but in your case there was only a likeness of death and sufferings, whereas of salvation there was not a likeness but a reality.[61]

Now let us look at what Cyril has to say about the sacrament of chrismation, to which he devotes the third of his mystagogical catechisms. The sermon takes as its text I John 2:20-28, "But you have been anointed by the Holy One, . . . the anointing which you have received from him abides in you, and you have no need that anyone should teach you; as his anointing teaches you about everything. . . ." What interests the preacher is that in the chrismation there is an imitation of Christ's messianic anointing. Christ means the anointed one, as was obvious to Cyril's Greek-speaking congregation. What could be more appropriate than that Christians be anointed too?

> Now ye have been made Christs, by receiving the antitype of the Holy Ghost; and all things have been wrought in you by imitation, because ye are images of Christ. He washed in the river Jordan, and having imparted of the fragrance of His Godhead to the waters, He came up from them; and the Holy Ghost in the fullness of His being lighted on Him, like resting upon like. And to you in like manner, after you had come up from the pool of the sacred streams, there was given an Unction, the anti-type of that wherewith Christ was anointed.[62]

---

60. Romans 6:5 (as understood by Cyril).
61. Cyril of Jerusalem, *Catechetical Lectures* 20.7.
62. Cyril of Jerusalem, *Catechetical Lectures* 21.1.

This anointing with perfumed oil after baptism Cyril clearly understands as a sacrament for the conferring of the Holy Spirit. Again we notice how important the concept of μίμησις is to Cyril.[63] It is by means of a ceremonial imitation of Christ's anointing that the Holy Spirit is conferred.

In regard to chrismation there is, in addition to the concept of μίμησις, a very clear statement that the chrism is in some sense consecrated. Like the bread and wine of the Eucharist, it is transformed by the invocation of the Holy Spirit so that it has the power to impart the divine nature.

> But beware of supposing this to be plain ointment. For as the Bread of the Eucharist, after the invocation of the Holy Ghost, is mere bread no longer, but the Body of Christ, so also this holy ointment is no more simple ointment, nor (so to say) common, after invocation, but it is Christ's gift of grace, and, by the advent of the Holy Ghost, is made fit to impart His Divine Nature.[64]

This approach to understanding a religious rite was only too familiar and only too easy for the newly converted Christians to grasp. The world they were brought up in was filled with religious rites of this sort.

Here we find another example of how literary imagery has been used to construct a liturgical rite. While some are convinced that this rite of chrismation went back to the primitive Church, the chances are that this is not the case. Chrismation far more likely owes its existence to a concern to make baptism and the first Communion which followed it into Christian mysteries more splendid than the rites of initiation so popular in the Hellenistic world. The rites were developed in order to make clear what those who celebrated them thought they accomplished. In this they differed considerably from the covenantal signs found in Scripture. A true covenantal sign is given by God, as was Noah's rainbow, as was circumcision, and as was the Passover meal. This is as true of the covenant signs of the New Covenant as it was of those of the Old Covenant. Baptism and Communion were both instituted of Christ, as the New Testament makes very clear.

If Cyril's treatment of baptism and chrismation put the emphasis on

---

63. The Greek text reads, καὶ πάντα εἰκονικῶς ἐφ' ὑμῶν γεγένηται, "And all things have been wrought in you by imitation." That we are still dealing with the concept of μίμησις is clear from *Catechetical Lectures* 20.5.

64. Cyril of Jerusalem, *Catechetical Lectures* 21.3.

these rites as μίμησις, the emphasis of the two sermons on the Eucharist is on μεταβολή, change, or very specifically the transformation of the bread and wine into the body and blood of Christ. This astounding miracle is far above and beyond anything the pagan mysteries had to offer. By participation in these "divine mysteries" the Christian became a partaker in the divine nature. E. H. Gifford in the preface to his edition of the mystagogical catechisms warns us against trying to read out of Cyril any of the eucharistic theologies of the Western Church. Cyril was not talking about transubstantiation as that idea developed in the Western Church. In Cyril we find a very early form of a eucharistic theology which developed in the Eastern Orthodox churches. Cyril speaks of the transforming of bread and wine into the body and blood of Christ, but ultimately what he is concerned about is the transforming of human nature. It is a very early attempt to speak of θέωσις, the transforming of sinful human nature into the divine nature, the nature of Christ himself. This transformation, according to Cyril, takes place through participation in the sacraments, through practicing ascetic disciplines, and through prayer.[65] Strangely enough Cyril does not mention at this point the reading and preaching of the Word of God. Unlike for Ambrose or John Chrysostom, for Cyril the reading and preaching of the Scriptures does not play a major role in this transformation; it is participation in the divine mysteries which initiates the transformation of mortal human nature into the incorruptible, immortal, divine nature.

Cyril begins the first sermon on the Eucharist by commenting on the Scripture lesson, taken from I Corinthians 11, in which the apostle Paul speaks of Christ's institution of the Lord's Supper:

> Even of itself the teaching of the Blessed Paul is sufficient to give you a full assurance concerning those Divine Mysteries, of which having been deemed worthy, ye are become of *the same body* and blood with Christ.[66]

We notice here, as frequently throughout these mystagogical catechisms, that participation in the Christian mysteries, like participation in the pagan mysteries, requires a certain degree of worthiness. The more Christians began to model their worship after the mystery religions, the more this

65. Cyril of Jerusalem, *Catechetical Lectures* 23.9.
66. Cyril of Jerusalem, *Catechetical Lectures* 22.1.

requirement of worthy participation was emphasized. Sad to say, this was often developed in such a way that the sacraments no longer seemed to be sacraments of grace. The requirements were so rigorous that they obscured the gratuitous nature of Christ's offer of salvation. The allusion to Ephesians 3:6, "The Gentiles are fellow heirs, members of the same body, and partakers of the promise in Christ Jesus through the gospel," does not quite say what Cyril wants it to say, but one can see, nevertheless, how Cyril comes to understand it the way he does.

Perhaps most indicative of how Cyril understands the Eucharist is the biblical "type" by which he would explain it. The Eucharist is not the Passover, nor the manna in the wilderness, nor the covenant meal on Mount Sinai. It is, in fact, not an Old Testament type at all, but rather the story of Jesus turning the water into wine at Cana:

> He once in Cana of Galilee, turned the water into wine, akin to blood,[67] and is it incredible that He should have turned wine into blood? When called to a bodily marriage, He miraculously wrought that wonderful work; and *on the children of the bridechamber,* shall He not much rather be acknowledged to have bestowed the fruition of His Body and Blood?[68]

Cyril speaks of the shewbread as a type of the Eucharist, but then he tells us that does not even begin to explain the Eucharist. The story of turning water into wine at the wedding of Cana gives Cyril what he wants, and that is the transformation of one substance into another. Even more, it is a miraculous transformation. For Cyril the essential thing is this miraculous transformation, and none of these more traditional Old Testament types involve a transformation.[69]

Many of us find θέωσις, divinization, very difficult to go along with, but that seems to be what Cyril is driving at. And besides, even if an American Protestant finds it difficult, Greek-speaking converts from the paganism of late antiquity probably found it quite easy to understand and to accept. θέωσις was a concept quite familiar to them. Cyril's strong point was that he communicated with the world in which he lived.

---

67. "Akin to blood" is the reading Gifford adopts; "Of his own will" is the reading suggested by Piédagnel. Piédagnel's reading is surely more convincing.

68. Cyril of Jerusalem, *Catechetical Lectures* 22.2.

69. See the note of Piédagnel on the significance of the Greek verb used for change, μεταβάλλειν. Piédagnel, *Catéchèses mystagogiques,* pp. 136ff.

Cyril's second sermon on the Eucharist begins with an explanation of two traditions which in the course of time had been ritualized, the washing of the hands and the kiss of peace. According to the Jewish Law, it was required to wash the hands before eating. We discover this even in the New Testament, where, however, it seems to be regarded as one of the ceremonies of the Law no longer binding on Christians (Mark 7:1-4). It was a natural thing to do, nevertheless, just as it was natural for people coming into the worship assembly to greet each other with an "abbraccio," or, as it is usually translated into English, a kiss of peace. For Cyril, once again these natural acts have been ritualized and a good amount of trouble has been given to explaining their spiritual significance. These natural actions have become allegorized so that the ceremonial of these rites of initiation communicates the essential religious truths. More and more it will be things like this that will take the place of preaching in Christian worship. It was true at the end of the fourth century, just as it is true today at the end of the twentieth.

With this Cyril turns to an explanation of the Eucharistic Prayer. Much could be said about Cyril's treatment which is not related to our subject but which is nevertheless of great interest to the historian of Christian worship. Still, we must aim at a certain brevity and select those features which most obviously are related to our subject.[70] For Cyril, to put it succinctly, the function of the Eucharistic Prayer is to transform the bread and wine into the body and blood of Christ so that the people of God are sanctified and transformed from sinful human nature to the eternal, incorruptible divine nature. One of the strangest things about Cyril's remarks at this point is the absence of comment about how this prayer gives thanks for God's mighty acts of redemption in Christ. We are told that the Eucharistic Prayer is a prayer of thanksgiving, but Cyril seems to be uninterested in the subject of the thanksgiving. Nothing is said about thanking God for the incarnation, the sacrifice on the cross, the resurrection from the grave, the ascension into heaven, or the pouring out of the Holy Spirit. What for many of us seems the central function of the prayer

---

70. On Cyril's eucharistic doctrine, cf. K. Baus, "Die eucharistische Glaubens-verkündigung," in *Die Messe in der Glaubensverkündigung*, ed. Franz Yaver Arnold et al., 2nd ed., Festschrift J. A. Jungmann (Freiburg im Breisgau, 1953), pp. 55-70; E. J. Cutrone, "Cyril's Mystagogical Catecheses and the Evolution of the Jerusalem Anaphore," *Orientalia Christiana Periodica* 44 (1978): 52-64; Mazza, *Mystagogy*, pp. 150-64; Johannes Quasten, "Mysterium tremendum. Eucharistische Frömmigkeitsauffassungen des vierten Jahrhunderts," in *Von Christlichen Mysterium*, ed. Anton Mayer et al., Festschrift Odo Casel (Düsseldorf: Patmos Verlag, 1951), pp. 66-75.

is ignored. No doubt this theme was found in the prayer traditionally used in Jerusalem, but Cyril was simply interested in other things. In the same way nothing is said about reciting the Words of Institution. As we will see, the reciting of these words was of primary importance for Ambrose, but for Cyril apparently this was not the case.

It is the epiclesis which is the high point of the Eucharistic Prayer. In fact, one gets the impression that the thanksgivings of the prayer are a mere preface to the central action:

> Then having sanctified ourselves by these spiritual Hymns, we beseech the merciful God to send forth His Holy Spirit upon the gifts lying before Him; that He may make the Bread the Body of Christ, and the Wine the Blood of Christ; for whatsoever the Holy Ghost has touched, is surely sanctified and changed.[71]

There is much to be said in favor of putting a strong emphasis on the epiclesis rather than on the reciting of the Words of Institution as a formula of consecration. When the Reformers thought about the arguments between the Orthodox and the Catholics on this matter, they understood the point the Orthodox had tried to make. But what Cyril has said here in such brief form does not seem to convey the deeper meaning which in the course of time Orthodox theologians developed. And of course the same thing will have to be said about Ambrose. At the end of the fourth century, however, what we have is a number of very distinctly different understandings of what happens in worship.

One thing here to which we need to draw attention is the way that, for Cyril, this transformation of bread and wine into the body and blood of Christ occurs and how offering these consecrated gifts to God is a mystery more divine and more spiritual than any of the pagan mysteries. Whereas the pagan mysteries involved bloody sacrifices, this sacrifice surpasses them because it is not bloody.

> Then, after the spiritual sacrifice, the bloodless service, is completed, over that sacrifice of propitiation we entreat God for the common peace of the Churches, for the welfare of the world; for kings; for soldiers and allies; for the sick; for the afflicted; and, in a word, for all who stand in need of succour we all pray and offer this sacrifice.[72]

71. Cyril of Jerusalem, *Catechetical Lectures* 23.7.
72. Cyril of Jerusalem, *Catechetical Lectures* 23.8.

30

The supplicatory, intercessory character of the eucharistic worship seems to be given a strong predominance. One gets the impression that one celebrates the liturgy not to celebrate Christ's full, perfect, and sufficient sacrifice which has atoned for all sins past, present, and future, but rather to win God's favor, or, as Cyril puts it elsewhere, to render God propitious. This impression is strengthened by the fact that it is at this point that Cyril chooses to give his explanation of the Lord's Prayer.

Finally, Cyril gives an explanation of the gestures with which one is to receive the Communion. Both the bread and the wine are to be received with gestures of adoration which, one senses, were not completely accepted at the time. Cyril seems to be urging his new converts to adopt them because they affirm his understanding of the eucharistic presence. Here again we find an obvious example of ceremonial being elaborated for the sake of developing a liturgical rite which can be read, or interpreted, by a mystagogical explanation. The intention which seems to be behind this is to use liturgical ceremonial as a means of communicating religious truth, a means Cyril imagined was much more effective than the reading and preaching of Scripture.

As we will see, Cyril's understanding of worship will have a great effect on the development of preaching. How ironic that this new approach to Christian worship seems to have developed in Jerusalem; from Jerusalem it seems to have spread very widely throughout the Church. But then, how could it have been otherwise? Churches like Antioch, Rome, and even Alexandria were so much more firmly set in genuine apostolic tradition that they would never have allowed such novelties to take root. The city of Jerusalem, on the other hand, was totally destroyed in A.D. 70. A few Christians remained in the neighborhood, but in 135, when Aelia Capitolina was founded to take its place, all Jews were banished from the area. The church of Jerusalem became a Gentile church and lost its continuity with the earliest Christian traditions of the city. Yet even at that Jerusalem had a sort of authority. From the time of Cyril on its liturgical forms would spread throughout Christendom.

When all is said, Cyril has much to his credit. Surely we must recognize him as the first great catechetical preacher. Surely it was he who first popularized this genre of Christian preaching and found for it a regular place in Christian worship. Catechetical preaching, especially as it was developed by Cyril, is an important genre of Christian preaching. At different times in the Church it has taken on quite diverse forms and functions. Here it is clearly evangelistic; it is aimed at preparing converts

31

from paganism for baptism and leading them through the Christian mysteries of initiation. This was how Cyril did evangelism. Recognizing that there were throngs of men and women in his day who wanted to be part of the new Christian empire, he taught them the faith of the Church and then initiated them into that faith. He had great confidence in the power of these rites to transform these people. This is an important element in Cyril's approach to preaching. He believed the sacraments would work miracles. The Greeks had for centuries tried to find sacred rites that would consecrate and sanctify human beings and elevate them to a higher divine life, and Cyril saw in the Christian sacraments the fulfillment of this search. If for the Christian preachers who had gone before Cyril Christ was the fulfillment of the Law and the prophets, for Cyril the Christian faith was the fulfillment of the philosophies and mysteries of the Hellenistic world. Baptism, chrism, and the Eucharist were the rites of initiation into the divine life that outshone all the sacred mysteries of Hellenism. Cyril's message was very simple, very clear, and very popular. He spoke to people's needs as they understood them. His message was what the ordinary men and women of his day wanted to hear; it was what they had been looking for. They understood it and thronged the Church of the Holy Sepulchre, the church the emperor had built, that they might be part of the Christian empire.

II. The Cappadocian Fathers

The three Cappadocian Fathers, Basil of Caesarea, his younger brother Gregory of Nyssa, and their lifelong friend Gregory of Nazianzus had all the advantages of being born into prominent and wealthy families. They were given the best education the world of classical antiquity could provide and knew the Greek poets and philosophers as they were so meticulously studied in the lecture halls of Athens and Alexandria. Above all they had studied classical rhetoric, which was expected of a young man of intelligence and good family who could be expected to come into public office some time in the future. Besides, oratory was something of an intellectual sport in the classical world, just as it was in former days at Princeton when all the students were divided into two debating societies and competition between them animated the whole university. After their studies abroad the three Cappadocians returned home and devoted their leisure to prayer and study. They must have studied the literature which the Church had produced up to that time quite thoroughly, for it was during these years of seclusion that they produced an anthology of the works of Origen. One might say that, having achieved the pinnacle of education as it was traditionally done in the Hellenistic world, they then similarly immersed themselves in the new Christian education as it was beginning to emerge. They had valuable connections and old friends in high places. They inherited their Christian faith from their families. Gregory of Nazianzus was the son of a bishop; Basil and his brother came from a family noted for its piety for several generations. These three Cappadocians may have come from a land of rather remote and forbidding terrain, but they were born and bred for leadership in the Church.

The three Cappadocian Fathers are, to be sure, at the center of one of the leading schools of Christian preaching. By all standards the preaching of the Greek Church attained an astounding brilliance at the end of the fourth and the beginning of the fifth Christian centuries. The Cappadocian Fathers were part of this school, and yet they can be regarded as a distinct school because they shared a very particular approach to preaching. It is rather unusual that a school of preaching lasts such a short time and is made up of so few preachers. Some of the schools we will study will last much longer, usually several generations, but this school depended to a large extent on three brilliant men who worked closely together and had a very distinct mission and most exceptional gifts. One of the reasons for the school's brief tenure was that these three preachers set such high standards that no one could really follow them. They outshone any who tried to do what they did. Especially in the Greek Church, their influence on succeeding centuries was enormous. Alas, their very stature discouraged imitators.

A. Basil of Caesarea

Basil (ca. 330-79) was born in Caesarea, the rough provincial capital of Cappadocia.[73] It was a town something like Lubbock, Texas — rich

---

73. For further information on Basil, see P. Allard, *Saint Basile* (1903); G. Bardy, "Basil de Césarée," *Dictionnaire d'histoire et de géographie ecclésiastiques* (Paris: Letouzy et Ane, 1912-95, 6: 1111-26; Hans Freiherr von Campenhausen, *Griechische Kirchenväter,* 3rd ed. (Stuttgart: W. Kohlhammer Verlag, 1955), pp. 86-100; M. M. Fox, *The Life and Times of St. Basil the Great as Revealed in His Works,* Patristic Studies, vol. 57 (Washington, 1937); Quasten, *Patrology,* 3:204-35; E. Venables, "Basilius of Caesarea," in *Dictionary of Christian Biography,* 1 (1877): 282-97; and J. W. C. Wand, *Doctors and Councils* (London: Faith Press, 1962), pp. 31-46.

enough, but hardly a cultural center. After attending what schools were available there, he went on to Constantinople to further his studies and to learn his way around the capital city of the Empire. Sometime after 351 he pursued his education in Athens, where he became the student of Libanius, one of the superluminaries of classical rhetoric. To study under Libanius in the fourth century was something like a modern cellist studying under Pablo Casals. Libanius, although he never became a Christian, was the teacher of three of the greatest preachers the Church has ever produced: Basil, his friend Gregory of Nazianzus, and later, when Libanius moved his school to Antioch, John Chrysostom. It was at the school of Libanius that Basil and Gregory of Nazianzus became such good friends.

Basil was above all a man of action, and yet he was an intellectual as well. Having decided to devote his life to the service of God, he established a monastic community at a remote spot on the family estates. This retreat from the world was obviously an advance for the Church. These years of solitude must have been filled with intellectual activity. It must have been there that he took the spiritual initiatives that made him the leader of orthodox Christianity in the next generation. This community prospered, and in time he was joined by his friend Gregory of Nazianzus and his brother Gregory of Nyssa. Eusebius, the bishop of his native city, eventually enlisted his services in administering his important diocese and above all in preaching. On the death of Eusebius in 370, Basil became his successor. Basil provided strong leadership to this important diocese and soon was recognized as a standard-bearer of Nicene orthodoxy.

Basil's literary legacy is considerable. While he was highly regarded as a preacher and seems to have preached frequently, the sermons which have come down to us form only a small part of that legacy. He does not seem to have occupied himself with finishing his sermons for publication. Evidently Basil, as many of the great orators of antiquity, had a high appreciation for the living word of public address. He realized that a sermon must be an encounter and that when it is reduced to a written document it is no longer a sermon. In the manner of the great orators of antiquity he carefully thought out what he intended to say, but he never wrote it out. Only in the pulpit in the course of worship, engaged in the sacred ministry to which God had called him, faced by the congregation gathered to hear the Word, could the sermon be put together. Living oratory was obviously an event for Basil, and that must be why he hesitated to turn the sermons into documents. Even at that, some of these sermons are indeed masterpieces and indicate that his reputation as a great preacher was well deserved. Particularly admired are his nine sermons on the six days of creation, the famous *Hexaemeron*. In addition, we have eighteen sermons on psalms, which apparently were taken down only sporadically by a stenographer from a longer series in which Basil may have preached through the whole book of Psalms. Some claim for Basil a series of sermons on the first sixteen chapters of Isaiah, but at present scholarly opinion denies the series to him. In addition, about twenty-three other sermons are attributed to Basil, including a sermon for the feast of the Epiphany, sermons commemorating a number of martyrs, and sermons commending works of piety and warning against various vices such as anger, jealousy, and avarice. Altogether we have enough to get a fairly comprehensive picture of Basil's preaching ministry.

1. Sermons on the Psalms and the Therapeutic Use of Scripture

Without a doubt the best example we have of the day-to-day preaching of Basil of Caesarea is his eighteen sermons on the psalms.[74] The sermons on the *Hexaemeron,* as we shall see, are a tour de force. They were preached early in his ministry while these sermons on the psalms come from later, after he had become the bishop of the church of Caesarea. We cannot imagine that Basil preached sermons like those on the *Hexaemeron* every Sunday, let alone every day. More than likely the sermons on the psalms are but a random selection taken down by a stenographer who happened to be in Caesarea while Basil was preaching through the book of Psalms; there seems to be no organizing principle behind the selection. Except for the sermon on Psalm 114 (LXX), they all come from the first half of the Psalter.[75] We do notice that the recurring theme in these sermons is the living of the Christian life. We imagine, however, that this emphasis was very strong in the preaching of Basil no matter which passage of Scripture was under consideration. A strong emphasis on this theme is apparently characteristic of Basil's preaching.

74. For the Greek text, see Migne, *Patrologia Graeca,* 29:209-494. For the English translation, see *Saint Basil: Exegetical Homilies,* trans. Sister Agnes Clare Way, C.D.P. (Washington, D.C.: Catholic University of America Press, 1963).

75. The sermons are preached on the Septuagint version and therefore the numbering reflects the Septuagint, rather than the Hebrew. While Psalms 1 and 7 are the same in both versions, Psalm 28 (LXX) equals Psalm 29 in the Hebrew. In most cases the Hebrew number is found by adding one to the Septuagint. With Psalm 114 (LXX), however, the Hebrew is counted as Psalm 116.

The sermons which have come down to us from this prince of the patristic pulpit indicate that Basil's strong suit is expository preaching. The sermons on the psalms make this most obvious, all of which follow closely the literary form of the expository sermon as it was developed in the synagogue and followed by the earliest Christian preachers. Basil goes through each psalm, commenting on the text verse by verse. Sometimes, as in his sermon on the first psalm, he does not get through the whole psalm, but then even with some obvious exceptions this was clearly his usual procedure. For the most part very little time is given to either introductions or conclusions, a rather surprising fact in view of Basil's long training in classical rhetoric. The sermons on the psalms, as the sermons on the six days of creation, would indicate that Basil followed the *lectio continua* for his regular preaching.

Basil kept to the usual practice of other Christian preachers in the patristic age in regard to sermon preparation. It has sometimes been claimed that Basil's preaching was impromptu, that is, completely without preparation or forethought. We will say more about this in regard to his famous *Hexaemeron,* but the sermons on the psalms surely indicate that most of the time Basil entered the pulpit well prepared. Having carefully studied the text, he thought out his interpretation of the passage and consulted commentaries. He did not, however, write out his sermons. What he did was fill his mind with all kinds of material and then, when he was in the pulpit, put it all together. It was extempore because it was put together at the time of delivery, addressed to a particular group of people for a particular occasion.

At several places in these sermons our preacher cites the sort of philological data that not even a genius could simply pull out of his hat. For example, in the sermon on Psalm 7 we find a long discussion on the way the word "judge" is used in Scripture.[76] For the subtle variations of meaning our preacher is able to cite examples all through the Bible. In the sermon on Psalm 33 (LXX) Basil tries to harmonize what is said in the psalm title about David and Abimelech, the king of Gath, and what is found in I Samuel 21:11-13, where we read that Achish rather than Abimelech was the king of Gath. The solution Basil suggests, which he buttresses with a number of texts, is that Abimelech was the title given to kings in the land of Canaan at the time, just as Pharaoh was the title given to the kings of Egypt. It is hard to imagine that he had information like

76. Basil, *Sermon on Psalm 7* 4 and 5.

this at his fingertips. In the sermon on Psalm 59 (LXX) Basil wants to explain the text "Gilead is mine; Manasseh is mine." He tells us that Gilead is the grandson of Manasseh. This information is to be gathered from the genealogical lists found in Numbers (Num. 26:29). Again this is not the sort of information even the most devoted biblical scholars are able to supply impromptu. Then a bit further on in the same sermon our preacher mentions how others have interpreted the passage under discussion.[77] It would seem quite clear from this that Basil had been studying his commentaries in preparation for his sermon.

On the other hand, some find in the sermon on Psalm 114 (LXX) evidence that Basil preached not only extempore but also impromptu. Basil begins the sermon by apologizing for arriving late for the service. Apparently the service in question was held at a chapel built over the tomb of a martyr some distance from the cathedral in the city,[78] and Basil had not begun his journey as early as he should have. The congregation which had started to assemble in the middle of the night occupied itself in singing psalms while waiting for the distinguished preacher, and when he finally arrived they were singing Psalm 114 (LXX). When Basil got up to preach he announced that he had decided to preach on that psalm, since they had just sung it. This, of course, implies that at least this sermon was impromptu, and a closer look at the sermon confirms that implication — it is short and does give the impression of being quite impromptu. The question is whether this sermon is typical or exceptional. It seems to me that the latter is the case. As Basil explains to his congregation, he had been burdened more than usual by the pressure of church business that day, and that was why he was late to the martyrium. Normally he would have prepared an eloquent panegyric in honor of the martyr, but he had not had time to collect his thoughts. And there he was, without a sermon. When he arrived and heard the congregation singing Psalm 114 (LXX), which speaks of God saving the faithful from death, it seemed an appropriate psalm from which to preach for the occasion. This seems even more likely if at this time Basil was in progress with his series on the psalms. The stenographer who was taking down these sermons happened to be there, took down this occasional sermon, and added it to the regular sermons he had collected. This sermon seems to have been impromptu, but in this regard it was not typical but rather exceptional.

77. Basil, *Sermon on Psalm 59 (LXX)* 4.
78. Basil, *Sermon on Psalm 114 (LXX)* 1.

The striking characteristic of these sermons is their pastoral quality. They are at one and the same time hymns of praise to God and instructions on how to live the Christian life. Basil's first sermon in the series makes it clear that this is the way he understands the psalms. He reminds us of the words of the apostle Paul, "All scripture is inspired by God and profitable for teaching, for reproof, for correction, and for training in righteousness" (II Tim. 3:16). Then he comments that the Bible is "composed by the Spirit for this reason, namely, that we men, each and all of us, as if in a general hospital for souls, may select the remedy for his own condition."[79] This is particularly the case with the book of Psalms. "The old wounds of souls it cures completely, and to the recently wounded it brings speedy improvement; the diseased it treats, and the unharmed it preserves."[80] For Basil psalms are above all psalms as they are sung in worship. They are at the same time doxological and therapeutic; their music gives them a remarkable healing quality. "The delight of the melody He mingled with the doctrines so that by the pleasantness and softness of the sound heard we might receive without perceiving it the benefit of the words, just as wise physicians who, when giving the fastidious rather bitter drugs to drink, frequently smear the cup with honey."[81] That Basil should speak of the healing quality of psalms seems to go back to the highest antiquity. In the book of Samuel we read how David was able with his harp to soothe the troubled spirit of King Saul (I Sam. 16:23). In much the same way Basil tells us, "A psalm implies serenity of soul; it is the author of peace, which calms bewildering and seething thoughts."[82]

Not only does psalmody have a pastoral function, it has an educational function as well. Basil tells us, "Oh! the wise invention of the teacher who contrived that while we were singing we should at the same time learn something useful; by this means, too, the teachings are in a certain way impressed more deeply on our minds."[83] Educational psychologists are more and more picking up this ancient insight. To use the modern lingo, they realize the force given to teaching that appeals both to the right side of the brain and to the left side. Psalms not only worship God; they teach the faithful as well. Where else, Basil asks, "Can you learn

---

79. Basil, *Sermon on Psalm 1* 1.
80. Basil, *Sermon on Psalm 1* 1.
81. Basil, *Sermon on Psalm 1* 1.
82. Basil, *Sermon on Psalm 1* 2.
83. Basil, *Sermon on Psalm 1* 2.

the grandeur of courage? The exactness of justice? The nobility of self-control? The perfection of prudence? A manner of penance? The measure of patience? And what ever other good things you might mention?"[84] There is something admirable about true morality; it has a winsome quality. In the end the good Christian is a truly beautiful person. This beauty of holiness is a spiritual beauty that glorifies God.

From what we are told about Basil of Caesarea, we gather that he was one of those beautiful people. His Christian morality was attractive. Among the young men of patrician class in the newly Christian empire he must have stood out as a spiritual prince, a true alternative to the playboys of Roman society who seemed dedicated to nothing so much as elegant debauchery. Basil demonstrated the value of a life filled with purity, truth, and honesty. Not only was he a master of classical rhetoric as it had been taught by the intellectuals of ancient Greece and Rome, he was as well the fulfillment of what the philosophers had taught about virtue. He was a Christian, and yet he lived a life of virtue which even the most enlightened pagan moralist could not help but recognize as truly wise. Men like Basil, John Chrysostom, and Gregory of Nazianzus, by the beauty of their virtues, led the most serious-minded men and women of their day to realize that the Christian fulfilled the highest ideals of the old pagan philosophies. When one catches sight of the sheer beauty of holiness, one has caught sight of the glory of God. What else can one do then but bow down before God in worship?

That the witness to the moral life is central to Christian worship may seem quite impossible to us after more than two hundred years of romanticism, but that was one of the most brilliant insights of the Christian faith. Holiness is beautiful.

But there is more to be said about how these sermons of Basil's are worship. The worship that concentrates on the glory of God has a therapeutic dimension for the faithful. As we have already mentioned, Basil found a strong therapeutic dimension to the psalms. Let us look at what Basil has to say about how this therapeutic dimension of the reading and preaching of Scripture in worship glorifies God.

In the sermon on Psalm 28 (LXX) we find an important passage on the relation of morality to worship. It is put rather negatively, but the point is clear nevertheless. Our preacher is commenting on the text "Bring to the Lord glory and honor." It is through the living of the Christian life

84. Basil, *Sermon on Psalm 1 2.*

39

that we honor God, Basil insists. Immorality, on the other hand, beclouds the glory of God. "He who worships and serves the creature more than the Creator does not bring glory to God, but to the creatures. . . . Let us fear lest, by bringing glory and occasions of exultation to the devil through our sins, we may be handed over to everlasting shame with him. That our sin becomes glory for him who effects it in us."[85] With one of the similes for which he is so well known Basil tells us it is like when two generals send their armies out to fight and one of the armies wins the battle. This victory glorifies the general who achieved the victory. So it is that God is glorified by our good deeds, but when we sin it is the devil who is honored. "For, when the mind wrestles with passion, if, indeed, it prevails through vigor and attention, it wins the prize of victory over the passion and by its own means, as it were, it crowns God."[86]

Basil goes on to the next verse, "Adore ye the Lord in his holy court." In a typical bit of Alexandrian exegesis we are reminded that it is only in the courts of Zion that true worship can be performed. This suggests to our preacher that we are to assume a higher meaning for the courts of the Lord. "It is possible to consider the court in a still loftier sense as the heavenly way of life."[87] In living the Christian way of life we reflect the heavenly glory and thereby worship God. A bit further on in this sermon our preacher tells us that when the word of God dwells in his people, then what they do magnifies God. "Therefore, they who entertain noble thoughts of God, contemplating sublimely the reasons for creation, and being able to comprehend to a certain extent at least the goodness of God's providence, and who besides are unsparing in their expenditures and are munificent in supplying the needs of their brothers, these are the magnificent men in whom the voice of the Lord dwells."[88] Those who truly live the Christian life magnify the glory of God; they reflect it and make it visible in the life of mortal beings. This is worship in the most basic sense of ethical monotheism; it is the alternative biblical religion proposes to idolatry. Because we ourselves are to be the image of God, we have been forbidden to fashion images of God in wood or stone or gold. Basil goes on to tell us that the true Christian despises all bodily things, judging them as of no account in comparison with the

85. Basil, *Sermon on Psalm 28 (LXX)* 2.
86. Basil, *Sermon on Psalm 28 (LXX)* 2.
87. Basil, *Sermon on Psalm 28 (LXX)* 3.
88. Basil, *Sermon on Psalm 28 (LXX)* 4.

unseen world.[89] The point is that the Christian who lives the life of the kingdom of God more truly reflects the invisible God in the visible world than the idol of the idolater.

The sermon on Psalm 29 (LXX) is another essay on the Christian life. It is to a large extent an example of how allegory was used in the ancient Church to interpret Scripture. The introduction tells us how the musical notations found in the psalms were understood allegorically. The human body is a harp which, when devoted to purity and charity, harmoniously offers up praises to God. "The physical structure of the body is, speaking figuratively, a harp and an instrument harmoniously adapted for the hymns of our God; and the actions of the body, which are referred to the glory of God, are a psalm, whenever in an appropriate measure we perform nothing out of tune in our actions."[90] One often notices this kind of allegory in patristic writings. Music frequently becomes a figure for spiritual harmony, and the use of musical instruments and the blending of voices were often seen as implying spiritual truths. It was a well-established allegory in the ancient Church. At that time Christians did not use musical instruments in worship, and so quite naturally the admonitions of the psalms were allegorized. Interpreting verse 5 of the psalm, "Sing to the Lord, O ye his saints," Basil comments, "All who send up the psalmody from a clean heart, and who are holy, maintaining righteousness toward God, these are able to sing to God, harmoniously guided by the spiritual rhythms."[91]

This particular sermon has an especially fine passage on spiritual beauty. If true virtue brings harmony to life, it also brings a beauty which is truly spiritual. Those who contemplate the truth as they meditate on psalms discover the beauty of God's truth. We, to be sure, can only perceive divine truth by the grace of God. Our souls must be purified to recognize the beauty of truth, but as we concentrate on this vision we begin to take on its radiance ourselves, just as Moses after his vigil on Mount Sinai came down the mountain with a glowing face.[92] Basil moves on to verse 12, "Thou turnest away thy face from me, and I become troubled." Basil comments that as long as the rays of the sun of God's watchfulness shine upon us we live a calm and untroubled life, but when God turns his face

89. Basil, *Sermon on Psalm 28 (LXX)* 4.
90. Basil, *Sermon on Psalm 29 (LXX)* 1.
91. Basil, *Sermon on Psalm 29 (LXX)* 3.
92. Basil, *Sermon on Psalm 29 (LXX)* 5.

away then come agitation and confusion. So it is that we must always pray for the face of God to shine upon us so that we might more and more become holy, gentle, and untroubled in every way.[93]

In the sermon on Psalm 61 (LXX) we find again several remarks about the therapeutic dimension of Christian worship. The sermon tells us that meditating on psalms helps cure us from the spiritual diseases of vainglory, love of riches, pride of physical prowess, dishonest business practices, and foul speech. Again we see that the medical metaphor plays a role in Basil's understanding of the ministry of the Word. At the beginning of the sermon we are told that David composed the psalm and gave it to one of his ministers, "that he might correct the passions of his soul, and also as a choral song to be sung in the presence of the people. Through it, also, God was glorified, and those who heard it amended their habits."[94] For Basil the ministry of the reading and preaching of the Scripture has a strong therapeutic dimension and, even considered from that dimension, is surely to be understood as worship. How is this?

We have already given part of the answer, but there is more. Whenever we fallible creatures turn to God in time of trouble, we honor God. In our very mortality we call on God's immortality. We can all understand that worship is eucharistic. No one doubts that we creatures owe thanksgiving to our creator. What is not so obvious is that worship is epicletic before it is eucharistic. Does God really want to hear about our troubles? Should we really bother the Eternal with the pains and agonies of our temporality? To this question Christians have unhesitatingly answered a firm "Yes!" It is the abiding witness of the psalms that when we cry to God we are worshiping him every bit as much as when we praise and glorify him. Even more, when worship heals us, when it sets life in order, and when it brings us salvation, God is worshiped. That our God is a saving God is his highest glory. To this we have the consistent witness of the Christian faith. The LORD is our Savior! That is the affirmation found in the very name Jesus. That was made abundantly clear by the Gospel of Matthew when we are told that an angel directed that the child was to be named Jesus, "'for he will save his people'" (Matt. 1:21).

---

93. Basil, *Sermon on Psalm 29 (LXX)* 6.
94. Basil, *Sermon on Psalm 61 (LXX)* 1.

2. Basil's Hexaemeron *and the Rediscovery of the Literal Sense of Scripture*

Basil's *Hexaemeron* is a series of nine sermons which were preached in the course of several days at morning and evening prayer.[95] It is often claimed that they were preached during Lent, but this may well be in error. There is a reference to fasting at the end of the eighth sermon, but this may refer to Friday fasting rather than Lenten fasting. Certainly the theme of the sermons does not suggest Lent, nor is there any indication that they were preached to catechumens. The sermons were evidently preached extempore, as discussed above, in the way classical rhetoric understood it should be done. Having been prepared and then preached without manuscript, the sermons were recorded by a stenographer and then written up with only light review by the preacher.

As we have already suggested, these sermons are a tour de force, but were they preached for a special event? One naturally asks how much these sermons reveal about the preaching schedule in the metropolitan church at Caesarea. Origen's sermons give us reason for believing that he preached daily at morning prayer, but did Basil and his colleagues regularly provide daily preaching in Caesarea, or was this series a special occasion? We cannot be sure, but perhaps the *Hexaemeron* was the beginning of the regular cycle of the reading through of the books of the Bible. One began at the beginning for such cycles, and perhaps this time it had been announced that the bishop's distinguished young assistant intended to give special attention to explaining the creation story. What made the occasion special was that Basil was scheduled to preach on this special passage of Scripture and give it sustained attention.

With the *Hexaemeron* we discover Christian preaching taking a different direction. The series is tremendously important because it shows a new day in preaching; after a century or more of strongly allegorical interpretation, we find in this series of sermons a reemphasis on the value of the literal sense of Scripture. At several points in the series Basil makes it clear that he intends to stay with the literal sense of the text rather than the spiritual sense. Surely, ever since the Alexandrian approach to the interpretation of Scripture

95. The following study is based on the edition of S. Giet: Basil of Caesarea, *Homélies sur l'Hexaéméron,* Greek text, introduction, and French translation by S. Giet, Sources chrétiennes, vol. 26 (Paris: Les Éditions du Cerf, 1968). Quotations are from the English translation of Agnes Clare Way, *Saint Basil: Exegetical Homilies,* mentioned above.

began to appear there were those who resisted it. With the appearance of Origen allegorical interpretation had an impressive champion, but even then there were voices of protest, and we need not imagine that all Christian preaching from the middle of the third century to the end of the fourth century rested on allegorical exegesis. Basil's reemphasis of the literal sense of Scripture is especially interesting because Basil must be regarded as one who grew up in the school of Origen; indeed, his grandmother had sat at the feet of Origen's most devoted pupil, Gregory Thaumaturgos. As we have already mentioned, Basil and his friend Gregory of Nazianzus had put together an anthology of passages from Origen early in their careers. This shift of emphasis was not a revolution against the teachings of Origen. Origen's approach was never explicitly rejected by the Cappadocian Fathers; in fact, they would often give the spiritual interpretation side by side with the literal interpretation. Probably more than anything else, the Cappadocian Fathers found that by sticking to the literal sense of Scripture they could so much more clearly defend the Christian faith from the attacks of Arianism, the various kinds of gnosticism, and other religious philosophies seeking to win over the Church.

If Basil's *Hexaemeron* indicates a new day in preaching, it also indicates a new day in theology. This series of sermons made explicit the value of creation. Even though some in the Greek world gave great attention to natural philosophy, to physics, to the study of the arts of medicine, to natural history, and to astronomy, there was always a tendency in Greek philosophy to deprecate the natural, material world. This carried over into the Alexandrian exegesis, which lost interest in the natural world at the same time it lost interest in the literal sense. This was not an absolute thing, to be sure, but a tendency. Origen always insisted on the value of the literal sense; it was just that he was so much more interested in the spiritual sense. The sermons of Basil's *Hexaemeron* reemphasize the importance of the natural world. In fact, the sermons rejoice in the goodness of light and earth and water; in the beauty of stars and trees, fields and seas; in the variety of fish, birds, and animals. "And God saw that it was good" constantly echoes through these sermons, just as it is the recurring refrain of the creation story found in the first chapter of Genesis.

Basil's *Hexaemeron* opens up another pathway in Christian theology. It points the way to a positive use of Greek learning. Basil is a preacher who shows how a knowledge of the natural world can be used to open up the meaning of Scripture. His knowledge of astronomy, zoology, and botany only increases his wonder and admiration for the greatness of God. He investigates the order, the vastness, and the variety of God's work of creation in such a way that God is praised. The various ways and habits of animals all point to moral lessons, and natural history becomes a source of edifying fables which point out the wisdom or folly of different kinds of behavior. Basil sees no reason not to use the insights of Aesop in his preaching.

Basil, no less than his brother Gregory of Nyssa and his friend Gregory of Nazianzus, felt the same way about other fields of Greek learning. The Cappadocian Fathers were well schooled in the literary arts. They had mastered the rhetorical forms of classical antiquity so that they knew how to present their message in a clear and interesting way. From classical rhetoric they learned how to be convincing, and how to win over their audience. They were the champions of orthodox Christianity in a day when Arianism was in the ascendency and was sponsored by the imperial court. They saw Greek learning as a means of advancing the cause of truth, and they succeeded in convincing the Church of the wisdom of orthodoxy through their brilliant literary activities. Their success in reestablishing Nicene Christianity had the effect of justifying their use of Greek learning in their theological endeavors as well as in their preaching.

3. Basil's Hexaemeron *and the Baptizing of Greek Rhetoric*

Let us focus in on this baptizing of Greek rhetoric.[96] With the preaching of Basil, Gregory of Nazianzus, and John Chrysostom, classical Greek rhetoric was born again after languishing for centuries for lack of a great cause. It was in Athenian democracy that Demosthenes had demonstrated the consummate value of the art of speaking well, the facility of persuading free men by a clear and forceful presentation of the truth. Great oratory arose in the service of a great cause. With the coming of autocratic rule, there was no longer a place for open discussion and, as the historians of rhetoric put it, the need for oratory dried up.[97] Christian worship, on the

---

96. On the rhetoric of Basil, see J. M. Campbell, *The Influence of the Second Sophistic on the Style of the Sermons of St. Basil the Great,* Patristic Studies, vol. 2 (Washington, D.C.: Catholic University of America, 1922); Y. Courtonne, *Saint Basile et l'hellénisme. Études sur la rencontre de la pensée chrétienne avec la sagesse antique dans l'Hexaéméron de Basile le Grand* (Paris: Firmin-Didot et cie, 1934).

97. Cf. George A. Kennedy, *Classical Rhetoric and Its Christian and Secular Tradition from Ancient to Modern Times* (Chapel Hill: University of North Carolina Press, 1980), and Edward P. J. Corbett, *Classical Rhetoric for the Modern Student,* 2nd ed. (New York: Oxford University Press, 1971).

other hand, with the enormous place it gave to the reading and preaching of the Scriptures, once more gave the orator a chance to deal with the essential issues of life and society. Given this opportunity, classical rhetoric came to life once more, and yet, it now had a completely different character.

a. Telos

Christian rhetoric as we find it in Basil's *Hexaemeron* has a very distinct purpose, namely, to serve the Word of God. It exists to serve the Word of God, to extol, to magnify, and to glorify the Word of God. For centuries one of the problems with rhetoric as it was practiced in the classical world was that it all too often served no purpose quite so clearly as the glorification of the orator. Public acclaim was lavished on orators, and all too often one became an orator that one might be showered with that public acclaim. For centuries rhetoric had been criticized because of this, and Plato's famous dialogue *Gorgias* criticizes Gorgias for this along with other faults. Gorgias was not a Demosthenes; he was not an enthusiast for a cause but a master of techniques. The purpose, the end, of rhetoric had a way of getting lost under the techniques. When rhetoric was made the servant of the Word, the ancient art was freed from its long slavery to egotism. Basil often makes this ministerial responsibility of his oratory clear. No doubt Libanius had taught his pupils all about Plato's criticism of rhetoric.

In the introduction to the opening sermon of the *Hexaemeron* we find Basil making it clear that Scripture is the authority under which his preaching serves. Our preacher introduces his text, "In the beginning God created the heavens and the earth," then after a few remarks he sets out:

> Before weighing the accuracy of these expressions, however, and examining how much meaning there is in these few words, let us consider who is speaking to us. For, even if we do not attain to the profound thoughts of the writer because of the weakness of our intellect, nevertheless, having regard for the authority of the speaker we shall be led spontaneously to agree with his utterances. Now, Moses is the author of this narrative. . . . So then, this man, who is made equal to the angels, being considered worthy of the sight of God face to face, reports to us those things which he heard from God. Let us hear, therefore, the words of truth expressed not in the persuasive language of human wisdom,

but in the teachings of the Spirit, whose end is not praise from those hearing, but the salvation of those taught.[98]

Several points are made here with the utmost clarity. The text of Scripture on which Basil wants to comment has divine authority, and it is for that reason that we accept its teaching. The teaching is from God, but God revealed it to Moses. And this obviously is significant. Moses was a man of great holiness and was therefore prepared to hear these divine teachings and to report them in a way that few others are. Moses was considered worthy to see God face-to-face. We who do not even approach such holiness are hardly in a position to judge his teaching with our human intellect. We would do better, as Basil sees it, to simply accept the report of Moses. It is the fear of the Lord rather than the sharpness of our intellect which is the beginning of wisdom. It is not the persuasiveness of human wisdom that matters for Basil, but rather, the convincing authority of God's Word. The allusion to the first chapter of I Corinthians is unmistakable. Basil intends to follow the teaching of the apostle Paul on the subject of revelation and reason, and Paul in the passage intends a criticism of a naked and self-centered rhetoric which seeks above all things praise for the speaker. Basil is clearly in agreement, but he also finds himself in the company of Plato and the tradition of philosophical rhetoric over against the more technical type of rhetoric represented by Gorgias. But one also notices that the authority of Scripture is not thought of in a merely formal way. It rests not only on the words of Moses but on the teaching of the Holy Spirit as well. The holiness of Moses made it possible to behold God face-to-face, to hear the divine teaching and to report it. In the same way it is the works of the Holy Spirit, making holy the hearers of the Word, which alone make possible a true understanding of the Word. The Word of revelation is a word of creation, a word of redemption, and also a word of sanctification.

Basil frequently speaks of the scriptural authority of Christian preaching in the introduction to his sermons. In the sixth sermon, on the creation of the lights of the heavens, our preacher begins his sermon by eliciting the active participation of his congregation in listening to the Word of God:

Because, since we are proposing to examine the structure of the world and to contemplate the whole universe, beginning, not from the wisdom

98. Basil, *Hexaemeron* 1.1.

47

of the world, but from what God taught His servant when He spoke to him in person and without riddles, it is absolutely necessary that those who are fond of great shows and wonders should have a mind trained for the consideration of what we propose.[99]

In Christian worship the reading and preaching of the Scriptures is not supposed to be merely a spectator sport, but rather, according to Basil, the whole congregation serves God in listening to his Word. Basil makes a major point in this sermon that God first created light and then the sun, the moon, and the stars. Almost in the same breath our preacher tells us that understanding comes from God, not from embellishment of words and melodiousness of sounds. His point is that a baptized rhetoric finds that "clarity of expression is more precious."[100] Once rhetoric finds the purpose of its existence and begins to exercise the ministry for which it was intended, then it is free to function properly. Basil's implied simile is that just as the sun, the moon, and the stars are ministers of the light, so is rhetoric the minister of the truth. But then Basil points out, just as the apostle teaches us, that there are certain lights in the world, but the light of the world is something else and by participation in it holy preachers become the lights of the souls they teach.[101]

In another place Basil speaks of himself as a minister of the Word.[102] If rhetoric is a minister of the Word, even more is the rhetor a minister of the Word. God has bestowed upon Basil this ministry, and it is through this ministry of the Word that the congregation is fed with spiritual food. For Basil there is obviously a very close relation between the Word of God which created the heavens and the earth and the Word of God as revelation. At the beginning of the last sermon of the series, Sermon 9, Basil tells us of the abiding nature of God's Word.

> (2) "Let the earth bring forth living creatures; cattle and wild beasts and crawling creatures." Consider the word of God moving through all creation, having begun at that time, active up to the present, and efficacious until the end, even to the consummation of the world. As a ball, when pushed by someone and then meeting with a slope, is borne downward by its own shape and the inclination of the ground and does

99. Basil, *Hexaemeron* 6.1.
100. Basil, *Hexaemeron* 6.2.
101. Basil, *Hexaemeron* 6.2.
102. Basil, *Hexaemeron* 6.11.

not stop before some level surface receives it, so, too, the nature of existing objects, set in motion by one command, passes through creation, without change, by generation and destruction, preserving the succession of the species through resemblance, until it reaches the very end. It begets a horse as the successor of a horse, a lion of a lion, and an eagle of an eagle; and it continues to preserve each of the animals by uninterrupted successions until the consummation of the universe. No length of time causes the specific characteristics of the animals to be corrupted or extinct, but, as if established just recently, nature, ever fresh, moves along with time.[103]

Basil's concept of the Word of God is dynamic. It is a word of creation, a word of redemption, and a word of revelation. It is that word which rhetoric serves, and in so doing achieves its telos. Having spoken of the purpose of Christian oratory as we find it in the work of Basil, let us look at some of the means Basil uses to bring about this end.

b. Schema

Classical rhetoric, as it was taught in the schools of ancient Greece and Rome, gave much attention to the arrangement of a speech. An orderly arrangement of one's thoughts, according to the teaching of rhetoric, was essential to a clear communication of one's thoughts. In its simplest form it was put this way: A well-constructed oration must begin with an *exordium,* or introduction. Having given a fitting introduction, one presents the main material first as *narratio,* or the statement of the *peroratio* proposition that one wants to maintain, then by its *confirmatio,* that is, the arguments in its favor, then by a *refutatio,* or refutation of arguments against it. Having put one's material in this orderly arrangement, one ends the presentation with a *peroratio,* or conclusion. The basically forensic cast of this schema is immediately apparent. This arrangement is best suited to proving one's case in court or attempting to persuade a deliberative assembly to adopt a specific policy or plan of action. The teachers of rhetoric always allowed for the adaptation of this basic schema to specific occasions and even provided special schemata for different genres of oratory. The funeral oration, the festival panegyric, and the congratulatory speech all had distinct schemata. Classical rhetoric offered no distinct schema, understandably, for the Christian sermon.

---

103. Basil, *Hexaemeron* 9.2.

The synagogue had, on the other hand, developed a schema for the expository sermon long before the Church was established, and we find Christian preachers such as Origen following the schema of the expository sermon quite faithfully. There were in fact a number of variations to the sermon schema as it was developed both in the Jewish synagogue and the Christian church.[104] For example, one could go through a passage verse by verse or even word by word, commenting on each as one went along. Or one could stay with one verse, drawing out one thought after another from it. Still another possibility was to start out with a text and then bring to it one parallel passage after another. What we find in Basil's *Hexaemeron* is a meticulous respect for the schema of the expository sermon combined with an appreciation for the value of good arrangement as it was taught by the rhetoricians of antiquity. Basil's introductions and conclusions are short and brilliant, but nevertheless his disposition of material respects the expository function of preaching. His introductions and conclusions never overpower the exposition of Scripture, which is at the center of the sermon. The focus in each sermon is the exposition of the text. Most often Basil moves through the text, although at times he will come back to the same text repeatedly to draw from it a variety of ideas. The picture we get from the nine sermons of the *Hexaemeron* is that Basil is committed to the expository schema as it was developed in the synagogue and the early Church, no matter how much he had learned from the Greek appreciation for schema.

The traditional disposition of the Greek rhetoricians has a distinct movement to it. It is a sort of dialectic. The material is presented, then the arguments are brought to support one's position, and finally the arguments against one's position are refuted. A schema of this sort has much to offer those who devote their sermons to theological disputation. It can make for a very lively presentation, and it can make things very clear, particularly if one is careful to respect the unities of Greek literary composition. The Greek orator was careful to make one point and only one point.

The expository sermon, on the other hand, has a different sort of movement. It is not as dialectical as it is descriptive. The Christian exposi-

---

104. One often calls this sermon schema a *homily*, intending to imply that the literary form is developed to emphasize that a sermon following this schema is a commentary on Scripture. One then distinguishes the homily from the sermon, which is supposed to be simply a religious address. In light of the more traditional use of these words this distinction seems confusing and so it has not been followed.

tor moves through a passage of Scripture, bringing out a variety of different ideas as they are found. This is one of the beautiful things about Basil's *Hexaemeron,* in terms of both the whole composition and each individual sermon. There is a very definite progression as our preacher goes from verse to verse through the text of the creation story, the division of the six days being symbolic of this progression. There is evening and there is morning each day. One is conscious of the movement from day to day as one moves from verse to verse. This movement is typical of the expository sermon. In the sixth sermon, for example, Basil begins with verse 14, "And God said, 'Let there be lights in the firmament of the heavens for the illumination of the earth, to separate day from night'" (Basil uses the text of the Septuagint). This verse, as Basil understands it, makes quite clear that the sun, the moon, and the stars are not deities. Light had already been created and only afterwards were the sun, moon, and stars created. After making this point he moves on to the second half of the verse: "'Let them be for signs and for seasons and for days and years,'" briefly explaining the usefulness of observing the heavens for signs of the weather, but then he quickly launches a lengthy attack on astrology. Astrologers misinterpret this verse, he says. The verse is more properly understood, according to our preacher, as a reference to the changing of the seasons. With this Basil presents us with a beautiful passage on how one season follows another according to the movements of the sun through the northern and the southern heavens. Moving on, our preacher takes up verse 16, "And God made the two great lights . . . ," and begins to expatiate on the vastness of the heavens and the wondrous size of the creation. The polemic first against astral deities and then against astrology does not mix very well with the doxological meditation on the wonder of the heavens. From the standpoint of Greek rhetoric this makes for a most problematic sermon outline, but from the standpoint of the Christian expository sermon it is quite acceptable.

As we shall see, Basil was not the only preacher during the golden age of Greek patristic preaching to face this problem of the difference between the schema of Greek oratory and the schema of the expository sermon. The Greek Fathers, at least when it came to expository preaching, maintained rather faithfully the schema of the expository sermon as it had become tradition in both synagogue and church. This is demonstrated again and again by the series of *lectio continua* sermons we have from one Father after another. It was another matter when it came to catechetical preaching and festal preaching, however. In the fourth and fifth centuries theological disputation was very popular — Greek rhetoric had, after all, been developed for public disputation. What could be more natural than for the Christian preacher to use all the arts of persuasion which Greek rhetoric could teach him? With the festal sermon the situation was somewhat the same. Greek rhetoric had developed several forms of festal oratory; these festal orations were called panegyrics. The eulogy was a panegyric delivered at the occasion of someone's death or on the anniversary of someone's death. There were congratulatory speeches for weddings and, above all, panegyrics delivered on holidays and festivals. Again it was only natural that Christian preachers should adopt the Greek rhetorical forms when they celebrated similar occasions. Even if Basil maintained the schema of the expository sermon for his regular preaching, he was quick to adopt the schema of the panegyric for the celebration of saints' days and festivals. Gregory of Nazianzus was even more enthusiastic in his use of the panegyric. There were, however, a number of preachers, like John Chrysostom and Hesychius of Jerusalem, who delivered expository sermons for festivals and saints' days as well.

c. Parallelism

Greek art idealized proportion. One readily recognizes this in Greek architecture and sculpture: The Parthenon was a symphony of proportion, and sculpture was based on an appreciation of the harmony of proportion in the human body. The same thing was true of the art of oratory. A well-delivered speech must have a sense of proportion; that is, it must have balance and symmetry, which one tried to achieve through different kinds of parallelism. The importance of parallelism is surely not unique to Greek literature — it is an important characteristic of Hebrew literature as well, as any student of the Psalms is well aware. The way Greeks worked this parallelism, however, is essential to an appreciation of Greek art prose. Already in the fourth century before Christ Gorgias had emphasized what came to be called the Gorgionic figures: *parison, paromoion,* and *antithesis.* Gorgias did not invent these figures; rather, his emphasis of them made them basic to Greek art prose from his time on. At the heart of these Gorgionic figures is the perception that there is a balance between two or more statements of equal length. The *isocolon* was a series of statements of exactly the same number of syllables, and sometimes an orator tries to achieve balance by this simple but mechanical use of an *isocolon.* One does find several examples of this in Basil's *Hexaemeron:*

> As the beginning of the road is not yet the road, and the beginning of the house, not yet the house, so also, the beginning of time is not yet time.[105]

It was more usually the case, however, that an orator attempted only a more general sort of balance between statements. This balance could be achieved primarily by a similarity of sound and rhythm, or sometimes by a similarity of grammatical structure. Parallelism helped give rhythm to speech, and when ideas were expressed with a pleasing rhythm the listener found it more pleasing to listen. Here is a beautiful passage filled with parallelism:

> And we, whom the Lord, the great Wonder-worker and Craftsman, has called together for a manifestation of His works, shall we become weary in contemplating or reluctant to hear the eloquence of the Spirit? Rather, shall we not, standing around this vast and varied workshop of the divine creation, and going back in thought, each one, to the times past, contemplate the orderly arrangement of the whole? The heavens standing, according to the word of prophecy, like a vaulted chamber; the earth, limitless in magnitude and weight, established upon itself; the diffused air, soft and fluid by nature, providing the proper and uninterrupted sustenance to all creatures that breathe, but yielding and parting around bodies in motion because of its softness, so that it presents no obstacle to moving bodies, since it always easily replaces itself, flowing around to the rear of the objects which cleave it, finally, the element of water, both that which sustains us and is provided for our other needs, and also that orderly gathering of it into the appointed places; all this you will clearly see from the words we have just read.[106]

First, one notices how God is described by parallel adjectives, "Wonder-worker" and "Craftsman." Although not apparent in English translation, in Greek they are quite parallel. One might convey this with a very free translation, "The Lord, the great construction-worker and miracle-worker." Then one notices the parallelism in his rhetorical question, "Shall we become weary in contemplating or reluctant to hear?" and the same sort of parallelism in his answer: "Rather, shall we not, standing around this vast and varied workshop of the divine creation, and going back in thought, . . . to the times past. . . ." Finally there is the larger parallelism

---

105. Basil, *Hexaemeron* 1.6.
106. Basil, *Hexaemeron* 4.1.

which speaks of earth, heaven, air, and water. A considerable amount of variation has been put in this parallelism, but the parallel structures are there, and it is they that give structure to the idea and clarity of the preacher's thought. One can hardly read a passage like this without sensing its beauty, which is appropriate because Basil wants to evoke the beauty of creation. Sensing the beauty of the Creator's handiwork is surely an element of worship. We find this repeatedly in Scripture. The art of this sermon is that the beauty of the sermon evokes the beauty of the creation. Basil has an amazing sense of beauty, the highest sort of beauty, the beauty of holiness.

Parallelism not only helped to achieve a sense of proportion, and therefore a certain beauty, it also was a very helpful means of getting across one's point. In the first sermon Basil wants to speak of the contradictory theories of natural philosophers on the subject of the foundations of the earth. The ideas Basil wants to get across are complicated. The clarity of Basil's thought is certainly helped by the parallelism of these sentences:

> Therefore, I urge you to abandon these questions and not to inquire upon what foundation it stands. *If* you do that, the mind will become dizzy, with the reasoning going on to no definite end. *If* you say that air is spread under the surface of the earth, you will be at a loss as to how its soft and porous nature, pressed down under such a weight, endures and does not slip through in all directions in order to escape from under the sinking weight and flow continuously over that which compresses it. Again, *if* you suppose that water is the substance placed under the earth, even so you will inquire how it is that the heavy and dense body does not pass through the water, but instead, although excelling in weight, is supported by the weaker nature. . . .
>
> (9) *If* you suggest that there is another body heavier than the earth to prevent the earth from going downward you will notice that, that too, needs some like support to keep it from falling down. And, *if* we are able to fashion some support and place it underneath, our mind will seek again the support for that, and thus we shall go on endlessly, always inventing other bases in turn for the bases found. Moreover, the farther we advance in our reasoning, the greater is the supporting force we are compelled to bring in, that will be able to withstand the whole superimposed mass. Set a limit, then, to your thoughts, lest the words of Job should ever censure your curiosity as you scrutinize things incomprehensible, and you also should be asked by him: "Upon what are its bases

grounded?" But, even *if* at some time in the Psalms you hear: "I have established the pillars thereof," believe that the sustaining force is called the pillars. As for the saying: "He hath founded it upon the seas," what else does it signify than that the water is spread around the earth on all sides? Now, how does water, which exists as a fluid and naturally tends to flow downward, remain hanging without support and never flow away? Yet, you do not consider that the earth, suspended by its own power, provides the same or even a greater need for a reason, since it has a heavier nature. Moreover, we must, even *if* we grant that the earth stands by its own power and *if* we say that it rides at anchor on the water, depart in no way from the thought of true religion, but admit that all things are kept under control by the power of the Creator. Therefore, we must say this to ourselves and to those asking us on what this immense and insupportable weight of the earth is propped up: "In the hand of God are all the ends of the earth." This is safest for our own understanding and is most profitable for our hearers.[107]

Here we have a long passage filled with several suggestions to explain what holds up the earth. In Basil's day science could only provide an endless procession of theories, which philosophers discussed interminably. As our preacher sees it, there is no point getting into these endless controversies, but nevertheless he wants to mention a few. By putting these ideas in parallel grammatical framework he helps to maintain clarity. One notices that each of these parallels is introduced by the word "if." The larger parallelism which gives clarity to these diverse ideas is the conditional sentence.

d. Antithesis

Sometimes parallelism is complementary and sometimes it is antithetical. It is often the case that ideas are made clearer by setting them off against their opposites. Greek rhetoric loved antithesis, and the paradoxes of Christian theology only encouraged this love. Antithesis can be achieved in a number of ways. Sometimes the antithesis involves whole paragraphs and sometimes it is contained within a single compound sentence. A simple antithesis is found in the passage in which Basil speaks about trees:

> But, the marvel is that you may find in plants the characteristics closely resembling those of human youth and old age. Around the young and

107. Basil, *Hexaemeron* 1.8-9.

thriving plants the bark is stretched smooth, but around the old it is as if wrinkled and rough.[108]

A more elaborate example is found in a paragraph which shows the antithesis between the wisdom of this world and the wisdom of God:

> Doubtless, their superfluous worldly wisdom will one day make their condemnation more grave because, while they are so keenly aware of vain matters, they have been blinded to the comprehension of the truth. They who measure the distances of the stars and register both those in the north, which are always shining above the horizon, and those which lie about the south pole visible to the eye of man there, but unknown to us; who also divide the northern zone and the zodiac into numberless spaces; who carefully observe the rising of the stars, their fixed positions, their descent, their recurrence, and the length of time in which each of the wandering stars completes its orbit; these men have not found one means from all this either to understand that God is the Creator of everything and the just Judge who gives the deserved reward for the actions of our life, or to acknowledge the idea of a consummation of all things consequent upon the doctrine of judgment, namely that it is necessary for the world to be changed if truly the state of the souls is to change to another form of life. As the present life has a nature akin to this world, so also the future existence of our souls will receive a lot consistent with its state. They, however, are so far from holding to these truths that they laugh broadly at us when we explain about the end of this world and the regeneration of life. Now, since the beginning naturally stands before that which proceeds from it, necessarily in talking about that which has its existence in time he placed this world before all others, saying: "In the beginning he created."[109]

There are, on close reading, several antitheses here. The larger subject is the antithesis between the beginning and the end, but worked into this is the antithesis between the judgment of the wise of this world who ridicule the wisdom of God and the Last Judgment, which will reveal the foolishness of worldly wisdom. The remarkable thing is the way the whole complicated structure of antitheses is kept lucid by parallelism.

It was recognized, of course, that parallelism, if worked out too rigorously, would only lead to monotony, and so the teachers of rhetoric

108. Basil, *Hexaemeron* 5.7.
109. Basil, *Hexaemeron* 1.4.

developed various ways of introducing variety into what was basically a parallel structure. One could use ellipsis, dropping easily understood terms from the parallel. One of the most popular of these variations was *chiasmus*, in which the parallel terms are crisscrossed. In such matters the ingenuity of the Greeks was unsurpassed! There were all kinds of schemes for bringing variety into the parallel structures of well-composed prose. One only begins a list by mentioning *parenthesis, apposition, asyndeton, polysyndeton, alliteration, assonance, anaphora, epistrophe, epanalepsis, anadiplosis,* and *polyptoton.* Here is a paragraph which has a basic parallelism, but which varies that parallelism in a variety of ways:

> (3) "Let the earth bring forth living creatures." Therefore, the soul of brute beasts did not emerge after having been hidden in the earth, but it was called into existence at the time of the command. But, there is only one soul of brute beasts, for, there is one thing that characterizes it, namely, lack of reason. Each of the animals, however, is distinguished by different characteristics. The ox is steadfast, the ass sluggish; the horse burns with desire for the mare; the wolf is untamable and the fox crafty; the deer is timid, the ant industrious; the dog is grateful and constant in friendship. As each animal was created, he brought with him a distinctive characteristic of nature. Courage was brought forth with the lion, also the tendency to a solitary life and an unsocial attitude toward those of his kind. Like a sort of tyrant of brute beasts, because of his natural arrogance, he does not admit an equal share of honor for the many. By no means does he accept yesterday's food or return to the remains of his prey. In him, also, nature has placed such powerful organs of voice that frequently many animals that surpass him in swiftness are overcome by his mere roaring. The leopard is violent and impetuous in attack. He has a body fitted for agility and lightness in accord with the movements of his spirit. The nature of the bear is sluggish and his ways peculiar to himself, treacherous and deeply secretive. He has been clothed with a body of the same type, heavy, compact, not distinctly articulated, truly fit for chilly hibernating in caves.[110]

One finds ellipsis in this list of the characteristics of animals: "The ox is steadfast, the ass sluggish." To avoid the monotony of the simple list the verb is simply left out. Then a phrase later the same thing is done, "The wolf is untamable and the fox crafty." Then with a bit of *chiasmus* the

110. Basil, *Hexaemeron* 9.3.

sentence order is crisscrossed, "Courage was brought forth with the lion." Some animals are characterized by a single word, "The deer is timid," while others are characterized by a whole cluster of adjectives — the bear is sluggish, treacherous, secretive, heavy, and compact. The variety with which these characteristics are listed is truly ingenious.

In recent times one has thought that a rich vocabulary should be avoided in the pulpit, but Basil's *Hexaemeron* is a beautiful example of how effective unusual, exotic, and even technical words can be. He seems to have ransacked the manuals of botanists, astronomers, geographers, and zoologists in preparation for this sermon:

> (2) "Let the waters bring forth crawling creatures of different kinds that have life." God orders the firstlings of each kind to be brought forth, seeds, as it were, for nature; and their numbers are controlled by successive progeny, whenever they must increase and become numerous. Of one kind are those which are called testaceans, such as mussels, scallops, sea snails, conchs, and numberless varieties of bivalves. Again, another kind besides these are the fish named crustaceans: crayfish, crabs, and all similar to them. Still another kind are the so-called soft fish, whose flesh is tender and loose: polyps, cuttlefish, and those like them. And among these, again, there are innumerable varieties. In fact, there are weevers, and lampreys, and eels, which are produced in the muddy rivers and swamps, and which resemble in their nature venomous animals more than fish. Another class is that of ovipara, and another, that of vivipara. The sharks and the dogfish and, in general, the cartilaginous fish are vivipara. And of the cetaceans the majority are vivipara, as dolphins and seals; these are said to readmit and hide in their belly the cubs, while still young, whenever they have for some reason or other been startled. "Let the waters bring forth the different kinds." The cetacean is one kind, and the tiny fish is another. Again, among the fish numberless varieties are distinguished according to species. Since their peculiar names and different food and form and size and qualities of flesh, all differ with the greatest variations from each other, the fish are placed in various classes. Now, what men who watch for tunneys are able to enumerate for us the varieties of its species? And yet, they say that they report even the number of fish in the great schools. Who of those who have grown old around the shores and beaches is able to acquaint us accurately with the history of all fishes?[111]

111. Basil, *Hexaemeron* 7.2.

Basil's sermons on the six days of creation have an architectural quality to them. This is found in both the symmetry of their form and the ingenuity of their interpretation of Scripture. Part of their beauty is that this symmetry is not merely the invention of the preacher. He discovers for us the symmetry of the six days, the manifold order of orders inherent in the work of the logos. Basil's parallelism is an order that bears witness to an even greater order.

e. Metaphor

Far from being mere word tricks, the tropes of classical rhetoric are the inevitable consequence of a creation endowed by its creator with meaning. "The heavens declare the glory of God, and the firmament proclaims his handiwork" (Ps. 19:1). The works of creation are witnesses to God's majesty and have both a doxological and a didactic function. Creation itself is metaphoric and parabolic. Things seen speak of things unseen. The natural order intimates the moral order. Basil finds moral lessons in everything from the movement of the stars to the instincts of animals. Basil did this, of course, to follow not only the teachings of Greek rhetoric but every bit as much the example of the prophets and psalmodists of the Old Testament as well as the apostles and, to be sure, Jesus himself. Scripture is filled with parable and metaphor.

Basil obviously understood the difference between *metaphor, simile, metonymy, synecdoche,* and *periphrasis.* He used all these figures with a constant eye to making his discourse vivacious and beautiful, yes, but even more, thought provoking. Basil's *Hexaemeron* is a treasure house of tropes. For example, speaking of the Greek cosmologists and their ideas on how the world came into being, we find this metaphor:

> Truly, it is a spider's web that these writers weave, who suggest such weak and unsubstantial beginnings of the heavens and earth and sea.[112]

A few sentences later we find a simile. Basil makes the point that the Creator did not exhaust himself in the work of creation:

> In fact, as the potter, although he has formed innumerable vessels by the same art, has exhausted neither his art nor his power, so also the

---

112. Basil, *Hexaemeron* 1.2.

Creator of the universe, possessing creative power not commensurate with one world, but infinitely greater, by the weight of His will alone brought the mighty creations of the visible world into existence.[113]

In the fifth sermon, speaking of the newly shaped earth putting forth its covering of vegetation, Basil says:

> the earth, chilled and barren, was . . . stirred up to productiveness, as if it had thrown aside some dark and dismal covering, had put on a more brilliant one, and, glorying in its own adornment, was presenting an infinite variety of growing plants.[114]

In the conclusion of this same sermon we find an artful combination of metaphor, simile, and metonymy. Basil tells us how the command "Let the earth bring forth" immediately produced

> an elaborate system which brought to perfection more swiftly than our thought the countless properties of plants. That command, which even yet is inherent in the earth, impels it in the course of each year to exert all power it has for the generation of herbs, seeds, and trees. For, as tops, from the first impulse given to them, produce successive whirls when they are spun, so also the order of nature, having received its beginning from that first command continues to all time thereafter, until it shall reach the common consummation of all things. Let all of us hasten, full of fruit and good works to this, in order that, planted in the house of the Lord, we may flourish in the courts of our God, in Christ Jesus our Lord, to whom be glory and power forever. Amen.[115]

The simile of how a child's top is like the creative work of God is then followed by an example of metonymy, the reference to the virtues of the Christian life as fruit. This is, to be sure, a very biblical figure (John 16 and Galatians 5) and is, in turn, followed by an equally biblical metaphor, "in order that, planted in the house of the Lord, we may flourish in the courts of our God." The whole thing, of course, is packed into an implied parable which sees in the fertility of plant life an admonition to Christian virtue.

One more thing needs to be said about Basil's *Hexaemeron*. It is surely one of the greatest series of sermons ever preached in the history of

113. Basil, *Hexaemeron* 1.2.
114. Basil, *Hexaemeron* 5.2.
115. Basil, *Hexaemeron* 5.10.

Christian worship, and yet it has a most obvious flaw: There should have been a final sermon devoted to the sixth day of creation, the day on which Adam and Eve were made. Somehow in the middle of the eighth sermon Basil realized he had left out the creation of the birds. He stopped for a moment and suddenly decided to change directions and began to speak of the creation of birds. How it happened that he left out the birds we don't know — he had obviously prepared quite a bit of material on the subject. Unfortunately the improvisation threw off his overall plan. Coming to the end of Sermon 9, he realized he was never going to do justice to the sixth day, so he made a few remarks on the subject, but the series was never completed. Like the missing arm of many a Greek statue, there is here an inexplicable flaw to an otherwise perfect work of Christian art.

And yet, this flaw tips us off to the whole character of patristic preaching. The question is why Basil published it just as his stenographer took it down. Why did he not patch it up before publishing it? And the answer is, because Basil realized that a sermon is an event rather than a document. The stenographer had recorded the event, but for him to rewrite the sermon for publication would have falsified the whole nature of oratory. It would no longer have been an oration; it would have become literature. Basil had a keen perception of the nature of the art of oratory. His study of rhetoric had made him abundantly aware that something is lost when a sermon is put down on paper and read as a manuscript. Part of the essence of a sermon is the spontaneous character of true oratory.

B. Gregory of Nazianzus

History has honored Gregory of Nazianzus (ca. 330–ca. 389) as the Christian Demosthenes.[116] The title is indeed apt, for he was an orator in the Greek style. The Greek Church particularly has venerated him as their great orator. Sometime after his death, a selection of his orations was put together which has come down to us almost as the canon of pulpit

116. For biographical information on Gregory of Nazianzus, see von Campenhausen, *Griechische Kirchenväter*, pp. 101-13; Paul Gallay, *La vie de S. Grégoire de Nazianze* (Lyon and Paris: E. Vitte, 1943); H. Leclercq, "Grégoire de Nazianze," in *Dictionnaire d'archaeologie chretiénne et de liturgie*, 15 vols. (Paris: Letouzey et Ane, 1907-53), VI/2:1667-1711; Friedhelm Lefherz, *Studien zu Gregor von Nazianz* (Bonn: Rheinische Friedrich Wilhelms-Universität, 1958); and Jean Plagnieux, *Saint Grégoire de Nazianze Theologien* (Paris: Éditions franciscaines, 1952).

eloquence. That these sermons have historically been referred to not as sermons but as orations surely has more than passing significance. The sermons selected for this collection were sermons for great occasions, which is what one would expect of a collection designed to show Gregory as the Christian Demosthenes. It belonged to the ethos of classical oratory that great speeches were born of great occasions. Unfortunately, we get no idea of how Gregory preached on an ordinary Lord's Day, and no series of expository sermons such as we have for Basil and Gregory of Nyssa has come down to us. The collection contains panegyrics in memory of the great Athanasius and the martyrs of the Eastern Church, funeral orations for members of his family, and a panegyric for his friend Saint Basil. There are sermons for the feast days of Christmas, Epiphany, Easter, and Pentecost. Finally there are the five Theological Orations.

1. The Theological Orations

The five Theological Orations are his most celebrated series of sermons.[117] Even more than outstanding oratory, these sermons have come to be loved as outstanding theology. They form one of the classical statements of Nicene orthodoxy. One thing that makes them interesting is that they are by no means academic, ivory tower theology. They are rather prophetic theology. As Gregory began his ministry, Christian theology was in confusion.[118] In the sixties and seventies of the fourth century Arianism struck the Church in full force. Unlike the great Constantine, so unswerving in his support of orthodox Christianity, the emperors of the sixties and seventies were theologically unstable. Julian, whom Gregory knew personally from their college days in Athens, reverted to paganism, and ever since has been known as Julian the Apostate. Valens was an open supporter of Arianism. Many of the leading bishops of the East had sided with the

117. The text used as the basis of this study is that of Paul Gallay: Gregory of Nazianzus, *Discours 27-31 (Discours théologiques)*, introduction, critical text, French translation, and notes by Paul Gallay, Sources chrétiennes, vol. 250 (Paris: Les Éditions du Cerf, 1978). English quotations are taken from the edition of Charles Gordon Browne and James Edward Swallow in the Nicene and Post-Nicene Fathers, 2nd ser., 7:280-328.

118. On the theological discussion in the last half of the fourth century, see Hans Lietzmann, *A History of the Early Church*, trans. Bertram Lee Woolf, 4 vols. (Cleveland: World Publishing Co., 1961), 4:35-49; and Jaroslav Pelikan, *The Emergence of the Catholic Tradition (100-600)* (Chicago and London: University of Chicago Press, 1971), pp. 200-225.

Arians or were at least willing to tolerate their views or make compromises in their direction. Even the bishop of Constantinople was an avowed Arian. While Rome and Alexandria stood solidly with Nicene orthodoxy, Antioch was racked with schism. It was a day when theological debate was popular; everyone knew the arguments of both the Arians and the orthodox. As Gregory himself laments in his introduction to the first sermon of the series, the arguments of the Arians were discussed everywhere from the kitchen to the barbershop. Gregory of Nazianzus began his theological career in the midst of this theological confusion, both as his father's assistant in the church of Nazianzus and in his long periods of monastic retreat with his two friends Basil of Caesarea and Gregory of Nyssa. Our great orator had been thinking about these theological issues for years before he finally mounted the pulpit of the Church of the Anastasia in Constantinople and in the course of five sermons gave one of the classic statements of the doctrine of the Trinity.

Gregory of Nazianzus came to Constantinople at a crucial moment in the history of theology. Two generations before, Constantine had made Constantinople the capital of his Christian empire. In 325 he called the first ecumenical council to meet in the nearby city of Nicaea, which at that time was in the heart of the most thoroughly Christianized region of the empire. The Council of Nicaea had established a thoroughly catholic Christology against the Neoplatonizing influences of Arianism. Unfortunately, several of Constantine's successors did not maintain his thoroughly orthodox position in church affairs any better than they maintained his vigorous civil authority or his military prowess. Finally Emperor Valens, who during his reign actively supported Arianism, came to his end at the disastrous defeat at Adrianople on 9 August 379. Gratian, in the weeks that followed, adopting a more lenient position toward the supporters of Nicene orthodoxy, allowed for a pastor to shepherd the orthodox minority in the capital city, and it was Gregory whom Basil and Melitius of Antioch, the leading orthodox bishops of the area, sent to represent their position at Constantinople. Sometime before the end of 379 Gregory was installed in the Church of the Anastasia, just outside the walls of the Capitol, in spite of the protests of Demophibes, the Arian archbishop of Constantinople. Like Amos in the king's sanctuary at Bethel, Gregory of Nazianzus became the prophet of Nicene orthodoxy at the imperial court.

Theological as they may be — yes, even doctrinal as they may be — the five Theological Orations of Gregory of Nazianzus are prophetic sermons because, like the sermons of the ancient prophets, they challenge God's people to new forms of obedience. Prophets are sent to those who ought to know; they are sent to those who have fallen away. Amos was sent to Israelites who had adopted Canaanite ways of worship, and Jeremiah to a Judah which had taken to worshiping idols. Gregory of Nazianzus was sent to the capital of a Christian empire which had begun to confuse the essential affirmations of Christian faith with the philosophies of ancient Greece. The essential error of Arianism was that it tried to explain the person and work of Christ as though the Christ were a Neoplatonic emanation from the divine. Arianism would explain the Christ as an intermediary between God and man who was neither fully God nor fully man. It had disastrous effects on Christian morality because the Arian Christ had become a Greek semidivine hero and was no longer a true example of what human beings could in fact be, and it had a disastrous effect on Christian theology because if Jesus was not really God, then there is nothing so very radical about God's love, who himself goes into the valley of the shadow of death to find the lost sheep. If the Son of God is not really God, then God did not really so love the world by offering up his only-begotten Son. It was Gregory's prophetic burden to reaffirm over against a revived pagan philosophy these fundamental Christian teachings.

The first of Gregory's Theological Orations sets out the methodology of theological discussion. Theological discussion must realize its limits, he tells us. The subjects to be discussed here are not to be bantered about in the marketplace or at dinner parties. Theological discussion must be entered upon with reverence by those who have meditated long on the subject and carried on with a sense of the limitations of human reason. For our contemporary sensitivities, it may be a bit of a surprise that Gregory so obviously considers that the place for theological discussion is in the pulpit and in the course of worship, but that is certainly the implication of what is said. After all, what greater function can the liturgy serve than to enthrone the divine Wisdom.

The second oration takes up the subject of our knowledge of God's existence. The whole spirit of the sermon is typified by the fact that it begins by invoking the illumination of the Father, the Son, and the Holy Spirit. Gregory both recognizes the limitations of human reason and affirms its value. "Thus reason that proceeds from God, that is implanted in all from the beginning and is the first law in us, and is bound up in all, leads us up to God through visible things."[119] Then Gregory speaks of Enoch, Noah, Jacob, Elijah, Isaiah, and Ezekiel and the intimations of

119. Gregory of Nazianzus, *Oration XXVIII* 16.

the knowledge of God which they had.[120] Even the apostle Paul, who was lifted up to the third heaven, tells us only that in this life we see through a glass darkly.[121] He continues to speak of how our knowledge of ourselves and other creatures gives us an intimation of God. We have to speak of those things which are visible to us and of which we have experience, even if they are not completely adequate. That is all we can do. From these things we get an intimation of the knowledge of God. He recalls the words of Job, who stood in awe before the wonders of God and confessed how little he knew of God.[122] The point Gregory obviously wants to make is that a reverent reason may assure us of God's existence even if it cannot really comprehend God, but if we are to go further in our knowledge we must be led by faith.[123] The spirit of the sermon emanates from that key text of the Wisdom theology, "The fear of the Lord is the beginning of wisdom and the knowledge of the holy is understanding." Doctrine and worship are held firmly together.

The third theological oration begins with a brief statement of the faith of the Church. It is the divine monarchy which the Church would proclaim against the teaching of Greek philosophy.

> It is, however, a monarchy that is not limited to one person, for it is possible for unity if at variance with itself to come into a condition of plurality; but one that is made of an equality of nature, and a union of mind, and an identity of motion, and a convergence of its elements to unity — a thing which is impossible to the created nature — so that though numerically distinct there is no severance of essence. Therefore unity, having from all eternity arrived by motion at duality, found its rest in trinity. This is what we mean by Father and Son and Holy Ghost. The Father is the begettor and the emitter. . . . The Son is the begotten, and the Holy Ghost the emission.[124]

The heart of Gregory's presentation is to make clear the unity of the three persons in their being alike eternal, powerful, and glorious. It is this which is the divine essence. The three persons differ from each other in that the Father is unbegotten, the Son begotten, and the Holy Spirit proceeds.

120. Gregory of Nazianzus, *Oration XXVIII* 18-19.
121. Gregory of Nazianzus, *Oration XXVIII* 20.
122. Gregory of Nazianzus, *Oration XXVIII* 28.
123. Gregory of Nazianzus, *Oration XXVIII* 28.
124. Gregory of Nazianzus, *Oration XXIX* 2.

These words have their meaning only as they express the relationships of the persons of the Trinity. The Father is the Father in an absolute sense. He is not also the son of some other father, nor does the Son become father of another son as is the case with human beings.[125] To be begotten or unbegotten is not the divine essence, not even a divine action, but the relation in which the Father stands to the Son and the Son to the Father.[126]

In the fourth oration we find a refutation of the Arian objections against Christ's divinity. Following the schema of classical rhetoric, our Christian orator develops his *refutatio*. Gregory takes up ten passages of Scripture which the Arians had called upon to show that Christ was not completely divine and in each case shows the Arians to have misunderstood the Scriptures. Having done away with the Arian proof texts, he takes up the names Scripture attributes to Christ and shows how they make clear his full divinity and full humanity.

The fifth oration concerns the Holy Spirit.[127] Gregory is very specific in making clear that the Holy Spirit is God just as the Father is God and just as the Son is God. "But we have so much confidence in the deity of the Spirit whom we adore, that we will begin his teaching concerning his Godhead by fitting to him the names which belong to the Trinity."[128] Just as it is correct to say both of the Father and of the Son that they were the true light which enlightens everyone who comes into the world, so it is correct to say the same of the Holy Spirit. There is one light and one God. And when David in Psalm 36:9 tells us, "In thy light we see light," we understand this in a trinitarian sense. It is in the light which is the Holy Spirit that we perceive the light who is the Son who is light of light, the Father.[129] Gregory tells us that just as the Son is distinct from the Father in that he is begotten, so the Holy Spirit is distinct in that he proceeds. The relation of the Spirit to the Father is not the same as the relation of the Son to the Father, as though the Holy Spirit were a second son or even a grandson. It is altogether a different relation. The Father sends the Holy Spirit and the Holy Spirit proceeds from the Father. The key passage for Gregory's understanding of the Holy Spirit is obviously John 15:26, " 'But

---

125. Gregory of Nazianzus, *Oration XXIX* 5.

126. Gregory of Nazianzus, *Oration XXIX* 16.

127. On the doctrine of the Holy Spirit in the late fourth century, see Pelikan, *Emergence of the Catholic Tradition*, pp. 211ff.

128. Gregory of Nazianzus, *Oration XXXI* 3.

129. Gregory of Nazianzus, *Oration XXXI* 3.

when the Counselor comes, whom I shall send you from the Father, even the Spirit of truth, who proceeds from the Father, he will bear witness to me.'"[130] Gregory admits that Scripture does not have as much to say about the doctrine of the Holy Spirit as we might wish, and yet for Gregory there is sufficient clarity that we can confess the Holy Spirit to be truly God. This he shows by drawing out what Scripture has to say about the works of the Spirit and the names given to the Holy Spirit.

Today even a well-trained theologian has to struggle over these sermons to understand them. One wonders how a congregation could possibly have understood them. Yet it was these sermons that won over the courtiers, the bureaucrats, and the church people of Constantinople. How was it that these sermons were so well received? For one thing, Gregory was speaking to a subject which was indeed spoken of from kitchen to marketplace, from dinner party to barbershop. Everyone knew the vocabulary of the discussion; everyone had the technical terms nailed down and knew just which proof texts were used by each side. When we read these sermons today, chances are we are not nearly as conversant on the subject as those who sat under Gregory's pulpit. Because they were so familiar with the subject, the words flowed into their ears much more smoothly. Surely this is the case, but this is not what interests us most.

What interests us much more is the way Gregory used classical Greek rhetoric to drive home rather complicated theological reasoning. It was for this reason that Greek rhetoric was born. Literary historians tell us that classical rhetoric goes back to the Greek colonies of Sicily where lawyers began to study ways of making complicated legal arguments clear to the judges and juries of the courts. Gorgionic rhetoric was particularly dedicated, even in the days of Gregory of Nazianzus, to the purpose of making one's point in court. It was forensic rhetoric, and this was the rhetoric Gregory used in these sermons. Unfortunately, not all these rhetorical forms come through in translation. Those who understand such things tell us that if we had heard these sermons preached in Greek and if we had been educated, as undoubtedly many of those who heard these sermons were, the words of Gregory would have dropped into our minds like gentle rain. These five Theological Orations are filled with parallel structures, carefully planned cadences and rhythms, rhymes and alliterations. So much of Greek rhetoric depended on sound and on timing; through movement and changes of mood the orator kept his audience

130. Gregory of Nazianzus, *Oration XXXI* 8.

spellbound. How cleverly Gregory uses rhetorical questions, irony, and invective. But then no sooner does Gregory deliver the Arians into the hands of the most cynical sarcasm than he mounts to the heavens in mystical rapture. Indeed, Gregory was a great orator. And the Greeks of Constantinople loved oratory, as much as they loved sports events and the theater. They understood all these rhetorical figures and would applaud even a preacher for a brilliant play, a deft bit of irony, or a sparkling word picture.

Gregory used the literary forms of forensic rhetoric for more than simply pragmatic reasons. Certainly, he knew that the Greek rhetors had mastered the techniques of communicating a complicated argument, but he also knew his congregation loved oratory and would probably be more receptive to a discourse in the style of courtroom oratory than in the form of a biblical sermon. No doubt Gregory remembered that the prophets before him often presented their messages in dramatic and unconventional forms. Isaiah's first oracle, for example, adopts the form of courtroom address. The five Theological Orations are far removed from the literary form of the biblical, expository sermon. There is no hint at a text in any of them, and we have no clue as to what might have been read as Scripture lessons before any of the sermons. Certainly none of the sermons is an attempt at explaining a passage of Scripture. The Scriptures are often mentioned and many passages are alluded to, but it is almost as though the Scriptures are admitted as witnesses to Gregory's courtroom. Surely they appear as the most important witnesses, but they are not the subject of the inquest. The subject is the faith, the faith of Nicaea.

But let us return to the subject we are discussing. Why were these sermons so convincing? Was it all a matter of rhetoric? Surely not! The rhetoric was only a means of getting the message across. Those who have studied all this very thoroughly assure us that Gregory's use of rhetoric was restrained, and that of course was what made it so effective. All the great rhetoricians understood that what one really needed for the greatest of oratory was a passion for a great cause. In the end great oratory must rest on great thoughts; great speech can only come from great ideas. That was exactly what made these sermons so fascinating to those who heard them. They are a magnificent presentation of the orthodox doctrine of the Trinity and a brilliant refutation of the Arian position. It was this that reconverted Constantinople and paved the way a year later for the calling of the Council of Constantinople, which finally formulated the doctrine of the Trinity as we know it today.

There are those, to be sure, who insist that the victory of the orthodox doctrine of the Trinity and of catholic Christology was really a matter of politics or, as others put it, of the economic forces of society. The reason the Cappadocian Fathers were able to win their case was not that Theodosius was at the gates of Constantinople and had for political reasons decided in favor of orthodoxy. In 381 Theodosius had not yet consolidated his power. On the other hand, these sermons of Gregory's gave orthodoxy a solid platform on which to stand. What made it solid was that it gave the orthodox a doctrine of the Trinity which really did explain the texts of Scripture better than the Arian position. If these sermons are court oratory rather than expository sermons that bring Scripture in merely as a witness, it is in the end the witness of Scripture that won the case.

2. Festal Sermons

With Saint Gregory's sermons for the feasts of Christmas, Epiphany, Easter, and Pentecost we find him using a different type of oratory.[131] The sermons we have just looked at were modeled on the oratory of the courtroom; they followed the principles of forensic debate. The sermons to which we now turn are modeled on the classical panegyric. The panegyric was an oration designed to celebrate a Greek feast and was traditionally delivered on religious holidays, on days commemorating the gods or the heroes of the past; its oratorical form was used for celebrations, memorials, funerals, and festivities. In Athens such speeches were delivered at national festivals or games and were supposed to inspire the people to follow the example of the heroes of the past. The great rhetors Gorgias, Lysias, and Isocrates all left classic examples of the form, so it was a natural thing for Gregory to compose panegyrics for the heroes and martyrs of the Church. His sermon honoring his friend Basil, like his sermon honoring Athanasius, the hero of Nicaean orthodoxy, has come down to us bearing the name panegyric. Likewise the festal sermons which have been preserved show the same influence, yet these sermons are something more. We want to look at these sermons from the standpoint not only of their

---

131. The following study is based on the edition of Claudio Mareschini: Gregory of Nazianzus, *Discours 38-41,* introduction, critical text, and notes by Claudio Mareschini, French translation by Paul Gallay, Sources chrétiennes, vol. 358 (Paris: Les Éditions du Cerf, 1990). Quotations are taken from the edition of C. G. Browne and J. F. Swallow in the Nicene and Post-Nicene Fathers, 2nd ser., 7:344ff.

rhetorical form but also of their hermeneutical intention. These sermons were preached in Constantinople at the time Gregory was trying to win the city for the faith of Nicaea. They have an evangelistic dimension.

Gregory's sermon for Christmas Day is regarded as a particularly fine example of Christian oratory. The introduction to the sermon is a brilliant burst of Asiatic rhetoric. He begins with a series of staccato imperatives. "Christ is born, glorify Him. Christ from heaven, go ye out to meet him. Christ on earth; be ye exalted . . . Christ in the flesh, rejoice with trembling and with joy."[132] This is followed by a series of paradoxical affirmations. "He that was without mother became without father. . . . He who was not carnal is become incarnate; the Son of God becomes the Son of Man."[133] After these initial trumpet blasts, Gregory makes a few remarks about the nature of the festival to be celebrated. This Christian festival is not to be celebrated as the Greeks celebrate their festivals, by decorating homes or streets or public places. It is not to be celebrated by a display of sparkling gems or shimmering gold, not with sumptuous feasts or luxurious clothing. But since the object of our rejoicing is the Word, let us make a feast of the Word. Let us rejoice by reading the Scriptures, especially those which have to do with the feast. It is a feast of the Word that Gregory would serve his guests.[134] This is a most interesting remark for our study because it shows us that on feast days such as Christmas, Scripture lessons were chosen which were appropriate for the feast. Yet, strangely enough, this sermon is obviously not based on those readings, and we cannot even discern from it which lessons might have been read for the occasion. The Greek panegyric was not supposed to be an exposition of Scripture. We see in comparison that Melito of Sardis, as much as he may have used Greek rhetoric, still feels obligated to expound the account of the Passover in Exodus in his sermon for Easter.

The main body of the sermon is a recounting of God's plan of salvation. It is done in such a way that the incarnation is the decisive moment in the story. First Gregory speaks of the infinity and incomprehensibility of God, then he expounds the doctrine of the Trinity. From this he goes into the doctrine of creation and tells how eternal goodness moves beyond itself and, pouring itself out, multiplies the objects of its benevolence.[135] He speaks of the creation of man and how man needs a

132. Gregory of Nazianzus, *Oration XXXVIII* 1.
133. Gregory of Nazianzus, *Oration XXXVIII* 2.
134. Gregory of Nazianzus, *Oration XXXVIII* 5.
135. Gregory of Nazianzus, *Oration XXXVIII* 9.

Savior.[136] Our preacher glories in the Savior through a series of honorific titles: He is before all worlds, the Invisible, the Incomprehensible, the Beginning of the Beginning, the Light of Light, the Source of Life and Immortality, the Image of Archetypal Beauty, the Immovable Seal, the Unchangeable who changed himself into that which had been made in his own image. It is this, the very Word of God, who was conceived by the Virgin, who first in body and soul was purified by the Holy Ghost.[137] At length he speaks of the incarnation of the Word and its significance. Using a series of dramatic paradoxes, he expresses his wonder at the incarnation. That which had always existed came into existence; he who was from all eternity was born of a virgin; the Uncreated became a creature; he who is the source of all riches became poor.[138] "He assumes the poverty of my flesh, that I may assume the richness of His Godhead."[139] Gregory then speaks of the humility of Christ, his suffering and his death, all of which was for our salvation. This is carefully put forth in terms of Nicene orthodoxy with careful distinctions on the two natures of Christ. Finally, concluding with the resurrection, Gregory marvels at all the holy mysteries there are in Christ. This long recounting of the plan of salvation is presented in vivid language, filled with the elegant paradoxes, rhetorical questions, hyperbole, periphrasis, and other rhetorical figures so loved by the audiences of his day. For example, at one point he addresses the Arians, "Dost thou at this point deem him lessened, because he girds himself with a towel and washes his disciples' feet and shows that humiliation is the best road to exaltation? . . . Why dost thou not also charge upon Him as a crime the fact that He eats with Publicans and at Publicans' tables, and that He makes disciples of Publicans, that too may gain somewhat . . . and that? . . . the salvation of sinners."[140] With such spice he seasoned the feast of the Word to which he had invited his congregation.

The conclusion of the sermon is a call to faith, the faith of Nicene orthodoxy. This call is given in the biblical imagery of the Christmas story. "Know as Isaiah bids thee, thine Owner, like the ox, and like the ass thy

---

136. Here it is essential that we not get tied up with feminist diction. Feminist diction is entirely too nominalist to express the idea of a culture where realist principles were so deeply imbedded. Whether for Plato or Moses, "man" was very real. Neither "humanity" nor "humankind" translates the thought of the patristic age at this point.

137. Gregory of Nazianzus, *Oration XXXVIII* 13.

138. Gregory of Nazianzus, *Oration XXXVIII* 13.

139. Gregory of Nazianzus, *Oration XXXVIII* 13.

140. Gregory of Nazianzus, *Oration XXXVIII* 14.

Master's crib . . . run with the star and bear thy gifts with the Magi. . . .
With the shepherds glorify Him; with Angels join in chorus; with Archangels sing hymns."[141] Here in this sermon we find the Greek rhetor at
his best, but even more we find the Christian evangelist who presents the
gospel story, that those who hear might believe unto their salvation.

One thing which needs to be pointed out about the sermon is that
in all probability it was the first Christmas sermon preached in Constantinople.[142] Up to this time Constantinople, typical of the Greek-speaking
churches of the East, did not celebrate Christmas on 25 December. For a
generation or so Epiphany, a feast very similar to Christmas, had been
celebrated in the night between 5 and 6 January. The two feasts were
essentially two different approaches to the celebration of the winter solstice.
Christmas had first been celebrated in Rome some fifty years before and
was unknown in the East until this time.[143] For evangelistic reasons
Gregory introduced the celebration of Christmas at Constantinople as an
opportunity to preach orthodox Christology. He saw in the rhetorical form
of the panegyric a perfect vehicle for his purpose.

A few days later for the eve of Epiphany Gregory preached his famous
sermon "On the Holy Lights." Here we find much the same thing. The
introduction links the celebration of Epiphany to Christmas. "Again my
Jesus, and again a mystery not deceitful nor disorderly, nor belonging to
Greek error or drunkenness (for so I call their solemnities, and so I think
will every man of sound sense); but a mystery lofty and divine and allied
to the glory above."[144] Gregory does not want his congregation celebrating
the feast days of the Christian faith as they once had the religious festivals
of paganism, and so our preacher once again wants to distinguish the way
the Greeks celebrated their mysteries from the way Christians should

---

141. Gregory of Nazianzus, *Oration XXXVIII* 17.

142. Paul Gallay in the introduction to the Sources Chrétiennes edition of Gregory
of Nazianzus, *Discours 38-41*, p. 14, traces this opinion to Anton Baumstark. See particularly Bernard Botte, *Les origenes de la Noël et de l'Épiphanie, Études historiques* (Louvain:
Abbaye du Mont César, 1932), pp. 27-28.

143. On the beginnings of the feast of Christmas, see Botte, *Les origenes de Noël et
de l'Épiphanie;* Oscar Cullmann, *Noël dans l'Église ancienne* (Neuchâtel: Delachaux &
Niestlé, 1949); Hieronymus Engberding, "Der 25. Dezember als Tag der Feier der Geburt
des Herrn," *Archiv für Liturgiewissenschaft,* II (1952); Hans Lietzmann, *A History of the
Early Church,* 3:314-22; and Thomas J. Talley, *The Origins of the Liturgical Year* (New York:
Pueblo Publishing Co., 1986), pp. 79-155.

144. Gregory of Nazianzus, *Oration XXXIX* 1.

celebrate the mighty works of redemption. The Christian emphasis should be on sound doctrine and on purity of life. It is from pagan debauchery that Christ has saved us; how can the Christian celebrate this salvation by a return to such impurities? Epiphany is a celebration of the baptism of Christ, the true light who enlightens everyone that comes into the world. This mystery is one of illumination of the mind and purification of life. "Therefore listen to the voice of God. . . . 'I Am the Light of the World.' Therefore approach ye to Him and be enlightened. . . . It is a season of new birth, let us be born again."[145] Again the evangelistic thrust of these festal sermons is clear. The feast of the Epiphany, as Gregory seems to understand it, is a time for evangelism.

Epiphany was a relatively new feast for Christians at the end of the fourth century, even for those in the East.[146] The feast seems to have originated in the East about the beginning of the fourth century; the first celebration that can be documented occurred about 360. This sermon was preached about twenty years later. It must therefore be among the oldest surviving Epiphany sermons to have been preached. Gregory was as much shaping a tradition as he was following one. From the beginning Epiphany was intended as a Christian substitute for a popular pagan feast held on 6 January. The exact nature of the pagan feast is not clear although it was in some way a celebration of the winter solstice. It is therefore quite natural that so much is made of the coming of the light. The earliest Christian observation of Epiphany celebrated the appearance of God in human form. Sometimes it remembered the birth of Christ, sometimes his baptism, and sometimes the beginning of his ministry at Cana. This sermon of Gregory's obviously commemorates the baptism of Christ, and just as obviously celebrates the appearance of Christ, the light of the world.

This introduction contains quite a bit of material regarding the theology of worship. As Gregory understands it, it is the Word both as it is read and as it is preached which in the Christian mysteries enlightens and purifies human life. For Gregory, the term "Christian mysteries" seems to stand for Christian worship in general. It has not yet come simply to mean the sacraments. The preaching of the Word is obviously central to

---

145. Gregory of Nazianzus, *Oration XXXIX* 2.

146. On the beginnings of the feast of the Epiphany, see Botte, *Les origines de la Noël et de l'Épiphanie;* Jean Leclercq, "Aux origines du cycle de Noël," *Ephemerides Liturgicae* 60 (1946): 4-26; and C. Mohrmann, "Epiphania," in *Études sur le latin des Chrétiens* (Rome, 1958).

Christian worship for Gregory. He bids the members of his congregation draw near to the light, to the illuminating Word, that they might become children of the light. "See the grace of this Day; see the power of this mystery. Are you not lifted up from the earth? Are you not clearly placed on high, being exalted by our voice and meditation? And you will be placed much higher when the Word shall have prospered the course of my words."[147]

After this powerful introduction Gregory begins to speak of the shadows of the pagan mysteries. It is interesting that for Origen, several generations before Gregory, the shadows were the shadows of the Law, but here, for Gregory, the shadows are the pagan mysteries. The pagan mysteries are shadows and darkness. Going through a whole list of these mysteries, he intimates the shame and folly of each. It is a fascinating catalogue. Gregory knows all the oratorical tricks for making this ridicule of paganism interesting. But this sermon is also an evangelistic sermon, a familiar feature of which is the polemic against paganism.

Having roundly attacked paganism, Gregory turns to propounding the essentials of Nicene orthodoxy. We have already spoken of the prophetic nature of Gregory's preaching the faith of Nicaea in the city of Constantinople. Now we need to speak of it as evangelistic. Here we have, indeed, both prophetic and evangelistic preaching on the feast of the Epiphany in the year 381, right under the nose of the Arian archbishop of Constantinople. This sermon contains one of Gregory's clearest expositions of the doctrine of the Trinity.[148] For Christians "there is but one God, the Father, of Whom are all things, and One Lord Jesus Christ, by Whom are all things; and one Holy Ghost, in Whom are all things."[149] There is no difference of nature between these three persons; they characterize the personalities of a nature which is one and unconfused. "The Father is Father, and is unoriginate, for He is of no one; the Son is Son, and is not unoriginate, for He is of the Father. . . . The Holy Ghost is truly Spirit, coming forth from the Father indeed, but not after the manner of the Son, for it is not by Generation but by Procession . . . for neither did the Father cease to be unbegotten because of his begetting something, nor the Son to be begotten because He is of the Unbegotten . . . nor is the Spirit changed into Father or Son because He proceeds, or because He is God — . . . There is then One God in Three, and these three are

147. Gregory of Nazianzus, *Oration XXXIX* 2.
148. Gregory of Nazianzus, *Oration XXXIX* 11ff.
149. Gregory of Nazianzus, *Oration XXXIX* 12.

One."[150] This is of the essence of the faith for which he would evangelize the people of Constantinople. All Christian feasts celebrate this central doctrine, Gregory tells us, but this particular feast celebrates also the baptism of Christ. And so our preacher tells the story of Christ's baptism and explains its meaning. At Christmas we celebrated the birth of Christ, but now we come to another celebration, the remembrance of Christ's baptism. This, too, is a mystery of our salvation. "Christ is illumined, let us shine forth with Him. Christ is baptized, let us descend with Him that we may also ascend with Him. Jesus is baptized; but we must attentively consider not only this but also some other points. Who is He, and by whom is He baptized, and at what time? He is the All-pure; and He is baptized by John; and the time is the beginning of his miracles."[151] Gregory elaborates these points, telling us what the Gospel accounts tell us about John the Baptist.[152] Then he turns to the subject of the descent of the dove and the voice from heaven.[153] He enlarges on the subject of the different kinds of baptism found in Scripture.[154] With this our preacher speaks at length about the way baptism washes away sin. This, too, is a classic evangelistic technique. Gregory beckons his unconverted listeners to baptism by making clear the grace that is to be received from the sacrament.

The conclusion of the sermon is an evangelistic appeal to be purified by the ministry of Word and sacrament.

> But let us venerate today the baptism of Christ; and let us keep the feast well, not in pampering the belly, but rejoicing in spirit. And how shall we luxuriate? "Wash you, make you clean." If ye be scarlet with sin and less bloody, be made white as snow; if ye be red, and men bathed in blood, yet be brought to the whiteness of wool. Anyhow be purified, and you shall be clean (for God rejoices in nothing so much as in the amendment and salvation of man, on whose behalf is every discourse and every Sacrament), that you may be like lights in the world, a quickening force to all other men; that you may stand as perfect lights beside that great Light, and may learn the mystery of the illumination of Heaven.[155]

150. Gregory of Nazianzus, *Oration XXXIX* 12.
151. Gregory of Nazianzus, *Oration XXXIX* 14.
152. Gregory of Nazianzus, *Oration XXXIX* 15.
153. Gregory of Nazianzus, *Oration XXXIX* 16.
154. Gregory of Nazianzus, *Oration XXXIX* 17.
155. Gregory of Nazianzus, *Oration XXXIX* 20.

It is the salvation of man in which God rejoices, and when men, women, and children are brought to salvation the feast is truly celebrated. In Gregory's pulpit the feast day has become the time for evangelism.

The "Oration on Holy Baptism" which followed the next morning on Epiphany Day is as much an evangelistic appeal as the sermon for Epiphany Eve. In fact, in this sermon, which is quite lengthy, Gregory urges the unbaptized not to delay their baptism. The delaying of baptism until old age was a common practice at the time, and our preacher comes up with every argument against it he can. One realizes, of course, that those who accepted the offer of baptism would not actually be baptized until Easter some three months hence, but they could, in the first few weeks following Epiphany, have their names inscribed and begin the required catechetical instruction. Gregory was obviously urging people to sign up for the catechetical instruction which would begin in a matter of weeks. No Bible Belt evangelist of our grandparents' day ever argued his hearers into the creek more unrelentingly than Gregory.

The practical evangelistic concern of these sermons to get people to sign up for baptism must not distract us, however, from noticing how Gregory finds in them an opportunity to press home the centrality of Nicene orthodoxy to genuine Christian faith. That in Jesus Christ we have an epiphany of God himself is an obvious argument against Arianism. Gregory is emphasizing the feasts of Christmas and Epiphany for strategic reasons. He sees it as a convenient weapon not only against paganism but against Arianism as well.

Let us turn now to a panegyric for the celebration of Easter. An Easter sermon preached in the last year of Gregory's active ministry gives us a splendid example of classical oratory in the service of the gospel. The sermon is very long, but it is filled with homiletical fireworks which must have kept the attention of his congregation down to the final sentence.

Immediately a note of drama is struck when our preacher tells his congregation that he intends to take his stand on the watchtower beside Habakkuk.[156] He, too, enlightened by the Holy Spirit, will scan the horizon to see what the future will bring. And, behold, he sees a man riding on the clouds. He is exalted and brilliant of countenance. He lifts his hand toward the east and cries with a loud voice. His voice is like a trumpet, and round about him is a multitude of heavenly host. Today, he proclaims, salvation is come to the world. Christ is risen from the dead;

156. Gregory of Nazianzus, *Oration XLV* 1.

let us rise with him. Christ is released from the tomb; let us be freed from the bonds of sin. The gates of hell are opened and death is destroyed. Then the heavenly hosts surrounding this brilliant messenger respond to his proclamation just as they did at the birth of Christ: "Glory to God in the highest, peace on earth, good will toward men." This is the Easter gospel Gregory would himself proclaim to his congregation.

After these stirring lines our preacher makes a few remarks about the celebration of Easter. In the first place it is the greatest of Christian feasts. According to Gregory, the proclamation of the gospel of the resurrection on Easter morning is at the heart of the celebration. It is even more important than the Easter vigil which had been celebrated with such dazzling illumination the night before. What our preacher wants to do at the Easter morning service is to make the appropriate sacrifice for Easter morning, and that sacrifice is nothing less than offering the fruit of the lips. When God created man he bestowed on him the gift of thinking, the gift of intelligent speech.[157] This is therefore the greatest offering which intelligent creatures can offer.[158] Apparently Gregory of Nazianzus had the highest appreciation of the preaching office. The idea that the ministry of the Word is a sacrifice specially acceptable to God is an idea firmly imbedded in Scripture, to be sure, but from this sermon we find quite clearly that the patristic period had in no way lost sight of it. At the conclusion of the sermon Gregory returns to this idea in an even more striking way. Addressing Christ as the Holy Passover, he offers his sermon to him as his festal worship.

The body of the sermon is a long recital of the history of redemption which begins with an explanation of the purposes of God in creating man as an intelligent being made in his image with the possibility of having communion with his Creator. Much of this is couched in the language of Greek philosophy. Much is said about the perfections of God on one hand and human fallibility on the other. The highly developed trinitarian doctrines of the Cappadocians are much in evidence as Gregory begins to mount to a climax in his exposition of the doctrine of the incarnation.[159]

Having reached his dazzling presentation of the doctrine of the incarnation, Gregory falls back to something a bit more traditional. He speaks of the derivation of the word *pascha* and the way different people

157. Gregory of Nazianzus, *Oration XLV* 2.
158. Gregory of Nazianzus, *Oration XLV* 2.
159. Gregory of Nazianzus, *Oration XLV* 3-9.

have understood it.[160] The Greeks have made a pun of it and have understood it as though it were the Greek word meaning suffering or passion. Originally *pascha* was the Hebrew word for Passover. With this Gregory turns to a discussion of the shadows of the Law, in this case, the ceremonial of the feast of Passover. This is, of course, central to the preaching of the Christian celebration of Passover. Explaining the Passover typology has been one of the most prominent features of the Easter sermon throughout the history of Christian preaching. Our preacher explains the significance of the Passover feast being held at night. The night is the primeval darkness in which all things come into being and chaos is brought to order. He goes on to treat the way the children of Israel fled from Egypt, the land of sin where Satan is the tyrant and Pharaoh rules over our lives. Gregory tells of the significance of the blood sprinkled on the lintels and doorposts of the houses, which is a type of the Christian life sealed by the precious blood of the Lamb.[161] Then he points out the typological significance of the requirement found in the Law of Moses that not a bone of the Passover lamb was to be broken.[162] And he explains the requirement that the Passover be eaten in haste, that it be eaten with bitter herbs and unleavened bread with shoes on the feet and staff in hand.[163] All of this was traditional Christian material which had been explained in Christian sermons every Passover for a good three hundred years. What is different here is the almost epigrammatic way in which it is recounted. The preacher realizes everyone knows all this material, so he recounts it very rapidly, suggesting more than he actually says. He helps us to recall material we already know, but he puts it in a very clever way so that the listener finds it new and interesting. Gradually the intensity of the sermon increases as our preacher uses the types of the Law to speak of the death and resurrection of Christ.[164] With the suffering of the Lamb of God the history of redemption comes to its climax. The Lamb that was slain is now highly exalted. The price of our redemption has been paid. Christ is risen from the dead. We are free to make the passage and enter the land of promise. Having recounted this triumphal story, Gregory delivers his invitation to receive Christ as Savior of the world at the Easter Communion. Let us

160. Gregory of Nazianzus, *Oration XLV* 10.
161. Gregory of Nazianzus, *Oration XLV* 15.
162. Gregory of Nazianzus, *Oration XLV* 16.
163. Gregory of Nazianzus, *Oration XLV* 17-19.
164. Gregory of Nazianzus, *Oration XLV* 13-22.

keep this feast by offering ourselves to Christ.[165] This Christian Passover is still to be received in types and signs, clearer than the types and signs of the Jewish Passover certainly, but they are still types. Gregory calls everyone to take part, whether one is a Simon of Cyrene, a thief on the cross, a Nicodemus, a Mary Magdalene, or a fallen apostle like Peter.[166] Here is a very classical Easter sermon. It tells how Jesus kept the feast of Passover by fulfilling the paschal ceremonial in his sacrifice on the cross. It announces that the passage has been made from this world to the Father and invites us all to follow. One is struck by the similarity between this invitation and the invitation of John Calvin found in his sermons for the week before Easter. Both Gregory of Nazianzus and Calvin see the invitation to Easter Communion in terms of evangelism.

Let us look at one more of Gregory's festal sermons. The sermon for the feast of Pentecost which has survived is supposed to have been preached in May 381, the same year as the Council of Constantinople. It was at that council that the definitions of the doctrine of the Holy Spirit were added to the creed. These definitions tell us that the Holy Spirit is "the Lord and Giver of Life, who proceedeth from the Father, who with the Father and the Son together is worshipped and glorified, who spoke by the prophets." The year 381 was, then, a particularly important year for the development of the doctrine of the Holy Spirit, and it is interesting to see just what was included in a sermon on the feast of Pentecost by a theologian who was particularly influential at this council.[167]

Once again the introduction to the sermon contains some significant words on how Christians should celebrate their feasts. "Let us reason a little about the Festival, that we may keep it spiritually. For different persons have different ways of keeping Festival; but to the worshippers of the Word a discourse seems best."[168] Gregory urges his congregation to maintain a spiritual celebration of the feast of the Spirit and suggests that the spiritual way of worshiping the Word is by listening to the preaching of the Word. What a striking statement of the Wisdom theology and its approach to worship! As we shall see, this sermon was well known to the

---

165. Gregory of Nazianzus, *Oration XLV* 23.

166. Gregory of Nazianzus, *Oration XLV* 24.

167. There is some discussion as to just when these points were added to the creed. On what actually happened at the Council of Constantinople, see Kelly, *Early Christian Creeds*.

168. Gregory of Nazianzus, *Oration XLI* 1.

Reformers in the sixteenth century and had a considerable influence in shaping the various Protestant calendars.

The body of the sermon is very theological for the most part. Gregory figures that this is an important opportunity to make clear to the orthodox of Constantinople the role of the Holy Spirit in the doctrine of the Trinity. Once again Gregory employs the festal sermon, clothed in the elegant rhetorical form of the panegyric, to contend for Nicene orthodoxy as it was understood by the Cappadocian Fathers and formulated by the Council of Constantinople in 381. Even at that, our preacher feels obligated at least to touch on some of the biblical themes of the feast of Pentecost. One of these themes goes back to the Jewish celebration of the feast of weeks where the fiftieth day marked the completion of the week of weeks. The Jews often called Pentecost the feast of weeks, and in the Old Testament it is the most common name for the feast (Exod. 34:22; Num. 28:26; Deut. 16:10). Sabbatarian speculation was much beloved by the ancient Jews. The ancient Church was very fond of it as well, as is evident both from the resurrection stories in the Gospels and from the book of Revelation. In this sermon Gregory catalogues the blessings which Scripture records in connection with the number seven. One is delighted with the prolixity and ingenuity of our preacher's list.[169]

But having acquitted himself of this very biblical theme, our preacher begins to present his somewhat philosophical arguments for the full divinity of the Holy Spirit.[170] As Gregory sees it, the Holy Spirit must be eternal just as the Father and the Son are eternal, for it is inconceivable that either the Father or the Son be without the Spirit, just as it is inconceivable that the Father be without the Son. If at the beginning he has no Son, then how could he have been the Father, but as it is he is the eternal Father. In the same way it is inconceivable that either the Father or the Son be without the Spirit, for the Spirit is the Spirit of Wisdom and of truth and of power.[171] Was there ever a time when God was without wisdom or truth or power? A second argument Gregory advances is that in all levels of existence, whether human or angelic, it is the Holy Spirit who sanctifies and perfects; the source of that holiness must be the Spirit of God himself.[172] It is only the Holy One who can make holy.

169. Gregory of Nazianzus, *Oration XLI* 3-4.
170. Gregory of Nazianzus, *Oration XLI* 6-7.
171. Gregory of Nazianzus, *Oration XLI* 9.
172. Gregory of Nazianzus, *Oration XLI* 11.

Again the sermon returns to the more biblical themes of Pentecost. Gregory comments on the tongues of fire which appeared when the Holy Spirit came upon the apostles gathered in the upper room on the Day of Pentecost. The very sign of tongues of fire is evidence that the Holy Spirit is the same substance as the Son who appeared as the Word of God. At the beginning of the Gospel of John we read that the Word of God appeared in the flesh of Christ, and at the beginning of Acts we read that the Spirit of God appeared in tongues of fire. To this our preacher brings another biblical theme of the Pentecost sermon: the reversing of the Tower of Babel and the coming together of the nations in a common understanding of the gospel.[173] This sermon combines two distinctly different approaches to the preaching of Pentecost, the most prominent of which is the theological approach. The sermon teaches a theology of the Holy Spirit. But there is behind this the more traditional approach — the explanation of the sign of Pentecost as it is recorded in the second chapter of Acts, the sign of the seven weeks of seven days, the sign of the tongues of fire, and the sign of the gift of tongues and the undoing of the curse of Babel. To the theological teaching there is added this element of exposition. The Cappadocian Fathers made a major contribution to our understanding of the Holy Spirit, and in this sermon we get an indication of the sort of doctrinal intensity which put across their theology.

On the basis of these four festal sermons, we have to say that the Christian Demosthenes ranks a place among the great evangelistic preachers of the Church. His evangelism was very theological and very doctrinal. He was urging his hearers to embrace orthodox Christianity. He obviously saw that the preaching of Christmas, Epiphany, Easter, and Pentecost gave him an opportunity to drive home the fundamental affirmations of Nicene Christology and the orthodox doctrine of the Trinity. Surely Gregory of Nazianzus should be considered one of those who shaped the whole idea of festal preaching as it has been developed in the Church ever since.

We wish we had a wider selection of Gregory's sermons. We wish we had a selection of sermons that revealed aspects of Gregory's sermons other than his oratorical prowess. We suspect that Sunday by Sunday, or perhaps even day by day, Gregory did the same kind of expository preaching Basil and Gregory of Nyssa did. That was the bread and butter, the meat and potatoes, of Christian preaching. In a time of crisis, Gregory could come up with a prophetic *chef d'oeuvre*. On the high holy days he

173. Gregory of Nazianzus, *Oration XLI* 16.

could produce a sumptuous feast of the Word with all the hors d'oeuvres of classical rhetoric. History unfortunately preserved only the forensic and panegyric orations, but somehow one suspects that Gregory cooked up some solid daily fare as well.

C. Gregory of Nyssa

Gregory of Nyssa (ca. 335–ca. 394) was the younger brother of Basil of Caesarea. He had had the same background of wealth and culture, yet he was not given the opportunity to study abroad as his older brother was. He himself considered his older brother Basil his teacher. His family encouraged him to enter the service of the church, but after being consecrated as a lector he decided to marry and follow a secular profession. This he did for a while, but when his wife died his brother and his friend Gregory of Nazianzus talked him into joining them in their monastic retreat in the wilderness of Pontus. When his brother became metropolitan of Caesarea in 371, he appointed Gregory as bishop of Nyssa. Gregory was a disappointment to his older brother, having no gift for church administration and seeming completely inept in matters of ecclesiastical politics. The Arians in his diocese were easily able to trump up charges against him, and in 376 he was deposed. Two years later with the death of the Arian emperor Valens, he returned to Nyssa and was welcomed back with jubilation. The following year his brother Basil died and he was called to take his place as metropolitan of Caesarea. At the ecumenical council held in Constantinople in 381 Gregory's superior gifts as a theologian were recognized. He and his friend Gregory of Nazianzus, the theologians with the backing of Emperor Theodosius I, were the victors for orthodoxy against the attacks of Arianism.

From that point on Gregory of Nyssa did a fair amount of traveling. He became the leading spokesman for the orthodoxy of the Council of Constantinople. It was in this capacity, we remember, that he visited Cyril of Jerusalem and vindicated his orthodoxy. Gregory's popularity as a preacher is indicated by the fact that he was chosen to preach at the funerals of both the only child of Theodosius I and, soon after, his empress Flaccilla.

Of the three Cappadocian Fathers, Gregory of Nyssa was the most systematic in theological formulation. He continued the work of his older brother Basil and their mutual friend Gregory of Nazianzus. As regards the Cappadocian tradition of preaching, we find much the same thing as we found with the others. We have from him a number of festal sermons, a collection of occasional sermons, and several series of expository sermons.[174]

Among the expository sermons we find a series on the book of Ecclesiastes; a series on the Song of Solomon, following in the tradition of Origen; and two New Testament series, one on the Lord's Prayer and one on the Beatitudes. Series of sermons on such key passages of Scripture, we will find, is a recurring feature throughout the history of preaching. Many preachers have done series on the Lord's Prayer or on the Beatitudes. A series on the Song of Solomon is always a particular challenge, and many preachers have given it elaborate attention, seeking to hand on the Christian tradition of its interpretation and to add their own insights as well. But also, the emphasis of these key passages is part of the job of interpretation. In our study of Saint Basil's *Hexaemeron* we saw an example of one of these classic series of sermons. For Basil to do a series on the creation story and for an Ambrose or a Bonaventure to follow this tradition points out the central importance of the passage to the life of the Church. Something is made very clear when century after century great preachers have one after another done their series on the book of Psalms or on the Gospel of John or on the Lord's Prayer or on the parables of Jesus or on the Beatitudes.

The series on Ecclesiastes is made up of eight sermons on the book's first three chapters. Ecclesiastes has always presented its particular problems, so much so that the rabbis had argued at length as to whether it should be counted as Holy Scripture. The book has a sort of skepticism and world-weariness that seems far removed from the Christian gospel and begs to be interpreted by the Christian preacher. In the opposite way the Song of Solomon with its erotic delight in sexual love challenges the Christian exegete to make sense of the book for the faithful. The fifteen sermons devoted to the book set out to show the necessity of interpreting the Scriptures spiritually. As Gregory understands it, the book speaks of

---

174. On Gregory of Nyssa in general, see von Campenhausen, *Griechische Kirchenväter*, pp. 114-24; Jean Daniélou, "Le mystère du cult dans les sermons de saint Grégoire de Nysse," in *Von christlichen Mysterium*, pp. 76-93; Jean Daniélou, *Platonisme et Theologie mystique* (Paris: Éditions Montaigne, 1954); P. Godet, *Dictionnaire de théologie catholique* (Paris: Letouzey et Ane, 1903-50), 6:1847-52; Vladimir Lossky, *Vision de Dieu* (Neuchâtel: Éditions Delachaux et Niestlé, 1962), especially pp. 70-74. E. C. E. Owen, "St. Gregory of Nyssa: Grammar, Vocabulary, and Style," *Journal of Theological Studies* 26 (1925): 64-71; Quasten, *Patrology*, 3:254-96; W. Völker, "Zur Gotteslehre Gregors von Nyssa," *Vigiliae Christianae* 9 (1955): 103-28.

the loving bond between God and the soul. The interpretation is more tropological than allegorical. As much as Gregory defends Origen's interpretation, he has gone beyond it. There is a certain responsibility of the great expositors of God's Word to treat a book like this, and so Gregory sets himself to the task.

Gregory's series on the Beatitudes is quite different from his series on Ecclesiastes.[175] For the most part it attempts to give a simple and straightforward literal interpretation of the text. We will give it special attention because here a great rhetor is bringing the Word of God to the Christian congregation, and we want to see how he made the Scriptures meaningful. In this series of sermons we see a Christian who was nurtured by Greek learning finding in the teachings of Jesus a more satisfying way of life than he had found in the wisdom of the Greeks. We see a Christian preacher availing himself of the literary culture of antiquity to proclaim the gospel. Yet the most fascinating thing about these sermons is the way they bring together the themes of Greek philosophy and biblical Christianity. One might almost say that in this series of sermons Gregory of Nyssa tries to baptize Plato.

The introduction to the first sermon reveals the preacher's overall purpose. He reminds his congregation of how Jesus went up on a mountain to teach the Beatitudes. Isaiah had spoken of how in the last days the mountain of the house of the Lord would be the highest of mountains and that all peoples would stream to it to receive divine teaching (Isa. 2:1-3). Surely when Jesus taught his Sermon on the Mount that prophecy was fulfilled. It is on the top of this mountain that all things are now visible; prior to this, as long as humanity was still in the cave, they were only perceived in shadows. The allusion to Plato's figure of the cave is unmistakable. It is a striking juxtaposition of imagery. The Greek philosopher's figure of our human quest for true understanding is brought next to the Hebrew prophet's vision of messianic fulfillment and used to affirm that they are both fulfilled in the teaching of Christ.[176] Having begun with this striking introduction,

---

175. The following study is based on the English translation of Hilda C. Graef: *Gregory of Nyssa: The Lord's Prayer, the Beatitudes,* Ancient Christian Writers, vol. 18 (Westminster, Md.: Newman Press, 1954), pp. 85-175; hereinafter Gregory of Nyssa, *Beatitudes.* References are the page numbers in this edition. A critical edition of the works of Gregory of Nyssa has been the life work of Werner Jaeger. Studies of Gregory of Nyssa have struggled under the lack of good critical editions of the extensive works of this prolific Father.

176. Gregory of Nyssa, *Beatitudes,* pp. 85-86.

the preacher turns to elucidating the text, and he begins by defining beatitude. Beatitude is having all things which are thought to be good with no essential element missing. Only God himself is truly blessed, but since man is created in God's image, man can participate in beatitude. Then the preacher makes his point even clearer with an example: A painter paints a portrait of a beautiful face. What makes the face beautiful is that it has all the essential features in beautiful symmetry. It is the face itself which is truly beautiful, but the portrait participates in the true beauty. In the same way the image of God participates in the beatitude of God.[177] What Gregory has done is explain evangelical blessedness in terms of the ultimate good of Platonic philosophy.

Following the order of the words in the verse, "Blessed are the poor in spirit, for theirs is the kingdom of heaven," Gregory comes to explain what is meant by "poor in spirit." "It seems to me that by poverty of spirit the Word understands voluntary humility."[178] What our preacher proposes to his congregation is the virtue of humility. Humility joins the classical virtues of wisdom, courage, temperance, and justice. For a Greek moralist, was this not a striking thing about Jesus, his humility? The apostle Paul is quoted, "For you know the grace of our Lord Jesus Christ, that though he was rich, yet for your sake he became poor, so that by his poverty you might become rich" (II Cor. 8:9). While Gregory's illustrative quotations are not nearly as frequent as those of many a contemporary preacher, they are strikingly appropriate. Our preacher goes on to develop the theme of voluntary humility. "But let no one imagine that humility can be achieved easily and without labour. On the contrary, it needs more effort than the practice of any other virtue."[179] Jesus is presented as the example of this virtue. Philippians 2:5-7 is quoted: "Have this mind among yourselves, which is yours in Christ Jesus, who, though he was in the form of God, did not count equality with God a thing to be grasped, but emptied himself, taking the form of a servant." Then the preacher comments, "What greater poverty is there for God than the form of a servant? What more humble for the King of Creation than to share in our poor nature? The Ruler of rulers, the Lord of lords, puts on voluntarily the garb of servitude. The Judge of all things becomes a subject of governors; the Lord of creation dwells in a cave; He who holds the universe in His hands finds

177. Gregory of Nyssa, *Beatitudes*, p. 88.
178. Gregory of Nyssa, *Beatitudes*, p. 90.
179. Gregory of Nyssa, *Beatitudes*, p. 91.

no place in the inn, but is cast aside into the manger of irrational beasts."[180] Oratory like this got the ears of Gregory's congregation. Even the common people of classical antiquity loved great public speaking, and the preachers who learned the art were well received by their congregations.

Gregory takes another approach to illuminating his text. He makes clear what he means by poverty of spirit by giving us two pictures of its opposite. The first is a character delineation of pride, and the second, of arrogance, both of which are vivid. He tells us of the pride of a handsome young man, dressed in the latest fashion, so that we can see the picture he paints, and then he skillfully calls us to contemplate the end of that pride. It is no more than the grave and its piles of earth-covered bones. This is followed by a second character sketch of a man of power and wealth riding in solemn procession to the sound of trumpets and fanfare. This vivid character delineation is given sparkle by a few skillful similes. The arrogant, like bubbles, are blown up by their own conceit.[181] But the powerful of this age are all too soon snatched away from their thrones and carried out to their graves, where the herald's trumpet is replaced by the mourner's wail.

The conclusion of the sermon returns to the words of Jesus, " 'Go, sell what you possess and give to the poor, and you will have treasure in heaven' " (Matt. 19:21). The poor in spirit are those who have freed themselves from the riches of this world for the sake of spiritual riches.

The second sermon takes up the beatitude "Blessed are the meek, for they shall inherit the earth." In the introduction Gregory suggests that "the Beatitudes are arranged in order like so many steps, so as to facilitate the ascent from one to the other. For if a man's mind has ascended to the first Beatitude, he will accept what follows as a necessary result of thought, even though the next clause seems to say something new beyond what has been said in the first."[182] Gregory often returns to this theme. It is an important part of his exposition to show a hierarchical arrangement of the virtues defined in the Beatitudes. While neither Jesus nor Matthew ever had any such thing in mind, Gregory's listeners understood many things in hierarchical order, and so it was a logical approach for our preacher to use. As most preachers who have preached on this text, Gregory feels a need to explain that Jesus is not talking about meekness as we usually

180. Gregory of Nyssa, *Beatitudes*, p. 51.
181. Gregory of Nyssa, *Beatitudes*, p. 94.
182. Gregory of Nyssa, *Beatitudes*, p. 97.

think of it. Look at the great heroes of Scripture; both Paul and David were vigorous in their approach to life.[183] Having said this, Gregory rather curiously accommodates meekness to the classical virtue of temperance or moderation. His congregation had been brought up on the Delphic proverb "moderation in all things." The meek are those, according to Gregory, who do not let the passions move the soul, but rather through reason keep themselves under control. To make his point our preacher uses two extended metaphors. The medical metaphor is a favorite of Gregory's, as is the athletic metaphor, and we find both kinds again and again in this series of sermons. The point which they make is the importance of discipline to the development of the spiritual life. For the Fathers of the Eastern Church the ascetic life became an athletic contest. The metaphor, as is often the case, was more than mere rhetoric.

The third sermon is on "Blessed are they that mourn, for they shall be comforted." The introduction again returns to the theme of the hierarchical arrangement of the Beatitudes: "We have not yet reached the summit of the mountain, but our minds are still at its foot. Even though we have already passed two hills and have been led up by the Beatitudes to blessed poverty and to the meekness that surpasses it, the Word now guides us to yet higher things. In orderly sequence He shows us through the Beatitudes the third height. To this one can ascend only, as the Apostle says, 'Laying aside every weight and sin which surrounded us,' and having thus come to the summit burdenless and light, our souls will approach truth in a purer light."[184] This theme of ascent, either in the figure of ascending the mountain or ascending Jacob's ladder, is a masterful device for tying together the whole series, but it is more than a device because it signals the way in which Gregory interprets the gospel as mystical ascent. Again we see that rhetoric is more than mere rhetoric.

As many preachers have done since, Gregory of Nyssa tells us that one can easily mistake the meaning of this beatitude. It would at first thought be ridiculous to think that Jesus "calls blessed those people whose life is spent enduring all manner of misfortune . . . the miseries of widowhood and the sad condition of orphans . . . financial losses, shipwrecks, . . . unjust judgments in lawcourts . . . and loss of one's honor."[185] One could of course understand this to mean that those are blessed who mourn

183. Gregory of Nyssa, *Beatitudes*, pp. 100-101.
184. Gregory of Nyssa, *Beatitudes*, p. 106.
185. Gregory of Nyssa, *Beatitudes*, p. 106.

their sins. But if that is what the Logos meant at this point, surely he would have said blessed are those who have mourned. Having set aside two insufficient interpretations of the text, Gregory delays getting to the heart of the matter yet again by constructing a parable of two men living in a dark cave. One has never known anything but living in darkness, but the other has lived in the light and knows the light and therefore mourns the light. This is the situation of man, who in the Garden of Eden knew the light. The reference to Plato's analogy of the cave is clear, but Gregory has changed Plato's story. The Christian preacher is still laboring with the problems recognized by the great Plato. Perhaps indeed the history of philosophy is a series of footnotes to Plato. "But lest our words should labour in vain in our effort to reach what is inaccessible, we will cut short our inquiry into the nature of the transcendent good; for it is impossible that such a thing should come within the scope of our comprehension."[186] So, having intimated his interpretation of what it means to mourn by means of a parable, Gregory now formulates it. "Hence when he calls mourning blessed, the underlying sense seems to be that the soul should turn to the true good and not immerse itself in the deceits of this present life."[187]

With this the sermon turns to the second half of the beatitude, "for they shall be comforted." "This kind of mourning is called blessed in reference to the comfort or consolation which comes from it." Gregory makes his point with two apt biblical examples. We find this in regard to the experience of Passover, for it is a feast of unleavened bread and bitter herbs. David well understood this, for although he was king, "yet he lavishly adds bitter herbs to his life, sighing and loudly lamenting his continued sojourn in the flesh."[188] David's heart cries out again and again for the Divine Tabernacle, "How lovely is thy dwelling place O LORD of hosts." At this point Gregory calls on the doctrine of the Holy Spirit to make the point, "Now the comfort comes through participating in the Comforter. For the gift of comforting is the special operation of the Spirit."[189]

The fourth sermon takes up the text "Blessed are they which hunger and thirst after righteousness, for they shall be filled." Gregory begins with a discussion of what hunger is from the standpoint of Greek medicine.

186. Gregory of Nyssa, *Beatitudes*, p. 112.
187. Gregory of Nyssa, *Beatitudes*, p. 114.
188. Gregory of Nyssa, *Beatitudes*, p. 115.
189. Gregory of Nyssa, *Beatitudes*, p. 116.

We have already mentioned the importance of the medical metaphor for spiritual health, and in this sermon Gregory elaborates it at great length. The healthy are hungry. A good appetite goes along with good health, and when one loses one's appetite the physician has reason to worry. Those who are healthy in spirit hunger for justice. One is immediately struck by the fact that the righteousness of the original beatitude is understood by Gregory in terms of the Greek concept of justice. Gregory tells us that "thinkers who have investigated these matters say that justice is the disposition to distribute equally to each according to his worth."[190] One does not need a doctorate in classical philology to recognize the source of this definition — it was one of the axioms of Greek moral philosophy. Gregory was coming up with a definition that everyone in his congregation who had any rudiments of an education knew well. He gives a few examples of the classical understanding of justice and tells us that Jesus had more in mind than that. What Jesus was talking about was hungering and thirsting after salvation. If Greek moral philosophy understood justice in terms of what we today call social justice, then Gregory would direct us to a transcendent justice which is over and beyond our society. Justice, our preacher tells us, stands for all the godly virtues. In fact, if we might venture a bolder interpretation, our text teaches us that those who make God himself the object of their desire are truly blessed.[191] To make this point our preacher brings in another of his well-chosen biblical quotations. This is what the psalmist means when he prays, "My soul thirsts for God."

The next sermon is on the text "Blessed are the merciful for they shall obtain mercy." The introduction to the sermon again speaks of the Beatitudes as a ladder. This time the ladder is specifically the ladder of Jacob's dream, which Gregory sees as a figure of our ascent to God. By means of this ladder God lifts us up to himself step-by-step.

Indeed, the next step taken by Gregory is momentous. As Gregory sees it, this parable teaches us about the divinization of the faithful. "So it seems to me that, through the effect that follows the Beatitude under consideration, He divinizes, as it were, His hearer, if he understands the word rightly."[192] Gregory's reason for saying this is rather interesting. Since mercy is a divine attribute, to receive mercy is to make us like God, hence to divinize us. Gregory defines mercy as a "loving disposition towards

190. Gregory of Nyssa, *Beatitudes*, p. 119.
191. Gregory of Nyssa, *Beatitudes*, p. 128.
192. Gregory of Nyssa, *Beatitudes*, p. 131.

those who suffer distress."[193] Mercy, he tells us, is intensified charity; to have mercy is to reach the summit of virtue. The point seems to be that for Gregory the basis of this divinization is moral virtue. But here Gregory leaves behind his literal understanding of the text and discovers mystical meanings. There is a secret meaning behind the use of the future tense in our text, "for they *shall* receive mercy," and if we meditate on this we penetrate the veil of the simple outward meaning. The merciful will have their reward reserved for later. He who made us in his own image endowed us with the principles of all goodness; it lies within us to have the good. Obviously the good here is the transcendent good, the *summum bonum* of Greek philosophy. After all, did Jesus not teach, "The Kingdom of God is within you"? Do we not read in the Gospels, "'Everyone who asks receives, and he who seeks finds, and to him that knocks it shall be opened'" (Luke 11:10 and Matt. 7:8)? For Gregory this means: "So it depends on us and is in the power of our own free will to receive what we desire, to find what we seek and to enter where we wish to be."[194] The Greek concept of free will has obviously made a strong impression on our preacher, for he goes even further in this vein: "Hence it is evident that the Lord of nature has endowed the nature of man with the power of ruling itself and willing freely. For all things, whether good or bad, depend on our choice. But the incorruptible and just sentence of the Divine Judgment follows the choice we have made according to our purpose."[195] He explains what he means with an example: Mirrors reflect faces as they are; some faces are miserable and some faces are joyful; the mirror cannot be blamed for reflecting the miserable face of those who are miserable. So it is with the judgment of God.[196] For those of us nurtured by classical Protestantism this is a rather surprising comment. One must ask if this example does not betray the message of the Beatitudes. Does this not make divine judgment very passive? Is God no longer the source of salvation? Is our salvation in ourselves? Greek philosophy had no concept of grace, and it would have been very difficult to explain grace to a congregation brought up on the popular philosophies of the ancient world. Greek philosophy was a philosophy of works every bit as much as Pharisaical Judaism was a religion of works. How does one explain grace to such

193. Gregory of Nyssa, *Beatitudes*, p. 133.
194. Gregory of Nyssa, *Beatitudes*, p. 135.
195. Gregory of Nyssa, *Beatitudes*, p. 136.
196. Gregory of Nyssa, *Beatitudes*, p. 136.

people? For those of us who follow a more Augustinian theology, Gregory of Nyssa seems terribly Pelagian here. Nowhere but in the Beatitudes does Jesus make more clear the surprising reversal of God's grace. The judgment of God is not passive but active. The biblical concept of God's judgment is that he makes the crooked straight, not that he impartially gives to each what each deserves.

Gregory goes on to speak of the feelings of mercy one might have for a friend who has suffered from misfortune. He develops a hypothetical story wherein this friend suffers banishment from his home and is finally sold into slavery. Surely one should have pity for such a friend. But then Gregory turns the story into a parable of the life of each one of us. We have all suffered this and need to have mercy on ourselves. We need to put aside the benefits of this life that we might receive mercy in the life to come. With that Gregory launches into a vivid presentation of the Last Judgment and the pitiful state of those who prefer the riches of this world to having mercy on the poor.[197] The point of the beatitude as Gregory understands it in the last sentence of the sermon is this: Therefore let us be merciful in this life, that we might receive mercy at the Last Judgment.

The sixth sermon takes up the text "Blessed are the pure in heart for they shall see God." Here Gregory gets involved in the contemplation of the transcendent Good so dear to Neoplatonic mysticism. Our preacher tries conscientiously to give a Christian answer to a philosophical problem. The text, he points out, makes very clear that the vision of God is promised to us, yet the Gospel of John tells us that no man has seen God at any time and the apostle Paul tells us that God is one whom no man hath seen, nor can see (John 1:18 and I Tim. 6:16). For the mystical theology of the Greek Church, the question of how these texts are to be resolved became a matter of intense debate. It became a central issue during the iconoclastic controversies in the eighth century and in the controversy between Gregory of Palymas and Barlaam in the fourteenth century. Gregory's attempt at a solution is summarized in the following words: "But since the promise of seeing God has a twofold meaning, on the one hand, that of knowing the nature that is above the universe, on the other, that of being united to him through purity of life, we must say that the voice of the Saints declares the former mode of contemplation impossible, whereas the latter is promised to human nature in our Lord's present

197. Gregory of Nyssa, *Beatitudes*, pp. 140ff.

teaching."[198] This sermon is very helpful in understanding Gregory of Nyssa's theology. It shows a Christian thinker trying to give some biblical insights to the questions of his day.

"Blessed are the peacemakers for they shall be called sons of God" is the subject of the next sermon. The introduction once more touches the theme of the mountain, but this time only briefly. The Tabernacle, Gregory tells us, had a Holy of Holies according to the plan God showed Moses on the mountain. This beatitude is a holy of holies. That mere human beings should be called the children of God is a thought of great majesty. Its majesty is emphasized by the preacher through a series of rhetorical questions. "For what do these words mean? What terms would suffice to exhaust the gift of so great a promise? What ever the mind may conceive, what is signified is completely above it. If you call that which the Beatitude promises good, or glorious, or sublime, yet what is made known is something more than these words mean: it is fulfillment that outstrips prayer, faith surpassing hope, grace transcending nature. What is man compared with the divine nature?"[199] The way Gregory uses these questions to intimate the ineffable makes the sermon doxological.

Having spoken of the reward at some length, Gregory now comes to speak of the work which needs to be done to receive the reward, namely, peace. Peace, he tells us, is surely a gift of God. For, even if one had all the good gifts of life, riches, good health, wife and children — his vivid description of these blessings must have captured the ears of his congregation — if war comes, the enjoyment of all this is cut short. In an equally vivid description he speaks of the horrors of war.[200] A bit further on we find Gregory at his most eloquent when he takes off on a long ridicule of hate,[201] another instance of the rhetorical technique of making clear a virtue by describing its opposite. Now Gregory returns to the positive description of peace by giving us a definition, "Let us first consider what peace is. Surely it is nothing else but a loving disposition toward one's neighbor."[202] To conclude the sermon Gregory comes back to his text, "Blessed are the peacemakers for they shall be called the children of God." What then are peacemakers? "Those who imitate the

198. Gregory of Nyssa, *Beatitudes*, p. 151.
199. Gregory of Nyssa, *Beatitudes*, pp. 154ff.
200. Gregory of Nyssa, *Beatitudes*, p. 158.
201. Gregory of Nyssa, *Beatitudes*, pp. 160-62.
202. Gregory of Nyssa, *Beatitudes*, p. 159.

Divine love of men, who show forth in their own the characteristic of the Divine energy."[203]

In reading this sermon, the modern biblical theologian is struck by the fact that Gregory has not really fathomed the biblical concept of shalom. Peace is the absence of war on the first level or, even better, the absence of envy, anger, and hate, as Gregory has put it in this sermon. Peace he presents as being free from the passions and reflecting the love of God in tranquillity. If this is not quite the biblical shalom, if this is not the peace that passes understanding, it was the peace that the thoughtful pagan of late antiquity yearned for, and Gregory assures such thoughtful and sincere pagans that by following the Christian way the peace for which they have yearned is indeed attainable.

The final sermon of the series is on the text "Blessed are those who are persecuted for righteousness' sake, for theirs is the kingdom of heaven." The sermon begins with a study of the significance of the number eight: It signifies the resurrection because it was on the eighth day that Christ rose from the dead, and so it is fitting that the eighth beatitude is the final rung in the ladder of ascent. The eighth beatitude speaks of the reinstatement in heaven of those who had fallen into servitude. Here we arrive at stability and permanence after all the variation and flux of earthly life.[204] Our preacher once again shows the Christian way of life as the answer to one of the great problems of classical antiquity.

Gregory develops the sermon by treating at length two biblical characters who attained blessedness through persecution: Joseph and Stephen.[205] He follows this with another of the athletic metaphors so dear to the classical moralists, and even to the apostle Paul. He tells us that the martyrs who run their valiant race are assisted by the judge of the contest. This development of the metaphor is a good insight into Gregory's theology of grace. The judge awards the crown to those who win the race, but the judge has also been the trainer who has assisted them to win the crown.[206] Here at least Gregory's doctrine of grace seems a bit stronger.

It is not easy to struggle against persecution, but the nature of human life is such that, throughout its course, we constantly have material attach-

---

203. Gregory of Nyssa, *Beatitudes,* p. 164.
204. Gregory of Nyssa, *Beatitudes,* p. 166.
205. Gregory of Nyssa, *Beatitudes,* pp. 169ff.
206. Gregory of Nyssa, *Beatitudes,* p. 170.

ments. Gregory introduces a fable from animal life, as the ethical teachers of classical antiquity loved to do to illustrate their teachings. We are like snails or shellfish who constantly drag along with us our covering of clay.[207] Then he gives us another example from the medical arts: "the bilious and those who suffer from superfluous humors readily drink the bitter medicine by which the cause of the disease might be removed."[208] It is in the same way that the persecuted accept the suffering as a means of destroying the power of pleasure. As Gregory sees it, sin entered into human life through pleasure, and therefore, when suffering does away with pleasure it frees us from sin.[209]

The conclusion of the sermon is an exhortation to bear affliction. "What we hope is nothing else but the Lord himself."[210] It is made powerful by a series of carefully formulated maxims. "He himself is the Judge of those who fight, and the crown of those who win. He it is who distributes the inheritance. He himself is the goodly inheritance. He is the portion and the giver of the portion. He makes rich and is Himself the riches. He shows you the treasure and is Himself your treasure."[211]

Certainly this is a most amazing series of sermons. They are fascinating for those of us who were schooled in Greek philosophy and the literature of classical antiquity. Not on first reading, perhaps, but surely with more sustained study it becomes clear that these are evangelistic sermons. They aim at the conversion of the heirs of Greek philosophy, at least as it was understood in late antiquity. Not only were the Cappadocian Fathers intent on baptizing Greek rhetoric, they were intent on baptizing Greek philosophy as well. For Gregory of Nyssa it was Plato he wanted most to convert. In this series of eight sermons Gregory makes it so easy for Plato and his heirs to see that it was to the Christian faith that their quest was inevitably leading them. This is a very distinct approach to evangelism. One explains the new faith in terms of the old faith. That was the way Gregory communicated, and in this series of sermons we see it very clearly. He made orthodox theology the obviously legitimate heir of none other than Plato.

207. Gregory of Nyssa, *Beatitudes*, p. 171.
208. Gregory of Nyssa, *Beatitudes*, p. 172.
209. Gregory of Nyssa, *Beatitudes*, p. 172.
210. Gregory of Nyssa, *Beatitudes*, p. 174.
211. Gregory of Nyssa, *Beatitudes*, p. 174.

D. The Festal Calendar of the Cappadocians

Although we have looked at five of the festal sermons of Gregory of Nazianzus which are especially brilliant, all three Cappadocian Fathers preached very similar sermons for the feast days. We now need to take a more general look at the festal calendar of the Cappadocians to learn about the development of this particular genre of Christian preaching.

Taking their work together, the three Cappadocian Fathers provide a comprehensive collection of Christian festal sermons. Among the works of the three, more than thirty sermons can be regarded as festal sermons. Bernardi gives us the following list.[212]

Basil
> Sermon for Epiphany
> Sermon for the beginning of Lent I
> Sermon for the beginning of Lent II
> Sermon for the Martyr Julitta
> Sermon for the Martyr Gordios
> Sermon for the Forty Martyrs of Sebaste
> Sermon for the Martyr Mamas

Gregory of Nazianzus
> Oration 1, On Easter
> Oration 21, Eulogy on Saint Athanasius
> Oration 24, Eulogy on Saint Cyprian
> Oration 25, Eulogy on Saint Maxime
> Oration 38, Christmas
> Oration 39, Epiphany Eve
> Oration 40, Epiphany Day
> Oration 41, Pentecost
> Oration 44, New Sunday
> Oration 45, Easter

Gregory of Nyssa
> Sermon 1, On the Forty Martyrs of Sebaste I
> Sermon 3, For Easter I

212. This list is taken from Jean Bernardi, *La Prédication des Pères Cappodociens* (Paris: Presses Universitaires de France, 1968).

Sermon 5, For Epiphany I
Sermon 6, For the Martyr Theodore
Sermon 12, Easter II
Sermon 13, Epiphany III
Sermon 14, On the Forty Martyrs of Sebaste II
Sermon 15, On the Forty Martyrs of Sebaste III
Sermon 20, Christmas
Sermon 21, Feast of Saint Stephen
Sermon 22, On the Holy Apostles (John and James)
Sermon 23, On the Octave of Christmas
Sermon 24, Easter III
Sermon 25, Ascension
Sermon 26, Pentecost

This is the first large group of festal sermons which has come down to us. We do have a number of festal sermons from John Chrysostom — he left us a sermon for Christmas, Epiphany, and Maundy Thursday, respectively; two for Good Friday; one apiece for Easter and Ascension; and two for Pentecost[213] — but his sermons probably come ten to twenty years after those of the Cappadocians.[214] While there may have been prior movements in this direction, it would appear that it was the festal preaching of the Cappadocian Fathers that popularized the genre.

Only with a counsel of caution would we embark on a study of these festal sermons as a basis for drawing conclusions about the festal calendar of the fourth century.[215] We wish we had more information, but it would appear from the evidence we do have that the last quarter of the fourth century saw the beginning of a cycle of festal sermons. To be sure, there had been several earlier attempts at drawing up a liturgical calendar.[216] A calendar of saints' days was apparently put together in Nicomedia about a decade

213. This is the list given by Quasten, *Patrology*, 3:454ff.

214. We would expect the festal sermons of John Chrysostom to show much the same tendency as those of the Cappadocians, especially in regard to the influence of Greek panegyric, for, as we shall point out, John Chrysostom had studied rhetoric under the same teacher as the Cappadocians, namely, Libanius.

215. Cf. Justin Mossay, *Les fêtes de Noël et d'Épiphanie d'après les sources littéraires cappadociennes au IVe siècle,* Textes et Études liturgiques, vol. 3 (Louvain: Abbaye du Mont Cesar, 1965).

216. Cf. P. Jounel, "Le culte des saints," in *L'Église en Prière*, ed. A. G. Martimort (Tournai: Desclée & Cie, 1961), pp. 777ff.

before the Cappadocian Fathers began their ministry, but it is only concerned with the annual memorials of martyrs.[217] As we have said elsewhere, saint's-day sermons really form a different genre, and have very different historical and theological roots. There is also a calendar from the city of Rome, dated 354, that shows that the birth of Christ was celebrated on 25 December and also gives dates for the feasts of a number of Christian martyrs,[218] but again, it tells us nothing about the sermons preached on these occasions. Other bits of information can be found here and there. However, the festal sermons of the Cappadocians give us our first picture of an annual cycle of Christian festal sermons. In fact, it may well be that these three outstanding orators came up with the idea of a festal calendar which bound the year together with a series of celebrations of the cardinal doctrines of Nicene orthodoxy. If we are very cautious not to read later ideas into an earlier time, we can get a fairly good picture of festal preaching as it first began to appear in the Greek-speaking church in Asia Minor toward the end of the fourth century.

Easter, the Christian celebration of Passover, is obviously the oldest and most important of the annual festivals,[219] at the center of which was the solemn proclamation that Christ is risen. The passing on of the witness that the tomb was empty and that Jesus appeared to his disciples was the essence of the apostolic ministry. In addition, there was another dimension to the earliest Christian celebrations of Easter: that the death and resurrection of Christ were according to Scripture, that is, according to the Scriptures of the Old Testament. Particularly at play here was the fulfillment of the Passover itself. In his death and resurrection Jesus had fulfilled the Passover. As we heard it in the Easter sermon of Melito of Sardis, the Passover narrative from the book of Exodus was read and interpreted in such a way that it was clear that Jesus had fulfilled the feast by passing from death to life. The passion and exaltation of the Messiah were the fulfillment of the Law and the prophets. Originally Christian Passover preached two themes: the passing on of the witness of the women and then the apostles who went to the tomb and found it empty, a witness that was confirmed by the apostles and others to whom Jesus appeared; and the opening of the Scriptures as Jesus had done on the road to Emmaus, showing that it was necessary for the

217. On the calendar of Nicomedia, see Lietzmann, *History of the Early Church,* 3:324ff.

218. See Lietzmann, *History of the Early Church,* 3:322.

219. Lietzmann, *History of the Early Church,* 3:314.

Christ to suffer and then to be exalted. By his innocent suffering Jesus was revealed to be the Passover lamb whose suffering atoned for the sin of the world. In the days of the Cappadocian Fathers these two dimensions of the Easter gospel were still essential to the preaching of the Christian Passover.

The Easter sermon of Gregory of Nazianzus is a good example of the opening of the Scriptures.[220] It retells the Old Testament account of Passover and explains how in the death and resurrection of Christ the Scriptures were fulfilled. Gregory of Nyssa has left us three Easter sermons.[221] One of these sermons, preached at the Easter vigil, tells how Christ is the fulfillment of the Old Testament types. The other two make the solemn proclamation of the resurrection; they pass on the apostolic witness to the empty tomb and to the resurrection appearances. They were apparently preached at the regular service on Easter Sunday morning.

Already, toward the end of the fourth century, there were several rather firm traditions about auxiliary observances. In the first place we find that the celebration of Easter lasted for seven weeks of seven days each and finally came to a conclusion with Pentecost, the fiftieth day. The earliest records seem to indicate that Pentecost was understood as the conclusion of the Easter season. We noticed this in the way Gregory of Nazianzus unfolded the sacred numerology of the Sabbath day.[222]

The picture we get of the celebration of Pentecost from the two sermons the Cappadocian Fathers have left us would indicate that not very much was made of Pentecost at the end of the fourth century. It was beginning to become more important as preachers were discovering that the feast day was a good time to emphasize orthodox doctrine. Controversy over the doctrine of the Holy Spirit was never as vigorous as controversy over the doctrine of the person of Christ, but problems inevitably arose. The Council of Constantinople in 381 felt obliged to make five definitions on the doctrine of the Holy Spirit, and the feast of Pentecost became an appropriate time for emphasizing those doctrines.

It is in Gregory of Nyssa's sermon for Ascension that we find the first evidence for the feast of the Ascension. It could not have been more than a few years afterward that John Chrysostom also preached a sermon

220. Gregory of Nazianzus, *Oration XLV.*
221. Five sermons are found in Migne's *Patrologia Graeca*, 46:599-690. Only the first, third, and fourth are considered genuine.
222. Gregory of Nazianzus, *Oration XLI.*

on this feast. Gregory calls Ascension a "great feast," but this does not mean it had been celebrated regularly before his time, especially when we realize that the day was ripe for the introduction of new festivities.

There is nothing in the way of a Good Friday sermon for the Cappadocian Fathers, although John Chrysostom provides two such sermons. At Antioch an all-day service was held at the cemetery, at which there was preaching, but this was a tradition unique to Antioch. Good Friday services were late in developing. The journal of Etheria tells us of the Good Friday services in Jerusalem.[223] Early in the morning, at the Church of the Upper Room, there was the viewing of the post to which Jesus was bound when he was scourged. Then in the middle of the morning there was the adoration of the true cross at the Church of the Holy Sepulchre. (This service would have originated at the time Helena discovered the true cross.) A three-hour service began at noon and featured the reading of the Old Testament prophecies of the Passion and the Gospel account of Christ's suffering and crucifixion. Most of these rites bear the imprint of Cyril's genius for creating liturgical rites appropriate to the Holy City but probably do not represent traditions of any antiquity. The readings during the three-hour service, on the other hand, may be fairly old, especially those of the Passion narrative. Even at that we find nothing similar from the Cappadocians.

Another auxiliary observance surrounding the Christian celebration of Passover is the forty-day fast, which we call Lent. Lent was then only beginning to take on the prominence it would later have. Basil, however, has left us two sermons for Lent, both of which were preached at the beginning of the forty days but during different years. This fact alone indicates that the beginning of the forty-day fast was considered a special occasion. Both sermons admonish the faithful to submit to the discipline of fasting for the forty days. They are, in short, archetypes of the whole tradition of Lenten preaching.

A most important thing to notice about the festal sermons of the Cappadocian Fathers is the preaching of Christmas and Epiphany. As the famous patristic scholar Anton Baumstark put it, Gregory of Nazianzus was the first to preach Christmas in Constantinople.[224] He fol-

---

223. Etheria, *Journal de Voyage*, Latin text, introduction, and translation by Hélène Pétré, Sources chrétiennes, vol. 21 (Paris: Les Éditions du Cerf, 1948), sec. 37.

224. See Paul Gallay's evaluation in his edition of the festal sermons: Gregory of Nazianzus, *Discours 38-41*, p. 14; and Botte, *Les origines de la Noël et de l'Épiphanie*, p. 28.

lowed that with an Epiphany sermon a few days later, the first Epiphany sermon which has come down to us from any quarter, East or West.[225]. One usually assumes that Constantinople had celebrated Epiphany, but there is no evidence of this. These sermons of Gregory's played an important role in his mission of restoring Nicene orthodoxy to the capital city.

A number of different theories on the origins of these two feasts have been presented.[226] The celebration of Christ's nativity developed for quite different reasons than did the Christian celebration of Passover. If Easter developed from a Christian interpretation of a Jewish feast, both Christmas and Epiphany developed as a Christian interpretation of two different pagan festivals for the celebration of the winter solstice.[227] In the East Epiphany was a Christian attempt to celebrate a solar festival on the night between 5 and 6 January, while in the West Christmas was an attempt to interpret the pagan feast of *Sol invictus,* the unconquerable sun, which celebrated the birth of the sun god as the pagans understood it.[228] This had been a festivity particularly dear to Constantine, who before his conversion had been dedicated to *Sol invictus.* The feast was held on 25 December because it was on that date that the days became noticeably longer after the winter solstice, which occurred on 21 or 22 December. This lengthening of days manifested the unconquerableness of the sun. With Constantine's conversion the feast took on a different meaning, and more and more 25 December became a celebration of Constantine's religious settlement, namely, Nicene orthodoxy.[229] Apparently the two feasts began to be observed in the Christian Church about the same time, namely, sometime before the middle of the fourth century. In the West Christmas

225. One assumes Epiphany originated in Egypt because of a passage in Clement of Alexandria that a Gnostic sect celebrated a feast of a similar sort during the night between 5 and 6 January. The evidence, however, for any kind of similar celebration among orthodox Christians is lacking.

226. For a review of the history of the discussion, see H. Frank, "Frühgeschichte und Ursprung des römischen Weihnachtsfestes im Lichte neuerer Forschung," *Archiv für Liturgiewissenschaft,* II (1952): 1-24; and Engberding, "Der 25. Dezember als Tag der Feier der Geburt des Herrn," pp. 25-43.

227. The recent attempts of Thomas Talley to deny this are hardly convincing. *Origins of the Liturgical Year,* pp. 87ff.

228. Botte finds it psychologically reasonable that Christians should celebrate the birthday of Christ on this date, once the emperor had become a Christian. *Les origines de la Noël et de l'Épiphanie,* pp. 66-67.

229. Lietzmann, *History of the Early Church,* 3:321ff.

was celebrated,[230] and in the East, Epiphany.[231] We can leave to others the discussion of the origins of Christmas and Epiphany and the history of the reconciliation of the two feasts in the liturgical calendar. What interests us are the homiletical traditions associated with these feasts. In the sermons of the Cappadocian Fathers we find a particular stage of that development.

The Cappadocian Fathers saw in preaching Christmas and Epiphany an opportunity to preach Nicene Christology,[232] to teach that the Lord Jesus Christ, the only-begotten Son of God, was begotten of his Father before all worlds, "God of God, Light of Light, Very God of Very God, begotten, not made, being of one substance with the Father by whom all things were made; who for us men, and for our salvation, came down from heaven, and was incarnate by the Holy Ghost of the Virgin Mary, and was made man." These doctrines needed to be preached, and the celebration of Christmas and Epiphany gave the defenders of orthodoxy the opportunity to do this.

Easter had been the only Christian feast of importance up to this time, but it emphasized the doctrine of Christ's redemptive work rather than his person. Easter emphasized a different part of the creed: "And was crucified for us under Pontius Pilate. He suffered and was buried, and the third day he rose again according to the Scriptures, and ascended into heaven, and sitteth on the right hand of the Father. . . ." It was the doctrine of the person of Christ which had become so controversial in the fourth century; the doctrine of the incarnation, rather than the mighty acts of redemption in the death and resurrection of Christ, had come to the center

---

230. Botte finds the first evidence for the celebration of Christmas on 25 December in the Roman calendar of 354. *Les origines de la Noël et de l'Épiphanie*, p. 32. He figures it was first celebrated in Rome in 336, that is, during the life of Constantine (p. 38).

231. Botte finds the first evidence for a feast celebrating the birth of Christ at Jerusalem in the journal of Etheria shortly before the end of the fourth century. *Les origines de la Noël et de l'Épiphanie*, pp. 13ff. For Egypt he finds no evidence of a Christian feast of the Epiphany before the end of the fourth century (p. 11). He finds no trace of either Christmas or Epiphany until the last quarter of the fourth century in either Asia Minor or Constantinople. In this case it is the Cappadocian Fathers who provide the most important information (p. 27).

232. Possibly Athanasius had seen the same possibility for Epiphany and encouraged its celebration in Egypt and then in Gaul. Cf. Lietzmann, *History of the Early Church*, 3:317-18. This would, of course, imply that the feast of the Epiphany was observed before 336 in Egypt. This is speculation, to be sure, for as Botte points out, we have no evidence of a Christian celebration of Epiphany in Egypt anything like that early.

of the stage. When Christians were thinking out their faith over against the Jews, the question of how the suffering of the Messiah won our salvation became the central theme of Christian theology. Now, thinking out their faith over against the pagans, the question was how God could reveal himself to us in his incarnate Son.

Just whose idea it was to introduce the celebration of Christmas at Constantinople we do not know for sure, but quite possibly it was Gregory of Nazianzus himself. From his Christmas sermon we learn that he wanted to keep the feast by reading appropriate Scripture lessons and preaching the affirmations that the feast celebrates.[233] If the Church was to hold the true doctrine of the incarnation, it needed to hear the incarnation preached on a regular basis. What better way to do this than to establish a Christian feast of the incarnation, a feast of the same magnitude as the Christian celebration of Passover. A feast lasting from 25 December to 6 January could give the preacher quite an opportunity to teach the full significance of the incarnation. If such a celebration could be established, then one could preach the doctrines of Nicaea to a full church.

It may well be that the Cappadocian Fathers saw in Christmas as it was celebrated in Rome a better foundation to emphasize the birth of Christ than they did in Epiphany as it was celebrated in the East. The celebration of the birth of Jesus to a human mother promoted more naturally the full humanity of the Christ than did the epiphany of the Christ. Many pagan gods granted to mortals an epiphany, but without an incarnation.

One of the most interesting things about these festal sermons of the Cappadocian Fathers is the way the celebration of the nativity began to be elaborated with the celebration of the feast of Saint Stephen, the protomartyr, on the day following Christmas, the feast of James and John on the day following that, and finally the octave of Christmas.[234] In each case these feast days celebrated the *dies natales* of the saints in question — the day the saint was born into eternity, that is, the day of the saint's martyrdom. This custom seems to have originated in Rome and may have evolved from the fact that the Roman Church had celebrated the martyrdom of Peter and Paul on 28 December well before the conversion of Constantine and the attempt to reinterpret the feast of *Sol invictus* in a Christian sense. The conjunction of these feasts was bound to make for

233. Gregory of Nazianzus, *Oration XXXVIII* 5.
234. Lietzmann, *History of the Early Church*, 3:326.

problems, though. But by explaining Christmas Day as the celebration of Christ's birth and the feast of Peter and Paul as the *dies natales,* the day of birth into eternity of the two saints, and adding the feast of Stephen, the first Christian to experience that birth, and then the feast of Saints John and James on 27 December, one was able to achieve a certain harmony out of obvious discord.[235] It is interesting to note that the calendar of Nicomedia already reports the celebration of Saint Stephen on 26 December, Saints John and James the following day, and Saints Peter and Paul on the day after that, and yet this calendar makes no mention of Christmas.

The festal sermons of all three Cappadocian Fathers include a number of sermons for saints' days. While we have chosen not to go into the question of saints'-day sermons at any length, we do feel it is important to notice that saints commemorated with festal sermons are for the most part local. Four sermons are devoted to the forty martyrs of Sebaste, and four other, presumably local, martyrs are also celebrated: Julitta, Gordios, Mamas, and Theodore. Gregory of Nazianzus, on the other hand, celebrated Athanasius, the champion of Nicene orthodoxy. Again it would appear that Gregory found feast days a good opportunity for doctrinal preaching. The oldest saints' days, by the very nature of this practice, were of a purely local nature.[236] It was only after the original intention of these celebrations had begun to fade that the calendar of saints began to include those of more than local significance. One notices that there are no Marian feasts at this point. It will take the controversies over the *theotokos* in the fifth century to bring these feasts into prominence.

There is another reason that the festal sermon has come to have special importance, but it is literary rather than theological. One gets the impression that it was under the influence of their training in Greek rhetoric that the people of this day thought of the sermons for feast days as something special. As we said above, Greek oratory gave a special place to the panegyric, the festive oration. It was for this reason that one might collect one's feast-day sermons, much as Isocrates published his *Panegyricus.* The older tradition of Christian preaching would have seen nothing special about preaching on holidays. A sermon was a sermon. It was an inter-

235. The best explanation I have heard of this material was in a series of lectures given by Hans-Dieter Altendorf, winter semester in Tübingen, 1965-66.

236. For more information on the origin of saints' days, see Lietzmann, *History of the Early Church,* 3:322-26; and Jounel, "Le culte des saints," pp. 766.

pretation of Scripture and that was what made it special. It was only when preachers had become orators that we begin to find collections of festal sermons.[237] It would appear that this is the first sizeable number of festal sermons that we have, and it is surely not without significance that the preachers of these sermons saw themselves as orators. The Cappadocian Fathers cultivated these Christian festivals and, as we have shown in regard to Gregory of Nazianzus, gave considerable attention to how the Church should celebrate these Christian feasts. As Gregory of Nazianzus makes clear, these feast days should above all be celebrated by a feast of the Word. They are fittingly remembered by special readings of Scripture which have to do with the feast and by an appropriate sermon. Gregory of Nyssa has left us a sermon for the feast of the Epiphany in which he makes much the same point. "Therefore let us leave the other matters of Scriptures for other occasions, and abide by the topic set before us, offering as far as we may, the gifts that are proper and fitting for the feast: for each festival demands its own treatment."[238] We take this to mean that the usual reading through of the Scriptures was suspended when a festival came along and was replaced by readings appropriate to the feast.

Yet here again we find it difficult from Gregory's Epiphany sermon to decide what the readings may have been. The sermon itself treats the theme of the feast rather than the lesson; it is not an exposition of the story of Christ's baptism in one of the Gospels. Very briefly the Old Testament types of baptism are recounted because, as Gregory tells us, "the festival season of necessity demands their recollection."[239] Perhaps these typological lessons had been read at the baptismal service, but we cannot say for sure. Toward the end of the sermon our preacher says, "And now we have spoken sufficiently for the holy subject of the day, which the circling year brings to us at appointed periods."[240] The sermon has done

237. It is not clear who might have collected the sermons of Basil, or those of Gregory of Nazianzus or Gregory of Nyssa. Particularly in the case of Gregory of Nazianzus it is clear that the collector intended to put together a collection of the best examples of the work of the Christian Demosthenes. It was quite the usual thing for a distinguished rhetor to leave a collection of examples for use in training orators — for example, the orations of Isocrates, Gorgias, and Lysias, and later the orations of Cicero. Cf. Kennedy, *Classical Rhetoric*, p. 35.

238. Gregory of Nyssa, "Sermon for Epiphany," in Nicene and Post-Nicene Fathers, 2nd ser., 5:518.

239. Gregory of Nyssa, "Sermon for Epiphany," 5:521.

240. Gregory of Nyssa, "Sermon for Epiphany," 5:524.

just that; it has spoken of the appropriate subject for the day. It is not an exposition of Scripture, as were so many of the sermons of the earliest Church and the synagogue before it, but a panegyric in honor of the feast, as were the festal sermons of Gregory of Nazianzus. It is a discourse on the love of God as it was manifested in the acts of redemption celebrated by the feast, offered to God in thanksgiving. It is "offering to Him a few words as the requital of great things."[241]

E. The Ministry of the Word as Worship

With the preaching of Basil, Gregory of Nazianzus, and Gregory of Nyssa we have a distinct school of preaching. In fact, it is usually regarded as one of the most brilliant schools in the whole history of Christian preaching. All three of these men must have done much preaching, for one can hardly develop such virtuosity without constant practice, and much of it must never have been recorded — only the masterpieces have come down to us. This school needs to be seen as a whole. While the homiletical legacy of each of the three Cappadocian Fathers tends to reveal different facets of sermonic activity, their preaching endeavors, we would imagine, were in actual practice much the same. All three were very successful in using Greek rhetoric in the service of Christian preaching. For both Basil and his brother Gregory of Nyssa we have noticed a renewed emphasis on the value of the literal sense of Scripture. In the sermons of Gregory of Nazianzus which have been preserved we did not find any pronounced interest in this subject, but this matter might appear very differently if a larger collection of his sermons had survived. In the same way, the surviving sermons of Basil do not show him to be a doctrinal preacher, but it hardly seems likely that one so devoted to the cause of doctrinal orthodoxy should not have taken this passionate concern to the pulpit. Gregory of Nazianzus we discovered to have been an evangelistic preacher, but we certainly would not want to claim that his colleagues were not interested in that facet of the preaching ministry. Taken together, however, the Cappadocian Fathers reveal a well-balanced homiletical activity.

For the Cappadocian Fathers preaching was an important aspect of worship. It was at the center of the service which the Church performed to the glory of God; this becomes very clear in the panegyric Gregory of

241. Gregory of Nyssa, "Sermon for Epiphany," 5:524.

Nazianzus composed for his friend Basil. In this elaborate sermon we learn that Basil's ministry of instruction was his greatest service to God. His eloquence, his intellectual power, his insight into the deep things of the Spirit, his ability to express in words the most profound truths were all divine gifts which made his ministry outstanding.[242] Gregory compares his friend Basil to the sower in the parable of Jesus who sowed the seed of the divine Word. That was the power of his ministry, the preaching of the Word of God.[243] Preaching was at the center of the ministry of Basil because, as Gregory explains it, it was the job of a minister to bring the people into the light of divine truth. As we said above, so often Gregory of Nazianzus himself begins his Theological Orations by calling on the Holy Spirit for divine illumination not only for himself but also for his congregation. It was through their preaching that the Cappadocian Fathers expected this illumination to take place. They had given special attention to developing the doctrine of the Holy Spirit, and their theology of preaching gave place to that doctrine. It was the Holy Spirit who illumined the mind and tongue of the preacher, and the hearts of those who listened. This illumination both taught and purified God's people. It brought them to salvation, and in that God took the highest pleasure. As we heard so clearly in Gregory's sermon on the holy lights, God is glorified when his creatures reflect his glory.

The doxological purpose of preaching is particularly evident in the sermons of the Cappadocian School. Here, too, we are at the core of Christian doxology. The Cappadocian Fathers were theologians and their theology of worship is richly developed. Basil's *Hexaemeron* is a paean of praise to the Creator of all things, and Gregory of Nazianzus says that whenever he read it he was brought into God's presence with ever more understanding and adoration.[244] The relation of praise and presence, as the theology of worship makes so clear, is very close. The psalmist tells us, "Enter into his gates with thanksgiving and into his courts with praise." The sort of doxological preaching we so frequently find among the sermons of the Cappadocian Fathers did indeed open the way to God's presence. Basil's *Hexaemeron* is surely a perfect example of this.

But one thing above all else about the *Hexaemeron* fascinates the liturgical theologian. There is an interesting similarity between the *Hex-*

242. Gregory of Nazianzus, "Panegyric on St. Basil," *Oration XLIII* 65.
243. Gregory of Nazianzus, "Panegyric on St. Basil," *Oration XLIII* 66.
244. Gregory of Nazianzus, "Panegyric on St. Basil," *Oration XLIII* 67.

aemeron and Basil's Eucharistic Prayer. In fact, one might go so far as to say that the first part of the Eucharistic Prayer is a drawing together, a summary or précis, of Basil's sermons on the creation offered up to God in prayer. Or put another way, the sermon is an amplification for the people of what is essentially a prayer to God. It is a sermon that is a prayer. It shares with the congregation what in prayer will be shared with God so that when the Eucharistic Prayer is prayed, it is indeed the prayer of the whole congregation. For the Cappadocian Fathers with their acute sense of the transcendent glory of God, the doxological dimension of the ministry of the Word is of the greatest possible importance.

The Cappadocian Fathers understood that preaching was a major part of the "spiritual worship" which the Christian Church offers to God. These three theologians, as we have pointed out, were significantly involved with the formulation of the doctrine of the Holy Spirit. Basil's treatise on the Holy Spirit remains today one of the fundamental patristic texts on the subject. The same can be said of the final theological oration delivered by Gregory of Nazianzus in Constantinople. The Cappadocian Fathers had a well-considered doctrine of the Holy Spirit and understood very well what was meant by the "spiritual sacrifices" mentioned in I Peter 2:4-10: It was the same thing as the "fruit of the lips" mentioned in Hebrews 13:15 and the "spiritual worship" mentioned in Romans 12:1. These phrases, found in so many levels of New Testament tradition, witness to a strong current of biblical thought which had developed in Judaism between the time of the exile and the beginning of the Church. This current saw in the ministry of prayer and praise and in the ministry of the Word as practiced in the synagogue the essence of true worship. It was the fulfillment of the sacrifices and ceremonial of the Temple. Several times in his festal sermons Gregory of Nazianzus makes the point that a Christian celebration of a festival should put the emphasis on this kind of spiritual worship.[245]

Gregory of Nazianzus even goes so far as to speak of his sermon as a spiritual sacrifice which he offers to God in preaching the feast.[246] It is the "fruit of the lips" which, according to Hebrews, as well as to the prophet Hosea before him, is the sacrifice most acceptable to God in the worship

---

245. Gregory of Nazianzus, "Sermon for the Feast of Holy Lights," *Oration XXXVIII* 5-6 and 20; "Sermon for Pentecost," *Oration XLI* 1 and 2; and "Second Sermon for Easter," *Oration XLV* 2 and 30.

246. Gregory of Nazianzus, "Second Sermon for Easter," *Oration XLV* 30.

of the New Covenant.[247] Gregory of Nyssa can also speak of preaching as a spiritual sacrifice.[248] The words of the sermon are offered to God as a sacrifice of thanksgiving for the abundant gifts God has showered upon us. It was in this same line, of course, that the apostle Paul had spoken of his preaching as the sacrifice of the gospel (Rom. 15:16).

Finally we want to point out that the Cappadocian Fathers had a strong sense of the Wisdom doxology. We have already spoken at length of the Wisdom literature of the Old Testament and its distinctive approach to the theology of worship. Early in the history of the Church a Wisdom Christology developed. Preaching was an important part of the worship that was to be offered to him who revealed himself as the Word of God. Fundamental to Cappadocian doctrine was the logos Christology found in the Gospel of John. These three theologians had a profound sense of the Wisdom theology of the Old Testament, so, quite naturally, they understood preaching the Word to be central to Christian worship. Gregory of Nazianzus put it very pointedly one time: Preaching the Word is appropriate service to him who is the Word.[249] When one has a strong appreciation of biblical Wisdom theology, especially as it is found in the Gospel of John, one will naturally make preaching a major part of worship, as the Cappadocian Fathers actually did.

III. Cyril of Alexandria

It is as the seal of the Fathers that Cyril of Alexandria (ca. 375-444) is honored by the Greek Church.[250] He is considered as the last word on the subject of Christology and the doctrine of the Trinity. The works which have come down to us fill ten folio volumes, making him one of the most prolific and best preserved of the Greek Fathers. A great theologian certainly, he has unfortunately suffered from a reputation as an inept eccle-

---

247. Gregory of Nazianzus, "Second Sermon for Easter," *Oration XLV* 2.

248. Gregory of Nyssa, "Sermon for Epiphany," 5:518 and 524.

249. Gregory of Nazianzus, "Sermon for Pentecost," *Oration XLI* 1.

250. For biographical material on Cyril, see G. Bardy, *Dictionnaire d'histoire et de géographie ecclésiastique* 13 (1956): 1169-77; von Campenhausen, *Griechische Kirchenväter*, pp. 153-64; J. Liébaert, "Saint Cyrille d'Alexandrie et la culture antique," *Mélanges de Sciences Religieuses* 12 (1955): 5-26; and Robert L. Wilken, *Judaism and the Early Christian Mind: A Study of Cyril of Alexandria's Exegesis and Theology* (New Haven and London: Yale University Press, 1971).

siastical leader. To what extent this ill repute is deserved is hard to say. Although he was the nephew of the patriarch Theophilus of Alexandria, and therefore certainly not of obscure origins, almost nothing is known of him until 412 when he succeeded his uncle. The rivalry between Alexandria and Antioch was well known, and Theophilus was zealous for the honor of Alexandria. It happened that when John Chrysostom, a priest of Antioch, was named patriarch of Constantinople, Theophilus felt threatened and actively promoted his exile. On the other hand, Theophilus was also an avowed enemy of Origen. At odds with both Origen and John Chrysostom — one can understand why Theophilus might be regarded as simply contentious. Apparently Cyril inherited not only the patriarchal throne but the reputation for contentiousness as well.

Cyril had been in office more than fifteen years when he embroiled himself in a controversy with Nestorius, who had shortly before been appointed the patriarch of Constantinople.[251] As Cyril saw it, Nestorius had compromised orthodox Christology by denying to the virgin Mary the title *theotokas*. Nestorius was quite willing to admit that Mary was the virgin mother of the Christ, the son of David, that she was the mother of the human nature of Christ, but he was not willing to regard her as the mother of his divine nature. Nestorius quite easily separated the divine nature of Christ from the human nature. It was to this that Cyril objected. We Protestants need to take care not to read into the discussion our own difficulties with the term "Mother of God" being applied to the Virgin. The term *theotokos* and the term "Mother of God" do not mean quite the same thing. For classical Protestantism the question of whether the virgin Mary should be invoked as the Mother of God has to do with the doctrine of prayer; it has nothing at all to do with Christology. But with Nestorius it was another matter. Nestorius was not a profound theologian, and it was probably somewhat unwittingly that he tended to speak of Christ as two beings, one the human son of David and the other the divine Son of God. In this Nestorius never went to the extremes Cyril thought he had, but, to put it

---

251. For background on Cyril and the christological controversies of his time, see D. Franses, "Cyrille au Concile d'Éphèse," *Studia Catolica* 7 (1931): 369-98; Charles Hefele and Henri Leclercq, *Histoire des Conciles d'apres les documents originaux* (Paris: Letouzey et Ane, 1908), II, 1, pp. 248-422; Gustave Neyron, "Saint Cyrille et la Concile d'Éphèse," in *Kyrilliana, Spicilegia edita Santi Cyrilli Alexandrini XV recurrente Saecuto (444-1944)* (Cairo, 1947), pp. 37-57; and Jaroslav Pelikan, *The Christian Tradition: A History of the Development of Doctrine*, 5 vols. (Chicago: University of Chicago Press, 1971-89), 1:226-66.

kindly, he did not do too well in the controversy. Cyril maneuvered him into the worst possible positions. Some have tried to explain the dispute in terms of provincial loyalties; Nestorius was an Antiochene, and one could expect Antiochenes and Alexandrians not to get along. Besides which, the Alexandrians looked on Constantinople as something of an upstart — for Antiochenes like John Chrysostom and Nestorius to control the new Rome was a bit hard for them to take. Surely there was some chauvinism involved, but that really does not explain the controversy. The truth is, Cyril was a brilliant theologian, and however the discussion may have gotten started, it sparked some brilliant insights in his mind.

Hardly a gifted writer, in fact a bit clumsy with words at times, Cyril is stimulating and thought provoking to read. His perception of the unity of the person of Christ is a real advance in Christology. The value of the so-called Cyrillian Christology is that it stressed the union of the divine and the human in the person of the Christ. It is not as though the incarnation produced some sort of split personality, nor is it a matter of Jesus being a balance of opposites, like yin and yang, nor again of Jesus being a hybrid between divinity and humanity. No one before Cyril had ever faced the question with the thoroughness and insight he did. It is his theology which engages us. It is difficult to read but worth the effort.

A. Cyril as Interpreter of Scripture

Not only is Cyril a great theologian, he is a remarkable interpreter of Scripture as well. While he certainly has to be included in the Alexandrian School, he is hardly a carbon copy of Origen; he departs from his school at a number of crucial points. This departure may have been related to the fact that the Alexandrian School underwent several changes late in the fourth century, with Diodore of Tarsus and Theodore of Mopsuestia having a far-reaching influence. Or perhaps something else made the Alexandrian become much more sober in his exegesis. Whatever the reason, there are in fact definite unique features to his exegetical work. At the time of the Protestant Reformation John Calvin regarded him as second only to John Chrysostom among the Greek exegetes. The Reformer particularly admired Cyril's commentary on the Gospel of John for its sober grammatical-historical interpretation. Intended as a theological study, the commentary was an exposition of the orthodox doctrine of the Trinity as it is found in the Gospel of John and has for centuries been regarded as a very convincing exposition. It is, no doubt, because this commentary is interested in doctrinal questions that it concentrates on a literal, rather than an allegorical, interpretation of the text.

On the other hand, Cyril produced some masterful interpretations of Scripture in the tradition of the great Alexandrians.[252] His *Adoration of God in Spirit and in Truth* is a Christian interpretation of the ceremonial law, the culmination of a long tradition, begun centuries earlier, of the "spiritual" interpretation of both the worship of the Tabernacle and the Temple and its ceremonial, its furnishing, its priesthood, and its festivals. The Alexandrian Jews had richly developed it, and the New Testament, especially in the Epistle to the Hebrews, used it to explain how Christ had fulfilled the Law. What is interesting about Cyril is that he keeps both the spiritual and the literal senses clearly distinguished and evenly balanced. Certainly one never gets the impression one gets from more than one of the Fathers that the literal interpretation is some sort of homely Leah that one must put up with for the sake of the beautiful Rachel. Cyril's literal sense is as interesting as his spiritual. Under Cyril's hand the literal interpretation is both fruitful and beautiful.[253]

Robert Wilken recently pointed out that Cyril of Alexandria needs to be seen first of all as an interpreter of Scripture. Most of his written work is in the form of commentaries, and only after 428 did he begin to turn his attention to matters of systematic theology. It is, of course, this strong grounding in Scripture which gives his theology such authority. According to Professor Wilken, much of Cyril's ability as an exegete was inspired by the dialogue between the Alexandrian church and the Alexandrian synagogue. A Christian of Alexandria had to be very clear about the Christian meaning of the Old Testament Scriptures. By Cyril's day this discussion already had a long history.

B. Cyril as Preacher

While Cyril is often praised as a great theologian, he has never been known as a Christian Demosthenes as Gregory of Nazianzus was. However, the

---

252. Cf. Alexander Kerrigan, *St. Cyril of Alexandria: Interpreter of the Old Testament* (Rome: Pontificio Istituto Biblico, 1952).

253. For a detailed discussion of Cyril's understanding of the literal sense of Scripture, see Kerrigan, *St. Cyril of Alexandria*, pp. 35ff.

sermons he left behind would indicate that his pulpit ministry was, in fact, of a very fine quality. We cannot be completely sure because his sermons have not been preserved as sermons but as commentaries. It would appear that many of his commentaries were originally series of sermons which were edited as commentaries. This is particularly transparent in his commentary on the Gospel of Luke, where the homiletical forms are still quite noticeable. It is for this reason that we will base our study of the preaching of Cyril on his sermons on the Gospel of Luke.[254]

Apparently this commentary is a series of more than 150 sermons based on a *lectio continua* of the Gospel of Luke which someone has attempted to turn into a commentary by eliminating strictly homiletical material and adding other material from the various writings of Cyril to complete it. This scissors-and-paste project may have been undertaken by Cyril himself and then continued after his death by another hand. About this we can only speculate. What is clear is that unlike the commentary on the Gospel of John, the work was never completed. All we really have, it would appear, is an extensive set of notes on a series of sermons taken down by a stenographer. Moreover, chances are that the stenographer did not take down the full sermon but rather reported it in abbreviated form; introductions, conclusions, and perhaps illustrations have been edited out, and in some cases whole sermons are missing. This work is hardly in finished literary form, but it does give us some idea of how Cyril's literary workshop operated.

Daily preaching must have been Cyril's theological workbench. It must have been in the day-by-day preparation of these sermons, going through one book of the Bible after another, that he thought out these theological issues. His exegetical studies as we find them in his sermons on the Gospel of Luke are careful and thoughtful. Cyril is gifted at finding parallel passages of Scripture to illuminate the text under consideration. And, especially in Cyril's day, without the concordances and lexical aids we have today, this gift demanded an extensive knowledge of Scripture. A scholar had to have the passages in his head. It could not be faked! Cyril was simply one of the best biblical scholars of the patristic age.

There must have been at one time a considerable number of Cyril's biblical commentaries, for in addition to the works on the Gospels of Luke and John we have an extensive commentary on Isaiah, a commentary on

---

254. Cyril of Alexandria, *Commentary on the Gospel of St. Luke,* trans. R. Payne Smith (n.p.: Studion Publishers, 1983).

the twelve minor prophets, and his famous work on the Pentateuch, *The Adoration of God in Spirit and in Truth*. Unfortunately the number of biblical commentaries Cyril is known to have published but which have since been lost is large. According to Johannes Quasten, numerous fragments of Cyril's commentary on the Psalms have survived.[255] The chains contain much material from Cyril's commentaries on the four books of Kings, Proverbs, the Song of Solomon, Jeremiah, Ezekiel, and Daniel. For New Testament commentaries the chains give us evidence of an extensive commentary on Matthew, which several Byzantine commentators mention, and from the material which has survived it is evident that it was much on the order of his commentary on John. The chains also make it clear that there were commentaries on Romans, I and II Corinthians, and Hebrews. This is a very impressive list. Not many commentators could even begin to match it. When one remembers that he was patriarch of Alexandria for more than thirty years and that he carried on a major theological dispute for which he wrote volumes of material, one has to ask when he got the time to produce all these commentaries. The answer lies close at hand: The commentaries are the literary remains of his sermons. Like both Origen and John Chrysostom before him, he preached daily, through one book of the Bible after another, and these sermons were taken down by stenographers and then edited into commentaries. This was a standard operation in the golden age of patristic preaching. The preacher carefully thought out his sermon, delivered it without notes, had it taken down by a stenographer, and then, with the help of the stenographer, edited it for publication. Much of this preaching Cyril may have done as his uncle's assistant, just as John Chrysostom did his bishop's preaching in Antioch. If Cyril had won a good reputation by doing his uncle's preaching for him, his being so easily selected as his uncle's successor would be more than understandable. Several of the commentaries that have come down to us appear to have been composed after the outbreak of the Nestorian controversy in 428, but the *The Adoration of God in Spirit and in Truth* and the commentary on Isaiah seem to have been written prior to that time.[256] Cyril must have given much attention both to the study

---

255. On the fragments of Cyril's biblical commentaries, see Quasten, *Patrology*, 3:122-25.

256. As early as 401 Cyril's uncle had begun to fulminate against Origen. Some of Cyril's Old Testament commentaries may have been an attempt to come to grips with the Alexandrian exegesis in light of his uncle's opposition to Origenism.

and the preaching of the Word throughout the whole length of his ministry. His preaching had no doubt been valued by his contemporaries, particularly by his own congregation.

An important moment in the preaching career of Cyril of Alexandria was at the Council of Ephesus, held at the Cathedral of Saint Mary during the summer of 431. A collection of eight sermons which are supposed to have been preached during the course of the Council has come down to us.[257] The fourth sermon is quite appropriately an encomium or panegyric on the virgin Mary. If I remember the story correctly, it was after the preaching of this sermon that the crowd, in imitation of their pagan ancestors who, stirred up by the opponents of the apostle Paul, had run through the streets shouting, "Great is Diana of the Ephesians," now four centuries later went through the streets shouting, "Great is Mary the *theotokas.*" If nothing else, this shows the ability of Cyril to stir up a crowd. Although this saint may have been somewhat volatile, he certainly was not boring.

C. Cyril's Sermons on Luke as Doctrinal Preaching

If Cyril of Alexandria's commentary on the Gospel of Luke indeed consists of his daily sermons on a *lectio continua* of that Gospel, and if this daily preaching was indeed the workbench of one of the leading theologians of the age, we are not surprised to discover that these sermons are often filled with doctrinal instruction. Cyril never missed the opportunity to point out the doctrinal implications of the passage under discussion. One must remark, of course, that this is quite in accord with the intentions of the Gospel writers themselves. One can hardly accuse Cyril of imposing doctrine on the simple story of the Gospels. He is clearly treating the Gospel texts as the original authors intended them to be treated. As the Gospel of John puts it, "These [things] are written that you may believe that Jesus is the Christ, the Son of God, and that believing you may have life in his name" (John 20:31). The Gospels intend to teach doctrine; particularly they intend to make clear who Jesus really was. That is, the Gospels are particularly concerned to teach Christology, the doctrine of the person and work of Christ. Actually Cyril could not have found a better way to preach his Christology than to

257. Cf. Quasten, *Patrology* III, pp. 131f.

preach through the Gospels one by one, which is apparently what he did. Let us look at several of these sermons taken from the early chapters of the Gospel, a section devoted to reporting the teaching and healing ministry of Jesus.

In the sermon on the temptation in the wilderness Cyril takes full advantage of the opportunity to show the implications of the Gospel story for the doctrine of the person and work of Christ. The introduction to the sermon is brief and weighty:

> The blessed prophets, when speaking of the Only-begotten Word of God — of Him Who is equal unto God in glory, and the sharer of His throne, and radiant in perfect equality unto Him — lead us to the persuasion that He was manifested as a Savior and Deliverer for those upon earth, by saying, *Arise, O Lord, help me.* He arose therefore and helped, having taken the form of a slave, and being made in the likeness of men; for so did He as one of us set Himself as an avenger in our stead, against that murderous and rebellious serpent, who had brought sin upon us, and thereby had caused corruption and death to reign over the dwellers upon earth, that we by His means, and in Him, might gain the victory, whereas of old we were vanquished, and fallen in Adam.[258]

The christological concerns of Cyril, stated briefly and simply, are obvious in this introduction, and the sober rhetoric is particularly obvious. When it comes to his approach to preaching, at least, he is still more Hebrew than Greek — for Cyril Greek oratory has not substantially changed the literary form of the Hebrew sermon. One notices here, as one frequently notices in Cyril's sermons, that the preacher begins by making a few remarks on a text of Scripture other than his principal text, in this case Psalm 44:26, "Arise, O Lord, help me." Perhaps these lines from Psalm 44 had been sung earlier in the service. More usually, however, such texts were taken from the regular Scripture lessons which had been read previously, and sometimes, one suspects, from a lesson specially chosen by the preacher as the key to his interpretation of the primary lesson. One finds this again and again in Cyril's sermons. One suspects that Cyril's practice reflects an old homiletical technique which the rabbis had used for centuries. We have already spoken of how Jesus used this technique in his Bread of Life Sermon in the sixth chapter of the Gospel of John. In this case the secondary text makes it possible to set in the clearest light the

---

258. Cyril, *Luke,* p. 85.

vicarious nature of Jesus' temptation in the wilderness. It was Jesus, a true man and therefore a representative of humanity as a whole, who met the temptations of Satan and overcame them.

The sermon continues with a few words which suggest how we might understand Cyril's theology of worship and how preaching fits into that theology. "Come, therefore, and let us praise the Lord, and sing psalms unto God our Savior; let us trample Satan under foot; let us raise the shout of victory over him now he is thrown and fallen; let us exult over the crafty reptile."[259] Preaching is doxological because it proclaims God's victory over the evil one. This is gospel for us because the victory has been won in Christ: "Therefore . . . human nature, as victorious in Him, wins the crown."[260] It is the dimension of proclamation, the kerygmatic dimension of preaching, which makes it worship. One cannot help but notice that this theology of worship develops quite naturally from Cyril's Christology.

From this sermon it is clear that the Cyrillian Christology gives considerable attention to the doctrine of the Holy Spirit. Our preacher calls attention to the text "Jesus being full of the Holy Spirit returned from the Jordan."[261] He comments that here we are to see human nature anointed with the grace of the Holy Spirit, an anointing that began with the anointing of Christ. He is the first fruit of this spiritual anointing; it is because of this spiritual anointing that he is crowned with the highest honors. Cyril has just preached, of course, on the story of the baptism of Jesus, which is recounted in the third chapter of Luke, and therefore the story of the temptation of Christ is seen in this context. In fact, the context, as we find it in Luke, throws considerable light on the story, and Luke by his introduction to the story even underlines the importance of this context: "Jesus being full of the Holy Spirit returned from the Jordan." Cyril, with his sensitivity to the profundity of the literal sense of Scripture, picks this up.[262] It is as the first fruit of human nature now anointed with the Holy Spirit that Jesus goes forth to defeat Satan.

It is not clear from the *Commentary on Luke* as we now have it where this sermon ends and where the next begins, for all of Homily 12 is included within the commentary section on Luke 4. In view of the rest

259. Cyril, *Luke,* p. 85.
260. Cyril, *Luke,* p. 85.
261. Cyril, *Luke,* p. 85.
262. Cyril, *Luke,* p. 86.

of the commentary it is unlikely that Cyril treated all of chapter 4 in one sermon. It would appear that this is an obvious example of the editor removing the homiletical character of his text in order to produce a commentary. One imagines that the story of Jesus preaching in the synagogue at Nazareth was treated by Cyril as a separate sermon. There is, however, no trace of a sermon introduction when Cyril takes up verse 16, which begins the passage. The matter of the anointing of the Holy Spirit is still prominent in our preacher's mind.[263] This, to be sure, is because the text demands it. Luke tells us that when Jesus preached at Nazareth he took as his text a passage from Isaiah 61, "The Spirit of the Lord is upon me, because he has anointed me to preach good tidings to the poor." Cyril comments "that the Son was anointed in no other way than by having become such as we are according to the flesh and taken our nature. For being at once God and man, he gives both the Spirit to the creation in his divine nature and receives it from God the Father in his human nature; while it is He who sanctifies the whole creation, both as having shone forth from the Holy Father, and as bestowing the Spirit, which he himself pours forth, both upon the powers above, as that which is his own and upon those who recognized his appearing."[264] Both of Luke's writings in the New Testament, the Gospel and the Acts of the Apostles, are rich in their teaching on the Holy Spirit, and Cyril has obviously appreciated those teachings and given full attention to the person of the Holy Spirit in developing his doctrine of the person of Christ. The biblical exposition we find in these sermons is inductive rather than deductive. I think it can be fairly said that Cyril does not begin with certain abstract christological doctrines and then interpret the text in light of those doctrines. He rather deduces his doctrines from his text. It is obviously Luke who has taught Cyril about the relation between the Son and the Holy Spirit.

Cyril goes on to make another important comment. Jesus took upon himself the humiliation of emptying himself of his glory. This is another dimension of the Cyrillian Christology. At this point Cyril does not indicate what specifically this emptying involved. Does the doing of mighty works fit in with this emptying? Perhaps it is in this sense that we are to understand what Cyril says in regard to the healing of Peter's mother-in-law a bit further on.[265] Christ's mighty works are performed

263. Cyril, *Luke,* p. 91.
264. Cyril, *Luke,* p. 92.
265. Cyril, *Luke,* pp. 99-101.

by an anointed humanity, and Cyril makes the point that she was healed by his hand of flesh.[266] The Jesus who healed Peter's mother-in-law had emptied himself of the divine prerogatives that would make it possible for him as a divine being to heal one of his creatures. It was as a human being that Jesus healed the woman. The Gospel of John would insist that "Greater works than these you will do." That is, the mighty works are all within the capability of an anointed humanity. The Spirit that was in him also descended upon him.[267] "He was anointed" befits the manhood. So, too, "He sent me" pertains to the same manhood.[268]

Cyril must have preached a number of sermons on the ministry of Jesus in Capernaum. Luke gave him abundant material for this. In verse 31 the Evangelist tells us about the preaching of Jesus in the Galilean metropolis, and Cyril picks up on the fact that even the Jews recognized that Jesus taught them with authority (v. 32). Quoting Isaiah 55:3, Cyril makes the point that the anointing of the Son of David will establish an everlasting covenant that will have authority over both Jews and Gentiles. While Moses had authority over the Jews but not the Gentiles, the authority of the Christ is to be over all nations. His is obviously an authority far beyond that of Moses.[269] For Cyril covenantal theology is still of the greatest possible importance. It is obviously a significant point for him that in Christ the covenant is opened up to the Gentiles. Jesus taught them as one having authority in that God had given him authority over a far greater sphere than Moses. But there is more than that. Moses and the prophets who followed him were ministers of the divine words. They spoke, "Thus saith the Lord." But our Lord Jesus Christ, Cyril tells us, spoke words most worthy of God. When he spoke, he spoke the Word of God. The rabbis discussed the various interpreters of Scripture; they even discussed the Scriptures. They discussed various authorities but they did not speak as having authority themselves. In this Jesus was quite different, for he spoke as one who himself had authority. Then Cyril sums up his thoughts in these two remarkable sentences:

> For His word was not of the shadow of the law, but as being Himself the lawgiver, He changed the letter into the truth, and the types into

266. Cyril, *Luke*, p. 100.
267. Cyril, *Luke*, p. 92.
268. Cyril, *Luke*, p. 93.
269. Cyril, *Luke*, p. 97.

their spiritual meaning. For He was a ruler, and possessed a ruler's authority to command.[270]

Cyril makes his point even more powerfully as he goes on to the story of the casting out of demons which follows in verses 33-36. Very skillfully our preacher brings in a parallel passage from the Gospel of Matthew which tells of how Jesus was accused of casting out devils by Beelzebub, the prince of devils, to which Jesus answered, "But if I in the Spirit of God cast out devils, then has the kingdom of God come upon you unawares."[271] It is this bringing in of parallel passages which is always Cyril's greatest art. Finally he sums up his commentary on this passage:

> For if, says He, I, Who have become a man like unto you, chide the unclean spirits with godlike power and majesty, it is your nature which is crowned with this great glory; for ye are seen both through Me and in Me to have gained the kingdom of God.[272]

The strength of Cyrillian Christology is its emphasis on the unity of the divine and human nature in Christ, and in this sermon he certainly makes this very clear.

Yet Cyril has another point to make on the authority of Christ in this sermon on the ministry of Christ in the synagogue of Capernaum. Cyril notices that it is by an authoritative command that Jesus heals this demoniac. He comments that Jesus wrought his miracles not by offering up a prayer, not by asking someone else with the power to accomplish them, but, by being himself the living and active Word of God the Father, he commanded the demons to be silent and depart.[273] They obeyed because his command was nothing less than the command of God himself.

No doubt there will be those who will abhor these heavily doctrinal sermons. Our day and age, still under the shadow of the Enlightenment, naively imagines that the doctrinal sermon is boring and that sermons like these must have been tedious. A less beclouded day will probably recognize this prejudice as a rather peculiar form of pietistic agnosticism. The history of preaching is filled with examples of great doctrinal preachers who drew enthusiastic, thoughtful, and, indeed, large congregations.

270. Cyril, *Luke*, p. 98.
271. Matthew 12:24-28, as quoted by Cyril, *Luke*, p. 98.
272. Cyril, *Luke*, p. 98.
273. Cyril, *Luke*, p. 98.

D. Cyril's Sermons on Luke as the Preaching of the Christian Life

As one reads through Cyril's sermons on the Gospel of Luke, one is impressed that the great systematic theologian is concerned as well with the teaching of the Christian life.[274] For any Christian preacher who wants to lead a congregation to a deeper understanding of the Christian life, the Sermon on the Mount as found either in the fifth, sixth, and seventh chapters of the Gospel of Matthew or in the sixth chapter of the Gospel of Luke offers a promising text. This collection of sayings on how the Christian should live is at the heart of Jesus' teaching. As one looks over the interpretations of the Sermon on the Mount that have been produced over the last two thousand years, one is impressed by their variety. They range from rigorous asceticism to the most accommodating liberalism. There are those who see the teaching of Jesus as some sort of elitist ethic for a chosen few and those who believe that if everyone would just live by the Sermon on the Mount all the problems of the world would be solved. In other words, they understand it as simple and practical rules for living. The monastic movement felt that to be serious about living by the Sermon on the Mount would eventually lead one to the cloister. Marxists are sure that in the Sermon on the Mount Jesus comes out on their side; both pacifism and liberation theology try to justify themselves from these very same sayings. Others see it as a radical and revolutionary call for a heavenly kind of life which unfortunately will not work in this world. One might expect Cyril to be one of the rigorists, but one is surprised.

The first sermon devoted to explaining the Sermon on the Mount begins with a reference to I Corinthians 11:1, "Be imitators of me, as I am of Christ."[275] Cyril comments:

> And how was the wise Paul like unto Christ? Did he establish the heavens, as did the Word of God? Did he set the earth upon its firm foundation, and bring forth the sun and moon, and the stars, and light? How, therefore, was he like Him? By being an imitator of that human virtue, which Christ showed forth for our example.[276]

---

274. On the way Cyril recognized a twofold purpose for the ministry of the Word, namely, the teaching of orthodox doctrine and instruction in the Christian way of life, see Kerrigan, *St. Cyril of Alexandria,* pp. 140-64.

275. We can assume that Homily 25 as it is now identified in the Syriac manuscript starts the series off, but again we find it difficult to decide where the sermons begin and end.

276. Cyril, *Luke,* p. 127.

As we have already suggested in regard to the beginning of another sermon, this would appear to be a remark on an auxiliary Scripture lesson. In this case the secondary lesson was from an epistle. What could be a better auxiliary text for a sermon on Christian morality! "Be imitators of . . . Christ."

Following the text as he finds it in the Gospel of Luke, Cyril takes up the subject of the calling of the disciples.[277] We will notice a slight tendency throughout his interpretation to apply these teachings very specifically to the twelve disciples, and by implication to ministers of the gospel, but our preacher does not seem to abuse this obvious dimension of the text. He does not come up with an elitist ethic. While Cyril applies certain aspects of the Sermon on the Mount very specifically to those to whom the apostolic ministry is committed, one also gets the impression that Cyril understands the moral teachings of Jesus to be generally applicable.

Having treated the call of the apostles, Cyril takes up the interpretation of the Beatitudes in their Lukan form.[278] The Lukan form is, of course, much shorter than the Matthean, giving us only four of the nine beatitudes found in Matthew. Cyril starts off with the text " 'Blessed are you poor, for yours is the kingdom of God' " (Luke 6:20) and then comments, "These are the Savior's words, when directing His disciples into the newness of the Gospel life after their appointment to the apostolate."[279] Nothing more is made of this theme at this point, and certainly nothing is said suggesting that this is an ethic for spiritual athletes. What interests Cyril at this point is the difference between the way Luke gives us the first beatitude and the way Matthew gives it. Matthew's version, Cyril tells us, makes it clear that God blesses those who have lowly thoughts of themselves, whose hearts are gentle and, being free from pride, are ready to yield to God. Cyril supports this with a quotation from Isaiah 66:2, " 'But this is the man to whom I will look, he that is humble and contrite in spirit, and trembles at my word.' " He finds the same teaching in Psalm 51:17, "A broken and contrite heart, O God, thou wilt not despise." Elsewhere in the Gospels, Cyril tells us, we find that Jesus made a point of being meek and lowly of heart himself (Matt. 11:29). On the other hand, according to Cyril, Luke reports a distinctly different teaching from

277. Cyril, *Luke,* pp. 127-28.
278. Cyril, *Luke,* pp. 129ff.
279. Cyril, *Luke,* p. 129.

that reported by Matthew. Matthew and Luke are not contradicting each other but simply bringing out different aspects of the teaching of Jesus. What Jesus teaches us in Luke is that it is those who care not for wealth, who are free of covetousness and the love of money and set no value on an ostentatious display of riches, who are blessed.[280] To support this approach to understanding the beatitude Cyril gives us his usual dazzling collection of parallel texts. We have no Ebionite reveling in poverty, no Marxist condemnation of the rich here. What Cyril condemns is materialism, and what he understands Jesus to have blessed is setting one's hope on the kingdom of God and the riches of his transcendent kingdom.

Next Cyril turns his attention to " 'Blessed are you that hunger now, for you shall be satisfied' " (Luke 6:21).[281] He notes the difference between Luke's version and Matthew's version, " 'Blessed are those who hunger and thirst for righteousness, for they shall be satisfied' " (Matt. 5:6). Cyril allows that it is surely an admirable thing to hunger and thirst after righteousness as we are admonished to do in the Gospel of Matthew. What this undoubtedly means, Cyril tells us, is habitually to take part in earnest endeavors after piety, but he suggests something even more admirable: cultivating a love of voluntary poverty that will enable us honorably and without distraction to practice the apostolic life.[282] One notices that Cyril's interpretation of this famous saying of Jesus is not ascetic; it is pragmatic. One leads a simple life so that one can devote one's energies to the service of the gospel. There is no glorification of poverty in itself, nor is there even a promotion of fasting as having spiritual value in itself.

When it comes to Luke's third beatitude, " 'Blessed are you that weep now, for you shall laugh' " (Luke 6:21),[283] Cyril is very brief; he simply tells us that our Lord pronounces a blessing on those who shun a life of merriment, vanity, and carnal pleasures. For Cyril, as for Christians of antiquity generally, there was a qualitative difference between the serious, sober, and simple life and the life of many pagans who devoted themselves to the pursuit of transient pleasures.

The final beatitude which Luke reports is " 'Blessed are you when men hate you, and when they exclude you and revile you, and cast out your name as evil, on account of the Son of man! Rejoice in that day, and

---

280. Cyril, *Luke*, p. 129.
281. Cyril, *Luke*, p. 130.
282. Cyril, *Luke*, p. 130.
283. Cyril, *Luke*, p. 130.

leap for joy, for behold, your reward is great in heaven'" (Luke 6:22-23). Here we notice that Cyril's interpretation particularly concerns the persecution which comes to those who, like the apostles, devote their lives to the preaching of the gospel. Just as the prophets were persecuted, so will the apostles be persecuted. The Scriptures, of course, provide no end of examples of the persecution of the prophets. But even if the preachers of the gospel will have to bear opposition and adversity, they can be sure that their work will bear fruit; in fact, their suffering is the pledge of their reward.[284]

One has to say that Cyril's approach to the interpretation of the Sermon on the Mount is very careful and conservative. It obviously rests on the literal sense of Scripture, and when one notes the importance Cyril gives to finding parallel passages it becomes clear that he gives great attention to the principle that Scripture is best interpreted by Scripture. One finds no trace of the sort of thing Gregory of Nyssa did with his series of sermons on the Beatitudes as they are found in Matthew, in which Gregory tried to make the Beatitudes understandable in terms of Greek moral philosophy. Plato rather than the Old Testament prophets and New Testament apostles was called on to explain the sayings of Jesus.

Next our preacher takes up the words of Jesus "'But woe to you that are rich, for you have received your consolation'" (Luke 6:24).[285] After reviewing his earlier remarks on poverty Cyril makes it clear that Christ asks this voluntary poverty of his apostles in order that they might be able to make the apostolic ministry more effective.[286] In other words, more is expected of the apostles than other Christians, but they also receive a greater reward. For Cyril it is quite legitimate that we be won to Christ's service by a desire to win a heavenly reward. On the other hand, by fear of punishment we may very prudently flee riches, luxury, and worldly merriment. "The rich have received their consolation," the text tells us. With this Cyril introduces by way of illustration the parable of the rich man and Lazarus found later in the Gospel of Luke. Commenting on the parable at length, Cyril draws the conclusion that the rich man had his enjoyment in this life. Lazarus, on the other hand, had a life of deprivation in this world but a life of fulfillment in the world to come.[287] Cyril then

284. Cyril, *Luke*, p. 131.
285. Cyril, *Luke*, p. 132.
286. Cyril, *Luke*, p. 132.
287. Cyril, *Luke*, p. 133.

moves on to speak of the virtues of almsgiving and works of mercy,[288] neighboring virtues to those our Savior has just commended to us. Our preacher would have us understand that according to the teaching of Jesus we are to be merciful even as our heavenly Father is merciful. Our Savior often exhorts us to give alms. Cyril notes that in the Sermon on the Mount this theme is clearly part of the context.[289] Now Cyril zeros in on his point. The rich man in the parable could have used his wealth to alleviate the suffering of Lazarus. If he had, things might have gone better for him. As Jesus put it in Luke 16:9, " 'Make friends for yourselves by means of unrighteous mammon, so that when it fails they may receive you into the eternal habitations.' " Obviously for Cyril the rich have a very specific ministry.[290]

Next Cyril turns to the saying of Jesus on turning the other cheek.[291] After an excursus on Christ's fulfillment of the Law and the greater spiritual maturity required by the gospel, Cyril explains that turning the other cheek teaches us patience. One notices that nothing resembling contemporary ideas about passive resistance or nonresistance to evil appears in his comments. In the New Testament Christians are frequently exhorted to patience, and patience was a highly prized virtue among early Christians as well, several Church Fathers producing works on the topic. The virtue of patience only makes sense, of course, if one has a high doctrine of providence and a strong commitment to the effectiveness of prayer. The modern revolutionary has neither and therefore finds patience a most worn-out virtue. For Jesus, as Cyril well understood, it was another matter. But, on the other hand, Cyril finds no suggestion that Jesus was really teaching some sort of mortification of the flesh. Mortification of the flesh was very important to asceticism, which, by the fifth century, had become quite influential in the Church. It is rather surprising, therefore, that Cyril does press this point.

Cyril's comments on the Golden Rule startle even the most jaded scholar. Jesus, he tells us, knowing well the ways of the human heart and understanding our perverse inclination, gives us in the Golden Rule a guide to virtue based on our tendency toward self-centeredness. But, Cyril goes on to say, the Christian ethic is really much more profound than the Golden Rule. It is a law written on the human heart, and when one has

288. Cyril, *Luke*, p. 133.
289. Cyril, *Luke*, p. 133.
290. Cyril, *Luke*, p. 135.
291. Cyril, *Luke*, p. 136.

that, a rule based on our self-centeredness is not really necessary.[292] For a theologian of the fifth century Cyril still has a strong appreciation of covenant theology, and the prophecy of Jeremiah on the coming and eternal covenant written on the tablets of the human heart played an important role in his understanding of the uniqueness of Christianity. The Jewish community of Alexandria was very old and very strong in Cyril's day, and a Christian theologian in that city had to be very clear as to just exactly what the difference was between the law and the gospel. One problem many Christian interpreters of the Sermon on the Mount have had is that they try to make it into a Christian law. During the Enlightenment this problem was doubly severe. It is clear that Cyril has no intention of making that error; whether he has discovered the Sermon on the Mount as gospel is another matter.

Agree with Cyril's interpretation of the Sermon on the Mount or disagree with it, one has to admit that what this preacher gave his congregation was a serious attempt at understanding the teaching of Jesus. Cyril was a teaching preacher of a very high order. His approach to preaching was very conservative as compared to the Cappadocians. The most ancient homiletical form of biblical preaching he maintained with great integrity. If only we had a more carefully preserved record of his preaching we might discover him to be the most classical of the preachers of that age when the preaching of the Greek Church came to its flowering.

IV. Hesychius of Jerusalem

It is only recently that this most prominent of fifth-century Jerusalem preachers has reemerged from the shadows. Never a bishop, nor a leader in the theological controversies of the day, Hesychius of Jerusalem (ca. 380–ca. 455) is not well known for having played the role of an ecclesiastical politician. His reputation was built entirely on his outstanding preaching ministry.[293]

---

292. Cyril, *Luke*, p. 137.

293. Michel Aubineau, *Les homélies festales d'Hésychius de Jérusalem*, 2 vols. (Brussels: Société des Bollandistes, 1978-80), pp. xiii-xviii; Klaudius Jüssen, *Die dogmatischen Anschauungen des Hesychius von Jerusalem*, 2 vols. (Münster im Westphalia: Aschendorff, 1931-34); J. Kirchmeyer, "Hésychius de Jérusalem," *Dictionnaire de la Spiritualité* (1968), vol 7, col. 399-408.

Jerusalem has always been the type of the Church, and, of course, it was at Jerusalem that the primitive Christian church was originally established, which first-generation Christians regarded as the mother church, or at least the home office to which missionaries and evangelists reported, as the apostle Paul did in the Acts of the Apostles. With the Jewish Wars and the fall of Jerusalem in A.D. 70 the Church left Jerusalem. The Romans were determined to destroy the city as they had Carthage at the end of the Punic Wars, and so the Holy City was plowed under. For the next two centuries Jerusalem had no particular significance for the Church other than typological, but with Constantine things began to change. The building of the Church of the Holy Sepulchre conferred on Jerusalem once more the role of pilgrimage center, and yet, even with the prestige of ancient memories, Jerusalem remained through the fourth century under the authority of the metropolitan of Caesarea. Caesarea on the Mediterranean coast, near modern Haifa, had long been the Roman provincial capital of Palestine. From the standpoint of ecclesiastical politics Jerusalem was a city of little importance. Even when it came to matters of tradition, Jerusalem had been eclipsed because, unlike the churches of Caesarea, Antioch, Alexandria, Ephesus, and others, the church of Jerusalem could not boast a continuity of apostolic tradition.

But once Constantine reestablished the Roman Empire on the spiritual foundations of the Christian faith, the church of Jerusalem began to recognize its advantages. We have already spoken of Cyril of Jerusalem's genius for attracting pilgrims to the new Christian Jerusalem through dramatic liturgical productions. Now we want to turn to another episode in this story. By the time of Cyril's death in A.D. 386 the Holy City provided an opportunity for Christian pilgrims from all over the world to deepen their religious experience through elaborate devotional exercises, which were most appropriately conducted in the city where Jesus had been crucified, buried, and raised. And one of the most prominent features of this intensified devotional life was a grand quantity of preaching. Hesychius, a presbyter of the church of Jerusalem in the first half of the fifth century, was one of a number of very good preachers who provided these thousands of pilgrims with preaching that made their trip to the city worth the effort. From the pilgrim Etheria, the Spanish nun who kept a journal of her pilgrimage to the Holy Land something like four or five years after Cyril's death, we get the impression that there was much preaching in Jerusalem and that this preaching made a very definite effort to bring out both the literal sense and the spiritual sense of

Scripture.[294] In other words, at the time of Etheria, the preachers of Jerusalem belonged to the Alexandrian School. When we remember that Origen spent his most productive years at Caesarea, we are hardly surprised at this. Perhaps the controversies over the Origenist interpretation of Scripture had moderated the exegetical climate by the time of Hesychius because, as we shall see, his remarkable series of expository sermons on the book of Job gives first priority to the literal sense of this difficult book. Even at that the interest in the "spiritual" sense of Scripture was still strong, as will become evident from the festal sermons of Hesychius. The Alexandrian spirituality, with its strong Neoplatonic tendency, loved to cultivate elaborate liturgical dramas.

Very little is known of the personal life, family background, or education of Hesychius.[295] Apparently he was a native of Jerusalem who early in life retired to a monastic community in the south of Palestine toward the Egyptian border. It must have been well before 412, the year Cyril of Alexandria became bishop of Alexandria, that Hesychius was called back to his native city to serve as teacher in the church of Jerusalem. By that time, according to one Byzantine historian, he already had a well-established reputation as a preacher. With the theological controversies which led to the Council of Ephesus in 435 and the Council of Chalcedon in 451, Hesychius took the part of Cyril of Alexandria over against Nestorius, thoroughly opposing Theodore of Mopsuestia. Apparently Hesychius opposed both the theology and exegetical method of the Antiochenes.

Hesychius, according to the oldest sources, was διδάσκαλος, that is, teacher, of the church of Jerusalem. In the Greek Church the *didaskalos* was a teacher of especially high rank, with a reputation both for learning and piety, and to be called a *didaskalos* of the church of Jerusalem might be roughly the equivalent to being called a doctor of theology. It was a term of real distinction. Indeed, sometimes he is referred to as Hesychius the Illuminated or Hesychius the Wise. The historians of following centuries tell us that he commented on all the books of the Bible, but his commentaries on Job, Leviticus, and the Psalms are all that have come down to us. Fragments preserved in the chains and other sources indicate

---

294. Etheria, *Journal de Voyage*, sec. 25 and 46.

295. For the most recent attempts at throwing some light on the life of this preacher, see the introduction to Aubineau's edition of his festal sermons, *Homélies festales*, pp. xiii-xviii.

that this claim was far from unfounded. He must have devoted his long life to a ministry of preaching and teaching of a sort similar to what we find in his homilies on Job. Some evidence suggests that he was still alive during the Council of Chalcedon (451), which would mean that his ministry lasted a good forty years.

A. Regular Expository Preaching in the Church of Jerusalem

More than likely at the beginning of the fifth century Jerusalem still had regular, daily expository preaching, just as Antioch did in the days of John Chrysostom or Caesarea in the days of Origen or, for that matter, Ephesus in the days of the apostle Paul. That this should happen in Jerusalem is no surprise. The Gospels tell us that Jesus taught daily in the Temple and Acts tells us that the apostles did the same thing. By the fifth century the Temple was long gone, but we can well imagine that there was daily preaching at the Church of the Holy Sepulchre, which was where the pilgrims would more than likely gather. No doubt morning prayers would have been held first, after which those who had the leisure settled in for a good long sermon which no one felt had to be hurried through in order to get to work. These daily sermons were for those who were devoting their time to spiritual matters, at least for the time they were on their pilgrimage. For Etheria this meant a good portion of the year, and this seems to have been fairly often the case. Pilgrims who went to Jerusalem in those days did not expect to "do" the Holy Land in two weeks. In fact, many came to the Holy Land to end their days of earthly pilgrimage in the city that was the type of the heavenly Jerusalem. Jerusalem had a high concentration of very pious people, the sort who were more than willing to follow a discipline of daily preaching.

From the sermons on Job which Hesychius has left us, it appears that regular preaching was conducted at other places in Jerusalem as well. Charles Renoux has shown quite convincingly that this series of sermons was preached at the Church of the Upper Room, which supposedly stood on the site of the Upper Room, just as the Church of the Holy Sepulchre was supposed to have stood on the site of the resurrection. Renoux also suggests that the sermons might have been preached during Lent, but he admits there is no concrete evidence for this hypothesis. There is, however, one very strong argument against it: The preacher makes no attempt to use his sermons to support the devotional disciplines of Lent that one would expect of a conscientious preacher in such a setting. It would seem more likely that Hesychius preached this series of sermons at a midweek preaching service at the Church of the Upper Room, and that it would have been quite similar to the daily service we imagine must have been held at the Church of the Holy Sepulchre. If we might be allowed a suggestion of our own, we would add that perhaps these daily services at the Church of the Upper Room might have been evening services. What place in Jerusalem would have been more appropriate for an evening service than the place where Jesus celebrated the Last Supper with his disciples on the night in which he was betrayed, and where, traditionally, Jesus also appeared to the disciples at the end of the day of the resurrection? Hesychius's sermons on Job may well have been preached after vespers on weekday evenings. They might also have been preached on Wednesday and Friday afternoons at the celebration of Communion, which we know to have been a regular feature of the worship of Jerusalem. And even beyond that, one might suggest that Hesychius occupied the same pulpit for a good many years, preaching through one book of the Bible after another. On the basis of what we have observed in regard to other preachers from this period, one thing seems clear: Somewhere in Jerusalem Hesychius did daily expository preaching year in and year out. It was this daily expository preaching which made it possible to produce the complete set of commentaries which he is supposed to have preached.

B. *The Sermons on Job*

In his sermons on Job Hesychius has given us a serious and learned attempt at a Christian interpretation of one of the most challenging and difficult books of the Bible.[296] It is clearly a Christian interpretation, and yet, at the same time, the literal sense of the text is given first attention. Very rarely does Hesychius go beyond this literal sense, and his interpretation is not at all far-fetched. There is much in these sermons which the Christian of today might well take to heart. A study of these sermons makes it quite clear that the exegesis of the Fathers was much more sound than we often imagine.

---

296. This study is based on the edition of Charles Renoux: Hesychius of Jerusalem, *Homélies sur Job*, Armenian text with French translation by Charles Renoux, Patrologia Orientalis, vol. 42 (Turnhout, Belgium: Brepols, 1983).

The original Greek text of this series of sermons has been lost. All we have is an Armenian translation, and at that, of only half the series: twenty-four sermons on the first twenty chapters of the book. Apparently the translator never finished his work. Even at that, it is a right sizeable volume — the sermons are not short. From fragments of the Greek text which have survived it is clear that the series originally covered the entire forty-two chapters of Job.

The overall interpretation Hesychius offers us follows the interpretation laid down in the Epistle of James:

> Be patient, therefore, brethren, until the coming of the Lord. . . . As an example of suffering and patience, brethren, take the prophets who spoke in the name of the Lord. Behold, we call those happy who are steadfast. You have heard of the steadfastness of Job, and you have seen the purpose of the Lord, how the Lord is compassionate and merciful. (James 5:7-11)

This early Christian interpretation of Job found in the Epistle of James presents Job as an example of patience, which is understood as a primary Christian virtue. The Christian, in view of the coming of the Lord, can afford to be patient, but even more, the Christian can be sure that God will fulfill his purposes. Hesychius finds a very strong doctrine of providence in the book of Job. God sets times and limits to our trials; he knows how much we can bear. Just as in the book of James the virtue of patience is based on a strong faith in providence, so it is with the book of Job.[297] The providence of God is compassionately disposed. The God who is in control is a loving God.

In a very tasteful and restrained way Hesychius brings in other biblical saints who have patiently borne suffering. Jeremiah would be an obvious example just taken generally, but Hesychius is able to quote laments of the tearful prophet which express exactly the same thoughts expressed in Job.[298] David's patient bearing of the persecution of King Saul is an important parallel for our preacher which enables him, of course, to view many psalms as parallel texts.[299] We might not approach it quite the same way, but the important thing is that Hesychius had the exegetical good sense to recognize the psalms of lamentation as parallel passages. The

297. Hesychius, *Homélies sur Job*, p. 377.
298. Hesychius, *Homélies sur Job*, p. 183.
299. Hesychius, *Homélies sur Job*, pp. 185, 203, 269, and 107.

patient waiting of Habakkuk becomes another parallel which our *didaska-los* carefully weaves into his colorful carpet.[300] But, of course, a Christian interpreter of Job could hardly do other than see in the trials of Job a prophetic type of the patient suffering of Jesus. And, one must ask, why not? As Hesychius interprets it, the sufferings of Job are a type of the sufferings of Christ.[301] Commenting on the text of Job 19:6, which tells us that it is the Lord who has brought the trouble on Job, Hesychius presents Job as another type of the righteous sufferer like the Suffering Servant of the fifty-third chapter of Isaiah.[302] Job was a blameless and upright man upon whom suffering came not because of his sin but because of the mysterious counsel of God. Job was an earthen vessel, an image of clay, and God would not have called him blameless and upright if it were not also that he was an image of the Christ. Though very conservative, this is clearly a Christian interpretation of Job.

The overall effect of this sensitive interpretation of the book of Job is to give to the Christian examples of how one can bear suffering. As Charles Renoux has pointed out, the sermons are clearly addressed to a congregation of many different kinds of people, not to a monastic congregation or a group of ascetics. Hesychius assumes that a good part of his congregation lives in the world, and it is to such people that he points out examples of patient suffering. What is surprising, given the time in which these sermons were preached, is that a spirit of *contemptus mundi* does not saturate them. Job is presented as a good man who lived in the world, a family man who delighted in his family, a man of enormous wealth and considerable power who used these blessings well. Being generous and charitable, he had won the respect of his contemporaries. And even beyond that, he was a man of wisdom who had been an inspiration to his generation. One never gets the impression that in the mind of Hesychius Job is really the model of the ascetic, for God restores Job's family and estate. Hesychius is aware of the danger of Manichaeism.[303] If Job despises this world, it is not the world God has created but the world as it has been perverted by human sin. This Hesychius makes quite clear.

Another noteworthy point about these sermons is that while they preserve the historic form of the expository sermon for the main body of

300. Hesychius, *Homélies sur Job*, p. 185.
301. Hesychius, *Homélies sur Job*, pp. 539ff.
302. Hesychius, *Homélies sur Job*, p. 540. Cf. as well p. 559.
303. Hesychius, *Homélies sur Job*, p. 183.

the sermon, Hesychius usually provides an introduction and a conclusion of the sort that the Greek-speaking world had come to expect. Hesychius was evidently trained in classical rhetoric, but he was confident that Scripture, plain and simple, is a lily which hardly needs to be gilded. Charles Renoux has put it very well: Hesychius has shown us how lively and interesting a rather straightforward expository sermon can be.

In the pulpit a surprisingly large portion of time was apparently given to reading the chapter on which the preacher intended to make his commentary. First it was read as the Scripture lesson, then section by section as the preacher progressed. When preaching from Job this must have been impressive. The simple text is of such beauty! Occasionally Hesychius can come up with an elegant *exordium* like the apostrophe at the beginning of Sermon 5 in which our preacher addresses the Church of the Upper Room and extols her spiritual wealth.[304] More often the introductions set the general theme of the particular chapter to be treated. For example, Sermon 9 gives us a brilliant introduction to the virtue of patience. With a magnificent extended metaphor it is called the throne of all virtues, the scepter which presides over life, the armor of Job in his spiritual warfare, more useful than any sword.[305] For an example of his more usual introductions let us take Sermon 21. This sermon begins very simply with a few remarks on the value of keeping our human mortality in mind. Being aware of our mortality keeps us from becoming too infatuated with the ephemeral pleasures of this world. It encourages us to set our mind on the end of life and the victory that is to come. This introduction puts the commentary which is to follow in a clear and more understandable light.[306]

While the main body of Hesychius's sermons is the verse-by-verse commentary on the text of one chapter after another of the book of Job, and while the body of the sermons may meander over a number of subjects, the introductions are brief and pointed. Usually the conclusions are even more sober. It is almost as though the preacher recognized this quality as a requirement for a well-ordered sermon, but, realizing the hour he has been expected to use was more than past, he quickly sums up his message. On the other hand sometimes his perorations, although very brief, are quite stirring, for example, his conclusion to Sermon 3. The last verse he

---

304. Hesychius, *Homélies sur Job*, pp. 149-53.
305. Hesychius, *Homélies sur Job*, pp. 235ff.
306. Hesychius, *Homélies sur Job*, p. 515.

treats is the famous text "'The Lord gave and the Lord has taken away; blessed be the name of the Lord'" (Job 1:21). His commentary on the text leads to a moving consolation for those who have suffered deprivation of the joys of life. These words of comfort then lead to the concluding doxology that one expects in sermons of this period.[307]

The conclusion to Sermon 8, which concerns the trials Job's friends have heaped upon him, gives us an example of the most eloquent brevity. It very fittingly gives a benediction of those who are put to the test. They have shared the sufferings of the prophets and apostles before them; they have filled the air with the scent of a sacred ointment of which we are aware, even in these later days, a sacred perfume which goes from life to life, from this life to the life of the Father, the Son, and the Holy Spirit, to whom be glory for ever and ever. Amen.[308]

We will have more to say about Hesychius in the chapter which follows, where we will show him to be a witness to the growing importance of festal, or liturgical, preaching. Here we emphasize that Hesychius is first of all a witness to the tradition of expository preaching which was so characteristic of the patristic age.

307. Hesychius, *Homélies sur Job*, p. 119.
308. Hesychius, *Homélies sur Job*, p. 231.

CHAPTER II

The Jerusalem Lectionary in the Fifth Century

It was not until the beginning of the fifth century that the public reading of Scripture in the church of Jerusalem had become so complicated that a special manual was needed to explain which portions of Scripture were to be read at the elaborate festivities of the Holy City. The calendar of Scripture lessons had begun to move in that direction, no doubt, when Cyril had been bishop and had presided over the Holy Week services in Constantine's magnificent Church of the Holy Sepulchre. It was probably Cyril more than anyone else who sensed the possibilities of staging in the streets of Jerusalem a Christian mystery play that would outdo anything Eleusius or Delphi could offer. By the close of the fourth century when the Spanish nun Etheria recorded her experiences as a pilgrim, the worship of Jerusalem was beginning to develop a liturgical calendar which took full advantage of the holy sites.[1] Etheria gives us a good picture of the

---

1. The following study is based on the text published by Hélène Pétré: Etheria, *Journal de Voyage,* Latin text, introduction, and translation by Hélène Pétré, Sources chrétiennes, vol. 21 (Paris: Éditions du Cerf, 1948). For an English translation, see G. E. Gingas, *Egeria: Diary of a Pilgrimage,* Ancient Christian Writers, vol. 38 (New York: Newman Press, 1970). Among the more important studies for our purposes: A. Bludau, *Die Pilgerreise der Aetheria,* Studien zur Geschichte und Kultur des Altertums, vol. 15 (Paderborn: F. Schoningh, 1927); P. Devos, "La date du voyage d'Egérie," *Analecta Bollandiana* 85 (1967): 165-94; and M. Féotin and H. Leclercq, *Dictionnaire d'archéologie chrétienne et de liturgie,* 15 vols. (Paris: Letouzey et Ane, 1907-53), 5:552-84; 7:2304-92; and 14:92-110.

liturgical dramas Cyril bequeathed to Christian Jerusalem. Let us look at Etheria's description of the cycle of annual feasts as Hesychius must have known it as a young man growing up in Jerusalem.

I. The Journals of Etheria

Etheria tells us first of the celebration of Epiphany.[2] On 5 January the Christians of the Holy City went in procession down to Bethlehem to the Church of the Nativity,[3] where they held a vigil very similar to the Easter vigil,[4] in which a long series of Scripture lessons was read, outlining the history of salvation. There is a missing leaf in the manuscript at this point, however, and we can derive from the document in its present condition only something about a return to Jerusalem. Once back in the Church of the Holy Sepulchre the pilgrims received a blessing from the bishop, and the monks spent the rest of the night in prayer at the church. At eight o'clock on the morning of 6 January there was a celebration of the Eucharist. This being a festive occasion, a number of the presbyters preached on the lessons, which were read before the bishop took the pulpit and preached his sermon.[5] For a full octave the feast of Epiphany was celebrated in the various sacred sites: the Church of the Upper Room, the Church on the Mount of Olives, and the church at Bethany.[6] Spreading the services out like this meant that an Epiphany service was held in each neighborhood, which gave pilgrims who were in Jerusalem for a shorter time a chance to get to all the sites.

Services for a major feast like Epiphany lasted all morning, and Etheria makes the point several times that a number of the presbyters took their turn at explaining the Scriptures before the bishop himself preached. Etheria emphasizes this collegial approach to preaching. It was apparently the regular custom in Jerusalem. She also emphasizes that the purpose of

2. On the celebration of Epiphany in the church of Jerusalem, cf. Bernard Botte, *Les origines de la Noël et de l'Épiphanie, Études historiques* (Louvain: Abbaye du Mont César, 1932), pp. 13-21.

3. Etheria, *Journal de Voyage* 25.

4. On the origins of the Epiphany vigil, see Anton Baumstark, *Nocturna laus: Typen frühchristlicher Virgilienfeier und ihr Fortleben vor allem im römischen und monastischen Ritus* (Münster im Westphalia: Aschendorff, 1967), pp. 26-33.

5. Etheria, *Journal de Voyage* 25.

6. Etheria, *Journal de Voyage* 25.

the preaching was to teach the people the Scriptures and to make clear to them the love of God.[7] That different elders should take their turn preaching and that a service of worship should have several sermons was surely a very old custom, especially in Palestinian congregations where the continuity with the synagogue was strong. On Sundays and surely even more so on holidays, the preaching could stretch the service out to as long as three hours. Preaching was obviously a big part of the celebration.[8]

Forty days after the feast of the Epiphany the church of Jerusalem celebrated the *Hypapante,* the feast of the presentation of Christ, or, as it became known in the West, the feast of the purification of the Virgin.[9] This feast is a prime example of the historicizing of the calendar. Etheria tells us it was marked by a special procession and celebrated with great honor,[10] and was, in fact, almost as big an occasion as Easter. The bishop, as well as the presbyters, would preach on the story as it is found in the Gospel of Luke of how Jesus was brought to the Temple forty days after his birth and received the blessing of Simeon and Anna (Luke 2:22). The original idea of this feast, as celebrated in Jerusalem, may have been to bring the nativity into the Holy City. As the one event surrounding the birth of Christ that took place in Jerusalem, we can understand why the church of Jerusalem made such an elaborate celebration of it: It was one more opportunity to develop the devotional value of a pilgrimage to Jerusalem. The chances are that it was at Jerusalem that this feast originated; it is fairly easy to imagine it as one more product of the fertile genius of Bishop Cyril. According to the liturgical historian Bernard Capelle, the report of Etheria, which gives it considerable attention, is the first mention of the feast.[11] As time went along the sermon for the feast of the *Hypapante,* just as the sermons for the feasts of the Annunciation, the Nativity, and the Dormition of the Virgin, became an important

---

7. "Sane quia hic consuetudo sic est, ut de omnibus presbyteris, qui sedent, quanti volunt, praedicent, et postillos omnes episcopus praedicat, quae praedicationes propterea semper dominicis diebus sunt, ut semper erudiatur populus in scripturis et in Dei delictione: quae praedicationes dum dicentur, grandis mora fit, ut fiat missa ecclesiae, et ideo ante quartam horam aut forte quintam missa non fit." Etheria, *Journal de Voyage* 25.

8. Etheria, *Journal de Voyage* 25.

9. Etheria, *Journal de Voyage* 26.

10. On the feast of *Hypapante,* see B. Capelle, "Les Fêtes Mariales," in *L'Église en Prière,* ed. A. G. Martimort (Tournai: Desclée & Cie., 1961), pp. 752ff., and G. Löw, "Festa della Purificazione," in *Enciclopedia cattolica,* 10:341-45.

11. Capelle, "Les Fêtes Mariales," in *L'Église en Prière,* p. 252.

homiletical convention. By the end of the fourth century in Jerusalem it was evidently well established.

In Etheria's day the liturgical observance of Lent was still quite modest. Its main concern, we gather, was the keeping of the fast; only after that was the preparation of candidates for baptism of interest.[12] Special catechetical sermons were still preached, as they had been in Cyril's day, and these, according to Etheria, consisted of two parts: a series of sermons going through the whole Bible, giving first the literal and then the spiritual meaning,[13] and an explanation of the creed, phrase by phrase.[14] Etheria makes special note of the fact that although Lent lasts eight weeks in Jerusalem, it does not include Saturdays and Sundays,[15] and no special Lenten sermons were preached on Sunday. Normally, all year long there was preaching at the Church of the Upper Room in the late afternoon, the Wednesday and Friday services of which concluded with the Lord's Supper.[16] But during the forty-day fast more time was given to preaching since Communion was not celebrated in consideration of those who fasted during the week. At least two sermons were preached at these services:[17] the usual evening sermon and then a special sermon by the bishop.[18] What apparently happened was that regularly there was a sermon following the *lectio continua* of some book of the Bible. This happened at least each Wednesday and Friday afternoon throughout the year. During Lent, however, another sermon appropriate to Lent was added, which may also have been a series of sermons on some appropriate book of the Bible such as the prophet Joel or Lamentations. What seems to be clear is that the observance of Lent was confined to midweek services.

12. Etheria, *Journal de Voyage* 27.

13. ". . . episcopus docet illos legem sici id est inchoans a Genese per illos dies quadraginta perurret omnes scripturas primum exponens carnaliter et sic illud soluens spiritualiter. Nec non etiam et de resurrectione, per illos dies; hoc autem cathecisis appellatur." Etheria, *Journal de Voyage* 46.

14. Etheria, *Journal de Voyage* 46.

15. Etheria, *Journal de Voyage* 27.

16. Possibly at one stage of the development this service was held every day while at another it was held only on Wednesday and Friday. The text is not completely clear. Etheria, *Journal de Voyage* 46.

17. "Diebus vero quadragesimarum, ut superius dixi, quarta feria ad nona in syon proceditur juxta consuetudinem totius anni et omnia aguntur, quae consuetudo est ad nonam agi praeter oblatio; nam ut semper populus presbyter praedicant assidue." Etheria, *Journal de Voyage* 27.

18. Etheria, *Journal de Voyage* 27.

One did not, even in Cyril's Jerusalem, drape the Lord's Day in penitential purple.

Much more important than the observance of the forty-day fast was the observance of Holy Week. The concern for the reenactment of the drama of the Savior's passion and resurrection at the sacred sites of the Holy City is obviously a strong force in shaping these traditions.[19] Lazarus Saturday made a lasting impression on Etheria.[20] She tells us of the procession which led out to Bethany, where Lazarus and his two sisters Mary and Martha had lived, and of the Scripture readings and psalmody appropriate to the place and the day. (Starting with Lazarus Saturday, each day had established readings from Scripture.) Besides mentioning the reading of the eleventh chapter of the Gospel of John, Etheria says that at the close of the service John 12:1 was read, which tells how Jesus was at Bethany six days before Passover. This retracing of the footsteps of Jesus fascinated our Spanish pilgrim because, she tells us, this is just the way it was, for from Lazarus Saturday to Maundy Thursday is six days.[21]

Palm Sunday put even more of an emphasis on dramatic reenactment. Sunday afternoon at one o'clock the faithful gathered on the Mount of Olives to hear appropriate Scripture lessons, psalms, and prayers. Since the service lasted all afternoon we can well imagine that again there was more than one sermon.[22] Specifically Etheria mentions the reading from the Gospel which tells of the entry of Jesus into Jerusalem. With this reading the procession begins. Children particularly were part of the crowd, with the younger ones being carried by their mothers. All carried branches of palm and olive and escorted the bishop into the city, winding through the streets and eventually ending up at the Church of the Holy Sepulchre where vespers was held at an hour considerably later than usual.[23]

---

19. Thomas Talley's attempt to deemphasize this is hardly convincing. *The Origins of the Liturgical Year* (New York: Pueblo Publishing Co., 1986), pp. 176-83.

20. Etheria, *Journal de Voyage* 29.

21. Etheria, *Journal de Voyage* 29.

22. "Hora ergo septima omnis populus ascendit in monte olivet, id est in Eleona, in ecclesia, sed et episcopus; dicuntur ymni et antiphonae aptae diei ipsi vel loco, lectiones etiam similiter. Et cum coeperit se facere hora nona, subitur cum ymnis in Inbomon, id est in eo loco, de quo ascendit Dominus in caelis, et ibi seditur; nam omnis populus semper prae sente episcopo, jubetur sedere, tantum quod diacones soli stant semper. Dicuntur et ibi ymni uel antiphonae aptae loco aut diei: similiter et lectiones interpositae et orationes." Etheria, *Journal de Voyage* 31.

23. Etheria, *Journal de Voyage* 31.

Surely these liturgical dramas engaged the whole population of the city. The crowds which took part in these processions could never fit inside the walls of one church building, and thus the processions from one site to another solved an important logistical problem. Also, one cannot help but detect an evangelistic dimension to these processions which went out into the streets and involved every passerby in these sacred mysteries.

On Thursday excitement must have mounted as the celebration traced the way of the Savior's suffering through the streets to the Mount of Olives, on to the sanctuary at Gethsemane, and then back into the city to the sanctuary of Golgotha where Jesus was crucified.[24] Now back inside the Church of the Holy Sepulchre, the bishop gives his flock a word of encouragement. Evidently the final sermon of the evening so impressed Etheria that she gives us a little summary.[25] It was a sermon admonishing the faithful who traced the way of Christ's suffering on this earth to put their faith in God above, who would faithfully repay them for their sufferings on earth by a far greater reward above. Apparently it was only at a later period that the more elaborate *via dolorosa* was developed, although the first signs of it are already beginning to appear. By this time Friday morning had dawned, and the people were sent home to get a little rest before the adoration of the cross began later that morning. The more fervent went to the Church of the Upper Room to see the column where Jesus had been scourged. At each stage of the procession the appropriate passages of Scripture were read and the appropriate psalms sung. In fact, the whole Passion narrative must have been read during the course of the week, chiefly from the Gospel of Matthew, although with supplementary passages from the other Gospels as occasion suggested.

On Saturday night the climax of the whole drama came when the faithful gathered for the Easter vigil at the Church of the Holy Sepulchre. With the congregation gathered around the tomb of Christ, the types of the resurrection were read as the faithful waited for the announcement that Christ is risen. Etheria does not tell us any of the details of these readings but simply mentions that it was done in Jerusalem just as it was back home.[26] These lessons must go back to very ancient times, for they were a well-established tradition throughout the whole Church by this time.[27] In one place

24. Etheria, *Journal de Voyage* 36.
25. Etheria, *Journal de Voyage* 36.
26. Etheria, *Journal de Voyage* 38.
27. Baumstark, *Nocturna laus,* pp. 34-48.

or another there might be variations, but there was always a reading of the story of the creation, Noah and the flood, the sacrifice of Abraham, the Passover and the passage through the Red Sea, and the stories of Jonah and Daniel.[28] At the end of the fourth century when these sacred mysteries were still fresh and vital and before the readings were abbreviated, one heard much Scripture read at that vigil — a veritable compendium of the history of redemption. After the reading of these types, new converts were baptized, and after the newly baptized had been brought back into the church, Easter Communion was celebrated and the Easter Gospel was read from the last chapter of Matthew. Apparently there was a second Easter Communion service held at the usual time for Sunday morning worship, but Etheria finds it unnecessary to describe the service further for it is much the same as what happened back home. She says nothing of the sermons which we know from other sources were preached; several preachers would have commented on the lessons for Easter Sunday morning, which by this time would have been firmly established by tradition. Then finally the bishop himself would have preached.

Finally in the evening, following the example of the first disciples, who on the evening of the first day of the week gathered in the Upper Room, the faithful gathered at the Church of the Upper Room and heard the reading of the passage from the twentieth chapter of the Gospel of John which told of the appearance of the risen Jesus to the disciples. Again Etheria makes the point that all is done just as the apostles had done it on the first resurrection Sunday and that the Scripture readings, the psalms, and the prayers are appropriate to the time and the place.[29]

Easter was celebrated for a full octave, with preaching every day for those who had been baptized. It was only now after the people had received them that the sacraments were explained to them.[30] The usual Sunday preaching continued the Sunday after Easter, but in the afternoon there was another long procession to the Mount of Olives and another trip to the Church of the Upper Room, at which the story of how Jesus appeared in the Upper Room eight days after the resurrection was read.[31] After the

28. Baumstark, *Nocturna laus,* pp. 46-48.

29. Etheria, *Journal de Voyage* 39.

30. Etheria, *Journal de Voyage* 47.

31. One wonders why on the octave of Easter there was another visit to the Mount of Olives. It is clear that every feast day included a procession to the Mount of Olives as well as to other sacred sites in and around Jerusalem. Processions were evidently popular. One reason was that they gave more people a chance to get into the central act of worship. They

Easter octave there seem to have been no special festivities until Ascension Day, which, following the Acts of the Apostles, was held forty days after Easter. One would have expected a special service on the Mount of Olives, but surprisingly, Ascension was celebrated in Bethlehem.[32] Then ten days after that Pentecost was celebrated, with services beginning at the Church of the Holy Sepulchre before dawn. By the middle of the morning the people moved to the Church of the Upper Room, and Etheria is quite explicit about the reading of the second chapter of Acts. Once again there is a long procession up to the Mount of Olives, then back down again, finishing up at the Church of the Upper Room about midnight. Etheria observes that it had been a long and exhausting day.[33]

Surely the arrangement of services in the church of Jerusalem from the feast of the Ascension to the feast of Pentecost is curious. It seems more than probable that what happened at a pilgrimage to Jerusalem was not a historicization of Christian doctrine but rather a reactualization of the history of salvation. The pilgrimage always began at Bethlehem; the main saving acts were "remembered" in the Church of the Holy Sepulchre at the site of the crucifixion and resurrection; the resurrection appearance was "remembered" at the Church of the Upper Room; there was the celebration at Bethany; and finally the pilgrimage experience ended at the celebration on the Mount of Olives where Christ ascended into heaven. It was the complete Christian mystery from rebirth to ascension, all of which one could experience in liturgical ceremonial just as one did in the Mithras cult or as one could in the mysteries of Delphi or Eleusius. Nowhere can one read this more clearly than in the liturgical celebrations of Ascension and Pentecost. About this we will have more to say further on.

Etheria gives us less information about the preaching which took place during Holy Week than she does about the Scripture readings. There must have been considerably more preaching than she mentions. For example, nothing is said about an Easter sermon; surely there was an Easter

---

tied together the various places of worship into one church. By moving around from one site to another one could accommodate a vast number of pilgrims who would never be able to fit into a single building.

32. Etheria, *Journal de Voyage* 42. The visit to Bethlehem at Ascension is explained by reasons other than the concern to retrace the steps of Jesus. It was on Pentecost afternoon that the story of the ascension was read at the site of the ascension. For various attempts to explain this, cf. Pétré, "Données Liturgiques et Ecclésiastiques," *Journal de Voyage*, pp. 66ff.; and Bludau, *Die Pilgerreise der Aetheria*, 15:155-62.

33. Etheria, *Journal de Voyage* 43.

sermon![34] But then, as we have noticed before, she tends not to tell about those things that happened in Jerusalem about the same way they happened at home. Reading through Etheria's account very carefully, one often suspects that there must have been some preaching at these stations or they would never have taken as long as they did. Besides that, as we shall see, we have from other sources sermons which were preached at these occasions. One of these sources is Hesychius himself. The point that needs to be made here, however, is that this kind of liturgical drama as it was beginning to develop in Jerusalem began to put heavier and heavier demands on the preacher. It began to establish conventions as to just what needed to be preached when and where. The liturgy set the theme of the sermon. What we find in the preaching of Hesychius of Jerusalem are two distinct kinds of sermons: the expository sermon and the festal sermon. While the expository sermon drew its themes directly from Scripture, the festal sermon drew its themes from the liturgy.

II. Scripture Readings for Feast Days

It was a generation after Etheria's visit that the first lectionary of Jerusalem appeared. This lectionary we know of from an Armenian translation, but it was originally, of course, a Greek lectionary.[35] The Armenian community in the Holy City has always been strong, and it is not at all surprising that this community should preserve some of the earliest documents of the Jerusalem church. The earliest form of this lectionary was drawn up in the first half of the fifth century, that is, during the ministry of Hesychius. It merits considerable attention on our part, particularly at this point in our story.

This Jerusalem lectionary is a list of Scripture lessons, psalms, and antiphons to be used at the various feast days and religious observances of the church of Jerusalem. It is one of the most important documents we have for the history of Christian worship. Several features stand out from

34. "Vigiliae autem paschales sic fiunt, quem ad modum ad nos; hoc solum hic amplius fit, quod infantes, cum baptidiati fuerit et vestiti, quemadmodum exierint de fonte, simul cum episcopo primum ad Anastase ducuntur. . . . et sic venit ad ecclesium majorem cum eis, ubi juxta consuetudinem omnis populus vigilat. Aguntur ibi, quae consuetudinis est etiam et aput nos, et facta oblatione fit missa." Etheria, *Journal de Voyage* 38.

35. Athanase Renoux, *Le Codex Arménien Jérusalem 121,* Patrologia Orientalis, vol. 36 (Turnholt: Brepols, 1969-71), pp. 141-388.

this document. First, one notices that this is a lectionary for the two major feasts of the year, Easter and Epiphany, each of which, by the beginning of the fifth century, has spawned a number of auxiliary celebrations. Easter particularly has spread out its observance over most of the springtime, while Epiphany still occupies a more modest portion of the midwinter calendar. This Jerusalem lectionary is then, first, a list of Scripture lessons for the Christian celebration of Passover and for the feast of the Nativity, and second, a calendar of saints' days.

Let us look for a moment at these saints' days, two or three dozen of which are observed. They are particularly interesting because they are so obviously artificial as compared to the saints' days of churches which had real continuity with the age of the martyrs — Rome, Antioch, or Caesarea, for instance. These Jerusalem saints' days exist for a different reason than the saints' days of other cities. Originally the saint's day was an annual memorial held at the grave of a martyr, much like the memorials Romans held for the departed members of their families each year at their graves. When the Church held these memorials for her martyrs, they began to take a much greater significance. They were understood as the *dies natales* of the martyr; that is, they celebrated the day at which the martyr had been born into eternal life. Some of these celebrations of martyrs' *dies natales* were very old, going back even as far as the first century. As time went along, it became customary for a church to keep a list of these *dies natales* and the dates at which these memorials were to be held, on which the bishop and his staff would proceed to the cemetery and hold the appropriate service. In churches like Rome and Antioch the list of martyrs whose memory was celebrated in this manner was rather long by the time Constantine finally brought an end to the persecution. But the situation was quite different in Jerusalem. Jerusalem had had her martyrs, to be sure. It was in Jerusalem that Stephen, the first Christian martyr, and a number of others had experienced their birth into the world to come, but since the church of Jerusalem had been dispersed during the Jewish Wars, there was not a continuing tradition of observing the *dies natales*. Yet, when the Christian emperors began to take an interest in rebuilding the church of Jerusalem, Jerusalem was not slow in discovering the relics of her most beloved saints. In time churches were built to house these relics and shrines to commemorate the spot where these martyrs passed from this life to the next. There were other factors at work as well, however. Jerusalem became home to Christians from many lands. As we have already mentioned, there was a sizeable community of Armenians in the city, as well as a large community of Latins — Saint Jerome and his friends Paula and

144

Marcella were not the only Romans who came to live in the Holy Land. From Constantinople the dowager Empress Eudoxia, widow of Theodosius II, had come to spend her last days on sacred ground, and then, of course, most important of all was Saint Helena, the mother of Constantine. These were only the most conspicuous of a whole host of pilgrims who spent a good part of their lives in Jerusalem. These pilgrims had particular devotion to saints who had no particular connection with Jerusalem but whom they wanted to commemorate nevertheless. With all the monks in Jerusalem, it was only natural that the feast of Saint Anthony should be celebrated. Romans naturally wanted to celebrate the martyrdom of Saints Peter and Paul. The list of saints' days found in the Jerusalem lectionary is, in effect, one of the first attempts at drawing up a calendar of saints which was of ecumenical rather than merely local interest.

Another noticeable feature of this lectionary is that Epiphany, rather than Christmas, is the feast of the Nativity.[36] Jerusalem was one of the last churches of the East to adopt 25 December as the feast of the Nativity. This no doubt was because the unique feature of Jerusalem's celebration of Epiphany was the journey to Bethlehem and the vigil in the Church of the Nativity, and for Jerusalem to do what other churches did — namely, to celebrate the nativity on 25 December and then save the celebration of the visit of the wise men, the baptism of Jesus, and the wedding at Cana for 6 January — would have demanded a much more radical rearrangement of established customs than in other churches. If Epiphany celebrated the baptism of Jesus or the marriage at Cana, there was no reason to go to Bethlehem. The visit of the Magi could be celebrated at Bethlehem, but that, in addition to being rather anticlimactic compared to the nativity, would have meant two trips to Bethlehem less than two weeks apart during winter, which might not have been too popular. One can understand why the church of Jerusalem was slow to adopt the celebration of the nativity on 25 December. Eventually Jerusalem did adopt that date, but during the ministry of Hesychius the birth of Christ was celebrated during the octave of Epiphany. Another thing one notices is that there is no trace of Advent. Advent was added to the liturgical calendar rather late, as a preparation for the Feast of the Nativity lasting four weeks. In Jerusalem the whole celebration takes not much more than a week; to be exact it is limited to the octave of Epiphany. The lectionary makes it clear that each day during the octave a different aspect of the nativity was celebrated.

36. Botte, *Les origines de la Noël et de l'Épiphanie*, p. 16.

The vigil at the Church of the Nativity in Bethlehem was characterized by a long series of readings from the Old Testament prophets which
told of the birth of the promised Messiah. The service began with the
pilgrims gathering at the shepherds' field just outside Bethlehem at four
o'clock on the afternoon of 5 January, where they heard a reading of the
story of the appearance of the angels to the shepherds (Luke 2:8-20).[37]
Afterward they moved into the Church of the Nativity and listened to the
following lessons:[38]

> Genesis 1:28–3:20
>> The Creation and Fall of Man
> Isaiah 7:10-17
>> "A Virgin Shall Conceive"
> Exodus 14:24–15:21
>> Song of the Sea
> Micah 5:1-6
>> The Messiah to Be Born in Bethlehem
> Proverbs 1:2-19
>> The Value of Wisdom
> Isaiah 9:4b-6
>> The Prince of Peace
> Isaiah 11:1-9
>> The Peaceable Kingdom
> Isaiah 35:3-8
>> The Desert Shall Bloom as a Rose
> Isaiah 40:10-17
>> "He Will Feed His Sheep Like a Shepherd"
> Isaiah 42:1-8
>> "A Bruised Reed He Will Not Break"
> Daniel 3:1-35a
>> Three Young Men in the Fiery Furnace
> Daniel 3:35b-51
>> The Song of the Three Young Men
> Titus 2:11-15
>> The Epiphany

37. Renoux, *Le Codex Arménien Jérusalem 121*, p. 211.
38. Renoux, *Le Codex Arménien Jérusalem 121*, pp. 211-15.

Matthew 2:1-12
The Birth of Christ

What we have here is a series of passages of the Old Testament which speak of the messianic hope. Some are straightforward prophecies while others are types or intimations. The passage from Micah which speaks of the birth of the Messiah in Bethlehem, the city of David, and several passages from Isaiah, such as those on the virgin birth of Immanuel, the Prince of Peace, the shoot from the root of Jesse, and the flowering of the rose in the desert (Isaiah 35), are among those "testimonies" which the ancient Church understood to speak most clearly of the coming of the Christ. They are beautiful passages of Scripture, so full of the biblical imagery of salvation,[39] and just hearing them read must have been inspiring. It certainly would appear that this Epiphany vigil is an attempt to do at Epiphany what had been so successful at Easter. Holidays have a way of copying each other. What people like to do at one feast they like to do at another. If people like a Christmas tree at Christmas, why not do an Easter tree at Easter and cover it with plastic colored eggs?

Once the Epiphany vigil was over the congregation returned to Jerusalem, going directly to the Church of the Holy Sepulchre for a solemn conclusion to their procession to Bethlehem. Back in Jerusalem there were services at which appropriate portions of Scripture were read each day:[40]

6 January (Church of the Holy Sepulchre)
　　Epistle: Titus 2:11-15 (The Epiphany)
　　Gospel: Matthew 1:18-25 (The birth of Jesus)
7 January (Church of Saint Stephen)
　　Acts 6:8–8:2 (The martyrdom of Stephen)
　　Titus 2:11-15 (The Epiphany)
　　John 12:24-26 (Jesus revealed to the Greeks)
8 January
　　Hebrews 1:1-12 (God's revelation to us in his Son)
　　Matthew 2:13-23 (Flight to Egypt)
9 January
　　Galatians 4:1-7 (God sent forth his Son)　·
　　Luke 1:26-38 (Annunciation)

---

39. Renoux, *Le Codex Arménien Jérusalem 121*, p. 213.
40. Renoux, *Le Codex Arménien Jérusalem 121*, pp. 215-23.

10 January (Church of the Upper Room?)
　　Hebrews 12:18-27 (You have come to Mount Zion)
　　Luke 1:39-56 (Visitation)
11 January (Church at Bethany)
　　I Thessalonians 4:13-18 (The resurrection of Christians)
　　John 11:1-46 (Resurrection of Lazarus)
12 January
　　Romans 1:1-7 (The Son of David)
　　Luke 2:1-7 (Birth of Jesus)
13 January
　　Colossians 2:8-15 (A circumcision made without hands)
　　Luke 2:21 (Circumcision)

The annunciation of the angel Gabriel to the Virgin, the visitation of Mary with her cousin Elizabeth, Joseph's dream, and finally, on the eighth day, the circumcision of the infant Jesus are all included. In time these celebrations will be spread out over the year. The annunciation was moved to 25 March, while the feast of the visitation was moved to 2 July, but in the days when the liturgical calendar was being organized the Gospel readings were chosen in such a way that the whole nativity narrative was read in the course of the octave. Appropriate readings from the Epistles, psalms, and antiphons were selected. There was one exception — the feast of the *Hypapante,* held forty days after Epiphany.[41] Other than that the celebration of Christ's birth was confined to the octave of Epiphany.

The most curious feature of this series of lessons is the reading of the story of the resurrection of Lazarus at the Church of Saint Lazarus at Bethany. Why during the octave of Epiphany is it significant that everyone process up to Bethany? Certainly what we are dealing with, once again, is not the historicization of the liturgy but rather an attempt to reactualize the history of salvation. In the course of the octave of Epiphany the pilgrim could imitate the whole progress of redemption, beginning with the reading of the creation narrative in Bethlehem on 5 January and seven days later on 11 January the reading of the resurrection of Lazarus at Bethany. Here again we very clearly see the attempt to make a mystery religion out of Christianity. One could come to Jerusalem and go through the whole experience. One could be born again in Bethlehem

41. Renoux, *Le Codex Arménien Jérusalem 121,* p. 229. We have already spoken above of the special meaning of this feast to the church of the city of Jerusalem.

and rise from the dead like Lazarus at Bethany all in the course of the octave of Epiphany.

Another marked characteristic of the early Jerusalem lectionary is how little effect Lent has on the selection of Scripture passages. The observance of Lent was strictly limited to weekdays. And, except for the second week in Lent when there were daily services, only two days of the week, namely, Wednesday and Friday, had special readings. The lectionary gives us the following readings for Lent:[42]

First Wednesday of Lent
    Exodus 1:1–2:10
    Joel 1:14-20
First Friday of Lent
    Deuteronomy 6:4b–7:10
    Job 6:2–7:13
    Isaiah 40:1-8
Second Week of Lent
    Monday
        I Kings 1:1-23a
        Proverbs 1:2-33
        Jeremiah 1:1-10
    Tuesday
        I Kings 1:23–2:26
        Proverbs 2:1–3:10
        Jeremiah 1:11–2:3
    Wednesday
        Exodus 2:11-22
        Joel 2:1-11
        Micah 4:1-7
    Thursday
        I Kings 3:21c–4:18
        Proverbs 3:11–4:14
        Jeremiah 2:31–3:16
    Friday
        Deuteronomy 7:11–8:1
        Job 9:2–10:2
        Isaiah 40:9-17

42. Renoux, *Le Codex Arménien Jérusalem 121*, pp. 239-55.

Third Wednesday of Lent
    Exodus 2:23–3:15
    Joel 2:21–3:5
Third Friday of Lent
    Deuteronomy 8:11–9:10
    Job 12:2–13:6
    Isaiah 42:1-9
Fourth Wednesday of Lent
    Exodus 3:16-22
    Joel 4:1-8
Fourth Friday of Lent
    Deuteronomy 9:11-24
    Job 16:2–17:16
    Isaiah 43:22–44:8
Fifth Wednesday of Lent
    Exodus 4:1-21a
    Joel 4:9-21
Fifth Friday of Lent
    Deuteronomy 10:1-15
    Job 19:2-29
    Isaiah 45:1-13
Sixth Wednesday in Lent
    Exodus 4:21b–5:3
    Zechariah 9:9-16a
Sixth Friday in Lent
    Deuteronomy 11:10-25
    Job 21:2-34
    Isaiah 46:3–47:4

It becomes apparent from this schedule of Scripture lessons for Lent that there are three sets of lessons: one for the Wednesdays, one for the Fridays, and one for Monday, Tuesday, and Thursday of the second week of Lent. The Wednesday set has a *lectio continua* of the first five chapters of Exodus and treats the birth of Moses, his call to deliver Israel at the burning bush, and his return to Egypt to begin his ministry. This is complemented by a *lectio continua* of the prophecy of Joel. Nothing could be more appropriate to the holding of a fast than these oracles of Joel. The Friday series contains three Old Testament lessons: a lesson from the Law, a *lectio continua* of Deuteronomy 6–11; a lesson from the Wisdom books, selected chapters from Job; and a lesson from the Prophets, a selection of prophetic oracles' from Isaiah announcing the ministry of the Suffering Servant. The set of lessons for Monday, Tuesday, and Thursday of the second week of Lent also provides for a lesson from each of the three types of Old Testament literature — Law, Wisdom, and Prophets — in the form of the beginning of a *lectio continua* of Kings, Proverbs, and Jeremiah. If we could understand just why these passages were selected for Lent, that would help us understand the approach to reading Scripture which was followed at this very formative period in the history of Christian worship. But figuring out the reasoning behind the lectionary selections of late antiquity is one of the favorite card tricks of liturgical scholars. So, only with a caution of modesty would we think of making a few suggestions.

First, we might try to explain the fact that there are three sets of lessons by the wealth of preachers in the city of Jerusalem who should be given an opportunity to preach. One preacher could be invited to preach through the first part of the Moses cycle in Exodus and another to preach through Joel. This would make one sermon per preacher each Wednesday for the six weeks of Lent. For Fridays a third preacher could be asked to do Deuteronomy, a fourth Job, and a fifth the prophecies of the Suffering Servant in Isaiah. The same could be done with the lessons for the second week in Lent.

Another question which presents itself is why, in these three sets, eight series of *lectio continua* lessons all begin new books but never, except for the reading from Joel, finish any. One implication seems to be that normally Scripture lessons were selected on the principle of the *lectio continua;* only for a limited number of special days were special lessons chosen. One also notices that if these eight *lectio continua* series were continued out over the period of a year at about the speed they are read during Lent, a very hefty portion of the Old Testament would be read. More likely, however, this was done for symbolic reasons. With these readings from all the different facets of the Old Testament one wanted to intimate the whole of revelation; one wanted the precepts of the Law, the wisdom of the wise, the ecstasy of the former prophets, and the proclamation of the later prophets.

After the first six weeks of Lent the picture changes. In Holy Week the Passion narrative was read through at the special Holy Week services, just as Epiphany was observed by reading the Nativity narrative. For the most part the Gospel of Matthew was read, although occasionally passages from other Gospels supplemented Matthew, and for the stories of Lazarus and the appearance of Jesus in the Upper Room the Gospel of John had to be used. During Lent there was catechetical preaching each morning during the week, a good part of which was done by the bishop at the Church of the Holy Sepulchre. As we have already suggested in regard to Etheria's pilgrimage journal, so we find in the Jerusalem lectionary: There was a considerable amount of preaching during Holy Week, and it was based on the reading of the Passion narrative. It started with the reading of the story of Lazarus the Saturday before Palm Sunday, continued through the reading of the resurrection gospel on Easter morning, and concluded with the story of the appearance in the Upper Room on Easter evening. We find the following readings for Holy Week:[43]

Lazarus Saturday
    I Thessalonians 4:13-18
    John 11:55–12:11
Palm Sunday
    Ephesians 1:3-10
    Matthew 20:29–21:17
Monday of Holy Week (meeting at 4:00 P.M. at the Church of the Holy Sepulchre)
    Genesis 1:1–2:24
    Proverbs 1:2-9
    Isaiah 40:1-8
    Matthew 20:17-28
Tuesday of Holy Week (meeting at 4:00 P.M. at the Church on the Mount of Olives)
    Genesis 6:9–9:17
    Proverbs 9:1-11
    Isaiah 40:9-17
    Matthew 24:1–26:2
Wednesday of Holy Week (meeting at 4:00 P.M. at the Church of the Holy Sepulchre)
    Genesis 18:1–19:30
    Proverbs 1:10-19
    Zechariah 11:11-14
    Matthew 26:3-16

43. Renoux, *Le Codex Arménien Jérusalem 121*, pp. 255-77.

Thursday of Holy Week (meeting at 1:00 P.M. at the Church of
the Holy Sepulchre)
Genesis 22:1-18
Isaiah 61:1-6
Acts 1:15-26 (followed by sermon)
I Corinthians 11:23-32
Matthew 26:17-30 (the congregation proceeds to the
Church of the Upper Room)
I Corinthians 11:23-32
Mark 14:1-26 (the congregation proceeds to the Church on
the Mount of Olives)
John 13:16–18:1 (the congregation proceeds to the top of
the Mount of Olives)
Luke 22:1-65
Mark 14:27-72 (the congregation proceeds to Gethsemane)
Matthew 26:31-56 (the congregation proceeds to the
Courtyard of the High Priest)
Matthew 26:57-75 (the congregation returns to the Church
of the Holy Sepulchre)

Presumably this service for Thursday of Holy Week took all afternoon and
way into the night. It is characterized by the reading of several very long
passages of the Passion narrative from all four of the Gospels, the longest
of which, the Upper Room Discourse, occupies more than four chapters
from the Gospel of John. In the course of that afternoon and evening one
heard a great amount of Scripture reading; one sang a good number of
psalms and offered a considerable number of prayers. One processed over
most of the Holy City, and with this constant moving about and constant
variety of prayers, psalms, and lessons the service maintained a considerable
amount of movement. One wonders, however, about preaching. Preaching
would give even greater variety to this very long service. One sermon is
indicated at the beginning of the service in the Church of the Holy
Sepulchre, but it is only mentioned in passing. The one who describes the
liturgy explains that the catechumens are dismissed immediately after the
sermon. One wonders if there were other sermons. A service lasting so
long and moving around so much might easily have had several sermons
at different points. It might be a welcome relief, for instance, to sit down
and listen to a sermon after climbing up to the top of the Mount of Olives.
On Good Friday the church of Jerusalem observed a service of

worship that commemorated the crucifixion, beginning at noon and lasting until four o'clock in the afternoon. Once again it is filled with readings from the Bible. First, there is the reading of the story of the crucifixion from each of the four Gospels:[44]

Matthew 27:1-56
Mark 15:1-41
Luke 22:66–23:49
John 19:16b-37

Second, a series of Old Testament prophecies of various aspects of the Passion story is matched up with passages from the New Testament Epistles which interpret the meaning of the crucifixion:[45]

Zechariah 11:11-14
Galatians 6:14-18

Isaiah 3:9b-15
Philippians 2:5-11

Isaiah 50:4-9a
Romans 5:6-11

Amos 8:9-12
I Corinthians 1:18-31

Isaiah 52:13–53:12
Hebrews 2:11-18

Isaiah 63:1-6
Hebrews 9:11-28

Jeremiah 11:18-20
Hebrews 10:19-31

Zechariah 14:5c-11
I Timothy 6:13-16

---

44. Renoux, *Le Codex Arménien Jérusalem 121*, pp. 287-93.
45. Renoux, *Le Codex Arménien Jérusalem 121*, pp. 281-91.

Some of these Old Testament prophecies, or, perhaps better, types of Christ's passion, are quite striking. The passage from Amos speaks of darkness at noon and the transformation of a feast day into a day of mourning for an only son. The passage about the Suffering Servant from Isaiah 52 and 53 is historically very significant, having been part of the earliest Christian proclamation that Christ suffered according to Scripture. The reading from Isaiah 63, "Who is this who comes from Edom in crimsoned garments?", was a favorite testimony of the patristic age. The three passages from Hebrews are among the most eloquent of the New Testament on the subject of the high priestly ministry of Christ. Some of the most arresting prefigurations of the suffering of the Messiah are found in the Psalms, but one notices that in the lectionary of Jerusalem psalms are never used as Scripture lessons — they are sung in the course of the worship. In fact, there is a generous use of psalmody with magnificent antiphons throughout the lectionary, but there is not a single use of a psalm for a lesson. Again one wonders if there must not have been some sort of interpretation of these prophetic figures. Would it not have been rather difficult to understand all this rich and elaborate typology without some preaching? Surely the four-hour service would have afforded plenty of time. In fact, as anyone who has ever conducted a three-hour Good Friday service with seven sermons on the seven last words from the cross will easily recognize, the Scripture lessons and psalms alone would hardly fill up four hours.

Even in Jerusalem, with the processions to the Church of Saint Lazarus, to the Mount of Olives, and to the Church of the Upper Room, walking along the streets Jesus himself would have passed over, the climax of the Christian celebration of Passover was still the paschal vigil.[46] Lazarus Saturday, Palm Sunday, the Maundy Thursday service, the tracing of the way of the cross on Thursday night, the veneration of the cross on Friday morning, and the long service on Friday afternoon were relative latecomers compared to the paschal vigil. Unlike the paschal vigil, they all sprang from this concern to develop a Christian mystery to reactualize the death and resurrection of Christ rather than find a Christian meaning of Passover. The oldest Easter sermon we have, the sermon of Melito of

---

46. Anton Baumstark, with his lifelong study of the history of Christian worship using the comparative approach, has shown the importance of this liturgical form in the ancient Church. For centuries in the Western Church this form fell into obscurity. For a full study, see his *Nocturna laus*, passim.

Sardis, is a sermon for this vigil. In the sermons preached for the paschal vigil we find a very different approach to the reading and preaching of Scripture in the worship of the Church. Instead of trying to reactualize salvation history, the earliest Christians aimed at reinterpreting the Passover Scriptures. As time went along the reading of the Passover narrative, which was the primary type of Christ's passage from death to life, was supplemented by a series of other types of Christ's work of redemption, such as Abraham's sacrifice of his only son, Jonah's three days and three nights in the belly of the whale, Joshua's passage over the Jordan, and a number of others.

Very important to the development of the paschal vigil was the final reading of the series, the story of the three young men in the fiery furnace from the book of Daniel. It may have been sermons attempting to interpret this story which gave rise to one of the most important preaching conventions of late antiquity, the *Christus Victor* sermon. This sermon presented Christ's death and descent into hell in terms of a spiritual warfare in which the Savior broke into the fortress of the underworld and released the captives of Satan and led them in a triumphal procession to eternal blessedness in heaven. As we will see in the preaching ministry of Romanos the Melode and other preachers of the following century, the *Christus Victor* sermon became a popular form of Easter preaching.

The readings for the paschal vigil which we find in the Jerusalem lectionary are as follows:[47]

1. Genesis 1:1–3:24
    The Creation and Fall
2. Genesis 22:1-18
    Abraham's Sacrifice
3. Exodus 12:1-24
    The Jewish Passover
4. Jonah 1:1–4:11
    The Whole Story of Jonah
5. Exodus 14:24–15:21
    The Song of the Sea
6. Isaiah 60:1-13
    "Arise, Shine, for Thy Light Is Come!"

47. Renoux, *Le Codex Arménien Jérusalem 121*, pp. 299-307.

7. Job 38:2-28
   God's Answer to Job
8. II Kings 2:1-22
   Elijah in the Fiery Chariot
9. Jeremiah 33:31-34
   The New Covenant
10. Joshua 1:1-9
    Joshua Succeeds Moses
11. Ezekiel 37:1-14
    The Dry Bones
12. Daniel 3:1-51
    Three Young Men in the Fiery Furnace

It was in relation to these readings that the first of the Easter sermons would have been preached. More than likely several sermons would have been preached during the vigil. We must remember that this service was supposed to last from sometime before midnight until daybreak when Easter Communion was celebrated. This gave ample opportunity for a variety of preachers to give their witness. Whether brief sermons followed each of the readings, culminated by a sermon from the bishop after the final reading, or whether all the readings were completed and then the different preachers were given an opportunity to preach one after another, we cannot say for sure. Etheria gives the impression that the preachers succeeded each other directly, but the need for variety and movement in the service would suggest that sermons followed lessons, or at least some of the lessons. These sermons would, of course, have been comparatively short, as is the one sermon from Hesychius which seems to have been preached at the paschal vigil. We shall look at that sermon in more detail shortly, but in the meantime we simply want to suggest that it was short sermons like this which elaborated the readings called for by the lectionary.

It was later on Easter Sunday, at the hour when the Lord's Day service was usually held, that the story of the resurrection from the Gospel of Mark was read.[48] Liturgical convention required for this service a sermon on the visit of the holy women to the empty tomb. In the Byzantine tradition this became the sermon on the Holy Myrrhophores, that is, on

48. Matthew 28:1-7 was originally read and preached by the bishop as the climax of the paschal vigil. On the Scripture reading for Easter Sunday, see Renoux, *Le Codex Arménien Jérusalem 121*, p. 313.

the women who carried myrrh to the tomb of Jesus on the morning of the resurrection and found it empty.

Of course, a considerable amount of biblical material on the subject of the resurrection was still to be read, and presumably there would be sermons on this material as well. On Sunday afternoon one would naturally return to the Church of the Upper Room and just as naturally read about the appearance of Jesus in the Upper Room. For the next week, that is, the octave of Easter, the remainder of the resurrection appearances were read. The list of lessons is as follows:[49]

Easter Monday
 Acts 2:22-41
 Luke 23:50–24:12
Tuesday
 Acts 2:42–3:21
 Luke 24:13-35
Wednesday
 Acts 3:22–4:12
 James 1:1-12
 Luke 24:36-40
Thursday
 Acts 4:13-31
 James 1:13-27
 Matthew 5:12 (1-12?
Friday
 Acts 4:32–5:11
 James 2:1-13
 John 21:1-14
Saturday
 Acts 5:12-33
 James 2:14-26
 John 21:15-25
Sunday
 Acts 5:34–6:7
 James 3:1-13
 John 1:1-17

49. Renoux, *Le Codex Arménien Jérusalem 121*, pp. 315-25.

Sunday Vespers at the Church of the Upper Room
John 20:26-31

Several very interesting things appear in these readings. First there is
the list of Gospel readings that finishes up the Gospel accounts of the
resurrection appearances. Clearly it is a principle of the Jerusalem lectionary that all this material must be read. Even more interesting is the way
the material from the Acts of the Apostles and the Epistle of James is
introduced. The obvious point of the material from Acts is to introduce
the testimony of Peter to the resurrection; the testimony of the two apostles
Matthew and John has been heard from the reading of their Gospels, and
it is important to hear the testimony of Peter. In the same way it is
important to hear the testimony of James, the Apostle of Jerusalem, the
first bishop of the Jerusalem church. The fact that his testimony to the
resurrection is more general in character than Peter's is not quite as important for the church of Jerusalem as the fact that James is clearly to be
numbered among the canonical witnesses of the resurrection (I Cor. 15:7).
This fine point might not be too clear from a simple reading of the three
lessons appointed for the day, and a preacher would no doubt have to
make this very lucid, especially to those who were visitors to the Holy
City. The beginning of a *lectio continua* of James on the Wednesday after
Easter was possibly continued in such a way that all the Catholic Epistles
were read through by Pentecost. In the same way, the reading of the
prologue of the Gospel of John on the Sunday after Easter — which
surprises a bit — is not so much an appropriate reading for that Sunday
as it is the beginning of a *lectio continua* of John that goes on every day
at the morning service at the rate of about two readings per chapter until
Pentecost.

If anything is made clear by a study of the Jerusalem lectionary as
we find it in the first half of the fifth century, it is how important the
simple reading of the Bible was to the church of that venerable city. It
was patently a major concern that the whole of Scripture be read through
in an orderly fashion. Even this lectionary makes it clear that normally
the Scriptures were read through on the basis of the *lectio continua*. The
feast days might demand special lessons for special days, but even at the
feast days the principle of the *lectio continua* appears and reappears. The
church of Jerusalem from the late fourth century when Etheria wrote
down her experiences to the middle of the fifth century gave considerable
time to both the reading and the preaching of Scripture, and the evidence,

159

when taken as a whole, indicates a good balance between the two. It was the whole of Scripture that was read and preached, not merely the New Testament; nor was the church of Jerusalem only interested in that part of the Old Testament which foreshadowed Christ. The church of Jerusalem was just as interested in the books of the Law and the books of Wisdom as in the Prophets. If Jerusalem at this time had other preachers who anywhere approached the quality of Hesychius, we would be inclined to say that the ministry of the Word was well exercised in the first half of the fifth century.

III. The Festal Preaching of Hesychius

With the careful scholarly work of Charles Renoux and Michel Aubineau the figure of Hesychius of Jerusalem has emerged as the leading preacher of the closing years of the golden age of Greek patristic preaching. What has come down to us is but an intimation of what must have been an extraordinary pulpit ministry. As we have said, Hesychius was above all an expository preacher who most of the year preached through one book of the Bible after another. His sermons were taken down by stenographers and worked into commentaries which were greatly appreciated in his time. The tragedy is that, gradually as biblical studies were more and more ignored in the Church, these commentaries fell into neglect and were eventually lost. Although best known as an expository preacher, on feast days Hesychius would devote his genius as an interpreter of Scripture and his talents as an orator to preaching the festal sermons which were so central to the festivities of Christian Jerusalem.

Our study of the Jerusalem lectionary has drawn for us the outlines of the cycle of annual observances maintained by the Jerusalem church. This Jerusalem lectionary is significant, not only because it was one of the first attempts at drawing up a liturgical calendar, but even more because it was very influential in establishing many of the conventions of festal preaching. This liturgical calendar provided settings for a whole series of festal sermons, and many of its features were in fact invented by the Jerusalem church. If only we had more of Hesychius's festal sermons we could probably draw in fairly clear detail the earliest conventions of festal preaching. As Michel Aubineau has put it, a great number of these sermons must have been preached by Hesychius and no doubt preserved at one time. We can regret this loss, but providentially we do have enough of these festal sermons to give us at least the outlines of the picture. Let us look at several characteristic festal sermons from this master.

The Christian celebration of Passover had developed a number of well-established conventions regarding preaching by the time of Hesychius. Perhaps the oldest of these was that at the paschal vigil a sermon should be preached on the institution of Passover and the passage through the Red Sea, giving the classic Christian interpretation of that crucial passage. Very closely related to this convention was the *Christus Victor* sermon, which, inspired by the story of the three young men in the fiery furnace, which was likewise read during the paschal vigil, spoke of Christ's descent into hell, his defeat of Satan, and his rescue of Adam and Eve. A third conventional Easter sermon was that preached at the Sunday morning service on the Gospel account of the women visiting the tomb and finding it empty. Unfortunately we do not have a full sermon from Hesychius for any of these conventional types of Easter sermons. It was probably also a liturgical convention at this time that the bishop had the responsibility of preaching these central messages. We know that in Jerusalem, however, it was the custom for a number of the presbyters to preach briefly and then for the bishop to give the final sermon. Hesychius was not the bishop and so, rather than a full-length Easter sermon, we have two very short sermons, one apparently preached at the Easter vigil and the other at the Easter morning service. In the first[50] we have the traditional themes of the *Christus Victor* sermon. In the same way the second gives us the themes of the traditional sermon on the empty tomb.[51]

We do, on the other hand, have among the homiletical remains of our preacher two examples of the Lazarus Saturday sermon, another of the conventional Easter sermons in Jerusalem. To this day the celebration of Lazarus Saturday is still cherished in Eastern Orthodox churches. Not too long before the beginning of the fifth century a church had been constructed at Bethany. In the days of Jesus Bethany had been a suburb of Jerusalem. It was there, the Gospels tell us, in the home of Martha, Mary, and Lazarus, that Jesus habitually stayed when he visited Jerusalem. It was there that Jesus had raised Lazarus, as the Gospel of John tells us. The way the Gospel of John arranges it, the raising of Lazarus becomes

---

50. Hesychius of Jerusalem, *Les homélies festales,* Greek text with French translation, ed. Michel Aubineau, 2 vols. (Brussels: Société des Bollandistes, 1978), 1:76-96.

51. Hesychius, *Les homélies festales,* 1:97-117.

the final sign of the ministry of Jesus which sums up both his work of teaching and preaching and his work of healing. As the story appears in John's Gospel the raising of Lazarus is also an intimation, a prophetic sign, of the resurrection which will culminate the Passion narrative. This is underlined by the report of the Gospel that when Jesus came to Jerusalem for his final Passover, he once more stayed at the home of Martha, Mary, and Lazarus. How long before that Jesus raised Lazarus is not clear from the story, but one gets the impression that it had only been a matter of weeks. John then reports that six days before the Passover Lazarus gave a festive dinner in honor of Jesus, and in the course of that dinner Mary, the sister of Lazarus, anointed the feet of Jesus. The prophetic nature of this anointing would hardly escape the notice of a careful reader, which, no doubt, is the way the author of the Gospel of John intended it. It was obviously a premonition of the death and burial of Jesus. Once a church had been built at Bethany, the opportunity to reenact that supper six days before Passover could hardly be ignored.

The two sermons for Lazarus Saturday are sumptuous examples of classical rhetoric, unlike the expository sermons Hesychius preached on Job at the Church of the Upper Room, which are plain and unadorned in comparison. Hesychius was surely pitching his oratorical style to his congregation in this case. The congregation that came to the Church of the Upper Room to hear his expository sermons at vespers was a more serious group of people than the crowds which filled the Bethany church and the fields and hillsides around it for the beginning of Holy Week.[52]

Perhaps the most interesting thing about these two sermons is the way our preacher brings variety to this conventional sermon and yet preserves the convention. The essence of the convention is the summing up of the ministry of Jesus and the introduction of the Passion and resurrection. In the first sermon Hesychius tells his congregation that the story of Lazarus is the prelude to the resurrection of the dead, the trumpet of Wisdom, the flute which cannot be silent, the lyre touched by the fingers of the Father, the harp held by God, the psalter spontaneously expressing divine harmony.[53] In view of this word spoken to Lazarus, "Lazarus, come forth," the whole destiny of the universe will change.[54] Hesychius takes up the theme of summarizing Jesus' ministry by intro-

---

52. Etheria implies a great crowd. Etheria, *Journal de Voyage* 29.

53. Hesychius, *Les homélies festales,* 1:404-5.

54. Hesychius, *Les homélies festales,* 1:408-9.

ducing an imaginative discourse with the inhabitants of Hades. Adam, Abel, Noah, Joseph, and David are all introduced in such a way that the whole history of salvation is recalled and one understands that we are at the verge of the climax of that history.[55] This variation of the essential theme was necessary to keep the interest of those who had heard a Lazarus Saturday sermon the year before, not to mention those who had heard one every year for as long as they could remember. The general populace of late classical antiquity was fairly sophisticated when it came to oratory and was capable of hooting the preacher of canned sermons right out of the pulpit. At the end of the sermon the theme of the foreshadowing of the resurrection recurs, as Hesychius has Jesus tell Lazarus that the reason he has been raised is that he might be the herald of new life.[56]

In the second sermon the theme of the summary of the work of redemption is particularly strong. The introduction of the sermon catalogues the mighty works of Jesus. Demons let those escape whom they had possessed, illnesses turn away from the bodies they enfeebled, the paralyzed begin to run, the blind lift up their eyes in sight, lepers are cleansed, the mute begin to speak, and the deaf suddenly recover possession of their ears.[57] The resurrection of Lazarus is the climax of all these signs and mighty works.[58] Hesychius begins to describe the resurrection of Lazarus, and although his description probably engaged the attention of the crowds of Jerusalem, to us it lacks respect for the mystery of the resurrection. Nevertheless, it does begin to intimate the resurrection of Christ. Toward the end of the sermon Hesychius takes up the theme of the raising of Lazarus as an intimation of the resurrection of Christ and, therefore, of the general resurrection of the faithful. The raising of Lazarus reminds us that Christ is the healing of our illnesses; he is the physician who heals even the dead of their corruption.[59] Again, according to our *didascalos,* the raising of Lazarus reminds us of the day when the earth shall be shaken and the graves shall give up their dead; as the Scriptures tell us, "The trumpet shall sound, and the dead will be raised imperishable . . ." (I Cor. 15:52).[60]

55. Hesychius, *Les homélies festales,* 1:410-17.
56. Hesychius, *Les homélies festales,* 1:424.
57. Hesychius, *Les homélies festales,* 1:448-51.
58. Hesychius, *Les homélies festales,* 1:450-51.
59. Hesychius, *Les homélies festales,* 1:458-59.
60. Hesychius, *Les homélies festales,* 1:460-61.

Another conventional sermon for which an example has survived in the works of Hesychius is the sermon for the feast of Saint Stephen.[61] We have already touched on the discovery of the relics of the first Christian martyr and the importance of this in the construction of a calendar of saints for the Holy City. Within the lifetime of Hesychius this would lead to the building of the Basilica of Saint Stephen.[62] The feast came to have particular importance in Jerusalem not only because Stephen was the first martyr but because he was Jerusalem's martyr.[63] During the ministry of Hesychius the liturgical commemoration of Saint Stephen shot into prominence. In 416, toward the beginning of his ministry, the relics of the saint were discovered by a monk in a spot just north of the city. On 26 December they were translated to the deacon's room of the Church of the Upper Room, the church, apparently, at which Hesychius did most of his preaching. And some thirty years later, toward the end of his ministry, the dowager Empress Eudoxia, widow of Theodosius II, built the Basilica of Saint Stephen, and Hesychius is known to have been present at the dedication, along with a number of other distinguished churchmen, not the least of whom was Cyril of Alexandria. The feast of Saint Stephen was a major event in the liturgical life of the Holy City and it demanded a festive sermon. It is just this kind of festival sermon which Hesychius produced.

The feast of the *Hypapante,* as we have said, was another major feast in the liturgical life of early-fifth-century Jerusalem. It celebrated, as we recall, the occasion when the baby Jesus was brought to Jerusalem forty days after his birth, that he might be presented at the Temple. When the holy family entered the Temple, two aged saints, Simeon and Anna, recognized that the Savior of the world, the one who would bring light to the Gentiles and glory to Israel, had finally come. This, the day the Savior made his first appearance within the walls of the Holy City, like the martyrdom of Stephen, was a special event for Jerusalem.[64] When Etheria made her pilgrimage to Jerusalem between 381 and 384 the feast of the *Hypapante* was celebrated on 14 February, forty days after 6 January, the day when the church of Jerusalem celebrated the birth of Christ, and *Hypapante,* like the celebration of Christ's birth, demanded festive oratory,

---

61. Hesychius, *Les homélies festales,* 1:287-350.

62. See Aubineau's introductory material, Hesychius, *Les homélies festales,* 1:315-19.

63. See Aubineau's introductory material, Hesychius, *Les homélies festales,* 1:291.

64. On the history of the feast of the purification, see Aubineau's introductory material, Hesychius, *Les homélies festales,* 1:2ff.

of which Hesychius has left us two carefully prepared sermons which he preached at the celebration of this feast in different years.[65] They are festive displays of the sort of oratory appropriate to the festive nature of the occasion.

It would be a mistake, however, to be carried away by our preacher's superb rhetoric and not notice his equally superb exegesis. In both these sermons our learned *didascalos* goes through the text of the Gospel passage phrase by phrase, bringing out the teaching of Scripture.[66] Admittedly, it is not the sort of exegesis that is popular in our day, just as Hesychius's rhetoric is not the sort that is popular today. Michel Aubineau has given us an analysis of both the rhetoric and the exegesis which we do not need to repeat here.

What needs to be pointed out is the growing demand of the festal calendar on the preacher. We have already spoken at length of the way the popularity of pilgrimages to the Holy City was encouraging the development of a liturgical calendar, and the feast of the *Hypapante* is but one more case in point. Here was a feast day that gave high priority to the city of Jerusalem and underlined its value as a center of devotional activity. Where could one more appropriately celebrate such a feast than in Jerusalem? What we see so clearly in these sermons is a distinct effort to produce a festive piece of oratory for the worship of the regular feast days of the calendar. During the time of Hesychius these feast days were increasing both in number and importance, and this was especially the case in Jerusalem, but as we shall see, other churches will follow the lead of Jerusalem.

The same point needs to be made here which we made in regard to the mystagogical sermons of Cyril of Jerusalem. When the liturgy becomes so complicated that it demands the sort of highly conventionized sermons we find it beginning to demand of Hesychius, the original purpose of preaching begins to fall from sight. Instead of explaining the Scriptures the sermon explains the liturgy. We begin to get sermons on the meaning of Septuagesima Sunday or on the message of the third Sunday in Advent. But there is something more here: The conventions encourage canned sermons. Canned sermons may be all right when nothing better can be had. They are better than the sermons of ignorant enthusiasts, and better than no sermons at all, but there is no reason why the Church has to

---

65. Hesychius, *Les homélies festales,* 1:1-75.
66. Hesychius, *Les homélies festales,* 1:6-9.

tolerate canned sermons for a prolonged period of time. The Church has to be willing to train her preachers, just as the Franciscans and Dominicans did in the Middle Ages and just as the Reformers did in the sixteenth century.

CHAPTER III

The Flourishing of Greek Preaching in the Christian Empire — the School of Antioch

The church of Antioch from the days of the apostles had been an important center of the Christian faith. It was here that the disciples were first called Christians, and it was from here that Paul began his missionary work among the Gentiles. Antioch was a center of Hellenistic civilization and culture, and yet it was the metropolis of Syria. From the end of the fourth century before Christ it was the capital of the Seleucid empire, and it was here that the infamous Antiochus Epiphanes had tried to impose Greek ways on all Syria. And yet, the golden age of Antioch was the age of the Christian emperors. Constantine built its great church and, during the reign of Theodosius, Libanius made Antioch the alma mater for the study of rhetoric. In addition to its Greek population, Antioch had a large Jewish community as well as a considerable segment of Syrians who were far more Semitic than Greek. Antioch was the gateway to the Orient where Romans, Greeks, Jews, and Syrians were in constant contact.[1]

---

1. On the history of Antioch, cf. Glanville Downey, *A History of Antioch in Syria from Seleucus to the Arab Conquests* (Princeton: Princeton University Press, 1961). See also D. S. Wallace-Hadrill, *Christian Antioch: A Study of Early Christian Thought in the East*

It was in the days when Antioch was in its flower that the city produced a school of Christian thought which was to have lasting influence on the Church. This school was based on a particular method of interpreting Scripture,[2] often called the grammatical-historical method. The preaching shaped by this school was sober. It had a high sense of the authority of the Word of God and a firm commitment to the moral integrity of the Christian life. Other schools of preaching down through the centuries have had these virtues, but what made Antiochene preaching of such special moment is that it approached its ministry schooled in the most cultivated classical oratory.

The School of Antioch came as a reaction against the School of Alexandria. From the middle of the third century until almost the end of the fourth century, Christian preaching in the East had been strongly influenced by Alexandrian exegesis. Origen had popularized the Alexandrian exegesis in the Church, and preachers such as Eusebius of Caesarea, Cyril of Jerusalem, and Hesychius of Jerusalem followed in this tradition. About these preachers we have already spoken.

By the end of the fourth century preachers had begun to turn away from Alexandrian exegesis. We mentioned this in regard to Basil's famous series of sermons on the six days of creation. The Cappadocian Fathers never made any polemic against Origen. Gregory of Nyssa's *Life of Moses* is in fact a superb example of allegorical exegesis, but it is not a series of sermons. His series of sermons on the Beatitudes, on the other hand, is primarily concerned with the literal interpretation of the text, even if from time to time the Alexandrian methods are used. With the Cappadocian Fathers there is certainly no rejection of Alexandrian exegesis, even if there is a growing interest in the literal sense.

We find a similar tendency in Jerome. Jerome developed an antipathy for Origen but never got away from allegorical exegesis, as much as he

---

(New York and Cambridge: Cambridge University Press, 1982), and the chapter "The Jews of Antioch" in Robert L. Wilken, *John Chrysostom and the Jews* (Berkeley, Los Angeles, and London: University of California Press, 1983), pp. 35-65.

    2. On the School of Antioch, see Jean Daniélou, *From Shadow to Reality: Studies in the Biblical Typology of the Fathers,* trans. W. Hibbard (Westminster, Md.: Newman Press, 1961); Jean Daniélou, *A History of Early Christian Doctrine before the Council of Nicea,* trans. J. A. Baker, 3 vols. (Philadelphia: Westminster Press, 1977), see especially vol. 1, *The Theology of Jewish Christianity;* Karlfried Froehlich, *Biblical Interpretation in the Early Church* (Philadelphia: Fortress Press, 1984); and Henri de Lubac, *The Sources of Revelation,* trans. Luke O'Niel (New York: Herder and Herder, 1968).

may have tried. His interest in Hebrew laid the foundations for a much more consistent grammatical-historical interpretation of the Old Testament. As we will show below, Jerome made significant progress toward developing a Christian interpretation of the Old Testament which was not based on allegory, but he never arrived at the ends to which he began to move. This movement away from the Alexandrian school of exegesis which we notice in several Fathers at the end of the fourth century became a systematic program in the school of Diodore of Tarsus, the outstanding biblical scholar at Antioch.

Diodore was born in Antioch during the reign of Constantine the Great.[3] He studied in the schools of Athens and evidently received the best literary education that highly cultivated city could offer. By the middle of the century Diodore presided over one of the monasteries in the vicinity of Antioch. His keen mind and theological interests drew him more and more into the debate over the teachings of Arius. Diodore was a firm supporter of Nicene orthodoxy, and his theological prowess won him the disdain of the emperor Julian the Apostate, who called him the high priest of the Christians and blamed him with inventing the deity of Christ. At one point when the Arians were in power he was exiled to Armenia, but then Theodosius came to power and recognized him as one of the pillars of orthodoxy. He ended his years as bishop of Tarsus, the native city of the apostle Paul. In only a few years his most celebrated pupil, John Chrysostom, would become the patriarch of Constantinople, the greatest of Christian preachers.

Professor Karlfried Froehlich has made the point that basically the Antiochene School was built on a method of interpretation rather than a theological tendency.[4] There have been numerous attempts to blame various heretical positions on the Antiochene School: Some insist that it inevitably produces Nestorianism, and others would compromise the school by claiming it is inescapably connected with Arianism — after all, Arius had studied under Lucian at Antioch. Arius may have been pastor of a church in Alexandria, but maybe he got his heretical ideas from

---

3. Johannes Quasten, *Patrology,* 4 vols. (Utrecht and Antwerp: Spectrum Publishers; Westminster, Md: Christian Classics, 1966-94), 3:397-401 (Quasten does not give much by way of recent bibliography); and E. Schweizer, "Diodor von Tarsus als Exeget," *Zeitschrift für die neutestamentliche Wissenschaft und die Kunde der älteren Kirche* 40 (1941/42): 33-75.

4. Froehlich, *Biblical Interpretation,* pp. 20ff.

Antioch — that's the way the Alexandrians argued it, at least. This attempt at slandering the school has never been able to beat down completely the obvious truth of what the school taught about the interpretation of Scripture. Although in the fifth century the opponents of the school were able to obtain an official condemnation of several of its leading representatives, such as Diodore of Tarsus and Theodore of Mopsuestia, today the value of the Antiochene School is widely recognized. Not even its most ardent opponents were ever able to becloud the reputation of John Chrysostom. John Chrysostom, faithfully practicing the methods of the School of Antioch, has been recognized not only as the greatest preacher the Church has ever produced, but also as one of the most reliable interpreters of Scripture in antiquity.

Diodore attacked allegorical interpretation because it did not respect the historical value of the text.[5] God revealed himself in history, and the words of Scripture had very definite meaning to those for whom they were originally written. It is also true that these words have a more general meaning for us as Christians as we try to live as Christ's disciples in our own day, but that more general meaning is based on the specific historical meaning. It is therefore important first of all to establish this historical or literal sense of Scripture. This is done by a careful study of the language, the grammar, and the rhetoric of the text. Before one asks what the text means to us, one must ask what the text originally meant to those who first wrote it and heard it. As Diodore understood it, the allegorical interpretation of the Alexandrian School had not given sufficient attention to the historical meaning of the text; all too quickly fanciful speculations developed as to what it must mean to the spiritually enlightened. All too often this method introduced ideas which came from Greek philosophy and were quite foreign to Scripture.[6]

Diodore understood his method as a middle road between the Alexandrian method of allegorical interpretation and what he calls the Jewish error of interpreting the text which does not recognize the higher sense that goes beyond the letter. The literal sense is not the same thing as the literalistic interpretation. An interpretation of Scripture which is thoroughly historical recognizes that Scripture uses similes, metaphors, and parables. Diodore was, after all, well schooled in Greek rhetoric, and he tells us that it is important to recognize that biblical rhetoric is different

---

5. For an English translation of several crucial passages from Diodore, cf. Froehlich, *Biblical Interpretation*, pp. 82-94.

6. Froehlich, *Biblical Interpretation*, p. 86.

from Greek rhetoric. Even if the apostle Paul uses the word "allegory" in Galatians 4:24, he does not mean by it what the Greeks meant.[7] The New Testament does not interpret the Old Testament allegorically, but it does find in the Old Testament higher and more profound meanings. This higher meaning of Scripture Diodore calls *theoria;* it is the "spiritual sense" of the Antiochene School. Yet these higher meanings are always based on the original meaning. As an example Diodore uses Psalm 30, which historically is a psalm of thanksgiving of King Hezekiah's after his recovery from illness and his delivery from the threat of Assyrian invasion. (Just where Diodore might have gotten this information is not clear.) The psalm gives thanks for his deliverance. By way of hyperbole the prayer praises God for deliverance from death. "Now these words fit Hezekiah when he was delivered from his ills, but they also fit all human beings when they obtain the promised resurrection."[8] The words had significant meaning at the time, and it is this meaning which is the basis of the spiritual meaning, that is, the meaning for us. "For this is the grace of the Spirit who gives eternal and imperishable gifts to human beings; I am speaking of the divine words which are capable of being adapted to every moment of time, down to the final perfection of human beings."[9]

The position of Diodore of Tarsus was really very well balanced. He was a prolific writer and is supposed to have written commentaries on all the books of the Old Testament, all four Gospels, Acts, and a number of New Testament epistles. Fragments of many of these works have been preserved even though his opponents were largely successful in suppressing his literary legacy. These fragments suggest that he was indeed a brilliant interpreter of Scripture. Unfortunately we know nothing of his preaching ministry, but as a biblical scholar of such note we assume that he must have preached regularly both to his monks and later, as bishop of Tarsus, to his congregation.

I. John Chrysostom

Without doubt the most universally respected of all preachers, the golden-mouthed John remains the crowning example of how the faithful

7. Froehlich, *Biblical Interpretation*, p. 87.
8. Froehlich, *Biblical Interpretation*, p. 92.
9. Froehlich, *Biblical Interpretation*, p. 91.

preaching of the Word of God ever purifies and enlightens the Church so that the Lord of the Church is glorified. Surely there is no one from whom we can learn more about preaching as worship.

John Chrysostom (ca. 347-407) was born in Antioch of a prosperous family.[10] It may well be that his father, who died in his son's infancy, was a Roman military officer of high rank. His devout mother raised her son in quiet and sincere piety and herself gave him his early education.[11] Nevertheless, as a young man he was sent to the famous school of Libanius.[12] One wonders why a Christian woman such as John's mother would send her son to the school of a famous pagan such as Libanius.[13] Nevertheless, we know that even Basil of Caesarea, who had also studied under Libanius, was on the friendliest of terms with him and recommended students to his school. John Chrysostom also studied under Diodore of Tarsus and from this distinguished biblical scholar learned the principles of biblical interpretation which distinguished the School of Antioch.[14] One of the reasons John Chrysostom achieved such distinction as a preacher was because he mastered both classical oratory as it was so brilliantly taught by Libanius and the principles of biblical interpretation as taught with no less luster by Diodore.

John Chrysostom is of special interest to us because of the variety

10. For bibliographical material, see Chrysostomus Baur, *John Chrysostom and His Time,* English translation by M. Gonzaga, 2 vols. (Westminster, Md.: Newman Press, 1959-60); Hans Freiherr von Campenhausen, "Johannes Chrysostomos," in *Griechische Kirchenväter* (Stuttgart: W. Kohlhammer Verlag, 1955); Glanville Downey, *Antioch in the Age of Theodosius the Great* (Norman: University of Oklahoma Press, 1962); and Bruno H. Vandenberghe, *Saint Jean Chrysostome et la Parole de Dieu* (Paris: Éditions du Cerf, 1961).

11. A. H. M. Jones, "St. John Chrysostom's Parentage and Education," *Harvard Theological Review* 46: 171-73. For further information on the education of John Chrysostom, see Jean Dumortier, "La culture profane de S. Jean Chrysostome," *Mélange de science religieuse* 8 (1953): 53-62.

12. Libanius, a native of Antioch, had won fame as a professor of rhetoric in Constantinople and in Nicomedia where he had taught both Basil of Caesarea and Gregory of Nazianzus. About 354 he was offered an endowed professorship by his native city and returned and established a school. Several volumes of his works on rhetoric are found in the Loeb Classical Library. For a short study of Libanius, see Baur, *John Chrysostom and His Time,* 1:16-21.

13. On the paganism of the schools in Antioch, cf. Wilken, *John Chrysostom and the Jews,* pp. 20, 24, 28, and throughout.

14. To what extent Diodore maintained a theological school in his monastery is not clear. Cf. Baur, *John Chrysostom and His Time,* 1:89-99.

of his preaching ministry. He has left us impressive examples of several genres of Christian preaching. First of all he was an expository preacher, leaving us extensive series of sermons on many books of the Old and New Testaments. We also have examples of his catechetical preaching and his sermons for feast days. His prophetic sermons were outstanding. John's reputation as a preacher who could proclaim the Word of God for difficult times was won by his series of sermons during the crisis over the desecration of the imperial statues in Antioch, when the whole city trembled before the threat of the emperor's reprisal for their rebellion. Few Christian preachers have been more prophetic than John Chrysostom was at the imperial court of Constantinople when he again and again called the leaders of society to turn away from their vain worship of luxury and power. Few preachers have done such a masterful job of polishing the many facets of the ministry of the Word.

By far the largest number of John Chrysostom's sermons were his expository sermons. Among his sermons on various books of the Bible we find the following series: 67 sermons on Genesis, 58 on selected psalms, 90 on the Gospel of Matthew, 88 on the Gospel of John, and 55 on the Acts of the Apostles. John was particularly fond of the epistles of Paul. His various series on separate Pauline epistles add up to over 200 sermons, including 34 sermons on the Epistle to the Hebrews, which our preacher, as one would expect, understood to come from the same apostle. The grand total comes to well over 500 sermons.

In both Antioch and Constantinople, John Chrysostom preached daily or almost daily. Apparently this was not only the case during Lent but during the rest of the year as well. Many of his long series of expository sermons show that the sermons followed each other day after day. To be sure, he may not have kept up this pace day after day, month after month throughout the whole year; surely other preachers relieved him from time to time. We also know that on occasion his series would be interrupted when he decided it was necessary to preach on some other subject. In principle, however, he preached the *lectio continua*, beginning each sermon where he had left off the sermon before.

The long series of sermons we have on individual books of the Bible are for the most part "finished" compositions. John studied the text beforehand and prepared his remarks but did not write out his sermons before preaching them. As was the custom in classical oratory, he went before the people with his mind prepared to engage his listeners and to bring out his thoughts in a lively exchange with those who were before him. A stenographer took down the sermon as it was delivered, and afterward the preacher would finish up the text for publication. Certain of the series that we have are not as well finished as others; perhaps this is because in his ministry at Constantinople he did not have the same amount of time to give to final editing that he had at Antioch. But even at that, the sermons were never so well finished that they became literature rather than oratory. If these sermons have come to us in literary form, they have never lost their character as recorded oratory. They have never been reshaped to fit the requirements of a written composition.

A. Sermons on Genesis — the Graciousness of God's Word

One of John Chrysostom's earliest and most interesting works is his series of sixty-seven sermons on the book of Genesis.[15] Begun during the forty-day fast in 388 while John was a presbyter at Antioch, the series was interrupted for the celebration of Easter and then concluded later in the year. These are very long sermons; they must have often taken well over an hour and sometimes may even have approached the two-hour mark. They are nevertheless vivacious and lively, the sort of oratory classical antiquity enjoyed. The congregation frequently applauded the preacher, which only inspired him to greater feats of eloquence. John often tells his congregation that their enthusiasm drove him on as the wind filling the sails of a ship.

These sermons, coming early in his career, are often characterized by a threefold arrangement. They begin with a long *exordium* in which any number of things, more or less connected with the text, might be discussed. Then there is an exposition of the lesson for the day, during which the preacher commented on several verses phrase by phrase. Finally there is a long exhortation to the living of the Christian life. The exhortation usually develops from the exposition, but the connection is sometimes less than obvious. One does not always find the sort of introduction, body, and conclusion, all developing a single theme, which today we are taught to expect of well-thought-out public speaking. It is often more like a three-course meal: salad, main course, and dessert. Each course is different, although they all complement each other.

15. This study is based on the recent translation of this work by Robert C. Hill: St. John Chrysostom, *Homilies on Genesis*, 3 vols. (Washington, D.C.: Catholic University of America Press, 1985-92); hereinafter Chrysostom, *Homilies on Genesis*.

His sermon on the fourth day of creation, for example, begins with an impassioned diatribe against those who have skipped church that day in order to attend the races at the hippodrome. Then he turns to an exposition of God's creation of the sun, the moon, and the stars and ends the sermon with an exhortation to spending our leisure time in the praise of God. Horse racing, he posits, is a waste of time. On the next day John opens with more complaints about horse racing: It is not very edifying for our non-Christian neighbors to see us Christians going off to the horse races. Then he takes up the text for the day, which just happens to be on the creation of the wild beasts, reptiles, sea monsters, and flying creatures. John marvels at them all. Each God made for some specific purpose. We may not always understand the reason for their existence, but we can be well assured nothing has been created without some reason. God blessed them, and in the ingenuity of their creation and their countless variety they are a witness to the majesty of their creator. The exposition is a beautiful sermon in itself, but an Antiochene sermon must have a moral exhortation, so John, in a clear attack on paganism, admonishes his congregation on the foolishness of worshiping beasts. In a city that was perhaps only one-third Christian, this attack was rather daring — there were plenty of pagans in the church before him. In those days anyone, regardless of religious persuasion, would show up to hear first-class oratory. Religious polemic of this sort added excitement to a discourse. No one thought of honest polemic as unfair, much less as bigotry. Much more, it was thought of as a straightforward intellectual criticism. Serious discourse in antiquity gave a legitimate place to polemic.

Strangely enough, not a word is said about God's purposes for creating horses, but the point comes across just the same. John Chrysostom often makes his point by skirting it, by not saying the obvious when everyone in the congregation knows the obvious. As we will see, George Truett understood the same secret when he preached against horse racing at First Baptist Church in Dallas so many centuries later. What John Chrysostom tells us is that in the sight of a galloping horse there is something which bears witness to the majesty of God, and that surely is good. Apparently our preacher leaves it to us to ask ourselves whether or not the right place to experience that is in the hippodrome.

What a strange juxtaposition of themes there is in these two sermons. How well John uses the advantage of painting on the big canvas. Here he is preaching on the goodness of creation at the beginning of the forty-day fast! What kind of asceticism is that going to develop? Would he not make a much stronger impression if he were obvious, short, and to the point? Would it not be so much more efficient? Could not one make a twenty-minute sermon on the evils of horse racing based on the text about God's creation of the beasts of the field and be done with it? Why all this meandering around about God's blessing of sea monsters, pagan abuse of worshiping animals, and even the purpose of God's creation of the sun, the moon, and the stars? To be sure, it all has its place, its magnificent order. The message of John Chrysostom has balance. He lays bare the antitheses, tensions, and dialectics of human existence, and it takes the big canvas to do this. The twenty-minute religious pep talk has to be simple, and all too often that simplicity is in fact simplistic, but when a truly great preacher has a sensitivity to a wide variety of themes, they have to be placed beside each other; they have to balance and interact with each other. It is this wide variety, this balancing, and this interaction which makes John Chrysostom the most catholic of all preachers.

One of the reasons we find John's sermons on Genesis so interesting is that here we have an example of how the School of Antioch, with its rejection of Alexandrian allegory and its insistence on a grammatical-historical interpretation of the text, actually came out with a sermon.[16] Did the method of Antioch mean that one would come out with an interpretation of an Old Testament book which was less than Christian? Certainly in the golden mouth of John this was not the case, as we often discover in these sermons. In his sermon on the text "'Let us make man in our image'" (Gen. 1:26), John affirms the traditional Christian interpretation that it was the Father who spoke these words to the Son. He takes some time refuting the Jewish claim that these words were spoken to the angels — the angels are ministering spirits, not creators. Then he turns to refuting the pagan philosophers who are offended at the anthropomorphism they find in these words.[17] Man is created in the image of God, John tells us, not that his bodily shape is to resemble the bodily shape of God, but that

16. On the exegesis of John Chrysostom, see the following: G. Bardy, "Interpretation chez les pères," *Dictionnaire Biblique,* supplement 4 (Paris, 1949): 569-91; Frederic Henry Chase, *Chrysostom: A Study in the History of Biblical Interpretation* (Cambridge: Deighton, Bell; London: George Bell, 1887); C. Hay, "Antiochene Exegesis and Christology," *Australian Biblical Review* 12 (1969): 10-23; Reiner Kaczynski, *Das Wort Gottes in Liturgie und Alltag der Gemeinden des Johannes Chrysostomus* (Freiburg, Basel, and Vienna: Herder, 1974); and A. Vaccari, "La theoria nella scuola esegetica de Antiochia," *Biblica* 1 (1920): 3-36.

17. Chrysostom, *Homilies on Genesis* 8.8.

he is to govern the creatures, as God does. This John tells us is clear from the context. " 'Let us make man in our image, after our likeness; and let them have dominion over the fish of the sea, and over the birds of the air, and over all the earth' " (Gen. 1:26). As we see, our preacher is very sober in his Christian interpretation. He brings none of the New Testament passages which so clearly speak of Christ's place in the work of creation into his interpretation of the passage. John 1:3 or Colossians 1:16, for example, could easily have been cited. For John Chrysostom the text of Genesis witnesses clearly enough to Christ. Those who truly believe Moses will believe in Christ as well.[18]

Let us look at another of John Chrysostom's sermons on a passage in Genesis which even in the fourth century had a well-established Christian interpretation. Christians have usually seen the story of Abraham's sacrifice as a type of the Father's offering up of the only-begotten Son. Already in the Gospel of John we find an allusion to this story from Genesis as a type of the love of the Father: "For God so loved the world that he gave his only Son, that whoever believes in him should not perish but have eternal life" (John 3:16). As more than one commentator has noted, this allusion to the story of Abraham's sacrifice is quite subtle but, nevertheless, hard to miss. John Chrysostom's treatment of the story is indeed chaste from the standpoint of its Christian interpretation. He tells the story much as it appears in the book of Genesis. For a Christian, of course, one of the primary interests of the story is what it says about the love of Abraham for his son, his only son. As John Chrysostom so often does, he portrays the saints as beautiful people, and surely one of the most beautiful things about Abraham as our preacher presents him is his love for Isaac. In fact, in his introduction to the sermon he tells us that "we will learn once again the patriarch's great virtue and the surpassing degree of God's lovingkindness."[19] One could go no further than saying that the love of Abraham for his son Isaac reveals the love of God for his children, and that might well be considered a sufficiently Christian interpretation.

John Chrysostom, to be sure, goes further than that. After having told the story in all its heart-tugging pathos, our preacher says, "All this, however, happened as a type of the Cross."[20] As Robert Hill puts it, only after exhausting the literal meaning does Chrysostom admit the typological

18. Chrysostom, *Homilies on Genesis* 8.6.
19. Chrysostom, *Homilies on Genesis* 47.1.
20. Chrysostom, *Homilies on Genesis* 47.14.

meaning.[21] We notice, however, that our preacher does not admit an allegorical meaning. He must have been well aware that the Isaac-Christ typology was firmly imbedded in the New Testament. He quotes the famous pun recorded in the Gospel of John, where Jesus says to the Jews, "'Abraham rejoiced to see my day'" (John 8:56). The Hebrew name "Isaac" was interpreted to mean Abraham laughed, or rejoiced, and so the pun means that Jesus claimed to be the true Isaac, the only-begotten Son. Chrysostom had no knowledge of Hebrew, but he had obviously learned this from those who did. He quotes the text from Matthew which tells us that at the baptism of Jesus a voice from heaven identified Jesus, "'This is my beloved Son, with whom I am well pleased'" (Matt. 3:17). Our preacher even quotes his beloved Paul to show how the Father's love as expressed in the sacrifice of Christ is prefigured by the story of Abraham's sacrifice: "He who did not spare his own Son but gave him up for us all, will he not also give us all things . . . ?" (Rom. 8:32).[22] These three quotations imply a rather thorough understanding of how the Isaac typology had been developed in the New Testament. Our preacher does not bring all this into the pulpit, but he obviously understood it.

Chrysostom had no trouble with typology, especially when the typology was so clearly to be found in the New Testament, as in the case with the Isaac typology. The New Testament typology belonged to a Christian interpretation of the Old Testament. But even beyond this, Chrysostom was willing to give an important place to a Christian understanding of the messianic prophecies of the Old Testament. There is not much in the way of messianic prophecies to be found in Genesis. One does, however, find one example of it at the very end of the book,[23] in the benediction of the patriarch Jacob, whom at this point Chrysostom identifies as a prophet:[24]

> "Judah, your brothers shall praise you;
> > your hand shall be on the neck of your enemies;
> > your father's sons shall bow down before you.
> Judah is a lion's whelp;
> > from the prey, my son, you have gone up.

---

21. Chrysostom, *Homilies on Genesis* 47.14. See Robert Hill's footnote in his translation of these sermons, 3:21 n. 20.

22. Chrysostom, *Homilies on Genesis* 47.14.

23. Chrysostom, *Homilies on Genesis* 67.8.

24. Chrysostom, *Homilies on Genesis* 67.4.

He stooped down, he couched as a lion,
   and as a lioness; who dares rouse him up?
The scepter shall not depart from Judah,
   nor the ruler's staff from between his feet,
until he comes to whom it belongs;
   and to him shall be the obedience of the peoples."

(Gen. 49:8-10)

Jacob blesses his son Judah in words that the Church has frequently understood in a messianic sense.[25] The Antiochene School firmly believed the affirmation of the creed of the Council of Constantinople that the Holy Spirit had spoken through the prophets.

    John Chrysostom's sermons on Genesis have a very definite evangelistic thrust. As we have already remarked, Antioch had a sizeable Jewish population and Christians and Jews were in constant discussion. John preached for the Jews' conversion, and he was convinced that what would convert them, as well as pagans, was the witness of a godly life. "Let us therefore, in all cases, give attention to teaching in action first and later in words."[26] This conviction is frequently expressed.[27] Nevertheless, there were Jews in his congregation who heard his sober interpretations of the Law of Moses and many more who would hear of his teachings indirectly. John knew that members of his congregation were in constant discussion about the claims of Christ, and he urges them to "argue the point in friendly exchange with the Jews, . . . showing them the words have reference not to some one of the ministering powers but to the only-begotten Son of God himself."[28] The point is that evangelism is in the last analysis a work of the Holy Spirit, not a matter of pressuring people into the kingdom of God. God uses the witness of lives that reflect the holiness of God, which is, to be sure, the most important means of bringing people to faith, but surely God also uses his Word. It is the word of Scripture itself which will convince the Jews. When the Spirit takes away the veil from their eyes, it will be by hearing Moses that they will hear Christ. The Antiochene exegesis has a missionary thrust. For John Chrysostom the sober exposition of Scripture is very effective evangelism.

    An important feature of the sermons on Genesis is the way John

---

25. Chrysostom, *Homilies on Genesis* 67.8.
26. Chrysostom, *Homilies on Genesis* 8.14.
27. Chrysostom, *Homilies on Genesis* 7.3 et passim.
28. Chrysostom, *Homilies on Genesis* 8.12.

interprets the patriarchs as guides to virtue. Their lives are examples for us, and therefore the preacher retells the stories of these heroes of godliness. This comes out with particular clarity in the sermons on the Joseph cycle.[29] From the very beginning Joseph as a seventeen-year-old boy is an example to us that youth does not constitute an obstacle to virtue;[30] indeed, Joseph had from youth an inclination to virtue. It was because of this that his father Jacob had such special regard for him. God had poured out on him "a kind of grace from on high that made the young man amiable and rendered him preferable to all the others on account of the virtue of his soul."[31] As Chrysostom sees it, virtue is a charisma that makes attractive those who are virtuous. When Joseph is betrayed by his brothers and sold into Egypt, our preacher marvels at Joseph's power of endurance[32] while at the same time filling in the villainy of Joseph's brothers, by contrast making the moral fortitude of Joseph even more conspicuous. One of the things which attracts us to these sermons is the way they make so clear the ugliness of sin and the beauty of virtue.

The exemplary character of Joseph becomes yet clearer when as a slave in the household of Potiphar, chief steward to the pharaoh of Egypt, he wins the favor of his master. Our preacher notes that God's grace had so anointed Joseph that Potiphar realized the Lord was with Joseph and that whatever Joseph did prospered,[33] so Potiphar gave Joseph increasing responsibility to the point where he became the steward of the steward of the pharaoh. Potiphar's wife also found Joseph attractive, although in a different way: She tried to seduce the young slave. But Joseph resisted her advances, and our preacher dwells at some length on the strength of Joseph in resisting temptation.[34] Not only was the young man beautiful in his physical appearance, he was beautiful in his moral character as well, and the ugliness of those who harassed him only made his strength of character more obvious. Potiphar's wife became more and more frustrated by Joseph's refusal to yield to her temptations and finally accused him of trying to seduce her. Joseph's innocence was not recognized, and yet it gave him strength even in adversity. Joseph was put into prison where the warden

---

29. Chrysostom, *Homilies on Genesis* 61-67.
30. Chrysostom, *Homilies on Genesis* 61.2.
31. Chrysostom, *Homilies on Genesis* 61.3.
32. Chrysostom, *Homilies on Genesis* 61.20.
33. Chrysostom, *Homilies on Genesis* 62.13-14.
34. Chrysostom, *Homilies on Genesis* 62.17-20.

of the prison recognized his talent for administration and once again Joseph prospered, albeit in prison. So it is, Chrysostom points out as he concludes his second sermon, that the grace of God makes it possible for the righteous to prosper even in the worst of circumstances. Virtue has its strength! Let us therefore "imitate this young man's self-control, his other virtues and noble attitude."[35]

In the next sermon our preacher begins to point out how the story of Joseph reveals the marvelous working out of divine providence.[36] Although Joseph is in prison for several years, we hear not a word of complaint from him. So complete is his faith in the providence of God that he wastes no time in self-pity. Finally the time comes for Joseph to be led into the court of Pharaoh, and our preacher recounts the story of how Joseph was able to understand the dreams first of his fellow prisoners and then of Pharaoh. And once again the wisdom of Joseph was recognized and he became one of the most influential men of Egypt. Chrysostom narrates the story well, storytelling being one of the first arts of the preacher, and then he draws his moral: "Do you see how important it is to bear trials thankfully? Hence Paul also said, 'Distress promotes endurance, endurance promotes character, character promotes hope, and hope does not disappoint us' (Romans 5:3-5). So take note: he bore distress with endurance, endurance gave him character, having character he acted in hope, and hope did not disappoint him."[37] As our preacher puts it, that is what faith is all about. God gives us a vision of the future just as he gave Joseph a dream as a young man. It was a promise of a blessed future, and Joseph believed that promise and unswervingly held to it. Contrary to all appearances, contrary to all discouragements and setbacks, Joseph believed God's promise and finally what was promised came true.[38]

The next sermon tells the story of how the famine Joseph had predicted came about and Joseph's brothers came down to Egypt to buy grain. The story as we find it in the Bible is beautifully told; in fact, it is one of the most beautiful narratives in Scripture. Understandably it makes for a long sermon. Again the noble virtue of Joseph is underlined. The sermon tells us how just as it was in the dream Joseph had had as a boy,

35. Chrysostom, *Homilies on Genesis* 62.24.
36. Chrysostom, *Homilies on Genesis* 63.13.
37. Chrysostom, *Homilies on Genesis* 63.17.
38. Chrysostom, *Homilies on Genesis* 63.21.

his brothers came to bow down before him.[39] But there is more to this story. God's kindly providence toward Joseph was not something to be enjoyed simply by Joseph himself; it was to issue in the salvation of his whole family. God's gifts are that way; they are to be passed on to others. The vision fulfilled, Joseph reveals his true identity to his brothers and reassures them of his love for them. "It was not so much from your malice in my regard as from God's wisdom and ineffable love that I should come here now and be in a favorable position to provide nourishment to you. . . . What has happened is by God's design."[40]

Sermon 65 treats the story of how Reuben returned to the land of Canaan and reported all that happened to the brothers' father, Jacob. Jacob is overjoyed that his beloved son had survived the ordeal he had gone through and had prospered in the land of Egypt, and in spite of his great age, he sets out on the long journey to see his son. The reunion of the two is a moving scene. The father's love for the son and the son's devotion to the father are at last in the providence of God rewarded, and John's admonition at the end of the sermon is: "If we were prepared to move on to all the stories contained in Scripture, we would find all those endowed with virtue passing through trials and thus succeeding in winning much grace on high."[41] The whole series of sermons on the Joseph cycle shows the attractiveness of those who are truly virtuous, but even more, these sermons again and again make the point that in the providence of God virtue has its rewards.

The next sermon treats Joseph's care for his father in old age. The tenderness of Joseph for the old man is very attractive. The modern reader of the biblical story is tempted to be distracted by some aspects of the story which would seem foolish to us today — for example, he might object that Jacob had been foolish in showing favoritism to his younger son. But our preacher skips over this and many things like it in the text. Robert Hill speaks quite candidly of Chrysostom's hagiographical interpretation of the patriarchs — by the time John gets through with him, Joseph is an Homeric hero — when in actual fact the saints of the Old Testament are much more human. The Bible is very candid about the sins of the patriarchs, and if we do not recognize this our interpretations too often go awry. This hagiographical tendency is a problem, to be sure, but the strength of these sermons is that they do intimate the beauty of

39. Chrysostom, *Homilies on Genesis* 64.5.
40. Chrysostom, *Homilies on Genesis* 64.28.
41. Chrysostom, *Homilies on Genesis* 65.18.

holiness. They show us that there is something admirable in human life and that those who live close to God come to reflect the very goodness of the Eternal. For an age addicted to the debunking school of history the biblical interpretation of Chrysostom seems naive and totally lacking in critical awareness. This may be true, but Chrysostom is aware of the power of godliness to be attractive. "Each of us, after all, has the knowledge of virtue set deep in our very own nature. . . . May it be the good fortune of us all to choose it, to practice it precisely, and to attain the blessings laid up in pledge for those who love him."[42] When we read these sermons very carefully it is clear that John Chrysostom's Joseph is less a reflection of Odysseus than a foreshadowing of Christ.

The final sermon in the Joseph cycle begins with a commentary on the blessing of the twelve patriarchs.[43] After conferring this final benediction, Jacob breathed his last breath. Throughout the land of Egypt there was general mourning, and Joseph, following the directions of his deceased father, accompanied his body to the land of Canaan and buried him with his fathers in the family crypt. After this had been done Joseph's brothers once again began to fear the revenge of the brother they had sold into Egypt.[44] For Chrysostom, this is still another occasion to point out the virtue of Joseph, who had indeed genuinely forgiven his brothers. They may have meant it for harm, but, as the text of Genesis puts it, God meant it for good (Gen. 50:19-20).[45] Providence has a way of bringing good out of evil — about this Chrysostom is quite certain. He even quotes his favorite biblical author, the apostle Paul, to make it abundantly clear. "You acted against me with evil intent, but God turned everything to good for me. Hence Paul also said, 'For those who love God all things work together for good' (Romans 8:28)."[46] God had poured out his grace on Joseph, giving him a vision of future blessings, and Joseph had believed the promise that had been revealed to him. In spite of every trial and every temptation Joseph was faithful to God. That was the heart of his virtue, his confidence in the faithfulness of God toward him. He was free to live the life of virtue because he knew God would support him. And God did support him far more abundantly than anything he ever imagined.

42. Chrysostom, *Homilies on Genesis* 66.16.
43. Chrysostom, *Homilies on Genesis* 67.4-14.
44. Chrysostom, *Homilies on Genesis* 67.18.
45. Chrysostom, *Homilies on Genesis* 67.19.
46. Chrysostom, *Homilies on Genesis* 67.19.

One can hardly read these sermons without being aware of the preacher's strong doctrine of biblical authority. In several passages John Chrysostom goes into the subject of just how it is that Scripture, and particularly the preaching of the Scriptures, is the Word of God.[47] John has a strong sense of God's being the author of Scripture. At the beginning of his series, he impresses upon his hearers the importance of listening to what Scripture has to say about creation rather than relying on the speculations of philosophers. "Since we therefore listen to these words not as the words of Moses but as the words of the God of all things coming through the tongue of Moses, so, I beg you, let us heed what is said and part company with our own reasoning."[48] Scripture obviously has authority which the reasonings of philosophers do not have. John Chrysostom lived in a world where the rationality of philosophy was accorded considerable authority, yet for him, as for Christians generally, revelation was something which was quite different and which had considerably more authority.

One thing we must be careful to note in Chrysostom's thought is that there is nothing static about his doctrine of the authority of Scripture. This authority is a living and abiding authority. The Scripture which has authority is the Bible as read and preached in worship. In the eighth sermon we read, "Come, now, let us see what it is today also the blessed Moses is teaching us through the text we've read, or rather what the grace of the Spirit has to say to us all through his tongue."[49] Surely in these lines there is no suggestion that the Scriptures committed to writing by the prophets and apostles are anything less than the Word of God. What is emphasized, however, is the authority of the Scriptures as read and preached in the worship of the Church. For our preacher the reading and preaching of the Scriptures in the Christian assembly of worship is the Word of God in its primary form. "Consider the dignity of this spiritual gathering and the fact that we are listening to God speaking to us through the tongue of the inspired authors."[50] It is not merely a matter of a printed book being the Word of God, but, even beyond that, it is a matter of a preached message

---

47. Robert Hill in a series of articles has recently pointed out the richness of John Chrysostom's doctrine of Scripture in these sermons. See Robert C. Hill, *St. John Chrysostom's Teaching on Inspiration in His Old Testament Homilies* (Sydney, 1981).

48. Chrysostom, *Homilies on Genesis* 2.5.

49. Chrysostom, *Homilies on Genesis* 8.3.

50. Chrysostom, *Homilies on Genesis* 15.3.

being the Word of God. To be sure, we need to affirm the authority of the written text before we can affirm the authority of the reading and preaching of that text. With John, as with many a great preacher, the conviction that the Scriptures are indeed the Word of God is the essential driving force of his ministry. The preaching of the Word of God is authoritative and efficacious because it is God's Word, not the preacher's. Here is the foundation of the passion and the power of great preaching. It is for this reason that the great preachers have preached and their congregations have heard them. In great preaching it is always clear that the authority of the preached Word comes from the author. The Word has authority because God is the author.

For John Chrysostom the inspiration of Scripture is a fundamental idea. It was less than a decade before these sermons were preached that the Council of Constantinople formulated that it was the Holy Spirit who spoke by the prophets. It is for this reason that John speaks of the human authors of the Old Testament as prophets, whether they be prophets in the usual sense, such as Isaiah or Jeremiah, or others such as Moses, David, or Solomon whom the Spirit inspired to write the various books. As Robert Hill has shown, "prophet" has, for Chrysostom, come to mean inspired author.[51] This inspiration is not understood in a general way but in a very exact and precise way. In the fifteenth sermon we read, "Let us act so as to interpret everything precisely and instruct you not to pass by even a brief phrase or single syllable contained in the Holy Scriptures. After all they are not simply words, but words of the Holy Spirit, and hence the treasure to be found in even a single syllable is great."[52] It is here, of course, that we moderns find the stumbling block. We figure that inspiration must have meant some kind of dictation theory for Chrysostom, as for other Church Fathers. This is probably true, although it is no doubt a mistake to read from this all that some more recent theologians would like. The Fathers were not the naive primitives some would imagine.

John Chrysostom often speaks of the exactness or preciseness of Scripture. Robert Hill tells us that our preacher delights in the precision of Scripture more than twenty times in these sermons.[53] According to Hill, the Greek word ἀκρίβεια is incorrectly translated "accuracy," whereas

---

51. Robert C. Hill, "Chrysostom's Terminology for the Inspired Word," *Estudios Biblicos* 41 (1983): 372.

52. Chrysostom, *Homilies on Genesis* 15.3.

53. Chrysostom, *Homilies on Genesis*, introduction, p. 18.

it should be translated "precision." This precision of Scripture is no doubt the logical corollary to our preacher's strong sense of inspiration. In the seventh sermon we read,

> For that reason the blessed Moses, inspired by the divine Spirit, teaches us with great precision, lest we fall victim to the same things as they, instead of being able to know clearly both the sequence of created things and how each thing was created. You see, if God in his care for our salvation had not directed the tongue of the biblical author in this way, it would have been sufficient to say that God made heaven and earth. . . . But lest he leave any grounds for excuse to those bent on folly, he explains in this way both the order of created things and the number of days, and he teaches us everything with great considerateness so that we may learn the whole truth and not turn our minds to the error of those uttering all these ideas from their own reasoning.[54]

What bothers the theologian of today about these words is the implication that God moved the tongue of the sacred author to utter truths of which he was unconscious. He taught doctrine he did not understand. This may or may not, however, be what John meant to convey. Sometimes his rhetoric leads him to put things in a way that is a bit too pictorial or too metaphorical, and perhaps what he is really talking about is the experience of ecstatic insight. Ecstatic insight is something preachers, poets, and writers have often described. Suddenly things become clear and the words begin to flow and one knows they have been poured out from some higher insight. They have come from that wisdom which is on high. As every artist knows, inspiration is gracious.

But there is something else at work here. The fourth-century Fathers were beginning to realize that in the literal sense of the creation story they had a strong defense against a number of heresies which had sprung up over the doctrine of creation. Marcionism, Manichaeism, and a number of brands of Gnosticism all taught doctrines of creation quite at odds with Genesis. In fact, John mentions these errors at the beginning of his series.[55] Because of these errors it was very important to pay attention to the exact and precise wording of the creation story. When one respects this precision of Scripture, then it will become clear that these other teachings are quite different from the teachings of Scripture. For example, after each thing

---

54. Chrysostom, *Homilies on Genesis* 7.10.
55. Chrysostom, *Homilies on Genesis* 2.10.

that was created the text says God saw that it was good. If we read the text with precision and realize that nothing is said in Scripture without a purpose, then it becomes clear that all those dualistic heresies which teach that matter is evil are contrary to Scripture.[56] The fact that a grammatical-historical interpretation of Genesis was so useful in refuting so many of these heresies may well explain why Genesis so frequently found a place in the preaching of the Church during the weeks when the catechumens were being prepared for baptism. It was important to get the catechumens straight on these matters. The precision of Scripture needed to be respected if heresy was to be avoided.

Perhaps John's most profound teaching on Scripture is his teaching on the condescension of God's Word. God out of his love for man comes down to us and speaks our language so that our minds, limited as they are, can grasp divine truth. Robert Hill suggests that a better translation of this Greek word, συγκατάβασις, might be "considerateness," because it avoids certain negative connotations the word "condescension" has in English. This considerateness of God in revealing himself to man meant that God "was speaking in a manner appropriate to his hearers."[57] Again speaking of a passage in Genesis, John tells us of the "considerateness employed by the blessed author, or rather the loving God through the tongue of the author, instructing the race of men to know the plan of created things. . . . The Holy Spirit accordingly explained every thing to us by moving the author's tongue in such a way as to take account of the limitations of the listeners."[58] The considerateness of God is true to the loving nature of God just as it is to the limitations inherent in human nature. For John Chrysostom the love of God for man, the divine φιλανθρωπία, is his supreme attribute, and therefore, for God to limit himself by expressing the divine wisdom in human words is no embarrassment. It is, if we may go a step further than Hill, a matter of God's grace. For Chrysostom the Word is supremely gracious. Just as we find in Karl Barth, the doctrine of revelation and the doctrine of grace are closely connected.

For the School of Alexandria, ever since Philo, the anthropomorphisms of Scripture were, on the other hand, an embarrassment. In fact, these anthropomorphisms were understood as one of the proofs that one

56. Chrysostom, *Homilies on Genesis* 6.18.
57. Chrysostom, *Homilies on Genesis* 2.10.
58. Chrysostom, *Homilies on Genesis* 3.7; see also 13.8.

had to understand Scripture allegorically. But for Chrysostom, it was not ἀνθρωπομορφία but φιλανθρωπία; it was not that God was shaped like man but that God loved man. Philo of Alexandria, to be sure, had no doctrine of the incarnation, and we could hardly expect him to have perceived what a John Chrysostom, who did have a doctrine of the incarnation, was able to perceive. To be sure, some of Philo's followers were Christians, but it sometimes takes a while for ideas like this to float to the top. The anthropomorphic language was a matter of God's considerateness in speaking to us human beings in a language that we would understand. In Sermon 12 we read, "After all, the words require the eyes of faith, spoken as they are with such great considerateness and with our limitations in mind. You see that the very remark, 'God shaped the human being, and breathed,' is properly inapplicable to God; yet because of us and our limitations Sacred Scripture expresses it in that way, showing considerateness to us."[59] In his sermon on the text "And they heard the sound of the LORD God walking in the garden" (Gen. 3:8), John remarks, "Let us not, dearly beloved, pass heedlessly by the words of Sacred Scripture, not remain at the level of their expression, but consider that the ordinariness of their expression occurs with our limitations in mind and that everything is done in a manner befitting God for the sake of our salvation."[60] It is because of Chrysostom's doctrine of God's considerateness in Scripture that he is able to stick with a literal interpretation and avoid an allegorical interpretation. His understanding of the literal sense admits a large degree of sophistication.

There is a certain balance between John Chrysostom's concept of the ἀκρίβεια of Scripture and the συνκατάβασις of Scripture. It may well be that if we moderns stumble over the former we can be lifted up by the latter. John did not of course have to wrestle with all the problems that the modern exegete must face — and face honestly — but it would be a mistake to think that his doctrine of God's considerateness in revealing himself in Scripture can simply be used to get around all the problems that historical criticism has raised. He did not develop his doctrine in this way, and we should respect that. On the other hand, his doctrine is certainly most suggestive as a starting point for recovering for our use his sublime sense of the authority of Scripture. When the Church does find a way to respect the full historicity of Scripture and the full humanity of

---

59. Chrysostom, *Homilies on Genesis* 12.12.
60. Chrysostom, *Homilies on Genesis* 17.3.

its human authors, and at the same time accepts their divine authority, then we will once again have preachers of the magnitude of John Chrysostom.

B. Sermons on the Statues

The systematic preaching through of one book of the Bible after another was the ordinary procedure in the pulpit at Antioch. It was this sort of preaching which produced volume after volume of John Chrysostom's expository sermons. There were occasions, however, that demanded a departure from this orderly system. One such occasion was the riot over taxation which occurred in 386 shortly before the beginning of the forty-day fast. The emperor Theodosius had imposed a new tax, and the resentment of the population was fanned into a riot which at its height led to the toppling of the statues of the emperor and the imperial family. Suddenly the city was sobered by the seriousness of their actions as the government instituted excessive measures to restore order. Arrests were made on any pretext, and even the most respected citizens were charged with high treason and on little or no evidence were condemned to death and swiftly executed.

The city was stunned with fear when John Chrysostom entered the pulpit to prepare his congregation to enter the forty-day fast.[61] Never was a congregation more ripe for repentance than the Christians of Antioch were at the beginning of the fast that year. The preacher lamented the sins of the city and challenged its citizens not merely to fast but to lay aside every form of sin, especially the sins of swearing and cursing. All through the twenty-one sermons John preached during the fast, this theme keeps recurring. Perhaps our preacher had planned to mount a special crusade against the making of oaths, the use of foul language, and other expressions of anger during the fasting season, or maybe he had intended this particular year to challenge his congregation to rid themselves of the sins of the

---

61. For studies of the Sermons on the Statues, see Mary Albania Burns, *St. John Chrysostom's Homilies on the Statues: A Study of Their Rhetorical Qualities and Form* (Washington, D.C.: Catholic University of America Press, 1930); J. M. Leroux, "Saint Jean Chrysostome, les Homélies sur les Statues," *Studia Patristica* 3, *Texte und Untersuchungen* 87 (Berlin, 1961): 233-39; and Frans van de Paverd, *St. John Chrysostom, the Homilies on the Statues: An Introduction* (Rome: Pontifical Institute of Oriental Studies, 1991).

tongue. We cannot be sure, but the theme keeps reoccurring. Surely the riot would never have grown to what it became if it had not been for excessive speech. Be that as it may, in this series of sermons it became clear that John was a prophet, a prophet who had come to call the Christians of Antioch to repentance.

While John Chrysostom did the best he could to lead the populace of the city to repentance from the pulpit, Flavian, the bishop of Antioch, decided to go to Constantinople himself to calm the emperor before he imposed the harsh reprisals the citizens of Antioch feared. If the local authorities had been severe in repressing the riot, how much more severe would the emperor be when he learned of the affront to his person! Flavian was a man of advanced years and would have to travel in haste, yet it was a good plan because Theodosius was known to be a devout Christian and the bishop of a church of such prestige would surely have weight with him. The only question was whether the elderly bishop could stand the rigors of such a journey. Would he be able to reach the ear of the emperor before the official military report which had already been dispatched?

In the meantime many fled the city fearing reprisals, and those who remained were deeply troubled. Their preacher well understood his pastoral responsibility and kept preaching that tribulation, if taken seriously and if used as a warning to turn away from sin, would lead to a far better life. These trials had fallen on Antioch to awaken the people to the importance of living an honest and sincere life. Instead of trusting in riches and influence and honor, the wise Christian should trust in God and cultivate a simple and sober life. The city had just experienced the vanity of worldly honors. The vengeance of the government had fallen on even the rich and the famous with unmitigated fury. Worldly wealth and power, political influence and family connections, had been no help in the reign of terror they were going through. Surely current events proved the futility of material security. Was it not far better, then, to strive for the treasures of the spirit?

Given the situation, it is not surprising that rumors racked the city, which our preacher constantly had to deal with from the pulpit. News came that the emissaries who had first been sent to report the riot were providentially hindered in their journey, and that Bishop Flavian had overtaken them. That at least was what had been reported, and John used the news to revive the hopes of his fellow citizens. Then came a rumor that the soldiers of the emperor were advancing on the city. The population converged on the churches hoping for asylum, and John had to enter the pulpit and assure them that it was only a rumor. He once again urged them to put their hope in God.

Finally reports began to reach Antioch that their bishop had reached Constantinople and had been able to appeal to the emperor's clemency. This time John was able to go to the pulpit with glad tidings. He told how their bishop had inspired pious sentiments in the heart of their Christian emperor. By Easter Bishop Flavian had reached home, and that year Easter became a celebration not only of the resurrection of Christ but of the salvation of Antioch as well.

The Sermons on the Statues have often been regarded as one of the outstanding monuments of Christian oratory. Even though they were preached only a year after John began his ministry in Antioch, the intensity of the situation evoked his greatest powers of eloquence. Let us look for a moment at the first of these sermons to discover some of the features of the rhetoric of John Chrysostom.[62] We need but a single sermon to make our point.

Although this first sermon might be described as a prophetic lamentation, it is indeed eloquent.[63] Our preacher opens with the following words:

> What shall I say, or what shall I speak of? The present season is one for tears, and not for words; for lamentation, not for discourse; for prayer, not for preaching. Such is the magnitude of the deeds daringly done; so incurable is the wound, so deep the blow, even beyond the power of all treatment. . . .[64]

This was an established way for someone well trained in Greek rhetoric to begin an oration of condolence. The speaker insists that no words will be adequate to express the grief appropriate to the situation:

> Scarcely am I able to open my mouth, to part my lips, to move my tongue, or to utter a syllable! So, even like a curb, the weight of grief checks my tongue, and keeps back what I would say.[65]

62. For a full analysis of the rhetoric of these sermons, see Burns, *Homilies on the Statues.*

63. The English text quoted in this study is the classic translation of W. R. W. Stephens in the Nicene and Post-Nicene Fathers, 1st ser., vol. 9 (Grand Rapids: Wm. B. Eerdmans Publishing Co., 1956), pp. 315-489; hereinafter cited as Chrysostom, *On the Statues.* One should note that the sermon which really begins the series is Homily 2 of the traditional collection as is explained by the notes on p. 331 of the above edition.

64. Chrysostom, *On the Statues* 2.1.

65. Chrysostom, *On the Statues* 2.2.

We notice the parallelism, the threefold repetition of grammatical structure, the recurrence of infinitives. All this is standard Greek rhetoric. A bit further on we find another feature of classical rhetoric, especially as it was taught by the Second Sophistic school, namely, *ecphrasis,* or the word picture. Here our preacher draws for us the city of Antioch traumatized with fear:

> We live in constant terror, . . . every one is pent up within the walls of his own house! And as it is not safe for those who are besieged to go beyond the walls, while the enemy without is encamped around; so neither, to many of those who inhabit this city, is it safe to go out of doors, or to appear openly; on account of those who are everywhere hunting for the innocent as well as the guilty; and seizing them even in the midst of the forum, and dragging them to the court of justice, without ceremony, and just as chance directs. For this reason, freemen sit in doors shackled up with their domestics; anxiously and minutely enquiring of those to whom they may safely put the question, "Who has been seized to-day; who carried off; or punished? How was it? and in what manner?" They live a life more wretched than any kind of death; being compelled daily to mourn the calamities of others; while they tremble for their own safety, and are in no better case than the dead; inasmuch as they are already dead with fear.[66]

This is followed by another picture of the streets, the forum, and the marketplace, all empty because the inhabitants dare not leave their houses for fear of arrest.

Classical rhetoric loved similes and metaphors, and John Chrysostom can come up with some magnificent examples. In this sermon he compares his responsibility to preach in the midst of such gloom to the sun, which must shine even when the earth is bedecked with clouds:

> And as when some dense cloud has formed, and flying under the solar rays, returns back to him all his splendour again, so indeed does the cloud of sadness, when it stands before our souls, refuse to admit an easy passage for the word, but chokes it and restrains it forcibly within. And this is the case not only with those who speak, but with those who hear; for as it does not suffer the word to burst forth freely from the soul of the speaker, so neither does it suffer it to sink into the mind of

---

66. Chrysostom, *On the Statues* 2.5.

those who listen, with its natural power. Therefore also the Jews of old time, while slaving at the mud and bricks, had not the heart to listen to Moses, while he repeatedly told them great things respecting their future deliverance; despondency making their minds inaccessible to the address, and shutting up their sense of hearing. I could have wished then, as to myself, to have put an end here to my discourse; but thinking that it is not only the nature of a cloud to intercept the forward passage of the nature of the sun's rays, but that often just the opposite happens to the cloud; since the sun continually falling upon it with much warmth, wears it away, and frequently breaks through the midst of it; and shining forth all at once, meets cheerfully the gaze of the beholders. This also I myself expect to do this day; and the word being continually associated with your minds, and dwelling in them, I hope to burst the cloud of sadness, and to shine through your understandings again, with the customary instruction![67]

A bit further on he assures his listeners that even in a time of calamity such as they now endure it is of great value to strengthen faith. "The believer hath his stand on the Rock; for this reason he cannot be overthrown by the dashing of the billows. For should the waves of temptation rise, they cannot reach his feet. He stands too lofty for any such assault."[68] Then commenting on the text "Neither trust in uncertain riches," John gives us the following metaphor:

For nothing is so faithless as wealth; of which I have often said, and will not cease to say, that it is a runaway, thankless servant, having no fidelity; and should you throw over him ten thousand chains, he will make off dragging his chains after him. Frequently, indeed, have those who possessed him shut him up with bars and doors, placing their slaves round about for guards. But he has over-persuaded these very servants, and has fled away together with his guards; dragging his keepers after him like a chain, so little security was there in this custody. What then can be more faithless than this?[69]

Metaphors and similes seem to come to this preacher all quite naturally and without the least sort of effort.

Having elaborated his text with a metaphor, he goes on to make it

67. Chrysostom, *On the Statues* 2.8.
68. Chrysostom, *On the Statues* 2.9.
69. Chrysostom, *On the Statues* 2.13.

even clearer with a paradox. If we are not to trust in riches because they are unfaithful, then it is also true that instead of trusting in them we should give them away, because it is in sharing our wealth that we enjoy it. "The rich man is not one who is in possession of much, but one who gives much."[70] To make his point he tells at length of Abraham, who lived in a nomad's tent but extended his hospitality to all. Even angels were honored to be his guests. They came to him not because of the richness of his dwelling but because of the magnificence of his soul. Abraham's investments had been made in virtue. His wealth was his piety.

The conclusion of this eloquent sermon is an ingenious piece of oratory. It is an invitation to the sacrament of the Lord's Supper. John invites his congregation to receive the sacrament as an assurance of God's saving presence. He speaks of Elijah the prophet, who lived through difficult times. Hunted by soldiers and despised by pagan priests, he resorted to the simplest kind of life. Daily he fasted in the brook Cherith, hidden away in the wilderness. Disdaining the life of luxury, he was protected by God. He had but one possession, his mantle — what a precious possession that was! But when at the end of his long ministry Elijah ascended into heaven in a fiery chariot, that one possession fell to his faithful follower Elisha. That mantle was a pledge of God's faithful protection in times of adversity and to those who lead a simple godly life. In the same way Christ has left us the sacrament as a pledge of the ultimate satisfaction and blessedness of a life of godly simplicity; therefore receive the sacrament of his body and blood as an assurance that he is with us.

Throughout these twenty-one Sermons on the Statues are many examples of all the figures of Greek rhetoric: beautiful parallel structures, such as *chiasmus* and *antithesis;* rhetorical questions; apostrophes; alliterations; and the rhythms and cadences so characteristic of classical oratory. We have spoken of this at some length in regard to Basil, who likewise was a pupil of the great Libanius, so it is not necessary to go over the same ground here.

There is, however, one thing about the rhetoric of John Chrysostom that does deserve our notice: Here is a preacher who has a profound sense of biblical eloquence as well. Just as the masterpieces of Greek oratory are filled with allusions to the Homeric epic and quotations of the classic dramas of Aeschylus, Sophocles, and Euripides, so the sermons of John are filled with allusions to the biblical epic, the psalms, and the prophets.

70. Chrysostom, *On the Statues* 2.15.

To be sure, he has mastered the classical rhetoric of the Greeks, but he has saturated himself with Hebrew rhetoric as well. One can hardly avoid the observation that if he was everything a Greek orator was supposed to be, he was also everything a Hebrew prophet was supposed to be. With all the passion of Elijah he confronted God's people with their sins; with all the eloquence of Isaiah he called his congregation to repentance. Right from the beginning of this sermon he recalls the complaints Job issued while sitting on his dunghill. He summons the Christian cities of the Empire to come and, like the counselors of Job, bewail the calamities of Antioch. The parallels to the Lamentations of Jeremiah are striking! The whole sermon breathes the spirit of Jeremiah every bit as much as the spirit of Demosthenes. In fact, John Chrysostom recites one of Jeremiah's lamentations:

> "Call for the mourning women, that they may come, and for the cunning women, and let them take up a wailing. Let your eyes run down with water, and your eyelids gush out with tears" (Jeremiah 9:17-18).[71]

He uses passages from Isaiah and Amos to much the same effect.

As far as we know the Hebrews never made a formal study of their rhetoric in the way the Greeks did, yet they obviously had a high sense of the beauty of the word. The art of the sermon was apparently carefully developed. Just how John may have picked this up is not clear. Perhaps he learned it from Diodore of Tarsus, or perhaps, during the years he lived as a monk, he saturated himself so thoroughly with the Old Testament prophets that he was able to come up with their kind of eloquence quite spontaneously. John may never have studied the doctrine of the perfections of Scripture as it was taught in the theological schools of Protestant orthodoxy, but he seems to have understood it just as well. One can learn much about eloquence from simply reading the Bible. The sufficiency of Scripture is well known by those who have in fact lived day by day from the Word of God.

For the specialist the techniques of rhetoric, be they Greek or Hebrew, have their interest, to be sure. And yet, we all know that as helpful as these techniques may be, the art of oratory must go beyond them. The sort of spontaneous eloquence John Chrysostom and Basil of Caesarea

---

71. Chrysostom, *On the Statues* 2.7.

developed had as its mainspring the development of a beautiful life. Eloquence of the tongue was but the outward manifestation of an inward spiritual beauty, an eloquence of the soul. To cultivate a simple life, to abound in generosity, and, like Abraham, to be rich in piety is the high road to the art of oratory. One notices how in these sermons so renowned for eloquence that the preacher constantly appeals to his congregation to make their tongues chaste. Avoid oaths! Clean up your language! Curse not! Mortify the anger within you! In our day it seems a trivial concern. How can we possibly understand the spiritual leader of a city in imminent danger of being plowed under out of political revenge pleading with the people to clean up their language? Is the purity of the word really all that crucial? Did he really believe that sanctity was the ultimate wisdom? Was holiness, even more, the ultimate strength and the ultimate beauty as well?

C. Catechetical Sermons

During the patristic period catechetical preaching appears as a clear and distinct genre of Christian preaching. We have today a number of distinguished series of catechetical sermons from this period; the mystagogical catechisms of Cyril of Jerusalem and Ambrose of Milan's *De sacramentis* are perhaps the most well known. Catechetical preaching, as we pointed out above, goes back to the command of Jesus to make disciples of all nations by baptizing them and teaching them to observe all things which he had commanded them (Matt. 28:19-20).

We have seen how the *Didache,* in its unfolding of the catechism of the two ways, understood this ministry of catechetical preaching.[72] It was an introduction to the Christian life, delineating the way of the children of light and the way of the children of darkness. The catechetical instruction outlined in the *Didache* is quite specific in teaching the beginner which practices are allowed Christians and which are not. By the time we get to the catechetical sermons of Cyril of Jerusalem, however, the emphasis has been placed on the explanation of Christian doctrine on one hand and, on the other, on the explanation of the Christian mysteries.[73]

Perhaps it is the understandable conservatism of the church of

72. On the *Didache* and the beginnings of catechetical preaching, see my first volume of this work, chapter 3.
73. On the catechetical sermons of Cyril of Jerusalem, see chapter 1 of this volume.

Antioch, the city where the disciples were first called Christians, which is responsible for John Chrysostom's approach to catechetical instruction, but whatever the reasons for it John did not follow the lead of Cyril. For John the emphasis of catechetical instruction is neither the teaching of doctrine nor the explanation of the liturgy but the explaining of the Christian way of life. His explanation of the rite of baptism is given before the sacrament is conferred on his converts, not after. His sermons cannot really be called mystagogy at all; like the *Didache,* they are concerned with Christian moral teaching. This was an important departure because, as we will see, Augustine takes the tradition even further in this same direction.

For a long time the approach of John Chrysostom was unrecognized. So few of his catechetical sermons had been published that the picture was fuzzy. In 1955 Père Antoine Wenger discovered in a manuscript of the monastery of Stavronikita on Mount Athos a complete series of John Chrysostom's catechetical sermons.[74] This discovery brought to light his approach to catechetical preaching. The sermons were apparently preached in Antioch about 390, by which time John's ministry was in full flower. Bishop Flavian had entrusted him with the major preaching responsibility of the cathedral.

The full responsibility of preparing the catechumens had not, however, been turned over to our popular preacher — the catechumens were taught by a number of other ministers, whom John mentions very specifically at one point.[75] Possibly even the bishop himself felt obliged to preach to the catechumens on the tradition of the creed and again on the tradition of the Lord's Prayer. Our preacher also tells us that the catechumens received thirty days of instruction prior to their baptism.[76] We do not know who performed this ministry nor what was taught during this period,

---

74. The following study is based on the edition of Antoine Wenger: St. John Chrysostom, *Huit catéchèses baptismales inédites,* French translation by Antoine Wenger (Paris: Les Éditions du Cerf, 1970; hereinafter cited as Chrysostom, *Catechetical Sermons.* There is an English translation by P. F. Harkins, *St. John Chrysostom: Baptismal Instructions* (Westminster, Md.: Newman Press, 1963). See the study by Enrico Mazza, *Mystagogy: A Theology of Liturgy in the Patristic Age,* trans. Matthew J. O'Connell (New York: Pueblo Publishing Co., 1989), pp. 104-49; Aldo Ceresa-Gastaldo, *Giovanni Crisostomo: Le catechesi battesimali* (Rome, 1982); and D. Sartore, "Il misterio del battesimo nelle catechesi di S. Giovanni Crisostomo," *Lateranum* 50 (1984).

75. Chrysostom, *Catechetical Sermons* 8.1.

76. Chrysostom, *Catechetical Sermons* 9.2 and 29, see note.

but we can presume that a good part of it was an explanation of the baptismal creed and the Lord's Prayer. There may also have been an introduction to the history of salvation, starting with the creation of Adam and Eve and continuing on through the patriarchal history, the exodus from Egypt, the promises of the prophets and their fulfillment in Christ. This was a fairly common pattern. Perhaps there were specially appointed catechists who carried out this instruction.

John was responsible for very specific sermons. He preached an introductory sermon at the time the candidates for baptism were enrolled in which he spoke of the momentousness of the occasion.[77] This was followed by a sermon at the end of thirty days of instruction in which he explained the rites and ceremonies of baptism.[78] After the candidates had been baptized very early on Easter morning, John preached to them again on the significance of what they had experienced.[79] Here our preacher's main point was that in the sacrament of baptism they had obligated themselves to live the kind of life Jesus had taught. Then during Easter week our preacher addressed the newly baptized each day on various aspects of the Christian life.[80]

Recently Father Auguste Piédagnel published a study of another series of catechetical sermons which throws additional light on the catechetical preaching of the church of Antioch.[81] These sermons had originally been published by the Byzantine scholar A. Papadopoulos in Saint Petersburg just before the beginning of the First World War. Understandably, they received little notice during those troubled times. Piédagnel's new edition of this other series shows us that one of the sermons published by Wenger, namely, the third sermon, really belongs to the series originally published by Papadopoulos.

What immediately strikes us about John Chrysostom's catechetical preaching is that it shows far greater interest in moral catechism than in either doctrinal or liturgical catechism. To be sure, these subjects are treated, but with far greater brevity than in the catechetical sermons of other preachers of the period. In regard to doctrinal instruction this is

77. Chrysostom, *Catechetical Sermons* 1.

78. Chrysostom, *Catechetical Sermons* 2. Wenger's Sermon 3 was preached on the same occasion but in a different year.

79. Chrysostom, *Catechetical Sermons* 4.

80. Chrysostom, *Catechetical Sermons* 5, 6, 7, and 8.

81. St. John Chrysostom, *Trois catéchèse baptismales,* introduction, critical text, French translation, and notes by Auguste Piédagnel (Paris: Les Éditions du Cerf, 1990).

probably explained by the fact that others had been charged with that facet of the instruction. In regard to an explanation of the sacraments, however, it is another matter. The sort of mystagogical catechism that we find in Cyril of Jerusalem is far removed from the interests of John Chrysostom. For John the sacraments are not Christian mysteries to be understood as the mysteries of Mithras or Eleusius were. Admittedly he uses the word "mysteries" in regard to the sacraments, but he has a much more biblical understanding of the word.[82] In the biblical sense the sacraments are covenant signs. They are like the biblical sign of circumcision, like the Passover feast and the covenantal meals of the Old Testament. John is always talking about baptism as a covenant.

At the center of baptism is the profession of faith. Our preacher quotes Romans 10:10, "For man believes with his heart and so is justified, and he confesses with his lips and so is saved," and says that is what happens in baptism.[83] As John understands it, the essence of the sacrament is making the covenant vows. One confesses one's faith and in so doing makes a contract or covenant with God.[84] To make his point very clear John tells his converts that the words they utter here below are recorded in heaven and the commitments they make in this sacrament are indelibly recorded with the Master.[85] He is constantly comparing baptism to a wedding and the baptismal vows to the wedding contract.[86] This is not at all the way Cyril understands the sacraments. Cyril's understanding demands mystagogical catechesis, but John's does not.

John's moral exhortations are based on baptism. Sermon 4, the first of the five sermons preached to the newly baptized during Easter week, is on the text "If any one is in Christ, he is a new creation; the old has passed away, behold, the new has come" (II Cor. 5:17). In baptism we have put on Christ, our preacher tells us, and therefore we must live a new life.[87] The apostle Paul in a number of places used the metaphor of taking off the soiled clothing of sin and being clothed in the righteousness of

---

82. Chrysostom, *Catechetical Sermons* 1.11-13.

83. Chrysostom, *Catechetical Sermons* 1.19.

84. Chrysostom, *Catechetical Sermons* 2.17.

85. Chrysostom, *Catechetical Sermons* 2.17. A very similar passage is found in 3.12. That John Chrysostom has the biblical concept of covenant in mind is clear from his commentary on Colossians 2:14, where he tells us that in our baptismal vows we make far more than a contract; we make a covenant.

86. Chrysostom, *Catechetical Sermons* 1.1-3 and 16-17.

87. Chrysostom, *Catechetical Sermons* 4.12-16.

Christ,[88] and our preacher develops this at length, exhorting the newly baptized to keep their white baptismal robes spotless.[89] He uses yet another Pauline metaphor: Christians, having become a new creation, are to bear the fruit of the Spirit (Gal. 5:22). Through baptism the Christian becomes a new creation and through Communion the faithful are nourished by spiritual food and spiritual drink; therefore, the Christian bears the fruit of the Spirit.[90] This sermon is not mystagogy but rather a covenantal understanding of the sacraments. The sacraments seal the promises of the covenant and obligate us to live by the covenant.

The theme of the sermons which follow is the new life that the baptized Christian is obligated to live. In Sermon 5 we have an instruction on the simplicity of the Christian life. The Christian should avoid luxury and should strive for temperance and moderation in all things. In Sermon 6, preached on the text "So, whether you eat or drink, or whatever you do, do all to the glory of God" (I Cor. 10:31), we have an instruction on the purpose of the Christian life. It is God who is glorified by the good conduct of his people, according to John.

The seventh sermon is based on the text "Seek the things that are above" (Col. 3:1). The sermon makes a great point of showing how the martyrs are a good example to us of those who courageously sought the kingdom of God and his righteousness above all the transient rewards of this life. The newly baptized should seek heavenly blessings, and to this end our preacher provides them with an instruction on the disciplines of prayer.

Sermon 8 is an instruction on the doctrine of providence. The Christian should follow the example of Abraham and seek spiritual blessing from God's hand through prayer. More is said about the disciplines of daily morning and evening prayer. If we seek first the spiritual blessings, we can count on God to supply our material needs, " 'for . . . your heavenly Father knows that you need them' " (Matt. 6:32). The Christian can be confident that God will be faithful to his promises.

These five sermons are a good introduction to the living of the Christian life which begins with baptism. It is because of the covenant

88. E.g., Galatians 3:27; Ephesians 4:22-24; Colossians 3:9-10. The Scripture lesson for that sermon had probably been II Corinthians 5:1-21. In that case the metaphor was already to be found in the lesson for the day.

89. Chrysostom, *Catechetical Sermons* 4.22-26.

90. Chrysostom, *Catechetical Sermons* 4.27.

promises made in baptism that we can live this new life. Our preacher exhorts the newly baptized, "The promises which you have exchanged with the Master, written not with ink on paper, but by faith and the profession of that faith, hold firm and uncompromised."[91] It is because of the covenant that we are obligated to live the Christian life, and because of the covenant we are free to live it. Here is the rationale for John's strong emphasis on moral catechism.

The significance of this has a much broader application that extends to the whole preaching ministry of John Chrysostom. John is recognized as a great preacher of the Christian life, and when we look for the connection of his preaching to worship in general, this must be recognized as one of the fundamental connections. His preaching is based on the baptismal covenant. As we have pointed out several times, catechetical preaching is essential to the celebration of baptism. Remembering the mighty acts of God which established the covenant as well as recounting the terms of the covenant were essential components of biblical worship from the beginning.[92]

John Chrysostom's moral exhortations take their logic from the sixth chapter of Paul's Epistle to the Romans, "Do you not know that all of us who have been baptized into Christ Jesus were baptized into his death, so that as Christ was raised from the dead by the glory of the Father, we too might walk in the newness of life" (Rom. 6:3-4).[93] Just as the epistles of Paul fall into two parts — an exposition of our salvation in Christ and an exhortation to live the Christian life — so do the sermons of John Chrysostom. First there is an exposition of Scripture and then an exhortation to the practical living out of the Christian faith.[94] The point is that the Christian life is the fruit of our salvation.

Christian morality flows from baptism, because in baptism we are united to Christ. This union is a covenantal union; it is a communion which sanctifies us and washes us from our sin. The Christian life is the

91. "Τὰς συνθήκας τοίνυν ἃς πρὸς τὸν δεσπότην ἔθεσθε, οὐ μέλανι οὐδὲ χάρτῃ ταύτας ἐγγράψαντες ἀλλὰ τῇ πίστει καὶ τῇ ὁμολογίᾳ, βεβαίους καὶ ἀκινήτους φυλάξαντες." Chrysostom, Catechetical Sermons 4.31.

92. We discussed this at several points in the first volume of this work, especially in regard to the worship of Israel at Mount Sinai recorded in Exodus 24.

93. Cf. John Chrysostom's two sermons on this passage, Sermon 10 and 11 on the Epistle to the Romans.

94. John Chrysostom specifically makes this point in the introduction of Sermon 11 on Romans.

realization of the sign of baptism. Baptism is a sign and a promise of our cleansing from sin, and in the pouring out of the Spirit upon us and in our living the new life in Christ the faithfulness of God to his promises is manifested. When this is done God is glorified.

No doubt the uniqueness of John's catechetical preaching has some foundation in the conservatism of the church of Antioch, as we have already suggested, but surely it is also due to our preacher's saturation with the theology of the apostle Paul. As we shall see even more clearly in Theodore of Mopsuestia, the biblical studies of the School of Antioch brought an increasing insight on the subject of worship.

D. Sermons on Colossians and Chrysostom's Social Hermeneutic

John Chrysostom's twelve sermons on Colossians were preached during the most heated days of his ministry in Constantinople.[95] Unlike his sermons on Romans, which were preached in Antioch where he had nothing of the ecclesiastical responsibilities or the political involvement he had as patriarch of Constantinople, the sermons on Colossians clearly show the strains and tensions of his tremendous responsibilities as leader of the imperial Church.[96] The sermons on Romans are commonly regarded as the best exposition of Romans to have come out of the patristic period. In them we find both solid biblical interpretation and magnificent oratory. The sermons on Colossians, while they often contain brilliant

95. For the Greek text of the sermons on Colossians, see Migne, *Patrologia Graeca* (Paris: Migne, 1857-66), 62:299-392, as well as St. John Chysostom, *Omelie sulla lettera di S. Paolo ai Colossei,* Italian translation by C. Piazzino (Turin, 1940). For an English translation, see J. Ashworth in the Nicene and Post-Nicene Fathers, 1st ser., vol. 13, pp. 257-321; hereinafter Chrysostom, *Homilies on Colossians.* This edition is edited by the eminent Southern Baptist homiletician of the last century, J. A. Broadus. Of special interest is his essay introducing this volume, "St. Chrysostom as a Homilist." References, contrary to our usual procedure, are to the number of the sermon and then to the page in volume 13 of the Nicene and Post-Nicene Fathers. Unlike most patristic works, these sermons are not divided into numbered sections.

96. For introductory material on the sermons on Colossians, cf. Quasten, *Patrology,* 3:448ff.; and Piazzino, trans., in *Omelie sulla lettera di S. Paolo ai Colossei.* See the chapter of Baur, "Chrysostom as Preacher in Constantinople," in *John Chrysostom and His Time,* 2:82-95; and Max von Bonsdorf, *Zur Predigtätigkeit des Johannes Chrysostomus. Biographisch-Chronologische Studien über seine Homilienserien zu neutestamentlichen Büchern* (Helsinki: Mercators tryckeri aktiebolog, 1922).

oratory, and while they often show clear insight into the meaning of the text, are not remarkable because of either. They are of interest to us because of the way the preacher applied the text to a variety of problems of Church and society. His social hermeneutic is fascinating and his courage in laying it out, inspiring. These sermons show John Chrysostom as a Christian orator who is both expositor and prophet; in fact, they show us so very clearly how prophetic expository preaching can be.

The first sermon begins with a few introductory remarks about the Prison Epistles, which, according to John, are of particular value because of the way they teach us to rejoice even in the midst of tribulations.[97] Perhaps it was because of this basic theme that our preacher chose to preach through Colossians at this time when both he and the church of Constantinople were experiencing so many trials. To be sure, one of the gifts of the great expository preacher is discerning what portions of Scripture are appropriate for a given congregation at a given time. Yet despite this time of trial for John and for orthodox Christianity in Constantinople, in these twelve sermons John constantly returns to the themes of praise and thanksgiving always appropriate to worship.

Also by way of introduction our preacher tells us that the immediate occasion of the apostle Paul's letter is that the Colossians had been troubled by certain people who taught doctrines of angelic intermediaries.[98] Along with this these teachers wanted to introduce a number of observances that were popular in both Jewish and Greek circles at the time which Christians up to that time had not accepted. As the series progresses, our preacher will use this theme of Paul's to attack a number of pagan practices common in fourth-century Constantinople.

The main theme of this first sermon, however, is the spiritual nature of Christian fellowship. After his introduction our preacher goes over the first eight verses of Colossians verse by verse, explaining the text. Paul commends the Colossians for "the love you have for all the saints"[99] and tells them that the faith they have is the very essence of Christian faith because it is "love in the Spirit." Epaphras had indeed preached to them faithfully.[100] They heard and received the true faith and, even more, they experienced in true Christian fellowship the fruit of that faith. The re-

---

97. Chrysostom, *Homilies on Colossians* 1, p. 257.
98. Chrysostom, *Homilies on Colossians* 1, p. 258.
99. Chrysostom, *Homilies on Colossians* 1, p. 258.
100. Chrysostom, *Homilies on Colossians* 1, p. 259.

mainder of the sermon draws the distinction between the friendships and convivialities of this world and true Christian fellowship. Here we find our preacher's rhetorical training being used to good advantage. We are asked to imagine two banquets.[101] The one is the sumptuous banquet so cultivated in the Hellenistic world whose keynote was luxury. As the banquet is described, one is fascinated by the rich vocabulary of the word picture: One can see the luxury as John describes the fine clothes of the guests and the ornate setting of the table. The dinner our preacher describes was no doubt typical of many which took place in Constantinople, but it could just as easily have taken place in Washington, D.C. Luxurious entertainments seem to be part of the political process, be it at the imperial courts of antiquity or in the democracies of our own day. The members of John's congregation knew only too well the follies of those who peddled political influences. Contrasted to this is a Christian agape to which the poor, the blind, and the barefooted have been invited. With the rich banquet there is not nearly as much pleasure as one imagines. One always has the social embarrassments, the unbearable vanity of social climbers, the burden of the heavy expense, the indigestion, and the hangover. Yet the joys of the simple fellowship meal of the Christian are far more lasting. One is satisfied with food but one does not suffer the discomfort of overindulgence, and, besides, one experiences the satisfaction of knowing one has helped those who are in need, and served God in the process. At the Christian fellowship meal there is also a feast of praise, the singing of hymns, and prayers of thanksgiving. The sermon is remarkable because it gives us a vision of what true Christian fellowship can be. While it shows the vanity of pagan revelry, it speaks of higher joys and higher bonds of fellowship which can unite a truly Christian fellowship.

The second sermon takes up Colossians 1:9-14.[102] In this passage the apostle makes two points very clear. First, the Colossians have indeed received the true Christian faith. The teachers who were troubling them had told them that what Paul and Epaphras had taught was only the introduction to much deeper teachings. Paul is therefore quite clear that what they have both believed and experienced is the essence of the Christian faith. The second point is that, while they have received the true faith, they do need, nevertheless, to grow in it. The apostle has not ceased to pray for the Colossians, ever since he heard that they had received the

---

101. Chrysostom, *Homilies on Colossians* 1, pp. 260ff.
102. Chrysostom, *Homilies on Colossians* 2, pp. 264ff.

gospel, that the faith which had been planted might mature. John goes through the text from verse to verse, as is his usual custom, bringing out Paul's basic points. He notices that the apostle speaks to the Colossians about being "filled with the knowledge of his will in all spiritual wisdom and understanding" (Col. 1:9). They have already received an appropriate portion; now they need to be filled to a greater degree of fullness with the same truth. Our preacher notices how often Paul uses the word "all." Paul prays "that you may be filled with the knowledge of his will in *all* spiritual wisdom . . . be strengthened with *all* power, . . . for *all* endurance and patience."[103] At the center of John's sermons is always this word-by-word analysis of the text, by means of which he makes as clear as possible what the text actually says.

This sermon begins to get interesting when our preacher underlines the apostle's doctrine of grace. John comments on the text "who has qualified us to share in the inheritance of the saints in light. He has delivered us from the dominion of darkness and transferred us to the kingdom of his beloved Son" (Col. 1:12-13). Our preacher tells us that God has given us citizenship in the kingdom, which, indeed, is a most gracious gift, but also he makes us worthy to receive such an honor, and this is an even more gracious gift. The preacher gives an example of a king who because of his authority gives to one of his favorite courtiers a governorship which he is quite unqualified to exercise competently. Unfortunately the king does not have the ability to make the favorite courtier capable of exercising the office, and in the end both the king and the unworthy courtier are made to look ridiculous.

The apostle Paul teaches us that God has not only given us the honor of the kingdom but has qualified us to exercise the responsibilities which go with the dignity.[104] This God does to show us that none of us inherits the kingdom by his own achievements. John goes on to speak of how God has delivered us from darkness and has transferred us to the kingdom of his Son. He makes the point that it is not a matter of picking us up bodily and then dropping us in the kingdom but of transforming us so that we actually belong in the kingdom.

We should not imagine, our preacher goes on, that this is a work of the Father alone. The whole thing is also the work of the Son, for we read, "He has delivered us from the dominion of darkness and transferred us

103. Chrysostom, *Homilies on Colossians* 2, p. 264.
104. Chrysostom, *Homilies on Colossians* 2, p. 266.

to the kingdom of his beloved Son, in whom we have redemption, the forgiveness of sins" (Col. 1:13-14). Our redemption consists in being brought into the kingdom of the Son through the work of the Son. Christ is the cause of our redemption, and it is through his redemptive work that our sins are forgiven. This whole redemptive act is attributed to the Son, just as it is attributed to the Father. Nothing is attributed to the mediation of angels. God's grace comes to us through Christ. Furthermore, we find most interesting that John Chrysostom's doctrine of God's grace demands our human works. In this he is a faithful interpreter of the apostle Paul. We do not receive the grace of God because our works have qualified us to receive it, but rather, the qualification is a work of grace just as well as the deliverance. Having received both the deliverance and the qualification by grace, we now owe the works. "Seeing we have come to enjoy so great a benefit, we ought to be ever mindful of it, and continually to turn in our minds to the free gift of God, and to reflect upon what we have been delivered from, what we have obtained; and so we shall be thankful; so we shall heighten our love toward Him."[105]

At this point John begins to exhort his congregation "to lead a life worthy of the Lord" (Col. 1:10). He rebukes Christians who are confident of God's grace and lazy about living the Christian life, comparing them, in a magnificent simile, to nestling swallows who remain too long in the nest and refuse to try their wings. They want to remain in the nest forever, but the longer they do the weaker they become, and when the winter rains come the nest is washed away and the nestlings perish.[106] The preacher then begins to speak of the Last Judgment. One can be sure that it will come just as the winter rains. The devil would have us ridicule the idea just as some taunted Noah when he was building the ark. But the rains came. Therefore, having received the grace of God, we ought to live a life worthy of this grace.[107]

The third sermon takes up Colossians 1:15-20, one of Paul's most eloquent passages on the divinity of Christ. The sermon begins almost without introduction, although the preacher does say that the day before he had begun to say something about this passage but wanted to concentrate on it as a whole because it refutes so many heresies; it deserves special attention. From this remark we gather that this series of twelve sermons

105. Chrysostom, *Homilies on Colossians* 2, p. 267.
106. Chrysostom, *Homilies on Colossians* 2, p. 267.
107. Chrysostom, *Homilies on Colossians* 2, pp. 269ff.

was preached continually, day after day, rather than only on Sundays, but any greater precision on how the series was set down on the calendar would exceed the evidence. One also notices that this series forgoes the long and elaborate introductions we so often found in the sermons on Genesis. In classical oratory the *exordium* was highly developed, and so for John Chrysostom to leave it aside is a step away from his training in rhetoric. As he grows older he is evidently less and less worried about this ability to grab the ears of his listeners.

So it is that the sermon begins almost abruptly with the text "He is the image of the invisible God" (Col. 1:15). With the aid of several rhetorical questions John makes the full weight of the text very clear. Christ is the image of God because he really is God. He is the image of God because he is the Son of God. About no angel can this be said. Angels are indeed invisible, but no angel can be called God, nor can any angel be called the Son of God. The visible Christ can be the image of the invisible God because he really is God, but Christ is truly man as well and therefore a created being. Even though Christ as man is a creature, because he is God he is the exact likeness of the Father.[108]

Our preacher moves on to the next phrase of the text, "the first-born of all creation" (Col. 1:15). He is not first created, but firstborn. This makes it clear that Christ is a brother to all of us. John alludes to Hebrews 2:17, "Therefore he had to be made like his brethren in every respect." Christ shares with us our essence. As Paul says elsewhere (Rom. 8:29), he is the firstborn from the dead, that is, he is the firstfruits of the resurrection. It is from him that we draw our existence as Christians. From the fact that Christ is the image of God we know that Christ is true God, and from the fact that Christ is the firstborn we know that he is true man.

John moves on to the next verse, "For in him all things were created, in heaven and on earth, visible and invisible, whether thrones or dominions or principalities or authorities — all things were created through him and for him" (Col. 1:16). What then of these angels, these thrones, dominions, principalities, and authorities which some would make so important? Is not Christ infinitely more important than they? What are the disciples of Paul of Samosata to say to this? Christ is the foundation of the very existence of these angelic powers. All these angelic beings were created through Christ and unto Christ. "He is before all things, and in him all things hold together" (Col. 1:17). If the subsistence of all these is in Christ,

108. Chrysostom, *Homilies on Colossians* 3, p. 270.

then if any of them should fall outside his providence they would cease to exist.

Taking up the verse "For in him all the fulness of God was pleased to dwell, and through him to reconcile to himself all things, . . . making peace by the blood of his cross" (Col. 1:19-20), John Chrysostom comments that Christ sanctified us and in his death on the cross offered us up with himself as a sacrifice. The word "fulness" makes it clear that the Son is not some sort of energy emanating from God but the substance of God himself. The words "he reconciles us to himself" make it clear that he exercises this office not as some sort of functionary or minister but as true God. The reconciliation he accomplished was through the blood of his own cross, through his own act of suffering. It was not through his speaking some sort of words but by his becoming a sacrifice for us. So it was that Christ accomplished everything for our redemption. It is Christ, therefore, that we should look to for our salvation, not some sort of angels or Neoplatonic emanations. This reconciliation has brought about peace. Jesus greeted his disciples, "'Peace I leave with you; my peace I give to you'" (John 14:27), and this peace prepares the way for love.[109]

From this point our preacher, who is by this time the archbishop of Constantinople, begins to speak of the office of the true minister of the Church. How often the one who presides at worship greets the assembly with the words "Peace be to you." Now, the bishop is a minister; unlike Christ he is a mere functionary. Nevertheless, his function is to keep peace in the Church, not to disrupt peace. "Many there are who rejoice at evil, who do rather rend in pieces the Body of Christ, than did the soldiers pierce it with the spear, or the Jews who struck it through with nails."[110] No doubt everyone listening to the sermon understood quite well at whom this bristling invective was aimed. Several bishops and archbishops were determined to do away with John Chrysostom once he became patriarch of Constantinople; Theophilus of Alexandria was only the most prominent of John's episcopal detractors. But we, almost fifteen hundred years after the fact, cannot be absolutely sure at whom it was directed, nor are we terribly interested, except to point out that John's classical rhetoric did not fail him when he was in the midst of the political intrigues of the Byzantine court. Classical oratory had cultivated invective to the point of making it an art, and here we see John using it. Some are always uncomfortable with

109. Chrysostom, *Homilies on Colossians* 3, p. 273.
110. Chrysostom, *Homilies on Colossians* 3, p. 273.

the use of invective in sermons, no matter against whom the invective might be hurled. We are not concerned here with deciding whether in this case John was justified in using it — that is hard to figure out almost fifteen hundred years later. What we do want to make clear is that the expository preaching of the patron saint of preachers was just as prophetic as preaching by Amos, Micah, and Jeremiah. John Chrysostom's invective was no less sharp or less timely than Isaiah's oracles against the house of Ahaz.

The fourth sermon treats Colossians 1:21-25. It takes up the question of why God waited so long to send Christ and to reveal the fullness of the gospel. Why is it that Paul could say, "I became a minister according to the divine office which was given to me for you, to make the word of God fully known" (Col. 1:25)? Why did God not make his Word fully known through Moses? John's answer to this question is that God does not do things all of a sudden. Out of God's love and his consideration for our human nature he works with us slowly and takes us one step at a time. This is the divine condescension of which John speaks so often.[111] We see in the ministry of Moses something of the divine pedagogic. As a wise teacher God began to train his people with the most rudimentary principles and patiently waited until they were ready for the next level of instruction to reveal the more profound truths. "In this way the wilderness was a school."[112] Here we see a very different way of looking at the Old Testament from the way Philo and the Alexandrian School had looked at it. For Philo it was important to defend the complete illumination of Moses; Moses had the full revelation even if it did come in allegories. Unlike Philo, John was not concerned with showing that the wisdom of Moses was greater than that of the Greek philosophers. He was perfectly willing to regard the revelation given to Moses as prefatory, as elementary instruction. What God taught his people through Moses was like the grammar and rhetoric which we teach children at school; in younger years we make no attempt to teach them profound doctrines. God did the same thing with the Jews, placing Moses over them as a schoolmaster.[113] He is even willing to call Moses a "nursing-father."[114] For John the fullness of

---

111. Perhaps as Robert Hill suggests, we should use the word "considerateness" rather than "condescension." See above in the section on Chrysostom's sermons on Genesis.

112. Chrysostom, *Homilies on Colossians* 4, p. 278.

113. Chrysostom, *Homilies on Colossians* 4, p. 277.

114. Chrysostom, *Homilies on Colossians* 4, p. 279.

wisdom is in Christ, and therefore neither he nor the Antiochene School were under the same pressure to justify everything they found recorded in the Old Testament. It is strange that Origen and the Christian interpreters of the Old Testament who followed him failed to recognize that as Christians they did not have the same problem that Philo had. In John's idea of the divine condescension we find a way of understanding that when God reveals himself he accommodates that revelation to our human capacities. One is not stuck with a doctrine of revelation which is filled with tricks like the oracles of Delphi. If God wants to reveal himself, then surely he wants to be clear and straightforward in his revelation. If God wants to be clear, then why should he speak in unfathomable allegories? God's graciousness is genuine, and therefore he speaks so we can understand.

The fifth sermon goes even further into the theology of revelation. Our preacher begins by going over the text of Colossians 1:26–2:5 in his accustomed manner. Here he notes with particular care what the text has to say about the revelation of the mystery. He has already spoken of the οἰκονομία of the divine revelation, the παιδαγωγία which God exercised toward Israel, and the συγκατάβασις or divine condescension in revelation. Now he applies these principles to Christian typology; note that John is not speaking about allegory. What interests us is the way he builds his understanding of typology into his doctrine of revelation. After speaking of the translation of Enoch and the taking up of Elijah as types of the resurrection of Christ, he says, "Behold how God schooleth us by little and little."[115] He speaks of how even in the Old Testament there is a progression of types, like a ladder that one must ascend one step at a time, moving from the more elementary to the more profound. John illustrates this by the types of Christ's virgin birth.[116] First there is the type of Eve being formed from Adam, then the frequent occurrence of barren women giving birth, and finally the type of the virgin birth of Christians by the work of the Holy Spirit. Here it is very clear that John does not have in mind allegories but types. These types suggest patterns by which God brings things about. When Sarah gives birth to Isaac, we do not have an allegory of the virgin birth but a type. We see the pattern of how faith in the promises of God brings about what is impossible by human power. This is a principle of spiritual birth. The children of God are born, "not of blood nor of the will of the flesh nor of the will of man, but of God"

115. Chrysostom, *Homilies on Colossians* 5, p. 283.
116. Chrysostom, *Homilies on Colossians* 5, p. 282.

(John 1:13). This principle is seen in the story of the creation of Eve, in children born to barren women, in the spiritual birth of Christians, and in the virgin birth of Christ. This is quite different from allegory. With allegory the inspired text is thought to contain truths which the enlightened can decode from the text. With typology, as opposed to allegory, the principles of God's redemptive work can be discerned from the literal sense of the text. Antiochene exegesis rejected allegory, but it did not reject typology because it recognized that something very different is at work in typology. The Antiochene School was well aware that the New Testament itself used typology and therefore had no problem using it when it clearly was already in the text.

The sixth sermon explains at length Paul's teaching on baptism as it is found particularly in Colossians 2:11 and 12. It is the moral imperative of the sacrament which catches John's attention. In a strong covenantal understanding of the sacrament he admonishes his congregation to mortify the sin which they still find within them. In baptism, as Chrysostom understands it, we are united to Christ in a covenant.[117] Before our baptism we were bound to Satan by our sin, but in baptism that bond was broken and we confess our faith in Christ, and instead of being bound to Satan and his pomp we enter into a covenant with Christ.[118] The new covenant is very different from the old bond; it is God's promise of eternal life.[119] Seeing that God's promise is so gracious, let us flee from the pomp of this world, from the devil, from all his services and all his angels and principalities.

The seventh sermon treats Colossians 2:16–3:4, where Paul attacks quite specifically the teaching of those who were troubling the Colossians:

> Therefore let no one pass judgment on you in questions of food and drink or with regard to a festival or a new moon or a sabbath. These are only a shadow of what is to come; but the substance belongs to Christ. Let no one disqualify you, insisting on self-abasement and worship of angels. . . . Why do you submit to regulations, "Do not handle, Do not taste, Do not touch" (referring to things which all perish as they are used), according to human precepts and doctrines? These have indeed an appearance of wisdom in promoting rigor of devotion and

---

117. Chrysostom, *Homilies on Colossians* 6, p. 287.
118. Chrysostom, *Homilies on Colossians* 6, p. 287.
119. Chrysostom, *Homilies on Colossians* 6, p. 287.

self-abasement and severity to the body, but they are of no value in checking the indulgence of the flesh. (Col. 2:16-23)

It would seem from the text that the apostle is attacking the rigorous asceticism of the false teachers in Colossae, but John Chrysostom evidently does not see this aspect of the problem or, at least, its importance. What speaks to us from a passage like this and what spoke to a preacher at the end of the fourth century can be quite different. At the end of the fourth century the Christian Church was developing its own kind of asceticism — an understandable reaction against the worldliness of the time. Then when the Church was supported by the imperial court the worldliness of the court was making inroads in the Church itself and the asceticism of those like Chrysostom was a defense against these inroads of pagan worldliness. But, then again, it has often been noticed that John has a way of backing away from asceticism even in its Christian forms.[120] For him it is a matter of being concerned with higher things. The ascetics against whom Paul argued made too much of material things in a negative sort of way. What they didn't eat and didn't touch was too important to them. In many ways John was very moderate in the matter of asceticism, but it is interesting that here he seems not to have caught Paul's polemic against asceticism.

What interests our preacher are the first four verses of the following chapter:

If then you have been raised with Christ, seek the things that are above, where Christ is, seated at the right hand of God. Set your minds on things that are above, not on things that are on earth. For you have died, and your life is hid with Christ in God. (Col. 3:1-3)

Here, incidentally, is a prime example of the way one's choice of where the lesson begins and where it ends has everything to do with how one interprets a passage of Scripture. Not noticing the apostle's polemic against asceticism, Chrysostom finds in this passage grounds for attacking the luxury of the imperial court. To be sure, the grounds of his attack are to be found in this passage, "Set your minds on things that are above, not

---

120. The subject of John Chrysostom's asceticism we will have to leave to others. The following might be helpful: A. Moulard, *Saint Jean Chrysostome, le défenseur du mariage et l'apôtre de la virginité* (Paris, 1923); J. Stiglmyr, "Zur Askese des hl. Chrysostomus," *Zeitschrift für Aszese und Mystik* (Würzburg, 1926-47), 4:29-49.

on things that are on earth" (Col. 3:2), and our preacher begins to speak of worldly honors and power and admonishes his hearers not to set their minds on these things for they soon perish. These are the pomps of the devil about which he had spoken in the previous sermon. He uses an example of the honors which a certain official of the imperial court so recently enjoyed. No doubt everyone in the congregation was aware that their preacher was speaking of Eutropius, even though he is not mentioned by name.[121] The description of the extravagant honors Eutropius claimed for himself is another brilliant word picture which shows the preacher's command of classical rhetoric:

> He who was yesterday up high on his tribunal, who had his heralds shouting with thrilling voice, and many to run before, and haughtily to clear the way for him through the forum, is to-day mean and low, and is of all those things bereft and bare, like dust blast-driven, like a stream that hath past by. And like as dust is raised by our feet, so truly are magistracies also produced by those who are engaged about money, and in the whole of life have the rank and condition of feet; and like as dust when it is raised occupies a large portion of the air, though itself be but a small body, so too doth power; and like as the dust blindeth the eyes, so too doth the pride of power bedim the eyes of understanding.[122]

Having exposed the vanity of power with such spellbinding oratory, our preacher goes on to speak of the vanity of luxury. "I will endeavor to prove clearly that opulence is a condition full of dishonor; it embases the soul."[123] He recounts a number of stories to show the senseless things that the wealthy do. He ridicules the lust for gold and silver that results in the extreme act of having one's chamber pot made of silver[124] and fulminates against the luxuries of the women of the court and their costly robes and cosmetics. How can a Christian pour such sums of money into these bizarre luxuries when the poor are hungry? The king of Persia, it is said, has his beard interwoven with golden thread. Our preacher goes on,

---

121. This passage, apparently referring to the fall of Eutropius, has been used by scholars to date this series of sermons quite exactly. It must have been preached in the summer of 399. Nothing is said of his violent death, which would seem to indicate that the events described happened very shortly before the sermon was preached. For a discussion of the incident, see Baur, *John Chrysostom and His Time*, 2:44-45.

122. Chrysostom, *Homilies on Colossians* 7, p. 290.

123. Chrysostom, *Homilies on Colossians* 7, p. 291.

124. Chrysostom, *Homilies on Colossians* 7, p. 292.

becoming more and more vitriolic in his exposé of luxury. As he describes these things his own blood begins to boil, and finally he threatens excommunication to those who continue in these senseless extravagances.

The sermon might well be found intemperate. Evidently the congregation found it so, for we read in the sermon on the following day that the preacher was aware of the offense of many in his congregation. One wonders how many courtiers of Constantinople had chamber pots of silver. Could it be that there was a story afoot that this was one of the luxuries of the imperial family? We cannot say for sure, but our preacher's invective was quite evidently more than explosive. When we read a sermon like this, John Chrysostom begins to step out of the stylized mosaics of hagiography and takes on the appearance of a modern social prophet. Surely when the patriarch of Constantinople preached against the luxurious ladies of the Byzantine court, we can even today hear an echo of Amos, "'Hear this, you cows of Bashan'" (Amos 4:1).

But the prophetic anointing of John Chrysostom was not spent in a single sermon. He was convinced that a Christian imperial court must be very different from a pagan court. The eighth sermon takes up Colossians 3:5-15, and one can imagine how the preacher felt as he began to go over the text for the next day. No doubt he was feeling a bit embarrassed about the way his anger had burst out in the morning's sermon, not unlike the father who is afraid he has whipped his child too hard. Not that the child did not have the whipping coming, not that severity was uncalled for, but rather, one's own anger is what one regrets. When he began to go over the text of the next morning's sermon, it became very clear to him that he must preach the same message again. There were the words before him:

> Put to death therefore what is earthly in you: fornication, impurity, passion, evil desire, and covetousness, which is idolatry. On account of these the wrath of God is coming. In these you once walked, when you lived in them. But now put them all away: anger, wrath, malice, slander, and foul talk from your mouth. Do not lie to one another, seeing that you have put off the old nature with its practices and have put on the new nature, which is being renewed in knowledge after the image of its creator. (Col. 3:5-10)

Again he would have to preach against the sins of the Byzantine court. That is the way it is with preaching the *lectio continua*. It has a way of getting the preacher engaged. The Word grabs the preacher and masters him so that he becomes its servant — which is how it should be if preachers are to be ministers of the Word. Everyone knew what he had to preach the next morning. For John Chrysostom it was a matter of providence. He begins his next sermon:

> I know that many are offended by the foregoing discourse, but what shall I do? Ye heard what the master enjoined. Am I to blame? What shall I do? . . . Heard ye what Paul proclaimed to day? "Mortify," he saith, "your members which are upon the earth; fornication, uncleanness, passion, evil desire, and covetousness which is idolatry." . . . Do not, I pray, take what I said amiss. . . . I was wishful ye should attain to such virtue. . . . So I said it not for authority's sake, not for imperiousness, but out of pain and of sorrow. Forgive me, forgive! I have no wish to violate decency by discoursing upon such subjects, but I am compelled to it.[125]

And so he proceeds to go over the text, making his usual exegetical comments. What suspense there must have been in the church as the congregation waited to see what lines would ignite the prophetic volley they knew was coming. Yes, the congregation knew it was coming just as the preacher knew it had to come. It was only that this time it could not come in anger; it could only come in love — critical, sorrowful, prophetic love. It was not that the Christian courtiers did not know the sins of the court, nor that all those bureaucrats, secretaries, and undersecretaries did not know about wickedness in high places. They knew all about it, and they detested it, too, but they needed to have a man of true holiness bring it to word, and bring it out in the right words. They needed to know there was an alternative. They needed someone with spiritual authority to tell them that God had something else in mind. It takes courage to be a prophet — everyone understands that. What everyone does not understand is that it takes holiness even more. Any knave can denounce. It takes holiness to see the vision of God's future, and that John Chrysostom had.

Beginning with the text "Put to death therefore what is earthly in you," our preacher recalls what he said two sermons earlier on baptism as mortification. He assures his congregation that even though they have been baptized and in their baptism have died to sin, they must continue

---

125. Chrysostom, *Homilies on Colossians* 8, pp. 293ff.

to die to sin. Then passing on to verse 8, "But now put them all away: anger, wrath, malice, slander, and foul talk from your mouth," he makes it clear that anger does not set things in order. It is rather the peace of God which sets things in order.[126] The text is very clear, "Let the peace of Christ rule in your hearts" (Col. 3:15). Even angry preachers must submit to the peace of Christ. He takes up other sins of passion: fornication, evil desires, covetousness. One could have expected the preacher to rip forth on any of these, but he does not. He says more on the subject of the peace of Christ than on any of the vices mentioned in the text.

It is on the subject of being thankful in the midst of adversity that John Chrysostom builds his admonition. "Let the peace of Christ rule in your hearts, to which indeed you were called in the one body. And be thankful" (Col. 3:15). At the beginning of his series our preacher had said this was the great lesson of the Prison Epistles, and now he brings this underlying theme to a more full expression. "Nothing is holier than the tongue, which in evil gives thanks to God; truly in no respect doth it fall short of that of martyrs: both are alike crowned, both this, and they. For over this one stands to force it to deny God, by blasphemy; the devil stands over it, torturing it with executioner thoughts, darkening it with despondencies."[127] To this marvelous bit of rhetoric our preacher adds a hypothetical story of a mother with a sick child who is tempted to employ pagan amulets and magical charms to induce health but resists the temptation to idolatry. The arts of medicine are of no avail and her friends encourage her to send for those who can drive away evil spirits by various incantations, but the mother is steadfast. The story of this mother who would rather have her child die than be subjected to pagan magic is told at great length and introduces, from Chrysostom, a whole string of biblical examples of parents who gave thanks to God even when their children suffered the worst adversities. Finally this very long and very moving sermon comes to an end with the assurance that God does support us in our adversity.

Here we see the pastoral genius of John Chrysostom. He knew his congregation. They loved great oratory as much as they loved the hippodrome and the theater, and they had come to church that day eager to hear another eloquent diatribe. What they heard instead was a hymn of praise to the faithfulness of God to those who hold to his righteousness. Again and again in his sermon the preacher touched the sensitive chords

---

126. Chrysostom, *Homilies on Colossians* 8, p. 296.
127. Chrysostom, *Homilies on Colossians* 8, p. 298.

of the sins of the people as well as his own, but he saved his eloquence for the faithfulness of God to those who fear him. If the sin of man abounds, the grace of God doth even more abound.

The ninth sermon takes up the text "Let the word of Christ dwell in you richly, teach and admonish one another in all wisdom, and sing psalms and hymns and spiritual songs with thankfulness in your hearts to God" (Col. 3:16). In this sermon John admonishes his congregation to give themselves to the reading of Scripture, to giving alms, and to singing psalms in their homes. He encourages the practice of family prayer that all might be spiritually strengthened and might thereby be prepared to meet adversities.

The tenth sermon takes up the apostle Paul's table of family responsibilities, "Wives, be subject to your husbands. . . . Husbands, love your wives. . . . Children, obey your parents. . . . Masters, treat your slaves justly . . . ," and so forth. Our preacher makes the standard remarks on the text and then passes on to the apostle's request that the Colossians keep him in their prayers that he might again have an opportunity to preach, "that God may open for us a door for the word" (Col. 4:3). This gives our preacher an opportunity to speak of the apostle's ministry of preaching. He speaks of the tremendous things Paul accomplished through preaching and of how even his prisoner's chains did not silence his preaching but were, in fact, a seal on it. When his enemies put him in prison they crowned him with those very chains. Yes, those chains were a crown of precious gems, John tells his congregation. "Come we, beloved, to emulate these bonds. As many of you women as deck yourselves with trinkets of gold, long ye for the bonds of Paul. Not so glitters the collar round your necks, as the grace of these iron bonds gleamed about his soul!"[128] Once again with his flashing sword of words the great preacher begins his duel with the luxury-loving courtiers of Constantinople. "Wouldst thou be convinced that those are ornament? Tell me which would more have won the notice of the spectators? Thou or Paul?"[129] His rhetorical questions come quickly, like the thrusts of a rapier. "And why do I say 'thou'? The queen herself who is all bedecked with gold would not have attracted the spectators so much; but if it had chanced that both Paul in his bonds and the queen had entered the Church at the same time, all would have removed their eyes from her to him; and with good

128. Chrysostom, *Homilies on Colossians* 10, p. 307.
129. Chrysostom, *Homilies on Colossians* 10, p. 307.

reason."[130] One wonders if the empress Eudoxia was present in the church at the time, that queen who was the virtual ruler of the Empire, who in no way was submissive to her husband. Could anyone mistake that the two-edged sword was being wielded against the empress? The prophetic message against the imperial court was clear. "Free both thy self from thy bonds, and the poor man from his hunger. Why rivetest thou fast the chains of thy sins? Some one saith, How? When thou wearest gold while another is perishing, when thou to get thee vain glory takest so much gold, whilst another hast not even what to eat, hast thou not wedged fast thy sins? Put Christ about thee, and not gold."[131] Yes, once again John Chrysostom had prophesied against the luxury of the court, in words that could hardly be mistaken. His oratory was as clear and sharp as it was flashing. Yet it was far more than an audacious critique; it had something in it of the white-hot incandescent light of holiness.

With preaching like this no one is surprised to learn that within a few years the patriarch was exiled to Armenia and there shared the bonds and the martyrdom of the apostle whom he so greatly admired. His martyrdom became a crown for him no less than it had for Paul. And yet he wears today an even greater crown. His sermons are the crown jewels of the Orthodox Church. It was he, as we shall see, who taught the Protestant Reformers to preach, and even Catholics venerate him as the patron saint of preachers. No preacher in the history of the Church is more universally honored.

E. The Liturgy of Saint John Chrysostom

What really was the liturgy of John Chrysostom? Scholars seem to agree that the venerable Byzantine liturgy which today goes by the name of the Liturgy of Saint John Chrysostom is the product of later centuries, as much as it may indeed preserve the liturgical heritage of that most eminent patriarch of Constantinople.[132] Certainly the cherished liturgy of the

---

130. Chrysostom, *Homilies on Colossians* 10, p. 308.

131. Chrysostom, *Homilies on Colossians* 10, p. 308.

132. On the history of the Byzantine liturgy, see the following: Frans van der Paverd, *Zur Geschichte der Messliturgie in Antiocheia und Konstantinopel gegen Ende des vierten Jahrhunderts: Analyse der Quellen bei Johannes Chrysostomos,* Orientalia Christiana Analecta, vol. 187 (Rome, 1970); Hans-Joachim Schulz, *The Byzantine Liturgy: Symbolic Structure and Faith Expression,* trans. Matthew J. O'Connell (New York: Pueblo Publishing Co., 1986), see especially pp. 8-10.

Orthodox Church in many of its features traces its lineage to the worship of the fourth-century Fathers. It seems, nevertheless, unlikely that John Chrysostom shaped or even codified any particular liturgical forms. Yet there is a very real sense in which he is, even today, one of the guiding hands behind Christian worship. Chrysostom has had a continuous influence on how Christians have worshiped all the way down through the history of the Church. This is especially the case in regard to the ministry of the Word.

Let us think for a moment about how John understood the reading and preaching of the Word of God as liturgy, that is, as service to God. The word λειτουργία, "liturgy," for John, as for the Hellenistic world in general, meant a public service, a service done for the good of the community.[133] When specifically applied to a religious service, the word meant something done to honor God. A liturgy was a public act intended to honor God.

We hardly need to say more about John as a prophet. The Sermons on the Statues and the Sermons on Colossians are among the outstanding examples of a prophetic doxology.[134] But there is more. Reading through his sermons, we note two prominent things which suggest how this outstanding preacher understood his ministry of the Word as worship: he understood it first in terms of a wisdom doxology and second in terms of a covenantal doxology.[135] Compared to his friend Theodore of Mopsuestia, what he says on this subject is much more subtle and much more practical. Theodore was the real theologian of the Antiochene School, as we shall see, yet John clearly had a theology of worship which again and again comes into view.

From the standpoint of a wisdom doxology we have noticed, particularly in the sermons on Genesis, the tremendous authority John Chrysostom gives to Holy Scripture. The preached Word of God has authority because it is God's Word. When God speaks, what can we do

---

133. J. M. Hanssens, *Institutiones liturgicae de ritibus Orientalibus* (Rome: Gregorian University, 1930), 2:21-41; A. G. Martimort, *L'Église en prière* (Paris, Tournai, Rome, and New York: Desclée, 1961), pp. 3ff.; and J. H. Miller, "The Nature and Definition of the Liturgy," *Theological Studies* 18 (1957): 325-56.

134. On the subject of a prophetic doxology, see my *Themes and Variations for a Christian Doxology: Some Thoughts on the Theology of Worship* (Grand Rapids: Wm. B. Eerdmans Publishing Co., 1992), pp. 91-100.

135. On the wisdom doxology, see my *Themes and Variations*, pp. 63-89, and on the covenantal doxology, see pp. 111-37.

but listen! The whole logos Christology, so influential in patristic thought, had made the point that God is by his very nature one who speaks. He is a communicating being. "In the beginning was the Word and the Word was with God and the Word was God." The way we relate to God, therefore, is by listening to that Word and believing that Word and living that Word. It is by means of his Word that God reveals himself. If we are to enter into God's presence we must listen to his Word. To understand Jesus, who in this world exercised a ministry of preaching, is to understand him as the Word of God. Jesus related to his disciples as a teacher and appointed his disciples to teach what he had taught. It was in terms of this that Chrysostom understood his own ministry.

One of the striking things about his essay *On the Priesthood* is the way he puts preaching at the center of the ministry.[136] In book 4 he speaks of the pastoral function of the minister being centered in the application of the Word to the problems of the faithful. He takes the apostle Paul as an example of how it is through the preaching of the Word that the work of the ministry is most effectively accomplished. "How do we find him employed at Thessalonica and Corinth, in Ephesus and in Rome itself? Did he not spend whole nights and days in interpreting the Scriptures in their order?"[137] Then Chrysostom goes through the admonitions Paul made to Timothy and Titus to make the point that the public reading, preaching, and teaching of the Scriptures are central to the ministry. He points out that the apostle emphasized that bishops must be apt teachers, skilled in their preaching and teaching.[138] Again we notice that for Chrysostom the reason the reading and preaching of Scripture are given such attention in worship is because it is inspired of God. It has authority because it is God's Word.[139] A bit further on the future patriarch of Constantinople makes the point that it is the learned preaching of the Scriptures which serves God. He speaks of "the expenditure of great labor

---

136. Cf. the edition by A. M. Malingurey: John Chrysostom, *Sur le sacerdoce (dialogue et homélie)*, ed. A. M. Malingurey, Sources chrétiennes, vol. 272 (Paris: Les Éditions du Cerf, 1980). English quotations are taken from the classic translation of W. R. W. Stephens: John Chrysostom, *On the Priesthood*, trans. W. R. W. Stephens, in Nicene and Post-Nicene Fathers, 1st ser. (Grand Rapids: Wm. B. Eerdmans Publishing Co., 1956), 9:25-83.

137. Chrysostom, *On the Priesthood* 4.7.

138. Chrysostom, *On the Priesthood* 4.8.

139. Chrysostom, *On the Priesthood* 4.8.

upon the preparation of discourses to be delivered in public."[140] It is, to be sure, necessary to work hard at mastering the skills of oratory, but it is more important to be able to make clear the Word of God. In fact, those who are skilled at oratory need to give themselves to "laborious study" that their preaching be not a vain display of technical skill but true teaching.[141] We gather from this as well as from the sermons themselves that our preacher spent much time in meditating on the meaning of the Scriptures. John Chrysostom did not do his expository preaching off the top of his head, as some have imagined, but before going into the pulpit he went over the passage of Scripture he was to treat and thought about its meaning for his congregation at that particular time in their lives; he also thought about other passages which taught similar or contrasting ideas. He chose his words and coined his phrases. He envisioned his congregation before him and planned his strategy for opening up their consciences. He may even have paced in his study and practiced his oratorical questions out loud. He would surely have prayed about the deeper meaning of the text. He returned again and again to the text itself. Then he preached on it. What a disgrace when a preacher who has neglected the preparation of the text first comes to meditate on it in the pulpit and "is forced in the midst of his efforts to meditate."[142]

Typical of a wisdom doxology is John's concern that his preaching please God. Preaching is not to entertain the congregation or to win human praise, but rather it is done to honor God. Just as we find in the book of Proverbs, God takes delight in wisdom, which daily rejoices before him (Prov. 8:30). Preaching is, to be sure, doxological! We find this again and again in the sermons of this master. Ministers should conscientiously prepare their sermons so that they may please God. If they win the approval of the congregation, well and good, but if not, they should not be discouraged. "For a sufficient consolation in his labors, and one greater than all, is when he is able to be conscious of arranging and ordering his teaching with a view to pleasing God."[143]

One cannot help but remark that John's famous work *On the Priesthood* is a magnificent commentary on what the apostle Paul meant by the phrase "the priestly service of the gospel" (Rom. 15:16). If we would know

140. Chrysostom, *On the Priesthood* 5.1.
141. Chrysostom, *On the Priesthood* 5.5.
142. Chrysostom, *On the Priesthood* 5.8.
143. Chrysostom, *On the Priesthood* 5.7.

what the liturgy of John Chrysostom really was, one answer at least is close at hand. His liturgy was to preach the Word of God.

When it comes to a covenantal doxology we find this theme developed in a most important way. We noticed in John's catechetical sermons how our preacher gave special attention to the development of what has come to be called "moral catechism." He made the point that when God's people live a simple life free of pretension and luxury, free of anger and the lust for power, filled with acts of mercy and generosity, then God is glorified. In purity of life, in genuine fellowship, and in words of peace God is praised. John's sermons are filled with exhortations to the Christian life, and for him this kind of teaching was clearly Christian worship. This is especially the case because John lived the kind of life he preached, and because he lived it, his preaching of it was a witness. In the true biblical sense of the word "witness" it was a public recognition of God's saving grace.

A covenantal theology of worship understands the witness of the righteous as the true sacrifice of thanksgiving. When God graciously intervenes and saves us from some threatening evil, from illness or from financial ruin; when God gives the nation of his people victory in time of war or when God gives a barren woman a child; when we cry to him and he delivers us; then we are obligated to thank God, to make a public witness to God's covenant faithfulness, and to confess the obligation we have to God. John was a man who had been saved from the vanity of a pagan life as it was understood in late antiquity. That he had come to live a simple life of Christian fellowship, that the grace of God had filled his life with Christian virtue, that he had come to know the truth and to rejoice in it — all this had given our preacher an overflowing sense of joy. When he taught his congregation about the victory of the Christian life, it was indeed a witness born of personal experience. This is true Christian witness. Such a witness from the standpoint of covenant theology is indeed worship.

This was what classical rhetoric was really supposed to be about. Eloquence was supposed to be the natural expression of a virtuous life. The trouble was that the teachers of rhetoric never seemed able to come anywhere near fulfilling their own ideal. Libanius was an unfortunate example — he was notoriously vain. It was very different with John Chrysostom. Because his life was just as eloquent as his preaching, his preaching was a true witness to the glory of God. The ultimate liturgy of John Chrysostom was the witness of a holy man that God saves us from our sin and renews our lives in righteousness and truth.

II. Theodore of Mopsuestia

Enjoying a high reputation as a preacher during his lifetime, much like his friend and colleague John Chrysostom, Theodore of Mopsuestia (ca. 350-428) is today recognized by many as the outstanding theologian of the School of Antioch.[144] Both John and Theodore were raised and educated in Antioch, and both studied in the same schools at the same time; in fact, it was in the school of Libanius that together they studied rhetoric and began their lifelong friendship. After they completed their training in the literary arts, they entered the monastery where Diodore of Tarsus was teaching his new approach to exegesis. What a great age that was in the history of theology! In 381 the Council of Constantinople was called and Arianism was finally defeated. The whole brilliant discussion of the divinity of Christ and the doctrine of the Trinity came to its climax at just about the time these two young men began their ministry. Theodore must have been in his early thirties when he was ordained by Bishop Flavian, who soon thereafter also ordained John, and the two young men worked side by side on the staff of the patriarch of Antioch. While John preached at the cathedral, Theodore lectured on theology at one of the leading monasteries. It was in 392, after some ten years of serving Flavian, that Theodore was made bishop of Mopsuestia, a small city in Cilicia. For the next thirty-five years he was an outstanding pastor, famed for his theological orthodoxy, his conscientiousness as a preacher, and above all his sobriety as a commentator on Scripture.

Strangely enough, a generation after his death he was declared a heretic, being regarded as one of the sources of the Nestorian heresy. Those determined to check the influence of the Antiochene exegesis were eager to blame the supposed heresies of Nestorius on an Antiochene theologian, and it seems Nestorius, as a young man, had studied under Theodore in Antioch. More recent scholarship, however, has recognized that Theodore was in fact an outstanding theologian and among the most well-balanced interpreters of Scripture the patristic age ever produced. He published a whole library of commentaries, including works on Genesis, the Psalms, the Minor Prophets, the Gospel of John, and one each on Paul's major

144. E. Amann, "Théodore de Mopsueste," *Dictionnaire de théologie catholique* (Paris: Letouzey et Ane, 1903-50), 15:235-79; Robert Devreesse, *Essai sur Théodore de Mopsueste* (Vatican City: Biblioteca Apostolica Vaticana, 1948); Froehlich, *Biblical Interpretation*, pp. 22ff.; R. A. Greer, *Theodore of Mopsuestia: Exegete and Theologian* (Westminster, Md.: Faith Press, 1961); and H. B. Swete, *Dictionary of Christian Biography*, 4:934-48.

and minor epistles. As happened to so much of the homiletical legacy of Origen, most of these commentaries were thought to have perished. Only recently has it been discovered that some of them were translated into Syriac by the Nestorians, who for centuries regarded Theodore as the most dependable of biblical interpreters. These commentaries, as is true of so many patristic commentaries, probably reflect in one way or another Theodore's preaching. In all probability he wrote them on the books of the Bible through which he was preaching at the time. No doubt he preached much the same way John Chrysostom did, but, alas, none of his expository sermons has come down to us in sermonic form.

The one example of his preaching which has come down to us is a series of sixteen catechetical sermons. It is usually assumed that these sermons were preached in Antioch sometime after his ordination in about 382, thus they would come after the Council of Constantinople (381) as well. The first ten sermons give an explanation of the Nicene Creed, which is followed by a sermon on the Lord's Prayer, three sermons on baptism, and two on the eucharistic liturgy. These catechetical sermons are a treasure! Here we have a fully developed theological statement produced by a theologian who had profited from the more enlightened biblical studies which Diodore was introducing in Antioch. It is the closest thing we have to a systematic theology from the Antiochene School. Although for centuries these sermons were believed to have been lost, a Syriac translation of them was discovered by Alphonse Mingana and published with English translation in 1932.[145] While we wish we were able to study the expository sermons of such a master exegete, we are generously compensated by the opportunity to study the catechetical sermons, for as we shall see, they will tell us much about the Antiochene theology of worship. What we found intimated in John Chrysostom will be brought out much more explicitly in these sermons of his friend and colleague, Theodore of Mopsuestia.

A. Catechetical Sermons

One does not have to read far into these sermons to discover that they are very serious sermons for a very mature audience. They assume that the

---

145. This study is based on the edition of Raymond Tonneau, O.P., in collaboration with Robert Devreesse, *Les homélies catéchétiques de Théodore de Mopsueste* (Vatican City: Biblioteca Apostolica Vaticana, 1949); hereinafter cited as Theodore, *Catechetical Sermons*.

listeners were accustomed to hearing theological matters discussed at a rather high level. It is not surprising that we find this in the city of Antioch at the close of the fourth century, for at that time Antioch was one of the centers of Hellenistic culture. As we have already said, Antioch had been a Hellenistic city ever since it was founded in 300 B.C. by Seleucus I, one of the heirs of Alexander the Great. The Seleucid dynasty had tried to impose Greek culture on Syria for centuries, one of the more infamous rulers of that dynasty, Antiochus Epiphanes, being ruthless in his insistence that Syria adopt Greek ways. In the five centuries that elapsed between Antiochus Epiphanes and Theodore of Mopsuestia Antioch had developed its own particular blend of Greek culture and Syrian blood. It became a Greek city open to the Orient, a city that was to the world of ancient Greece and Rome somewhat like San Francisco is to America today, a gateway to the Orient, which, in Antioch's case, was primarily the Semitic world of the Near East. Many Semitic traditions and attitudes were perpetuated even after centuries of Greek rule, and Antioch had a large and articulate Jewish population. But it was equally the case that the heirs of Moses and the prophets, whether Jew or Christian, could be very sensitive about guarding Scripture from the encroachments of Greek paganism. Philosophical approaches to the interpretation of Scripture were looked over very carefully, and theological subjects at issue between Christians and Jews were vigorously discussed by a wide section of the population. It is hardly surprising that catechetical sermons preached in this city would be especially mature and well thought out.

No doubt because the church of Antioch was in such close connection with the Semitic world, we discover that these sermons are marked by a strong sense of the transcendence of God. In the opening sermons one finds that Theodore is just as interested in teaching the unity of God as the trinity of God. Already in the first sermon our preacher urges us to flee the error of polytheism.[146] Quoting the Shema, he insists, "'The Lord your God alone is Lord'" (Deut. 6:4).[147] To make his point he quotes the text from Jeremiah, "'The gods who did not make the heavens and the earth, let them perish from off the earth and from under the heavens'" (Jer. 10:11). Theodore reminds us that it was Moses who taught us that God and God alone is the cause of all things. It is he and he alone who truly exists from all eternity and to all eternity; he and he alone is God.

146. Theodore, *Catechetical Sermons* 1.13.
147. Theodore, *Catechetical Sermons* 1.15.

Altogether different are those gods who have not existed from all eternity, who do not exist in truth because their existence is derived from another. They have been made and the cause of their existence is elsewhere than in themselves. Again Theodore quotes the Old Testament prophets, " 'It is I who am God, the first and the last, nothing was created before me and after me there is nothing at all' " (Isa. 44:6).[148] As Theodore understands it, it is not possible for one who is created to become God.[149] For the pagans the gods are of great number and great variety — some are young and some are old, some have one power and some another, some disappear while others become greater and more powerful. But from the Scriptures of the Old Testament we learn something quite different. We learn from the prophets who spoke by the Holy Spirit that the gods of the heathen are false; they are no gods at all. Theodore elaborates this with a variety of Old Testament quotations and allusions and finally sums up by telling us that the divine nature is unique. It exists in a unique way. It exists from all eternity and needs no other in order to exist. God in himself is the cause of all things. God is unique.

Theodore puts so well at the end of the fourth century what Karl Barth put so well in the twentieth: God is totally other. On the other hand, that which is made and derives its existence from some other source can by that fact never become God.[150] It is because of this uniqueness of God that we owe him worship. He exists of himself, but we exist from another; therefore God and man are radically different from one another in nature. He exists of himself, and we owe our existence to him; therefore, we owe him worship. It is because of the unity of God that we owe him worship, and because of the trinity of God that we can give him what we owe him.

The tension between the Antiochene type of theology and the Alexandrian type of theology is one of those things that keep recurring in the history of Christian thought. The Antiochene theology we find in Theodore is a good corrective to the sort of popular Neoplatonism of his day, which tended to think of a hierarchical progression which ascended from humanity to divinity. The Antiochene theologians with their strong emphasis on grammatical-historical exegesis never could quite go along with the sort of humanism that sprang from Greek culture. Greek pa-

---

148. Theodore, *Catechetical Sermons* 1.15.
149. Theodore, *Catechetical Sermons* 1.15.
150. Theodore, *Catechetical Sermons* 1.16.

ganism saw man and God in very similar terms, which was what so offended the Antiochenes about Arianism. Orthodox theology has never been willing to go all the way with Neoplatonism, and to a large extent that is because of the Antiochene Fathers. The Antiochene theologians were always suspicious of a sort of theology which tended to make God not so much totally other as totally absorbing. With Alexandrian theology, taken to extremes, humanity seems to lose its significance, while Antiochene theology takes humanity much more seriously. In these sermons we notice how Theodore is careful to make clear the true humanity of Christ as well as his true divinity. In the third sermon Theodore tells us, "Our fathers quite correctly considered it very important not to neglect the doctrine of the humanity of our Lord which had an ineffable association with the divine nature."[151]

In the fourth sermon Theodore goes into the question of what it means for Jesus to be called the only-begotten Son of God, "who is born of the Father before all the world." Theodore makes the point that Jesus really is the Son of God by his very nature. He is not merely called the Son of God by imputation, nor is he a son by grace as the rest of us are.[152] He is very God of very God; that is, he is God in the same sense that God is God, not in the sense that some human beings are called divine or godly or in the sense that Psalm 81 says that we are all gods.[153] Jesus is God in the sense that we find in the Gospel of John where Jesus says, " 'I and my Father are one' " (John 10:30).[154] The Son is one in authority and one in power with the Father.[155]

In the fifth sermon Theodore takes up the question of the "economy of his humanity," or dispensation of his humanity. Here again we notice how carefully our Antiochene theologian guards the true humanity of Christ. Jesus came to save men since they were lost and under the control of evil. By his grace and unspeakable mercy he gave us life and delivered us from evil. It is therefore that the creed tells us that the Son of God for us men and for our salvation descended from heaven and became man.[156] Theodore insists that in the incarnation the Son took upon himself a

151. Theodore, *Catechetical Sermons* 3.4.
152. Theodore, *Catechetical Sermons* 4.3.
153. Theodore, *Catechetical Sermons* 4.9-10.
154. Theodore, *Catechetical Sermons* 4.13-14.
155. Theodore, *Catechetical Sermons* 4.15.
156. Theodore, *Catechetical Sermons* 5.3.

human body, a human mind, and a human soul,[157] yet although completely human, he did not sin.[158] It is this insistence on the integrity of Christ's humanity which makes the ethical teaching of the Antiochenes so strong. No doubt the reason the Antiochene preachers underlined the humanity of Jesus is because they put such strong emphasis on grammatical-historical exegesis. The Bible itself makes Jesus very human. Here in these catechetical sermons of Theodore's we find the theological key to the sermons of John Chrysostom, which were at one and the same time so expository and so ethical.

Much else could be pointed out about these catechetical sermons. They are certainly an impressive statement of the monotheistic faith in terms of a profoundly trinitarian unfolding of that faith. But let us move on to what these sermons tell us about the Antiochene theology of worship and the light it throws on the ministry of the Word as it was so brilliantly practiced by this school.

B. Antiochene Theology of Worship

Included in this series of catechetical sermons, in addition to the ten sermons on the text of the Nicene Creed, are several sermons on the sacraments.[159] They bear important similarities to several other collections of sermons on the sacraments which were preached at about the same time, including those of Cyril of Jerusalem and John Chrysostom, which we have already looked at, and the *De sacramentiis* of Ambrose of Milan and Augustine's sermons on the First Epistle of John, which we will examine later. These sacramental sermons of Theodore's deserve careful attention — more than we can give them here, sad to say — for they are among the most important documents on the history of Christian worship that have come down to us. Here we see a theologian of more than ordinary insight trying to explain the liturgical practices of his day by the text of

---

157. Theodore, *Catechetical Sermons* 5.15.

158. Theodore, *Catechetical Sermons* 5.18.

159. On the significance of these sermons for our understanding of Christian worship, see Mazza, *Mystagogy;* Johannes Quasten, "The Liturgical Mysticism of Theodore of Mopsuestia," *Texte und Untersuchungen* 15 (1954): 431-39; Francis Joseph Reine, *The Eucharistic Doctrine and Liturgy of the Mystagogical Catechisms of Theodore of Mopsuestia* (Washington, D.C.: Catholic University of America Press, 1942); and Schulz, *The Byzantine Liturgy.*

the New Testament. What makes them of special interest is the deeper insight projected by the School of Antioch into the task of biblical interpretation. Because the Antiochenes were so perceptive in regard to Scripture, their theology of worship was less influenced by the Neoplatonic approach to worship which was beginning to appear in Christian churches. As philosophical and as poetic as the insights of the School of Alexandria may have been, they often missed the deeper insights of Scripture itself. The liturgical practices of the late fourth century had moved a long way from the simple observances of New Testament times, but those liturgical practices are not what interests us here. What we want to look at are Theodore's insights into the nature of worship which he has won from his biblical studies. Interestingly enough Theodore seems to be commenting on the text of a church constitution or directory of worship. This text, which is not identified, gives the framework of the sermons, although in each sermon Theodore calls on half a dozen biblical passages to explain the rites described in his directory of worship.

The first thing we notice, and we notice it throughout the series of sermons, is that our worship is demanded by the transcendence of God. It is because God is totally other that we must worship him, and it is in awe that we must stand before him. We can do nothing else. Worship is the appropriate way for the finite to relate to the infinite; it is the relationship the Bible so often calls the fear of the Lord. It is the awe and wonder from which comes true understanding, as we find in Proverbs, "The fear of the LORD is the beginning of wisdom" (Prov. 9:10). Some have recently spoken with a certain amount of embarrassment about the appearance of holy fear in these sermons of Theodore's. The up-to-date liturgists of our day have been scandalized by it. But there is no reason to be so offended by Theodore's recurrent reference to "fearful" mysteries and "dreadful" liturgical observances. Holy fear has always been an element of biblical worship. Theodore was neither the first nor the last to discover the experience of Isaiah in the year that King Uzziah died to be an important part of Christian worship (Isa. 6:1-13). The sixth chapter of Isaiah is a most important text for Theodore as he tries to explain worship.[160] "Holy, holy, holy Lord God of Hosts, heaven and earth are full of thee; Glory be to thee O Most High" is a hymn that expresses our sacred fear, our awe and wonderment before God. When we are confronted by the transcendence of God, it is only appro-

---

160. Theodore, *Catechetical Sermons* 16.6-10.

priate to fall down in worship before him.[161] This is a fundamental biblical insight as to the nature of worship, an insight Theodore as a careful student of the Scriptures understood.

This has an obvious implication for preaching. If God is the *hagia sophia,* the Holy Wisdom from on high, then how can there be any more fitting way to relate to him than to become a disciple, to study the word of the Word of God? If Christ is the Word, how better to relate to him than to listen to that Word? From Isaiah's experience of this holy fear in the worship of the Temple came Isaiah's call to be a preacher. Theodore tells us the story of how the glowing coal was brought from the altar fires to sanctify the prophet's lips.[162] It is the heavenly liturgy itself which sanctifies the preacher's lips and calls us to hear the Word of God. If God has revealed himself as the Word, then the appropriate way to relate to the Word is to hear it and receive it, and to study it and obey it. The Wisdom doxology is indeed quite logical.

We cannot help but notice that Theodore has a strongly covenantal approach to worship. This is first of all apparent in sermons for those who are about to be baptized at the beginning of the series on the creed. At the center of the rite of baptism covenant vows are to be made and sealed; these covenant vows take the form of a profession of faith in the one God, Father, Son, and Holy Spirit. It is therefore that these sermons treat the new covenant which God has concluded with the human race.[163] For Theodore we are saved by faith and at baptism we make a profession of that faith.[164] This baptismal profession of faith is engagement in the covenantal relationship.[165] We find much the same thing when we get to Theodore's sermons on baptism. At baptism one makes one's professions of faith and engagements to God which are, in effect, a promise to be faithful to God.[166] In explaining this Theodore uses a rather full array of synonyms for the covenantal nature of baptism. In baptism we conclude a contract to serve God; we make a pact to be faithful to God's love toward us.[167] Theodore also has a covenantal understanding of the Lord's Supper. Quite appropriately, it is when Theodore gets down to speaking of the

---

161. Theodore, *Catechetical Sermons* 1.13-17.
162. Theodore, *Catechetical Sermons* 16.36ff.
163. Theodore, *Catechetical Sermons* 1.3.
164. Theodore, *Catechetical Sermons* 1.5 and 6.
165. Theodore, *Catechetical Sermons* 1.7 and 8.
166. Theodore, *Catechetical Sermons* 12.26.
167. Theodore, *Catechetical Sermons* 12.27.

actual Communion, that is, the sharing of the bread and wine, that the covenantal dimension of the sacrament comes out.[168] We all become the one body of Christ through sharing in the same loaf and the same cup. It is through this food that the grace of the Holy Spirit nourishes us.[169] Here Theodore calls on that key text for the covenantal understanding of the Lord's Supper, I Corinthians 10:16-17, for as it is one loaf of bread, so we, although many, become one by sharing in it. It is communion with him that we receive by means of this nourishment. As Theodore sees it, the apostle Paul teaches us that by receiving the body and blood of Christ we are joined to him and enter into communion with him.[170]

Especially when it comes to catechetical preaching does a covenantal theology of the sacraments have much to say about why we preach and what we are to preach. If in the sacraments we are entering into a covenant relationship and nourishing a covenant relationship, as Theodore so clearly teaches, then making clear the terms of the covenant is of the greatest possible importance. That has been clear ever since Jesus gave the apostles the Great Commission — we are to baptize and to teach all that Christ has commanded us. Theodore's sermons proclaim the faith that is the basis of new life in Christ; this is what Theodore unfolds in his sermons on the creed. In the sermon on the Lord's Prayer Theodore takes up what it means to live the Christian life, and in the sermons on the sacraments he teaches us the nature of the worship which we owe to God by virtue of our being the covenant people of God.[171] This is most obvious in the relation of preaching to baptism, but it is just as true in the relation of preaching to the Lord's Supper. If one understands the Supper as spiritual food which nourishes us in the new life of the kingdom of God, then the reading and preaching of the covenant are essential to a faithful celebration of the Supper.[172] It is solid biblical theology to understand Christian preaching and Christian teaching as spiritual nourishment and to understand the sharing of a meal as a sign of the spiritual nourishment which comes through the Word of God. This is taught throughout Scripture but especially in the Bread of Life Discourse in the sixth chapter of the Gospel of John, a discourse to which Theodore gives

168. Theodore, *Catechetical Sermons* 16.24.
169. Theodore, *Catechetical Sermons* 16.24.
170. Theodore, *Catechetical Sermons* 16.24.
171. Theodore, *Catechetical Sermons* 16.29.
172. Theodore, *Catechetical Sermons* 15.5-6.

quite a bit of time.[173] He understands the Bread of Life as nourishment for immortality. This essential relationship of solid preaching to a true celebration of the Eucharist was something realized by the Italian Franciscans in the fifteenth century just as it was realized by the Scottish Covenanters in the eighteenth century. In both cases the faithful preachers of those days devoted a whole season of sermons to preparing their congregations for the sacrament beforehand and to considering the implication of their participation afterwards.

Even beyond sacramental or catechetical preaching, a covenantal understanding of worship has much to say about how we carry out the regular task of preaching to the assembled congregation week by week or even day by day. Theodore frequently speaks of worship as a memorial.[174] This has always been a fundamental concept for the biblical understanding of worship. Ever since Moses gave the fourth commandment, "Remember the Sabbath day to keep it holy," God's people have felt the obligation to worship God by remembering his mighty acts of creation and redemption. Ever since Jesus said to his disciples, "Do this in remembrance of me," Christians have understood that in celebrating the sacrament of Communion they were observing a sacred memorial of Christ's death and resurrection. If in worship we are celebrating a memorial, then it is fitting that there be a festive setting forth of that which the memorial commemorates. It had always belonged to the liturgy of the covenant renewal to read the book of the covenant. When Moses did this at the foot of Mount Sinai, it may not have taken all that long; when Ezra read through the book of the covenant and gave its sense, it took the better part of a week; and by the time of Jesus this reading and preaching of the covenantal literature had been arranged so that it was read through in course — each Sabbath a portion was read and preached on. Behind it was the same basic understanding. Worship is a memorial or remembrance of the saving acts of God on which the covenant relationship is based.

Another important biblical concept of worship we find in Theodore's sermons is that worship is an experience in the here and now of a transcendent reality which in heaven is fulfilled but which is yet to come here on earth. Worship is a foretaste of that transcendent reality. One might say in Eastern terms that worship is a participation in heavenly mysteries, but one could put it in Western terms as well: Worship is a sacrament, an

173. Theodore, *Catechetical Sermons* 15.11-12.
174. Theodore, *Catechetical Sermons* 15.15, 20, and 35; 16.5 and 10.

outward and visible sign of an inward and invisible reality. Theodore often uses the words "figure," "image," "symbol," and "sign" in regard to the sacraments,[175] but most often he uses the word "type," and in a rather unusual way. While so many patristic authors use it particularly to denote the Old Testament types of Christ and his works of redemption, Theodore uses it in a way that almost suggests that "type" is his word for sacrament. For Theodore the word has a sort of eschatological thrust. In baptism we are born again in type. The experience of the sacrament is a sort of down payment of being born into the kingdom of God at the resurrection; it is a sign of our renewal and ultimate purification in the Last Day. In the same way the nourishment we receive in the Supper is a food which we enjoy in this world but which is a sign of the wedding feast of the Lamb in the world to come.

In fact, the clear sacramental thinking of Theodore is one of the most interesting features of these sermons. One of the places where it comes out most clearly is in regard to the subject of the eucharistic sacrifice. There is no question that by the end of the fourth century the celebration of the Lord's Supper was often thought of as a sacrifice. Many of the patristic writers felt the need to show that it was a sacrifice more awesome than the sacrifices of the pagans. However, there were those such as Theodore and John Chrysostom who had hesitations about this view.[176] Because of the passage of the Epistle to the Hebrews which taught that the sacrifice of Christ was once and for all, that it was unique and never needed to be repeated, these two Antiochene preachers preferred to speak of the Lord's Supper as a memorial of Christ's sacrifice.[177] Theodore gives a great deal of attention in this discussion to the eighth, ninth, and tenth chapters of Hebrews,[178] which were obviously of particular importance for his understanding of worship.

As interesting as it might be to discuss Theodore's understanding of sacrament at great length, we will have to leave it to others. What is important for our discussion is that Theodore's understanding of the sacramental dimension of worship demands a strong preaching ministry.

---

175. Theodore, *Catechetical Sermons* 14.3, 5, 6, 7, and 22; 15.3, 6, 7, 11, 14, 15, and 21; and 16.26, 28, 30, and passim.

176. On John Chrysostom's understanding of the Lord's Supper as a memorial of Christ's sacrifice, see Chrysostom, *Homilies on Hebrews* 17.6, in Nicene and Post-Nicene Fathers, 1st ser., 14:449.

177. Theodore, *Catechetical Sermons* 15.15 and 20.

178. Theodore, *Catechetical Sermons* 15.15-19.

To describe it as mystagogy is misleading.[179] It is not popular Platonism which is behind Theodore's understanding of worship so much as it is some very basic biblical concepts which Theodore has been able to bring into focus better than many of his contemporaries.

We have tried to resist the temptation to study Theodore as a theologian, because we are properly concerned with him as a preacher. Unfortunately, we don't have all the documents we really need to study him as a preacher. All we know is that in an age of pulpit giants he had a reputation for being among the best. We suspect that the catechetical sermons we have studied have been edited for publication, and that his commentaries are really series of expository sermons edited for publication as commentaries. But even so, one thing comes through very clearly: Theodore was a serious preacher whom people listened to. Theodore was way ahead of his time. Tragically, he was misunderstood, but even at that he is a witness to the integrity of the ministry of the Word; he shows us the value of a serious study of Scripture as the foundation of serious preaching. For the modern biblical preacher he is an encouragement. We can relate to his exegesis in a way that we can't relate to the exegesis of Origen. Theodore was obviously a great biblical scholar who could preach as well. Not only that, he was a true theologian in a way that John Chrysostom was not. Theodore was a systematic theologian. He shows us an important dimension of the preaching of the School of Antioch which we might have missed if we did not have his catechetical sermons. The systematic preaching of Christian doctrine has a place in the Christian pulpit, just as the systematic preaching of the Bible does. Here is an especially fine example of the value of careful study, clear thinking, and articulate public speaking in the worship of God.

III. Theodoret of Cyrus

Theodoret of Cyrus (ca. 383–ca. 460) is another example of learned, studied preaching. He was a preacher of moderation and balance, and a man of wit and personal charm as well.[180] The Antioch in which he grew

179. Here I find myself at considerable odds with the excellent book of Mazza, *Mystagogy*.

180. This comes out particularly in his letters: Theodoret of Cyr, *Correspondence*, ed. Y. Azéma, 3 vols., Sources chrétiennes, vols. 40, 98, and 111 (Paris: Les Éditions du Cerf, 1955-65).

up was in its golden age, with John Chrysostom preaching daily in the great church built by Constantine and Theodore of Mopsuestia teaching in its monastery schools. As a young man Theodoret devoted himself to a monastic life, entering a community of Syriac-speaking monks at Nicerte. In 423, when he was perhaps forty years old, he was chosen bishop of Cyrus, a town east of Antioch which, together with the surrounding area, had a considerable Christian population. A vigorous supporter of the Antiochene theology, he wrote early in his career an attack on Cyril of Alexandria's anathemas against Nestorius, which brought him into the vigorous theological debates which led up to the Council of Chalcedon in 451. Not an extremist by nature, he submitted to the compromise which was finally worked out even to the point of reluctantly anathematizing Nestorius. There has frequently been something of a cloud over Theodoret's reputation as a systematic theologian. The rigid supporters of Cyril of Alexandria were never quite satisfied with his affirmations of loyalty to Nicene orthodoxy.[181] Today most scholars feel he was treated with less than the objectivity he deserved. He was in fact one of the best Christian thinkers of his day, and apparently one of the best preachers of his day as well.

A. Learned Preaching

Theodoret must have lived in his library, and it must have been a very large and rich library. His literary legacy is both extensive and varied, and he produced a good number of commentaries. In addition to works on the historical books of the Old Testament, he left us commentaries on all the prophets and a work on the Psalms that is outstanding. Theodoret tells us in the preface of this latter volume that he studied a number of commentaries both from those who wished to understand the Psalms allegorically and from those who wished to understand them historically, and saw value in both approaches. It depended on the particular psalm in question. What he regards as Jewish skepticism is to be avoided. While he could not go along with the allegorical interpretations of the Alexandrians, he basically supported the older Christian interpretation of the Old Testa-

181. On the question of Theodoret's relation to Nestorianism, see H. M. Diepen and J. Daniélou, "Théodoret et le dogme d'Éphèse," *Recherches de Sciences Religieuses* 44 (1956): 243-48.

ment. Theodoret also produced commentaries on the New Testament, but all that has survived is his commentary on the Pauline Epistles. Considering only what has come down to us, he deserves to be regarded as a major biblical commentator. What is to be admired about his commentaries is their balance. As a member of the School of Antioch Theodoret follows a grammatical-historical approach to the interpretation of Scripture, and yet he accepts the well-established Christian interpretations of many passages in the prophets, and of such books as the Song of Solomon, as well as many of the traditional messianic psalms.

In addition to these commentaries he has left us three major works on church history. His history of the monastic movement is of value because it preserves material about Syrian ascetics and hermits who were contemporaries or near contemporaries of Theodoret. In some cases Theodoret knew them or people who had known them. Simon Stylites, for example, was a well-known figure in Syrian church life of the time. Theodoret's supplement to the *Ecclesiastical History* of Eusebius is highly regarded because of his use of source documents. He takes up the story in 323 and continues it for another century, until 428, that is, just before the beginning of the Nestorian controversy. Finally there is a history of heresies, in which he again used a variety of source documents, some of which have been lost, that included Justin Martyr, Irenaeus, Hippolytus, Clement of Alexandria, Eusebius of Caesarea, and Eusebius of Emesa. One is constantly amazed at how rich Theodoret's library must have been.

Theodoret's apologetical works are also highly regarded. In fact, his *Cure of Pagan Maladies* is often praised as the last and the best patristic apology. The work, in a very learned fashion, takes up one theological or philosophical theme after another and compares the Christian teaching to various pagan teachings on the subject. The series of sermons at which we are about to look is sometimes thought of as a popularization of one of the chapters of this work. Theodoret also wrote a polemic against the Persian magi as well as a work defending Christian faith against Jewish criticism.

Theodoret's primary dogmatic work, *Eranistes,* is a dialogue between an orthodox Christian and a Monophysite. The author's purpose is to show that Monophysitism is nothing more than a revival of many older heresies. Again it is a rich collection of citations from over eighty different authorities, which, apparently, he had not gathered himself. Over the years, under the leadership of several of the bishops of Antioch, an anthology had been put together of *testimonia* supporting the Antiochene position, and Theodoret gave the collection of *testimonia* an attractive literary form. Some have criticized Theodoret's originality, but in a day when manuscripts were copied by hand, a manuscript filled with brilliant feathers from other birds was considered all the more valuable. Florilegia were popular in those days. Even at that, Theodoret must have studied whole works of many of these writers, especially those who were considered orthodox.[182]

Theodoret also left us one of the great collections of letters which has come down from antiquity. These letters give us a personal look at the first half of the fifth century and reveal the charm of a delightful Christian personality. Although an accomplished scholar, Theodoret is utterly free of pretentiousness. His letters show him to be simple and direct. Besides that, they are an important source for the history of the times.

It is to be regretted that few of Theodoret's sermons have been preserved. But, as his commentaries surely attest, he must have preached long series of expository sermons, much like his contemporaries. One does not produce the wealth of commentaries that the Antiochene School produced unless a good number of preachers are doing the sort of daily expository preaching John Chrysostom did. Careful verse-by-verse study of Scripture obviously had an audience in the Syrian church. The commentaries only came into being because this kind of preaching was a prominent feature in the church life of the time. But, alas, none of these expository sermons has come down to us, at least not in homiletical form. The single example of Theodoret's preaching which has survived is a series of ten sermons on providence. They are among the most sparkling gems of the patristic treasury and suggest the hand of a master craftsman, one who had long experience at maintaining the attention of a congregation.

B. Sermons on Providence and the Antiochene Theology of Evangelism

For a long time Theodoret's *On Divine Providence* was practically unknown to the English-speaking world. With the magnificent translation of

---

182. See the work of Pierre Nautin, "La valeur des lemmes dans l'*Éranistes* de Théodoret," *Revue d'Histoire Ecclésiastique* 46 (1951): 681-83; M. Richard, "Notes sur les florilèges dogmatiques de Ve et du VIe siècle," *Actes du Congrès d'Études Byzantines* (Paris, 1948): 307-18; and L. Salet, "Les sources de l'*Éranistes* de Théodoret," *Revue d'Histoire Ecclésiastique* 6 (1905): 289-303, 513-36, 741-54.

Thomas Halton, so beautifully annotated, this should change.[183] These sermons easily belong on even the shortest lists of the pulpit classics of Christian antiquity.

Scholars have often wondered whether they are real sermons that were actually preached. From a literary standpoint they are splendid! Could they be purely literary compositions which only adopted the form of the sermon? One of the strongest arguments against this is that the sermons seem to be a popularization of one of the chapters of the *Eranistes*, in which Theodoret compares the biblical idea of providence with those found among various pagan authors. In the sermons the references to the pagan authors are dropped; only the authoritative texts of Scripture are used in the pulpit. This seems to have been a fairly widespread convention in those days — one did not discuss the ideas of pagan philosophers in the pulpit. If these sermons were not actually intended for the pulpit, there would be no reason to abide by the convention.

Actually the homiletical form of these sermons is rather unusual for the patristic period. While they seem to be real sermons, they probably were not typical sermons. Perhaps some special occasion called for them. From the standpoint of literary form these sermons are polemical. They are defenses of Christian doctrine cast in the literary form of a philosophic discourse. Greek rhetoric had developed definite forms for philosophical disputation, which were very similar to the forms they developed for argumentation in the courtroom. In this respect Theodoret's sermons are similar to the Theological Orations of Gregory of Nazianzus. These sermons are cast in the literary form of the philosophical discourse rather than the literary form of the expository sermon. The expository sermon, with plenty of exceptions certainly, was the sort found most often in the pulpit, the usual fare of the Sunday service as well as the weekday service. Gradually, however, under the influence of Greek rhetoric the preachers of the Church began to develop Christian panegyrics as well as Christian philosophical discourses. The old literary forms were used, but they were infused with Christian content.

There must have been a good amount of apologetical preaching during the patristic period. It was the way the Greek mind would have understood evangelistic preaching. To preach apologetically was, so to speak, to enter into a courtroom and attempt to win the case for the

183. Theodoret of Cyrus, *On Divine Providence*, trans. Thomas Halton (New York and Mahwah, N.J.: Newman Press, 1988).

Christian faith. It was quite different from going into the synagogue and interpreting the Scriptures in a Christian sense as Jesus had done in Nazareth or as Paul had so often done in the synagogues of the Diaspora. These were all attempts at evangelism tailored to the Jewish mentality. In the same way apologetical preaching was a type of evangelistic preaching tailored to the Greek and Roman mentality of late antiquity.

A strange thing about these apologetical sermons of Theodoret's is the way the arguments taken from the pagan philosophers which are so learnedly developed in his *Cure of Pagan Maladies* are passed over in silence when he mounts the pulpit. This, as I have suggested, would argue for their being real sermons. These sermons probably were preached at the regular weekday morning service but with the intention of answering pagan arguments against the Christian faith. If this is indeed the case, then the *Eranistes* shows us the kind of studies that were behind Theodoret's preaching. Here was a preacher who went into the pulpit well prepared.

Theodoret's whole ministry took theology very seriously. His biblical studies account for a large portion of his literary output, but his apologetical and doctrinal works show the same meticulous attention. Apologetical preaching must have been a major facet of his ministry. His zeal for right doctrine, for orthodoxy, was thoroughly evangelistic. We are told that twenty years after he began his pastorate, he had successfully won over any who had been affected by heresy. Heresy for Theodoret was a sort of lingering paganism. People were heretics because they had not been fully converted — the intellectual dimension to conversion had been neglected. Too many people had been baptized and brought into the fellowship of the Church whose minds had not yet been transformed, and they needed to be evangelized intellectually. It was to this problem that Theodoret devoted a good part of his preaching ministry, just as it was to this problem that he had devoted a good part of his literary ministry. Quite possibly, then, if we might venture a suggestion, the ten sermons on providence are only a sample of a much more extensive ministry of apologetic preaching. If these ten sermons are a popular form of one chapter of his classic apology *The Cure of Pagan Maladies,* then there may have been similar series of sermons on the other chapters. To use Paul Ramsey's remark about the preaching of Jonathan Edwards, Theodoret's pulpit may have been the workbench at which he fashioned his published literary works. The reason Theodoret's *Cure of Pagan Maladies* attained such excellence is that it was all preached before it was written. Anyone who is familiar with how preachers do their work, week after week, will understand the force of this argument.

But, having spoken about the ministry of apologetic preaching of which these sermons on providence are such a beautiful example, we need to look at what Theodoret has to say about the doctrine of providence. The annotations which Halton has made for his translation help us to see Theodoret's teaching on this subject in the intellectual landscape of late antiquity. Providence was a well-defined term in classical philosophy. The Stoics spoke of it frequently. The Stoic concept of πρόνοια had to do with divine governing of the creation, with the maintaining of the order of nature, with natural law, with the rewarding of the good and the punishing of evil. One of the sermons, Sermon 3, is devoted to showing how the marvelous organism of the human body was so created by God that every need was provided for. As Halton shows in his notes, much of this material was taken from the Greek natural philosophers. Greek medicine was a highly developed art at the time and had produced an extensive literature, and Theodoret, studious saint that he was, had apparently read fairly widely in this field. Galen was appreciated by Christians because he saw in the order of the human body evidence of the wisdom of divine providence. Our preacher spins out this line of thought in some detail.

In Sermon 6 Theodoret goes into the question of why in the providence of God some are rich and some are poor, and particularly why it is that often the wicked are rich and the good are poor. The pagan philosophers had discussed this problem at length, and here is one place where our preacher might be accused of getting too involved in pagan philosophy at the expense of biblical theology. Sometimes one gets the impression that Theodoret is more interested in the Stoic concept than the biblical concept, for he often illustrates Stoic ideas with biblical texts. Somehow he exhibits a sort of social fatalism which seems to fall short of the Christian understanding of providence. The aspect of God calling us to a certain service or ministry and then equipping us to perform that vocation seems to be missing. At times one gets the impression that Theodoret does not recognize the distinction between philosophical fatalism and the Christian doctrine of election. On the other hand, he discusses at some length the story of Joseph, which illustrates a strong doctrine of election. Joseph was called to a very specific service and was equipped with the means of carrying it out.[184] Here Theodoret is much closer, it would seem, to the biblical concept of providence. The story of Joseph is surely a major witness to a biblical doctrine of providence. For Theodoret,

---

184. Theodoret, *On Divine Providence* 8.

however, the Christian faith in providence is the fulfillment of the teaching of the best pagan philosophers. It is the Christian faith in the resurrection which justifies the seeming inequities of this life.[185] In the resurrection the poor are rewarded and the enslaved are freed from their burdens. Finally it is in the incarnation of Christ that God's providential care for both Jew and Gentile is most fully revealed.[186] We are tempted to go on at considerable length discussing our preacher's insights on the subject of divine providence, but we must move on.

No one can read this series of sermons without rejoicing in the sheer beauty of Theodoret's rhetoric. It has the same oratorical majesty as Basil's sermons on the six days of creation. One could almost use it as a textbook of pulpit eloquence. Let us note very briefly one of the more outstanding features of Theodoret's oratory.

Theodoret understood very well that variety is the spice of preaching, just as it is the spice of life; therefore, he used a variety of rhetorical figures. Especially noticeable is his variety of sentence structure, which would be especially important in his oral delivery. It seems a bit contrived in written form, but again we maintain that these were true sermons, actually preached to a congregation. This variety of sentence structure gives rhythm and flow to the spoken word, the importance of which Greek orators understood thoroughly. In the first sermon Theodoret speaks of how the providence of God is to be observed in nature. We notice the variety of his sentence structure.

> 32. Now that you have seen the utility of sun and moon, the regular successions of night and day, and the benefits that accrue to men from them, consider next the very delightful and beneficial succession of the seasons of the year. The Creator did not just divide the circle of the year into two, giving us winter and summer simply. We do not go from one extreme to another without any intermediate stage. Instead, spring and autumn afford us a mean temperature between the icy cold and the burning heat.
>
> 33. An excessively wet, cold winter does not succeed a very dry, warm summer, but spring, which participates in the heat of one and the cold of the other, effects the best mixture of the extremes and taking in hand, so to speak, these contrary elements — the cold of winter and the heat of

---

185. Theodoret, *On Divine Providence* 9.
186. Theodoret, *On Divine Providence* 10.

summer — brings complete enemies into friendly agreement. As a result, our transition from winter to summer is made without difficulty. In a short time we get away from the cold of winter and approach the heat of summer without experiencing any injury from the rapid transition.

34. Likewise in changing from summer to winter, autumn intervenes to prevent us from reaching the extreme of winter all at once and also to temper the extremes of heat and cold, providing another mean temperature and conducting us to this extreme by easy stages. Such is the care of the Creator for us. And thus He makes the changes of the seasons pleasant as well as endurable for us.

35. But perhaps some ungrateful creature will rise to criticize these excellent provisions and blame this wise, beneficent economy in these terms: Why, pray, these changes at all? What use to us are those changes of season? I ask you, my smart, clever critic of providence, what blessings come to us without the seasons?

36. For at the beginning of winter we sow the seeds. He who taught us how to do so nourishes them, raining on them from the clouds, drawing up sea water by His word, carrying it aloft and gently changing its briny nature, distilling it, and letting it down at one time in small drops and at another in a downpour of big drops as if He were separating these products of the clouds with a sieve. Accordingly the season of winter exists to provide you, you wretch, with nourishment, and to supply you, you ungrateful creature, with your needs.

37. When spring comes round again, some of the farmers cut the vines, others plant new ones, and the shoots that are burst by the heat of the atmosphere are forced to put forth their buds. At the peak of summer, when the sun causes a steep rise in temperature, the wheat calls the farmer to reaping, grapes turn black, olives in full bloom ripen as do the various kinds of fruit. Then the harvest comes and offers these in full maturity to the harvesters. And they, as soon as the harvest is done, prepare once more for the sowing.

Stop being ungrateful, then, stop using His gifts in an attempt to slander providence, stop throwing back His gifts in His face. Recognize in all that has been said the providence of God directing and governing you, and ensuring for you an abundance of every blessing.[187]

This passage begins with a number of declaratory sentences. After the transitional sentence we find two declaratory sentences expressed nega-

187. Theodoret, *On Divine Providence* 1.32-37.

tively. "The Creator did not just divide the circle of the year into two, giving us winter and summer simply. We do not go from one extreme to another without any intermediate stage." This is followed by a third declaratory sentence put positively, "Instead, spring and autumn afford us a mean temperature between icy cold and the burning heat." The next paragraph begins with a long compound sentence joined with an adversative conjunction. This is followed by a sentence introduced by an adverbial phrase expressing result and then another simple declarative sentence. A bit further on the rhythm of the speaker is again varied by three interrogative sentences, "Why, pray, these changes at all? What use to us are those changes of season? I ask you, my smart, clever critic of providence, what blessings come to us without the seasons?" Once more we have a simple declarative sentence. Then there is a long sentence filled with participial phrases. "For at the beginning of winter we sow the seeds. He who taught us how to do so nourishes them, raining on them from the clouds, drawing up sea water by His word, carrying it aloft and gently changing its briny nature, distilling it, and letting it down at one time in small drops and at another in a downpour of big drops. . . ." Theodoret's sentence structure is never monotonous! A bit further on we find the passage brought to a dramatic conclusion by a series of imperatives. "Stop being ungrateful," then, "stop using His gifts in an attempt to slander providence, stop throwing back His gifts in His face." These staccato negative imperatives are finally resolved in a positive imperative which summarizes the point of the whole sermon. "Recognize in all that has been said the providence of God directing and governing you, and ensuring for you an abundance of every blessing." The rich variety of Theodoret's syntax only reflects the rich insights of the sermon itself.

Theodoret is a master of parallelism. We find a number of skillfully constructed sentences which convey a great deal of information rapidly and easily because of their parallel structure. In the ninth discourse, for example:

> Yet though the potter and the clay are of the same nature one does not find the same function in each. The one moves, the other is moved; one fashions, the other is fashioned; one mixes, the other is mixed; one shapes, the other takes shape, and the potter changes its shape whatever way he wishes. If, when the nature is the same, the function is different, there will be a greater difference still in function when the natures are different. For it is impossible to compare things that are incomparable.

How then could you compare what is created from nothing with what existed from all eternity? Or the temporal with the eternal? Or what is made of clay with the Creator of heaven and earth?[188]

A bit further on in the same sermon we find another striking bit of parallelism:

Nevertheless, this useless, insignificant, inanimate matter that lacks a spirit and is altogether devoid of sensibility becomes man at the will of God, and, despite its uniformity, assumes many forms, some tough and durable, others soft and supple, others loose and porous, others compact and dense, others stout and smooth, others slender, reticular, and fibrous, others tubular and porous, others solid and without any pores.[189]

Sentences like this, of course, also add to the variety of our preacher's sentence structure.

In the eighth discourse we find our preacher giving variety to his rather philosophical sermons by reciting at length several biblical illustrations. God's providence is illustrated by the story of Joseph, who was sold as a slave into Egypt by his brothers that years later he might provide for the whole family during the seven-year famine. The story is told with so much imaginative detail that it takes up something like half the sermon. In the ninth discourse our preacher introduces two highly imaginative monologues: one dealing with what the soul might say to the divine judge if it alone were punished at the Last Judgment, the other of what the body might say in the same circumstance. Given the usual sobriety of patristic preaching, these two monologues might almost be considered humorous. This rather unusual rhetorical device is one more indication of Theodoret's appreciation of the importance of variety in the pulpit.

Finally we need to say something about Theodoret's theology of worship. No doubt Theodoret would follow along with most of the ideas which the older Antiochene theologians had expressed. There is, however, a most interesting passage in one of these sermons which expresses a very different theology of worship — a theology of worship influenced by Stoicism. This is especially remarkable when one considers that so many

188. Theodoret, *On Divine Providence* 9.34.
189. Theodoret, *On Divine Providence* 9.40.

of the Greek Fathers were much more influenced by Neoplatonism when it came to worship, particularly those who followed closely in the train of Origen. Others, like Cyril of Jerusalem, were swayed by the Hellenistic mystery religions. This is not to say that biblical concepts of worship were absent. In some of the Fathers they came through quite strong, notably in the Antiochene Fathers, as we have maintained. Yet, it is still the case that Neoplatonism had a marked influence on the way fourth- and fifth-century Christians understood their worship. The Stoic approach to worship, however, is not found as often — Clement of Alexandria comes to mind here, and one finds it in Lactantius among the Latin Fathers. This is surprising because there is much in the Stoic approach to worship which has a close affinity to some of the biblical approaches.

Theodoret's seventh discourse begins with a passage obviously influenced by Stoicism:

> The Creator of the universe does not need mortal tongue to chorus His praise. Nor does He listen to the chant of angels as though He needed it; but when He sees creatures well disposed He treats them with indulgence. When people made their customary offerings to God they did so, of course, not as if they fulfilled some need on God's part, but in thanksgiving for countless benefits received.[190]

This is very similar to the sort of thing we find in the prophets,[191] or with considerable ardor in Psalm 50. What is of special interest for us is how Theodoret relates this to preaching. In our preaching we offer "our worthless sermons," not in the hope of adding to the depths of wisdom with our tiny drop of truth, but in an attempt to show how thankful we should be. This thankfulness, moreover, is expressed in obedience to God.[192] Preaching, for Theodoret, is an act of praise and thanksgiving on the part of the preacher which kindles the praise and thanksgiving of the congregation.[193] As Theodoret presents this idea, especially in the context

190. Theodoret, *On Divine Providence* 7.1.
191. On specific passages of the prophets which voice similar ideas, see my article, "John Calvin and the Prophetic Criticism of Worship," in *John Calvin and the Church: A Prism of Reform*, ed. Timothy George (Louisville: Westminster/John Knox, 1990), pp. 230-46.
192. Theodoret, *On Divine Providence* 7.2.
193. Theodoret, *On Divine Providence* 8.59.

of this series of sermons, the Stoic ring is easily detected, but it would be hard to argue that it could not just as easily come from the Old Testament prophets or the Psalms. The fact that Theodoret had published commentaries on all the prophets would surely indicate that the prophetic doxology could easily have gotten through to him.

One could follow out at considerable length this theme of a Christian theology of worship which has such similarities to Stoic philosophy on one hand and to the liturgical theology of the prophets on the other.[194] We will have more to say on this subject further on.

194. On the relation of Stoicism to the prophetic theology of worship, see my *Themes and Variations,* pp. 97-100.

CHAPTER IV

The Syriac Church

The worship of the Syriac church helps us see the worship of the Greek and Latin Churches in a certain cultural perspective. The Syriac-speaking church thrived in a group of Semitic cities at the edge of the Roman Empire, a Roman Empire which had taken up into itself the culture of ancient Greece in all its many dimensions and held sway over a number of provinces where different Eastern civilizations had flourished. At one time or another Rome ruled over the ruins of Greece, Egypt, Babylon, and Assyria. Already before the coming of the Romans, the Hellenistic world had absorbed much that was Oriental. By the time Christianity began Antioch had become one of the centers of Hellenistic civilization. In Antioch Greek was the predominant language; in fact, Antioch was a sort of Greek colony in Syria, a center for the dissemination of Greek culture. In western Syria, along the Mediterranean coast, many Syrians adopted Greek ways and Greek was widely spoken, but Eastern Syria was another matter. It was old Syria, the heartland of Semitic culture, where Syriac was still the predominant language. Although the Roman province of Syria was a blend of the Greek and the Oriental, eastern Syria remained quite remote from the culture of the Hellenized cities of the West.

Ever since the fourth century before Christ, the Seleucid empire with its capital at Antioch not only spread the culture of Alexander the Great in the East but brought the culture of the East to the West. By the fourth century after Christ the Roman Empire had absorbed much that we call Oriental, and when the Church moved from Jerusalem to Rome it was hardly beating a new path, as Rome was already filled with Oriental cults.

Rome took on many of the ways of the East, but things went in the other direction, too. Christianity particularly adopted the ways of Greece and Rome, and yet the Westernizing of Christianity in those early years has always raised the question of what Christianity would have been like if it had not been Westernized. The Syriac church gives us some ideas.[1] It was a Christian church which remained in the East. The worship of the Syriac-speaking church retained certain features and developed certain tendencies which to a large extent disappeared in the churches of the West.

It is in the Acts of the Apostles that we first hear of the Church in Syria. Already when Saul had his Damascus road experience, there were disciples of Christ in Damascus. It was to rid the Damascus synagogue of these disciples that Saul was going to that Syrian city. From Acts we also learn of a strong Christian church at Antioch. These were Syrian churches but probably not Syriac-speaking churches, for the Syriac-speaking church was in eastern Syria between the Tigris and Euphrates Rivers, the center of the old Assyrian empire. The ancient kingdom of Edessa, right in the middle of this area, was one of the first countries of the ancient world to embrace Christianity. Here was a kingdom which had an independent existence but from an early date had allied itself with Rome as a defense from the encroachments of the Persians. There was an old tradition that the king of Edessa had corresponded with Jesus, a tradition which probably bore witness to the venerable and ancient origins of the Syriac church.

The Syriac-speaking church was probably never very large, at least not compared to the Greek-speaking church or the Latin-speaking church. It embraced the churches of Edessa, Nisibis, Sarug, Mabbug, and perhaps a dozen other cities. In time, one branch of the Syriac church, the Nestorians, did extensive missionary work in Persia, central Asia, and China. In India a Syriac church was established in the second or third century, and even today maintains its existence. Yet even at that the Syriac-speaking church never embraced the great variety of tribes and nations that the Latin or Greek Church did. One is surprised, however, at what a tremendous amount of literature it produced. In fact, the sheer mass of the

---

1. The Syriac church preserved, as R. Draguet puts it, "a Christianity of a special type, still not subject to Greek influence." "Syriac Language and Literature," *New Catholic Encyclopaedia*, 17 vols. (Washington, D.C.: Catholic University of America Press, 1967), 13:395. For more general information on Syriac language and literature, cf. Norman M'Lean, *Encyclopaedia Britannica*, 11th ed., (New York: Encyclopedia Britannica, Inc., 1910-11), 26:309-17.

material has made the task of publishing it, let alone translating it, seem insurmountable. Evidently there are thousands of Syriac manuscripts catalogued in various libraries which have never been studied.

In this chapter we will look at three Syriac preachers. We are somewhat limited in our selection because of what has been published. Nevertheless, with the material which has been available for our study we can demonstrate something of the range of Syriac preaching. First we will look at Ephrem's *Hymns on Paradise,* one of the classics of Syriac literature, a perfect example of what homiletical poetry can be. Then we will study a Christmas sermon of Narsai to get an idea of Syriac festal preaching. Finally for an example of catechetical preaching we will look at the spiritual catechisms of Philoxenus of Mabbug.

I. Ephrem of Nisibis

Ephrem (306-73) was the Shakespeare of Syriac literature, the incomparable poet of the language, but unlike Shakespeare, he was a saint, and even a theologian. Among the preachers of the Christian Church Ephrem ranks as one of the poets; he preached in poetry, in poetic stanzas and metrical lines. This homiletical poetry is usually divided up into two distinct types, *madrashe* and *memre.* One might say that the *madrashe* is a homiletical hymn. The poet-preacher chants a stanza and the congregation responds with a refrain or antiphon. The *memre,* on the other hand, has less the character of a hymn and more the character of a discourse. It is not divided into stanzas and there is no refrain. If the *madrashe* is a homiletical hymn, the *memre* is a hymnic sermon. In both cases these literary forms served as sermons, yet in different ways they added the dimension of poetry. This sermonic poetry has been treasured by the Syriac-speaking church for centuries.

When Ephrem was born in Nisibis, that thoroughly Oriental city was within the borders of the Roman Empire.[2] The Empire was still pagan, but within a few years Constantine would establish the Christian Church

---

2. For biographical information on Ephrem, see Anton Baumstark, *Geschichte der syrischen Literatur* (Bonn: A. Marcus und E. Weber, 1922), pp. 31-52; E. Beck, "Ephrem of Nisibus," *Dictionnaire de la Spiritualité* (Paris: Beauchesne, 1937-90), vol. 4, cols. 788-800; Kathleen McVey, *Ephrem the Syrian: Hymns* (New York and Mahwah, N.J.: Paulist Press, 1989), pp. 3-28; Arthur Vööbus, *Literary, Critical, and Historical Studies in Ephrem the Syrian* (Stockholm: ETSE, 1958).

as the official religion of the state, an event Ephrem would have witnessed. He may have been a Syrian and a Semite, but he was devoted to the new Christian empire. A story is told that he attended the Council of Nicaea as the assistant of his bishop, and another that he had met Gregory of Nazianzus and that the two of them were devoted friends, but both stories are probably apocryphal. However, they do indicate that while Ephrem may have lived on the far eastern borders of the Roman Empire, he was in no way out of touch with what was happening in the heart of the new and Christian Roman Empire.

Early in his life Ephrem became the disciple of James, the bishop of Nisibis. He was his student and then his assistant and, in time, was ordained a deacon, a position he held the rest of his life, probably because he was so devoted to the music of the church, which was a peculiarly diaconal concern. Even in these early years in Nisibis he won a reputation as a teacher in the school of Nisibis. This theological academy was particularly remarkable, but it was not the only theological school in Nisibis. There was a rabbinical school as well, which evidently served as a challenge to Christian theological thought and led to the most vigorous sort of exegetical reflection.

Ephrem was a mature man in 346 when Bishop James died and was succeeded by Bishop Vologeses, who was highly respected for his blend of culture and asceticism. Under his pastoral care the ministry of Ephrem flourished. Ephrem must have preached frequently for the number of sermons which has come down to us from this period is considerable. Ephrem was in his mid-fifties when Julian the Apostate came to the throne of his uncle, Constantine the Great, and to the embarrassment of Christians all over the Empire rejected the Christian faith of his predecessors and tried to revive the old Greco-Roman religion. In Syria he encouraged the Oriental cults and publicly offered worship in pagan temples as he marched through the country on a campaign to recover the territory the Persian emperor Shapur II had wrested from Rome. One day Ephrem watched the Apostate lead his army past Nisibis to engage the Persian forces, and only a few weeks later, after the Apostate's campaign had been disastrously defeated, Ephrem watched the funeral cortege of the emperor he so despised pass by Nisibis on the return. The ignominious defeat of the apostate emperor had dire consequences for the Christians of Nisibis, however. The Roman Empire lost the city, and its new emperor, Shapur II of Persia, was even more hostile to the Christian Church than Julian had been. The whole Christian community of Nisibis was exiled and, quite naturally, turned to Edessa, a Syriac-speaking city still safely within the Roman Empire, for refuge. Barses, the bishop of Edessa, received the refugees kindly and encouraged Ephrem to reconstitute the school of Nisibis in Edessa. It is not clear whether Edessa already had a school at this time. What is clear is that Ephrem brought the school to great renown. Like his younger contemporary Diodore of Tarsus, Ephrem had little love for the Alexandrian school of exegesis and cultivated a grammatical-historical interpretation of Scripture at the school. Another ministry Ephrem cultivated in Edessa was liturgical music. According to Kathleen McVey, Ephrem trained a choir of women which provided music for the services of worship. Our preacher was obviously a man of varied talents. He not only wrote hymns; he trained a choir to sing them as well.

Ephrem was a devoted ascetic. In fact, all the leaders of the Syriac church during this period were ascetics. It is one of the most difficult aspects of their religious expression for us to understand, but it was of the essence of their piety. This asceticism, however, seemed to be not the least bit embarrassed about the cultivation of good literature. Whether Ephrem lived in a monastic community is not at all clear. Apparently he preached for the cathedral church rather than in a monastery or school chapel, and we have no hint that he went into the wilderness; in fact, all indications would suggest that he participated fully in the life of the Christian community of Edessa. It was during an epidemic that Ephrem, himself once again exercising his diaconal ministry by caring for the sick, fell victim to the pest and died.

A. Ephrem as Biblical Scholar

In our day we find Ephrem of interest because of his poetry, but in his own day he was esteemed primarily because of his biblical studies. Ephrem's commentaries were highly prized. They were translated into several other languages, with Greek translations appearing already in his own lifetime. A number of fourth-century Western theologians such as Theodoret of Cyrus seem to have been familiar with his work. Ephrem's commentary on the Gospels claims our attention because it treats the text as it was found in Tatian's *Diatessaron,* an arrangement and harmonizing of the four Gospels into a single narrative which was commonly accepted in the Syriac church instead of the four separate Gospels. In addition Ephrem did commentaries on Acts and the Pauline Epistles. He originally produced a number of Old Testament commentaries, but only those on Genesis and Exodus have survived in the original Syriac. Some of these commentaries have come down to us in the form of long series of sermons on particular books of the Bible. Apparently, not all of Ephrem's sermons were in poetry. Even at that, the sermons which have been edited into formal commentaries surely reflect his normal preaching and teaching both at Nisibis and Edessa.

One should not imagine that Ephrem's approach to the study of Scripture was simply a reflection of the School of Antioch. Diodore of Tarsus was a younger contemporary of Ephrem and, of course, his two students John Chrysostom and Theodore of Mopsuestia were even younger still, John being forty years Ephrem's junior. Thus, Ephrem's approach was not simply borrowed from Antioch but quite original. Surely his Christian interpretation of the Old Testament reflected the polemic between the rabbinical school at Nisibis and Ephrem's own school. This rabbinical thought must have been quite different from the thought of Alexandrian Judaism, as Babylon and Alexandria were at opposite ends of the Jewish intellectual world. Just as Origen, Ephrem was in constant contact with the synagogue, but the synagogue with which Ephrem was in contact was no doubt quite different.

While one does find typology in Ephrem's understanding of Scripture, one does not find allegory. Ephrem was not faced with the problem of reconciling the biblical worldview with the Greek worldview in the way that Origen and the Alexandrian Jews were. Ephrem understands Scripture by living within the biblical world — he does not have to translate. This, of course, is always the best way of understanding Scripture, no matter what culture one lives within or what language one speaks on the street. Ephrem understands Scripture naturally and simply. This is not to say that there were not foreign elements which Ephrem had to face. He gave generous attention to the refutation of the heretics of the day, the Manichaeans and several types of Gnostics. As a Semite who lived in a largely Semitic world, the biblical worldview made sense to him. It was not that there were no other ways of looking at things around him, nor was he unfamiliar with anything else; it was more that he devoted himself to looking at things from inside the biblical world. Perhaps it came more easily for Ephrem, living as he did in the Semitic homeland. No doubt, more importantly, it was because he chose to look at things that way.

B. The *Hymns on Paradise*

The most remarkable series of sermons which has come down to us from Ephrem is the *Hymns on Paradise.*[3] Comprising fifteen *madrashe*, or metrical sermons, the series treats the account of the creation of Adam and Eve in the Garden of Eden. As with Milton's *Paradise Lost* and *Paradise Regained*, the series tells us of the purpose of human life as we move from the paradise in which we were created to the paradise for which we were created. The means the preacher intends to use are set forth in the first three stanzas:

> 1. Moses, who instructs all men
>   with his celestial writings,
>   He the master of the Hebrews,
>   has instructed us in his teaching —
>   the Law, which constitutes
>   a very treasure house of revelations,
>   wherein is revealed
>   the tale of the Garden —
>   described by things visible,
>   but glorious for what lies hidden,
>   spoken of in few words,
>   yet wondrous with its many plants.

> Response: Praise to Your righteousness
>   which exalts those who prove victorious.

> 2. I took my stand halfway
>   between awe and love;
>   a yearning for Paradise
>   invited me to explore it,
>   but awe at its majesty

---

3. This study is based on the Sources chrétiennes edition of the *Hymns on Paradise:* Ephrem of Nisibis, *Hymnes sur le Paradis*, translated from Syriac to French by René Lavenant, introduction and notes by François Graffin, Sources chrétiennes, vol. 137 (Paris: Éditions du Cerf, 1968). English translations are quoted from Ephrem the Syrian, *Hymns on Paradise*, trans. Sebastian Brock (Crestwood, N.Y.: St. Vladimir's Seminary Press, 1990); hereinafter Ephrem, *Hymns on Paradise*.

restrained me from my search.
With wisdom, however,
   I reconciled the two;
I revered what lay hidden
   and meditated on what was revealed.
The aim of my search was to gain profit,
   the aim of my silence was to find succor.

3. Joyfully did I embark
   on the tale of Paradise —
a tale that is short to read
   but rich to explore.
My tongue read the story's
   outward narrative,
while my intellect took wing
   and soared upward in awe
as it perceived the splendor of Paradise —
   not indeed as it really is,
but insofar as humanity
   is granted to comprehend it.[4]

The story as it is found in Scripture and as it has been interpreted by God's people ever since is quite transparent. The beginning, the source of our existence, is intended to be an intimation of our destiny. Where we have been is a hint about where we are going.

    Once we fully understand the purpose of these sermons we understand why they are poetry. The whole purpose of poetry is to intimate more than is said, and it is quite clear that Ephrem understands very well that this is what needs to be done when one is talking about a subject like this. Poetry must always have a certain reserve, one might almost say, a certain modesty. Ephrem tells us again and again of the impossibility of describing explicitly the eternal realities:

7. The tongue cannot relate
   the description of innermost Paradise,
nor indeed does it suffice
   for the beauties of the outer part;

4. Ephrem, *Hymns on Paradise* 1.1-3.

for even the simple adornments
    by the Garden's fence
cannot be related
    in an adequate way.
For the colors of Paradise are full of joy,
    its scents most wonderful,
its beauties most desirable,
    and its delicacies glorious.

8. Even though the treasure
    that adjoins the fence is lowly,
yet it surpasses all other treasures
    in the world entire;
and by as much as the slopes, too,
    are lowly in comparison
with that treasury
    of the summit on high,
so the blessed state by the fence
    is more glorious and exalted
than all that we experience as blessed,
    who live in the valley below.[5]

As we shall see a bit further on, it all has to do with the outward meaning and the inward meaning, the literal sense and the spiritual sense of Scripture.

C. Ephrem's Doctrine of Scripture

The vitality of Ephrem's approach to Scripture is remarkable. Even in the patristic period when the Church was so obviously animated by Scripture, Ephrem's perception of biblical inspiration demands our attention. Since the purpose of these volumes is to discover what the reading and preaching of Scripture is really all about, we will want to look at what Ephrem has to say because his exercise of the ministry of the Word has some rather unique aspects. One is tempted to suggest that Ephrem's devotion to Scripture has some sort of ethnic basis, or that it springs naturally from

5. Ephrem, *Hymns on Paradise* 1.7-8.

255

the Semitic languages. Ephrem, after all, preached in the same language, or almost the same language, as Jesus did.[6] It is probably better to recognize the biblical character of Syriac worship as something which is profoundly Christian and transcends the effects of ethnic culture. Be that as it may, the Bible and the study of the Bible play a central role in the worship of the Syriac church.[7] Ephrem takes it for granted that the worshiper comes to church to be taught the Word of life:

25. With love and instruction,
     commingled with truth,
   the intellect can grow
     and become rich with new things,
   as it meditates with discernment
     on the treasure store of hidden mysteries.
   For my part, I have loved, and so learned,
     and become assured
   that Paradise possesses
     the haven of the victorious.
   As I have been held worthy to perceive it,
     so make me worthy to enter it![8]

One gathers from these lines that the worship assembly is not only a fellowship of love but also a fellowship of truth. In worship the congregation "meditates with discernment / on the treasure store of hidden mysteries." Both in the sermon and in the sacraments meditation is an essential element to worship.

28. Who has ever beheld gatherings of people
     whose sustenance is the giving of praise?
   Their raiment is light,
     their countenance full of radiance;
   as they ruminate
     on the abundance of his gift

---

6. A century ago there was quite a bit of excitement about this, but more recently one has distinguished between Aramaic and Syriac. Cf. Norman M'Lean, *Encyclopaedia Britannica*, 26:309-17, and R. Draguet, *New Catholic Encyclopaedia*, 13:395-97.

7. Ephrem, *Hymns on Paradise* 6.1-2.

8. Ephrem, *Hymns on Paradise* 6.25.

there burst forth from their mouths
    springs of wisdom;
tranquility reigns over their thought,
    truth over their knowledge,
reverence over their enquiry,
    and love over their offering of praise.[9]

That praise gives us spiritual "sustenance" is no doubt understood to be the case because the psalmody and hymnody of the Syriac church has so much teaching in it. The radiance of those gathered for worship is explained by their "ruminating" on the reading and preaching of the Scriptures. The congregation is a conclave of "wisdom." Here once more is expressed the Wisdom doxology of the patristic age, of which we have often spoken. In the ministry of the Word as well as in the prayers and hymns wisdom flows into the lives of the faithful. The reading and preaching of Scripture have a central role in worship because it is in Scripture that God reveals his love to us. This is something we are incapable of understanding on our own. But God is gracious and because of his love for us he wants us to understand; therefore, he speaks to us in our language. Ephrem has a strong sense of the necessity of revelation. We could never understand about God if God did not take the initiative to reveal himself to us.[10] For Ephrem there is clearly a revelation in nature.[11] The art of the creation reveals the artist, and yet it is a secondary way of knowing God. It is completely dependent on God's self-revelation in Scripture, which is confirmed by the revelation of God in nature. Nature is filled with parallels and examples which support the truths we find in the Bible.[12]

One of the most obvious features of Ephrem's doctrine of Scripture is that it moves from promise to fulfillment.[13] Scripture is to be understood covenantally; it is the book of the covenant, the book of the Old Covenant and the New Covenant. To understand Scripture is to see this movement from the promise of redemption made to the patriarchs all the way to its fulfillment in Christ. In Ephrem's *Hymns on Paradise* the movement from the paradise of the Garden of Eden to the transcendent paradise of heaven

9. Ephrem, *Hymns on Paradise* 6.28.
10. Ephrem, *Hymns on Paradise* 1.1-3 and 17.
11. Ephrem, *Hymns on Paradise* 5.2 and 6.1.
12. Ephrem, *Hymns on Paradise* 5.1-2.
13. Ephrem, *Hymns on Paradise* 14 passim.

is the central theme of the whole series. The paradise that is lost is a picture and premonition of that which is to come,[14] and in the same way the paradise that is above explains and justifies the paradise below. The one is understood by the other. Also, the types which appear throughout the whole history of redemption keep reminding us of the promise. They are hints and premonitions of the fulfillment of the promise. They keep reminding us that the covenant is eternal and that the God who gave the covenant is faithful to the covenant. First the Tabernacle and then the Temple are types of the heavenly dwelling, reminding us of the place being prepared for us. The ascent of Mount Sinai and descent of the Holy Spirit on the Day of Pentecost both beckon the faithful toward the promised land.

An important insight into the nature of worship which one finds in Ephrem is that the study, reading, and preaching of Scripture brings us into the presence of God.[15] In Scripture one is confronted with God. We see in the *Hymns on Paradise* how the reading of the story of Eden becomes a personal encounter with paradise. Ephrem picks up the book of Genesis and as he begins to read he trembles with joy. The lines and verses of the text open their arms to him. The very words kiss him and lead him into the center of the mystery of Scripture, which is paradise itself:

> 3. I read the opening of this book
>   and was filled with joy,
>   for its verses and lines
>   spread out their arms to welcome me;
>   the first rushed out and kissed me,
>   and led me on to its companion;
>   and when I reached that verse
>   wherein is written
>   the story of Paradise,
>   it lifted me up and transported me
>   from the bosom of the book
>   to the very bosom of Paradise.[16]

The doctrine of verbal inspiration is tame compared to this. The Enlightenment could never go along with anything like this. What is being

14. Ephrem, *Hymns on Paradise* 15.17.
15. Ephrem, *Hymns on Paradise* 6.2.
16. Ephrem, *Hymns on Paradise* 5.3.

affirmed here is the vitality of the Word. In our previous volume, in regard to I Peter 1:23-25, we spoke of the ability of the Word to reach out to us even above and beyond the ability of the preacher. It is of the very nature of God's Word that it reaches out to us. The Word of God is neither static nor passive; it is a revealing Word, a Word of power, a Word of life. Ephrem in the same sermon goes on to tell us that his eyes and his spirit pass over the lines as though they were a bridge. The eyes have their work and the spirit has its work, and together they arrive at Eden, whereupon the eyes repose and the spirit toils.[17] Finding paradise, one enters the inner meaning. In order to find paradise one must pass over the bridge which is Holy Scripture and enter through the gate, which likewise is Holy Scripture. Even if the eyes remain outside, the spirit penetrates the intimate and interior meaning of Scripture.[18] This is not, of course, the imagery contemporary theologians commonly use to speak about it, but they nonetheless have been talking about this. Particularly modern theologians influenced by existentialism have been concerned to draw a distinction between the idea that Scripture reveals certain concepts and that in the experience of revelation we are confronted by God's Word. It is a helpful distinction to make, but one must be careful not to drive a wedge between the two. Sound doctrine is surely a means to a truly profound communion.

This brings us to the whole matter of the literal interpretation of Scripture and the spiritual interpretation of Scripture. In one way or another, all the way through the history of the Church, it has been affirmed that there is an outward meaning to Scripture and an inward meaning of Scripture. This is one of the loci of the classical doctrine of Scripture. To be sure, this theme is developed in one way by Origen in his *De Principiis* and in quite a different way by Augustine in his *De Spiritu et littera*. And one finds the basic idea just as clearly in the Reformers as in the Fathers. The Reformers were worried about affirming the perspicuity of Scripture and shied away from allegorical interpretations, and yet they recognized well-established Christian interpretations of certain passages of the Old Testament, certain psalms, the Song of Solomon, and much else. They carefully studied rhetoric and recognized the use of tropes and figures. Ephrem's doctrine has its own particular stripe, but he clearly is getting at the same thing.

To interpret Scripture spiritually is to enter into genuine worship, according to Ephrem. It is to stand before the presence of God in awe and

17. Ephrem, *Hymns on Paradise* 5.4.
18. Ephrem, *Hymns on Paradise* 5.5.

wonder and, hearing his Word, to be transformed by that Word in the image of the Son of God. The spiritual interpretation is something which is experienced. It is to experience both justification and sanctification. The spiritual interpretation is the experiencing of that about which Scripture speaks. In the *Hymns on Paradise* we find a magnificent elaboration of this idea. Ephrem presents the winds of the Garden of Eden as a figure of the Holy Spirit, and it is these winds which nourish the Garden and all that is in it.

7. Scented breezes blow
          with varied force;
    like Martha and Mary,
          they hasten with delicate foods,
    for the guests at this banquet
          never have to depart at all.
    Weary Martha
          made so bold
    as to complain to Him
          who invites us to His Paradise
    where those who minister
          never weary in their service.

8. The breezes of Paradise
          hasten to attend to the just:
    one blows satiety,
          another quenches the thirst;
    this one is laden with goodness,
          that one with all that is rich.
    Who has ever beheld breezes
          acting as waiters,
    some offering foods,
          others diverse drinks,
    one breathing dew,
          another fragrant scents?

9. In a spiritual way do these breezes
          suckle spiritual beings:
    this is a feast where no hand labors
          or ever grows tired;

the teeth do not weary,
    the stomach never grows heavy.
Who has ever reclined and enjoyed himself
    without anyone slaving away?
Who has eaten to satisfaction without any food,
    or drunk and become merry without any drink?[19]

We gather from this that these breezes are what Reformed theology speaks of as the inner testimony of the Holy Spirit. It is the inner testimony of the Holy Spirit which makes the outward word the inward word. These breezes of the Spirit are the Mary and Martha of the wedding feast of the Lamb, the waitresses of the spiritual banquet who bring us the bread of life. Without the Holy Spirit there is no feasting on the Word, no *manducatio spiritualis*. It is in our being justified and our being sanctified that we interpret Scripture spiritually.

    It is the breath of the Spirit which makes Scripture alive; it is also the breath of the Spirit which makes the Church alive. Breath, breeze, wind, spirit — they are all the same. Just as on the Day of Pentecost the Church was enlivened by a mighty wind, so Eden was vivified by the cool breezes of the evening.[20] The different winds bring different blessings — one brings food, another drink, another the refreshing dew, and still another the perfumed ointment.[21] These breaths of air nourish the breath of life in each of us, feeding, refreshing, and strengthening our spirits. They provide spiritual food.[22] The perfumed breezes of paradise perform the function of bread, and the breath of life the office of a drink. By their delights they revive the senses, that they might rejoice in the presence of God:

17. Instead of bread, it is the very fragrance of Paradise
      that gives nourishment;
  instead of liquid,
      this life-giving breeze does service:
  the senses delight
      in its luxuriant waves

19. Ephrem, *Hymns on Paradise* 9.7-9.
20. Ephrem, *Hymns on Paradise* 11.14.
21. Ephrem, *Hymns on Paradise* 9.8.
22. Ephrem, *Hymns on Paradise* 9.9.

which surge up
    in endless variety,
with joyous intensity.
    Being unburdened,
the senses stand in awe and delight
    before the divine Majesty.[23]

Even more the human spirit hungers and the Holy Spirit provides the appropriate food, and to understand Scripture spiritually is to feed upon this food.[24] All this is to the end that the creature be renewed after the image of the Creator.[25] This renewal takes place in worship, in the celebration of the sacraments, in prayer and praise, in the reading and preaching of the Word. To read and discern, to discern and to be moved with devotion, that is worship.

As with many of the preachers of the patristic age, Ephrem's theology of preaching is closely related to the Wisdom theology of the period. The Christian is nourished by the divine Wisdom.[26] Through the disciplines of the Christian life we purify our spiritual eyes so that we can behold the truth. In the reading and preaching of Scripture we open our ears to the truth. It is as one opens one's ears that one is able to embrace the Wisdom of God:

26. Accordingly as each here on earth
        purifies his eye for Him,
    so does he become more able to behold
        His incomparable glory;
    accordingly as each here on earth
        opens his ear to Him,
    so does he become more able to grasp
        His wisdom;
    accordingly as each here on earth
        prepares a receptacle for Him,
    so is he enabled to carry
        a small portion of His riches.[27]

23. Ephrem, *Hymns on Paradise* 9.17.
24. Ephrem, *Hymns on Paradise* 9.18-20.
25. Ephrem, *Hymns on Paradise* 9.20.
26. Ephrem, *Hymns on Paradise* 9.23.
27. Ephrem, *Hymns on Paradise* 9.26.

One obviously participates in worship to receive wisdom. It is for this reason that the Syriac church gave so much time to such ample readings of Scripture. As we shall see, the Syriac lectionaries provided long lessons from the Law and the Prophets and the Epistles and Gospels. Here is a church which cultivated expository preaching, as we can tell from the commentaries which survived. And biblical Wisdom theology is behind it all.

In a way similar to John Chrysostom, Ephrem speaks of the divine condescension. God provides spiritual food without measure to his people, and yet he measures it out to us according to our need. He adopts the vision of his glory to our eyes, his voice to our ears, his benediction to our hunger, and his knowledge to our language.

27. The Lord who is beyond measure
    measures out nourishment to all,
adapting to our eyes the sight of Himself,
    to our hearing His voice,
His blessing to our appetite,
    His wisdom to our tongue.
At His gift
    blessings swarm,
for this is always new in its savor,
    wonderfully fragrant,
adaptable in its strength,
    resplendent in its colors.

28. Who has ever beheld gatherings of people
    whose sustenance is the giving of praise?
Their raiment is light,
    their countenance full of radiance;
as they ruminate
    on the abundance of His gift
there burst forth from their mouths
    springs of wisdom;
tranquility reigns over their thought,
    truth over their knowledge,
reverence over their enquiry,
    and love over their offering of praise.[28]

28. Ephrem, *Hymns on Paradise* 9.27-28.

Characteristic of Christian Wisdom theology, Ephrem's *Hymns on Paradise* exhibits a strong continuity between the Word of God written and the Word of God incarnate in Jesus Christ.[29] Ephrem does not drive a hard-and-fast distinction between the two, as contemporary theologians are wont to do, and one is never too sure in reading a text if the terms he uses for the divine Wisdom refer to Christ, to Scripture, or to the proclamation of the gospel.[30] It may well be that Ephrem intends to think of all these senses — poets have a way of doing this sort of thing. Besides, this is of the essence of Christian Wisdom theology. The striking thing about the dictum "In the beginning was the Word and the Word was with God and the Word was God" is that it ties the doctrine of the incarnation and the doctrine of revelation closely together. The doctrine of the Trinity is a theology of revelation.

D. Homiletical Poetry

The fact that a substantial number of Syriac preachers delivered their sermons in poetry invites us to stop for a moment and think about what homiletical poetry might, in fact, be. One way to look at it would be to recall that in school we all learned that for English poetry there are three genres: epic poetry, lyric poetry, and dramatic poetry. For Syriac poetry one would have to add a fourth genre, homiletical poetry. It is not only the Syriac language but the Semitic languages generally which produced homiletical poetry. The canonical prophets preached in poetry — the oracles of Amos, Micah, Isaiah, and Jeremiah are in poetic verse — and these sermons, set down centuries before the Christian era, remain the classic poetry of the Hebrew language. In the seventh century after Christ, Muhammad uttered the Koran in what was apparently extemporized verse, and from the standpoint of Arabic poetry nothing written since has begun to approach it. It is in the context of the poetry of the prophets and the poetry of the Koran that the homiletical poetry of the Syriac-speaking

29. This is especially evident in the French translation of Lavenant:

"C'est selon que chacun
　　Ouvre ici ses oreilles
Qu'il pourra embrasser
　　La sagesse (de Dieu)." (*Hymnes sur le Paradis* 9.26)

30. Ephrem, *Hymns on Paradise* 5.1 and 6.1, 2.

Christian Church does not really look all that eccentric. When we see it in this context we are not quite so apt to regard it as a terribly stilted liturgical form or as a stiffly formalized religious expression, which we might otherwise be tempted to do.

Although it may not come to mind so quickly, there is also something similar in the history of English and American poetry. During the eighteenth century, in those circles particularly influenced by Pietism, a great amount of homiletical poetry was produced. The preacher would compose the poetry in the course of his sermon preparation and then, at the conclusion of the sermon's delivery, would line out the hymn for the congregation to sing. Charles Wesley seems to have composed his hymns this way, at least in the beginning, as did Samuel Davies, the leader of the Great Awakening in Virginia. These were not, of course, sermons preached in poetry, but sermons which issued in poetry; nevertheless, one could call these hymns homiletical poetry and, in so doing, come much closer to understanding what that kind of poetry really is. Some very fine religious poetry has been written in the English language which had as its express purpose the complementing of the pulpit. Unfortunately this poetry has often been misunderstood by secular literary authorities as a sort of misdirected lyric poetry. Nothing could be less the case! Just as hymnology is an art in itself, so homiletical poetry is a distinct genre of poetry.

Well, then, what is homiletical poetry? Or to be more specific, wherein consists the poetry of the *Hymns on Paradise,* this magnificent series of poetic sermons preached by Ephrem of Syria in the middle of the fourth century after Christ? There is, of course, the obvious fact that these sermons are preached in metrical lines which are arranged in stanzas. After each stanza the congregation is to respond by singing a refrain or, since we are dealing with liturgical poetry, perhaps we should call it an antiphon. It is this which distinguishes the *madrashe* (hymns) from the *memre* (discourses). While the *memre* is an unbroken series of metrical lines, the *madrashe* groups the lines into stanzas and follows each stanza with an antiphon. The fact that the preacher chants the stanza and the congregation joins in only with the antiphon is surely one of the things which clearly identifies it as a sermon and distinguishes it from what we usually understand as a hymn sung by the congregation. In addition to these basic poetical forms, the homiletical poetry of Ephrem uses all the alliterations, plays on words, rhymes, and antitheses familiar to the poetry of other times and places. Very little of this can be translated into another language, and we can only take the word of connoisseurs of Oriental languages that

Ephrem uses all these devices to achieve a high sonority, a fascinating variety, and a rich harmony, as Professor McVey so nicely put it.

Certain poetic elements do come out even in translation, however, the most important of which is thought rhyme. Those who have studied the Psalms will be familiar with the parallelism of Hebrew poetry, and what we find in the Psalms comes out very clearly in Syriac homiletical poetry. Ephrem brought the whole of Scripture into thought rhyme. He shows us the harmonies of ideas, perceptions, and reflections which run through the whole of Scripture. This is what typology is really all about, and no one has ever understood typology so well as Ephrem — he understood it far better than Origen, in fact. Typology is the poetry of the Bible; it is thought rhyming in its broadest dimension, taken to its most splendid expression.

It is this thought rhyming which is the great beauty of the *Hymns on Paradise*. There is the rhyme between Eden, the paradise at the beginning, and the heavenly Jerusalem, the paradise at the end. Then there are types which reflect this theme all through Scripture: for example, the congregation gathered in Noah's ark and the Church gathered in the upper room on the Day of Pentecost; the fruits of paradise and the fruits of the Spirit — love, joy, peace, etc.; the fruits of the Song of Solomon and the fruits differing each month of the year as we find it in the Revelation of John. The winds of paradise are a premonition of the winds heard in the upper room at the birth of the Church. It is they which breathe the breath of life into the apostolic community.

A particularly beautiful development of typology is found in the fifth hymn, where Ephrem reminds us of the well-known type of the rock which poured forth water in the wilderness to refresh the children of Israel (Exod. 17:6), and which the apostle Paul tells us is a type of Christ (I Cor. 10:4). He develops this well-known type by showing us that this rock is not only a type of Christ but a type of Christ as the Word of the Creator:

> I considered the Word of the Creator,
>   and likened it
> to the rock that marched
>   with the people of Israel in the wilderness.[31]

We have already spoken of the way Ephrem assumes a continuity between the Word of God as Christ and the Word of God as Scripture. Here

---

31. Ephrem, *Hymns on Paradise* 5.1.

Ephrem brings in a third element. He points out the continuity between the Word of creation, the Word revealed to Moses, and the Word incarnate in Christ. Here again we see how Ephrem's thoughts are under the influence of Wisdom theology. The point that he wants to make is that Scripture is a never ending source of truth to those who meditate on it:

> There was no water in the rock,
>   yet oceans sprang forth from it;
> Just so did the Word
>   fashion created things out of nothing.[32]

This counterpoint of types and antetypes is of the essence of homiletical poetry.

Closely related to the Old Testament types of Christ and his works of salvation recognized in the New Testament are the Old Testament types of the Christian life. A number of the saints of Israel are seen as prototypes or ancestral forms of Christian sanctity. Hymn 6 mentions several, but the one who is specially developed is Elijah, who, in the Epistle of James, is spoken of as an example of the life of prayer. The monks of the Eastern churches have long claimed Elijah as the prototype or foreshadow of the life of the Christian ascetic. The way Ephrem develops this is to see Elijah's translation into heaven in a chariot of fire as, first, a type of Christ's ascension and, second, a prototype and example of how a life of prayer, fasting, and celibacy is crowned above in paradise.[33]

This rhyming of thoughts can go far beyond types and prototypes in the strictest sense of these terms. A true type is recognized by Scripture, which is one of a number of criteria which distinguishes types from allegories. Yet one can find a certain parabolic meaning in many of the biblical stories, and this, too, belongs to thought rhyming. Many of the classic biblical illustrations are parabolic in nature. Jesus himself was a master of parabolic preaching, and sometimes, as in his sermon in the synagogue in Nazareth, he shaped his parables out of biblical materials, but sometimes he did not. In Hymn 13 Ephrem uses the story of King Nebuchadnezzar in a parabolic way, showing how the king of Babylon repeated the mistake of Adam by exercising kingship in a way that pro-

---

32. Ephrem, *Hymns on Paradise* 5.1.
33. Ephrem, *Hymns on Paradise* 6.22-25.

voked God. "The king of Babylon resembled Adam king of the universe."[34] Nebuchadnezzar returned to his kingdom showing us the way. We see here how parallelism and thought rhyming are important elements in the structuring of homiletical poetry.

Another beautiful example of thought rhyme is found in the seventh hymn where Ephrem speaks of the saints being clothed in light. These garments of light have taken the place of the fig leaves with which Adam and Eve clothed themselves after they had fallen:

> Both men and women
>   are clothed in raiment of light;
> the garments provided to cover their nakedness
>   are swallowed up in glory.[35]

Here the parallelism of promise and fulfillment is the basis of explaining the meaning of the text. The apostle Paul had exhorted Christians to clothe themselves in Christ, and in another passage we read of being clothed in the righteous deeds of the saints. All this has its meaning not so much in what is said as in what is intimated. That, of course, is the very soul of the art of poetry. The beauty of homiletical poetry lies in its power to intimate heavenly reality.

Homiletical poetry opens up the beauty of Scripture. It is in this sense that it is exposition. Ephrem's *Hymns on Paradise* is an example of this. It presents the destiny which God has appointed to man in all of its eternal beauty, in all its desirability. Nothing could be more evangelistic than these sermons. As the poet-preacher goes on and on the listener realizes that this is the destiny to which he or she is called and can do nothing else than aspire to it.

II. Narsai

High on the list of Syriac preachers is Narsai, "the Harp of the Holy Spirit."[36] As the reverential epithet would indicate, Narsai (ca. 399-503)

---

34. Ephrem, *Hymns on Paradise* 13.4.

35. Ephrem, *Hymns on Paradise* 7.5.

36. For biographical information on Narsai, see Baumstark, *Geschichte der syrischen Literatur,* pp. 57-121; H. Leclercq, *Dictionnaire d'archéologie chrétienne et de liturgie* 12/1 (1935): col. 884-88.

has won a reputation for his homiletical poetry.[37] From a literary standpoint his preaching is of the highest order, and from a theological standpoint he is regarded as one of the most accomplished of the Nestorian
thinkers. There was a time when Narsai's Dyophysitism was regarded as
heretical, just as the Monophysitism of Philoxenus of Mabbug was regarded as heretical in the opposite direction. Today one is more inclined
to regard Narsai's christological doctrine as orthodox, but in the fifth
century it was the cause of considerable controversy. Teaching in the
theological school of Edessa, perhaps as early as 437, Narsai became a
disciple of Theodore of Mopsuestia in his approach to biblical interpretation and a supporter of Antiochene Christology. More and more he found
himself one of the leading opponents of Alexandrian Christology; his
opposition was not limited to the extreme Monophysites, for he opposed
Cyril of Alexandria as well. As head of the theological school at Edessa at
the time of the Council of Chalcedon (451), he had to bear the brunt of
the controversy. Finally he fled Edessa and settled in Nisibis, where,
encouraged by the bishop, he reestablished a theological school. Being
outside the territory of the Byzantine Empire, this school was able to give
guidance to the Nestorians of Asia for many centuries to come.

What attracts our attention to Narsai, just as to Ephrem, is his ability
to bring together poetry and theology. Narsai is another homiletical poet.
Somehow in our culture poetry and theology seem to be like the oil and
water which cannot be made to mix. Were it not for Jacob of Sarug, who
obviously continued the tradition, we could regard Ephrem and Narsai as
some sort of brilliant exceptions, but then, as we begin to look around we
discover other homiletical poets. In another chapter we will have occasion
to study Romanos the Melode, who, although a native of Syria, was able
to develop homiletical poetry in Greek. So homiletical poetry apparently
is not simply a matter of the genius of a particular language. Even further,
we will eventually come to Charles Wesley and Samuel Davies, who, as
we have said, did something quite similar in their homiletical poetry.
Narsai, however, has one characteristic which among the great preacher-

---

37. Among the modern editions of sermons the most easily available are the
following: *Homélies de Narsai sur le Creation,* French translation and introduction by
Phillipe Gignoux, Patrologia Orientalis, vol. 34 (Turnhout: Brepols, 1968); *Liturgical
Homilies,* English translation with introduction by R. H. Connolly, *Texts and Studies* 8
(Cambridge, 1909); Frederick G. McLeod, trans., *Narsai's Metrical Homilies on the Nativity,
Epiphany, Passion, Resurrection, and Ascension,* Patrologia Orientalis, vol. 40 (Turnhout:
Brepols, 1979-81).

poets is particularly noteworthy: Narsai could preach highly polemical sermons in poetry. There may well have been other Syriac preachers who could do the same thing, but so little of the Syriac homiletical poetry has been translated, or even edited for that matter, that we cannot be sure. Frederick G. McLeod's edition of Narsai's festal sermons gives us some highly polemical sermons preached on the major Christian festivals.

As we have seen in relation to the Cappadocian Fathers, the major Christian festivals have often had a polemical function. For the first few centuries the celebration of festivals played a very small part in the worship of the Church; the emphasis was on the celebration of the Lord's Day rather than festivals. But because of the polemical necessity of making clear the Christian meaning of Passover, Easter was developed. The earliest Easter sermon we have, the sermon of Melito of Sardis, is solidly polemical. Taking the Jewish Passover as a type of redemption in Christ, Melito presents the Christian gospel as the fulfillment of the Law and the prophets. The uniqueness of the Christian celebration of Passover pointed to the centrality of Christian soteriology. It was the saving work of Christ which was the heart of Christian teaching. It was not until the time of Constantine that Christmas began to be celebrated. In the East there had been a celebration of Epiphany, and the two began to develop as a pair. The celebration of Christmas and Epiphany immediately became very popular because they reflected the shift of emphasis from the soteriology of the death and resurrection of Christ to the ontological concerns of the doctrine of the incarnation. Christmas, as it has been often put before, is the celebration of Nicene orthodoxy every bit as much as it is the celebration of the birth of Jesus. That Narsai should choose Christmas as a time to make clear one of the central doctrines of the Christian faith is hardly surprising.

Let us look at one of these homiletical celebrations of Christian doctrine, the sermon on the feast of the Nativity. The formal introduction to this sermon is lengthy — more than a hundred lines, or about a fifth of the sermon. It is a weighty and momentous theological statement. There is a sort of august splendor about it:[38]

> Refrain: Blessed be the Messiah who on the day of his birth
> gladdened the earth and made heaven rejoice.

---

38. McLeod, *Narsai's Metrical Homilies*, p. 37, lines 1-10.

My Brothers:

The Coming of the Divine Word

In love and mercy the Creator was pleased to give life to the universe,
    and (so) He sent His Son to restore the universe to His knowledge.
There went forth from the Father the Word of the Father — though
    He did not depart;
    and He came to our dwelling place, though He was in our
    dwelling place and in all things.
There went forth His (good) pleasure, and He came in His love to
    earthly beings;
    but His Nature remained unchanged in what It was.
(It was) not according to His Nature (that) the Almighty went forth
    or departed,
    because there is no place for the (Divine) Essence to go to within
    what It has fashioned.
For He does not go forth in (the sense of) moving away from what
    He is,
    because, in what He is, He remains forever unchanged.

In the Syriac the lines are perfectly balanced; the words are carefully chosen. All the art of the poet is used to make the cadences of the language appropriate to the high seriousness of the thoughts expressed. That high dogma can be poetry is inconceivable to some, but there are plenty of examples — T. S. Eliot's introduction to *The Wasteland,* for one. In this hundred-line introduction Narsai gives us the whole divine plan for the creation and redemption of the human race. Man was created to be the image of God so that God's image might dwell within him and thereby reflect and magnify his glory.

Having set forth the divine plan, Narsai takes up his story with the annunciation. The central portion of the typical Syriac homiletical poem is the recounting of the biblical narrative. A great portion of these metrical sermons might be seen as epic poems in the Western tradition. As much as they may begin with a statement of dogma and as much as they often turn to doctrinal reflection or moral admonitions, the core of the sermon is more than likely the telling of a story. Here we begin with the story of the archangel Gabriel visiting the virgin Mary. Mary is pictured as the new Eve who believes the word Gabriel announces to her: that she is to become the temple of human flesh in which the image of God is to take human form. The whole passage resonates with typology. It is as though the types play a continual counterpoint to the melody which is played in the Gospel narrative. One thing is clear, for Narsai as for the Syriac preachers generally, typology is of the essence of homiletical poetry.

Having pursued the narrative for a while, Narsai now takes up the theological implications. He openly attacks Eutychus; Cyril of Alexandria, whom he disparagingly calls the Egyptian; as well as any who have trod a road tending toward Monophysitism. The annunciation is, to be sure, one of the crucial points in the controversy between Nestorius and his opponents. Being patriarch of Constantinople, Nestorius had registered his doubts about the appropriateness of calling the virgin Mary Θεοτόκος, theotokos, or "God-bearer." This had triggered strong reactions, particularly from theologians of the Alexandrian School. Gabriel's salutation, "Hail Mary, full of grace . . . ," is, of course, one of the texts which is particularly significant to those who would ascribe to Mary the title Θεοτόκος. This passage, as Narsai understands it, has to be understood properly.[39] With this he explains the true meaning of this much-discussed text.

A second time our preacher picks up the narrative, recounting at length the visitation, the birth of Jesus in Bethlehem, the announcement to the shepherds, the journey of the wise men, the fear of Herod, the slaughter of the innocents, and the presentation in the Temple. The story is told with a considerable amount of rhetoric. Irony and paradox are used extensively. Of particular interest to Narsai is God's gracious condescension in revealing himself to the Assyrian astrologers in terms their astrology could understand. The symbolism of the gold, frankincense, and myrrh is elaborated. One gets the impression that Narsai sees in the three wise men his own people. Finally the story comes to its conclusion with the story of the presentation in the Temple. We notice that it is Mary who is once more in the center of the stage of the nativity narrative, just as she was at the beginning of the story.

With this Narsai begins his conclusion, which is just as long as the introduction, about a hundred lines, and just as theological. Narsai now asks who it is who has presented Jesus at the Temple. The question so dear to the Nestorians is once more broached: who is Mary? The Nestorians

---

39. As we have already said, Θεοτόκος is not quite the same thing as "Mother of God." One should take care not to confuse the objections of the Nestorians with those of classical Protestantism. For a balanced Protestant approach to the question, see David F. Wright, *Chosen by God: Mary in Evangelical Perspective* (London: Marshall Pickering, 1989).

wanted to affirm the confession that Christ is both true God and true man, but they could not go along with calling Mary the Θεοτόκος. The way Narsai tries to solve the problem is by interpreting the whole nativity narrative with the text of John 1:14. It is not that the eternal Word became flesh in such a way that the Word lost its characteristics or divine nature, but rather that it became flesh in the sense that it dwelt in human flesh, the flesh of Jesus.[40]

> The Word of the Father has abased Himself by means of His (good) pleasure;
>> and His power dwelt in the pure body which Mary bore.
> (It was) not in His (Divine) Essence (that) He abased Himself and came to a birth;
>> the (good) pleasure of His love abode in another and called him by His name.
> (It was) not the (Divine) Essence which is hidden from all that Mary bore;
>> a man she bore who is entirely like the members of his race.
> (It was) not the spiritual One who has no structure (that) hands have circumcised;
>> it was a corporeal being whom the hands of corporeal beings circumcised.
> Mary is a human being from the humanity of Adam's race;
>> and like to her is the child who is from her in body and soul.
> Mary is equal to (other) females because of her fashioning;
>> her offspring, on the other hand, is greater than all the offsprings of the daughters of Eve.
> Her offspring is like to (other) corporeal beings in body and soul,
>> but holier and more glorious than corporeal beings because of his fashioning.
> His nature is like that of his mother from whom he exists,
>> but he is more exalted than she because it is not from seed (that he has acquired) his (bodily) structure.
> He is entirely a man because of the wholeness of (his) body and soul;
>> but he is also God because he became the dwelling place for the God of the universe.
> He is the son of a woman because from her is the nature of his (bodily) structure,

40. McLeod, *Narsai's Metrical Homilies,* pp. 61-63, lines 415-34.

> but he is the Son of the (Divine) Essence because he is equal to
> this by the power of his Assumer.

Narsai is quite willing to honor the virgin Mary. For him the doctrine of the virgin birth is of major importance, for Mary plays a key role in the history of salvation. From the standpoint of Christ's humanity she is the woman who brought the Savior into the world. Besides this Narsai is willing to recognize the biblical types for Mary: Mary is the second Eve, and the temple enshrining the divine presence. The basic concern of the whole Antiochene School was to emphasize the true humanity of Christ. Not wavering on the Trinity, not wavering on the divinity of Christ, not even wavering on the doctrine of the virgin birth, Narsai, as Nestorianism generally, had a gospel of the humanity of the Son of God. For many years to come the Nestorians would preach that gospel into the far corners of Asia. The Nestorians were great missionaries, and great missionaries are made by the hot, burning fire of conviction. Whether we agree or not with Narsai or with his Nestorianism, one thing is clear from these sermons: They show us how beautiful doctrinal preaching can be.

III. Philoxenus of Mabbug

One of the classical writers of Syriac literature, Philoxenus of Mabbug (ca. 440-523) is regarded as a saint and doctor of the Monophysite churches of the East.[41] A heretic he was not. He was opposed to Nestorianism, but by going off in the opposite direction he came to be regarded as one of the founders of the Monophysite, or Syrian Jacobite, church. Philoxenus must have been a student in the year 451 when the Council of Chalcedon convened and decided against both the Nestorians on one hand and the Monophysites on the other, but the discussion went on for generations, especially in Syria. Apparently Philoxenus was a well-rounded theologian

---

41. This study is based on the following work: Philoxenus of Mabbug, *Homélies*, French translation by Eugène Lemoine, Sources chrétiennes, vol. 44 (Paris: Les Éditions du Cerf, 1956). The most recent edition of these sermons is in *La lettre a Patricius de Philoxene de Mabbug*, ed. and trans. René Lavenant, Patrologia Orientalis, vol. 30.5 (Paris: Firmin-Didot, 1963), pp. 725-894. There is also an English translation by Budge: *The Discourses of Philoxenus*, ed. and trans. E. A. Wallis Budge, 2 vols. (London, 1894). For biographical material, see André de Halleux, *Philoxène de Mabboug, sa vie, ses écrits, sa théologie* (Louvain: Imprimerie Orientaliste, 1963); and E. Tisserant, *Dictionnaire de Théologie Catholique* 12/2:1509-32.

— some eighty major works have come down from him, ranging from important exegetical works to doctrinal treatises. He left us collections both of his sermons and his letters. He is one more witness to the vitality of the Syriac church.

Born at Tahal, within the confines of the Persian empire, Philoxenus went to study at the famous school of Edessa, where the controversies between the Nestorians and the Monophysites had become increasingly bitter. It must not have been long after Philoxenus had finished his studies there that the Nestorians gained control of the school, and he departed for Nisibis. How early in his life he accepted his monastic vocation we are not sure, but we gather that by the age of fifty he was well known in the numerous monastic communities of eastern Syria. Apparently he had preached in many of these communities, and the series of sermons he left us is a summary of his preaching ministry in these monasteries. They seem to have been preached before 485, the year of his elevation to the episcopate of Mabbug. By this time he had considerable influence in the Syrian church; he was one of those who had helped Peter the Fuller to the see of Antioch and a few years later, in 512, brought the anti-Nestorian party to its zenith by helping Severus of Antioch gain that same prestigious see. With the accession of the orthodox emperor Justin I, he himself was exiled to Thrace where he died in 523.

The chief interest of the sermons of Philoxenus is that they show us how catechetical preaching developed. They help us see the transition from rabbinical teaching in the Jewish schools as we find it reflected in the Mishnah and the Talmud to the sort of moral catechism which became more and more part of Christian preaching. In the intellectual centers of the Syriac world the rabbinical schools were greatly respected and naturally tended to keep Christian learning from developing in the direction of Hellenistic learning. We have already given considerable attention to the primitive Christian catechism and its origins in the New Testament Church. Here we find a very similar kind of teaching, in that Christian teaching is approached systematically, that is, subject by subject, rather than exegetically, going through the Bible book by book, chapter by chapter. This was the way rabbis did it in their schools, and it was also the way Christian teachers did it. We find Christians doing this even in the New Testament, where, as we have shown, this method is used in the last half of I Peter, the last half of Ephesians, as well as in the whole of I Timothy and James. It is often pointed out that the regular preaching of the Church was handled quite differently but that side by side with the proclamation of the gospel and the preaching through of the Scriptures there was also this teaching of the Christian life. Philoxenus gives us a good example of classical catechetical preaching.

The sermons of Philoxenus are finished sermons which record in concentrated form the substance of the preacher's message. They had been preached many times and in many monastic communities before they were put down in writing and are catechetical sermons not in the sense that they are introductory, but in the sense that they are a systematic presentation of the moral teachings of the Christian life, particularly as it concerned members of a monastic community, and thus represent what more and more has come to be called "spiritual" catechism. They were preached to those who sought to attain a more advanced spiritual life. The first of the thirteen sermons that constitute this series is introductory in nature but is followed by two sermons on faith, two on simplicity, and two on the fear of the Lord. It is with these that one begins serious Christian discipleship. Advancing along the path of Christian perfection, Philoxenus preaches two sermons each on the renouncing of the world, the struggle against gluttony, and the struggle against fornication. The sermons, as these topics indicate, are moral catechism through and through.

Also of particular interest is the way these sermons handle Scripture. In treating each subject our preacher has selected a wide variety of biblical sayings as the basis of his remarks. In his two sermons on faith, for instance, he has collected a series of biblical maxims on the subject. He begins, appropriately, with the saying found in the Epistle to the Hebrews, "For whoever would draw near to God must believe that he exists and that he rewards those who seek him" (11:6). After a few comments on this verse he moves on to the saying of Jesus that those who would receive the kingdom must receive it with childlike faith (Mark 10:14 and Matt. 19:14). He then mentions the saying of Jesus about the power of faith the size of a mustard seed and the apostle Paul's maxim about faith coming from hearing. As we have already pointed out, this method of organizing a sermon was greatly beloved in the synagogue. The rabbis called such sermons "a string of pearls." This is not proof texting, nor do the biblical quotations serve as some sort of pious decoration, but actually, they form the framework of the discourse. Our preacher moves from one saying to another in order to develop many different aspects of his subject. In the same way he mentions a whole series of examples of faith, again like a string of pearls, one following another. Elijah was a particularly fine example of faith, and Philoxenus discusses the nature of his faith at length.

He also holds up Joshua as an example of faith and the mighty works of Jesus to show the power of faith. One is constantly amazed at the insights of Philoxenus, and at the many facets of faith which he illumines. The work is indeed a classic and can be read today with profit.

What impresses one most about these sermons is the serious moral character of Syriac Christianity. While few of us today would emulate the asceticism which so obviously appealed to that age, we can admire the genuine purity of life which they strove to attain. Holiness of life was an essential dimension of their worship.

IV. The Syriac Lectionaries

The Syriac lectionaries are of interest to us because they come from a Christian community which took great delight in the public reading of Scripture. The Syriac-speaking churches of Mesopotamia regularly had four Scripture lessons at the least, and some had six, and on the major feast days perhaps even more. Possibly the four lessons go back to the primitive Church when the earliest Christians read the Law and the Prophets and then added to this twofold reading of the Old Testament a twofold reading of the New Testament: a reading from the Gospels and another from the Epistles. The Syriac lectionaries give us another strong piece of evidence that in the first three or four centuries of Christian history the reading of the Old Testament occupied an important place in Christian worship. Whereas in the West the Old Testament lessons had a tendency toward atrophy, the tendency in the East was the opposite. One reason for this was because the Syriac church was in constant conversation with the synagogue. If in the more Hellenized religions of the Mediterranean coast the Greek-speaking Syrian church was constantly at pains to explain its worship as the celebration of mysteries more spiritual than those of paganism, in the more Semitic sections of the country the Church was eager to show that its worship came not to destroy the Law but to fulfill it. We have noticed how prominent this theme was in Antiochene preachers such as Theodore of Mopsuestia. It was even more prominent in Syria once one crossed the mountains of Lebanon and descended into the valley of the Tigris and Euphrates. There one entered into a Semitic world in which the concerns of the Church were different.

A thorough study of the Syriac lectionaries will have to be left to specialists, but enough work has been done by such people as Arthur Maclean and Anton Baumstark that we can get an inspiring impression of the vitality of the ministry of the Word as it was maintained in the Syriac church of the fifth, sixth, and seventh centuries.[42] While in western Syria these centuries witnessed the fall of the Roman Empire, the churches of eastern Syria, outside the border of the old Roman Empire, flourished. Both of the non-Chalcedonian branches of the Syriac church, the Nestorians and the Jacobites, carried out impressive missionary work as far east as China and India. As the Church grew and spread out and as more and more people came to church leadership who had not been brought up in the liturgical traditions of the Church, a need to codify the worship was felt. One finds an amazing exuberance in these lectionaries. Syriac Christians must have found deep significance in the public reading of Scripture.

A good number of liturgical manuscripts have survived. In fact, more Syriac liturgical manuscripts are available in Western libraries than scholars have been able to study. All we can do is report on some of the material uncovered by the scholars who have worked this rich vein. Let us look first at the material brought to light by Anton Baumstark on the Nestorian lectionary of the Upper Monastery of Mosul.

A. The Lectionary of Mosul

Today Mosul is one of the major cities of Iraq. Located on the right bank of the Tigris River, across from the site of ancient Nineveh, some three hundred miles north of Baghdad, its population is overwhelmingly Arabic and Moslem. There was a time, however, when it had a sizeable Aramaic population, much of which was Christian; indeed, from the sixth to the tenth centuries Mosul flourished as a Christian city. The Nestorian patriarch maintained his seat in the city, but there was a number of Syrian Jacobites in the city as well. With the eleventh century a decline set in, but it was not until the Mogul invasions of the thirteenth and fourteenth centuries that Christianity lost its majority. It is from this golden age of Syriac Christianity, from this center of Nestorianism, that this lectionary

---

42. Anton Baumstark, *Nichtevangelische syrische Perikopenordnungen des ersten jahrtausends* (Münster im Westphalia: Aschendorff, 1921); Arthur J. Maclean, *East Syrian Daily Offices* (London: Rivington, Percival and Co., 1894); Arthur Vööbus, *Handscriftliche Überlieferung der Memre-Dichtung des Ja'qob von Serug,* Corpus scriptorum christianorum orientalium, vols. 184 and 197 (Louvain: Secrétariat du Corpus SCO, 1973).

came. We hesitate to assign a definite date to it, but the lectionary would appear to have been formulated several centuries after the lectionary of Jerusalem which we studied in a previous chapter.

Baumstark finds three sections of this lectionary to be of special interest. The first of these is the lectionary for Lent. He gives the following list:[43]

First Week of Lent
    Monday
        Genesis 1:1-19
        Joshua 1:1-11
        Romans 1:1-25
        (Matthew 5:17-38)
    Tuesday
        Genesis 1:20–2:7
        Joshua 1:17–2:11
        Romans 1:26–2:5
        (Matthew 5:38-48)
    Wednesday
        Genesis 2:8-25
        Joshua 2:12-24
        Romans 2:6-27
        (Matthew 6:1-19)
    Thursday
        Genesis 3:1-19
        Joshua 3:1-13
        Romans 2:28–3:26
        (Matthew 6:19-34)
    Friday
        Genesis 3:20–4:16
        Joshua 3:14–4:9
        Romans 3:27–4:25
        (Matthew 7:1-15)

43. Baumstark, being consistent with the purpose of his inquiry, does not give the Gospel lessons. These have been filled in from Maclean, *East Syrian Daily Offices*. What this may lack in scholarly method is hopefully compensated by what it adds to giving a more complete picture of the public reading of Scripture. The matter of the reading of the Gospel in Syriac worship is complicated by the widespread use of the *Diatessaron* as late as the fifth century.

Second Week of Lent
  Sunday
        Genesis 5:18-31a
        Joshua 4:15-25
        Romans 5:1-21
        (Matthew 7:15-28)
  Friday
        Genesis 5:31b–6:22
        Joshua 5:1-12
        Romans 7:1-13
        (Mark 11:27–12:12)

Third Week of Lent
  Sunday
        Genesis 7:1-24
        Joshua 5:13–6:5
        Romans 7:14-25a
        (Matthew 20:17-29)
  Friday
        Genesis 9:8-29
        Joshua 6:6-26
        Romans 7:25b–8:11
        (Mark 12:13-35)

Fourth Week of Lent
  Sunday
        Genesis 11:1-32
        Joshua 6:27–7:9
        Romans 8:12-28
        (Matthew 21:23-46)
  Monday
        Genesis 12:1-9
        Joshua 7:16-26
        Romans 9:1-13
        (John 5:1-19)
  Tuesday
        Genesis 12:10–13:7
        Joshua 8:1-17
        Romans 9:14-29
        (John 5:19-47)

280

Wednesday
>Genesis 13:8-18
>Joshua 8:18-29
>Romans 9:30–10:16
>(John 6:51-70)

Thursday
>Genesis 14:1-17
>Joshua 8:30-35
>Romans 10:17–11:12
>(John 7:1-14)

Friday
>Genesis 14:18–15:15
>Joshua 9:1-14
>Romans 11:25-36
>(John 7:14-37)

Fifth Week of Lent
Sunday
>Genesis 16:1–17:27
>Joshua 9:15-27
>Romans 12:1-21
>(John 7:37–8:21)

Friday
>Genesis 18:1-19
>Joshua 14:6-15
>Romans 13:1-14
>(John 8:31-59)

Sixth Week of Lent
Sunday
>Genesis 19:1-26
>Joshua 21:43–22:9
>Romans 14:10-23
>(John 9:39–10:22)

Friday
>Genesis 19:27-38
>Joshua 22:10-20
>Romans 15:1-13
>(John 11:1-45)

Holy Monday
          Genesis 37:1-22
          Joshua 22:21-29
          Hebrews 1:1–2:18
          (John 11:47–12:12)
Holy Tuesday
          Genesis 37:23-35
          Joshua 22:30–23:1a
          Hebrews 4:14–6:8
          (John 12:12-44)
Holy Wednesday
          Genesis 39:7–40:23
          Joshua 23:1b-13
          Hebrews 9:11-28
          (John 13:1-18)

The first thing we notice is how long these lessons are. A minimum of around fifty verses seems to be the rule, and sometimes the count comes in at over eighty. The reading of the lessons alone could well have taken as much as twenty minutes or even half an hour, by the time the accompanying benedictions and doxologies were offered. What this means is that a good part of the service of worship was devoted to the public reading of Holy Scripture.

The second thing we notice is the strong use of the *lectio continua.* For the reading from the Law Genesis is read, or actually, only the first half of the book.[44] We learn from several sources starting at the end of the fourth century that preaching on Genesis was considered especially appropriate to Lent.[45] The custom perhaps comes from the idea of acquainting the catechumen with the cardinal events of salvation history. The same reason may help explain the selections from the book of Joshua,

44. The material at our disposal gives us no hint about why the remainder of the book was not read. In contrast, John Chrysostom continued his series on Genesis after Easter. Perhaps the *lectio continua* of Genesis was taken up where it had been left off the following year. Perhaps on the principle of *pars pro toto* it was considered sufficient to have read what was read.

45. We have to reckon with the possibility that what we have here is the reading of the beginning of the first book of the Law; the reading of the first book of the former prophets, that is, Joshua; the reading of the first epistle, Romans; and finally the reading of the first Gospel. This does not seem to fit in with the rest of the lectionary.

which also follow in a *lectio continua*. From a typological standpoint the book of Joshua could be understood as a figure for starting out the Christian life. While normally we do not think of Joshua as a prophet, Baumstark claims there seems to be some inclinations in this direction on the part of the Babylonian Jews with whom Syrian Christians were in such close contact.[46] The lesson from the prophets was sometimes understood as a lesson from some part of the Old Testament canon other than the Pentateuch. Most of Romans is covered in a *lectio continua* except for certain passages which have been taken out for use on special days. For example, the sixth chapter of Romans is skipped but then, because it speaks of our resurrection with Christ, is read on Easter Sunday.[47]

A third thing we notice is that the reading of Genesis and Romans is particularly appropriate for the baptism of converts from Judaism. Not only is there the typology of the old creation and the new creation, but also the typology of the old Adam and the new Adam so prominent in Romans 4 and 5 and the matter of Abraham being the father of faith which is so thoroughly discussed in Romans. The juxtaposition of Genesis and Romans would give the preacher ample material for instructing candidates for baptism. This is particularly the case if one only takes the first twenty chapters of Genesis.

The chances are that behind this fixed *lectio continua* of the first half of Genesis, the story of entering the Promised Land from Joshua, and Paul's epistle to the Romans was a more flexible *lectio continua*. At the point in the history of worship when this lectionary for Lent was drawn up the reading through of Scripture on the principle of the *lectio continua* was the normal way of doing things. There was no attempt to get through the whole Bible in a year, nor was there any date at which the church year had to begin over again. Special lessons were by this time a well-established principle, but they were read only on a few special days. Filling out the whole calendar was something new. It was a very definite innovation. We noticed a very similar situation with the lectionary of Jerusalem when it first appeared; originally the *lectio continua* was not attached to the calendar. This was true both in the Church and in the synagogue. In the synagogue, it was not until Masoretic times (that is, from the sixth to the

---

46. Baumstark, *Nichtevangelische syrische Perikopenordnungen des ersten jahrtausends,* p. 21.

47. Baumstark, *Nichtevangelische syrische Perikopenordnungen des ersten jahrtausends,* pp. 20-21.

tenth centuries) that the *lectio continua* of the Torah was attached to the calendar so that the whole thing was read through in either a year or three years. The original idea of the *lectio continua* was that one proceeded from service to service, beginning each time where one had left off the service before. The schedule would have been different in every synagogue, and it would have been different every time one went through it, taking from a year and a half to about four years. It was a later development that established *parashoth* or pericopes and assigned them to a particular date. Originally the *lectio continua* needed no lectionary, but with the growth of the festal calendar and the establishing of liturgical seasons the drawing up of a lectionary became necessary. This lectionary, like the Jerusalem lectionary of the fifth century, shows us something of the transition from one system to the other.

The second part of the Nestorian lectionary which Baumstark finds particularly interesting is the section which follows Pentecost and continues until one begins to anticipate Christmas. This makes up roughly half the Sundays of the year. These Sundays, along with the Sundays following Epiphany, were the last to be assigned specific pericopes and, therefore, the last to lose the *lectio continua*. Baumstark gives the following:[48]

> Third Apostle Sunday
>> Deuteronomy 1:3-17
>> Isaiah 1:1-9
>> I Corinthians 7:1-7
>> (Luke 10:23-42)
> Fourth Apostle Sunday
>> Deuteronomy 1:16-33a
>> Isaiah 1:10-20
>> I Corinthians 9:13-27
>> (Luke 6:12-47)
> Fifth Apostle Sunday
>> Deuteronomy 1:33b–2:1
>> Isaiah 1:21-31
>> I Corinthians 14:1-19
>> (Luke 12:16-35)

48. Baumstark, *Nichtevangelische syrische Perikopenordnungen des ersten jahrtausends*, pp. 24-25. The Gospels are taken from Maclean, *East Syrian Daily Offices*, pp. 262-81.

Sixth Apostle Sunday
> Deuteronomy 4:1-10a
> Isaiah 2:1-22
> I Corinthians 10:14-32
> (Luke 12:57–13:18)

Seventh Apostle Sunday
> Deuteronomy 4:10b-24
> Isaiah 5:8-25
> I Corinthians 15:58–16:24
> (Luke 13:22-35)

First Summer Sunday
> Deuteronomy 4:25-31
> Isaiah 2:22–3:15
> II Corinthians 1:8-14
> (Luke 14:1-15)

Second Summer Sunday
> Deuteronomy 4:32-40
> Isaiah 3:16–4:6
> II Corinthians 3:4-18
> (Luke 15:4-32)

Third Summer Sunday
> Deuteronomy 5:1-16
> Isaiah 5:1-7
> II Corinthians 7:1-11
> (John 9:1-39)

Fourth Summer Sunday
> Deuteronomy 5:16–6:3
> Isaiah 9:8-21
> II Corinthians 10:1-18
> (Mark 7:1-24)

Fifth Summer Sunday
> Leviticus[49]

---

49. Curiously the readings from Deuteronomy suddenly break off after introducing the Ten Commandments (Deut. 6:1-3). For the next three Sundays it is replaced by the reading of something from Leviticus. The passages are not identified. Then on the fourth Sunday the readings of Deuteronomy are resumed at 6:20. The effect is to skip over the second version of the Ten Commandments. Then, as we will notice, the readings continue only up to the beginning of chapter 13.

Isaiah 28:14-22
II Corinthians 12:14–13:13
(Luke 16:19–17:11)

Sixth Summer Sunday
Leviticus
Isaiah 29:13-24
I Thessalonians 2:1-13
(Luke 17:5-20)

Seventh Summer Sunday
Leviticus
Isaiah 30:1-15
I Thessalonians 2:14–3:13
(Luke 18:2-15)

First Elijah Sunday
Deuteronomy 6:20–7:6
Isaiah 31:1-9
II Thessalonians 1:1-12
(Luke 18:35–19:11)

Second Elijah Sunday
Deuteronomy 7:7-11
Isaiah 30:15-26
II Thessalonians 2:5–3:18
(Matthew 13:1-9)

Third Elijah Sunday
Deuteronomy 7:12-26
Isaiah 32:1–33:6
Philippians 1:12-25
(Matthew 13:24-44)

Fourth Elijah Sunday
Deuteronomy 8:11-20
Isaiah 33:13-24
Philippians 1:27–2:12
(Matthew 4:12–5:17)

Fifth Elijah Sunday
Deuteronomy 9:1-8
Isaiah 25:1-8
Philippians 3:1-14
(Matthew 17:14-27)

Sixth Elijah Sunday
    Deuteronomy 9:13-22
    Isaiah 26:1-19
    Philippians 4:4-23
    (Matthew 15:21-39)
Seventh Elijah Sunday
    Deuteronomy 10:12-22
    Isaiah 28:23–29:12
    I Corinthians 14:26-40
    (Matthew 18:1-19)
First Moses Sunday
    Deuteronomy 11:1-12
    Isaiah 40:1-17
    II Corinthians 1:23–2:16
    (Matthew 20:1-17)
Second Moses Sunday
    Deuteronomy 11:13–12:1
    Isaiah 40:18–41:7
    Galatians 11:13–12:1 (sic)
    (Matthew 12:46-50)
Third Moses Sunday
    Deuteronomy 12:1-28
    Isaiah 41:8-20
    Galatians 6:1-18
    (John 5:1-19)
Fourth Moses Sunday
    Deuteronomy 12:29–13:5
    Isaiah 41:21–42:4
    I Timothy 5:1-16
    (Matthew 8:23–9:10)

The first thing Baumstark points out about these selections is that there is an attempt at a *lectio continua* of Deuteronomy for the lesson from the Law.[50] Why the *lectio continua* only goes up to chapter 13, he does not explain. The reason, we suggest, is that this first half of Deuteronomy, made up of two long sermons of Moses, is one of the high points of the Pentateuch. It is well

---

50. Baumstark, *Nichtevangelische syrische Perikopenordnungen des ersten jahrtausends*, pp. 25-26.

suited for a public reading of Scripture, whereas much of the material from the beginning of chapter 12 on is taken up by the Deuteronomic Code, which is material less suitable for liturgical reading. While Baumstark does not go into this, it would seem that we have here a clear example of the freedom with which the *lectio continua* could be used. Following the *lectio continua* did not mean one had to read everything from the particular books in question. Obviously those responsible for drawing up this series of lessons have made an attempt to emphasize the most edifying portions of the Pentateuch. As we have pointed out before, deciding what needs to be read and what does not is an important part of the job of interpretation.

The second thing Baumstark points out about the Scripture lessons for the Sundays after Pentecost is that someone back in the history of the Nestorian lectionary filled in all the Sundays not otherwise designated as feast days with portions of a *lectio continua* of the book of Isaiah.[51] Again we notice that it is a fixed *lectio continua*. The Sundays after Pentecost begin the series and take Isaiah up to chapter 42. The Sundays after Epiphany take it up at chapter 44 while chapter 60 is read on Easter and several following passages during Easter week. A number of the choice portions of Isaiah have been assigned to special days — portions of chapters 7 and 9 were read at Christmas and chapter 53 on Good Friday — and have thus been taken out of the *lectio continua*. Chapters 13–27 have been left out, as have chapters 34–40. These passages were no doubt considered less edifying and therefore have been skipped over. Again we would want to point out that the drawing up of a lectionary makes some very important decisions about what is more important in Scripture and what is less important. Isaiah is one of the richest books in Scripture, and whoever shaped this lectionary wanted to be sure that the best of the oracles of Isaiah were frequently heard by the people.

Having looked briefly at these numerous survivals of the *lectio continua* in this lectionary of the Upper Monastery of Mosul, let us take an equally brief look at the selections for feast days. We begin with the selections for Easter, starting with Palm Sunday and continuing through the beginning of the week following:[52]

---

51. Baumstark, *Nichtevangelische syrische Perikopenordnungen des ersten jahrtausends,* pp. 26-27.

52. Again Baumstark describes the selections other than the Gospel. We assume that during this time the lesson from the Gospels would treat the story of the passion and resurrection of Christ. This is indeed what we find in the reconstruction of the Nestorian lectionary published by Maclean. As above, we add the Gospel lessons given by Maclean in parenthesis.

Palm Sunday
> Genesis 49:1-12, 22-26
> Zechariah (selections)
> Romans 11:13-24
> (Matthew 20:29–21:23)

Maundy Thursday
> Exodus 12:1-28
> Zechariah (selections)
> I Corinthians 5:6-8
> I Corinthians 10:15-17
> I Corinthians 11:23-34
> (Matthew 26:17-25)
> (John 13:22-28)
> (John 13:3-16)
> (Matthew 26:26-31)

Good Friday
> Isaiah 53
> Daniel 9:20-27
> Galatians 2:17–3:14
> (Matthew 27:1-3)
> (Luke 23:27-31)
> (Matthew 27:33-44)
> (Luke 23:39-44)
> (Matthew 27:45-55)
> (John 19:31-38)
> (Matthew 27:57-62)

Holy Saturday
> Genesis 22:1-19
> Jonah 1 and 2
> I Corinthians 1:18-31
> I Corinthians 10:1-13
> I Corinthians 15:20-28
> (Matthew 27:62-66)

Easter Sunday
> Isaiah 60:1-7
> I Samuel 2:1-10
> Romans 5:20–6:23

Hebrews 13:20-25
(Matthew 28)
(Luke 24:1-13)
(John 20:1-10)

Easter Monday
Isaiah 60:9-22
Acts 2:14-36
Ephesians 6:10-24
(John 14:18–15:15)

Tuesday
Isaiah 61:1-9
Acts 2:37-47
I Corinthians 15:1-22
(Luke 24:13-36)

Wednesday
Isaiah 61:10–62:5
Acts 4:23-31
Ephesians 4:1-16
(John 15:1-26)

Thursday
Isaiah 54:1-16
Acts 6:1-7
Colossians 2:8–3:4
(Matthew 10:1-16)

Sunday after Easter
Isaiah 55:4-13
Acts 4:32–5:11
Colossians 1:1-21
(John 20:19-31)

The first thing that catches our attention in these selections is the appearance of some of the gems of the Old Testament prophets. For the most part they are the classics one would expect: for example, the reading of the opening lines of the sixtieth chapter of Isaiah on Easter Sunday:

Arise, shine; for your light has come,
    and the glory of the LORD has risen upon you.

In fact, the reading of Isaiah 60 is continued on Easter Monday; then chapter 61 is continued on Tuesday of Easter week.[53] Perhaps this is a trace of an older practice of reading the final chapters of Isaiah during Easter week. On Good Friday Isaiah 53 is read, the most obviously appropriate passage for this day. It is a mighty passage that did much to shape the way the first Christians understood the Passion of the messianic Servant of the Lord. This is clear from so many passages of the New Testament. In fact, as we have already said, one is tempted to think that this interpretation goes back to Jesus himself.

The reading of two of the four chapters of Jonah is another one of those well-established typologies which may well have gone back to Jesus. Baumstark figures that originally all four chapters of the short book would have been read, and only later did the Church feel obliged to shorten the reading of this colorful lesson.[54] Twice we find that the prophetic lesson is devoted to reading an anthology of the prophecies of Zechariah.[55] This no doubt is suggested by the account of the triumphal entry in the Gospels which quotes from Zechariah, and yet the Passion narrative as a whole makes frequent use of Zechariah. Again, these are colorful, imaginative selections. They so obviously come from a Church which delighted in the reading of Scripture.

The readings from the Law on the other hand are a bit disappointing. So little is done with the Passover narrative — the institution of the Passover feast (Exod. 12:1-28) is read on Maundy Thursday, but that is it. The readings for the Easter vigil are a different matter.[56] There we find the story of Abraham's sacrifice as well as generous selections from the Passover narrative. These lessons are much older and explain why this material was not read over again in the week after Easter.

The celebration of the fifty days from Easter to Pentecost goes back much further than any of the other so-called liturgical seasons. It owes its existence not to the penitential preparation for baptism during Lent but

53. Baumstark, *Nichtevangelische syrische Perikopenordnungen des ersten jahrtausends*, p. 30.

54. Baumstark, *Nichtevangelische syrische Perikopenordnungen des ersten jahrtausends*, p. 45.

55. Baumstark, *Nichtevangelische syrische Perikopenordnungen des ersten jahrtausends*, pp. 42ff.

56. See Anton Baumstark, *Nocturna laus: Typen frühchristlicher Virgilienfeier und ihr Fortleben vor allem im römischen und monastischen Ritus* (Münster im Westphalia: Aschendorff, 1957), pp. 46-48.

to the recognition that Easter begins a new epoch in salvation history. There was an old tradition going back to the time when most of the lessons were still selected on the basis of the *lectio continua* which called for a reading through of the Acts of the Apostles from Easter to Pentecost. Evidently this had replaced the reading of the Law, so that by the time this lectionary was drawn up the four lessons read from Easter to Pentecost were as follows: first, a lesson from the Prophets; second, a lesson from Acts; third, a lesson from the Pauline Epistles; and finally a lesson from the Gospels.

The readings from the Pauline Epistles have been appreciably multiplied during the Easter season. On Easter Sunday the whole sixth chapter of Romans is read, and to that is added a reading from Hebrews, which was no doubt thought of as a Pauline epistle. On Maundy Thursday three selections are read from First Corinthians. On Holy Saturday we find the same thing.

B. The Lectionary of Athanasius V

Another lectionary which Baumstark describes at length was put together under the Syrian Jacobite patriarch Athanasius V. Although this patriarch was active in the tenth century, Baumstark is of the opinion that he used much material from the seventh century. No doubt, older material was used as well.

The first section of this lectionary Baumstark draws to our attention is a number of Sundays which he believes preserve the oldest level of the Syriac tradition regarding the reading of Scripture lessons:[57]

Second Sunday after Epiphany
    Exodus 34:22–35:19
    Jeremiah 50:4-16
    Romans 7:22–8:11
Fourth Sunday after Epiphany
    Exodus 35:30–36:5
    Jeremiah 51:1-12
    Romans 9:14-26

57. Baumstark, *Nichtevangelische syrische Perikopenordnungen des ersten jahrtausends,* pp. 101-2.

Sixth Sunday after Epiphany
    Exodus 36:23-38
    Jeremiah 51:15-29
    Romans 7:4-13
Second Sunday after Easter
    Exodus 2:11-29
    Ezekiel 3:22–4:3
    I Corinthians 2:6–3:3
Third Sunday after Easter
    Exodus 3:13-22
    Ezekiel 5:5-15
    Romans 10:17–11:2
Fourth Sunday after Easter
    Exodus 5:1-9
    Ezekiel 6:1-9
    Romans 13:12–14:3
Fifth Sunday after Easter
    Exodus 5:10–6:1
    Ezekiel 8:14–9:10
    Romans 6:12-23
First Sunday after Pentecost
    Exodus 16:9-26
    Job 6:1-30
    I Corinthians 6:1-11
Second Sunday after Pentecost
    Exodus 18:1-12
    Job 7:1-21
    Colossians 3:1-17
Third Sunday after Pentecost
    Exodus 18:13-27
    Job 8:1-22
    I Thessalonians 1:2-10
Fourth Sunday after Pentecost
    Exodus 20:1-20
    Job 9:1-28
    I Corinthians 7:1-15
Fifth Sunday after Pentecost
    Exodus 20:21-21b (sic)
    Job 9:29–10:22

293

II Thessalonians 1:3-12
Sixth Sunday after Pentecost
    Exodus 21:26–22:4
    Job 11:1-20
    I Timothy 4:11–5:8
Seventh Sunday after Pentecost
    Exodus 22:5-20
    Job 12:1–13:1
    II Thessalonians 2:15-39

One of the things which mark these selections as being especially old is the fact that they provide but two Old Testament lessons. As time went on the Syrian Jacobites moved toward a threefold Old Testament lesson, with readings from the Law, the Prophets, and the Wisdom books, respectively. Corresponding to this they developed a reading from a Pauline epistle, a catholic epistle, and a Gospel. These selections just listed were made before the Syrian Jacobites had moved to a third Old Testament lesson. Another thing which indicates the antiquity of these selections is their witness to a *lectio continua* of several different books. There are traces of a *lectio continua* of Exodus which must have taken the better part of a year, a *lectio continua* of Jeremiah which may well have taken just as long, and a reading of the prophet Ezekiel which may have at least started during the Easter season. One wonders if these pieces of evidence are contradictory to the lectionary of Mosul, or whether perhaps they might dovetail with it. Is it possible that what we have here is evidence that during one year the *lectio continua* from the Law was taken from Genesis, during another year from Exodus, and during still a third year from Deuteronomy? The same thing could have been done with the Prophets. We saw how a year was given to Isaiah in the lectionary of Mosul; now we see evidence that a year was given to Jeremiah and perhaps Ezekiel as well. On the other hand, Ezekiel may have become a favored prophet for Easter time just as the book of Acts was favored for between Easter and Pentecost. While Acts spoke of the evangelism of the primitive Church, Ezekiel was prophetic of the worship of the restored messianic community. One thing seems to be indicated by the evidence which has so far come to light: The Syriac lectionaries were very fluid. One wonders if they felt a strong compulsion to do everything just the way it was done last year. Surely there were old favorites, like reading the fifty-third chapter of Isaiah on Good Friday or the sixtieth chapter on Easter Sunday, but perhaps in regard to other readings there was more play in what could "traditionally" be read. Perhaps one year one could read through Jeremiah or the book of the twelve prophets. One year the first half of Genesis could be read during Lent and another year the second half, planned so that the Joseph cycle could be read during Holy Week.

Only as the tradition of the *lectio continua* was more and more neglected in favor of prescribed pericopes assigned to specific points on the liturgical calendar did one begin to tailor the *lectio continua* to fit into the liturgical calendar. Tailoring the *lectio continua* to the calendar is a rather late development in the history of the liturgical reading of Scripture. In fact, when this tailoring occurs and the *lectio continua* becomes fixed, the real spirit of this ancient principle is largely lost.

Much time could be given to the study of these Syrian lectionaries. They give us an important look into the time when the public reading of Scripture was more flexible than it later became. The great number and variety of the lectionaries suggest that whatever rules and precedents there might have been were not really all that hard and fast. Passages of less interest could be dropped and other passages could be added. One year one thing could be done and the next year something else could be done. No matter how one may wish to interpret this, one cannot help but be impressed by the fact that so much of the Bible is included. The enthusiasm of the Syriac-speaking church for the public reading of Scripture is evident.

CHAPTER V

The Latin Fathers

With the age of Theodosius, Latin preaching began to flourish. Ambrose of Milan, true to the best tradition of classical antiquity, recognized the importance of personally addressing the people. He was one of those literate patricians who understood the need of making clear to the people the direction in which he wanted to lead them. Augustine was his disciple, and being schooled in classical rhetoric, he developed the homiletical tradition of the West with practical good sense. No one could have been more Roman than Augustine! With all his philosophical brilliance he never lost sight of the popular orientation of Christian preaching. Even Jerome, who in his literary activity was often fastidious, preached to his monks in Bethlehem in a simple, direct, and practical way. His masterpiece was the Vulgate, the Word of God in the language of the common people. Among the Latin Fathers there was, however, neither a John Chrysostom nor a Gregory of Nazianzus. The Latin Fathers never produced great oratory in the same way the Greek Fathers did but were much more pragmatic, much more popular in their approach.

The Romans shared with the Greeks much the same sort of culture, and it was Hellenistic culture which bound together the empire of the Caesars. The subjects of that vast empire shared many of the same attitudes toward life and many of the same values. Greece and Rome had in common the same pantheon and honored the same deities. They recounted many of the same epics, together admiring the heroes of the Trojan War. The grandeur that was Rome was heir to the glory that was Greece. Even at that, though, Rome had its own distinct character, and in many ways the Latin Fathers exemplified that character in their preaching.

Latin Christianity inherited much from Roman civilization, much that was distinctly different from what Greek Christianity inherited from Greek civilization. This is particularly clear in the distinction between Platonism and Stoicism. While Platonism and Neoplatonism had a wide attraction in Greece, Rome was much more attracted by Stoicism. The Christian gospel had to address the cultural heritage of the peoples it evangelized, and as one would expect, the Church Fathers did just that. Those to whom they preached were attracted by different aspects of the Christian faith, depending on what their old faith, be it Platonism or Stoicism, had taught them to admire. It might be a bit too simplistic to say that those brought up in Platonism admired the otherworldliness of Christianity while those brought up in Stoicism found the practical moral teachings of Christianity attractive. It was much more complicated than that, but there is something to it, nevertheless. Rarely was the average Roman a pure Stoic or the average Greek a pure Platonist. By the time the Christian faith began to appeal to the masses of the Roman Empire Platonism had become Neoplatonism and Stoicism was in its late period. The popular Platonism of the fourth Christian century was a long way from Plato, and Stoicism a long way from Zeno. The majority of people were eclectic when it came to the philosophical schools. They may have been influenced by an amalgam of the views of the old philosophers, but they also were influenced by all kinds of superstitions and in time of need turned to amulets, omens, and divination. The Hellenistic mystery religions had a strong influence in the Roman Empire in the third and fourth centuries. In fact, the mysteries probably had a stronger influence than faith in the old Homeric gods.

There is no question but that Stoicism had a particularly strong influence on Roman civilization. Stoicism caught the imagination of the Roman aristocracy especially from the time of Cicero to the time of Marcus Aurelius, that is, from just before Christ to just before Constantine. It was to the serious minded of Roman antiquity that Stoicism appealed. Quite different from Epicureanism, Stoicism fostered an earnestness about life to which the Christian preacher could appeal. It was the simple life that the Stoic admired; the luxurious and the dramatic tended to be thought of as decadent. It is therefore that we find the Latin Fathers advocating a simpler rhetoric. The more elaborate orations and panegyrics of the Cappadocian Fathers were simply not as effective where Stoicism had made its influence felt. Often it is said that the Romans were a very practical people, a people who loved to build highways and bridges, while the Greeks were much more philosophical and loved to speculate about metaphysics. One might say the Romans were better engineers than philosophers. The Romans were interested in philosophy, but they were above all interested in moral philosophy. Stoic philosophy had appealed to this strain in the Roman temperament and encouraged it, and when the Romans were converted to Christianity they retained this tendency. We will find the Latin Fathers preaching frequently about the practical living of the Christian life.

Stoicism gave much attention to the community. To use a well-worn phrase, Stoicism taught the brotherhood of man, a concept upon which it was easy for Christian preachers to build. Slave or free, Roman, Greek, or barbarian — all human beings were equal. Again and again the Stoics compared the different classes of society to the members of the human body, and for the body to function all the members must work together. The apostle Paul was not the only Christian who saw the truth in this metaphor. For the well-run state all classes were important, and therefore the state must exist as a commonwealth for all. Here was a philosophy which gave a major role to the state. Patriotism was among the highest of spiritual values, and nothing could be more honorable than service to that state. The emperor Marcus Aurelius ranked among the saints of Stoicism. Involvement in public affairs was important for Stoic piety. As we shall see, Christians like Ambrose of Milan were able to fulfill the highest ideals of Stoicism in the course of their preaching ministry. If Gregory of Nazianzus was a Christian Demosthenes, Ambrose was a Christian Cicero. Just as Cicero was an orator in the service of the Senate and people of Rome, so Ambrose was a preacher in the service of the Christian Church.

When it came to worship there were many ways in which the Stoics provided a good foundation for developing the understanding of worship found in the New Testament. Put another way, biblical concepts of worship found a fertile field in the presuppositions of Stoic philosophy. They thrived in this field far better than in the field prepared by the mystery religions or the popular Platonism of the day. The best example we have of this is the work of Lactantius. Lactantius was not a preacher, but he wrote a most important chapter, "On True Worship," in his famous *Divine Institutes*. As Lactantius saw it, Christian worship in its simplicity, in its rejection of ostentation and ceremonial, honored God far more than the elaborate rituals of paganism. Nothing could serve God more than the hymns and praises of a holy people and sermons which taught people how to live an earnest and honest life. "On True Worship" helps us understand many of the most important features of the preaching of the Latin Fathers.

I. Ambrose

Ambrose was a man of ten talents, all of which he dedicated to God with complete sincerity and single-mindedness. Brought up in the best traditions of the Roman nobility as well as in the most solid sort of Christian piety, Ambrose can well be regarded as a prototype of Christian leadership.

Ambrose (339-97) was born in what today is Trier, Germany.[1] There his father was the Roman governor of Gaul, which by that time, four hundred years after Julius Caesar, was a solid Roman province. He must have been still a boy when his father died, after which his mother returned to Rome with him and his brother and sister. The two boys received a very fine education and solid training in the liberal arts. Greek was evidently spoken at home, which may indicate that the family had some Greek ancestry or some other Greek connection, and they learned to speak the language fluently. Perhaps the father or grandfather of the family had done service in a Greek-speaking province. As they grew older they studied law and prepared to follow their father into the Roman civil service. They must have been given a solid Christian education at home and maintained a disciplined Christian life from childhood because Marcelline, the sister of Ambrose, entered a convent in Rome while Ambrose was still a teenager.

About 370 Ambrose was appointed governor of the Roman provinces of Liguria and Aemilia. Milan was at the time serving as the administrative center of the region, and it was there that the emperor maintained his residence. Ambrose quickly won a reputation as a governor of high principles and integrity. The story is often told of how he was called to arbitrate

---

1. For biographical material on Ambrose, see the following: Hans Freiherr von Campenhausen, "Ambrosius," in *Lateinische Kirchenväter*, 2nd rev. ed. (Stuttgart: W. Kohlhammer, 1965), pp. 77-108; Hans Freiherr von Campenhausen, *Ambrosius von Miland als Kirchenpolitiker* (Berlin and Leipzig: W. de Gruyter, 1929); Frederick Homes Dudden, *The Life and Times of St. Ambrose*, 2 vols. (Oxford: Clarendon Press, 1935); Maria Grazia Mara, "Ambrose of Milan," *Patrology*, vol. 4, ed. Angelo di Bernardino, English translation by Placid Solari (Westminster, Md.: Christian Classics, 1994), pp. 144-79; Angelo Paredi, *St. Ambrose*, trans. J. Costello (Notre Dame, Ind.: University of Notre Dame Press, 1963).

in a dispute over the election of a new bishop for Milan and in the course of trying to settle the situation was surprised to find himself elected to the position by acclamation. Being a sincere Christian, he accepted and applied himself conscientiously to fulfilling his new responsibilities. An important part of his preparation for his new ministry was devoting himself to a thorough study of the Christian literature of the time. We assume this included such works as those of Tertullian, Cyprian, and Lactantius. Under the guidance of the able theologian Simplicianus, he carefully read through the writings of a number of Greek theologians — Origen, Athanasius, Didymus the Blind, and Basil. Ambrose is usually regarded as a politician turned preacher, but he was well read in theology just the same.

A. Sermons on Luke

Typical of the preaching of Ambrose of Milan is a series of sermons on the Gospel of Luke which has come down to us in the form of a commentary on the Gospel.[2] It is quite easy to see that this is really a transcript of a series of sermons. Sometimes, but not always, introductions or conclusions enable us to recognize individual sermons. Apparently some material of a more homiletical sort has been left out, but much has been retained in the published version. As was Ambrose's custom, the editorial work was not done with a heavy hand. His *De sacramentis*, which we will study below, is an example of a stenographic report of a series of sermons which has come down to us with no editorial revision, while his *De mysteriis* is a fully revised edition of the same material.

To get an idea of how this outstanding pastor exercised the ministry of the Word, let us look at his sermons on the fourth and fifth chapters of the Gospel of Luke. In these chapters Luke tells us of the beginning of Jesus' ministry, starting out with the story of the temptations in the wilderness and the sermon in Nazareth, continuing with Jesus' ministry of healing in Capernaum, and concluding with the story of the conversion

2. This study is based on the text of Gabriel Tissot: Ambrose of Milan, *Traité sur l'Évangile de S. Luc*, ed. Gabriel Tissot, Sources chrétiennes, vols. 45 and 52 (Paris: Les Éditions du Cerf, 1956 and 1958); hereinafter Ambrose, *On Luke*. See as well *Patrologia Latina*, 15:1607-1944. For studies of this work, see August Engelbrecht, *Studien über den Lukaskommentar des Ambrosius* (Vienna, 1903); and D. Ramos-Lisson, "La doctrina de la 'salus' en la 'Expositio Evangelii secundum Lucam' de s. Ambrosio," *Scripta Teologica* 5 (1973): 629-66.

of the tax collector Levi, who eventually became the apostle Matthew. A good variety of subjects is covered in the passage — there are dialogues, healing stories, and teachings. Ambrose probably devoted at least six sermons to this material.

The sermon on the temptation in the wilderness shows mature insight regarding the nature of the Christian life. It has sometimes been claimed that from the standpoint of biblical interpretation Ambrose offers little that is original. Supposedly he is strongly under the influence of Origen's commentary on the same Gospel.[3] Although Ambrose is passing on much material he has learned from Origen or from other Christian teachers, it is material which has obviously passed through his own experience and is therefore truly his own.[4] This is of the very nature of the pastoral office; Ambrose as a minister of the Word has learned from the tradition how the Scriptures are to be understood. He has lived out these same Scriptures in his own life, and now as a preacher gives witness that these Scriptures are the Word of God.

The material as we now find it begins with a long introduction about the temptations of Ulysses.[5] As Gabriel Tissot suggests, this material may have been added to the sermon in the process of editing it, but then again it would certainly be appropriate to the sermon. A Victorian homiletician would have been delighted with Ambrose for using his extensive knowledge of the literary traditions of his day to embroider his sermon. On the other hand, if this account of how the hero of the Trojan War was tempted again and again in the course of his odyssey was recounted in the sermon as it was actually preached, it must be admitted that it was not something that a Christian congregation in that day was accustomed to hearing in a sermon. The similarity and the contrast between the temptations of Ulysses and Christ are certainly striking and indeed instructive, but the Christian congregation was more accustomed to hearing the contrast between the temptation in the wilderness and the temptation in the Garden of Eden. The text of the sermon as it has come down to us brings this out, to be sure.[6] That was classic Christian material, as Ambrose no doubt learned

---

3. Only the sermons Origen preached on the first two chapters of Luke's Gospel have survived. For details, see volume 1 of this work, the section on Origen's sermons on the Gospel of Luke.

4. On the sources used by Ambrose, cf. Tissot's edition of Ambrose's *Traité sur l'Évangile de S. Luc*, pp. 15-18.

5. Ambrose, *On Luke* 4.2.

6. Ambrose, *On Luke* 4.7.

from Origen as well as from the sermons of countless other Christian preachers of the time.

Ambrose presents this material in the best rhetorical style of his day. At one place he contrasts the old Adam and Christ the new Adam in a series of those terse antithetical phrases which so delighted the devotees of Roman literature:

> From the virgin earth came Adam;
>> from the Virgin Mary came Christ.
> Adam was made in the image of God;
>> Christ was the image of God himself.
> Adam had authority over all animals;
>> Christ had authority over all creation.
> Adam was made foolish through woman;
>> Christ was made wise through the Virgin.
> Adam tasted death through a tree;
>> Christ brought life through a Cross.[7]

Ambrose had had the kind of Roman education which made it easy for him to be eloquent when the occasion arose.

In actual fact, Ambrose, and the early Christian exegetical tradition that preceded him, probably understood Luke correctly here. Luke seems to have understood the scene of the annunciation earlier in the Gospel as the reverse of the temptation of Eve, and now in the fourth chapter Mary's child triumphs over the ancient serpent by standing fast against the temptations of Satan.[8] Ambrose may not have gone through the usual theological training in his day, but this sermon certainly shows that he had in some way or another gotten a good hold on the tradition of exegesis which the Church had built up in the three and a half centuries since Jesus began it in his own preaching.

We also see from this sermon that Ambrose was no flyweight theologian. One of the major points he makes is that Jesus went through temptation because, as the Son of God who had been born a true man, he suffered all the hardships, all the disappointments, all the pressures,

---

7. "Ex terra uirgine Adam, Christus ex uirgine, ille ad imaginem dei factus, hic imago dei, ille omnibus inrationabilibus animalibus, hic omnibus animantibus antelatus — per mulierem stultitia, per uirginem sapientia, mors per arborem, uita per crucem. . . ." Ambrose, *On Luke* 4.7.

8. Ambrose, *On Luke* 2.3.

and all the frustrations that we suffer. Again we find this truth expressed in a series of terse phrases:

> That he might win the infirm,
> he became infirm.
> That he might win the poor,
> he became poor.
> To win the rich,
> he was rich.
> To win the weeping,
> he wept.
> To win the hungry,
> he hungered.
> To win the thirsty,
> he thirsted.[9]

There was nothing conformist about the orthodox Christology of our preacher. He understood the issues quite thoroughly. He realized that it had always been Nicene orthodoxy which understood the essence of the Gospel.

Another thing we find in this sermon is the obvious evidence of our preacher's pastoral good sense. In this particular case we see how Ambrose recognizes the temptations which most readily come the way of the sincerely devout. Religion has its own temptations, and these temptations are particularly strong for those who are put in positions of church leadership. Serious theological error is a strong temptation for the devout.[10] The irreligious hardly consider such things. The truly chaste are tempted to condemn marriage.[11] Rigorism is a constant temptation to celibate Christians.[12]

From the standpoint of literary form this sermon follows the tradition of the classic expository sermon as it had been developed first in the synagogue and then in the Church. Our preacher has chosen a passage of about a dozen verses which follows directly the passage on which he had preached the service before and continues the passage to its logical con-

---

9. "Factus est infirmibus infirmus per corporis passionem, ut lucrifaceret eos, omnibus postremo omnia factus est, pauper pauperibus, diues diuitibus, flens flentibus, esuriens esurientibus, sitiens sitientibus. . . ." Ambrose, *On Luke* 4.6.

10. Ambrose, *On Luke* 4.10.

11. Ambrose, *On Luke* 4.10.

12. Ambrose, *On Luke* 4.10.

clusion. Just where the passage begins and where it should end is part of his job of interpretation, and how fast or how slow he goes is a matter of his wisdom in deciding what the congregation is able to absorb from the material being treated. For these two chapters we would suppose there to have been at least six sermons. That would be approximately three sermons per chapter, which would seem about right for a Sunday morning preaching-through of one of the Gospels. Starting at the beginning of the passage that serves as the text, our preacher quotes the line or lines from Scripture and then comments on them, after which he moves on to the next line or phrase on which he wants to comment, drawing conclusions or applications when appropriate. Our preacher moves on in like manner through the text until he has reached the end of the passage he has selected or, perhaps, until he has reached the end of the hour or so the preacher was usually allotted. The organization of the sermon carefully followed the arrangement of the text. This arrangement was markedly different from the sort taught by the schools of rhetoric. The fact that in his expository sermons Ambrose followed quite carefully the literary form of the Hebrew expository sermon rather than that of the Greek panegyric or even the philosophical discourses of the Stoic philosophers such as Cicero and Seneca is an indication of his careful adherence to the homiletical traditions which the Church had by this time developed. In this regard he is quite different from, say, Gregory of Nazianzus, but quite similar to John Chrysostom. On the other hand, as we shall see, when he preached his sermon against Auxentius he followed closely the example of Cicero.

We move on to the next passage in the fourth chapter of the Gospel of Luke, the story of Jesus preaching in the synagogue of Nazareth.[13] This passage allows Ambrose to address a number of subjects, but he makes no attempt to draw them together into a single theme. First there is the matter of how the scene as it is found in Luke illustrates the orthodox doctrine of the unity of the persons of the Trinity. The fact that Jesus picks up the Old Testament and reads from the book of Isaiah about his being anointed by the Holy Spirit should be sufficient to refute the claims of the Marcionites, who insisted that the God of the Old Testament was different from the God of the New Testament.[14] The scene shows clearly, according to our preacher, that Jesus saw a continuity between the Word of God as it was proclaimed by the Old Testament prophets and the Word of God as

13. Ambrose, *On Luke* 4.43-56.
14. Ambrose, *On Luke* 4.44.

Jesus himself proclaimed it. The same Holy Spirit who had anointed Isaiah, anointed Jesus to preach.[15] In the story of the baptism of Jesus the unity and cooperation of the persons had been even more evident. There the Holy Spirit had descended in the form of a dove and the voice of the Father was heard from heaven claiming Jesus as his Son. Here in the synagogue there is the same thing, albeit not as clearly demonstrated; nevertheless, it is an obvious reality. Ambrose devotes much of his sermon to discussing the theme of why the Jews rejected their own Messiah. Jesus' choice of text alone, our preacher tells us, made the messianic claim patent: "The Spirit of the Lord has anointed me." What particularly catches the attention of Ambrose are the stories from the book of Kings which tell how in the ministry of Elijah and Elisha the Gentiles often received the blessings of God when the Jews were too hard-hearted to receive God's Word.[16] Because they would not listen they could not be blessed. Even from the beginning of his ministry the Jews rejected Jesus, and yet Jesus still preferred to do his work among them rather than the Gentiles.[17] The long-suffering of God's grace toward his people is a mystery at which we can only be amazed.[18]

What appears to be a third sermon deals with two episodes from Jesus' ministry in Capernaum, the healing of a man with a withered arm in the synagogue and the healing of the mother-in-law of Simon Peter (Luke 4:31-44).[19] In this case the stenographic report of the sermon was either thoroughly condensed or sharply abbreviated, but there does seem to be a unity to the material that suggests it formed a single, complete sermon.

Right away Ambrose suggests, *"Vide clementiam domini salvatoris,"* that is, "Notice the clemency of the Lord of Salvation!"[20] To a congregation of Romans recently turned Christian this had a familiar ring. Clemency was one of the four virtues of classical antiquity. This was a different value system from the biblical value system, a value system which would be worked into Scholastic moral theology. What is interesting here is the way Ambrose, one of the most perceptive of the Latin

---

15. Ambrose, *On Luke* 4.45.
16. Ambrose, *On Luke* 4.48-49.
17. Ambrose, *On Luke* 4.56.
18. Ambrose, *On Luke* 4.55-56.
19. Ambrose, *On Luke* 4.57-67.
20. Ambrose, *On Luke* 4.57.

Church Fathers, is already claiming the best of pagan moral philosophy for the Christian faith. Jesus is an example of the noble Roman virtue of clemency.[21]

Even at that, however, Ambrose seems most concerned to show that in Jesus and his works of healing it is the grace of God himself which is revealed. Grace is not the same thing as clemency, similar as they may appear, but a uniquely biblical concept. The unifying theme which Ambrose finds both in the story of the healing of the man in the synagogue and in the healing of Peter's mother-in-law is clearly the biblical understanding of grace. Provoked by their injustice, offended by their evils, moved by indignation, Jesus could simply have left the Jews to their own devices, but that, Ambrose points out, he did not do. Instead, he was mindful of his mercy, sometimes teaching them, sometimes delivering them from demons, sometimes healing their bodies; by whatever means he could he softened the hearts of unbelievers. Jesus was determined to win the devotion of his people.[22]

Right from the beginning of his ministry Jesus was concerned to show that he had come to heal both men and women, for he delivered a man in the synagogue from an unclean spirit, and then later on that same day he delivered a woman, Peter's mother-in-law, from a fever.[23]

Ambrose finds significance in the fact that these healings took place on the Sabbath. He makes particular note of the fact that the first healing recorded by Luke took place on the Sabbath; it was on the Sabbath that the healing work of the Lord's Day was begun.[24] This was to show that the work of the new creation had started. It is clear that from the beginning the Son of God was not under the Law but was rather superior to the Law, and yet he did not destroy the Law but fulfilled it. It was not through the old written Law that this man was healed, but through the very Word of God himself, incarnate in Jesus Christ. Just as at the beginning, this was the case even for the old creation: "By the word of the LORD the heavens were made" (Ps. 33:6). The Law was not abolished but fulfilled that the humanity which had once been desecrated might be restored.[25] The two miracles side by side teach us the same principle we find taught

21. Ambrose, *On Luke* 4.57.
22. Ambrose, *On Luke* 4.57.
23. Ambrose, *On Luke* 4.57.
24. Ambrose, *On Luke* 4.58.
25. Ambrose, *On Luke* 4.58.

by the apostle Paul: "For as in Adam all die, so also in Christ shall all be made alive" (I Cor. 15:22).[26]

Following the direction of Alexandrian exegesis, Ambrose presents the man with the unclean spirit whom Jesus healed in the synagogue at Capernaum as an allegory of the Jewish people. We know that Ambrose had studied Origen's commentary on the same Gospel. We wish we knew exactly what Origen had to say about this story, but, apart from the first two chapters, Origen's commentary on Luke is among the many works of the Alexandrian master which have been lost. Ambrose asks who this man possessed by an evil spirit might be, and suggests he is none other than the people of the Jews. The reason he has an unclean spirit is because he had lost the Holy Spirit, for the devil entered when Christ left.[27] Even at that, the unclean spirit was not to have the victory, for Jesus commanded the demon to leave the man and he did. First the man's spirit was healed, then his body.

From a story about the healing of a man's spirit Ambrose takes us to a story about the healing of a woman's body. Somewhat hesitatingly Ambrose proceeds to give an allegorical interpretation to the story of the healing of Peter's mother-in-law. She should perhaps be regarded as a figure of the fever which our flesh suffers from different desires, our preacher tells us, for the desires of the flesh are a fever, as we learn from the apostle Paul's comments to the Corinthians that it is better to marry than to burn (I Cor. 7:9). Luxury is another one of our fevers; still another is anger. With this our preacher launches into a long discussion of the fevers of desire and how they can destroy our spiritual health.[28] In all this Ambrose makes it quite clear that what these two stories teach us is the surprising goodness of God, who so patiently and tirelessly works for our salvation and whose efforts, because he is our almighty Lord, will not be frustrated.[29] This sermon is a good example of how one of the Church Fathers, strongly influenced by Origen, uses his principles of allegorical exegesis to interpret the New Testament. The allegorical method can come up with some strange ideas, but there is never any question but that in the pulpit of Ambrose the grace of God in the work of Christ is clearly proclaimed. Again and again we find the sermons of Ambrose marked by hermeneutical good sense.

26. Ambrose, *On Luke* 4.61.
27. Ambrose, *On Luke* 4.61.
28. Ambrose, *On Luke* 4.64-65.
29. Ambrose, *On Luke* 4.65.

The next sermon, if we have taken the right hints from our text, has to do with the mighty works of Christ on the Sea of Galilee. Again we find this of particular interest because the interpretation is strongly allegorical. In this case, however, it seems to be justified. The story as we find it in the Gospel of Luke is about a miraculous catch of fish, and Ambrose compares it with the account of the stilling of the storm found in Matthew 8, as the two stories are quite similar. He makes the point that while in the beginning the Church goes through difficult storms, in the end the mission of the Church is successful.[30] The boat is understood as an allegory of the Church. So far the allegorizing of the story may be quite in line with the intention of the author. One can imagine that when Luke wrote the story into his Gospel, the ship was already understood as an allegory of the Church. One might even go so far as to say that in the event itself there was an element of the acted-out parable which was so significant in the ministry of the Old Testament prophets. Jesus may have himself handled the event as a prophetic sign of the evangelical ministry he intended his disciples to continue in the world. Ambrose found in the story a sign of the divine authority of Jesus to command the wind and the sea and thereby protect the Church in times of trouble.[31]

Up to this point the allegorical interpretation of Ambrose seems appropriate enough, but as is often the case with allegorical interpretations, his imagination carries him a bit too far. Peter's boat is allegorized as the Church, but the boat of John and James in the story is allegorized as well.[32] As much time as Ambrose takes in developing some of these bizarre allegorical flourishes, he brings the sermon back into focus by concentrating on Peter's reaction to this sign: He falls down before Jesus, confessing himself to be a poor sinner. As Ambrose understands it, Peter's humility is exemplary. We ought to say the same thing, our preacher exclaims, in order that we might hear from our Lord his words of consolation, *noli timere,* Fear not! We need not be afraid, Ambrose assures us, to bring our faults and offenses to the Lord, confessing our sin, for he is not one to be envious or fly into a rage about our wrongdoings. He is neither unresponsive nor distant. Ambrose assures his congregation, Come see how good the Lord is! He is gracious to us, even to the point of giving his life for us![33]

30. Ambrose, *On Luke* 4.68.
31. Ambrose, *On Luke* 4.69.
32. Ambrose, *On Luke* 4.70 and 77.
33. Ambrose, *On Luke* 4.79.

A fifth sermon appears to begin with Ambrose's interpretation of the story of the healing of a leper found in Luke 5:12-16 and continues through the story of the healing of the paralytic let down through the roof in Luke 5:17-26.[34] This is suggested by the conclusion at the end of the interpretation of the latter story which closely links the two stories.[35]

Ambrose begins by observing that it is appropriate that the text "While he was in one of the cities . . ." (Luke 5:12) is a bit vague as to the locality of this healing, because that indicates that this healing could have happened in any city. Even more, the healing of this one leper was a sign of the healing of all lepers and, in fact, a sign of the healing of all peoples everywhere by the gospel of Christ.[36] Furthermore, this cleansing of this particular leper is one of those signs which demonstrates how Jesus came not to destroy the Law but to fulfill it. This is particularly clear when one compares it to the version of the story found in Matthew. The Law only excluded lepers from society, but Christ healed the leper and restored him to the community. The story, according to Ambrose, teaches much about grace which is over and above the Law. That grace which we find in Christ is able to wash away the spots of leprosy. In this story we see on one hand the power and authority of our Lord, but we also see in the man who approached Jesus with his plight a firm and steadfast faith. Ambrose notes that this leper was a very devout and pious man. He came up to Jesus and bowed down, touching his face to the ground. This indicates his humility and his modesty. He knows full well the shame and fallibility of the human situation, but he also knows that in God there is the hope of salvation. If you will, he pleads, you have the power to heal me.[37]

What Ambrose finds edifying in this story is that the man attributes effective power to the bare will of Christ. He has no doubt that Christ can heal him, but he is not sure that Christ will want to heal him. It is not that he doubts the goodness of the Lord but only that he is so conscious of the shame of his situation that he does not want to presume on the goodness of God. How well Ambrose understands the hesitation of so many of us! Even more Ambrose understands the love of God. He affirms that in the simple response of Jesus, "I will. Be clean," the man was healed and the divine love was revealed.

34. Ambrose, *On Luke* 5.1-15.
35. Ambrose, *On Luke* 5.15.
36. Ambrose, *On Luke* 5.1.
37. Ambrose, *On Luke* 5.2.

Nothing came between the work our Lord performed and the Word he gave. He spoke and it was done.[38] The very will of God has within it the power of God. For Ambrose this makes it clear that in Jesus is the unity of will and power which belongs to the Trinity, the divine will and the divine power in perfect cooperation. In this single story from the Gospel of Luke Ambrose sees three major heresies refuted, that of Arius, that of Photin of Sirmium, and that of the Manichaeans.[39] For Ambrose the Word of God had its own power — it healed the leprosy directly. It was as the words recorded in the Gospel of John attest: "'You are already made clean by the word which I have spoken to you'" (John 15:3). If therefore the medicine for leprosy is receiving the word with faith, then receiving the Word with contempt is a leprosy of the mind.[40]

For Ambrose this story of the healing of the leper teaches us about the nature of true faith. It shows the value of spontaneous faith, for it was with spontaneous faith that he approached Jesus, and it was with spontaneous faith that he received the healing words of Jesus. It was not a calculated faith called into existence in order to win a cure; he simply believed the Lord, who said, "Be healed." It is this kind of faith, Ambrose assures us, which receives the blessing of God.[41] Ambrose has an evangelical understanding of the saving power of faith, just as he seems to have a deep appreciation of the Pauline doctrine of grace. One often says this about Augustine rather than Ambrose; in fact, Augustine is famous for his appreciation of these central Christian doctrines. A study of these sermons on the Gospel of Luke, however, might well suggest that Augustine learned these doctrines from the preacher he so often heard and so much admired, Ambrose of Milan.[42]

Ambrose's commentary on the story of the healing of the paralytic let down through the roof seems to be a continuation of the same sermon. Our preacher finds in this story an important teaching on the corporate nature of Christian faith, as it is really the friends of the paralytic who have faith. Ambrose suggests that here we see an example of how those who need help are well advised to seek the intercession of their Christian

38. Ambrose, *On Luke* 5.3.

39. Ambrose, *On Luke* 5.4.

40. Ambrose, *On Luke* 5.5.

41. Ambrose, *On Luke* 5.5.

42. P. Rollero, "L'influsso dell'Exposito in Lucam di Ambrogio nell'esegesi agostiniana," in *Augustinus Magister,* 2 vols. (Paris: Études augustiniennes, 1954-55), 2:211-20; P. Rollero, *La Expositio Evangelii secundum di Ambrogio come fonte dell'esegesi agostiniana* (Turin, 1958).

friends.[43] One gathers that the fourth-century bishop of Milan well understood what we sometimes imagine is a more contemporary insight. Indeed, the supportive help of the fellowship of the Church is a significant element in Christian healing.[44]

Much of the body of this sermon is taken up by a discussion of the way the scribes and the Pharisees objected to Jesus' forgiving the man's sin and Jesus' answer that it is not much harder to say your sins are forgiven you than to say rise up and walk. Again Ambrose comes up with an observation which we think of as very modern. As he sees it, it is the whole man which needs to be healed.[45]

Ambrose concludes the sermon by tying together these two healing stories with a very sobering thought. He observes that Jesus, the Great High Priest, saw the leprosy in the hearts of the Jews, a kind of leprosy worse than that of the leper who had come to him for healing. Those sick from this kind of leprosy Jesus sent away lest they contaminate others.[46] From that sermon the congregation must have gone home with something to think about.

Now we turn to a masterpiece! The sixth sermon we find on the fourth and fifth chapters of Luke is on the conversion of Levi. The sermon has been preserved in a relatively full form, and yet the stenographic report has noticeably condensed the material. It must have been a long sermon. Here again we have a good example of the classical expository sermon, going from verse to verse explaining the text as it comes.

The sermon is introduced by a description of the call of Levi. It could be the call of any one of us. Levi was a man who had formerly devoted his life to the amassing of a fortune, but when he heard the call of Christ to come and follow him, he rose up and did just that. Levi the tax collector became Matthew the Evangelist. Here again we have a masterpiece of terse Latin prose. It is the story of one who heard the mystical call of Christ and, free from the attachments of the flesh, followed the inclination of his heart.[47] Quitting the infamous bureau of the tax collector, he followed his new master with all the ardor of his soul. He put on his festal robes and prepared a great banquet for his Lord. That is the

---

43. Ambrose, *On Luke* 5.11.
44. Ambrose, *On Luke* 5.10.
45. Ambrose, *On Luke* 5.13.
46. Ambrose, *On Luke* 5.15.
47. Ambrose, *On Luke* 5.16.

nature of conversion. Those who receive the Christ in the secret chamber of their hearts, Ambrose tells us, are fed on heavenly delicacies.

With the idea of conversion as a spiritual feast in which the soul of the believer enters into communion with Christ, Ambrose fashions together the whole sermon in an artistic unity. Even if the sermon does follow the literary form of the classical expository sermon, Ambrose is sufficiently the master of his material that he is often able to give a unifying theme to his discourse. This seems to come quite naturally to Ambrose, who had been trained in the literary classics. However, he did not feel he had to follow some kind of artistic canon or convention that forced him to forge a unifying theme for his material even when no such unifying theme legitimately followed from the material. Sometimes he found no such unity, but often he was able to weave together the different subjects treated in the course of his exposition into a very natural thematic unity.

The Gospel account tells us not only that Levi got up from his counting table and followed Jesus but that he prepared a great feast in his home. It is this feast and the conversation at this feast which form the body of the sermon. Freely the Lord enters into the home of those who believe in him. Happily he abides there. But for those who will not believe, there is no feast. There is only fasting. Ambrose cites his text. He explains the questions which are raised. The scribes and the Pharisees are very critical of Jesus because he eats and drinks with common people. They could admire the spirituality of John the Baptist, who was an ascetic, but the worldliness of Jesus offended them. This is the difference, Ambrose comments, between those who insist on living by the Law and those who live by grace. Those who live by the Law are subject to a fast and are eternally hungry,[48] but those who have received the Word of God in the secret places of their hearts are renewed by the abundance of God's house and the eternal fountain of life, and they cannot hunger or thirst. And that is why those who from a spiritual standpoint are perpetually fasting murmur about Jesus' eating and drinking with publicans and sinners.[49] Our preacher proceeds to the next line of his text, " 'Those who are well have no need of a physician, but those who are sick' " (Luke 5:31). This murmuring of the scribes and the Pharisees is the voice of the serpent. It is only right that Jesus eat with tax collectors and sinners because it is they who need him most.[50]

48. Ambrose, *On Luke* 5.17.
49. Ambrose, *On Luke* 5.18.
50. Ambrose, *On Luke* 5.18.

Ambrose moves on to another line in his text, " 'The days will come, when the bridegroom is taken away from them, and then they will fast in those days' " (Luke 5:35). He comments that Christ, however, has promised to be with us until the end of the age; he has promised not to leave us as orphans (Matt. 28:20 and John 14:18). No one can take Christ from us, neither Caiaphas nor Pontius Pilate. No one can separate us from Christ unless we ourselves leave him through our boasting and our arrogance.[51] Ambrose is a persuasive evangelist in his classical expository preaching, just as Origen was. He warns that if we do not accept Christ we find the contrary — we end up living by law rather than by grace. The scribes and Pharisees we read about in this passage invented their own righteousness. They usurped the righteousness of God and therefore never heard Christ's call to grace. The call to grace was, of course, a call to repentance, and so, despising repentance, they renounced grace.

Our preacher takes up still another line of his text, " 'No one tears a piece from a new garment and puts it upon an old garment; if he does, he will tear the new . . .' " (Luke 5:36). This parable, Ambrose says, is addressed to the friends of the groom, that is, the friends of the Word, who through baptism have been joined to the people of God.[52] As long as the groom is with them they are not able to fast. Now, Ambrose asks, how can it be that the disciples are kept from fasting when in fact their Master himself fasted? As the sermon is reported, Ambrose never really gives the answer that in the actual sermon he must have given. Fasting, as Ambrose no doubt recognized, is of value as a devotional discipline, but it is corrupted when it is imposed as a sort of rigorism or legalism, as in fact many did. Alluding to Colossians 3:9-10, Ambrose tells us that what we need to understand by this passage is that the works of the old man are not to be mixed with the works of the new man.[53] The festal garments of the friends of the groom should be of the same color as that of the groom. They should not be soiled or spotted. The festal garments of the Christian should be peace of soul, purity of heart, and clarity of mind, for the groom is none other than the Lord Jesus.[54]

The conclusion of the sermon is a fine apostrophe in the best tradition of classical rhetoric. "No more will I hear about the old Levi.

51. Ambrose, *On Luke* 5.20.
52. Ambrose, *On Luke* 5.23.
53. Ambrose, *On Luke* 5.23.
54. Ambrose, *On Luke* 5.23-24.

Off with the old Levi! On with Christ! I flee from my old life. You only, O Lord Jesus Christ, would I follow! You have healed my wounds! Who shall separate me from the love of God which I have found in you, O Christ! Shall tribulation, or distress, or famine take me from you? With nails of faith I am joined to you. I am held fast to you by the gentle claim of your love."[55] No one who knows the classics of American evangelistic preaching will fail to recognize this sinner's prayer. Its echo was heard in the revivals of Dwight L. Moody, Sam Jones, and George Truett from one end of America to the other. If Augustine was converted under the ministry of Ambrose and produced as a result his famous spiritual autobiography, *The Confessions,* the classic on the subject of conversion, it is certainly more than clear from these sermons who pointed to him the way.

B. The Sermon against Auxentius

While for the most part the sermons of Ambrose are, in terms of literary form, classical biblical expository sermons, there are some, however, which follow more closely the literary forms of Greek and Roman oratory. In the sermon "Against Auxentius" we find a pulpit address which is modeled after the orations of Cicero.[56] Cicero's famous orations against Cataline had been held up as models of public address for some four hundred years when Ambrose mounted his pulpit in Milan to declaim against Auxentius, the Arian bishop who had demanded that Ambrose turn over his basilicas to the Arians.

The situation which demanded this sermon was as follows: The empress Justina, being a staunch Arian, had demanded that Ambrose turn over at least one church in Milan to the Arian bishop Auxentius. At first she demanded a church outside the walls, but as time passed she increased her demand. In January of 386 she finally demanded that Ambrose turn over the Cathedral and had her son the young Emperor Valentinian

---

55. "Iam non publicanum gero, iam non porto Leuin. Exui Leuin, postquam Christum indui. Odi genus meum, fugio uitam meam; solum te sequor, domine Iesu, qui sanas uulnera mea. *Quis* enim *me separat a caritate dei,* quae in te est? Tribulatio an angustia, an famis? Ligatus sum fide clauis quibusdam et bonis conpedibus caritatis innexus sum." Ambrose, *On Luke* 5.27.

56. For the English text, see the translation of H. de Romestin, in the Nicene and Post-Nicene Fathers, 2nd ser. (Grand Rapids: Wm. B. Eerdmans Publishing Co., 1976), 10:430-36. For the Latin text, see *Patrologia Latina,* 16:1049-53.

summon Ambrose to the palace to answer for his refusal. Ambrose refused to go and wrote a letter to the emperor explaining himself. In the meantime he preached a sermon to his congregation attacking the Arian bishop Auxentius.

One of the things that makes this sermon such an interesting document for the history of Christian worship is that three of the passages of Scripture used at the service are identified. The Gospel lesson was taken from the nineteenth chapter of Luke and included the story of Christ's entry into Jerusalem and perhaps the cleansing of the Temple. Nothing is said about an epistle being read, but a selection from the Psalms is mentioned. There was also a reading from the book of I Kings in which the story of Naboth's vineyard is recounted. The sermon makes good use of the three passages mentioned, especially the story of Naboth's vineyard. What we particularly notice is that Ambrose tells us that these three lessons had not been specially selected for the occasion but had come along by chance. Possibly the Gospel selection was demanded by virtue of its being Holy Week, but it would be hard to explain the reading from I Kings if that were the case. The more natural explanation would be that the Old Testament lesson as well as the New Testament lesson just happened to come up in the course of reading through those books in the *lectio continua*.

Even at that one cannot say that this sermon is an expository sermon based on Scripture readings which had been read earlier in the service. This sermon developed out of our preacher's recognition of the need of bringing the Word of God to bear on a crisis which had arisen in the church of Milan. This, as we have often noticed in this study, is of the essence of prophetic preaching. The right word is given for the right time. How often we as preachers discover that in the providence of God. God provides the right word when the need arises.

What that morning's Gospel lesson said to Ambrose was that God has a way of making the demands of truth and justice clear to people even if established authority does not recognize it. As Jesus entered Jerusalem on a donkey the children cried out, "Blessed is he who comes in the name of the Lord." There were those who were scandalized at the way the children gave messianic honors to Jesus, but Jesus answered by saying that if the children were silenced, the stones themselves would cry out to acclaim him. So it is, Ambrose assured his congregation: Auxentius may have the weight of established authority behind him, but what he intends to do is contrary to divine justice, and divine justice will be vindicated.

Ambrose finds even greater support in the story of Naboth's vineyard.

There King Ahab, instigated by his pagan wife Jezebel, uses his royal power to seize the vineyard of Naboth. Naboth protests that the vineyard was his patrimony and he could not give it up, and so Ambrose insists that the basilicas are the patrimony of the Church and the state had no right to them. Ambrose brings in a number of other passages of Scripture to support his argument, but the use he made of the story of Naboth's vineyard is a classic. Ever since the story has been retold in support of private property against a rapacious government.

It is as a defender of the rights of the Church against the claims of the state that Ambrose is most often remembered. In Christendom this has often been an important function of the Church. Yes, to be sure, it has often happened that the Church has succumbed to the seductions of a totalitarian state, but it is also true that many times the Church has effectively frustrated the ambitions of all kinds of princes and presidents, führers and dictators.

C. Preaching as Mystagogy

Ambrose of Milan's collection of six catechetical sermons, *De sacramentis*, is one of the most fascinating works in all of patristic literature.[57] It gives a picture of the initiation mysteries of the Christian Church during the reign of Emperor Theodosius, an age when the Church was highly respected and people were eager to become members. These sermons were preached by one of the most admirable leaders the Church has ever had. A member of the Roman aristocracy who had been brought up in a Christian family, Ambrose flung wide the doors of the Church to those who were eager to enter. He knew how to speak the language of the educated, serious-minded Roman of his day. He knew how to tell his converts that their new faith was the fulfillment of their spiritual Aeneid. He knew how to give meaning to their experience.

That Ambrose is explaining Christian worship in terms of the initia-

---

57. This study is based on the following text: Ambrose of Milan, *De sacramentis, des mystères. Nouvelle édition revue et augmentée de l'Explication du Symbole,* text established, French translation, and annotation by Dom Bernard Botte, 2nd ed., Sources chrétiennes, vol. 25 (Paris: Les Éditions du Cerf, 1961). For an English translation, see Ambrose of Milan, *On the Mysteries and Treatise on the Sacraments,* trans. T. Thompson, reedited by J. H. Srawley (London: SPCK, 1950).

tion mysteries so popular in the Hellenistic world is clear from the opening words of the first sermon. He tells his converts that now he wants to give them a discourse on the sacraments they had just received. This would not have been appropriate earlier, as one had to have faith before one was baptized, but in Milan, just as in Rome, one is called a Christian only when one has been baptized. So, having been baptized, they are now entitled to an explanation of the mysteries they have experienced.[58] This was exactly the approach of a mystagogue when explaining the mysteries to a neophyte. Ambrose follows the whole process beginning with the *effeta* exorcism, the anointing of the candidates before they enter the font, the renunciation of Satan, the blessing of the font, the actual baptism itself, the postbaptismal anointing and benediction, and finally the first Communion, which included the first use of the Lord's Prayer. All these rites are carefully gone over and explained as though one had been initiated into the Christian mysteries.

What is of special interest to us at this point in our story is that this series of sermons exemplifies a new approach to preaching. It might be called liturgical preaching or perhaps mystagogical preaching, by which we mean that the function of the sermon is to explain the liturgy. It is the liturgical rites themselves which become the center of attention. The sermon, which is auxiliary to worship rather than at its center, explains these rites. In this case it is the rites of initiation which are explained.

As we have already seen, Christian preachers have developed a number of different facets to their catechetical ministry. At the end of the fourth century catechetical preaching was very important to the celebration of baptism. We have already seen several approaches to it. Let us review them very briefly. One of the most basic of these facets is the recounting of the history of salvation. This facet belongs to the ministry of evangelism as much as it does to the catechetical ministry. It is the most basic aspect, the most introductory of introductory instructions. Already we find this being done in the Acts of the Apostles (13:16-21). As we shall see later in our study, Augustine wrote at length about this in his *De catechizandis rudibus*, and Caesarius of Arles, later in the fifth century, would publish

---

58. "De sacramentis quae accepistis sermonem adorior cuius rationem non oportuit ante praemitti. In christiano enim uiro prima est fides. Ideo et Romae fideles dicuntur qui baptizati sunt et pater noster Abraham ex fide iustificatus est non ex operibus. Ergo accepistis baptismum, credidistis. Nefas est namque me aliud aestimare; neque enim uocatus esses ad gratiam nisi dignum te Christus sua gratia iudicasset." Ambrose, *De sacramentis* 1.1.

a whole series of sermons in which he would recount the history of salvation for the instruction of new converts. This was a well-established component of the preaching or teaching which was given to the catechumen of Milan, as Ambrose himself tells us.[59] It had, however, by this time become one of those traditions that were well established even though most people had forgotten why they were done. They simply knew that in the weeks before Easter one preached through Genesis, or one preached on the lives of the patriarchs at the daily catechetical services.

A second facet of the catechetical ministry was moral catechism. This was also already fairly well developed in New Testament times, and is evidenced by the primitive Christian catechism found in I Peter 3–5, in I Timothy, and in Ephesians 5. The *Didache,* one of the oldest Christian documents which has come down to us, is often called the catechism of the two ways. From earliest Christian times it was felt that converts needed some instruction in the Christian way of life, particularly in its moral and ethical dimensions. In the New Testament this took the form of what is sometimes called the *Haustafel,* or house rules, a list of different relationships showing the duties of husbands to their wives, parents to their children, servants to their masters, and so forth. Later it often took the form of a Christian interpretation of the Ten Commandments, of which Thomas Aquinas has given us a very fine example. Ambrose speaks of a series of sermons on the Proverbs of Solomon being preached to the catechumen, which must have been another approach to moral catechism.[60]

More recent in its development was doctrinal catechism, which in the fourth century became a major facet of catechetical preaching. Its roots were very ancient, however, because it must have begun as an explanation of the profession of faith that the candidate was expected to make at the time of his or her baptism. It explained what it meant to believe in God the Father, God the Son, and God the Holy Spirit. In the baptismal rites of Milan at the end of the fourth century a time was set aside for teaching the candidates the creed. The bishop would give a special sermon, the *traditio symboli,* explaining the creed, then the candidates would return the next day and recite it, which was called the *redditio symboli.* The rite

59. Ambrose, *De mysteriis* 1. "De moralibus quoticianum sermonem habuimus, cum vel patriarcharum gesta vel proverbiorum legerentur praecepta, ut his informati atque instituti adsuesceretis maiorum ingredi uias eorumque iter carpere ac diuinis oboedire oraculis, quo renouati per baptismum eius uitae usum teneretis quae ablutos deceret."

60. Ambrose, *De mysteriis* 1. See quotation above.

was understood as the time when one made the vows of faith. With the controversies over the doctrine of the Trinity in the fourth century this facet of catechetical instruction became crucial, as we saw in the catechetical sermons of Cyril of Jerusalem and Theodore of Mopsuestia. Ambrose, nevertheless, was content to leave this facet of catechetical instruction to a single sermon, an example of which we have in his *explanatio symboli.*[61]

It was another facet of catechetical preaching to which Ambrose gave his most careful attention, a facet which would be particularly significant to converts from paganism who were coming over to Christianity from the Hellenistic mystery religions. These mystery religions had been popular in the declining years of Greek and Roman antiquity. They had found a very effective way of inculcating their beliefs in their converts: They developed elaborate initiation rites, and after leading their converts through these initiation rites they taught them the meaning of the rites. This explanation of the mysteries was called mystagogy. We have already spoken of the mystagogical catechisms of Cyril of Jerusalem; now we need to take a look at this very similar work of Ambrose of Milan, the famous *De sacramentis,* which in its finished form is significantly called *De mysteriis.* As the modern Italian theologian Enrico Mazza has shown, the *De sacramentis* is one of the most important expressions of a very distinctive approach to worship.

The question has been discussed at length as to whether Ambrose is the originator of this approach or whether he is dependent directly or indirectly on Cyril of Jerusalem. If the mystagogical catechisms traditionally attributed to Cyril are not the work of Cyril but rather his successor, John of Jerusalem, this would place them too late to have influenced Ambrose. I tend to agree with Auguste Piédagnel that the mystagogical catechisms are the work of Cyril and that therefore they could have and probably did influence Ambrose. As we have already pointed out, Ambrose was an attentive reader of the Greek Christian theologians. This does not mean he simply copied out Cyril's ideas and read them out in his own pulpit — Ambrose was a more creative thinker than that. Instead, it appears to be the case that Ambrose provided the Latin Church with his interpretation of three classics of Greek homiletical literature: Basil's *Hexaemeron,* Origen's sermons on the Gospel of Luke, and finally Cyril's mystagogical catechisms.

Ambrose and Cyril of Jerusalem were not the first Christian pastors who tried to explain the sacraments. This practice goes as far back as the

---

61. A modern edition of the text of this document by Dom Bernard Botte is found in the same volume as his edition of the *De sacramentis* cited above.

New Testament Church. One of the interesting things is that already in the New Testament the sacraments were being explained by typology. Baptism was explained by the Old Testament rite of circumcision and by various rites of purification which involved washing or the sprinkling of blood (Col. 2:11-17 and Rev. 1:5-6), and by the great flood in the days of Noah and the passage through the Red Sea (I Pet. 3:20-21 and I Cor. 10:1-5). The Lord's Supper was explained in relation to Passover. In fact, the first Lord's Supper seems to have been celebrated at the Passover feast, at least according to the Synoptic Gospels (Matt. 26:17-29 and par.). It was also explained in terms of the feeding with manna (John 6:1-70) and the covenantal feast on the mountain (I Cor. 11:25), and in terms of the wedding feast in the Song of Solomon (John 2:1-11). Ambrose particularly gave ample attention to explaining the sacraments in terms of typology. As Mazza has recognized, this typological explanation of the sacraments is of the soul of a true liturgical theology.[62] In this Ambrose was following a well-established Christian tradition. Tertullian had generously used typology in his treatise on baptism at the end of the second century, and even before that it seems to have been the practice of Christians to read through the Old Testament types of our redemption in Christ at the long vigil service on the night before Easter. The stories of the Passover and the exodus from Egypt were prominent in these readings, as were other stories that were regarded as types of baptism. It was after the reading of these Old Testament types that new converts were baptized. Explaining the sacraments by means of typology is a tradition of long standing.

A noteworthy feature of the *De sacramentis* is .the types Ambrose chooses to emphasize in his typology. While he certainly mentions some of the more traditional types, those he emphasizes are often very different from those which were most important in the New Testament. The crossing of the Red Sea and the great flood are mentioned,[63] but much more important is the cleansing of Naaman, the Syrian whom Elisha sent to wash in the Jordan River (II Kings 5:1-27). What impressed Ambrose was why the waters of the Jordan healed Naaman. Seeing the rather unimpressive waters of the Jordan, Naaman had asked if there were not better rivers in Syria which could do just as well. The important thing was that because of the blessing of God the waters of the Jordan had the power to cleanse Naaman, whereas the waters

---

62. Enrico Mazza, *Mystagogy: A Theology of Liturgy in the Patristic Age,* trans. M. J. O'Connell (New York: Pueblo Publishing Co., 1989).

63. Ambrose, *De sacramentis* 1.12, 20, and 2.1.

of Syria did not have that power.[64] Only the water which has the grace of Christ can heal us from our sins. The water is one thing; the consecration it receives is another.[65] Not all water heals, only that which has been consecrated by the grace of Christ.[66] Here we see Ambrose struggling against magic. He wants to make clear that it is the Word of Christ which consecrates the font, not some magician's secret formula of consecration. He will attempt to make much the same point in regard to the Lord's Supper a bit further on. Eventually Scholastic theology will turn its attention away from the consecration of the baptismal font, but in Ambrose's *De sacramentis* the idea of the consecration of the water of baptism was at the center of attention. This is clear from a second typology to which Ambrose gives special attention, a type that also comes from the Elisha cycle in the book of Kings. The story recounts how one of the prophet's servants, while cutting wood, lost the head of his axe in the river (II Kings 6:1-7). The servant complained to the prophet about the loss of what in those days was a very valuable tool. The prophet invoked the name of the Lord, as Ambrose tells it, and then threw the handle into the water, which of itself recovered the metal axe head. As Ambrose understands it, the wooden axe handle is a figure of the cross.[67] The story explains how the cross of Christ frees us from our infirmities.[68] Again Ambrose seems to be taking great care to skirt anything which might be interpreted as magic, but even at that, it is clear that this story is chosen because it suggests how the invocation of the Trinity in the words of Christ, "Go baptize the nations in the name of the Father and the Son and the Holy Spirit," sanctifies the waters of baptism.[69] This idea is supported by yet another type, the sweetening of the bitter waters of Mara which Moses healed by throwing wood into the water.[70] The two types from the Elisha cycle have become so prominent because for Ambrose the meaning of baptism has

64. Ambrose, *De sacramentis* 1.15.

65. Ambrose, *De sacramentis* 1.15.

66. "Vidisti aquam, sed non aqua omnis sanat, sed aqua sanat quae habet gratiam Christi. Aliud est elementum, aliud consecratio, aliud opus, aliud operatio. . . ." Ambrose, *De sacramentis* 1.15.

67. Ambrose, *De sacramentis* 2.11.

68. "In cruce Christi omnium hominum levatur infirmitas." Ambrose, *De sacramentis* 2.11.

69. "Idem itaque dominus Iesus in evangelio suo dicit ad apostolos: *Ite, baptizate gentes in nomine patris et filii et spiritus sancti.* Sermo hic salvatoris est." Ambrose, *De sacramentis* 4.10.

70. Ambrose, *De sacramentis* 2.12.

changed from what it was in New Testament times. The focus of baptism is the power of the rites of initiation to save those who go through them. Quite conscientiously he insists that this power to save comes from the sacrifice of Christ, but still he holds onto the idea that the Christian rites of initiation, far better than the initiation rites of the Hellenistic mystery religions, have the power to save those who receive them.

There is something else here which must be recognized. Strictly speaking these two stories from the Elisha cycle are not types at all, as they are never mentioned in the New Testament as types of baptism, which is an essential criterion for genuine biblical typology; they are allegories in the tradition of the Alexandrian School. Ambrose was a faithful disciple of Origen, as we have already remarked, so it was only natural for a disciple of the Alexandrian exegesis to turn types into allegories. Ambrose interpreted the little girl who suggested Naaman seek the aid of Elisha as a figure of the Church.[71] That the wooden handle of the axe or the wood thrown into the waters of Mara be a figure of the cross is allegory pure and simple. What we have in the *De sacramentis* is one of the earliest examples of an allegorical interpretation of worship. Examples can be found earlier, but here is a fully worked-out allegorical interpretation of the mysteries of Christian initiation. It spoke powerfully to the convert from the Hellenistic mystery religions of the far greater mysteries to be found in Christ. Surely the Christian mysteries of initiation were more profound than anything the Greeks had to offer. This strategy of explaining Christian worship in terms of pagan mysteries will have a tremendous effect on how Christians would worship for centuries to come.

The eucharistic typology we find in the *De sacramentis* is equally interesting. The most obvious type of the Lord's Supper, the Passover meal, is not even mentioned. Neither is the covenant meal on top of Mount Sinai where Moses and the elders of Israel ate and drank and beheld God. On the other hand, the meal in the wilderness where the children of Israel ate manna and drank the water from the rock is treated,[72] and the wedding feast from the Song of Solomon is spoken of in considerable detail.[73] What is puzzling is the use of the sacrifices of Abel and Melchizedek as types of the Lord's Supper.[74] This goes well beyond the types mentioned in Scrip-

71. Ambrose, *De sacramentis* 2.
72. Ambrose, *De sacramentis* 4.9-10.
73. Ambrose, *De sacramentis* 5.5-11 and 14-15.
74. Ambrose, *De sacramentis* 4.10-12 and 27.

ture. While the Epistle to the Hebrews speaks of Melchizedek as a type of Christ, there is no suggestion that the bread and wine he shared with Abraham was a type of the Lord's Supper. Besides that, the Genesis account of the story does not tell us that Melchizedek offered a sacrifice (Gen. 14:17-24 and Heb. 7:1-10). Just as Ambrose was eager to show that the baptismal waters were consecrated by the Word of Christ, so he wants to make the point that it is the Word of Christ which consecrates the bread and wine at Communion. As Enrico Mazza points out, the older, more traditional typology does not present him with the story he wanted, so in order to make this point he calls on the same types, or more correctly, allegories, as he did in regard to the consecration of the baptismal waters, namely, the healing of the waters of Mara and the story about Elisha and the axe head. To this is added the story of Moses opening the Red Sea by striking it with his rod.[75] In all three cases the wood is an allegory for the cross of Christ. The point Ambrose makes of it is that by reciting the words of Christ the miracle of confecting the sacrament occurs.[76]

As we can see here, it came quite naturally for a disciple of Alexandrian exegesis to allegorize the rites of baptism and the Lord's Supper and present them to the recently converted pagans as the rites of a Christian initiation. Surely these new converts understood very well the explanation Ambrose gave them. But, as we noticed in regard to Cyril of Jerusalem, the important thing is that a whole new approach to worship is beginning to set in, an approach that will make the celebration of the rites more important than the preaching. Preaching will be understood as mystagogy. More and more preaching will be thought of as the explanation of the rites; more and more it will be imagined that it is the rites themselves which communicate; and eventually it will come to the point where the rites will be celebrated without any preaching at all. They will be thought of as sufficient in themselves. They will no longer seal the preaching of the Word but will replace the preaching of the Word. We can well imagine that Ambrose would have quickly jumped back from this path had he possessed even the slightest premonition of where it would lead. But, then, this happens to so many of us. We can never be sure what our heirs will do with the treasures we leave behind. One thing is sure: Augustine was the first heir of the bishop of Milan, and in his hands the ten talents of

---

75. Ambrose, *De sacramentis* 4.18.
76. Ambrose, *De sacramentis* 4.14 and 19.

Ambrose made ten talents more. Ambrose was, to be sure, one of the most conscientious and effective preachers the Church has ever known.

II. Jerome

The preaching of Jerome (ca. 347–419 or 420) interests us for very different reasons than the preaching of Ambrose and Augustine. Jerome was a biblical scholar. He was not a bishop nor pastor of a church, as Ambrose and Augustine were, nor was he a theologian in the strictest sense of the term. His gifts were not in the field of speculative thought.[77] His great accomplishment was the translation of the Hebrew Old Testament and the Greek New Testament into a very clear and popular Latin. He was a pioneer in the field of biblical scholarship. Jerome got his education in the city of Rome. It was the best kind of education. He was schooled in the Latin classics. Grammar and rhetoric were important to him. He knew how to write in such a way that he was clear, interesting, and persuasive. That was at the heart of a good Roman education — learning to use the Latin language with power and authority. Perhaps no Christian scholar of his period searched out more thoroughly and more systematically the meaning of Scripture. He asked the kind of penetrating questions about the interpretation of the Scriptures which distinguishes solid scholarship from speculation. He carefully studied the original languages.[78] He critically studied questions of authorship, textual criticism, and canonicity. He was well read in the commentaries of earlier generations of Christians and was acquainted

77. For biographical material, see von Campenhausen, "Hieronymus," in *Lateinische Kirchenväter*, pp. 109-50; Ferdinand Cavallera, *S. Jérôme: Sa vie et son Oeuvre* (Louvain: "Spicilegium Sacrum Lovaniense" Bureaux; Paris: E. Champion, 1922); Jean Gribomont, "Jerome," in *Patrology*, 4:212-46; Harald Hagendahl, *Latin Fathers and the Classics* (Göteborg: Elanders Boktr. Aktiebolag, 1958); J. N. D. Kelly, *Jerome, His Life, Writings, and Controversies* (London: Gerald Duckworth and Co., 1975); Angelo Penna, *Principi e carattere dell'esegesi di S. Gerolamo* (Rome: Pontificio Istituto Biblico, 1950).

78. Recently the question has been raised as to whether Jerome really knew as much Hebrew as he pretended to know. Kelly has shown that Jerome frequently pretended to know much more about different subjects than he really did, but to claim that he really could not handle Hebrew does not seem to be seriously entertained by the most recent research. Cf. Gribomont's section, "Jerome: The Philologist of Oriental Languages," in *Patrology*, 4:222ff. and 244ff.

with the interpretations of Jewish scholars. Because he was a biblical scholar of such ability, we are specially interested in how he interpreted Scripture in his preaching.

Unfortunately we do not have enough information to be able to piece together Jerome's preaching schedule. From the information we have, however, we are able to say that Jerome preached on a fairly regular basis at his monastery in Bethlehem. He traveled often and was sometimes in Caesarea or in Jerusalem, where he often preached as well, but normally when he was at home in his monastery in Bethlehem he preached to his monks in the monastery chapel both at Sunday and midweek services. Evidently his congregation expected to hear more than one sermon at a service. In a single service there might be a sermon on the lesson taken from the Gospels, a sermon on the lesson taken from the Epistles, and a sermon on one of the psalms which had been chanted. Apparently Jerome also preached in town, at the Basilica of the Nativity, and on at least one occasion he preached there at the feast of the Nativity.

At the beginning of this century Dom Gérard Morin was able to recover almost a hundred of Jerome's sermons,[79] fifty-nine of which were preached on individual psalms which had been sung during the course of the liturgy. Why we do not have sermons on the other ninety-one psalms is not completely clear. It may simply be that Jerome was ill or out of town when these psalms were sung. In fact, he explains at the beginning of his sermon on Psalm 7, "Last Sunday, we read the sixth psalm; because of my illness, we could not interpret it; today, however, we have read the seventh, which likewise, is sung after the Alleluia."[80] The impression one gets is that after the reading of the regular Scripture lessons, a psalm was sung by the congregation before the sermon began.[81] The more usual

---

79. For the Latin text of these sermons, see *S. Hieronymi presbyteri opera, pars II, opera homiletica,* ed. Gérard Morin, Corpus Christianorum, series Latina, vol. 78 (Turnholt, Belgium: Brepols, 1958). For an English translation, see *The Homilies of Saint Jerome,* ed. and trans. Sister Marie Liguori Ewald, 2 vols. (Washington, D.C.: Catholic University of America Press, 1964 and 1966). See as well Gribomont's article in *Patrology,* 4:236.

80. English translations are taken from the edition of Marie Liguori Ewald, *The Homilies of St. Jerome.*

81. The singing of psalms after the Scripture lessons must have been a practice that went back to the synagogue. Sometimes there was a psalm after each lesson, and sometimes there was but a single psalm. The practice could differ considerably from place to place. Cf. Josef A. Jungmann, *Missarum Sollemnia,* 5th ed., 2 vols. (Vienna, Freiburg, and Basel: Herder, 1962), 1:539-65.

practice, however, was probably to preach on one of the Scripture lessons rather than on the psalm sung between the lessons and the sermon.[82] Be that as it may, evidently our preacher at one point in his ministry decided to preach on psalms. Since these psalms were chosen on the basis of a *lectio continua,* it would have amounted to preaching through the whole book of Psalms. One of Jerome's stenographers, perhaps at his own initiative, decided to record the sermons. Unfortunately Jerome was prevented by ill health from preaching each day, or perhaps the stenographer was unavailable for one reason or another, but the liturgy went on and the psalms were chanted in course whether sermons were recorded or not. The result was that we have only a sporadic collection of psalms.

Whatever the reason for our having sermons for only fifty-nine psalms, we are grateful to have these, because they give us a candid look at how Jerome actually preached. It seems fairly certain that Jerome himself never laid eyes on these transcriptions of his sermons, for they are filled with all kinds of mistakes: inexact quotations, faulty references to authors, contradictions, ambiguities, infelicities of style, and even grammatical errors. He always had a number of projects going at the same time and was only too willing to delegate details to his secretaries. It is usually said that these sermons were extempore. Possibly that is the case or almost the case for some of them, but for others one gets the impression that they were preceded by a certain amount of forethought and organization. These sermons may well have been thought out in the early morning before worship, with Jerome giving them an hour's preparation, perhaps more. He no doubt gave them considerably less time than Ambrose gave his sermons, but then Jerome was constantly involved in biblical scholarship. Also, it was uncommon in antiquity for an orator to write out a speech beforehand. Preachers during the patristic age meditated on the Scriptures for hours beforehand, but they did not write out their sermons before preaching them. Although Jerome's preparation was not so extensive as it might have been, we find it hard to believe, at least in regard to many of these sermons, that they were completely off the top of the saint's halo.

Having made these general remarks, let us take a more detailed look

---

82. Apparently the psalms were never read as Scripture lessons. There was no question as to whether they were considered Scripture, however. It was just that they were sung as praise and prayer even if occasionally they were preached. We have already spoken of how Basil preached on the psalms sung in the service. As we will see, Augustine sometimes did the same thing.

at three representative sermons from this series. We begin with Jerome's sermon on the first psalm, which is an introductory psalm, as Jerome notes. He begins his sermon with a very nice simile: The Psalter is like a stately mansion. A main door leads into the house, but inside the house are many doors leading into different rooms. One needs a key to get into the house, but one also needs other keys to get into separate rooms. The first psalm is the key to get into the whole Psalter. This opening remark, as a good introduction should, tips us off as to Jerome's whole approach to the interpretation of the Psalms. This psalm is a psalm of moral instruction which admonishes us to turn away from sin and to study God's Law and live by its teachings. For Jerome the Psalter is not so much the hymnbook of the Temple as it is a manual of moral discipline and spiritual meditation. To be sure, that is about the way the author of this psalm understood the purpose of the Psalter as well. Today many scholars claim that the author of the first psalm was the one who collected the psalms together, and that he wrote it as a preface to the Psalter. One may also say there is more to the psalms than this particular editor of the Psalter understood, but surely Jerome has caught the message of the first psalm.

Our preacher is familiar with the line of interpretation which would make Christ the key to this as well as to every other psalm. Such a line of interpretation would suggest that Christ is the blessed man who walks not in the way of the ungodly but delights in the Law of God. Jerome rules out this analysis and prefers a more general interpretation. The blessed in the first psalm could be anyone who is just and upright. Those who are blessed are those who live according to the eight beatitudes about which Jesus spoke in the Sermon on the Mount.[83] Jerome's interpretation of this psalm is a very sober and conservative Christian interpretation, but it is a Christian interpretation nevertheless.

According to Jerome, the psalm speaks of three ways of committing sin: walking in the counsel of the ungodly, standing in the way of sinners, and sitting in the seat of scoffers. This means that we sin when we entertain sinful thoughts, commit sinful acts, or teach sinful ways.[84] We are all sinners, but we do not have to persevere in our sin. When we leave our sin behind, then we are happy.

Having spoken of three things we must not do, the psalmist then speaks of two things we must do if we are to be blessed with happiness:

83. Jerome, *On the Psalms,* p. 3.
84. Jerome, *On the Psalms,* pp. 4ff.

First we must delight in God's Law, then we must meditate on God's Law. To meditate on God's Law is to do it. If one does what the Law of God teaches, one is in fact praying with one's whole body.[85]

Jerome goes on to the next verse, "He is like a tree planted by streams of water." There are those who interpret this very simply, our preacher tells us. They say this verse means that just as a tree planted near water prospers, so those who meditate on the Law of God will derive strength and life from their meditation. But there is more here than that, according to Jerome. Our preacher goes on to speak of the tree of life planted in the Garden of Eden. This tree of life is the wisdom spoken about by Solomon. "She is a tree of life to those who lay hold of her" (Prov. 3:18). At this point Jerome expresses his doubts about Solomon being the author of Proverbs, but, not lingering on this subject, he goes on to tell us that Christ is the wisdom spoken of here, for indeed Christ is the Wisdom of God, as the apostle Paul tells us. Now we see why it is difficult to say that Christ is the blessed man spoken of by this psalm. This blessed man is compared to the tree of life, that is, to Christ, and if the blessed man is compared to Christ, then the blessed man must be someone other than Christ. Alluding to Ephesians 2:6, Jerome says that the Christian who turns away from sin and lives the Law of God is raised up together with Christ and seated with him in heaven.[86]

Continuing his exposition of this passage, Jerome brings up the vision from Revelation of the tree of life planted by the river of life (Rev. 22:1-3). At this point he gives us a little excursus on the canonicity of the Revelation, commending its canonicity in spite of the opinion of the church of Jerusalem. Returning to his subject, he points out that in this vision the tree of life bears twelve kinds of fruit, one for each month, and from this we learn that the grace of the Holy Spirit comes to us through the Scriptures.[87] It is because the grace of God is contained in the Scriptures that the blessed delight in meditating on the Scriptures. There is something very moving in the way Jerome has brought to these words about the tree planted by the rivers of water a number of biblical developments of this same poetic image. Here he is interpreting Scripture by Scripture with the highest art.

The sermon takes another turn with the next verse, "The wicked are

85. Jerome, *On the Psalms*, p. 6.
86. Jerome, *On the Psalms*, p. 7.
87. Jerome, *On the Psalms*, pp. 3ff.

not so, but are like the dust which the wind drives away." A distinction is made between the wicked who deny God altogether and sinners who acknowledge God even though they commit sin. Jerome often makes it clear by distinctions such as this that there is hope for sinners if they turn away from their sin. The wicked are those who give themselves up to sin. The psalmist, Jerome tells us, compares the wicked to dust because they have no substance; having denied God, they are scattered about by their delusions wherever the breath of the devil sends them.[88] Taking up John 3:18, "He who believes in him is not condemned," Jerome tells us that it is faith which gives us substance and stability. When we sin it is because we waiver in faith.[89] Those who have faith need not fear the judgment of God. In the judgment of God "the way of the wicked will perish." Jerome draws attention to the fact that the text does not say that the wicked will perish but rather the *way* of the wicked. Just as Jerome holds out hope for sinners, so he even holds out hope for the wicked. The apostle Paul, he points out, before he was converted and sent out as an apostle, during the time he was persecuting the Church, was wicked, but he repented and turned from his wickedness. There is always a chance that the wicked will repent, and when they do the wickedness vanishes. Jerome ends his sermon with the prayer that we be like the just and blessed, like the tree of life, rather than dust blown about by the winds of the devil.

Now let us look at Jerome's sermon on Psalm 84. The psalm with its magnificent poetic imagery is one of the most beautiful in the Psalter. While it is a pilgrimage psalm which speaks of going up to Jerusalem for one of the pilgrimage feasts, clearly the author of the psalm himself saw this outward pilgrimage as a sacrament of our spiritual ascent to God. Jerome's sermon is surely in touch with the deepest insights of the psalm.

Jerome begins with a few remarks on the psalm title, noting that the psalms of the sons of Korah are generally joyful hymns. This is a very common way for our preacher to begin his sermons.[90] Instead of an explosion of oratorical eloquence immediately demanding the attention of the congregation, Jerome most often begins his sermons with a few quiet, scholarly observations of this sort. Taking up the opening verses:

88. Jerome, *On the Psalms*, p. 11.
89. Jerome, *On the Psalms*, p. 11.
90. Jerome, *On the Psalms*, p. 118.

How lovely are thy tabernacles, O Lord of Hosts!
   my soul longs, yea faints for the courts of the Lord. . . .
Blessed are those who dwell in thy house
   ever singing thy praise. . . .

Jerome makes a distinction between tabernacles, courts, and houses. Although he does not draw out his distinction clearly at any one point in the sermon, he returns to it several times in the course of the sermon. In fact, he is inconsistent in the way he uses the three words. On the verse "How lovely are thy tabernacles, O Lord of Hosts" he says,

> The sole ambition of some people is to possess property; others long to be enriched by the wealth of this world; still others wish to hold prominent places at conventions and be esteemed among men. But for me, there is only one longing: to see Your eternal dwelling places *(tabernacles)*. To me, those are the lovely dwelling places *(tabernacles)* where the virtuous and not the vicious congregate. My soul yearns and pines for the courts of the Lord *(atria)*. This is my desire, this my only love, that I may see Your courts *(atria)*. Notice the order. First, he longs for the tabernacles, tents without a foundation and easily portable. A tent moreover, is always on the move, folded up and carried hither and thither. Courts, on the other hand, although certainly not houses, do have a kind of foundation, and from the court we enter the house. Our psalmist, therefore, at first longs for a tabernacle, and then afterwards pines and yearns with love to see Your courts; and when he is in Your court, then he cries out: Happy they who dwell in Your house! *(domo)*.[91]

Notwithstanding the rather vague and inconsistent way in which he develops this distinction between tabernacle, court, and house, Jerome does communicate by means of it something which the poetic imagery of the psalm does indeed intimate. Jerome, after all, as a master philologist, is very sensitive to the way the psalmist uses words.

We find a very similar thing in his comments on the verse "Even the sparrow finds a home and the dove a nest in which she puts her young." Literally this verse speaks of our yearning for rest, but, our preacher tells us, there is a higher meaning. Jerome alludes to several passages of Scripture to show that birds are often used as a poetic image of the holy desires of

---

91. Jerome, *On the Psalms*, pp. 119ff.

the soul.[92] Like the dove in the Song of Solomon, this dove brings to mind our higher nature which yearns for heaven. Our higher nature yearns not merely for a tabernacle or even for the courts of pilgrimage, but for the house of the Lord. We long to dwell in God's house where God permanently resides. Again we find that Jerome brings out the poetic intimations which are imbedded in the psalm. This is not allegorical interpretation, but rather a sensitivity to the poetry of Scripture.

Taking up the verse "Blessed are the men whose strength is in thee," Jerome comments, "Truly, do we long for Your tabernacles, and Your courts, and Your house, but to attain our heart's desire is not within our power; it does not depend on our strength, but upon Your help."[93] The way Jerome addressed these lines to God, something he often does in these sermons, makes eloquent his passionate sense of grace, which many who have studied him have felt to be lacking in his more controversial writings. But then Jerome, as is equally well recognized, is not primarily a systematic theologian, and often his rigorous asceticism appears to overshadow his doctrine of grace. Even in this sermon he follows this strong emphasis on grace with an insistence on the discipline of the Christian life. The Christian must make daily progress and must have a wholehearted desire to advance steadily. We have to begin our pilgrimage in the vale of tears. God has set us in a contest as athletes. "He has willed that this place be set for us as an arena that He may reward our victory with a crown."[94] As Jerome sees it, God has willed us to contend that he may give us a blessing. "The psalmist did not say, they shall go from weakness to strength, but from strength to strength. Do you want to be a man of fortitude there? Then be one here first. Do you want to be crowned there? Fight here."[95] With this subject Jerome's eloquence mounts. "'They go from strength to strength.' We can say this in another way: 'Christ the power of God and the wisdom of God.' He who has power here, there will possess Power himself. 'They go from strength to strength.' What gain will they have when they go from strength to strength? What will be their reward? 'They shall see the God of gods in Sion.' Reward enough for the victors in the face of Christ, reward enough for those who have fought! To see God is an infinite crown."[96]

92. Jerome, *On the Psalms*, p. 121.
93. Jerome, *On the Psalms*, p. 122.
94. Jerome, *On the Psalms*, p. 123.
95. Jerome, *On the Psalms*, pp. 123ff.
96. Jerome, *On the Psalms*, p. 124.

Continuing in the same line, Jerome takes up the verse "Behold, O God, our Protector, and look upon the face of your Christ." The modern preacher would no doubt have problems translating this verse with such an overt reference to Christ, preferring a translation such as, "Look upon the face of your anointed," but Jerome of course knew both the Greek and Hebrew texts and knew as well that the Christ literally means the anointed one. He also knew that the New Testament Church had already understood that the anointed one mentioned in the Psalms was the Christ (cf. Acts 4:26). While to us this seems a rather extreme Christianizing of the text, Jerome is following the historic Christian interpretation of the Psalms which is already well established in the New Testament.

Moving on to the verse "For a day in thy courts is better than a thousand elsewhere," Jerome tells us that many would simply interpret this to mean that it is better to have a little in the kingdom of heaven than to possess everything here that this world offers. "That is a true and good interpretation," says Jerome. "Let us say however: If it were possible for anyone to be in the kingdom of heaven for a single day and after that be cast out, rightly would he say, I had rather one day in Your courts. Actually this is the meaning of 'one day': the kingdom of heaven is one day; there is no night, nor darkness, but always light. Whoever is in the kingdom of heaven for one day is there forever."[97] Jerome's interpretation here is not literal, to be sure, but then it is not a "spiritual" or allegorical interpretation either. It is profound insight into the meaning of this psalm for the Christian.

In this sermon Jerome put before his congregation the hope of eternity. The psalm as it was originally written had done the same thing. What the psalmist's doctrine of heaven may or may not have been, we really do not know, but he spoke of a transcendent life with a poetic imagery that has remained accessible to the faithful ever since. Jerome caught the message of the psalm as the author intended it and opened it up to his monks so that they too were inspired with the hope that was set before them.

Finally let us look at Jerome's sermon on Psalm 147:1-11 (Psalm 146 in the Septuagint and Vulgate). Again we find a few remarks about the title of the psalm, which, as Jerome reads it, is Alleluia. "Ja," he tells us, "is one of the Hebrew names for God. Theodosian, the very literal translator of the Hebrew Bible, translates this as αἰνεῖτε τον Ἰά, or,

---

97. Jerome, *On the Psalms*, pp. 124ff.

quite literally, "Praise the LORD." This is both the title and the theme of the psalm.[98]

Addressing himself to the first verse, "For it is good to sing praises to our God," Jerome points out that the text is not speaking of a good psalm but is declaring the goodness of psalms in the absolute sense. It is a good thing to sing a sacred song. From this point of grammar Jerome insists that we should take care to sing with a pure heart and a good conscience. "How many there are who have good voices but because they are sinners, their singing is bad. He sings well who sings in his heart, who sings to Christ in his conscience. 'It is fitting to praise him in joyful song.' It is fitting to praise Him with joyful song, not with the voice but with a good conscience."[99] It is really not good unless it is pleasing to God. That is, after all, the purpose of sacred music, and unless sacred song comes from a pure heart it will never please God. It was because Noah made his sacrifices to God with a pure heart that God found the odor pleasing. This is a point that Jerome makes frequently in these sermons on the Psalms. If worship is to glorify God, it must come from a pure heart.

Going on to verse 3, "He heals the brokenhearted and binds up their wounds," Jerome recalls Psalm 51:17, "A broken and contrite heart, O God, thou wilt not despise." Evidently for Jerome God's redemptive care of his people makes possible their worship because it purifies their hearts. That God binds up the wounds of the repentant heart is confirmed by the story of the Good Samaritan, who bound up the wounds of the man he found on the road.[100]

Jerome's commentary on the next verse, "He determines the number of the stars, he gives to all of them their names," no doubt sounds very strange to us today. Our preacher asks what the connection is between healing the brokenhearted and giving names to the stars, and then tells us that after God heals the souls of the penitent he changes them into stars. Recalling the story of Abraham being shown the stars and being promised that his descendants would be as numerous as the stars, and of how God gave Abraham a new name, Jerome tells us that when Abraham was made a star, his name was changed. It was the same with the apostle Paul and others. Jerome goes on to another verse but then, coming to the verse "The Lord lifts up the downtrodden," he returns to the subject of the

---

98. Jerome, *On the Psalms,* p. 400.
99. Jerome, *On the Psalms,* p. 401.
100. Jerome, *On the Psalms,* p. 402.

faithful being changed into stars. He quotes Daniel 12:3, which tells us that the righteous shall shine as stars. It is the wisdom of God, Jerome says, to exalt the humble.[101] This chain of comments was much more edifying to Jerome's listeners than we might imagine. The teachings of astrology were widespread in antiquity, and these teachings worked against the biblical doctrine of providence, inspiring a kind of fatalism which is quite different from the Christian doctrine of providence. Here we find Jerome arguing for the doctrine of providence. God's wisdom and redemptive care embrace all his creatures. Neither the stars nor the lives of the most humble human beings are beyond his knowledge or his concern. The God who made the stars, far from being unaware and unconcerned for the humble, is indeed their savior. It was no doubt this message which Jerome communicated in this sermon and, we might go on to say, it was no doubt much the same message which the psalmist had in mind.

Jerome's comments on the verse "Make melody to our God upon the lyre" are typical for the patristic period. The musical instruments used in the worship of the Temple were all parables of godly virtues, with stringed instruments suggesting the importance of all the Christian virtues sounding in harmony.[102] The ancient Church did not use musical instruments in worship. That was all part of the ceremonial of the Law which Christians interpreted spiritually.

Taking up the verse "He gives to the beasts their food and to the young ravens which cry," Jerome brings out several references to ravens in Scripture: the raven sent out from Noah's ark, Elijah being fed by ravens, and even a text from Proverbs, "The eye that mocks a father and scorns to obey a mother will be picked out by the ravens of the valley" (30:17). Jerome is not simply displaying his ability to act as a living concordance, nor is he running into the ground the principle that Scripture should be interpreted by Scripture; rather, he is giving us an analysis of biblical imagery, making the point that in Scripture ravens, unlike doves or sparrows, are rather sinister and despicable creatures. When they serve a useful purpose it is rather surprising. Even more amazing is that God's providential care and redemptive purpose are extended even to their young.

As one looks over the current literature on Jerome, one notices that his sermons have received very little attention. Jerome himself seems not to have given any attention to their publication. This is unfortunate

---

101. Jerome, *On the Psalms*, pp. 402ff.
102. Jerome, *On the Psalms*, p. 403.

because these sermons are of considerable substance. One has to make allowances for the fact that what we have has not been edited. His comments on some days never really came off as sermons but were taken down nevertheless. Jerome made no attempt to turn them into the literary monuments he was so capable of doing if he had wanted. Aside from all this, one has to say that there is some very solid homiletical material here. This is particularly evident when one looks at these sermons in the context of the whole history of preaching. These sermons have a number of strong points.

First of all, Jerome's knowledge of Greek and Hebrew served him well. He was often able to give his congregation a fresh and precise translation of a text of Scripture. It is, alas, too often the case with those who know the Scriptures almost by heart that the words become so shopworn and blunt that they no longer penetrate the mind. This is particularly so when the translation is inadequate — there is so much more implied by the original text than the translation can convey. Jerome's knowledge of the original languages was profound, the sort of knowledge of a second language one acquires when one lives in the land where the language is at home and one is forced to use it bargaining in the marketplace and arguing through the theological controversies of the time and place. Jerome's monks prayed the Psalms every day and must have known many of them by heart, and Jerome's ability to deepen their appreciation of the meaning of these lines, which indeed they knew so well, must have been gratefully received.

Jerome's knowledge of the original languages also enabled him to penetrate into the biblical thought world far more profoundly than most of his contemporaries. To be sure, there were plenty of things he missed and plenty of things about which he was confused, like his comments about the righteous becoming stars that we noted above. But Jerome's constant dwelling on God's concern for sinners, his strong doctrine of providence, his thorough familiarity with the Wisdom theology of the Old Testament, and his recurring insistence on the moral dimensions of worship all show him to be in touch with the biblical thought world to a much greater degree than many of his contemporaries.

Jerome's knowledge of the history of interpretation gave him perspective in developing his own interpretations. How often we hear in his sermons a remark about the interpretations of others. He is familiar with Jewish interpreters, particularly those of his own day. We get the impression from his remarks that many of the Jewish interpreters whom he knew had reacted strongly against the Alexandrian exegesis of an earlier period and were, in Jerome's day, eager to maintain the literal sense even to the point of reductionism. J. N. D. Kelly has pointed out that Jerome is much more dependent on Origen than he admits. True, Jerome is always familiar with Origen's interpretations of any given passage, but he is also familiar with a number of other early Christian biblical interpreters. Didymus the Blind, Apollinarius, Eusebius of Emesa, Theodore of Heraclea, and John Chrysostom are mentioned in regard to his New Testament commentaries.[103] In reference to his Old Testament studies we know that, in addition to Origen, he used Hippolytus on Zechariah, Gregory Thaumaturgos on Ecclesiastes, and Didymus of Alexandria on Zechariah.[104] Knowing the wide possibilities of interpreting any given passage sometimes gave a sort of discipline to Jerome's comments. It challenged him to think more deeply and to investigate more thoroughly the text before him.

Another strong point of Jerome's preaching is his sensitivity to the literary forms of the Bible. Jerome had been schooled in classical philology. He understood the importance of grammar, syntax, style, and rhetoric. He understood how writers use figures of speech and how poets intimate things and convey their feelings. He understood something of the way a writer can speak symbolically. He understood the problems of transmitting a text and how mistakes of copying manuscripts could come about, how the tradition could become confused about authorship, and how editors could emend a text they did not understand. Jerome's knowledge of literature made it possible for him to get into the mind of the biblical writers in a way that not all preachers seem to be able to do.

This ability to get into the biblical way of looking at things was no doubt sharpened by his wide travels. Being a Westerner who was schooled in the city of Rome, Jerome spent some years on the German frontier and lived in Antioch and even the Syrian desert before finally settling in Bethlehem. This gave him an experience which must have sharpened his appreciation for the uniqueness of biblical thought. He seems to have appreciated the fact that the biblical authors did not think the way the typical Roman citizen of his day thought. To be sure, this insight is not developed in Jerome anything like as clearly as we have developed it today, but Jerome seems to have at least begun to get a feel for this dimension of biblical interpretation. Jerome, the *vir trilingus,* was a pioneer in crossing what today we call cultural barriers. He was one of the first to sense that a preacher must bring the spiritual insights of one

103. Kelly, *Jerome,* pp. 144-49.
104. Kelly, *Jerome,* p. 292.

culture to the men and women of a very different culture. His translation of the Latin Bible, the Vulgate, remains to this day a great monument to his ability to bring an ancient message to a later age, but his sermons, although often hastily prepared and unfinished, show the same genius.

Jerome's sermons are often dismissed as being allegorical by those who find no value in the allegorical interpretation of Scripture. To be sure, there is much allegorical interpretation in these sermons. Jerome did not, any more than the better part of the Antiochene school, make a radical departure from the Alexandrian school of exegesis. He did, however, lay a very firm foundation for a more solid kind of grammatical-historical exegesis, particularly in his emphasis on the study of Hebrew, which is the most obvious value of his approach to exegesis. He opened the way to the Hebrew text for the Christian preacher. What is perhaps not so evident until one carefully reads the sermons is that he began to demonstrate the usefulness of a grammatical-historical interpretation. Basil, Gregory of Nyssa, and above all John Chrysostom had begun to do this, but, because of his knowledge of Hebrew, Jerome was able to go even further. In his sermons he took seriously the value of the literal sense of the Hebrew psalms and, in most cases, conveyed that literal sense very clearly. In the three sermons discussed above, we attempted to show how he did this. To be sure, Jerome, as any Christian preacher must, is concerned to make the meaning of the psalm clear to a Christian congregation. He is aware of how the ideas found in the Psalms are developed in the New Testament and even how particular psalms were interpreted in the New Testament. For Jerome this is all part of a legitimate Christian interpretation of a psalm and belongs to an expository sermon on a psalm. When we look at other sermons on psalms from this period, we get the impression that Jerome does a far better job than most in making clear the meaning intended by the author. Jerome, we would claim, has brought us several giant steps back from the excesses of Alexandrian exegesis and made significant progress toward a Christian interpretation of the Psalms.

Jerome's understanding of the reading and preaching of the Scriptures in worship is particularly interesting because he was aware, during his age, of many of the critical problems which today make it difficult for us to formulate our own doctrine. It is interesting that Jerome's appreciation of the value of Scripture for the life and worship of the Christian is in no way hampered by his awareness of the problems involved in its human origin. In fact, Jerome accepts in a surprisingly straightforward way the weaknesses of the human authors of Scripture side by side with the divine authority of Scripture.

Jerome is very fond of reminding his congregation that Christ is the Wisdom of God (I Cor. 1:24). Jerome gave much time to the Wisdom literature of the Old Testament and seemed to have a feel for what today we call the Wisdom theology. He appreciated the important place the Wisdom theology gave to ethical and moral teaching. This is not surprising for one schooled in Cicero and the Roman Stoics. But for the Jewish rabbis, whom Jerome also knew very well, study was worship and Jerome's devotion to biblical scholarship was for him a devotional act. The line in Psalm 1 which tells us of the blessed whose delight is in the law of the Lord applies to Jerome as well as anyone. For Jerome the Scriptures were a never ending source of divine healing and spiritual nourishment, but in the end it is always Christ who is the wisdom of God. Scripture is centered in Christ; all of its prophecies, all of its mysteries, all of its moral teachings lead to Christ. When the Scriptures are read and preached in the worship of the Church, Christ is truly present. In Jerome's sermon on Psalm 147:12-20 he comments on the text "He will fill you with the finest of the wheat":

> Happy is the man who perceives the richness of this grain. We have read the Sacred Scriptures. I think the Gospel is the body of Christ; Holy Writ, His teaching. When He says: "He who does not eat my flesh and drink my blood," although the words may be understood in a mystical sense, nevertheless, I say the word of Scripture is truly the body of Christ and His blood; it is divine doctrine. If at any time we approach the Sacrament — the faithful understand what I mean — and a tiny crumb should fall, we are appalled. Even so, if at any time we hear the word of God, through which the body and blood of Christ is being poured into our ears, and we yield carelessly to distraction, how responsible are we not for our failing? . . . The divine word is exceedingly rich, containing within itself every delight. Whatever you desire is found in it, just as the Jews recount that when they were eating the manna each one tasted the kind of food he liked. . . . We, in the flesh of Christ, which is the word of divine doctrine, or the interpretation of the Sacred Scriptures, received manna in accordance with and in proportion to our desire.[105]

Clearly Jerome has in mind both the reading and the preaching of the Word of God in worship. We found the doctrine that Christ is present in

105. Jerome, *On the Psalms*, p. 410.

the worship of the Church when the Word of God is preached in the *Didache,* and we will find it again. Christians have often spoken of the kerygmatic real presence in much the same way as the eucharistic real presence.

III. Maximus of Turin

About Maximus of Turin (ca. 350–ca. 420) we have very little information. He is not mentioned in any documents of his time, although toward the end of the fifth century Gennadius of Marseilles, in his work on famous men, indicates that he was bishop of Turin, knowledgeable in the sacred Scriptures, and gives us a partial list of his sermons. A manuscript from about the year 500 gives us a selection of some sixty of his sermons. His sermons, although sometimes incorrectly attributed to Ambrose or Augustine, were well known in the early Middle Ages because many of them were included in the homiliaries of the Carolingian period.

In 1962 Almut Mutzenbecher published a critical edition of an ancient collection of eighty-nine of his sermons, most of which appear to be genuine.[106] To this he added some twenty more from other sources. The original collection was no doubt a selection from the sermons of our preacher, and the fact that other sermons were preserved suggests there was originally a much larger collection available. Sermons for the major feasts and fasts as well as for saints' days figure prominently in the collection. The preponderance of this genre may reflect the interests of those who preserved the sermons, but about this we cannot be sure. One gets the impression that Maximus preached very frequently, almost daily, rather than only on red-letter days, for often his sermons begin with a remark about last Sunday's sermon or yesterday's sermon. About a third of the sermons are expositions of texts of Scripture, although there is no indication of any order or plan behind these sermons. They may be based on a *lectio continua,* but this is not discernible from the sermons which have come down to us. Bardenhewer interprets the words of Gennadius, *"de capitulis evangeliorum et actum apostolorum multa sapienter exposuit,"* to mean that he knew of longer series of sermons on the Gospels and the

---

106. Maximus of Turin, *Collectionem sermonum antiguam, nonnullus sermonibus extravagantibus adjectis,* ed. Almut Mutzenbecher, Corpus Christianorum, series Latina (Turnholt, Belgium: Brepols, 1962).

Acts of the Apostles.[107] No catechetical sermons have come down to us, but this does not mean he did not preach such sermons.

The texts we have appear to be the preacher's written draft of the sermon rather than a stenographer's transcript, such as we have for Jerome, Ambrose, and Augustine. They do not appear to be finished sermons written up after being preached. The preacher's draft of a sermon tends to be briefer than a sermon finished up for publication.

Maximus was a popular preacher who addressed himself to the practical concerns of piety. Matters of doctrine, which might concern the more intellectual and speculative Christians of the time, do not particularly interest Maximus. Unlike Augustine, he rarely does battle with the heresies of his day. Nor does he address himself to the ascetic or those who had committed themselves to a more intense or rigorous spiritual life. Unlike Jerome, he makes no attempt to call the true Christian away from the world into a monastery. His main concern is to teach the artisan, the merchant, the mistress and her maid, the landsman and his landlord, the elderly widow, and the aspiring man of affairs how to be a Christian right in the middle of life.

A particularly fine example of these sermons on practical piety is one Maximus preached at the beginning of the forty-day fast. He begins the sermon by reminding the congregation that on the previous Sunday he made the point that keeping the forty-day fast is an important work of faith, and that it is kept not simply by abstaining from food but by devoting energy to doing good works. What he would like to do in this sermon, Maximus says, is look into the question of what form fasting ought to take, how useful it is for the Christian, and how pleasing it is to God.[108] Referring to Isaiah 58:4-5, he formulates the question he would like to address in his sermon, What is the fast which the Lord would have us keep? The passage from Isaiah is indeed the key to the sermon. Although Maximus does not simply give us a running commentary on the text as we find in Origen, Chrysostom, or Jerome, the leading ideas of the text come to clear expression in the sermon. In other words, while the sermon is not expository in form, it is in content. Although Maximus does not quote verse 3 of chapter 58, "'Behold in the day of your fast you seek your own pleasure and oppress your workers,'" it is obviously the basis of

---

107. O. Bardenhewer, *Geschichte der altenkirchlichen Literatur,* 5 vols. (Freiburg im Breisgau: Herder, 1913-32), 4:612.

108. Maximus, Sermon 23, in *Collectionem,* p. 141.

the following remarks. Maximus tells us that there are far too many in the fasting time who abstain from food but seek their own pleasure.[109] Instead of going to church the first thing in the morning, they gather their servants together to prepare their hunting nets and romp through field and forest chasing wild game. This is not fair to the servants who may want to go to church; they, too, are in need of the forgiveness of sins. The fast that the Lord will have is a matter of abstaining from sin as well as from food. One fasts in order that one might make room for prayer;[110] indeed, verse 5 makes clear that a season of fasting is a season of prayer. Then Maximus elaborates further the passage from Isaiah that if one oppresses one's workers, God is not honored no matter how rigorous the fasting might be. He laments that there are those who take better care of their hunting dogs than they do of their servants.[111] The purpose of a fast is not to win God's favor but to pray for one's household, including one's servants, but if one would win God's favor, one should remember that God's mercy rests on the merciful. With this he quotes Luke 6:38, "'The measure you give will be the measure you get.'" By condition of life your servant may indeed be your servant, but by grace he is your brother.

This long example of the hunter and his servants serves very well to make the teaching of Isaiah vivid to the congregation. The literal sense of this Old Testament passage is made clear and applied to the experience of the congregation. The sermon is concluded with an admonition, as Maximus tells his flock that the fast which pleases God chastens the body by abstaining from food, but even more it puts on a humble spirit. Let us therefore be gentle with our servants, considerate to strangers, and merciful to the poor. Let us get up early in the morning, hasten to church, and devoutly pray. Let us spend the whole day in prayers, in readings, in giving alms.[112] Again, all this comes quite directly from the passage in Isaiah.

Maximus of Turin gives us several examples of what in the fifth century might be called evangelistic sermons. One such is a sermon inviting non-Christians to receive catechetical instruction and baptism. It bears the title "On the Grace of Baptism"[113] and may have been preached in connection with the feast of the Epiphany when the Church celebrated the baptism of

---

109. Maximus, Sermon 23, in *Collectionem*, p. 141.
110. Maximus, Sermon 23, in *Collectionem*, p. 142.
111. Maximus, Sermon 23, in *Collectionem*, p. 143.
112. Maximus, Sermon 23, in *Collectionem*, p. 143.
113. Maximus, Sermon 13, in *Collectionem*, pp. 50-52.

Christ. Beginning with an invitation to receive the sacrament, it outlines the benefits of the sacrament. What is interesting here is that apparently Maximus made his evangelistic appeal to his usual congregation. He may have made it at the feast of the Epiphany when he could count on a large congregation, but apparently he did not go outside his church to address the masses of unconverted but made his appeal to those who already had some inclination toward the Christian faith.

Even more interesting is another pair of sermons which probably should be thought of as evangelistic as well.[114] Maximus knew that although Christianity had officially been adopted by the Empire, paganism was still strongly rooted in Italian soil. At one time an eclipse of the moon had provoked a reappearance of pagan practices, and the bishop of Turin took to the pulpit to launch a two-sermon polemic against paganism. In the first of these sermons Maximus began by reproaching the foolishness of those who thought they could control the changes of the moon by magic incantation.[115] The whole affair resembled nothing so much as drunken revelry. Maximus takes up a text from Sirach, "The talk of the godly man is always wise, but the fool changes like the moon" (Sir. 27:11). When Christian people act like this they are foolish; they waiver from the fullness of faith to the emptiness of faithlessness.[116] Faith does not wax and wane as the moon but rather remains, as the psalmist says, steadfast as the sun (Ps. 72:5). The moon, Maximus tells his congregation, is a creature of God and serves his purposes as other creatures do. He quotes the apostle Paul, "We know that the whole creation has been groaning in travail together until now" (Rom. 8:22). This is a very happy choice of texts. Not only does it make very clear God's lordship over the natural order, it also makes clear that the natural order suffers from the fall. Natural catastrophes happen even though God is lord over them, and we should not despair at them because even nature will share in the final redemption of the world, "because the creation itself will be set free from its servitude" (Rom. 8:21). The moon is a servant of God and is bound to obey God, not the incantations of magicians. It goes through its changes not of its own will but according to divinely established statutes.[117] The sermon ends

114. Maximus, Sermons 30 and 31, in *Collectionem*, pp. 116-23.

115. Maximus, Sermon 23, in *Collectionem*, p. 117.

116. Maximus, Sermon 23, in *Collectionem*, p. 118.

117. Here we find a passage which suggests that possibly the text as we have it is the preacher's preliminary draft of the sermon. The thought is not put down on paper with the fullness it would need to be followed by a congregation.

with an admonition to the congregation to imitate the moon not in its darkness but in its fullness. Be, then, Maximus tells his congregation, citing the psalmist, "Be then like the full moon in heaven, a faithful witness forever" (Ps. 89:37).[118]

Maximus was hardly a prince of the patristic pulpit, but he was a good, solid preacher. There must have been many good preachers like him spread over Italy, Gaul, and North Africa. Without this general high level of preaching one would not find the genuises like Ambrose, Jerome, and Augustine.

IV. Augustine

A. Eloquia Dei

The ministry of the Word as it was carried out by Augustine of Hippo (354-430) is of surpassing interest to us, not because he was a great orator but because he fulfilled his service as a minister of the gospel with such faithfulness. Augustine probably could have been among the greatest orators of antiquity. He had a masterful grasp of rhetoric, that art which Roman antiquity so admired and cultivated. He was, we remember, regius professor of rhetoric in Milan. Yet, great oratory was not his aim.[119] His preaching was worship, a service to God. He carried out his apostolic ministry of preaching in obedience to God that the people of God might be nourished by the Word of God.[120] To him the apostolic ministry was

---

118. Maximus, Sermon 23, in *Collectionem*, p. 119.

119. The literature on Augustine is extensive. Among the most helpful in regard to biographical material and general interpretation is the following: Gustave Bardy, *Saint Augustin, L'homme et l'oeuvre*, 7th ed. (Paris: Desclée & Brouwer, 1948); Gerald Bonner, *St. Augustine of Hippo: Life and Controversies* (Philadelphia: Westminster Press, 1963); Peter Brown, *Augustine of Hippo: A Biography* (Berkeley and Los Angeles: University of California Press, 1967); von Campenhausen, "Augustin," in *Lateinische Kirchenväter*, pp. 151-222.

120. R. J. Deferrari, "St. Augustine's Method of Composing and Delivering Sermons," *American Journal of Philology* 43 (1922): 97-123 and 193-219; Adalbero Kunzelmann, "Augustines Predigttätigkeit," in *Festschrift der Görres-Gesellschaft* (Cologne: G. P. Bachem, 1930), pp. 155-68; A. D. R. Polman, *The Word of God according to St. Augustine* (London: Hodder and Stoughton, 1961); Maurice Pontet, *L'exégèse de S. Augustin prédicateur* (Paris: Aubier, 1944); F. Schritzler, *Zur Theologie der Verkündigung in den Predigten des hl. Augustinus* (Freiburg, Basel, and Vienna: Herder, 1968); Wolfgang Wieland, *Offenbarung bei Augustinus* (Mainz: Matthias Grünwald Verlag, 1978).

an act of love for God and for the people of God. The words of Jesus to the apostle Peter summed up his own understanding of the ministry, " 'Do you love me . . . feed my lambs' " (John 21:15). He was concerned that the congregation understand the Scriptures, and so he preached without the artificial eloquence which was popular in his day. His preaching might have been more literary had he been preaching in Rome or Constantinople or one of the cultural centers of the day, but he was preaching in Hippo, a rather unimportant provincial city of North Africa. To be sure, his facility with words was put to good use, and how often, even now, fifteen hundred years later, we read his Latin prose with delight. But Augustine was not so much concerned with producing great human literature as he was with the exposition of the Word of God. It was God's Word which fascinated him. He was content that his own eloquence should fade before the *eloquia Dei*.

In Augustine's own day he was thought of as a great preacher. In addition to his lengthy series of sermons on the Gospel of John and his equally lengthy series on the Psalms, some five hundred of his sermons have come down to us — far and away the largest collection of sermons we have from Latin antiquity. Augustine preached very frequently, some- times even daily, and if an editor had collected his fifty best sermons, as was the case with Gregory of Nazianzus, we might have a much higher opinion of his preaching. Nonetheless, his preaching was so highly valued that much of it was taken down by stenographers, sometimes in full, sometimes in a more abbreviated form. That was the way stenographers worked in those days. Sometimes the preacher went over the stenographic reports carefully, but more often they were published pretty much as they were taken down. With a few exceptions, we do not get the impression that Augustine gave too much time to finishing up his sermons for pub- lication. This very relaxed approach is not what wins the senior preaching prize, but it does meet the spiritual needs of the Church, and it was at this that Augustine aimed.

B. Expository Preaching

In his homiletical work, Augustine gave first importance to expository preaching. This was quite consistent with his whole theological system. Augustine had a strong theology of grace, and a strong theology of grace leads to a strong emphasis on revelation. Sermon after sermon we find our preacher intent on nothing so much as explaining the Holy Scriptures, for there it was that God revealed himself. Let us look first, then, at three groups of Augustine's expository sermons: a series of sermons on the Gospel of John, sermons on the Psalms, and finally a series on the First Epistle of John.

Each of these groups gives us a different perspective on Augustine as an expository preacher. The series on John shows him as the artist at work on the big canvas. It gives us a look at the art of doing a prolonged cycle of sermons on a single major book of the Bible. It is rather straightforward grammatical-historical exegesis; Augustine, like Basil before him, has discovered the value of this kind of exegesis, especially when one is trying to make a theological point. These sermons are not only expository sermons but also theological sermons. The sermons on the Psalms are quite different. Here we see Augustine's fruitful imagination. What an inventive man he was! So full of play and fantasy! Here we often see Augustine using allegorical methods of interpretation. These sermons should not be regarded as a series, but rather as a collection of individual pieces preached at different times throughout Augustine's long ministry in Hippo. The series on the First Epistle of John offers us yet again something quite different. It shows Augustine's strong sense of hermeneutic. For a group of new Christians, just baptized, he interprets I John with the intention of introducing them to the Christian life. It is a life of faith, hope, and love, and so he approaches his exposition with a very distinct hermeneutical purpose. Let us look at each of these three groups of sermons.

1. Sermons on the Gospel of John

Preaching on the Gospel of John is like being hired as the gardener of a large plantation. The gardens were laid out long ago by a renowned landscape architect. One approaches the splendid house down an allée of live oaks under which are plantings of white azaleas. There are rose gardens and kitchen gardens and orchards. Every season produces its fruit. Daffodils have been planted to bloom in the spring, and for the fall asters and chrysanthemums. Trees have been planted over the whole estate with a view to fall coloring. Behind the house is a terrace from which one takes in a breathtaking view of the mountains. Everything is in the garden, and it is the job of the gardener to make what is there blossom and bear fruit. That can be done with proper cultivation, planting, pruning, watering, and harvesting. Gardening is among the finest of the fine arts; it is the art of showing the beauty of the creation. The art of the preacher is very similar. The preacher has the responsibility of showing us the beauty of revelation, of bringing it both to flower and to fruit.

If we be allowed to extend our simile a bit further, we could say that the prologue of the Gospel is the magnificent approach, the allée of live oaks. Then comes the book of signs like so many specialized plantings, each with its own seasons and colors. The discourse on being born of the Spirit in chapter 3, the discourse on the worship that is in spirit and truth in chapter 4, the discourse on the bread of life in chapter 6, and the discourse on the resurrection and the life, in chapter 11, are like so many well-delineated, separate gardens. Finally comes the Passion narrative with its vista of eternity. No artist could ask for more. To preach through the Gospel of John gives the preacher an opportunity to be an artist, to treat the highest themes of the ministry of the Word.[121]

So many of the masters of the art of preaching have done cycles of sermons on the Gospel of John: Origen, John Chrysostom, Cyril of Alexandria, Bonaventure, Luther, Thomas Chalmers, William Temple, and James Boice, only fragments of which, in some cases, have come down to us. Sometimes we have broad sketches and sometimes we have cycles which were never completed, but for a project of this size we must expect that. A great garden is never complete. Generation after generation of talented gardeners do what they can, but the garden itself is greater than any one of them. There is always more to do, and nothing has been done so well that it cannot be done again quite differently another time. The daffodils are never so splendid but that one wants them to be splendid again. The cherries are so sweet and abundant one season, yet the following year it is

121. For the Latin text of Augustine's sermons on the Gospel of John, see Augustine, *In Iohannis evangelium tractatus CXXIV,* ed. Radbodus Willems, Corpus Christianorum, series Latina, vol. 36 (Turnholt, Belgium: Brepols, 1954). For an English translation, see Augustine, *Homilies on the Gospel of John,* trans. John Gibb and James Innes, Nicene and Post-Nicene Fathers, 1st ser., vol. 7 (Grand Rapids: Wm. B. Eerdmans Publishing Co., 1974), pp. 7-452; and Augustine, *Tractates on the Gospel of John,* trans. John W. Rettig, The Fathers of the Church, vol. 92 (Washington, D.C.: Catholic University of America Press, 1995). For studies on these sermons, see Marie Comeau, *Saint Augustin, exégète du quatrième évangile* (Paris: Gabriel Beauchesne, 1930); Richard P. Hardy, *Actualité de la Révélation divine* (Paris: Beauchesne, 1974); Richard P. Hardy, "The Incarnation and Revelation in Augustine's 'Tractatus in Johannes Evangelium,'" *Église et théologie* 3 (1972): 193-200; Maurice Pontet, *Saint Augustin: Sermons sur Saint Jean* (Namur, 1958); D. F. Wright, "The Manuscripts of St. Augustine's 'Tractatus in Evangelium Iohannis,'" *Recherches Augustiennes* 8 (1972): 55-143.

the plums which most delight us. It is the same when different preachers approach a major book like the Gospel of John. When we compare the way different preachers have handled it, we begin to see the beauty of interpretation. The text is always the same, and yet each preacher brings different fields to fruit and different beds to flower.

But before turning into the gates of our homiletical plantation, we must make a few introductory remarks. First, we need to point out that while we have 124 sermons on the Gospel of John, only the first 50 or so are full reports; the rest are heavily abbreviated. Different scholars have understood this differently.[122] What seems to me to be the case is that Augustine preached through the whole of the Gospel day after day, starting sometime after Christmas about the year 400. As the Easter season approached he interrupted his series but then resumed it later in the year. The only trouble was that when he had preached 50 sermons and saw how many pages of manuscript he had, and that he was only halfway through the Gospel, he began to realize that this was going to be an enormous work, much too extensive to be practical. Publishing it would be more expensive than he could afford, and so he began to have his stenographer record the remaining sermons in an abbreviated form. This was a common practice among stenographers. That is one of the differences between a tape recorder and a stenographer — a stenographer can condense the material as it is taken down. The preached sermons as they were delivered from the pulpit continued in all the rich detail and rhetorical brilliance with which they had begun, but the last half of the series has come down to us in an abbreviated form.

One of the beauties of Augustine's sermons on the Gospel of John is that they show us how one of the most profound theological thinkers the Church has ever produced preached theology to a very average, very provincial sort of congregation. Here we have beautiful doctrinal preaching. These 124 sermons form a cycle of discourses which explores the whole mystery of the doctrine of Christ's divinity, investigating all kinds of moral and philosophical implications of this central Christian teaching.

An interesting feature of these sermons is their literary form. Augustine often refers to them as discourses. The use of this term is significant, just as it is significant when Basil of Caesarea or Gregory of

---

122. See the introductory material in Corpus Christianorum, series Latina, p. xii, for the theory of Radbobus Willems. For another theory, see M. Le Landais, "Deux années de prédication de S. Augustin," in *Études Augustiniennes* (Paris, 1953).

Nazianzus refer to their festal sermons as panegyrics. The discourse, as the Latin term *discursus* suggests, refers to a very particular kind of speech. The idea of the discourse is to give a complete, systematic treatment of a subject; it is to make the complete course, going around the whole topic. It is the speech of a philosopher in which he completely treats a subject. When Cicero discusses the subjects of old age, friendship, or the nature of the gods, we have a discourse, and when Seneca holds forth on mercy, on anger, or on providence, we also have a discourse. These are pagan literary compositions, to be sure, but the discourse is not unique to the pagan literature of ancient Greece and Rome. Surely Augustine noticed that much of the teaching of the Gospel of John is framed in discourses — indeed, the Fourth Gospel itself might be called a series of discourses. Surely Augustine has this model before him, but just as surely has he been influenced by the more traditional literary form of the Christian expository sermon, which ultimately goes back to the traditional synagogue sermon. These sermons of Augustine's are discourses on religion, to be sure, but even more basically they are expositions of Scripture. There is an important difference between a sermon and a discourse in the literary, philosophical sense of the term: A sermon is first of all an exposition of Scripture. Augustine makes this clear again and again, especially in the introductions of these sermons where he mentions the reading of the lesson which has just taken place and announces that he intends to explain the text of that lesson. In the opening sentences of the first two sermons our preacher makes this particularly clear.[123] The introduction to the twelfth sermon tells us that the discourse he intends to present to his congregation is an explanation of the lesson from the day before. Our preacher had evidently been unable to finish his discourse, so he had the Gospel lesson read over again in order to complete his explanation.[124] What we have, then, in these sermons on John is Christian expository discourses, and what makes them Christian discourses is that they are expositions of Scripture. Here we see a clear case of how Augustine is much more conservative in his use of classical rhetoric than Gregory of Nazianzus. He maintains the literary form of the primitive Christian sermon in a way Gregory of Nazianzus did not.

When it comes to the content of this series of expository discourses, it is quite clear that Augustine has given us a comprehensive treatment of

---

123. Augustine, *In Iohannis Evangelium* 1.1 and 2.1.
124. Augustine, *In Iohannis Evangelium* 12.1.

the gospel of Christ's divinity. The Gospel of John lends itself very well to a series of discourses on this subject. It is often said that Matthew presents Jesus as the promised Messiah, that Mark presents him as the Servant of the Lord, that Luke presents him as the Great Physician, but the Gospel of John presents Jesus as God, or, to use the words of the Council of Nicaea, God of God, Light of Light, Very God of Very God. From beginning to end the Gospel of John makes that point. Augustine well understands this, and in one sermon after another he unfolds this basic affirmation, showing its manifold implications for the Christian way of life.

The Gospel of John has a definite structure, which Augustine uses to delineate his exposition. The Evangelist has developed a series of discourses which are introduced as explanations of various signs performed by Jesus. The Gospel begins with the sign of Cana and the sign of the cleansing of the Temple, which are followed by the discourse with Nicodemus on the new life; the discourse on the bread of life, following the sign of the feeding of the five thousand; the discourse on the light of the world and the healing of the man born blind; the discourse on the resurrection and the life woven into the story of the raising of Lazarus; and finally the discourse in the Upper Room, which prepares the way for the ultimate sign of the lifting up of the Son of Man. The fundamental themes of the Gospel are announced in the prologue. Augustine takes full advantage of this, constantly quoting these fundamental texts throughout the series: "In the beginning was the Word" (John 1:1), "All things were made by him" (1:3), "The true light that enlightens every man was coming into the world" (1:9), "And the Word became flesh and dwelt among us" (1:14). The constant recurrence of these themes gives artistic unity to the whole cycle.

Having made these introductory remarks, let us turn into the entrance to our homiletical plantation. Three sermons are devoted to the prologue. The first starts out with the opening sentence of the Gospel, "In the beginning was the Word, and the Word was with God, and the Word was God." As Augustine interprets it, the Gospel presents Jesus as the divine Wisdom from on high, who is ultimately God himself.[125] The divine Wisdom is the design found from all eternity within the heart of God, the design for our creation, redemption, and glorification.[126] Our

125. Augustine, *In Iohannis Evangelium* 1.16. See also 1.2-4 and 16-19.
126. Augustine, *In Iohannis Evangelium* 1.9.

preacher alludes to some of the classic texts of Old Testament Wisdom literature as well as the familiar text from the apostle Paul which speaks of Christ as the Wisdom of God (I Cor. 1:24).

In the second sermon Augustine goes on to show that the divine Wisdom is the light that enlightens all life.[127] Christ is himself the light that comes into the world and enlightens everyone. He is the light who needs no enlightenment because he is the source of all enlightenment, just as the Wisdom of God is in himself Wisdom and the source of all Wisdom. Then our preacher tells us that it is the Wisdom of God to create sons and daughters for God, and it was therefore that the Word became flesh.[128] The eternal Son became a son that we might all be sons of God.

In the third sermon Augustine returns to the first two fundamental texts he dwelt upon in the two previous sermons: "In the beginning was the Word" and "the Word became flesh. . . ." He makes the point that the Word of God is the eternal Wisdom of God. The Word of God is from the beginning. The Word was God and always was God. It was through this divine Wisdom that God made all things.[129] To this he now adds a third text, "And from his fullness we have all received grace upon grace." We received grace in that we were given faith that we might walk in faith and thereby live in grace.[130] Here our preacher opens up the phrase "grace upon grace." Having obtained the gracious gift of faith, we are justified. We are justified by faith, but even our faith is a gift of grace.[131]

These are the three keys which Augustine uses to unlock the whole Gospel. For Augustine the doctrine of Christ's divinity as he finds it in John implies God's saving grace; Christology leads to soteriology. In these three sermons Augustine lays bare the theological principles which are the foundation of the Gospel of John. It is a very imposing entrance to the most theological of Gospels. Today we read these sermons and wonder how the preacher of a small provincial city in North Africa, preaching well over an hour on subjects like this, could hold the attention of his congregation. These sermons may be brilliant but they are certainly not simple.

Skipping over the sermons on the second chapter, we survey the two sermons devoted to the discourse on the new life in the third chapter of

127. Augustine, *In Iohannis Evangelium* 2.6-7.
128. Augustine, *In Iohannis Evangelium* 2.13.
129. Augustine, *In Iohannis Evangelium* 3.4.
130. Augustine, *In Iohannis Evangelium* 3.8.
131. Augustine, *In Iohannis Evangelium* 3.9.

John.[132] Here is a very distinct garden, a garden where one can sit in the evening and discuss far into the night what we don't quite understand. It was the visit of Nicodemus, who came by night to speak with Jesus, which prompted this discourse. Most of us are accustomed to hearing the third chapter of John developed in terms of the doctrine of justification by faith, but Augustine shows us here that salvation comes about by the work of God's Spirit in our lives, which is a concept of the greatest possible importance. Given the time of year when Augustine preached this sermon, that is, two or three months before Easter, there were a good number of catechumens in the congregation, and so our preacher speaks at considerable length about baptism, particularly about the peculiar problems the Donatist controversy had raised about the validity of the sacraments ministered by unworthy ministers.[133] Given the theological questions and concerns of his congregation, it is easy to understand why in these sermons Augustine emphasizes the work of the Holy Spirit in our baptism. Baptism depends upon neither the worthiness of the candidate nor the minister but rather upon the faithfulness of God's Holy Spirit.[134] It is the Spirit of God who brings about what is signified by the sacrament. To be spiritually born is to be born by the Holy Spirit, who brings about this spiritual birth through the ministry of the Word and sacrament.[135] This is a most important principle in worship, which Augustine brought out with particular clarity in his controversy with the Donatists. The minister of Word and sacrament is neither a magician nor a shaman. The power is in God's Spirit alone.

It is of the essence of expository preaching that one interprets the needs and concerns of the congregation just as one interprets the Scriptures. We have already spoken of this quite often, and we will often speak of it again. Here we are dealing with hermeneutic, the transition from the text to the congregation. If we may again have recourse to our simile, how the gardener does his work has much to do with the changes of the seasons of the year. When the seasons change, the gardener has to adapt his work accordingly, for different seasons require different kinds of work. The third chapter of the Gospel is bound to look very different when Augustine preaches it in North Africa during the Donatist controversy than when

132. Augustine, *In Iohannis Evangelium* 11-12.
133. Augustine, *In Iohannis Evangelium* 12.13-15.
134. Augustine, *In Iohannis Evangelium* 12.5.
135. Augustine, *In Iohannis Evangelium* 12.5.

Jean Daillé preached it in Paris during the reign of Louis XIV. The way Charles Stanley would preach on this chapter in Atlanta, Georgia, today, at the end of the twentieth century, is bound to be different still. What Augustine had to say about regeneration may sound like terribly involved theology to us, but it apparently filled his church, even on a weekday morning. At several points in these sermons our preacher remarks about the fact that attendance has been especially good for this series of sermons.[136] Yes, Augustine draws a crowd. Expository preaching which is truly seasonal has a way of doing just that.

The seven sermons Augustine preaches on the story of the healing of the man at the pool of Bethesda and the discourse which follows it give us another example of how our gardener does his work. Here is a very specialized garden; perhaps we might see it as an herb garden. The seven sermons all revolve around a special text, John 5:19, "'Truly, truly, I say to you, the Son can do nothing of his own accord, but only what he sees the Father doing; for whatever he does, the Son does likewise.'" This text claims Augustine's special attention because it brings out a very particular dimension of the doctrine of Christ's divinity, namely, that the Father works in and through the Son. This is a major theme of the Gospel of John, a theme intimated in the prologue, "All things were made through him, and without him was not anything made that was made" (John 1:3). Throughout these seven sermons our preacher keeps coming back to John 5:19, as is evidenced in the way the Scripture passages are arranged:

1. Sermon 17   John 5:1-18
2. Sermon 18   John 5:19
3. Sermon 19   John 5:19-30
4. Sermon 20   John 5:19
5. Sermon 21   John 5:20-23
6. Sermon 22   John 5:24-30
7. Sermon 23   John 5:19-40

In the first sermon, Sermon 17, Augustine takes the story of the man who was healed by the pool of Bethesda and goes through the narrative itself, giving particular attention to the numerology in the story. There is an important meaning in the fact that the pool was surrounded by five porches

---

136. Augustine, *In Iohannis Evangelium* 6.1 and 7.1. This was especially the case with sermons on the third chapter of John. *In Iohannis Evangelium* 12.1.

and that the man was thirty-eight years old.[137] This the modern reader finds rather artificial, but when Augustine preached this sermon, as, in fact, when John wrote the Gospel, sacred numerology was taken quite seriously. The numerology leads Augustine to make the point that without love the Christian life is immature. At thirty-eight years this man was two years short of forty, the age of maturity. After being healed, the man must take up his bed and walk; that is, he has to begin living the Christian life. For Augustine Christian preaching must always end up exhorting us toward love for God, love for the neighbor, and specific acts of Christian charity.[138] The application seems a bit forced here, but one has a hard time objecting. Finally Augustine mentions that John makes quite a point of the fact that this healing took place on the Sabbath.[139] As Augustine understands it, the Sabbath is a sacrament, a sacred, God-given sign of eternal reality.

The second sermon, Sermon 18, is a very exacting look at the text which so interests Augustine, John 5:19. He is concerned that an Arian interpretation not be given the verse. The Arians claimed that in these words Jesus made it clear that he did not really claim to be equal to the Father nor to be of the same substance of the Father.[140] What the text really teaches us is that the Father works through the Son.[141] In Sermon 19 Augustine shows that his interpretation is borne out by the discourse which follows; in fact, it is demanded by the context. The following verse, John 5:20, makes it clear that it is because of the Father's love for the Son that the Father shows everything to the Son so that whatever the Father does is done through the Son.[142] Then in John 5:23 we read, "'Whoso honoreth not the Son, honoreth not the Father that sent Him.'" To honor God truly is to honor God as Father, but how can one honor God as Father if one does not believe in the Son?[143] It is above all in the resurrection that we see the Father at work in the Son, a point Jesus makes very clear in his discourse in the fifth chapter of John.[144] Those who hear the word of the Son are raised up to eternal life.[145] This shows us that the

---

137. Augustine, *In Iohannis Evangelium* 17.4-6.
138. Augustine, *In Iohannis Evangelium* 17.8.
139. Augustine, *In Iohannis Evangelium* 17.13.
140. Augustine, *In Iohannis Evangelium* 18.3.
141. Augustine, *In Iohannis Evangelium* 18.6.
142. Augustine, *In Iohannis Evangelium* 19.3.
143. Augustine, *In Iohannis Evangelium* 19.6.
144. Augustine, *In Iohannis Evangelium* 19.8.
145. Augustine, *In Iohannis Evangelium* 19.10.

Son is the source of eternal life, that is, he is of the same substance as the Father. "'For as the Father has life in Himself, even so hath He given to the Son to have life in Himself' (John 5:26)." Nowhere else but in himself is the source of his living.[146] The whole point of this discourse in John 5 is that it is in the resurrection that the Sabbath is kept. It is, to be sure, the Christian Sabbath, the eighth day, that is in mind. Healing, the ultimate healing, is the proper work of the Sabbath. Surely here Augustine has come as close to understanding the Gospel as anyone who has ever preached on this passage.

Rarely content with his finished product, Augustine takes a fourth sermon, Sermon 20, to return to verse 19 and try to do an even better job of making his point. Then he takes two more sermons, Sermons 21 and 22, to go over the discourse again and show even more convincingly that the orthodox interpretation of the passage is much sounder than the Arian interpretation. Finally, in a seventh sermon, he recapitulates the whole discourse. One of the beautiful things about this series of sermons is the way one sermon builds on another. This is a constant feature of first-class expository preaching as we shall see again and again.

One wonders if Augustine's congregation found this all a bit tedious. Chances are that they did not because, after all, Augustine was a master of the art of rhetoric. Rhetoric was supposed to show a speaker how to go through a complicated argument and convince one's hearers of the validity of the argument. For a rhetorician the worst of faults was to put one's audience to sleep. One notices again and again how Augustine keeps his listeners engaged through the use of rhetorical questions. This is a means of keeping the dialectical tension at its height wherein the objections and the questions of the listeners were anticipated, expressed, and then answered. The rhetorical question was developed in forensic debate, and it was in the courtroom that the teachers of rhetoric had proven the value of their art. In fact, classical rhetoric was used in the courtroom long before it was used in the pulpit. Augustine learned the rhetoric of the lawyer as well as the rhetoric of the philosopher, and this is particularly clear in these sermons on the Gospel of John.

But there is something else here — the secret of classical oratory in fact — and that is that Augustine is thinking all this out on his feet. He did not go into the pulpit with a prepared text which he read out of his memory; he was thinking with his congregation all the while. Of the

146. Augustine, *In Iohannis Evangelium* 19.11.

essence of oratory is the play back and forth between the speaker and the audience. Genuine oratory is like a game of tennis between preacher and congregation, and in these sermons we see this game being played with consummate skill. We detect the intellectual vitality of the struggle as Augustine serves his interpretations of Christian doctrine and the congregation returns them. What the stenographer has gotten down is only half the game, but it is enough for us to realize it was a keen display of theological wit. The chances are that the Christian people of Hippo were thoroughly engrossed in the intellectual competition in which their preacher had engaged them.

The sixth chapter of the Gospel of John tells the story of the feeding of the multitude with the five loaves and the two fishes. It is followed by the discourse on the bread of life. Here is another splendid garden in the plantation that is the Gospel of John. So many gifted interpreters have worked this garden! Augustine's interpretation of this difficult chapter is quite consistent with what he has to say in the rest of the series. It takes up the theme of the way the ministry of Word and sacrament brings us into the new life of the kingdom of God, of how Word and sacrament, in relation to each other, together bring us into communion with God. These sermons exhibit a very strong covenantal understanding of worship,[147] which is why the sixteenth-century Reformers particularly cherished Augustine's sermons on John 6. To understand Jesus as the Word, as the self-revelation of the divine Wisdom, is bound to lead to a strong doctrine of Word and sacrament.

As Augustine puts it, the meal Jesus served the multitude on the mountain was a visible word. The act of his feeding that great multitude made the word visible.[148] It made it a sacrament.[149] The discourse which follows the meal explains that Christ in his divinity is the meat and drink of the new life. In Sermon 25 Augustine comments on the text " 'This is the work of God that ye believe on Him whom He has sent' " (John 6:29), telling us that it is by faith in Christ that we feed on Christ.[150] By faith we feed on the food that does not perish but which endures to eternal life.[151] Again and again in this series of sermons Augustine underlines

---

147. Augustine, *In Iohannis Evangelium* 26.13.
148. Augustine, *In Iohannis Evangelium* 25.2.
149. Augustine, *In Iohannis Evangelium* 24.2-3.
150. Augustine, *In Iohannis Evangelium* 25.12.
151. Augustine, *In Iohannis Evangelium* 25.12-14.

what the Gospel has to say about faith, about the essential role of believing in Jesus Christ as the divine Son of God. It is the divine Christ, our Lord and our God, who as the Lamb of God has taken away our sin. It is the divine Christ who is our Savior, and it is by faith that we appropriate his salvation.[152] As Augustine understands it, the fundamental theme of the Gospel is the saving divinity of Christ, and so in his preaching of this Gospel he often comes to speak of the ministry of Word and sacrament because it is through them that faith appropriates this salvation.

An important point made in these sermons on the bread of life is that it is with God himself that we deal in the ministry of Word and sacrament. Here we have a spiritual food which supports the spiritual life. Both the preaching of the Word and the celebration of the Lord's Supper are to be understood in terms of spiritual food.[153] Just as the new birth is the work of God in John 3, so here in John 6 the new life of the Christian is nourished and sustained by none other than God himself. It is the teaching of the Word of God in the person of Christ which sustains the new life. In Sermon 26 our preacher sets himself to interpret the text " 'They shall all be taught by God' " (John 6:45). Here, by quoting this text from the prophets, Jesus makes a strong claim of his own divinity. He is the Word made flesh, who was in the beginning with God and is indeed God himself.[154] One does not have to meditate on these sermons very long before one realizes that they imply a profound understanding of the office of preaching. Preaching is worship, just as the Lord's Supper is worship, because it is thereby that we stand before the presence of God. Biblical Wisdom theology as we find it in the Gospel of John, as we have found it in many of the early Fathers, and especially in Origen, is obviously very strong in these sermons on the Gospel of John. For Wisdom theology nothing is more central to worship than listening to God's Word. Hearing the Word of God and obeying the Word of God are at the center of communion with God. They are of the essence of worship.

When one steps back and looks at this very long series of 124 sermons, one realizes it is a major work of art. In its original form, that is, as it was preached, it must have been superb. The record that has come down to us only gives us a hint of what it must have been like. But that is the way it is with the art of oratory. The record has, however, communi-

---

152. Augustine, *In Iohannis Evangelium* 26.1-3.
153. Augustine, *In Iohannis Evangelium* 26.11.
154. Augustine, *In Iohannis Evangelium* 26.7.

cated how this series of sermons was impressive for its vastness. For a painter there is nothing like painting the big canvas. It gives one the opportunity to explore so many different harmonies and contrasts! So many different colors, shades, and tones! It is the same way with a gardener who is given the opportunity to cultivate a large estate — to work with meadows, with woods, with ponds and streams, with sunny gardens and shady gardens. And it is the same thing when a preacher has the opportunity to preach through a major book of the Bible like Genesis, the Epistle to the Romans, or the Gospel of John. We could spend much more time looking at these sermons on John, but what we have already seen should at least give us an intimation of the grandeur of its design.

2. Sermons on the Psalms

Another important series of expository sermons is his *Enarrationes in Psalmos*.[155] Most of these sermons were preached in worship, although some are clearly literary compositions. The series as it now stands treats all of the 150 psalms. In some cases we have several sermons on the same psalm — 3 sermons on Psalm 37, 4 on Psalm 104, and 22 on Psalm 119 — and in other cases we have both a written commentary and a preached sermon on the same psalm. Augustine worked on this project from 392 to 418, a period of over twenty-five years. Although any attempt to work out a chronology is more than precarious, a few parts of the series can be dated. Psalms 120 to 134 were preached in Carthage in December of 412, and other psalms were preached at special occasions and appear to be isolated from any series. Most often Augustine preached on the psalm that had been sung in the liturgy. One sermon, the sermon on Psalm 120, begins by saying that the cantor had sung the psalm and the congregation had sung the antiphon. On one occasion Augustine decided on the spot

---

155. For the Latin text, see Augustine, *Enarrationes in Psalmos*, ed. Eligius Dekkers and Iohannes Fraipont, Corpus Christianorum, series Latina, vols. 38 and 39 (Turnholt, Belgium: Brepols, 1978 and 1981). For an English translation, see Augustine, *St. Augustine on the Psalms*, translated and annotated by Dame Scholastica Hebyin and Dame Felicitas Corrigan, Ancient Christian Writers, vols. 29-30 (Westminster, Md.: Newman Press; London: Longmans, Green and Co., 1960-61). Particularly helpful for understanding this most difficult work are: Maurice Pontet, *L'exégèse de S. Augustin prédicateur*; T. Delmare, "Lorsque St. Augustin expliquait les Psaumes," *La Vie spirituelle* 82 (1950): 115-36; and J. F. Cordelier, *La pédagogie de saint Augustin dans les "Ennarationes in Psalmos"* (Dijon, 1971).

to preach on the psalm that had been sung rather than the Gospel, but on other occasions he may well have appointed the psalm to be sung because he intended to preach on it. Finally, having accumulated sermons on most of the psalms in the course of time, he decided to finish the collection by writing commentaries on the missing psalms in the literary form of a sermon. For example, he did not have a sermon on Psalm 119 in the collection he had accumulated, so, he tells us, he dictated a "sermon" to his stenographer which he never preached from the pulpit but which served to complete his commentary. The twenty-two sermons on Psalm 119 were therefore literary compositions rather than real sermons.

What system of selecting psalms for worship might have been used at Hippo in the days of Augustine, we do not know for sure. More than likely the whole Psalter was sung through in course, service by service, some of the longer psalms being divided up over several services. Then again, perhaps the choice was left to the bishop or even the cantor. There were probably no hard-and-fast rules about such things, and the bishop could always change things around when it seemed appropriate. The important thing was that the whole Psalter should be sung through in the course of time. For feast days there were probably already certain psalms which were traditionally sung. We gather that Psalm 118 was sung at Easter, and from his sermon on Psalm 42 we learn that it was customary to sing this psalm in connection with the preparation of catechumens for baptism. If the psalms were sung through on a regular basis, Augustine would have many occasions to work on his series of sermons. No doubt he preached many sermons on psalms which were not preserved. What was preserved in this commentary were his better efforts.

Augustine's sermons on the Psalms are difficult for the modern reader, for in them the preacher's love of allegory often leads him far from the literal sense. His understanding of the psalm titles had a tendency to encourage him to the wildest excesses of allegorical interpretation. The Latin translation he used was often so misleading that even the ingenuity of an Augustine was taxed to make some sort of spiritually edifying sense out of the text. Yet, nevertheless, this collection of sermons is a fascinating mural of theological and devotional insight. More even than a mural, perhaps it should be compared with a complete city, with its marketplaces, its fortresses, its courtyards, its tenements and sacred sanctuaries. Augustine's cycle of sermons on the Psalms is a veritable theological Jerusalem of heavenly meditation and celestial praise. It has fortresses of moral instruction, luxurious palaces of rich doctrinal theology, brilliant vistas of typological insight, pious parks and playgrounds of allegory. For the theologian, yes, even for the modern theologian, reading these sermons is like a vacation in Venice. It is a marvelous fantasy, a very classical fantasy, which somehow points to a reality beyond the fantasy and which is so much more true than the more mundane type of reality; it is a reality everyday shopping-center reductionists will never understand.

3. Sermons on the First Epistle of John

If Augustine's series of sermons on the Gospel of John may be compared to an immense plantation, and his series on the Psalms to a city with its intricate variety and great extent, his series of ten sermons on the First Epistle of John may be compared to a single, very well designed house.[156] One would not want to compare it to the symmetrical house of the Enlightenment but to the functional house of modern architecture. Like the masterpieces of Frank Lloyd Wright, it knows what services it needs to perform. Its beauty is the way it fits into the site, and there brings grace by doing its work simply and directly.

The series was conceived as a whole. It was intended to be preached in the week following Easter, as an introduction to the Christian life to those who had just been baptized, but Augustine did not get through the series during the octave of Easter, so the last two or three sermons had to be fitted in a few days later.[157] The theme of the series is Christian love. After they had been baptized and had made their confession of faith, Augustine sees it as his pastoral responsibility to exhort the newly baptized to the practice of Christian love. Their faith must now bear fruit, and that

---

156. This study is based on the edition of Paul Agaësse: Augustine, *Commentaire de la première épître de S. Jean,* Latin text and French translation with introduction and notes by Paul Agaësse, Sources chrétiennes, vol. 75 (Paris: Les Éditions du Cerf, 1961). By way of interpretation, see: O. Roy, "L'expérience de l'amour et l'intelligence de la foi trinitaire selon saint Augustin," *Recherches Augustiniennes* 2 (1962): 415-45; Suzanne Poque, "Les lectures liturgiques de l'Octave pascale à Hippone d'après les Traites de saint Augustin sur la Première Épître de S. Jean," *Revue Bénédictine* 74 (1964): 217-41.

157. Attempts to put these sermons precisely on the calendar have not been successful. One would expect that Augustine would have continued the unfinished series during the following week, but some are of the opinion that it may not have been finished until sometime between Ascension and Easter. I find this hard to accept because with Sermons 8 and 9 the series reaches a climax which would have been hard to maintain with such a long break.

fruit is love for God and love for the neighbor. One might call these sermons catechetical sermons; they certainly performed a catechetical function, even if in terms of literary form they are expository sermons.

The most striking thing about these sermons is that they are not anything like the mystagogical catechisms of Cyril of Jerusalem or Ambrose of Milan. This is even more striking when we remember that Augustine himself was baptized in Milan by none other than Ambrose. Why does Augustine not follow the example of his spiritual father and offer his converts an explanation of the Christian mysteries? Could it be that he saw in this practice a compromise with paganism? Or that he found the comparison between the Christian sacraments and the rites of the mystery religions misleading? Perhaps he sensed the direction in which this approach would take the worship of the Church and stepped back from it.

We have already spoken of the fact that John Chrysostom took a very different approach from Cyril and Ambrose. Of the five major series of catechetical sermons which appeared between A.D. 380 and 415, Augustine's bears the closest similarity to that of John Chrysostom. He, as Chrysostom, puts the emphasis on moral catechism once converts have been baptized. It is hard to say whether John Chrysostom deliberately departed from the precedent set by Cyril of Jerusalem, or whether he even knew of the catechetical preaching of Cyril. We don't know. One thing is clear, however: The catechetical sermons of John are not mystagogical. With Augustine there is no question but that he knew this practice of Ambrose, and while he made no scandal of it, he simply did not follow it. Perhaps there was no precedent for that sort of thing in North Africa and Augustine did not consider it wise to introduce the practice. But then, Augustine's whole approach to worship is completely different. He does not understand Christian worship in terms of the rites of the mystery religions. For Augustine Christian worship is to be understood in terms of the communion between God and his people.

The centrality of the bond of love between God and his people to the living of the Christian life is insisted upon again and again in these ten sermons. This is the ultimate principle for Augustine's theology of worship, and it is the primary theme of the catechetical instruction he would give his converts. The theme these sermons unfold is exactly that, the nature of Christian love.

After a study of these sermons, one is tempted to call them one of the finest examples of expository preaching that has come down to us. The book is preached through as a whole so that its literary integrity is respected and the author's central message is brought to light. It is preached through verse by verse so that each detail is brought into relation with the major theme of the whole book. They are good expository sermons because they aim to convey very simply what the text of Scripture would convey. The genius of the preacher is in recognizing the appropriateness of this particular portion of sacred Scripture to the situation he had before him. To be sure, not every book of the Bible has such a clear unity of theme, nor is every book of the Bible so short, so simple, so direct. But to recognize this particular feature of I John, as well as to recognize its opposite in the Psalms, is essential to Augustine's insight. He obviously understood both that not every book of the Bible is to be treated the same way and that not every juncture in the Christian life requires the same message.

In this series of sermons we see the genius of Augustine's hermeneutic. Hermeneutic is the art of moving from Scripture to congregation, of recognizing which Scripture is appropriate to a congregation at a particular time in its life. Whether it is an art or a science has often been discussed, and Augustine, of course, approached it as an art. Be that as it may, the series of sermons is a masterpiece of hermeneutic.

Augustine's ten sermons on I John repay a careful analysis.[158] Let us look at these sermons to see just what made them so effective. First of all we notice that these sermons focus on the great religious questions. Augustine appreciated more than most that the human heart has a passionate desire for God and for the blessing of God. In spite of all man's rebellion, all his rejection, and all his denial, the religious question is the basic, the most persistent, and the ultimate question which he poses. If a preacher treats these central religious themes with integrity, imagination, and intelligence, that preacher will always win a hearing. When in Sermon 3 Augustine speaks of the Christian hope of eternal life, he obviously catches the attention of his congregation for one gathers from the text that they applaud him mightily at that point.[159] How magnificently Augustine convinces us in Sermon 4 that the Christian hope is a reality upon which we can set our hope.[160] How forthrightly he takes up the question of the remaining vestiges of sin in the life of the Christian. We all sin and yet we would be holy; indeed, we have the name of Christian but not the full

158. The following study is based on the Latin text of Paul Agaësse: Augustine, *Commentaire de la première épître de S. Jean.*
159. Augustine, *In Epistolam Joannis* 3.11.
160. Augustine, *In Epistolam Joannis* 4.3-6.

reality. Augustine knows what a gnawing problem this is to every sincere Christian, and so he treats it at full depth and great length.[161]

Second, we find that the effectiveness of these sermons rests on the preacher's sense of the divine authority of his message. It is God's Word that he is preaching. Therefore, it is the text of Scripture which he presses upon his congregation. Again and again Augustine recites the text so that the listener has a strong sense of hearing Scripture. At the beginning of the third sermon he takes up the text "Children, it is the last hour" (I John 2:18) and tells his congregation of recently baptized Christians that even though they are children, it is important that they make haste to grow because the time is short. He urges them to seek out the breasts of their mother eagerly, that they might grow rapidly. Their mother is the Church and her breasts are the two Testaments of Holy Scripture — there they will suck the mysteries of eternal salvation.[162] At the end of the same sermon Augustine turns to the text "His anointing teaches you about everything" (I John 2:27) and asks what the use of preaching is if the inner illumination of the Holy Spirit is what really teaches us. He answers his question by telling us that God works through outward means to bring about inward results. Just as God used the outward means of having the apostle John write the epistle, so God uses the preacher that the word might be heard. The sounds of the preacher's words strike the ears, but the teacher is within. Outward teaching on earth is but an aid;[163] he who instructs the heart has his pulpit in heaven.[164] The outward words which we preach here on earth are like a farmer growing a tree. The farmer waters and cultivates, but it is God who gives growth to the tree. As Paul put it, "I have planted, Apollos watered, but God gives the increase" (I Cor. 3:6). In the apostolic ministry of preaching, it is Christ who is the Word and his Spirit who makes the Word fruitful. Augustine's understanding of preaching is based on a strong doctrine of grace. He is confident that it is God who is speaking through him. The Word is not merely his word but God's Word.

If the members of Augustine's congregation listened to him with confidence, it was because they were satisfied with his faithfulness in listening to the Word himself. Augustine obviously gave great amounts

161. Augustine, *In Epistolam Joannis* 5.
162. Augustine, *In Epistolam Joannis* 3.1.
163. Augustine, *In Epistolam Joannis* 3.13.
164. Augustine, *In Epistolam Joannis* 3.13.

of time to studying the Bible, and his sermons show a profound under-standing of the Scriptures. While his breadth of understanding those Scriptures may grasp our attention, it is his depth of understanding which interests us. To be sure, sometimes his mystical mathematics and his delight in imaginative flights of allegory impress us as being contrived and artificial, but all this is more than compensated for by his ability to explain Scripture by Scripture. He knows the Scriptures well enough to identify where Paul has spoken clearly about a subject John mentions only briefly. Commenting on I John 3:2-3, "Beloved, we are God's children now; it does not yet appear what we shall be, but we know that when he appears we shall be like him, for we shall see him as he is. And everyone who thus hopes in him purifies himself as he is pure," he assures his congregation that the whole life of the good Christian is a holy desire.[165] What one desires one does not yet see in this life, but this desire makes us capable of accomplishing what we desire, that when Christ comes the hope will be fulfilled. He then quotes Paul, "For in this hope we were saved. Now hope that is seen is not hope. For who hopes for what he sees? But if we hope for what we do not see, we wait for it with patience" (Rom. 8:24-25). Augustine knows Scripture well enough to pinpoint exactly where the great themes of Scripture are most clearly unfolded, to identify precisely where central themes are found in their most perfect expression.

Augustine has a wonderful sense for the way biblical stories illustrate biblical teachings, and he uses this sense to make his sermons interesting and accessible. For example, he explains I John 2:16, "For all that is in the world, the lust of the flesh and the lust of the eyes and the pride of life, is not of the Father but is of the world," by the story of the three temptations of Christ in the wilderness. The temptation to turn the stones into bread was the lust of the flesh; the temptation to work a fantastic miracle was the lust of the eye; and the temptation to worship the devil in return for power over all the kingdoms of the world was the pride of life.[166] It was by these temptations that the devil would have led Jesus astray, and it is by these same temptations that he would lead us astray.

Several times Augustine uses the story of Christ's restoration of Peter to illustrate the theme that the way we love God is by serving our

165. Augustine, *In Epistolam Joannis* 4.6.
166. Augustine, *In Epistolam Joannis* 2.14.

neighbor. If Peter did indeed love Christ, he was to express that love by feeding the sheep of his Shepherd's flock.[167] Even today, with all the progress that has been made in the understanding of Scripture and all the historical and linguistic aids which stand at our disposal, we read the sermons of Augustine with a sense of amazement at how someone who had so little of our technical sophistication could again and again get to the heart of Scripture. His preaching is a beautiful example of what he himself taught about Scripture: that it is the grace of God that is at work in the reading and preaching of the Word. God indeed avails himself of human means and the ministry of his servants, but the Word illumines our hearts because it is God's Word. It is in the end because it is God's Word that it is clear and powerful and life-giving. Augustine's brilliance as a preacher was his recognition that in Scripture itself is a far greater brilliance.

A third reason for the effectiveness of Augustine's preaching is the way he was involved in a dialogue with his congregation. One never gets the impression of monologue or soliloquy in these sermons. Classical rhetoric had understood how, by using rhetorical questions and other devices, one could engage one's listeners in the dialectic of one's thinking. We will have occasion to speak of this again, but here we want to emphasize that it was Augustine's pastoral concern that so deeply engaged him with his congregation. It is this pastoral concern which saves him from making his preaching a personal display, an individualistic performance or a work of oratorical art or self-expression. Augustine was quite capable of soliloquies and even of introspective confessions, but we find none of this in his sermons. His rich use of rhetorical questions clearly illustrates his constant engagement with his congregation. Commenting on the text "He who says he abides in him ought to walk in the same way in which he walked" (I John 2:6), Augustine addresses his congregation, "How is that then, Brethren? How is it that we are admonished? 'He who says he abides in him,' that is in Christ, 'ought to walk in the same way in which he walked.' Is John telling us to walk on the sea? Certainly not! Surely what we are being told to do is walk in righteousness."[168] We find this sort of dialogue between the preacher and the congregation all through these sermons.[169]

167. Augustine, *In Epistolam Joannis* 5.4 and 7.9.
168. Augustine, *In Epistolam Joannis* 1.9.
169. Cf. Bardy, *Saint Augustin,* pp. 233-36.

A fourth reason for the effectiveness of Augustine's sermons is the simplicity of his speech. Latin literature had a tendency to admire complicated, sometimes even contrived, diction; Latin had the equivalent of a very *hoch Hochdeutsch.* With the exception of a few early Christian writers such as Tertullian, the Latin Fathers struggled against the current. With Jerome there was always an ambiguity. He loved his Cicero and wrote letters that cultivated the traditional style, but he had the good sense to use a more simple and direct style for his translation of the Vulgate. It was the Latin of his Vulgate, not the Latin of his letters, which shaped the Latin language for the next thousand years. Augustine, too, particularly in his sermons, was aware of the importance of speaking a clear, simple, and direct Latin. Ever since the Renaissance the Church has been inclined to deprecate the Latin of Augustine. Erasmus and his disciples regarded the Christian Latin of the Middle Ages with disdain and wanted to recover the highly stylized literary Latin of antiquity. Now we realize that, unfortunately, the success of Erasmus spelled the death of Latin. It just may be that Jerome and Augustine knew what they were doing far better than Erasmus did. Augustine has never gotten the appreciation he deserved for his part in creating a simple and direct Christian Latin, but these sermons show important progress in that direction.

Something, no doubt, must be said about Augustine's use of rhetoric.[170] As we have already remarked, he was by professional training a rhetorician. While he appreciates the importance of using the language well, and while he makes a point of showing that Scripture contains many fine examples of beautiful language, he tells us that he has no interest in developing a Christian rhetoric, probably because as a Christian he is much more interested in inner meaning than in outward form. In fact, this was one of the foundations of his theology. This emphasis on the inward, all in being quite Platonic to be sure, is profoundly Christian. Be that as it may, he was a fine public speaker and used many of the rhetorical forms of antiquity with very good taste and moderation. One often finds good metaphors and similes in his sermons. He uses paradox effectively. At antithesis he was a master.

Augustine's use of sermon illustrations is moderate. Many of his illustrations are a bit mundane, some a bit homely, or even shopworn, but occasionally we find a brilliant illustration. We have spoken of his biblical illustrations, but he often used illustrations from everyday life as

170. Cf. Bardy, *Saint Augustin,* pp. 233-45.

well. Commenting on the text "But perfect love casts out fear," he tells us that the fear of God prepares a place in our hearts for love of God, but when it has done that, the love of God enters our hearts and the fear is removed. He compares this to a needle entering a cloth and, passing through, bringing with it the thread which sews the cloth together. The thread cannot enter without the needle, but for the thread to enter the needle must pass out of the cloth.[171] This is a magnificent illustration, yet it is very simple. Augustine's illustrations give the impression of being spontaneous. One never suspects that he has gone to any effort to search them out. If they occurred to him he used them; if not, he did not worry about it.

A fifth reason for the effectiveness of Augustine's sermons is their variety. He exhibits variety in his method of presentation, but much more significant is his variety in subject matter. This is particularly exemplified in this series of ten sermons on I John. Sometimes Augustine addresses the practical moral question of how one is to love one's neighbor. Sometimes he treats the transcendent realities, the hope of eternal life and the ultimate vision of God. At other times he does battle with the schisms and heresies of the day. At times he is doctrinal, at times polemic, and still at other times he is pastoral. Few moral preachers have done such a great job of explaining how much the Christian's love for one's enemy is a means of making the enemy one's brother.[172] Augustine's polemic against the Donatists makes so clear that schism is a sin against Christian love[173] that, when understood in that way, it clearly belongs in a series of sermons on Christian love. On the other hand, how different in tone is his mystical sermon on the beauty of Christ and how our love for God will make us beautiful as Christ is beautiful.[174] One can hardly find a more rapturous passage in all the sermons of the recognized mystical preachers. Some have criticized these sermons for meandering over the whole theological landscape, yet when one is preaching an hour a day to the same congregation over a period of ten days or two weeks, variety can be an important aid to holding the attention of one's listeners. Not many preachers down through the history of the Church possessed the breadth of vision or the fullness of insight that Augustine did. The balance of moral, mystical, and

171. Augustine, *In Epistolam Joannis* 9.4.
172. Augustine, *In Epistolam Joannis* 8.
173. Augustine, *In Epistolam Joannis* 1.12.
174. Augustine, *In Epistolam Joannis* 9.9.

doctrinal is one of the most attractive features of the preaching ministry of the bishop of Hippo.

Finally we would suggest a sixth reason for the effectiveness of Augustine's preaching. These sermons are effective because of their vitality. In one of Augustine's sermons on the Psalms he says that a preacher must be on fire himself if he is to ignite others. Augustine's vitality is hard to put a finger on, but as one goes through these ten sermons one's sense of it begins to mount. The vitality of a preacher is sensed in many ways, not least of which is in his personal presence. To experience this fully, one would have to be in attendance in the congregation; the recorded sermon may well miss it completely. John Chrysostom's vitality must have been communicated through the purity of the man, his passion for holiness. With Origen it must have been felt in his imagination and his inventiveness. Augustine's listeners must have sensed a magisterial personality over and above what today we read in his words, but even if we cannot see him, the written words we have before us still carry a clue to his vitality. Those written words convey an overpoweringly devout intelligence which even today sparks the minds of those who can come no closer to him than the written page.

C. Festal Sermons

The festal sermons of Augustine were collected at a rather early date. Writing in the middle of the fifth century, Possidius lists over fifty, although considerably more have survived. The Maurists, at the end of the seventeenth century, had a collection of eighty-nine of his festal sermons. In that list we find the following items:

> thirteen sermons for Christmas
> six sermons for Epiphany
> seven sermons for the Forty-Day Fast
> one sermon on the Passion of the Lord
> five sermons for the Paschal Vigil
> five sermons for the Christian Passover
> twenty-nine sermons for the Paschal Days
> two sermons for the Paschal Octave
> five sermons for Ascension
> one sermon for the Vigil of Pentecost
> six sermons for Pentecost

A generation after Augustine's death preachers began to make homiliaries, or collections of sermons, of famous preachers, not for literary
purposes but for very practical reasons — they intended to preach these
sermons from their own pulpits. As we have often said, the Romans
expected a significant word from the leaders of their society on any great
occasion or high feast, and bishops, being leaders themselves, were also
expected to deliver a masterful, festive sermon at least on the high holy
days, when their churches would be especially full. The problem was that
as the fifth century progressed education became more and more difficult
to obtain; as the barbarian tribes overran the old centers of culture fewer
and fewer men received the kind of literary education needed to produce
good preaching. It was therefore that they began to borrow the sermons
of the leading preachers of earlier days. Augustine had a reputation as a
learned and literate preacher, and so bishops from all over the Latin-speaking world began to send their assistants to Hippo to copy out the festal
sermons of Augustine. Although Augustine himself never published a cycle
of festal sermons, the cathedral library of Hippo contained the manuscripts
of the stenographers who had taken them down, and these assistants could
go through these and copy out what looked like it might be suitable to
be used back home. For this reason a number of different collections of
Augustine's festal sermons were current in western Europe from an early
date.[175]

These festal sermons provide us with much interesting information.
What claims our attention at this point is the information they provide
on how the liturgical calendar was understood about the beginning of the
fifth century in the Latin-speaking West. One notices first of all the
overwhelming preponderance of Easter; it was clearly the primary feast.
No other celebration or observance demanded anything like a series of
eight sermons the way Easter did. There was a special sermon for the
beginning of Lent, but that was all. One Lenten sermon each year was
sufficient. The Sundays in Lent did not have special lessons or special
sermons. There was, however, a sermon on the reading of the Passion
narrative during Holy Week. The first Sunday after Easter, that is, the
Easter octave, demanded a special sermon, as did Ascension and Pentecost.
This brought to a conclusion the fifty days of Easter.

A study of these sermons shows that festal sermons were thought

175. Cf. A. Wilmart, "Easter Sermons of St. Augustine," *Journal of Theological
Studies* 28 (1926): 113-34.

appropriate for Christmas and Epiphany.[176] There were no Advent sermons, however; in fact, the observance of Advent did not come until well after the time of Augustine. Only in the generation after Augustine, when the barbarian invasions changed the whole temper of Christian devotion, did the penitential seasons begin to overshadow the evangelical feast days. The festal calendar, as we see it reflected in these collections of Augustine's festal sermons, was really very simple. Easter was preeminently the central feast. Lenten preaching had not yet begun to usurp the primacy of Easter preaching. In the church of Hippo during Augustine's pastorate, the week following Easter was a time of rich homiletical development. It was a time for expressing the Easter joy with frequent preaching.

Let us look, then, at what Augustine preached at Easter.[177] Unfortunately most of the Easter sermons which have come down to us have been detached from their historical setting. For the most part, what we have is a number of sermons for the Easter vigil, Easter Day, and the week following Easter which come from different years, although occasionally we can determine that two or more of these sermons belonged to the same year. Some larger collections, the most important of which is the *Homiliary of Fleury*, start with Easter Day and give us a sermon for each day of the octave of Easter.[178] As we have seen, the series on I John was preached during the Easter octave as well, but it was preached in addition to the usual sermons such as those in the *Homiliary of Fleury*. The sermons which have come down to us for the Easter vigil and for Easter Day are a bit disappointing. None of them really seems worthy of the occasion. One can only guess as to the reason for this. Perhaps the fatigue of the preacher explains it; perhaps the stenographer was not in sufficiently good health to record sermons preached in the middle of the night; perhaps the baptism

176. We notice that there are sermons for New Year's Day, but they were to warn Christians not to celebrate the pagan festivities of the day. Perhaps there were sermons for the feast of Saint Stephen and the feast of the holy innocents, but they would be found in the collection of sermons for saints' days. There are also a number of sermons to the catechumens at the time of their baptism which might be classified as catechetical sermons rather than festal sermons.

177. This study is greatly facilitated by the volume of Suzanne Poque, *Augustin d'Hippone, Sermons pour la Pâque,* introduction, critical text, translation, and notes by Suzanne Poque, Sources chrétiennes, vol. 116 (Paris: Les Éditions du Cerf, 1966); hereinafter Poque, *Sermons pour la Pâque.* This study is based on the Latin text of this edition; nevertheless, the traditional method of citing Augustine's sermons has been followed.

178. Cf. Poque, *Sermons pour la Pâque,* pp. 10ff.

of large groups of converts as well as their admission to their first Communion took so much time that the preaching had to be postponed; or perhaps Augustine was never sufficiently satisfied with his proclamation of the Easter gospel that he would allow any of his attempts to be published. We can only speculate.

The evidence would seem to indicate that somewhere back in the tradition the primary Easter sermon would be on the story of the resurrection as it is found in the Gospel of Matthew. But, although we have numerous sermons on the resurrection stories in the other Gospels, we have only one sermon on the story as it is found in Matthew,[179] and that hardly seems to be a major effort of our most able preacher. For that matter, we do not have sermons on other classic types of Easter preaching either, on the Passover from Exodus 12–14 or on the classic text I Corinthians 5:7, "Christ our Passover has been sacrificed, therefore let us keep the feast."[180] While I Corinthians 5:7-8 is mentioned in a few other sermons for the Easter vigil, none of these sermons seems to be a major homiletical effort. Surely we would be justified in asking whether we have the real Easter sermons of Augustine. But there is another way of looking at it. What appears to have happened is that these primary types of Easter proclamation — the announcement that the tomb was empty on the basis of Matthew 28, the Christian interpretation of the Passover narrative in Exodus 12–14, and the identification of Christ as the Passover Lamb in I Corinthians 5 — had simply atrophied. This often happens to the best of liturgical traditions. As classical as a tradition may indeed be, it is repeated so often and becomes so conventional that it loses its vitality.

If these primary traditions of Easter festal preaching had atrophied by Augustine's time, they did reemerge in his preaching, but in a different form. The reading of the resurrection narratives in all four Gospels during the week following Easter became a major feature of the Christian celebration of Easter; thus the resurrection was proclaimed through the reading and preaching of all four Gospels. Augustine evidently found this tradition well established in North Africa. He recognized its value and developed it vigorously, as the sermons we find in the *Homiliary of Fleury* attest. For example, the sermon for Easter Monday opens with the words, "The story of the Resurrection of our Lord Jesus Christ is customarily read during

---

179. Poque, *Sermons pour la Pâque,* p. 81.

180. There is a very short sermon on this text, Sermon 220, delivered at the Easter vigil, but there is no attempt to unfold the paschal typology here.

Easter week from all of the Gospels."[181] At the close of the Easter vigil the series begins with the reading of Matthew 28, and it is this reading which announces the resurrection. On Easter Monday the resurrection narrative from the Gospel of Mark is read. The somewhat longer passages from Luke are divided up over Tuesday and Wednesday, and passages from John fill in the rest of the week. What is interesting here is that when the old traditions were lost, Augustine returned to Scripture itself to find the heart of the Christian message.

Suzanne Poque identifies four different "orders" for the reading of the Gospels during the Easter octave, all of which start with the reading of Matthew 28 at the conclusion of the Easter vigil and continue with the reading of John 1:1-14 at the Easter morning service. This latter reading, of course, is not of the resurrection narrative and does not figure in Augustine's remarks at this point.[182] The reading for Monday can be either from Mark or Luke, while the reading for Wednesday can be from Mark, Luke, or even John. From Thursday on the readings are from the last two chapters of John.[183] Apparently Augustine did not figure that the lectionary was so fixed that he could not change it from time to time.

Let us look very briefly at three examples. Sermon 231 is on the resurrection as it is recorded in the Gospel of Mark. Interestingly enough, our preacher begins by explaining that it was the custom at Hippo on Easter and the week following to read the story of the resurrection from all of the Gospels.[184] Then he points out that in the Markan account Jesus chided his disciples because they did not believe (Mark 16:14). "They were the fathers of the faith, but not yet were they believers. They did not yet believe, although they were made teachers so that the whole world might believe."[185]

---

181. "Resurrectio domini nostri Iesu Christi ex more legitur his diebus ex omnibus libris sancti euangeli." Augustine, *Sermo CCXXXI* 1.

182. The reading of the prologue to the Gospel of John on Easter morning is probably inspired by the long reading of the creation narrative from Genesis at the Easter vigil. Here we find an important theme of the Easter typology. With the resurrection of Christ a new creation begins to appear. The prologue to the Gospel of John is a fitting proclamation of the beginning of the age which is begun with the resurrection of Christ.

183. Cf. Poque, *Sermons pour la Pâque*, pp. 85ff.

184. In a number of his sermons Augustine mentions this custom. In Sermon 247 he explains in detail that because Luke and John give longer accounts, more than one sermon is devoted to each of these Gospels. Poque, *Sermons pour la Pâque*, p. 203.

185. "Patres fidei nondum fideles, magistri ut crederet totus orbis terrarum quod praedicturi fuerant et propter quod fuerant morturi, nondum credebant." Augustine, *Sermo CCXXXI* 1.

With this striking paradox Augustine emphasizes how little even the apostles were by their own efforts. The preacher then, on the basis of this text, makes several reflections on the subject of the new life in Christ. "Moreover, the Resurrection of our Lord Jesus Christ is a new life for those who believe in Jesus."[186] First Augustine makes the point that Christ's death was a vicarious atonement. "He was crucified, so that on the cross He might show the destruction of our old man; and He rose again so that He might point out the newness of our life. For thus the apostolic teaching expresses it: 'He was delivered up for our sins, and rose again for our justification' (Rom. 4:25)."[187] What Augustine has drawn from the resurrection narrative in the Gospel of Mark is the surprising nature of God's grace. The fathers of the faith, when they were shown the empty tomb, were found to have no faith. Our preacher delineates the offense of the empty tomb and the fear of the disciples. Certainly Augustine has caught the central vision of Mark's account of the resurrection; that is, the simple awesomeness of the empty tomb. The simple fact that God by his grace raised up Jesus, however, turned the whole thing around. The faith of the apostles was a gift of God's grace just as the resurrection was. The Gospel of Mark does not really tell us very much about the resurrection. It simply shows us the empty tomb and the fact that the disciples reacted with fear instead of faith.[188]

For Augustine this paradox is a witness to the surprising fullness of God's grace. Only from death can new life come.[189] From this point Augustine develops the theme of the new life which is in Christ. In the new life we must first die to the old life and then set our minds on heavenly things that are above. He quotes Colossians 3:1-5 at length, which makes exactly this point:[190]

> Let us hear the Apostle when he tells us, "If you have been raised with Christ. . . ." When were we raised, we who have not yet died? What is it

186. "Resurrectio autem domini nostri Iesu Christi nova vita est credentium in Iesum." Augustine, *Sermo CCXXXI* 2.

187. "Ergo crucifixus est ut in cruce ostenderet veteris hominis nostri occasum et resurrexit ut in sua vita ostenderet nostrae vitae novitatem. Sic enim docet doctrina apostolica: *Traditus est, inquit, propter peccata nostra et resurrexit propter justificatum nostram.*" Augustine, *Sermo CCXXXI* 2.

188. Augustine must have had only the shorter form of the final chapter of the Gospel of Mark.

189. "Non enim sine causa vita venit ad mortem, non sine causa fons vitae, unde bibitur ut vivatur, bibit hic calicem qui ei non debetur." Augustine, *Sermo CCXXXI* 2.

190. Augustine, *Sermo CCXXXI* 3.

then that the Apostle wants to say to us when he says, "If we have been raised with Christ? . . ." Can anyone rise again unless he first has died? . . . Those who have died to sin have been raised up. . . . If we live a godly life we have both died and have been raised. If we live in sin we have not really lived at all. Therefore let us die that we might not die.[191]

The empty tomb makes clear the emptiness of the godless life. Our preacher talks about some of the things we think will make us happy — the riches, the honors, and the pleasures of this life — and tells us that this is not at all what will make us happy.[192] The empty tomb shows us what we need to know if we would be happy. We can't be truly happy in this life — no one can. We seek good things, but this land is not the place where the things we seek are to be found.[193] The apostle Paul makes clear that the blessed life that we all seek is not in this life here below but in the life that is above. That is what the angel made clear to the disciples who saw the empty tomb. He is risen! He is not here! Augustine's juxtaposition of the two texts is masterful. " 'He is not here' " (Mark 16:6) is interpreted by "Set your minds on things that are above, not on things that are on the earth" (Col. 3:2). "If Christ had found the good life here, you could have found it here, too . . . but what did he find? . . . Sorrow and death. . . . He came to your dwelling place and ate with you. He shared with you the misery that is so abundant here."[194] Then our preacher elaborates on the things that are above which will make us

191. "Audiamus apostolum dicentem: *Si resurrexistis cum Christo.* . . . Quando resurgemus, qui nondum mortui sumus? Quid est ergo quod uoluit dicere apostolus: *Si resurrexistis cum Christo?* Numquid ille resurrexisset nisi prius mortuus fuisset? Viuentibus loquebatur, nondum morientibus et iam resurgentibus. Quid sibi uult? Videte quid dicat: *Si resurrexistis cum Christo, quae sursum sunt sapite, ubi Christus est in dextera dei sedens; quae sursum sunt quaerite, non quae super terram. Mortui enim estis.* Ipse dicit non ego et tamen uerum dicit et ideo dico et ego. Quare illud dico et ego? *Credidi propter quod locutus sum.* Si bene uiuimus, mortui sumus et resurreximus; qui autem nondum mortuus est nec resurrexit, male adhuc uiuit; si male uiuit no uiuit; moriatur ne moriatur." Augustine, *Sermo CCXXXI* 3.

192. Augustine, *Sermo CCXXXI* 4.

193. "Ostendit tibi quid debeas sapere, si vis beatus esse. Hic enim esse non potes. In hac vita beatus esse non potes. Nemo potest. Bonam rem quaeris sed terra ista non est regio eius rei quam quaeris." Augustine, *Sermo CCXXXI* 5.

194. "Si habuit hic illud Christus, habebis et tu. In regione mortis tuae, quid ille inuenit? adtende: ueniens de alia regione quid hic inuenit, nisi quod hic abundat: labores, dolores, mortem, ecce quod hic habes, quod hic abundat. Manducauit tecum, quod abundabat in cella miseriae tuae. Acetum hic bibit, fel hic habuit. Ecce quod in cella tua inuenit." Augustine, *Sermo CCXXXI* 5.

happy. The life that makes us happy is a life of communion with God; it is the heavenly banquet; it is companionship with Christ. To his great table he has invited us, to the table of heaven, to the table of the angels, where he himself is the bread. The themes of the paschal Eucharist are unmistakable. Christ, having descended to our dwelling place and having scorned not our paltry table, has promised us a place at his table. What is it that he says to us?

> "Believe, believe that at last you will come to my table spread with every good thing for I scorned not your poor table." If he bore our sorrows will he not bestow upon us his joys? Certainly he shall give them! He has promised to us his life, but it is unbelievable what he has brought to pass. His death he has given to us as a down payment. It is as though he had said, "To my life I invite you, where no one dies, where one is truly blessed, where the food does not disappoint us, leave us hungry, or give us indigestion. See the place to which I invite you; it is the habitation of angels; it is the fellowship of the Father and the Holy Spirit; it is the eternal banquet. It is fellowship with me; it is to be my brother; it is to share my life. Do you not wish to believe that I shall give to you my life? If you do, then hold on to that pledge I have given you of my death. . . ."[195]

This sermon is a proclamation of the empty tomb and an invitation to the wedding feast of the paschal lamb. In fact, the empty tomb in all the starkness in which Mark presents it is surprisingly enough the invitation to the wedding feast of the lamb who was slain and lives forevermore.

The sermon for Tuesday of Easter week, Sermon 232, treats the resurrection story as we find it in the Gospel of Luke.[196] It is the first of

---

195. "Et ad magnam mensam suam te inuitauit, mensam caeli, mensam angelorum, ubi ipse panis est. Descendens ergo et ista mala inueniens in cella tua et non dedignatus est talem mensam tuam et promisit suam. Quid nobis dicit? 'Credite, credite uos uenturos ad bona mensae meae, quando non sum dedignatus mala mensae uestrae.' Malum tuum tulit et bonum suum dabit? Vtique dabit. Vitam suam promisit nobis, sed incredibilius est quod fecit: mortem suam praerogauit nobis. . . . 'Ad uitam meam uos inuito, ubi nemo moritur, ubi uere uita beata est, ubi cibus non corrumpitur, ubi reficit et non deficit. Ecce quo uos inuito, ad regionem angelorum, ad amicitiam patris et sancti spiritus, ad cenam sempiteram, ad fraternitatem meam, postremo ad me ipsum. Ad uitam meam uos inuito. Non uultis credere quia dabo uobis uitam meam? Tenete pignus mortem meam.'" Augustine, *Sermo CCXXXI* 5.

196. Augustine, *Sermo CCXXXII.*

two sermons on the Lukan resurrection narratives. Again Augustine begins his sermon by reminding his congregation that his plan during Easter week is to read through the resurrection narratives in all four of the Gospels. Clearly, Augustine himself sees these sermons on the resurrection narratives as a series. Having begun with the story of the women finding the tomb empty in Matthew 28, then passing to the story of how an angel told the women that he was not to be found in the tomb but that he had risen, Augustine explains that he now takes up the story as it is found in Luke. Furthermore, he tells them that he is doing it this way because that is the order of the Gospels themselves.[197]

Once more our preacher notices that the eyewitnesses themselves did not at first have faith. There is a great advantage to this as Augustine understands it. It helps us realize how much more blessed it is to hear and to believe what we have heard. Apparently seeing is not all that much of an advantage when it comes to faith. One really does not have to see in order to believe.[198]

What our preacher finds unique in Luke's report is that the Evangelist understands the story of the resurrection as a reversing of the story of the fall. That the fall of Adam and Eve has been turned around and that the curse has been broken is of the essence of the good news proclaimed at Easter. Yet for Augustine there is a tragic irony about it, for the disciples could not at first believe. When Jesus rose from the dead, the disciples he had called, taught, and lived with here on earth, before whose eyes he performed so many miracles, could not believe that in his flesh he had indeed been raised up. When the women came to the tomb and did not find the body in the tomb, they heard from the angels that Christ was risen, which news they announced to the men. And what does Scripture tell us happened then? The men did not believe them.[199] Adam believed Eve when she was influenced by Satan; why did not the disciples believe the faithful women when in obedience to the angel they reported to them Christ's resurrection? That, according to Augustine, is the sorrow of the human condition. But here we notice the balance of divine providence,

---

197. "Resurrectio domini nostri Iesu Christi et hodie recitata est sed de altro libro evangelii, qui est secundum Lucam. Primo enim lecta est secundum Mattheum, hesterna autem die secundum Marcum, hodie secundum Lucam, sicut habet ordo evangelistarum." Augustine, *Sermo CCXXXII* 1.

198. Augustine, *Sermo CCXXXII* 1.

199. Augustine, *Sermo CCXXXII* 2.

which arranged things so that the women were the first to believe and so that the angel told them to report the resurrection to the men. "As through the female sex man fell, so through the female sex the fall was reversed. As Christ was conceived through the Virgin so woman announced the Christ to have risen. Just as death came through women, so life came through woman."[200] The fall had been reversed. The curse that Eve had brought on the whole human race had been wiped away. Woman was no longer man's undoing but his blessing.

Having briefly spoken of the reversing of the fall, our preacher moves on to the story of the appearance of Jesus to the two disciples on the road to Emmaus.[201] As the two walked along and discussed the unhappy events of the last few days, a third traveler joined them. The two disciples, not recognizing that it was Jesus who, unbeknown to them, had risen and was now walking with them. They told their fellow traveler about the hopes they and the other disciples had had that Jesus of Nazareth was the long-promised Messiah. At this point Augustine discusses Peter's confession of faith (Matt. 16:16) that Jesus had been the Messiah.[202] Again, Scripture is best explained by Scripture, as Augustine so often teaches us. Even at the time Peter made this confession Jesus had made it clear that true faith in Jesus as the Messiah was only possible when God reveals it to us. Flesh and blood had not revealed this truth to Peter, but rather the Father in heaven (Matt. 16:17). We cannot come to that faith by our own understanding, for it is a gift of God's grace.[203] Again Augustine would have his congregation understand that it was not seeing Jesus which brings us to faith, but hearing the gospel of Christ's victory over death and believing it.

For Augustine the experience the disciples had of Jesus' appearing to them on the road to Emmaus was a great sacrament.[204] They walked along the road together; they stayed together at the same inn; he broke bread with them and only then did they recognize him. We think we have never seen Christ, yet we have. We have seen if we believe. In fact, not only do

---

200. "Quia per sexum femineum cecidit homo, per sexum femineum reparatus est homo: quia virgo Christum peperat, femina resurrexisse nuntiabat. Per feminam mors, per feminam vita." Augustine, *Sermo CCXXXII* 2.

201. Augustine, *Sermo CCXXXII* 3.

202. Augustine, *Sermo CCXXXII* 3.

203. Augustine, *Sermo CCXXXII* 4.

204. "Diende iam, carissimi, magnum sacramentum cognovimus." Augustine, *Sermo CCXXXII* 7.

we see him if we believe, we *have* him if we believe. They had Christ when they lived with him, but we have him when he is in our souls. It is far more to have Christ in our hearts than in our houses.[205] Having recounted this episode of the resurrection narrative as found in Luke, Augustine exhorts his congregation to receive the gospel by faith and to live by faith. Particularly he exhorts those who have failed to follow the moral disciplines of the faith to reform their lives. The Easter gospel is not only for the pagan but also for those who once believed but have lost their faith. In fact, when one looks at the resurrection narratives as closely as Augustine has in these sermons, it is clear that the good news is that God's grace is specially given to those whose faith had failed. Here we have a good example of how Augustine understood the perseverance of the saints. The risen Christ went out and found the disciples whose faith had broken down and who were leaving Jerusalem.

For Augustine Easter is a time to preach faith. It is not that seeing is believing but rather that believing is seeing. The disciples on the road to Emmaus did not see until they believed, but once they believed their eyes were opened and they discovered that Christ is risen and living in their hearts even when their faith failed. To preach the resurrection is to preach that God is faithful.

Let us look now at a third sermon in Augustine's series on the resurrection narratives of the Gospels. On Thursday of Easter week Augustine took up the Gospel of John and preached a sermon on the appearance of Jesus to Mary Magdalene. The lesson read to the congregation started with the beginning of the twentieth chapter, which speaks of Peter and John finding the empty tomb, and continued through the story of Jesus' appearance to Mary Magdalene. Our preacher treats the first part of the story very briefly.[206] Augustine has a particular point he wants to make with this sermon. The sermon on the previous day had treated the passage in Luke where Jesus appeared to the disciples in the Upper Room and they supposed they had seen a spirit. It would have been very easy for someone of late antiquity to have believed in a "spiritual interpretation" of the resurrection stories, as that sort of thinking was very popular back

205. "Ambulabat cum illis, suscipitur hospitio, panem frangit et cognoscitur. Et nos non dicamus quia Christum non nouimus: nouimus si credimus. Parum est, nouimus si credimus; habemus si credimus. Habebant illi Christum in conuiuio, nos intus in animo. Plus est Christum habere in corde quam in domo." Augustine, *Sermo CCXXXII* 7.
206. Augustine, *Sermo CCXLVI* 1-2.

then. Augustine recognizes that the text emphasizes that the risen Jesus was not merely some sort of phantom, some sort of eternal essence. The Greeks believed in the immortality of the soul but the earliest Christians believed in the resurrection of the body, and Augustine fully understands how important it is to distinguish between the two. In the sermon on Luke Augustine makes clear that when his Gospel tells us that Jesus ate with the disciples in the Upper Room, it was making clear that a spiritualist interpretation of the resurrection is not sufficient. Immortal spirits don't eat food.[207]

The story of Christ's appearance to Mary Magdalene was frequently appealed to by those who pressed for a spiritualist interpretation of Christ's resurrection. They imagined that Jesus forbade the Magdalene to touch him because one cannot touch a "spiritual" body. Our preacher shows his congregation that the Gospel of John has nothing of the sort in mind.

Mary Magdalene's problem was that she wanted to hold on to things as they were, which she thought she could do by embalming the body of Jesus. Augustine tells us that was not what needed to be done.[208] "O Woman, you think what you need is the dead Christ, but what you really need is to know that he lives. . . . A dead Christ had done nothing for us unless he had risen. The one who is sought dead shows himself alive."[209] With this the risen Jesus calls Mary by her name, Mary. And here Augustine, firm believer that he is in predestination, makes the remark, "He called her by the name with which he had called her into the kingdom of heaven. He called her by her own name, that name which he had already written in his book."[210] The old relationship Mary had had with Jesus had to be transcended. Mary was devoted to Jesus because he had healed her, she wanted to hold on to him because he was her beloved physician, but now she needed to relate to the ascended, glorified Christ who brought her into communion with her God and Father. Now Mary was to know Jesus as her redeemer.

When Mary reached out to hold on to Jesus, he said to her, "Touch

---

207. Augustine, *Sermo CCXXVII* 4.

208. Augustine, *Sermo CCXLVI* 3.

209. "O mulier, necessarium tibi putas mortuum Christum, vivum agnose. . . . Nihil autem nobis mortuus prodesset nisi a mortuis resurrexisset. Et quaerebatur mortuus, vivum se ostendit." Augustine, *Sermo CCXLVI* 3.

210. "Nomen ipse appelavit qui ad regnum caelorum vocavit. Hoc nomen dixit quod in libro suo ipse scripserat." Augustine, *Sermo CCXLVI* 3.

me not, for I have not yet ascended to my Father."[211] With a rhetorical question Augustine asks his congregation what Jesus meant by this. Why could not Mary touch him? Here, of course, was where the spiritualist interpretation thought it was clear that Mary could not touch Jesus because he was only a spirit. Augustine answers, "If she was not able to touch him standing on the earth, she would be able to touch him seated in heaven. It was as though he had said to her, 'For now don't touch me, but then when I shall ascend to the Father.'"[212] Our preacher reminds his congregation that in his sermon on the previous day, commenting on the passage of Luke where Jesus appears to the disciples in the Upper Room, he had remarked on how Jesus, realizing they thought they saw only a spirit, had invited them to look at his hands and feet and to feel them.[213] Our preacher distinguishes between feeling, *palpandum,* the hands and feet of Jesus, and touching, *tangendum,* them. As Augustine understands it, touching Jesus is nothing less than believing in Jesus.[214] To touch Jesus is not really all that important — all sorts of infidels touched him when he was crucified — but for the faithful, for good catholic Christians, the important thing is to touch him by faith. To touch him by faith is to believe in him as the Son of the Father. It is only when we realize he is ascended to his Father that we — or Mary or anyone else — can touch him by faith. "If you think that Jesus was a man and nothing more, you have touched him on earth. If you believe Jesus to be the Lord, equal to the Father, then you have touched him when he has ascended to the Father."[215]

With this Augustine shows how the passage makes clear both the true humanity and true divinity of Jesus. Jesus told Mary he was going to ascend to his Father and to her Father. It was because Jesus was really the

211. "Noli me tangere, nondum enim ascendi ad patrem meum" (John 20:17). Augustine, *Sermo CCXLVI* 4. At this point the Latin translation used by Augustine, which here reads the same as the Vulgate, is not a particularly good rendering of the original Greek. The RSV, "Do not hold me," translates the Greek far better.

212. "Si non illum poterat tangere in terra stantem, poterat tangere in caelo sedentem, tanquam diceret: 'modo me noli tangere, tunc me tange cum ascendero ad patrem?'" Augustine, *Sermo CCXLVI* 4.

213. Augustine, *Sermo CCXLVI* 4.

214. "Quid est ergo tangere nisi credere? Fide enim tangimus Christum et melius est manu non tangere et fide tangere quam manu palpare et fide non tangere." Augustine, *Sermo CCXLVI* 4.

215. "Si Christum tantum modo hominem putaveris, in terra tetigisti. Si Christum dominum credideris aequalem patri, tunc tetigisti quando ascendit ad patrem." Augustine, *Sermo CCXLVI* 4.

Son of the Father that he was God. He was Son of the Father by nature, but we are children of the Father by grace,[216] made so by God when we put our faith in Christ. But then Jesus adds "to my God and your God." This makes clear that Jesus is truly a man, a creature of God in addition to being the Son of God.[217] Christ can be our Savior because he shares our human flesh.

Augustine was not really finished with this sermon, but he ends it nevertheless, reminding his congregation that the Gospel of John has much more to say about the resurrection than any of the other Gospels, and that he has several more sermons to preach before he finishes his series.[218] The three sermons we have described give us a good taste of the Easter preaching of Augustine. The proclamation of the resurrection of Christ was central to the preaching of Augustine, and in preaching it, as we have seen, he preached faith. For Augustine the resurrection was the proof of God's faithfulness. For the congregation to hear that and believe it was worship at its most profound. Augustine exhorted his hearers to hear the Easter Gospel and believe it that it might be the basis of a new and eternal life, a life that would glorify God.

Two things remain to be said about Augustine's Easter sermons. The first is the obvious contrast between the elaborate festal sermons of the Greek Fathers, most notably Gregory of Nazianzus, and the simple, straightforward sermons of Augustine. None of Augustine's Easter sermons which we have looked at could be called a panegyric. As a rhetorician Augustine would have known this artistic form very well, but he has obviously not chosen to use it, sticking instead with the form of the expository sermon as it was developed in the synagogue and in the early Christian Church. He used what he inherited from the biblical tradition rather than the artistic forms of Hellenistic culture. These sermons are not sermons on the feast days but rather sermons on the resurrection narratives.

The panegyric as it was developed in the rhetoric of ancient Greece and Rome was an attempt at high art. Not only was the message festive, the artistic form was festive as well. We do not find this in these Easter sermons, as Augustine makes no attempt at elegance. Evidently, for Augustine, one does not have to decorate the Word of God. Holiness has its own beauty.

---

216. "Illius pater per naturam, noster per gratiam." Augustine, *Sermo CCXLVI* 5.
217. "Quia et creatura Christus secundum hominem." Augustine, *Sermo CCXLVI* 5.
218. Augustine, *Sermo CCXLVI* 6.

The second point about these sermons is that they are not only expository but also evangelistic. They are preached to strike the spark of faith. The sacred accounts of the mighty acts of God are read and preached because they are the basis of the faith and life of the children of God. God's victory over sin in the death and resurrection of Christ is the foundation of the new covenant, the ratification of which is celebrated in the Christian celebration of Passover. It is when the chosen people of God hear the recounting of the mighty acts of salvation that faith is engendered. This is worship, to hear the story in faith. As we have noticed repeatedly in these sermons, Augustine insists that, more than seeing or touching, it is those who hear the gospel of the resurrection and believe it who are blessed. For Augustine, as for the apostle Paul, faith cometh by hearing and hearing by the Word of God. Surely it is because of this that the reading and preaching of that Word is worship. It serves God by inspiring the adoration of our hearts.

D. Introducing the Faith

Augustine's treatise *De catechizandis rudibus* informs us of the sort of introductory instruction that should be given to what might be called rough recruits, that is, those who first approach the Church to be received as members.[219] How this treatise came to be written is as follows: Carthage was, of course, a large city in those days, and Augustine, as the bishop of Carthage, most likely delegated a number of special tasks to his assistants. One such assistant, a deacon of the church by the name of Deogratias,

---

219. For the Latin text, see Augustine, *De catechizandis rudibus,* ed. Joseph B. Bauer, Corpus Christianorum, series Latina, vol. 46 (Turnholt, Belgium: Brepols, 1969), pp. 121-78. For English translations, see Augustine, *First Catechetical Instruction,* trans. Joseph Christopher, Ancient Christian Writers, vol. 2 (Westminster, Md.: Newman Bookshop, 1966); and Augustine, *On the Catechising of the Uninstructed,* trans. S. D. F. Salmond, Nicene and Post-Nicene Fathers, 1st ser., vol. 3 (Grand Rapids: Wm. B. Eerdmans Publishing Co., 1976), pp. 282-314. Among the many studies of this work, see the following: J. P. Belche, "Die Bekehrung zum Christentum nach des Augustinus Büchlein 'De catechizandis rudibus,'" *Augustiniana* 27 (1977): 26-69, 333-63, and 28 (1978): 255-87; D. Grasso, "Saint Augustin évangélisateur," *Parole et Mission* 6 (1963): 357-78; G. Oggioni, "Il 'De catechizandis rudibus' di S. Augustino, catechesi per i lontani," *La Scuola Cattolica* 91 (1963): 117-26; C. Przydatek, *L'annucio del Vangelo nello spirito del dialog. Studio storico theologico sulla predicazione missionaria secondo l'opuscolo di S. Augustino "De catechizandis rudibus"* (Rome, 1971).

was asked by him to take on the responsibility of introducing pagans to the faith, evidently because of his knowledge of Christian theology and his ability as a public speaker. And Deogratius, in turn, asked Augustine to set down for him some principles to help him in fulfilling this responsibility.[220] What Augustine had asked Deogratias to do was, essentially, to be an evangelist, although not quite in the same way as we understand the term. In those days the Church did not have to go out looking for people; people came to the Church asking how they could become Christians. The situation, interestingly enough, was much as it is in Korea today (we will consider Korea in the last volume of our study). At the beginning of the fifth century in Roman North Africa the job of evangelism was usually a matter of preaching the gospel to those who had already decided they wanted to become Christians. It did not entail preaching on street corners or in marketplaces and trying to convince people to come to church. They came to church and wanted to be told how to become Christians. Evangelism then became a matter of instruction.

It is not too clear from this treatise just how this initial instruction of catechumens was organized in North Africa. Did Deogratias prepare these people individually to enroll as catechumens, or did he conduct classes?[221] Was Augustine really talking about a single session or a series of sessions? We know that different churches organized their catechetical instruction quite differently, so perhaps Augustine, in an effort to be helpful to other catechists besides Deogratias, is being rather vague on purpose in order that other readers might be encouraged to fit it into the local practice. However, our theologian does make it quite clear that what he has to say would apply both when the catechist is dealing with a single convert and when he is dealing with a group. He also makes it clear that what he has to say needs to be adapted to both the educated and the uneducated, to both city people and country people.[222] Adaptation is obviously assumed throughout the work.[223]

What, then, do we really have here? It is certainly not a manual for catechetical instruction. Too many essential features of catechetical preaching as they had become firmly established have been left out.[224] As a

---

220. Augustine, *De catechizandis rudibus* 1.
221. Augustine, *De catechizandis rudibus* 15 and 26.
222. Augustine, *De catechizandis rudibus* 8.
223. Augustine, *De catechizandis rudibus* 26.
224. Augustine, *De catechizandis rudibus* 26.

matter of fact we might regard this more as a manual of evangelism than a manual of catechetical instruction. That is the way the missionary preachers of the next few centuries understood the work. As we shall see, this treatise had a strong effect on the evangelistic preaching of such missionaries as Martin of Braga and Pirmen of Reichenau.

One of the most interesting features of this work is that it recognizes the importance of personal interaction between the prospective convert and the preacher.[225] In fact, Augustine seems to assume a rather informal sort of instruction that might be as much a conversation between two people as a sermon or series of sermons to a group of people. The instructor or preacher should ask those to whom he is about to present the gospel how it is that they come to seek admission to the Church, attempting to discover something of their motives as well as their educational and cultural background.

Having discovered where his listeners are coming from, the preacher is supposed to recount the history of salvation, beginning with the creation.[226] He narrates the creation at length, making clear some of the uniquely biblical insights, especially in relation to the creation of Adam and Eve. God created us human beings to have communion with himself, but we turned away from this destiny. God, being a loving and merciful creator, developed a plan for winning us back, and to this end he called Israel to be his chosen people. God delivered Israel again and again, from bondage in Egypt, from captivity in Babylon.[227] During all these tribulations and deliverances God slowly revealed a final plan of salvation whereby man was to be renewed by the grace of God and restored to perfect fellowship with him. To this end God sent us a Savior, born of a virgin.[228] The life and ministry of Jesus is explained at length as well as his Passion and glorious resurrection. This resurrection was followed by his ascension into heaven, which opened the way for us to follow. The hope of eternal life is central to the Christian faith as Augustine presents it. Fifty days after the resurrection the ascended Christ sent forth his Holy Spirit in order that his followers might be filled with love toward one another and enabled to live according to God's commandments.[229] This sending forth of the

---

225. Augustine, *De catechizandis rudibus* 5.
226. Augustine, *De catechizandis rudibus* 18.
227. Augustine, *De catechizandis rudibus* 20-21.
228. Augustine, *De catechizandis rudibus* 22.
229. Augustine, *De catechizandis rudibus* 23.

Holy Spirit established the Church where even here on earth God's people might live this new life of fellowship with God.[230] Augustine then speaks at length of the life Christians live in the Church, the coming of the Last Judgment, and the joy of heaven which awaits those who are faithful.[231]

After this thorough presentation of the history of salvation, the inquirers are to be asked if they believe this and earnestly desire to live the Christian life.[232] If they agree, they are to be received with the sign of the cross and prepared for baptism. One might call this the first commitment, and it is after this that catechetical instruction began. Having gone through the discipline of catechetical instruction, having studied the tenets of the faith, one makes a formal profession of faith which is sealed by the sacrament of baptism. This baptismal profession of faith is therefore well informed, conscious, and public.

The long address Augustine describes is essentially the presentation of the gospel to those who have never heard it before. Possibly the candidate has heard the regular preaching of the Church, which, of course, was directed to baptized members, or possibly the candidate has done a certain amount of reading or study on his or her own or has engaged in long discussions of Christian doctrine with friends or neighbors. If this is the case, Augustine tells us, the preacher should make allowances for this in his presentation.[233] The essential thing, however, is that those who first approach the Church get the basic message of the gospel. This, then, is evangelism proper, that is, the recounting of the good news that is the gospel.

One wonders to what extent Augustine is directing Deogratias to do something that was the common practice of the Church at that time. Was there a special time and place for evangelistic preaching at the close of the fourth century or the beginning of the fifth? Perhaps what Augustine is telling Deogratias is better regarded as a corrective to the practice of the day which had neglected evangelistic preaching in favor of catechetical preaching. However that may be, this kind of evangelistic sermon will occupy a more important place as the Church begins to accept the responsibility of winning the barbarians to Christ as they more and more begin to overrun the Roman Empire.

230. Augustine, *De catechizandis rudibus* 24.
231. Augustine, *De catechizandis rudibus* 25.
232. Augustine, *De catechizandis rudibus* 26.
233. Augustine, *De catechizandis rudibus* 26.

E. On the Art of Christian Teaching:
Exegesis, Hermeneutic, and Rhetoric

No one could have summed up better what preaching was supposed to be for the Latin Christian of late antiquity than Augustine. As a young and precocious pagan he was appointed professor of rhetoric in Milan, a most prestigious position. Only in mature life was he converted to Christianity, but once a Christian he went on to become one of the outstanding preachers of the Church. His masterful *De doctrina christiana* is in fact the classic Christian rhetoric, although at one point Augustine insists he is not writing a Christian rhetoric.[234] It is, to be sure, much more than a Christian rhetoric. It is an essay on hermeneutics and on exegesis as well, discussing both the purposes and principles of interpretation. The title of this most influential book might be translated into English as *On the Art of Christian Teaching*, as in this case the Latin word "doctrina" means teaching rather than doctrine. Probably no other book on preaching has had so strong an effect on how Christian preachers have preached. To be sure, just as Augustine tells us, this book is not a comprehensive textbook on the various techniques of the art of rhetoric but rather a guide to the Christian use of that art so much beloved by classical antiquity. Working back and forth through the history of Christian preaching, one sees how often the principles of this venerable classic have been invoked. Let us look at some of these ideas as Augustine originally developed them.

In the first book Augustine speaks at length of the purpose of Christian preaching. As Augustine sees it, it is love of God and love of our neighbors for the sake of God which is the whole point of our trying to understand

234. The Latin text used in this study is that of J. Martin: Augustine, *De Doctrina christiana,* ed. J. Martin, Corpus Christianorum, series Latina, vol. 32 (Turnholt, Belgium: Brepols, 1962), pp. 1-167. There are numerous English translations. Those consulted in this study are: *St. Augustine's On Christian Doctrine,* trans. J. F. Shaw, Nicene and Post-Nicene Fathers, 1st ser., vol. 2 (Grand Rapids: Wm. B. Eerdmans Publishing Co., 1979), pp. 519-97; *Christian Instruction,* trans. J. J. Cavigan, Fathers of the Church, vol. 2 (Washington, D.C.: Catholic University of America Press, 1985), pp. 19-235; Augustine, *On Christian Doctrine,* trans. Durant Waite Robertson (New York: Macmillan, 1958). There are numerous studies of this work. Among the more recent: U. Duchrow, "Zum Prolog von Augustins 'De Doctrina Christiana,'" *Vigiliae Christianae* 17 (1963): 165-72; M. D. Jordan, "Words and Word, Incarnation and Signification in Augustine's 'De doctrina christiana,'" *Augustinian Studies* 11 (1980): 177-96; E. Kevane, "Augustine's 'De doctrina christiana,' a Treatise on Christian Education," *Recherches Augustiniennes* 4 (1966): 97-133; and G. A. Press, "The Subject and Structure of Augustine's 'De Doctrina Christiana,'" *Augustinian Studies* 11 (1980): 99-124.

Scripture and of our trying to teach what we have come to understand.[235] Worship, as our theologian understood it, is an experience of that covenant relationship between God and his people which brings us together in the household of faith to enjoy the love of the Father in the fellowship of the Church.[236] Worship is entering into this covenant relationship, restoring it, and nourishing it. For Augustine worship in general is an expression of our love for God which is experienced in the bond of Christian fellowship.[237] Whenever he talks about what worship is, he goes back to Christ's summary of the Law and the prophets: We are to love God with all our hearts, all our minds, and all our souls, and our neighbor as ourselves. That for Augustine is the focus of Christian ethics, the focus of Christian doctrine, and the focus of Christian worship. To this the great Latin theologian comes back again and again. Indeed, it is in order that we might do this that God has given us the Scriptures, and to use the Scriptures properly we must use them to this end.[238] This is a very classical hermeneutical principle. Our preaching of the Scriptures should be guided by a concern to strengthen the bond of love which unites the Church. The unity of the Church was very important for Augustine. How Roman! One finds it again and again as one reads his writings. Unity is the fruit of love. How Christian! He constantly returns to Christ's interpretation of the first and greatest commandment: You shall love the Lord your God with all your heart, with all your soul, and with all your mind.[239] In matters of worship, particularly, he keeps returning to the instructions of the apostle Paul in I Corinthians 10–14. Love should be the aim of our preaching. This is the foundation of Augustine's hermeneutics. "Make love your aim" (I Cor. 14:1).

We notice that Augustine begins his treatise by speaking about loving God and, very specifically, about loving God in terms of worship, in terms of rejoicing in his praise and enjoying his Wisdom.[240] God is to be enjoyed in himself, not as a means to attain something else. It often happens, Augustine tells us, that we are distracted by other enjoyments, but the triune God is the ultimate enjoyment.[241] For Augustine it is the Wisdom of God in which he specially delights. Augustine obviously enjoys being

235. Augustine, *De doctrina christiana* 1.36.
236. Augustine, *De doctrina christiana* 1.30.
237. Augustine, *De doctrina christiana* 1.5.
238. Augustine, *De doctrina christiana* 1.35.
239. Augustine, *De doctrina christiana* 1.22.
240. Augustine, *De doctrina christiana* 1.5-6.
241. Augustine, *De doctrina christiana* 1.22.

a theologian; he is a happy man, and what makes him happy is his delight in God's Wisdom. That we should enjoy the divine Wisdom is a miracle of God's grace that constantly amazes him. While this Wisdom is ultimately beyond our understanding, God accommodates himself to our understanding.[242] Augustine puts it in a way very similar to the way John Chrysostom had put it. This divine accommodation is the key to understanding the nature of revelation, the nature of Scripture, and ultimately the nature of preaching. The divine Wisdom is incarnate in Jesus Christ, who is the Word of God made flesh,[243] and God accommodates himself to us by reaching out to us, by coming to us in the person of Jesus Christ. God accommodates himself to us by reaching out to us in his Word in the preaching of the gospel of Christ, in the Word of Scripture.

The study and teaching of God's Word is enjoyable not only for those who preach but for those who hear as well. Hearing the Word of God preached delights us. In it God is reaching out to us in love, and when we recognize this we are filled with love. The joy which comes from the knowledge of the divine Wisdom does not pass away quickly, but rather is an abiding joy, for God is himself everlasting. Even more this divine Wisdom is a healing medicine for the whole human race.[244] Jesus is the incarnate Wisdom of God that he might be the Savior of the world. Quite obviously Augustine's theology of preaching is thoroughly based on biblical Wisdom theology, especially as found in the Gospel of John.[245]

Having established that the purpose of preaching is to strengthen the bond of love between God and his people as well as the bond of love between Christians, Augustine moves on to speak of how the preacher is to go about the interpretation of Scripture, for the work of the preacher consists of two parts: first, to ascertain the meaning of Scripture, and second, to communicate that meaning once it is ascertained.[246]

In the second book we discover Augustine as philosopher. Philosophically Augustine was always a Platonist. In much of his thought he was a Stoic — a thoroughly Christian Stoic, to be sure, but a Stoic

---

242. Augustine, *De doctrina christiana* 1.6.

243. Augustine, *De doctrina christiana* 1.13.

244. Augustine, *De doctrina christiana* 1.14.

245. For a full discussion of this, see my chapter on the Wisdom doxology in *Themes and Variations for a Christian Doxology: Some Thoughts on a Theology of Worship* (Grand Rapids: Wm. B. Eerdmans Publishing Co., 1992).

246. Augustine, *De doctrina christiana* 4.1.

nevertheless — and, as we have seen, one can even hear from him some of the themes of Epicureanism. But as the Romans tended to be, he was very pragmatic and very eclectic. When it came to understanding society he was a Stoic, but when it came to a theory of knowledge he was a Platonist. When he was converted to Christianity, many of his philosophical presuppositions helped him understand the gospel; indeed, one might say he was converted because Christianity fulfilled many of the expectations the education of classical antiquity had taught him. So much of Greek and Roman philosophy assumes that reality is perceived in terms of two levels of existence: the everyday, commonsense level and the transcendent or spiritual level. To use a term common in our day, Augustine assumed a three-story universe. Such a way of looking at things may be anathema to the modern existentialist, but that was what Plato was all about. What interested Plato, and most of those trained in Greek and Roman philosophy, was a higher reality which he somehow sensed was to be found in everyday human existence; they believed in some sort of transcendent reality. It is in this sense that Augustine was so obviously a Platonist, and it is therefore that he has much to say about appearance and reality, *signum* and *res,* the sign and the thing signified.

Augustine begins his second book by discussing language in these terms.[247] The Scriptures provide us with an intimation of divine reality. The words of Scripture are divinely given signs which, while earthly in themselves, signify a heavenly truth. Words are not the only signs of transcendent reality, as one may speak of the sacraments and the other visual or tactile signs which Scripture tells about, but words are the chief signs which convey to us the realities of the spirit.[248] Here we have a very strong affirmation that Christianity is quite legitimately a verbal, literary, preaching religion. This has been discussed at great length recently. The whole emphasis on liturgy we find in certain circles is an attempt to flee the verbal tendency of Christianity. It would de-emphasize preaching, making it merely auxiliary to worship rather than putting it at the center. One imagines it would be better to give more room to visual and tactile ways of experiencing reality. Obviously Augustine does not lead us in this direction. Quite unabashedly he explains Christianity as a religion of the Word, and that is why he gives such attention to the reading and preaching of Scripture in worship.[249]

247. Augustine, *De doctrina christiana* 2.1-3.
248. Augustine, *De doctrina christiana* 2.3.
249. Augustine, *De doctrina christiana* 2.3.

With this very philosophical point on the nature of language Augustine lays down a number of more practical points on how we are to approach the interpretation of Scripture.

1. Any particular passage of Scripture is best interpreted in terms of the whole of Scripture; therefore, those who have a thorough knowledge of the whole of Scripture are best prepared to interpret any particular passage. One should be careful to study all the books of both the Old and New Testaments.[250]

2. Those who want to do the work of interpretation should study both Greek and Hebrew. If one cannot handle the original languages, one should consult a variety of translations, always remaining sensitive to the fact that one is studying a translation.[251] Augustine did not know Hebrew, and although he made an effort throughout his life to improve his Greek, he was not a first-class philologist. Even at that, he recognized the importance of the original languages. He probably figured his conversion came too late in life for him to master Greek and Hebrew.

3. The Christian preacher should have a wide acquaintance with secular learning. One must be careful, however, because the knowledge accumulated by the secular world is a mixture of truth and superstition. Pagan myths are found everywhere. The Christian must avoid astrology, divination, and fear of demons wherever they are found, but even at that, there is much in the knowledge which non-Christians have discovered which is valuable. Every Christian should well understand that wherever truth is found it belongs to the God of truth.[252]

4. History is a particularly important subject for the Christian preacher to master.[253]

5. The study of the natural sciences such as zoology, botany, and geography are likewise helpful for the interpreter of Scripture.[254]

6. To this should be added the formal study of classical logic and rhetoric and the meaning of numbers.[255]

Augustine was a forthright advocate of what we have come to call a liberal arts education. In this he was, of course, simply following in the

---

250. Augustine, *De doctrina christiana* 2.8.
251. Augustine, *De doctrina christiana* 2.11.
252. Augustine, *De doctrina christiana* 2.20-24.
253. Augustine, *De doctrina christiana* 2.28.
254. Augustine, *De doctrina christiana* 2.28.
255. Augustine, *De doctrina christiana* 2.31-38.

train of the classical civilization of ancient Greece and Rome. As Augustine saw it, this kind of education was of the highest possible value for the preacher. Now, fifteen hundred years later, we realize that Augustine would hardly be put in his grave before the barbarians would lay waste to that classical civilization and the kind of education it had developed. Still, wherever and whenever the Church recognized the importance of preaching, this kind of education would be cultivated. On the authority of Augustine the liberal arts education would be revived by the universities of the High Middle Ages. When the preaching orders, notably the Franciscans and Dominicans, began to think about how preachers were to be trained, they carefully studied Augustine's *De doctrina christiana* and tried to give their young friars exactly this kind of education. The Puritans, upon arriving in America, did the same thing, founding colleges and seeing to it that they gave the same kind of education in liberal arts which Augustine recommended. Even in the Midwest in the last century the typical Christian college was a liberal arts college. Kentucky, Tennessee, Ohio, Indiana, Illinois, Iowa, Kansas — the whole American heartland is filled with small Christian liberal arts colleges. If the Church needed preachers it had to provide the sort of education that produces preachers.

In the third book of this classic Augustine turns to the more difficult problems of interpreting the text. He has already spoken of the importance of mastering grammar, but now he must address some of the more advanced questions of rhetoric, the matter of tropes and figurative expressions. This is fundamental to understanding Scripture.[256] Here again we detect the philosophical bent of Augustine's mind. For him it is a matter of the letter of the law and the spirit of the law. The apostle Paul had warned that the letter of the law kills but the spirit gives life, and Augustine often wrote about the problems of law and grace, letter and spirit. He saw the problem in terms of classical philosophy and what it had to say about appearance and reality. It was the same problem about which the apostle Paul had spoken when he taught that the Law of the Old Testament was a schoolmaster to prepare us for the gospel.[257] Here is where Christianity bears a similarity to the philosophies of Plato and Aristotle: both recognize a difference between the reality which is seen and the reality which is unseen; both can talk about *signum* and *res*, sign and reality. The visible world is full of signs of the transcendent world. The same is true with language. Language often has a

---

256. Augustine, *De doctrina christiana* 3.5.
257. Augustine, *De doctrina christiana* 3.6.

double sense: a simple, obvious sense and a higher, less obvious sense. Much that the pagan poets had to say about this Augustine cannot accept. When put philosophically by Plato, Aristotle, and others it was quite acceptable, but when the poets and dramatists began to recount the myths of ancient Greece and Rome it was another matter. Their attempts to spiritualize these myths only made paganism more subtle. In the end it was still spiritual fornication.[258] Spiritual interpretation does not always lead us to the truth. When it comes to the Homeric gods no amount of spiritual interpretation will make these traditions edifying.

It is a very different matter with the signs which God appointed under the Law of the Old Testament. We now understand their meaning because they pointed to Christ, and now that Christ has come these signs have been fulfilled. Here Augustine takes up a theme we find frequently in the Fathers of the ancient Church. Under the old dispensation there were a great number of elaborate signs, but under the new dispensation brought in by Christ there are only a few, and they are much simpler. Our Lord himself has handed down to us a few rites, such as baptism and Communion, which are much simpler and more straightforward than the rites of the Law.[259] The Christian interpretation of the liturgical rites of the Old Testament was a subject of particular interest to the preachers of the patristic age. It was only a generation after Augustine that Cyril of Alexandria produced his famous interpretation of the Levitical rites, *On Worship in Spirit and in Truth,* but many of these ideas already had a wide currency which went far back in the Alexandrian school.

It was Philo, Alexandria's Jewish philosopher, who had popularized the spiritual interpretation of the Law of Moses. There was much, perhaps too much, in this philosophical interpretation of Scripture that Augustine was willing to go along with, but even at that, he thought spiritualizing Scripture can go too far. In Augustine's time, even as in our own, spiritualizing can lead to relativizing. Philosophers often make the mistake of being so confused by the variety of customs from one nation to another that they adopt a kind of moral relativism. In the end they imagine that there is no such thing as right or wrong.[260] This is something Augustine would have us avoid.

There is another danger in spiritualized interpretation. A spiritual or

---

258. Augustine, *De doctrina christiana* 3.8.
259. Augustine, *De doctrina christiana* 3.9.
260. Augustine, *De doctrina christiana* 3.15.

tropological approach to a passage should never lead us to an interpretation of Scripture which contradicts the law of love. An allegorical interpretation of the ceremonial law of the Old Testament is one thing, but spiritualizing the gospel is quite another. The fundamentals of the gospel must always lead our interpretation and application. In fact, if a passage seems in an outward way to contradict the central teachings of the gospel, there is reason to think that it is a figurative passage and should be interpreted accordingly. Here, of course, is a principle the Alexandrian school of exegesis had often laid down.

Many people take offense at certain passages in the Bible because they have not taken care to study the context. One always needs to ask to whom a passage is addressed, by whom it is spoken, and by what authority that person has spoken. Some commands are given to special groups of people for a particular time; others are given to all in general.[261] Other people take offense at passages which quite frankly speak of the sins of the saints. These passages are there to keep us constantly mindful of our need of grace.[262] None is perfect; none is beyond temptation; none can stand alone against Satan. Even the strongest must depend upon the power of God and God alone.

Once more Augustine reiterates the classic principle that Scripture is to be interpreted by Scripture. Passages which are obscure are to be interpreted by passages which are more clear on any particular subject. This, of course, is one of those principles of biblical interpretation which goes back as far as the Bible itself. Here Augustine warns us against trying to interpret Scripture from the standpoint of some principles of reason as understood by one philosophical school or another. In the end revelation is a gift of God's grace. It is not as though our reason is going to save us when grace fails. God's revelation as we find it in Scripture is sufficient. It is important that we approach it in prayer. We read in Proverbs:

> For the LORD gives wisdom;
>   from his mouth come knowledge and understanding.

> (Prov. 2:6)

It is because God is ultimately the source of wisdom that in the beginning and in the end we must seek it from him in prayer.

261. Augustine, *De doctrina christiana* 3.17-20.
262. Augustine, *De doctrina christiana* 3.23.

The last of Augustine's four books, *On the Art of Christian Teaching,* has to do with how the preacher is to use the art of rhetoric in communicating the Word of God as it is found in Holy Scripture. As Augustine understands it, his job is not to teach rhetoric. That is something the conscientious Christian preacher needs to learn, but the place to learn it is in the schools.[263] On the other hand, the art of public speaking is a talent; some people have a natural inclination for it and some do not. Augustine quotes a saying of Cicero's that people learn rhetoric quickly or not at all.[264] As a matter of fact, Augustine insists that one learns the arts of eloquence not so much from teachers and lessons as from hearing the addresses of eloquent speakers. Eloquence begets eloquence. Those who have the talent can pick it up by observation.

Ever since Plato's famous dialogue *Gorgias,* philosopers have criticized the vanity of rhetoricians who stress the eloquence of oratorical form rather than the wisdom of the inner message the speaker was supposed to convey. Intelligent people have a natural antipathy to the facile tongue, to the slick salesman, and to the fast-talking politician. Yet there is an eloquence which is consistent with wisdom. What makes the difference is that for the Christian preacher wisdom is in the end more important than eloquence. We find this exemplified by the writers of Scripture, who so often join eloquence to wisdom, and from Scripture itself we learn that there is a certain kind of eloquence appropriate to those who justly claim the highest authority and who are quite evidently inspired of God.[265] The prophets and apostles have a sort of eloquence which is distinctly their own, and yet they use that rhetoric so naturally that one is hardly aware of either its presence or absence. And it is that which Augustine most admires, this eloquence which is not obvious and, in fact, is scarcely detected. It is a sort of eloquence which does not detract from the beauty of Wisdom itself.[266] To make his point about the relation of wisdom and eloquence, Augustine gives us a superb figure of speech. It is as though Wisdom were going forth from her house, and eloquence, like an inseparable attendant, followed her without having to be summoned.[267]

With this our preacher shows us how first the apostle Paul and then

---

263. Augustine, *De doctrina christiana* 4.1.
264. Augustine, *De doctrina christiana* 4.3.
265. Augustine, *De doctrina christiana* 4.5.
266. Augustine, *De doctrina christiana* 4.6.
267. Augustine, *De doctrina christiana* 4.6.

the prophet Amos had a natural sort of eloquence which, even when measured by the canons of classical oratory, shows the unmistakable marks of genius. Both in regard to Paul and in regard to Amos Augustine gives us detailed examples.

For a Christian rhetoric, perspicuity is the foundation of all the canons of style.[268] Clarity of thought must always be the preacher's aim. Clarity is the basic beauty of eloquent oratory and the driving power that persuades one's listeners.[269] The beauty of teaching is making clear the truth, for it is in the truth itself, rather than in the words about truth, in which beauty is found.[270] The truth itself, Augustine tells us, when presented in simplicity, gives pleasure because it is the truth. This is one of Augustine's best insights. Here, a thousand years before the Protestant Reformation, one easily detects the guiding principle of Protestant plain style. Here is the foundation of the Protestant understanding of beauty. In what contrast it stands to the artiness which is so often passed off as beauty! And yet it is an approach to beauty which is consistent with the Christian faith.

Spontaneity is another fundamental feature of true oratory. This is something which may not be caught by those unacquainted with the oratorical arts of antiquity. The great orators of Greece and Rome never wrote out their speeches beforehand. This does not mean they preached extemporaneously, however. They carefully studied the passage of Scripture on which they were to preach; they meditated on its meaning and application and prepared their material very carefully beforehand; but only when they were in front of their audience did they put it together. They were very much dependent on the reaction of their listeners, and, depending on their audience and the response of their audience, they served up what seemed appropriate from what they had prepared. If today we have records of the orations of Demosthenes and Cicero, it is because they were taken down by a stenographer or written up afterwards by the speaker or one of his assistants. During the actual delivery the orator needed to read the audience, and he could hardly do that if he were reading a manuscript. The spontaneous quality of oratory is of its essence. It is fundamentally an encounter between speaker and listener. That is what makes the difference between oratory and literature. In public worship the Scriptures are to be read, but the sermon is to be preached.

268. Augustine, *De doctrina christiana* 4.10.
269. Augustine, *De doctrina christiana* 4.26.
270. Augustine, *De doctrina christiana* 4.11.

Augustine learned much from Cicero, and, of course, that is one reason why Christian schools all down through the centuries have taught Cicero to those whom they prepared to fill their pulpits. Cicero has nurtured as many good preachers as he has good lawyers. It was some four hundred years after Cicero that Augustine taught the principles of that ultimate Roman orator. It is, of course, Cicero that one hears when Augustine says that an orator must speak so as to teach, to delight, and to persuade. To teach is a necessity, to delight is a beauty, and to persuade is a triumph.[271] Those who were privileged to read Cicero's orations in their high school Latin classes understand quite well what this is all about. Strangely enough, a generation after Cicero was taken out of the curriculum of the typical American school our preachers began to have a hard time holding the attention of a congregation.

By way of conclusion Augustine brings his strong theology of grace to bear on his use of rhetoric. Christian preaching must be borne of prayer. When the hour is come for the preacher to mount the pulpit, he must lift up his thirsty soul to God, to drink in what he is about to pour forth and to be himself filled with what he is about to distribute.[272] The study of rhetoric and the careful application of its rules are of value if God gives his Holy Spirit. It is this giving of the Holy Spirit that produces fruit in our lives. God can save us without human help and is not dependent on preachers, but when his Holy Spirit anoints the work of the preacher, then it is a means of grace which brings us into communion with God. Augustine ends his treatise with a biblical simile. Just as Queen Esther devoted herself to prayer before entering the presence of Ahasuerus, so the Christian preacher must commit his work to God before facing his congregation.[273]

The preaching ministry of Augustine had a tremendous influence on the preaching of the Western Church, down through the Middle Ages, in the Reformation, and even to our own day. His manual on preaching, *De doctrina christiana,* is still regarded as a classic. His actual sermons were collected, memorized, and preached all over the Latin world. As fewer and fewer ministers were capable of composing sermons themselves, homiliaries were collected so that priests or even bishops could at least read a sermon to their congregations. Augustine in his own lifetime encouraged

---

271. Augustine, *De doctrina christiana* 4.12.
272. Augustine, *De doctrina christiana* 4.15.
273. Augustine, *De doctrina christiana* 4.16.

this development. In his commentary on Psalm 119 he tells us that his colleagues urged him to complete his series of sermons on the Psalms so that they might have a complete commentary. At that point Augustine had preached or commented on all the psalms except the longest, Psalm 119. He set to work writing a commentary on the psalm but decided to write it in the form of a series of sermons. Therefore, Augustine tells us, "I have at length decided to set it out in sermons, . . . which may be preached to the people."[274] Obviously Augustine was beginning to realize that if the ordinary congregation was to hear regular preaching, it would have to hear read sermons. No doubt Augustine had no idea how extensively this would be practiced in the centuries to come. Surely, if he had realized how many of his sermons would be preached, in how many pulpits, and for how many centuries, he would have given far greater care to their editing and publication. But, be that as it may, Augustine has left us enough to give us a fairly good idea of what the art of Christian teaching really ought to be. We can be thankful that the foremost theologian of Latin antiquity was also a very practical practicing pastor.

F. Theologia Verbi Dei

For the Western Church, at least, Augustine was the premier preacher of the patristic age. The example he set would shape the homiletical patterns of the Latin-speaking church for centuries to come. Having gone through a good number of his sermons, what can we conclude about this ministry which he performed? What can we say about the ministry of the Word as worship?

For Augustine the purpose of the ministry of the Word of God is to establish and nourish the bond of love which unites us to God. This is not only the purpose of the reading and preaching of the Word, it is the purpose of worship in general. The purpose of all that we do in God's service is first to love God and second to love the neighbor. As we have seen again and again, Augustine always gets back to the first commandment as Jesus interpreted it — Thou shalt love the Lord thy God. It is by the Word that we are called into the covenant community, and it is by the Word that we are instructed in the life of the covenant community. To love God implies loving the neighbor. Love is the essence of the

274. Hebyin and Corrigan, St. Augustine on the Psalms, p. 3.

covenant relationship, the glue that binds us together, and preaching encourages and strengthens it. Again Augustine's commentary on the sixth chapter of the Gospel of John makes the point that worship is supposed to nourish the bond of love which unites the Church, the household of faith. The sacrament of this nourishing is the Lord's Supper. It is a sign of what is happening in preaching, but it is also a seal of what is promised in the preaching of the Word. For Augustine worship is to feast on the Word in the fellowship of the Church.

Augustine is well known for his dictum that the sacraments are the Word made visible. For him they both presuppose the Word and entail the Word. Baptism was just as closely connected to the Word as was the Eucharist. The catechetical sermons on I John which we studied showed how the sacrament of baptism entailed the teaching of the Christian way of life. Baptism not only seals the promises proclaimed in the gospel, it demands a systematic, lifelong study of God's Word. The whole preaching ministry of the Church is founded in the sign of baptism.

One cannot help but notice as one reads through the sermons of Augustine that here is a preacher who takes great delight in preaching. If the *Westminster Catechism* teaches us that man's chief end is to glorify God and to enjoy him forever, Augustine would underline worship as enjoying God. The wisdom of God is a sacred delight to the Christian. We find the Wisdom theology all through Augustine because in Scripture he finds the treasures of divine wisdom. For him preaching is an opportunity to display these treasures and thereby to enjoy them. But even more, preaching glorifies God. Here is where a Wisdom theology links up with a covenantal theology. It is in the reading and preaching of the Word that God reveals himself. He reveals his wisdom; that is a delight. He reveals his love, his covenant faithfulness; that is glorious! And when that happens, what else can we do but bow down in love, in wonder, in obedience? When we do this, God is worshiped.

CHAPTER VI

The Eternal Gospel in a Dying Culture

It was in the year 410 that Rome fell to the barbarians, when Alaric and his Visigoths sacked the capital city of the Roman Empire. Not everyone realized it at the time, but that was the undeniable sign of the end of an age. The culture of classical antiquity was living its last days. Nor did everything stop all of a sudden; in fact, things sputtered along for several generations. In 455 Valentinian III was murdered, which, as far as Rome was concerned, brought the dynasty of Theodosius to an end. Finally in 476 the Roman Empire became extinct when the barbarian Odoacer proclaimed himself king of Italy. While he formally recognized the Byzantine emperor, everyone knew it was a fiction. The old Roman Empire was finished.

Ambrose, Jerome, and Augustine grew up in a world in which the supremacy of Rome was assumed. It was another matter with Leo, Peter Chrysologus, and Gregory. The Theodosian revival in which Ambrose played such a vital role was nothing like the Augustan Age, but one could still recognize it as the Roman Empire. By the end of Leo's life, however, it was clear that the Roman Empire had finally fallen. More than a century later Gregory succeeded Leo, and to Gregory it was evident that the Byzantine Empire was no longer the Roman Empire but something quite different and quite remote. With whatever vestiges of Roman culture the Goths, the Vandals, and the Lombards may have invested themselves, they were not Romans; they were barbarians and they were in control.

The barbarians had managed to subdue the Roman Empire, but they brought very little to take its place. They had no vision of what society could be and, sad to say, very little sense of what life was really all about. The Christian Church, on the other hand, had a vision. Augustine had made that very clear in his classic *The City of God.* In fact, the more the old Rome began to unravel, the more the disheartened Romans became interested in the Christian vision of a transcendent city of God. Christian preachers had an important function from the end of the fifth to the beginning of the seventh centuries. Almost alone they were able to give some hope in an age of discouragement.

For the history of Christian worship one might say that this was the age in which the hatches were battened down. The most perceptive Christian leaders of the time realized they had to prepare the Church to carry on through the Dark Ages. As a classical education became harder and harder to come by, fewer and fewer of the young men entering the ministry, through no fault of their own, had been trained in the literary arts. As a result, more and more men like Leo and Gregory would codify the liturgy so that those who had had little training in the literary arts could conduct public worship which had some sort of integrity. Prayers were written and put into sacramentaries, lectionaries began to take shape, and the sermons of the better preachers were collected and put into homiliaries.

Surely one of the best things which happened during this period was the evolution of the Benedictine Order. In a move that was symptomatic of his age, Saint Benedict, in about 500, retreated from the city of Rome to follow a simple life of contemplation in the wilderness, eventually building a monastery at Monte Cassino. This monastery became the cornerstone of a new movement that grew to the point that, by the end of the century, Gregory was one of its strongest supporters. As Benedictine monasticism developed, it became a powerful institution for the development of sacred learning. Dom Jean Leclercq, in his perceptive study *The Love of Literature and the Desire for God,* has shown us what Benedictine monasticism was really about. Apart from monasticism, Christian literary culture, if not Christianity itself, might well have completely perished in the Western world. That Gregory the Great did so much for the movement was surely one of his most valuable achievements.

If the Church was to continue to worship as it always had, there needed to be a steady supply of young men who knew how to speak in public, how to use words, and how to read and understand a written text. If there was to be a ministry of the Word, then the culture of words, the arts of literature, and the preservation and distribution of books had to be cultivated. Benedictine monasticism was a powerful instrument for doing just this.

There was something very courageous about the preachers to whom we now turn. In a very dark day when the world seemed to be coming to an end they were able to preach that the God of Abraham, Isaac, and Jacob, the God and Father of our Lord Jesus Christ, is not the God of one age or another but the eternal God, to be worshiped by all peoples, of all cultures, in all places, and for all ages.

I. Leo the Great

Leo the Great (ca. 400-461) was a most brilliant ray in the sunset of classical civilization.[1] The virtual successor to the Roman Caesars, now filling the office of Roman pope, he was a consummate statesman who more than once saved the Eternal City. It was Leo who, with no army behind him but brandishing only the arms of faith, met with the barbarian chief Attila the Hun and convinced him not to attack Rome. In the best Roman tradition he was an able politician, a capable thinker, an articulate spokesman for his program, and an orator of proven gifts. In him the tradition of Cicero, Julius Caesar, and Marcus Aurelius once again came to expression. Leo the Great was, like those who had gone before him, an architect of society. The society he intended to build was a Christian society, yet this Christian society was not an end in itself — it had its eyes on a heavenly glory. The society here below was crumbling, but the city of God was gathering her own within her that they might depart for an eternal kingdom.

Leo was a firm supporter of the Chalcedonian faith. According to the Christology of the Council of Chalcedon, human nature is neither consumed nor destroyed by the incarnation; it is rather transformed and glorified. Humanity has significance and, therefore, human society has

1. For biographical information, see O. Bardenhewer, *Geschichte der altenkirchlichen Literatur,* 5 vols. (Freiburg im Breisgau: Herder, 1913-32), 4:617-23; Trevor Jalland, *The Life and Times of St. Leo the Great* (London: SPCK, 1941); Hans Lietzmann, "Leo I," *Pauly-Wissowa-Kroll, Realencyklopädie der klassischen Altertumswissenschaft,* 12/2 (1925): 1962-73; Basil Studer, in Johannes Quasten, *Patrology,* vol. 4, ed. Angelo di Bernardino, English translation Placid Solari (Westminster, Md.: Christian Classics, 1994), pp. 586-612.

significance. But if because of the incarnation of Christ human society has significance, then Leo understood himself, as the vicar of Christ, to have great significance for society. Leo was one of those responsible for developing the doctrine of papal authority. His excellent political and theological leadership gave substance to his theories, and, to a large extent, he was able to win the authority he claimed.

A. Leo's Festal Cycle

Leo preached as pope. His style is authoritative and majestic, his words few but weighty. Because the same style is found in many of the prayers of the Roman sacramentaries, not a few liturgical scholars are convinced that he is indeed the author of much of the liturgical work which has been preserved in these sacramentaries.[2] Ninety-six of his sermons, all carefully finished, have come down to us.[3] No doubt Leo gave much attention to editing his sermons before allowing them to be published. For the most part they are short and show an amazing economy of words and precision of statement. Convinced of having great authority, he is careful to speak clearly in pronouncing the faith of the Church. Yet one wonders if the congregation was able to follow his sermons. They are so ingeniously terse that one would be surprised if a congregation could pick up all his meaning from the living voice that came from the papal chair. It is possible that these sermons have been heavily edited and the homiletical expansions eliminated, and yet the style in which they have come down to us has a definite logic. They are the august pronouncements of the heir to the throne of Saint Peter delivered at the great solemnities of the Roman Church.

Leo preached only at solemnities,[4] which was evidently the custom in

2. Arthur Paul Lang, *Leo der Grosse und die Texte des Altgelasianums* (Steyer: Verlagsbuchhandlung, 1957).

3. For editions of Leo's sermons, see Leo the Great, *Tractatus septem et nonaginta,* ed. Antoine Chavasse, Corpus Christianorum, series Latina, vols. 138 and 138A (Turnholt, Belgium, and Paris: Brepols, 1973); *Léon le Grand, Sermons,* ed. René Dolle with introduction by Jean Leclercq, Sources chrétiennes, vols. 22, 49, 74, and 200 (Paris: Les Éditions du Cerf, 1949-73); hereinafter Dolle, *Léon le Grand.* The English translation is taken from *The Letters and Sermons of Leo the Great,* trans. C. L. Feltoe, Nicene and Post-Nicene Fathers, 2nd ser., vol. 12 (Grand Rapids: Wm. B. Eerdmans Publishing Co., 1976). Where Leo's sermons are quoted, the classical method of citation is used.

4. Dom J. Leclercq, in Dolle, *Léon le Grand,* 1:19.

the Roman Church in the fifth century. One is not surprised at this, for it follows the long-established customs of classical oratory.[5] Leo's sermons are not expository sermons in the tradition of the early Church and the synagogue but are much more like the panegyrics of classical oratory. We find sermons for Christmas, Epiphany, the beginning of Lent, Transfiguration, Passion Sunday, the Wednesday of Holy Week, Easter, Ascension, Pentecost, the feasts of Saint Peter and Saint Paul, the feast of Saint Lawrence, and the Ember Days.[6] These were the great solemnities, the holy days of the Roman Church, upon which Romans expected a word from their bishop.

When understood this way, the sermons of Leo have a specific place in Christian worship. Dom Leclercq has made the point that these are liturgical sermons, which they are indeed, in a very particular understanding of the term. These sermons fit into the worship of the Church quite differently from the way most of the sermons of John Chrysostom or Augustine fit into worship. For Leo the liturgy is the celebration of the Christian mysteries, and the sermon is an expounding of those mysteries. They are mystagogy in the sense that Cyril of Jerusalem's mystagogical catechisms were mystagogy. Leo's sermons are not an exposition of the sacred Scriptures in the way in which the sermons of Origen, Basil, or Ambrose were. In these sermons there is a definition of the doctrines which the mysteries celebrate. One could almost say that Leo's sermons on the solemnities form a volume of systematic theology. The cycle of feasts and fasts has become the schema on which the substance of Christian doctrine can be explained. With the preaching of Leo the festal sermon has become the chief sermon genre. This needs to be noted very carefully, for it is a pivotal development in the history of Christian worship.

For the celebration of Christmas ten sermons have been preserved, each of which was preached at a different Christmas during Leo's twenty years as bishop of Rome. The first of these begins with a jubilant proclamation of the birth of Christ: "Our Savior, dearly-beloved, was born today. Let us be glad. . . . No one is excluded from sharing in this happiness. . . . Our Lord, the destroyer of sin and death, finds none free from charge, so is He come to free us all."[7] This intense burst of joy is

---

5. From the liturgical traditions of the Christian Church, on the other hand, it was a distinct departure. Cyril of Alexandria, Leo's contemporary, preached each Lord's Day if not daily.

6. Cf. Dolle, *Léon le Grand,* 1:64.

7. Leo, *Sermo XXI* 1.

followed by a precise unfolding of the doctrine of the incarnation. "For the Son of God in the fullness of time which the inscrutable depth of the Divine counsel has determined, has taken on Him the nature of man, thereby to reconcile it to its Author: in order that the inventor of death, the devil, might be conquered through that which he had conquered."[8] Each sentence of this sermon Leo fills with marvelous paradoxes, parallelisms, and antitheses, all in the best tradition of classical oratory. Our preacher continues with this arresting thought by saying God carried out the struggle for us with a wondrous sense of justice. Our Lord waged this war against the devil, not in his majesty but in our humility; he shared our mortality but not our sin.[9] Leo's doctrine is indeed very close to Scripture even if he is not expounding a particular passage of Scripture. We recognize many allusions to Scripture rather than specific quotations of the text of Scripture.[10]

Having laid this theological groundwork, our preacher comes to speak of the birth of Jesus. He tells us of how God chose a virgin from the line of David to bear a child both human and divine. She conceived this child not so much as a bodily function but as an act of faith. Although she could hardly have understood what God was going to do, she was not terrified by the unusual circumstances of the child's birth, for in perfect faith she heard from the voice of an angel that what was happening to her was the work of the Holy Spirit.[11] One of course recognizes that this is a very brief interpretation of the nativity narrative from the Gospel of Luke. Next Leo alludes to the prologue of the Gospel of John, telling us that the Word of God who is God, even the Son of God, who was in the beginning with God, in order to liberate man from eternal death, was made man. Thus he took on our humility without lessening his majesty. Remaining what he was he took on what he was not. This union of the divine and the human was of such a kind that neither was the lesser nature consumed by being glorified nor the greater diminished by taking on the more lowly.[12] In reading this sermon we easily recognize that Leo is giving us pure Chalcedonian doctrine. The sermon becomes almost a confession of faith, almost a creedal formulation.

8. Leo, *Sermo XXI* 1.
9. Leo, *Sermo XXI* 1.
10. Leo, *Sermo XXI* 1.
11. Leo, *Sermo XXI* 1.
12. Leo, *Sermo XXI* 2.

Having given us this virile statement of Christian doctrine, Leo continues, "Let us then, dearly beloved, give thanks to God the Father, through His Son, in the Holy Spirit, Who for His great mercy, wherewith He has loved us, has had pity on us: . . . that we might be in Him a new creation."[13] Here again the wording is strongly influenced by the apostle Paul — typically Leo's conclusions are Pauline. He exhorts his congregation to put aside the works of the old humanity and take up the new life in Christ. "Christian, acknowledge thy dignity, and become a partner in the Divine nature."[14] For those who enjoy theological statements, these Christmas sermons are a delight. It was of course during Leo's pontificate that the Council of Chalcedon met, and one is aware as one reads these sermons that one is hearing in almost poetic form the affirmations of the age of Chalcedon.[15]

There are twelve sermons for the beginning of Lent. Leo obviously considered the beginning of the forty-day fast a major solemnity, among the highest, in fact, of the high holy days. Indeed, with Leo one begins to sense the increasing importance of fast days for the newly emerging liturgical calendar. He also preached on the fast days of Pentecost, the fast days of September, and the fast days of December, giving them an increased importance in Christian devotional life. This growing penitential cast which now begins to shape the liturgy, and particularly the rapidly developing Christian calendar, must surely be related to the troubles of the times. As the barbarian tribes began to pour over the Alps — first the Visigoths, then the Huns, and then the Vandals — all Italy trembled before the enemy. In 452, midway in the pontificate of Leo, the Vandals actually occupied the city of Rome. Surely seasons of lamentation and fasting would have been particularly important in such a period of history. We will have more to say about this in a moment.

These sermons for the beginning of Lent preach Lent; that is, they encourage the faithful to keep the spiritual disciplines of the season. Our preacher tells us that Lent is a time for more serious practices of piety and often spells out these disciplines very clearly: works of charity, the pardoning of offenses, the giving of alms, fasting, frequent prayer and study of

13. Leo, *Sermo XXI* 3.

14. Leo, *Sermo XXI* 3.

15. On the role played by Leo at the Council of Chalcedon, see Jaroslav Pelikan, *The Emergence of the Catholic Tradition (100-600)* (Chicago and London: University of Chicago Press, 1971), pp. 256-66.

Scripture. One should particularly avoid gluttony, drunkenness, and luxurious living. Leo often makes the point that Lent is a time of spiritual warfare, and the devil, our adversary, would seduce us from these pious observances by various temptations. Sometimes these sermons mention the Scripture lessons which have been read, namely, the story of Christ's temptation from the fourth chapter of Matthew and the sixth chapter of Second Corinthians. In the fourth sermon he makes an extended commentary on the reading from the Epistle, but many of these sermons, appropriate as they are to Lent, do not even mention the Scripture lessons of the day. These sermons are not expositions of Scripture; instead, they offer the congregation encouragement and direction for the keeping of Lent.

The keeping of Lent reached its high point, in the practice of the Roman Church of that period, with Passion Sunday and the observances of Holy Week. Lent was understood as a preparation for the Christian celebration of Passover, as we often hear in Leo's Lenten sermons. It was Passion Sunday, not Palm Sunday, which in that age began Holy Week. There was a lengthy reading, begun on Sunday and completed on Wednesday, of the Passion narrative from the Gospel of Matthew. From the sermons that have come down to us we get the impression that neither the preparation of candidates for baptism nor the Easter vigil demanded a sermon from the bishop. There is no sermon for the tradition of the creed or the Lord's Prayer and no catechetical sermons introducing the converts to the sacraments. The ministry to the catechumens and the sacrament of baptism was beginning to lose its importance in the observance of both Lent and Easter.

As we have said, two sermons each year were devoted to the preaching of the Passion. We have these sermons on the Passion in nine sets of two. Let us look at the third of these sets, the fifth and sixth sermons on the Passion.[16] The fifth sermon begins with a noble proclamation of Christ's saving work on the cross in which we are told that the creator and Lord of all things, our Savior, Christ, having been born of the Virgin in a manner most marvelous and extraordinary, having received the homage of the Magi at his manger, having proclaimed the heavenly teaching and through his efficacious words brought about marvelous healings, has now brought to consummation the dispensation of all sacred mysteries by his all-saving Passion. Indeed, most beloved brethren, Leo continues, the cross of Christ

16. Leo, *Sermo LVI* and *Sermo LVII*.

is the inner reason and fundamental cause of the Christian hope. Let the cross of Christ be a stumbling block to the Jews and foolishness to the Gentiles; to us, on the other hand, it is the power of God and the wisdom of God.[17] Leo goes on to say that most assuredly we should always cherish this sacrament of divine mercy, yet at this time it is particularly appropriate not only because the time of its remembrance has returned but also because the reading of the Gospel has spoken to us once again of the work of our redemption. Leo's Christology comes to expression when he tells us Christ suffered on the cross both with humility and with exaltation. Even if this world views this as impossible for man and unworthy for God, both are to be received, both are to be believed, for no one can be saved apart from both.[18]

After this weighty introduction our preacher passes to the story of Christ's agony in the garden. He tells what happened in the briefest words, then quoting the text "'My Father, if it be possible, let this cup pass from me; nevertheless, not as I will, but as thou wilt'" (Matt. 26:39), he comments that in this prayer of Jesus we have two petitions.[19] The first is a prayer of human infirmity and weakness; the second is an affirmation of divine power. We find in this prayer both the human anguish which is natural and appropriate to our human nature and the divine resolve to suffer for the sake of man.[20] Once again we notice in these words of Leo something typical of his sermons: a doctrinal statement put in the most concise manner possible. What verbal economy! This is particularly evident in the Latin text. It is a terse expression of one of the most brilliant insights of the Chalcedonian Christology. Again, one wonders if a congregation could follow and understand all that is said in this concisely stated sermon, without something more in the way of homiletical elaboration. But perhaps they could. After all, these ideas were in current discussion during the age of Chalcedon.

Our preacher then passes on to the treason of Judas and Christ's arrest.[21] Leo comments that here we see that the Son of God delivered himself into impious hands and that by the power of suffering he lovingly fulfilled those actions which were done to him out of a hateful savagery.

17. Leo, *Sermo LVI* 1.
18. Leo, *Sermo LVI* 1.
19. Leo, *Sermo LVI* 2.
20. Leo, *Sermo LVI* 2.
21. Leo, *Sermo LVI* 2.

This is a sacrament of piety for us, the preacher continues, because Christ submitted to injuries he could have restrained had he been willing to reveal his divine power. If he had done this, however, he would have displayed the divine power instead of curing the human weakness. In bearing human cruelty he bore away human sin; he exercised his priesthood for the expiation of our sins. That nature which in us is captive was in him free. In the perfect freedom of his innocent suffering he bore away our guilt, so that now we are free from that by which he suffered. He was the sacrificial lamb who made of himself the sacrifice, joining himself to our nature in substance while yet being distinct from us by his spiritual origin.[22] Promising to continue his sermon on the Passion the following Wednesday, the preacher ends with a doxology.

Leo begins the sixth sermon on the Passion by recalling very briefly the events about which he had spoken in the previous sermon.[23] Then he tells us that the Lord Christ was captured by the crowd in order that he might fulfill the divine plan; he limited his power and commanded Peter to abstain from the sword.[24] It was superfluous of him who could have commanded the heavenly hosts to want to be defended by a single disciple. Indeed, the power of him who was captured was greater than those who captured him. Christ took the way of suffering, that by his suffering all might be saved.

Now Leo turns to the trial of Jesus before Caiaphas.[25] Jesus was led before the high priest and false witnesses were brought forth, but Jesus chose to be silent. Then Caiaphas said, "'I adjure you by the living God, tell us if you are the Christ, the Son of God'" (Matt. 26:63). Jesus responded with such truth and prudence that, with the same words, he both blinded the unfaithful and confirmed the faithful.[26] Here our preacher quotes the words of Jesus from the Gospel of Matthew: "'But I tell you, hereafter you will see the Son of man seated at the right hand of Power, and coming on the clouds of heaven'" (Matt. 26:64). At this, Leo tells us, the high priest tore his robes, not realizing that by this act he deprived himself of priestly honor. For in the Law we read that the high-priestly vestments were not to be torn (cf. Lev. 21:10). In this act he

22. Leo, *Sermo LVI* 2.
23. Leo, *Sermo LVII* 1.
24. Leo, *Sermo LVII* 1.
25. Leo, *Sermo LVII* 2.
26. Leo, *Sermo LVII* 2.

demonstrated the end of the old Law, as the rending of the veil of the Temple would also soon show.[27]

Next the preacher takes up the trial of Jesus before Pilate. He comments on the hypocrisy of the Jews in insisting that Pilate execute him physically when the crowd, crying "Crucify him, crucify him," had already executed him with their tongues. Pilate sinned in doing what he did not wish, but the Jews sinned no less by making Pilate bend to their will.[28] The preacher now goes on to speak of the crucifixion. Christ was crucified on Golgotha, he says. He who fell beneath the weight of the wood was now lifted up on the same wood that he might draw all to himself. At some length the preacher speaks of how at the death of Christ all creation mourned. Leo concludes the sermon by exhorting the congregation to the practice of good works and faithfulness.[29]

For the feast of the Resurrection, only two sermons of Leo's have been preserved. Let us look at the first of these.[30] Our preacher begins by telling his congregation that they have participated in the cross of Christ through the celebration of the paschal mysteries. Surely they have found useful the long fast, the frequent prayers, and the generous alms. Having observed the forty-day fast, they are now made participants in the resurrection of Christ and pass from death to life while indeed still in this life. Through this experience the Christian is in a certain way changed by a sort of conversion, so that Christians are now what before they were not. As Christians, Leo tells us, we have died to what we were, and that dying is the cause of our now being alive with a new life.[31] One notices here the strong influence of the mystery religions. The Christian celebration of Passover has become the celebration of the Christian mysteries.[32]

Leo quotes from I Corinthians 15:47-49. He tells us that we should rejoice in this transformation which has come about because of the mercy of him who descended into this world that we might be raised up. The resurrection of Christ has changed both human nature and the human condition.[33] For Leo this transformation or conversion of man is of great

27. Leo, *Sermo LVII* 2.
28. Leo, *Sermo LVII* 3.
29. Leo, *Sermo LVII* 5.
30. Leo, *Sermo LXXI*.
31. Leo, *Sermo LXXI* 1.

32. See the careful and meticulous study of Dom Marie Bernard de Soos, *Le mystère liturgique d'après saint Léon le grand* (Münster im Westphalia: Aschendorff, 1958).

33. Leo, *Sermo LXXI* 2.

interest. He tells us that the resurrection of our Lord does not bring the end of human flesh but rather its transformation. Again we notice the doctrinal concerns of the Council of Chalcedon, for, Leo says, the resurrection appearances show us that the properties of the divine and human nature remain undivided in the risen Christ.[34] Its quality is changed but its nature is not done away with; the body which could be crucified has been transformed and is now impassible. What could be killed has become immortal, and what could be wounded has become incorruptible. This is our basis for the hope of eternal life. What happened in Christ is the pattern of what happens to us, and what we believe happened to him has already begun in us.[35] Again Leo ends his sermon with an exhortation: Let the people of God know that in Christ they are a new creation. Do not fall back into the vices from which you have been raised. The way of salvation is to imitate the resurrection which in Christ has already begun. The healing of the sickness of sin is long and difficult, but let us be swift in applying the remedy that we might rise in Christ.[36]

Two things stand out about this Easter sermon. On the one hand we cannot help but notice that it is quite different from the traditional types of Easter sermons which had developed up to that time. This sermon is not a passing on of the apostolic witness that the tomb was empty, nor is it a Christian interpretation of the Passover narrative. It is neither a sermon on the Holy Myrrhophores nor a *Christus Victor* sermon. It is rather a discussion of the theology of the resurrection in terms of the doctrinal concerns of the Council of Chalcedon. To be sure, the doctrinal point that Leo is able to clarify because of the discussions of Chalcedon is of the greatest importance, but one also notices that there is so much in the traditional proclamation of the resurrection which Leo does not get around to. In reading through the collection as it now exists, we go through all these sermons on the first Sunday in Lent and then all these sermons on the Passion, but Easter comes up rather short. There may be perfectly good explanations for this, but one cannot help but wonder if the basic problem might simply be that Easter had begun to lose its priority. Had the same thing happened to Easter that had happened to the Lord's Day? One cannot help but wonder, if Leo did not preach every Lord's Day but only at solemnities, whether the weekly celebration of the resurrection had

34. Leo, *Sermo LXXI* 3.
35. Leo, *Sermo LXXI* 4.
36. Leo, *Sermo LXXI* 6.

lost ground to the liturgical calendar. Even worse, in this liturgical calendar which was in the process of being hammered together at this very time, it would appear that the feasts were losing ground to the fasts.

B. The Predominance of a Penitential Approach to Worship

There is still more to say about Leo's sermons for Lent. The fact that we have twelve of these sermons as opposed to only two for Easter could perhaps be explained circumstantially. It seems more likely, however, that the sermons for Lent give us a look at the beginnings of an important development in the history of Christian worship. While Leo was accustomed to preach a single sermon on the observance of Lent at the beginning of the forty-day fast, the time would come when Lent would be regarded as the preaching season of the year. As we shall see, there were times in the history of the Church when the paucity of preaching at regular worship through most of the year would be supplemented by an annual Lenten preaching mission. In fact, in some places Lent would occasion the major devotional emphasis of the year. In this we find yet another instance where Leo's approach to the ministry of the Word has proven pivotal to the history of Christian worship. While Leo comes toward the end of the patristic period and, to be sure, certainly belongs to the patristic period, he nevertheless does point the way to the medieval period. This is even more true of Leo's successor, Gregory, but certainly in Leo's work we begin to find the first signs of the transition from the ancient Church to the medieval Church.

Lent has usually been explained as a period of forty days during which those preparing for baptism at Easter were instructed in the essentials of the faith and, along with the rest of the Church, observed a more intense discipline of prayer and fasting. That those preparing for the sacrament should submit themselves to the disciplines of repentance had been an essential dimension of baptism from the beginning. Repentance had been at the heart of the ministry of John the Baptist, and for the ancient Church the baptism of Jesus by John had been the prototype of Christian baptism. While the penitential disciplines of Lent had been directed primarily at catechumens it had been considered appropriate from earliest times that the whole Church join the catechumens in these disciplines. As early as the *Didache* this principle is clearly expressed. It was a way of supporting the catechumens in these disciplines and of extending to them the bond of fellowship.

411

It must have been about Leo's time that the baptism of adults in Rome became more and more infrequent and the baptism of infants became more regular. With this transition to infant baptism the penitential disciplines of Lent would have lost their significance had not the threat of barbarian invasion, at this same time, imbued them with new importance. After all, one could hardly ask infants to fast for forty days. On the other hand, Christians saw in the threat of barbarian invasion a reason to intensify their self-examination and the disciplines of penitential prayer. Surely the importance of penitential preaching in Leo's pulpit ministry is obvious; in fact, it is rather heavily weighted in that direction, which the troubled days in which he preached surely help explain. It was in these troubled days that the liturgical calendar began to develop and take its place as the primary principle for organizing worship. As the Dark Ages progressed, Lent soon became the most important liturgical season of all. From very early in its development the liturgical calendar was stamped with a penitential cast.

The connection between the preeminence of Lent in the liturgical calendar and the barbarian invasions is clear right from the introduction of the first of these Lenten sermons. Reading these penitential sermons, one finds no direct reference to these invasions, but one does not need very much imagination to read between the lines. In the first sermon for Lent Leo speaks about the combat of the Christian with spiritual enemies. Yet what he has to say seems even more appropriate in regard to the preparation of the Christian to meet those very real political enemies who were invading Italy at that moment:

> In former days, when the people of the Hebrews and all the tribes of Israel were oppressed for their scandalous sins by the grievous tyranny of the Philistines, in order that they might be able to overcome their enemies, as the sacred story declares, they restored their powers of mind and body by the injunction of a fast. For they understood that they had deserved that hard and wretched subjection for their neglect of God's commands, and evil ways, and that it was in vain to strive with arms unless they had first withstood their sin. Therefore abstaining from food and drink, they applied the discipline of strict correction to themselves, and in order to conquer their foes, first conquered the allurements of their palate in themselves. . . . And so we too, dearly beloved, who are set in the midst of many oppositions and conflicts, may be cured if only we will use the same means.[37]

37. Leo, *Sermo XXXIX* 1.

It is rather hard to miss the parallel between the tyranny of the Philistines and the invasions of the barbarians.

There is another fact that needs to be examined. In the course of one of his sermons Leo tells us that not only is Lent a time to prepare for one's baptism, it is also a time for those who have seriously failed in their Christian faith to be reconciled with the Church. Presumably he has in mind that those who had been excommunicated would be reconciled and admitted to Easter Communion, but he is also probably directing this toward those whose straying from the Church was not quite so obvious, not quite so objective. Such people may not have formally been excommunicated, but they, nevertheless, were aware of their failings and therefore approached Easter Communion in a spirit of repentance. But Leo's message encompasses even more than these. Leo calls to repentance every baptized Christian who has failed to be a perfect Christian to once again go through the disciplines of prebaptismal repentance. It is to such people primarily that Leo addresses his Lenten sermons. Those before his pulpit were for the most part serious Christians whom Leo wanted to call to repentance. They were not the unbaptized pagan or the notorious sinner but the faithful who were nevertheless in need of repentance. Like the revivals so popular in America a generation or two ago, one had to get saved all over again every year. Again and again we hear from these sermons that not even the best of us are so good but that we could not be better. Sin and repentance have been allowed to become cyclical.

For American Protestants accustomed to hearing frequent commentary on current events from our pulpits, it is surprising how rarely Leo's sermons refer to the troubling events of the time. Leo's sermons are not unique in this respect; they are representative of Christian antiquity. That the Fathers spoke of eternal things when they preached was in total accord with the idealism of classical culture, which worked against the discussion of current events in the pulpit. Unless a preacher had absorbed a strong dose of the prophetic spirit, as, for example, John Chrysostom had, he was not apt to become entangled in temporal issues. It is not that the Fathers were unaware of what was going on in the world — they were very much aware — it is that they saw in the events of the world around them the realities of eternity, and it was about these eternal realities that they spoke. Here is one of those places where the presuppositions of the Greek world and the Hebrew world were quite different. If Leo only occasionally mentions the troubles of his day, it certainly does not mean that he was blind to them or that they did not have a tremendous effect on the way he shaped the worship of the Roman

413

Church. What it does mean is that we should underline the few places he does mention it in red.

Closely connected with the idealism of Greco-Roman culture is Leo's cyclical approach to the ministry of the Word. While cataclysmic events such as Alaric's invasion of Italy or Genersic's siege of Rome may have occasioned particular sermons, such sermons, if preached, were not recorded. A cyclical approach to reading and preaching the Word was adopted because the troubled times nourished a predominance of penitential preaching in the cycle of the liturgical year. If a problem recurred constantly, it had to be worked into the cycle of eternal realities. Given Leo's predilection for understanding worship by means of the concepts of the Greek mysteries, one is hardly surprised that Leo moved in this direction.[38] The Greek mystery rites were frequently understood in terms of yearly cycles. Lent came around every year, and every year Leo preached essentially the same message, with the same Scripture lessons and the same auxiliary texts used to develop his sermon. This is in direct contrast to the prophetic approach, which is the proclamation of a very particular word for a very particular time. One has often noticed that Leo's sermons are redundant. He has a message for Christmas, a message for Lent, a message for Passion Sunday, and so forth. Even today redundancy is one of the problems of lectionary preaching, just as it was in fifth-century Rome. Leo was a good orator, but when preachers of lesser ability take this approach the repetition becomes monotonous. Alas, the age of Leo the Great was an age in which Christians began to conventionalize their worship. Their creative thrust was losing its strength and so to preserve it they canonized it. To put it in popular parlance, they canned their sermons just as they canned their prayers. Sad to say, canned sermons, no matter how good they once were, get sort of tiring after a while.

Yet another characteristic of Leo's Lenten preaching is his understanding of Christian asceticism. One cannot help but find in these sermons what might be called the gospel of asceticism. A passage such as the following comes to mind:

> But, beloved, in this opportunity for the virtues' exercise there are also other notable crowns, to be won by no dispersing abroad of granaries, by no disbursement of money, if wantonness is repelled, if drunken-

---

38. On Leo's understanding of worship as a Christian mystery, see the work of de Soos, *Le mystère liturgique d'après saint Léon le Grand.*

ness is abandoned, and the lusts of the flesh tamed by the laws of chastity: if hatreds pass into affection, if enmities be turned into peace, if meekness extinguishes wrath, if gentleness forgives wrongs, if in fine the conduct of master and of slaves is so well ordered that the rule of the one is milder, and the discipline of the other is more complete. It is by such observances then, dearly-beloved, that GOD's mercy will be gained, the charge of sin wiped out, and the adorable Easter festival devoutly kept.[39]

We find much the same point in another sermon:

Being therefore, dearly-beloved, fully instructed by these admonitions of ours, which we have often repeated in your ears in protest against abominable error, enter upon the holy days of Lent with godly devoutness, and prepare yourselves to win GOD's mercy by your own works of mercy. Quench your anger, wipe out enmities, cherish unity, and vie with one another in the offices of true humility. Rule your slaves and those who are put under you with fairness, let none of them be tortured by imprisonment or chains. Forego vengeance, forgive offences: exchange severity for gentleness, indignation for meekness, discord for peace. Let all men find us self-restrained, peaceable, kind: that our fastings may be acceptable to GOD. For in a word to Him we offer the sacrifice of true abstinence and true godliness, when we keep ourselves from all evil: the Almighty GOD helping us through all, to Whom with the Son and Holy Spirit belongs one Godhead and one Majesty, for ever and ever. Amen.[40]

It is this gospel of asceticism which is the whole basis of the celebration of Lent. As Leo understands it, the grace of God in Christ is the giving of an example of how we, too, may obtain salvation. As Christ was saved through suffering, so we can be saved through suffering. If we follow the example of Christ and resist the temptations of the devil, if we deny the appetites of the flesh as Christ did, then we, too, will be worthy of making the passover from this life to life eternal. To many of us this sounds at least mildly Pelagian. And it is this air of Pelagianism which makes Protestants very uncomfortable with Lent. Certainly one has to take seriously Leo's warnings about the desires of the flesh, and his encouragement of

---

39. Leo, *Sermo XL* 5.
40. Leo, *Sermo XLII* 1.

the yearnings of the spirit. Certainly one must listen most attentively to Leo's encouragements toward a simpler style of life, his appeal for alms, and his exhortations to works of mercy. All this is of the essence of Christianity. What bothers a Protestant is the idea that by faithfully keeping these Lenten disciplines we will be worthy of salvation.

The pivotal nature of Leo's ministry of reading and preaching the Word in the worship of the Christian Church is obvious, but whether we should rejoice or lament over the directions in which he pointed the ministry of the Word is a question we would do well to ponder. Given the times, perhaps he did as well as any human being could. Perhaps he did what he could with the options he was given. The question we need to ask is whether in our day the canonizing of the liturgy and the reintroduction of a liturgical calendar would be a true reform of the worship of American Protestantism.

II. Peter Chrysologus

The sermons of Peter Chrysologus (ca. 406-450) are best heard against the background of the mosaics of Ravenna. Some of the churches of Ravenna were built during his episcopate, and today one can still see the chapel of Peter Chrysologus in Ravenna's Archepiscopal Palace with its star-spangled mosaic ceiling. San Giovanni Evangelista was built by Princess Galla Placidia, the daughter of Theodosius and the regent mother of Valentinian III. She was a devout lady, having built the church in fulfillment of a vow, and the chances are that Peter Chrysologus preached at its dedication. She died during Peter Chrysologus's pastorate, and her tomb was decorated with one of the treasures of early Christian art. It was not more than two or three years after Peter's death that his successor, Neon, built the Baptistry of the Orthodox with its splendid mosaics. They cover the inside of the dome and portray the apostles clothed with senatorial authority. How majestically Roman they are! In the midst of these apostles, these very Roman apostles looking like the high officials of the emperor's household, we see the imperial throne, and on the imperial throne is the gospel. For fifteen years Peter Chrysologus expounded the gospel in Ravenna with such effectiveness that when his ministry was finished the church of Ravenna recognized the imperium of the gospel.

Ravenna had become the residence of the imperial family in 404 when Honorius, alarmed by the advances of Alaric in northern Italy, felt the need of retreating to a more easily defended location. Located on the marches along the Adriatic coast, protected by a network of canals and backed up to the sea, Ravenna offered an easy escape if all else failed. It was from this place that the Emperor Honorius and his sister Galla Placidia watched the sack of Rome in 410. They somehow knew the barbarians were not going to disappear back over the Alps. If only they could preserve a little of old Rome in Ravenna! And so they dug their canals and built up their city, their garrisons, their palaces, and their churches — a modest bit of late antiquity. It was to such a city that Peter Chrysologus preached, a city filled with soldiers, sailors, courtiers and bureaucrats, bricklayers, builders, and architects. Ravenna could hardly afford the pride of Rome. It was a realistic city which had settled for its role. Its soldiers had no illusions of invincibility; its architects knew they had to build with lots of brick and little marble; its bureaucrats scrambled to control the diminished revenues of a shrunken empire. The imperial court of Ravenna was no longer glorious and arrogant. It was realistic, practical, and often myopic.

Just when Peter, the fifth-century archbishop of Ravenna, was given the honorific "Chrysologus" is not clear. It is obviously an attempt to claim him as the Italian John Chrysostom. The large collection of sermons which come down to us appears to consist of sacred orations the collector regarded as stellar examples of sacred oratory. The literary critics of the Renaissance did not think highly of Peter Chrysologus because his Latin did not measure up to their canons of high Latin style. We see things a bit differently today, however; we are beginning to discover that his preaching often attained both power and eloquence.

One hundred sixty-eight sermons of Peter Chrysologus have been preserved for us.[41] For the most part they are sermons on the four Gospels as they were read in the regular worship of the church, on which Peter commented verse by verse.[42] Occasionally our preacher expanded one of

41. For the Latin text, see the edition of Alexander Olivar, *Sancti Petri Chrysologi, Collectio sermonum a Felice Episcopo parata sermonibus extravagantibus adjectis,* ed. Alexander Olivar, Corpus Christianorum, series Latina, vol. 24 (Turnholt, Belgium: Brepols, 1975). For an English translation, see Saint Peter Chrysologus, *Selected Sermons,* trans. George E. Ganss, S.J., The Fathers of the Church, vol. 17 (New York: Fathers of the Church, 1953). English translations are quoted from this edition.

42. For a very helpful study of the preaching of Peter Chrysologus, see Gottfried Böhmer, *Peter Chrysologus, Erzbishof von Ravenna, als Prediger* (Paderborn: Ferdinand

these readings into a short series, preaching on the same reading two, three, or even as many as five times. The parable of the prodigal son, for example, he preached on five times. First he preached on Luke 15:11-16, treating the younger son's departure; then Luke 15:17-19, the younger son's repentance; followed by Luke 15:20-24, God's mercy to the repentant; then Luke 15:25-30, the jealousy of the elder son; and finally he preached on the story as a whole, showing that it teaches us about the relation of the Jewish synagogue and the Gentile church. One gets the impression that the same lesson was read on five successive Sundays, but it could have been read on five successive days of the week as well. At any rate the preacher seems to have had the liberty to determine the length of the lessons as the Gospel was read through, and even to decide that a particular passage was to be read over again. We find three sermons each on the call of Matthew from Matthew 9:9-13 and the story of the woman who anointed the feet of Jesus while he was dining with the Pharisees (Luke 7:36-50).

These sermons as they have come down to us are all very short. If they were preached as they were recorded, they would have been no more than twenty minutes long. The chances are, however, that they have been condensed. We will find this increasingly as literary facility recedes during the Dark Ages.[43]

For the most part the sermons draw a moral lesson from the Gospel stories, although Peter frequently preaches first on what he calls the literal sense, drawing a moral teaching from the story, and then in a subsequent sermon he draws out what he calls the allegorical sense. However, what Peter calls allegory is often not allegory at all, but rather what today we would recognize as the theological intention of the author. And what he calls the literal sense is what today we would consider moralizing. For example, the first of his five sermons on the parable of the prodigal son

---

Schöningh, 1919). For more recent studies, see Basil Studer, "Peter Chrysologus," in *Patrology*, 4:575-77; Alexander Olivar, *Los sermones de san Petro Crisólogo* (Monserat, 1962); Alexander Olivar, "La duración de la predicación antigua," *Liturgica* 3 (Monserat, 1966): 143-84; Franco Sottocornola, *L'anno liturgico nei sermoni de Pietro Crisologo. Ricera storico-critica sulla liturgica de Ravenna antica* (Cesena: Centro studi e recerche sulla antica provincia ecclesiastica ravennate, 1973); M. Spinelli, "L'eco delle invasioni babariche nelle omelie di Pier Crisologo," *Vetera Christianorum* 16 (1979): 87-93.

43. There is some difference on the length of the sermon in the fourth and fifth centuries. On the relevance of Peter Chrysologus to this question, see Olivar, "La duración de la predicación antigua."

treats the foolishness of the younger son in leaving home; the second treats the repentance of the younger son; the third tells us of God's mercy to the repentant; the fourth is an admonition against jealousy; and finally in the fifth sermon our preacher takes up the theological question of how the Jew and the Gentile have reacted to the preaching of the gospel. One is tempted to remark that if it were not for these supposedly allegorical treatments of the Gospels, these sermons would seem rather moralistic. This may, however, be due to the concerns of the editor of the collection.

Among the sermons of Peter Chrysologus we find the fragments of a series based on a *lectio continua* of Paul's letter to the Romans. We find the following sermons:

> Sermon 111, Romans 5:12-14
> Sermon 112, Romans 5:15-21
> Sermon 113, Romans 6:1-14
> Sermon 114, Romans 6:15-21
> Sermon 115, Romans 7:1-6
> Sermon 116, Romans 7:7-12

Several of these sermons make quite explicit that the preacher is regularly preaching through the book of Romans as it is read in the course of the liturgy. Sermon 114, for example, begins with the following remark:

> A traveler always finds it sweet and pleasant to return to his own home. The courtyards of his ancestral house are attractive to him after an absence. Similarly, after these intervals, I find it sweet to return to my series of passages from the Apostle. Some necessity of religion often compels us to depart from the order of discourses which we had intended, and from the straight path which our discourse was to follow. For we must so control the sequence of our instruction that one matter does not hinder another. Wherefore, let us hear what the Holy Apostle has told us today.[44]

Several conclusions can be derived from these comments. In the first place, when our preacher again took up his series of sermons on Romans after a break of several weeks or so, he continued where he left off. The reading of the lessons in the service of worship was flexible enough to allow for

---

44. Chrysologus, *Sermon 114*, pp. 184-85.

interruptions. Second, the series of sermons was interrupted by sermons on other subjects which no doubt called for other Scripture lessons. We can only speculate about what might have come up that required the archbishop to depart from his usual course of lessons and sermons. Maybe he was out of town that week, or possibly he was interrupted by the Christmas or Easter season, but the text seems to imply something unexpected. What seems more likely is that his series was interrupted by some natural catastrophe; a serious drought, for example, might have suggested a series of penitential sermons, or some political situation might have demanded a special warning or admonition. We remember that John Chrysostom had interrupted his usual series of sermons to deliver his famous series on the desecration of the imperial statues.

The next sermon in the series likewise begins with some remarks about the relation of the liturgical lessons to the sermons:

> After we have soothed your minds and hearts by playing upon the Davidical harp with a plectrum of spiritual understanding and an accompaniment of rhythmical chant, and after we have expounded awesome principles of the resounding Gospel to quicken your powers of perception, we have thought that we should soon come back to the teaching of the Apostle. Thus, each section of our threefold division of the preaching of Christian doctrine can retain and impart its salutary instruction. For the chant relaxes your minds from constant effort, the authority of the Gospel refreshes them again and stirs them up to labor, and the Apostle's vigor does not permit your minds to be drawn off the direct road and to wander.[45]

From this passage it is quite clear that at least two sermons were preached in the service, perhaps even three. In addition to this sermon on the Epistle, there was clearly a sermon on the lesson from the Gospels for Peter tells us that we *expounded* the principles of the Gospel. Apparently there was also a sermon on the psalm which was chanted. "Playing upon the Davidical harp with a plectrum of spiritual understanding" is not a reference to musical accompaniment but to preaching. Besides that, according to the archbishop of Ravenna, there is a threefold division of Christian preaching: the preaching of the Epistles, the Psalms, and the Gospels. This certainly sounds as if the service of worship contained a reading from the Epistle, the chanting of a psalm, and the reading of a passage from the Gospel,

45. Chrysologus, *Sermon 115*, pp. 189-90.

each of which was followed by a sermon. In a previous chapter we called attention to the fact that the church of Jerusalem often had several sermons in the course of a single service. We also spoke of this in regard to Origen and Jerome.

Curiously, the passage seems to imply that both the psalm and the Gospel have been read and preached upon before this sermon on the Epistle. That is not the usual sequence of lessons as we find it fairly frequently at the beginning of the fifth century, the more usual sequence being Epistle, psalm, and Gospel. Why is this order changed? Perhaps the bishop had decided he wanted to preach on the apostle for long enough to get through his series and, as it was the long-established custom that the bishop preach last, he delivered his sermon on the Epistle after other presbyters had preached on the Gospel and the psalm. Or it could be that on a given occasion the bishop himself decided to preach on more than one of the lessons. In Sermon 120, on Romans 12:2-21, Peter implies that the reading and preaching of a passage from the Gospel is to follow the sermon on the Epistle.[46] This may indicate that he himself intended to preach on the Gospel passage as well. On most occasions, however, when the bishop preached on the Epistle, someone else preached on the Gospel beforehand. This seems to be the order followed when Sermons 115 and 116 were preached. In the latter we read, "Consequently, after the prophetical song and the astonishing miracles worked by Christ's powers, let us return to the series of readings from the Apostles."[47] A church of the size and importance of Ravenna no doubt had several presbyters who could preach and should have been given the opportunity to do so. We found this was the case in Jerusalem, and there is no reason why it could not have been the case elsewhere.

Normally the bishop preached on the Gospel, but there was no reason why he could not preach on the Epistle or even the psalm if he wished. It would appear, for instance, that Peter's Sermon 6 on Psalm 100 was preached quite appropriately during his series on the prodigal son.[48] That was his prerogative, just as it was his prerogative to decide where the lesson began and where it ended, or that a lesson could be read over again if he had yet another sermon to give on it. Without that prerogative, how can one interpret the Holy Scriptures? Peter's freedom in choosing his

---

46. Chrysologus, *Sermon 120*, p. 203.
47. Chrysologus, *Sermon 116*, p. 194.
48. Chrysologus, *Sermon 6*, p. 52.

lessons is rather striking, but we suspect he was not at all unique in this, for we found the same thing in regard to Augustine. The bishop, as pastor of the flock, had that kind of authority. Such an important part of the interpretation of Scripture is deciding what is needed for one's congregation at any particular time. Peter Chrysologus obviously understood this very well. He had a good sense of measure, appropriateness, and just plain good timing. Leo I, Peter's more famous contemporary, seems to have neglected expository preaching. Sad to relate, much of Leo's preaching was left to convention, but as we shall often see in the history of preaching, what Leo overlooked Peter provided. Rarely, it seems, does God anoint a single minister with all the gifts of ministry.

Let us look very briefly at Peter's festal sermons. In addition to the regular preaching through of the four Gospels and the apostles, that is, the Epistles and other New Testament books, Peter Chrysologus preached sermons for the major feast days and saints' days. We find sermons for the feast of the Annunciation, for the feast of the Nativity, and for the saints' days immediately following Christmas. There is a sermon for New Year's Day and several for the feast of the Epiphany, Passion Sunday, Easter, and Pentecost. Twelve sermons were delivered on the resurrection of Christ, which may indicate that our preacher was accustomed to preach on resurrection stories for some time after Easter. In addition to the saints' days connected with Christmas, we have sermons for the *dies natales* of the apostle Peter; John the Baptist; Apollonarius, the founder of the church of Ravenna; Cyprian; Andrew; Felicity; Lawrence; and Adelphius.[49]

Peter Chrysologus has left us a number of catechetical sermons — a set of seven sermons on the creed and a set of six on the Lord's Prayer. These sermons are clear and simple expositions of basic Christian teaching directed toward new converts to the Christian faith. The church of Ravenna, unlike the church of the city of Rome in this same period, was evidently accustomed to baptizing a large number of converts each Easter, a fact which is clear from both these sermons and from the large baptistry Peter's successor built. The preparing of the converts for baptism at Easter and the elaborate baptismal service demanded so much of the archbishop's time that he evidently suspended his usual preaching schedule to devote himself to his catechetical preaching.[50]

49. On the calendar of feasts used in Ravenna at the time of Peter Chrysologus, see Böhmer, *Peter Chrysologus*, pp. 36-43.
50. Chrysologus, *Sermon 74*, p. 123.

The sermons of Peter Chrysologus have been regarded very differently over the centuries.[51] We leave to others the evaluation of his oratory, but we must admit that his theology was not particularly profound. On the other hand, he may well have had a pulpit presence which gave weight and authority to his word; about this we can hardly judge since history provides no testimonies to his effect on his hearers. Be that as it may, we get the impression that he was a good, solid preacher with considerable pastoral sense. His sermons are a conscientious attempt to interpret the Scriptures and apply them to the lives of the men and women who came to worship in the church of Ravenna. If they do not have the mystical fire of a Bernard of Clairvaux or the evangelical fervor of a John Wesley, they do have pastoral warmth.

What has been overlooked in evaluating the sermons of Peter Chrysologus is how appropriate his message was to his congregation. His sermons show an awareness of the problems of his day which does not commonly appear in the sermons of the patristic period. His solid knowledge of Scripture makes it possible for him to speak the Word of God to the situation in a way that is prophetic. Peter was above all a pastoral preacher.

The strong pastoral bent of Peter's preaching is noticeable, for example, in the Christmas sermons which have come down to us. Sermon 149, on Luke 2:8-14, to which someone has given the title "The Birth of Christ and the Peace of Christians," speaks of the song of the angels proclaiming peace on earth. Peter tells us that Christ has brought peace to the earth. One almost wonders if the sermon were perhaps preached to celebrate a military victory over some barbarian tribe which had penetrated the Italian peninsula, but it probably was not. Our preacher often had to preach peace to his garrison, which was so precariously perched on the shores of the Adriatic. War was a constant threat in Ravenna. So many in his congregation were the soldiers and the wives and children of soldiers who would fall in those ultimately futile battles with the barbarians. On the feast of the holy innocents Peter preached against brutality — the brutality of Herod in putting so many innocent children to the sword. This is not a frontal attack on militarism but rather a portrayal of brutality that makes very clear that it is wrong. On the calends of January Peter preached against the pagan revelry with

---

51. Cf. Böhmer, *Peter Chrysologus,* pp. 30-35, for a survey of opinions on the preaching of Peter Chrysologus.

which the New Year had been celebrated. He decries the cruelty with which pagans worship Mars, and the sexual license with which they worship Venus. Those who participate in the pagan theater, with its obscenities, copy pagan practice with its beastomorphic gods; those who attend the gladiatorial contests with their brutal competitions do nothing but turn themselves into beasts. This is not an expository sermon although it refers most appropriately to the first chapter of Romans. No doubt the good bishop departed from his usual preaching schedule because of the need of the day. Paganism was far from dead in Christian Ravenna.

Once again in Sermon 156, which was preached for the feast of the Epiphany, he takes up his attack on lingering paganism, this time preaching against astrology. The wise men were not fatalistically moved through life by the motions of the stars when they discovered the Christ who is the Lord of the Stars. One notices that Peter Chrysologus, with his strong pastoral concerns, has clearly perceived what was no doubt the message of the original author in this story. Surely the story of the Magi was included in the Gospel of Matthew to make clear that the Christian faith was the true wisdom and Christ the true guide in life which the astrologers had hoped to find in the stars. For our preacher this was far from a theoretical point of exegesis. The popular religion of late antiquity had a strong dose of astrology in its mix, and a good pastor in those days had to make clear that the fatalism of the astrologers was inconsistent with the Christian doctrine of providence.

We have spoken of the preaching ministry of Peter Chrysologus at greater length than one might have expected. He deserves to be better known. It is generally admitted that he was not a particularly significant theologian, or even a distinguished ecclesiastical statesman, but he is a fine example of pastoral preaching. Peter has left us a rather large collection of sermons which shows us how a conscientious pastor read and preached the Scriptures in those difficult days. Peter Chrysologus was not a genius like Augustine, but he was a competent preacher and teacher who gave time and thought to the ministry of the Word. If there were other bishops in that day who exercised their ministry as conscientiously as he, and no doubt there were, we can understand why Christianity survived the catastrophes of the fifth century.

III. Gregory the Great

When the Dark Ages were at their darkest, Gregory the Great (ca. 540-604) was a man of exceeding brilliance. He was the evening star of the patristic age, the last of the Fathers of the Western Church. The son of an old senatorial family which had already placed two of its scions on the papal throne, Gregory was one of the last Romans to enjoy a classical education.[52] This meant, as it had meant for Ambrose before him, that he would have been schooled in the arts of language and public oratory. With his family background, it is not at all surprising that he entered the civil service. As a relatively young man he became prefect of Rome, which at that time meant that he was chief executive officer of the city. He had been in office about five years when his father died, and Gregory, being freed from family responsibilities, retired from the world. Benedictine monasticism was still in its initial flush of creativity when he entered the order. His beautiful home on the Monte Celio he turned into a monastery, and on the family estates in Sicily, which he evidently inherited, he established a number of monastic communities. Inspired by Saint Benedict, he organized these communities according to the Benedictine Rule. His first few years in the monastery must have been devoted to study, because it is clear from his sermons that somewhere along the line he had stored up a considerable reserve of biblical knowledge. Besides that, he often speaks of the importance of study and meditation on the Scriptures, and one would imagine from these passages that he himself loved to do exactly that.

Gregory's obvious gifts for administration could not long be left in retirement. He was soon made one of the seven deacons who administered the ecclesiastical affairs of the city. In 579 he was sent to Constantinople to represent the bishop of old Rome at the court of the emperor of new Rome. It was a rather difficult role to fulfill, for, although being quite polite about it, Constantinople found it convenient to ignore Rome. Gregory seems to have restricted himself to his house and to the company

---

52. For biographical information, see the following: Pierre Batiffol, *Saint Grégoire le Grand* (Paris: J. Gabalda, 1928); English translation *St. Gregory the Great*, trans. John Stoddard (New York: Benziger, 1929); Frederick Homes Dudden, *Gregory the Great: His Place in History and in Thought*, 2 vols. (London: Longmans, Green and Co., 1905); A. C. Rush, "Gregory I (The Great), Pope, St.," *New Catholic Encyclopaedia* (Washington, D.C.: Catholic University of America Press, 1967), 6:766-70; H. Schwank, *Gregor der Grosse als Prediger* (1934).

of the small monastic community he brought with him during this time. At any rate he never learned Greek. The Byzantine court was not too interested in hearing from him, and so again he must have spent the seven years he carried out this office in the study of the Scriptures. He regularly preached to his monks, and a summary of these sermons, his famous *Moralia on Job,* has come down to us. It is what one would expect — an interpretation of the book of Job in terms of the tradition of the old Roman moralists. It owes as much to Seneca, Cicero, and Marcus Aurelius as it does to the prophets and apostles. Gregory was, like the Roman moralists, a man of action who thought deeply. Those years in Constantinople must have been frustrating to him as he observed the futility of the political situation and meditated on the meaning of the gospel. As he himself often tells us, God usually calls us to contemplation before he calls us to preach.

Recalled to Rome in 586, he served as counselor to Pope Pelagius II. Four years later Pelagius died and Gregory was selected as his successor. His pontificate was rather short, from 590 to 604, but in that time he set the foundation stones of a new civilization that would last a thousand years. If Gregory was the evening star of the patristic age, he was also the morning star of the Middle Ages. One often regards Gregory as the founder of the papacy, and not without reason — he made very high claims for the authority of his office. But in a way it is good that he insisted on the authority of the Roman papacy; if he hadn't the politicians of the day would have swallowed the Church whole and turned all Christianity into the compliant chaplain of the state. But Gregory was far more than the architect of the papacy; he was a man who had a profound understanding of spiritual authority. He gave the West an appreciation of true leadership, both spiritual and terrestrial, both political and religious, and at the center of that was his deep understanding of the office of preacher.

The influence Gregory had on the Reformation is interesting. The papacy was one of the first things the Reformers attacked, but Gregory's preaching was considered exemplary; in fact, the preaching of the Reformers followed the example of Gregory, at some points, as much as Augustine or John Chrysostom. This is particularly true of Calvin, who regarded Gregory as one of the last exemplary pastors and preachers of the ancient Church. One cannot read very far into the works of Gregory without being delighted by his practical, profound wisdom. One does not often find the profound so practical, but that was the essence of Roman learning and the genius of Gregory. Gregory's works had been well preserved during the Middle Ages and were among the first to appear in printed editions.[53] The Reformers knew him well and deeply respected him, even if he was one of the principal architects of the papacy. They realized he was a great preacher, and for the Reformers that was more important.

Gregory has left us three major series of sermons, each of which comes from a different genre of preaching. We have a collection of forty sermons preached on the Gospels for Sundays and feast days which, although never completed, is probably an attempt at providing a cycle of festal sermons. We also have a series of expository sermons on the book of Ezekiel and the *Moralia on Job,* a good example of monastic catechetical preaching. This latter series comprised very informal discourses, relaxed and voluminous, given to a small group of friends and running to thirty-five books. We are told they were delivered to the monks who made up Gregory's household in Constantinople. Monastic catechism would develop into a major genre of Byzantine preaching, of which Theodore the Studite and Symeon the New Theologian, as we shall see, will be regarded as the masters. The sermons are a discussion of the Christian way of life as understood from the point of view of a monastic community. In fact, the theologians of the Middle Ages regarded it as the primary patristic treatise on Christian ethics. It is unfortunately clouded by an attitude of *contemptus mundi,* a disregard for the vanities of this life, but that was part of the times. It was, after all, the unshakable legacy of classical philosophy.

One of the most interesting things about the sermons on Job is Gregory's use of what has sometimes been called the "accommodated sense" of Scripture. It was not really that Gregory drew his ideas from the text of the Old Testament book of Job so much as that Job is the springboard which gets him into the subject he wants to discuss. Put in a more positive way, Job is the grain of sand around which our preacher secretes his pearl. Job serves as the example of the point Gregory wants to make. We will have more to say about the accommodated sense in regard to Gregory's sermons on Ezekiel. Yet, more than the sermons on Job, both the sermons on Ezekiel and the sermons on the Gospels are of interest to us for what they have to show us about preaching in general. We will center our attention, therefore, on these two collections of sermons.

53. See Hughes Oliphant Old, *The Patristic Roots of Reformed Worship* (Zurich: Theologischer Verlag, 1975), p. 167.

A. Sermons on the Roman Lectionary

A collection of forty of Gregory's sermons on the Gospels has been preserved.[54] Scholars are of the opinion that for the most part these sermons were preached in the year 593, that is, toward the beginning of his pontificate.[55] These sermons have a different character from the meandering sermons on Job, and, as we shall see, they are in marked contrast to the very profound sermons on Ezekiel. The sermons on the Gospels were preached to the crowds which gathered in the churches of Rome for the celebration of feast days. They tend to be markedly shorter than Gregory's other sermons and decidedly more popular in style. In his book on the pastoral office Gregory had emphasized the importance of suiting one's preaching to the audience, and in these sermons he is obviously aware that his audience is large and varied. It is for this reason, no doubt, that he limits himself to preaching on the Gospels rather than more difficult books such as Job and Ezekiel.

Generally, but not always, each sermon makes a few simple, clear points. In this these sermons are different from those on Ezekiel, which, following the text from verse to verse, treat as many subjects as the text might suggest. These sermons, on the other hand, are so lean that one is tempted to imagine that what we have is a draft of the sermons Gregory intended to preach. Indeed, some of them may have been taken down in abbreviated form by Gregory's stenographer. Gregory tells us in the preface, as well as in some of his sermons, that many were written out beforehand and read by one of his notaries rather than being preached by himself.[56] These sermons give the impression of being a distilled essence. The best of Latin authors prided themselves on a sort of Stoic brevity, and Gregory's style in these sermons is simple, sparse, and pungent. Also, the collection is apparently incomplete, for the order of the sermons sometimes appears haphazard and one gets the impression that not all of the pieces are finished. They are not so much a collection of exemplary sermons as a record of what Gregory preached during a particular year when he preached

---

54. For the Latin text, see Migne, *XL Homiliarum in evangelia libri duo*, in *Patrologia Latina* (Paris: Migne, 1853-66), vol. 76. References are to sermons as they are numbered in this edition. English translations are taken from Dom David Hurst's translation, Gregory the Great, *Forty Gospel Homilies* (Kalamazoo, Mich.: Cistercian Publications, 1990).

55. Dom Hurst would put them as early as 591-92. *Forty Gospel Homilies*, p. 1.

56. Gregory, *Homiliarum in evangelia* 21 and 22.

through the major solemnities of the liturgical calendar. The chances are that Gregory intended to provide a cycle of model sermons for the special occasions of the liturgical calendar. He, too, recognized the need of providing homiletical material for preachers who had not received the benefits of a literary education. He realized that in his day it was unrealistic to expect even bishops to obtain the sort of education required for serious preaching. The project, however, was never finished.

Gregory has a gift for oratory that is seen not only in his style but also in the literary form of his sermons. They are often beautiful examples of exposition. Unlike the panegyrics preached by Leo, these sermons are expository sermons in the tradition of the early Church. With only the briefest introduction or conclusion he gives us a running commentary on the text, going through six to a dozen verses, commenting on each verse as he goes. His major method of exposition is the classic approach of explaining Scripture by Scripture. He quotes supporting texts from other portions of the sacred writings and supplies us with a colorful array of biblical illustrations. Occasionally he makes use of current events or other kinds of illustrative material, but not often. Such illustrative material is not typical of his preaching, and one has to be a bit skeptical about the suggestion that the *exempla* so popular in the preaching of the late Middle Ages had their roots in the sermons of Gregory the Great. Gregory is much more apt to use biblical illustrations than stories drawn from other sources. Even more than his illustrative material, however, Gregory's ability to make a clear point is the fundamental strength of these sermons, and this is surely the greatest of literary gifts.

The Roman lectionary had grown vigorously from the time of Leo the Great to the time of Gregory the Great. The church calendar had become more elaborate. As a matter of habit one tended to use the same lessons one had used the year before as these new solemnities were worked into the calendar. The habitual lessons of the fourth century soon became the traditional lessons of the fifth century, and yet even by the end of the sixth century those traditions had not become so rigid that Gregory could not institute extensive changes in those traditions. We will say more about this further on.[57] The calendar of appointed lessons was still fairly fluid when Gregory began his work, with plenty of Sundays and special occasions for which there were no appointed lessons. In some cases Gregory

---

57. Cf. the chapter section on the Gregorian lectionary which will appear in the third volume of this work.

may have filled up these spaces in the liturgical calendar himself, but in other cases he had some precedents for his work. This very creative Christian leader understood himself as a definer of the tradition rather than as an innovator. Gregory's usage, however, was to set these traditions more solidly than they had ever been set before. In fact, in the popular imagination Gregory was to become the final authority on the liturgical traditions of the Roman Church. This was true generally, but it was particularly true for the lectionary, the calendar of appointed lessons.[58]

Gregory's festal sermons are found in several clusters gathered around the major Christian observances. The most important of these clusters is, as one would expect, Easter, which starts with the vigil on Holy Saturday and continues for eight days through the octave of Easter.[59] Several things stand out about Gregory's Easter sermons. First we notice an attempt to preach through the Easter narratives in all four Gospels. We remember that Augustine made a point of doing the same thing. To be sure, the six sermons that have come down to us do not cover all the narratives the Gospels provide. Some traditional sermons are missing. For this one can think of several explanations. First, one has to say that six sermons in one week is a rather impressive feat for any preacher, and second, Gregory was recovering from an illness during that particular year which had kept him out of the pulpit for some time, but just how much time we do not know.[60] In fact, on Easter morning he reentered the pulpit for the first time after his illness. This no doubt explains why the sermon on the appearance of Christ to the disciples on the road to Emmaus can best be described as short to the point of being perfunctory.[61]

One wonders the same thing about the absence of the sermon on the Easter Gospel from Matthew (Matt. 28:1-10). In studying the Easter sermons of Augustine we suggested that the absence of a sermon on the women discovering the empty tomb as it is recorded in the twenty-eighth chapter of Matthew may have been due to either practical considerations or the fact that the Easter vigil was beginning to atrophy. The lesson on the resurrection from Matthew was still read at the Easter vigil, but Gregory

---

58. As we have noted, the collection of festal sermons which has come down to us comes from early in Gregory's pontificate. These sermons do not always reflect the reforms he made later in his ministry.

59. Following the arrangement of the *Patrologia Latina*, this would include *Homiliarum in evangelia* 21, 22, 23, 24, 25, and 26.

60. Gregory, *Homiliarum in evangelia* 22.

61. Gregory, *Homiliarum in evangelia* 23.

did not preach on it. Since mostly children were being baptized rather than adult converts, this service was beginning to lose its centrality. It was no longer so important for the bishop to preach at the vigil, especially if he was not in very good health.

Something else we notice in these sermons is that two of the most traditional themes of Easter preaching have been tacked onto sermons on the resurrection narratives where they really do not belong. The sermon on the Christian understanding of Passover is added at the end of the sermon on John 20:1-9.[62] Having finished his explanation of the text of the Gospel which had been read, our preacher tells us that he would like to address the subject of the celebration of Easter as a whole. This is the greatest of feasts; it is the feast of feasts, the solemnity of solemnities. Having recovered from his illness, Gregory decides to make up for what he had earlier treated in such brief form or had missed entirely. He takes up I Corinthians 5:7, the famous verse which tells us that Christ our Passover has been sacrificed, then he explains the meaning of the Passover narrative from the twelfth chapter of Exodus. He goes over the institution of the feast as it is found in the Law of Moses, explaining each detail as it has been fulfilled in the death and resurrection of Christ. In Christ the Passover is fulfilled as he moved from this world to the Father. It is a way which we can follow, the prototype of our passage to heaven. Traditionally this was the message preached at the Easter vigil when the long series of the types of the resurrection was read. Here in this sermon, at last, is the Easter Gospel as it was proclaimed in the earliest Christian Church. It is the same message we found in the Easter sermon of Melito of Sardis, the oldest Easter sermon we have.

As we have often noticed, the *Christus Victor* theme had become a traditional theme of Easter preaching, and Gregory apparently feels it needs to be treated, although he somewhat artificially introduces it into his exposition of Mark 16:1-7.[63] The more logical place for this theme is in the sermon on the exposition of the story of the empty tomb in Matthew 28, but regrettably, as noted above, this collection does not have a sermon on this passage. Again, this rearrangement may have been due to our preacher's health in that particular year. However one is to explain some of the peculiarities of Gregory's six Easter sermons for the year 593, one thing is clear: He obviously intends to preach through all of the resurrection narratives as they are found in the four Gospels.

62. Gregory, *Homiliarum in evangelia* 22.
63. Gregory, *Homiliarum in evangelia* 21.

For Gregory, as for Augustine, the major attention given to proclaiming the gospel of the resurrection is striking. For a full week this message is drawn out. It is apparently understood as the central core of the preaching ministry of the Christian Church; indeed, this is the essence of preaching. If nothing else is preached, this must be. It is the passing on of the witness of the apostles, and as long as the ministry does this, it is truly the apostolic ministry.

Gregory celebrated Ascension and Pentecost by preaching sermons on the Scripture lessons which had already become traditional for those two feasts.[64] The sermon for the feast of the Ascension takes as its Scripture lesson the long ending of the Gospel of Mark, which Gregory treats as the last of the resurrection narratives. The ascension is the final evidence of the resurrection. The Christ who rose from the dead and ascended into heaven was a true human being of flesh and blood as well as being truly God, the Son of the Father. Following the long ending of Mark (Mark 16:14), our preacher makes the point that it was while Jesus was eating with the disciples that he was lifted up. From this the reality of his body was evident.[65] The sermon goes on to speak of the Great Commission, making the point that although we are saved by faith we have the responsibility to do the works our Savior has commanded us to do. Of special interest for Gregory are the Old Testament types of the ascension, among which he reckons both the translation of Enoch and the ascent of Elijah in his fiery chariot. Unlike the types, the ascension of Jesus was not assisted by angels, for Jesus had divine power in himself.[66]

The sermon for Pentecost is first an exposition of the lesson from the Gospel, John 14:23-27, and second an exposition of a passage read from the Acts of the Apostles, the traditional story of Pentecost.[67] The point Gregory wants to make is that when the Holy Spirit came upon the disciples, they were completely transformed. Their hearts were set on fire; gently the love of God enflamed them. God is love, as John so often tells us. When the Holy Spirit comes upon us, he unites us to God in that same love which unites the Father to the Son. Pentecost is the celebration of God's coming to us to be a guest in our hearts.[68]

---

64. Gregory, *Homiliarum in evangelia* 29 and 30.
65. Gregory, *Homiliarum in evangelia* 29.
66. Gregory, *Homiliarum in evangelia* 29.
67. Gregory, *Homiliarum in evangelia* 30.
68. Gregory, *Homiliarum in evangelia* 30.

If Gregory had not been ill that year, these sermons from Easter to Pentecost would no doubt have been quite exemplary. What this collection offers for Lent and Holy Week is another matter, however. There are no sermons for Holy Week. One's first reaction is to explain this by his illness; after all, he mentions this at the beginning of his Easter sermon.[69] But he also explains elsewhere that his notaries sometimes read sermons he had written. Why had this not been done during Holy Week? We can only guess. Perhaps he was too ill even to dictate. We would certainly want to believe that Gregory normally did preach on the Passion during Holy Week. But if we are to go by the collection of sermons which has come down to us, it would appear that Gregory did not preach at all during Holy Week, nor did he supply his notaries with sermons they could read for him. Be that as it may, one thing is clear from the lectionaries: During Holy Week the whole of the Passion narrative was read from each of the four Gospels.[70] Matthew was read on the Sunday before Easter, Mark on Tuesday, Luke on Wednesday, and John on Friday. Reading through the Passion narrative in any one of the Gospels would take a good amount of time. Could it be that preaching was eliminated to make room for more extensive Scripture readings? This, it seems to me, is a definite possibility. In Gregory's day the public reading of the Scriptures occupied a much more important place than it does today because for most people hearing the Bible read at church was the way they were most apt to become familiar with it. The number of people who had their own Bibles and could read them privately was limited. The public reading of the whole of the Passion narrative was, therefore, an important feature of the celebration of Christ's saving work. As we have seen, this was an important consideration in the celebration of Holy Week in Christian Jerusalem. If this is indeed the case, Gregory may not have been responsible for the fact that there are no sermons for Holy Week. Gregory did not like to be an innovator. He may simply have been following the practice of his predecessors.[71]

What Gregory has left us for Lent is a bit troubling, at least for an American Protestant, for he seems to be preaching the gospel of asceticism.

---

69. Gregory, *Homiliarum in evangelia* 21.

70. Stephan Beissel, *Entstehung der Perikopen des römischen Messbuches* (Rome: Herder, 1967), pp. 62-63.

71. If Gregory had been following a precedent, it would not have been a precedent of long standing. As we showed in our study of Leo I, Leo preached twice on the Passion narrative during Holy Week.

In the sermons of Gregory that have come down to us, for the first and fifth Sundays,[72] he more or less follows Leo in his Lenten emphasis. By this time it was a well-established custom that on the first Sunday of Lent the story of the forty days of temptation in the wilderness was read and the congregation was urged to maintain the Lenten fast. In fact, the six weeks of Lent were generally understood as a time for calling people to repentance. In sixth-century Rome the people had been largely converted and baptism was administered to infants without catechetical preaching; thus the preparing of candidates for baptism was no longer a major concern of the Church. Lent, therefore, changed its character and became a time devoted to penitential devotions for those who were already baptized. These penitential devotions tended to be strongly ascetic, and fasting was the most important one. This was made clear by reading the Gospel about the forty-day fast of Jesus. While fasting was central to the observance, other forms of mortification were practiced as well. At one point Gregory tells his congregation, "We . . . try every year during Lent to afflict our bodies by fasting."[73] A bit further on in the same sermon we read, "Let each one, as far as his strength allows, vex his body and afflict his desires. Let each one put to death his base desires, so that, in the words of Paul, he may become a living sacrificial victim. . . . A pleasure-loving body had drawn us to sin; let an afflicted one bring us to pardon. The author of our death broke the commandments by eating the fruit of the forbidden tree of life. Let us who have fallen away from the joys of paradise through food, rise up to them again, so much as we can, through fasting."[74]

In fact, asceticism became more and more common as the Christian approach to repentance. Doing penance was looked on as the way to repent. One does not get the impression that Gregory was particularly responsible for this unhappy development. It was just part of the age. As we mentioned above in regard to Leo, the gospel of asceticism won a big following in those days. It was more than natural that the Dark Ages should be particularly given to penance, being constantly wracked with the ravages of war as it was, with one barbarian tribe after another pillaging its way through the land. Life became short and painful, and many Christians presented the disciplines of penance as the best way of escape.

Gregory's remarks are typical of his age. Because this world was

---

72. Gregory, *Homiliarum in evangelia* 16 and 17.
73. Gregory, *Homiliarum in evangelia* 16; Hurst, *Forty Gospel Homilies*, p. 104.
74. Gregory, *Homiliarum in evangelia* 16; Hurst, *Forty Gospel Homilies*, p. 105.

passing away, it seemed so much better to turn away from it and embrace the world to come. In a sermon for the fifth Sunday in Lent Gregory admonishes us to desire the world to come which is our true heavenly home, to deny our physical desires, our worldly pleasures, and the glories of this world. It is in the world to come that we will find our happiness.[75]

Much of this is true, of course. Surely there is something of the Christian message here, and denying the world has its place in the Christian life. As Christians we are not to conform to the world. But more than that, as Christians we are to be transformed and live in this world as God intended us to live in it (Rom. 12:1-2). Penance as we find it preached in the Dark Ages all too often emphasized the condemnation of the world rather than its redemption.

In Gregory's Lenten sermons one misses a solid preaching of the cross. While Gregory guards against the extremes of Pelagianism, there is certainly a Pelagian drift to his message. This, too, was part of the age in which he lived. The Christianity of late antiquity was still influenced by a strong current of Neoplatonism, which tended to encourage the denial of the material world, and in the development of Lent both Neoplatonism and Pelagianism came to full expression. The message of Lent, even today, is Pelagian through and through. In fact, Pelagius is somewhat symptomatic of the way much of Christian spirituality developed when the barbarian invasions began to threaten the Roman world. Pelagius was a British Christian who left the British Isles for Rome when the Romans withdrew and the Anglo-Saxons began their invasion, and when the barbarians threatened Rome he moved on to North Africa. His asceticism was a way of fleeing a world doomed to destruction.

With Gregory's sermons for Advent we have a more complete picture of how Gregory preached the season, for, unlike the picture we have of Easter and Holy Week, obscured as it is by missing sermons, here we have the full set. Advent was just beginning to take its place in the liturgical calendar when Gregory began his pontificate. Sad to relate, it was in the spirit of this same prevailing penitential mood that this season also developed. Gregory has left us one sermon on the coming of the end of the world and three on the penitential ministry of John the Baptist to be preached on the Sundays of Advent.[76] Why, one wonders, are there no sermons on the messianic hope as we find it in the Old Testament prophets

---

75. Gregory, *Homiliarum in evangelia* 17.
76. Gregory, *Homiliarum in evangelia* 1, 6, 7, and 20.

or on the annunciation as we find it in Luke, but three on John the Baptist? The collection which has come down to us gives us a sermon on Luke 21:25-33, intended for the first Sunday in Advent.[77] This passage tells of the signs of the end of the world: earthquakes, wars, pestilence, the darkening of the sun and the moon. When Christians see these signs, our preacher tells us, we are to rejoice that our redemption is near. Christ will soon return. Our preacher elaborates the lesson by speaking of its context, not only in the Gospel of Luke but in the other Gospels as well. Similar apocalyptic sayings of Jesus are found from the other Gospels. Not surprisingly Gregory is able to speak of the catastrophes of his age by way of illustration. War seems to have choked the life out of that generation. One need only read the books of history, Gregory tells his congregation, to learn that it was not always so. Just the day before yesterday, he says, we heard of a whole city, right here in Italy, destroyed by a mighty wind.[78] By such events the Christian should be warned not to love the world or the things of this world, for they will all pass away. The judge of the world is coming, and those who are wise will take warning and live godly lives that when the world is destroyed they be not destroyed with it. Here again we cannot help but read between the lines. The current events of the sixth century have, not surprisingly, shaped Gregory's perception of the gospel.

Let us look at another of Gregory's Advent sermons. This one interprets the ministry of John the Baptist as it is found in John 1:19-27.[79] The purpose of his ministry, as Gregory interprets it, was to call Israel to repentance. Repentance is the way we prepare for the coming of Christ. Those who are spiritually proud can never receive the blessing of God. John the Baptist was the consummate example of the humility we must have if we are to be blessed by the coming of Christ. Everyone in Gregory's congregation well understood humility because Rome had been so thoroughly humiliated in the sixth century, but in that very fact there was hope. As Gregory sees it, humility is the only way for a Christian to meet an impossible situation, for to embrace humility is to cast one's hope completely on God. The beauty of Gregory's message is his fearless affirmation of the transcendent. Here was a very practical politician who understood the abiding value of the things of God. This is certainly true enough, but one wonders if the Church of the sixth century did not

77. Gregory, *Homiliarum in evangelia* 1.
78. Gregory, *Homiliarum in evangelia* 1.
79. Gregory, *Homiliarum in evangelia* 7.

imagine that if the people of Italy could just be humble enough, the course of history might change. If people would just do more penance, then a new society might be born. One sometimes wonders to what extent fasting and other ascetic practices are an attempt to twist God's arm, as it were.

Explain it as you will, for the next thousand years asceticism would become the essence of being religious and the church calendar would become a fasting schedule. Advent and Lent would become the religious seasons of the year and the weekly celebrations of the Lord's Day would no longer set the tone of Christian worship.

B. Sermons on Ezekiel

With Gregory's sermons on Ezekiel we have a magnificent example of expository preaching.[80] The sermons were preached daily,[81] just as the sermons on Job were, with one difference: While the sermons on Job were preached to a small group of monks, the sermons on Ezekiel were preached *ad populum,* to the whole congregation. It was, no doubt, not as large a congregation as the one that gathered on Sunday morning. The preacher clearly assumes a congregation of more committed Christians than he assumes on Sunday morning, but it is not a congregation made up only of trained theologians or the professionally religious. This is preaching which is aimed at the faithful, but which is at the same time a thorough and careful exposition of Scripture. Apparently Gregory did such expository preaching fairly regularly on weekday mornings.

These sermons were published because years later there were those who remembered that they were among his best efforts, so Gregory, finding that the notaries had taken them down, reworked them and had them published. We might not even bother trying to study them had our preacher not engaged two topics in them that are of the greatest possible interest. In the first place they were preached to address a most difficult crisis: The Lombards had invaded Italy and were marching toward Rome.

---

80. This study is based on Gregory the Great, *Homiliae in Hiezechihelem prophetam,* ed. Marcus Adriaen, Corpus Christianorum, series Latina, vol. 142 (Turnholt, Belgium: Brepols, 1971); Gregory the Great, *Homélies sur Ézéchiel,* Latin text with French translation, notes, and introduction by Charles Morel, S.J., Sources chrétiennes, vols. 327 and 360 (Paris: Les Éditions du Cerf, 1986; hereinafter Gregory, *In Hiezechihelem.*

81. The fact that these sermons were preached daily is clear from Gregory, *In Hiezechihelem* 5.1.

In the second place, but perhaps even more importantly, these sermons, especially the first twelve, are in fact a treatise on the preaching ministry. For our purposes this is of paramount interest. The first twelve sermons follow a *lectio continua* of the prophet Ezekiel up to chapter 4, and then, with the Lombards at the gates of the Eternal City, suddenly Gregory jumps to chapter 40, in which the prophet tells of the heavenly Jerusalem. It is not exactly the sort of homiletical tack we would consider relevant, but we would do well to look at it nevertheless.

Half the genius of great *lectio continua* preaching is selecting the right book or portion of a book at the right time. There is, to be sure, a parallel between the days of Ezekiel and the days of Gregory. In the days of Ezekiel a military power came down upon Jerusalem from the north as punishment to a worldly and apostate religious establishment, and yet God sent Israel, through the prophetic ministry of Ezekiel, a vision of the transcendent kingdom which by the grace of God was coming. It was that which Gregory heard as the Word of God for his time, the promise of transcendent heavenly order, which was not of this world but of God, a kingdom which was not of the power of this world but of grace.

The beautiful thing about this series of sermons is that the basic exegetical structure is a grammatical-historical understanding of the text. Gregory understood well that what Ezekiel had preached was hope in the face of a barbarian invasion and the promise of a transcendent kingdom. Gregory realized the importance of preaching repentance to his generation, but even more he perceived the urgency of proclaiming the promises of the heavenly Jerusalem. In an age in which the old stabilities of the Roman world had all but disappeared, Gregory perceived the urgency of giving that age a vision of a transcendent order which was eternal. Rome, which one liked to think of as the eternal city, had fallen before, and it was about to fall again, just as Jerusalem had in the days of Ezekiel, but there was a transcendent reality behind the earthly Rome just as there was behind the earthly Jerusalem, and that reality is not only established but also nourished by the preaching of the Word. These sermons on Ezekiel are great preaching because at a time when the world was falling apart Gregory gave hope to the people of God by assuring them that there is indeed a transcendent reality which is not falling apart, which never has and never will. Gregory's greatest contribution was to assure an age that was at the edge of chaos that there is an ultimate order.

Gregory's emphasis on contemplation explains why so often his interpretations of Scripture seem to be based not so much on either the literal sense or the spiritual sense of Scripture but on what is sometimes called the accommodated sense. By the accommodated sense one usually means the use of a biblical text to support a traditional teaching of the Church, even if that is not what the text originally meant. It is not the same as allegorizing the text; that is something quite different. The accommodated sense depends on some sort of analogy between the text and the tradition. The analogy may rest on vocabulary or grammar. For example, in discussing the time it took God to create the world one often quotes the verse from Psalm 90, "For a thousand years in thy sight / are but as yesterday . . ." (Ps. 90:4). The original intention of the psalmist was not to speak about how long it took God to create the world, although the psalmist does say something about the relation of our time to God's time. This line from the psalm certainly suggests something about the matter under discussion. One can accommodate the one to the other quite justifiably, but the literal meaning of the verse from the psalm does not really speak to the problem of how long it took God to create the world. Gregory's sermons on Job make wide use of the accommodated sense of the text "For I know that my redeemer liveth. . . ." This text does not teach the Christian doctrine of the resurrection, although for centuries Christians have accommodated it to the traditional teaching.

While the overall interpretation of Ezekiel which is fundamental to this series of sermons is all quite literal, a good number of the details are not. One of Gregory's important uses of the accommodated sense is his interpretation of the four living creatures which figure so prominently in the first chapter of Ezekiel. Ezekiel 1 is infamous for its obscurity, so obscure in fact that in certain Jewish circles it was forbidden to preach on it or even read it in public. To make any sense of Ezekiel's introductory vision is quite a challenge, and Gregory really does an amazing job of cutting through the difficulties (which we will explore momentarily). These four living creatures are found elsewhere in Scripture, and there have been other attempts to interpret them. Christians have commonly understood them to signify the four Gospels, but it is not likely that the prophet understood them that way. On the other hand, this accommodation which is perhaps already found in the Revelation has a long tradition behind it and does seem to make sense and communicate (Rev. 4:6-9). Gregory uses the accommodated sense of Scripture very often. We will see this frequently in the Middle Ages where the contemplation of Scripture is emphasized even if the biblical scholars of the time did not have the best tools of exegesis.

Another beautiful thing about these sermons is the way they witness to the importance of holiness in the ministry of the Word. Gregory, like

Origen or Basil or John Chrysostom, had a tremendous sensitivity to holiness. Surely this is one of the reasons he chose to preach on Ezekiel in those dark days, as an important part of Ezekiel's message was his vision of holiness. The holiness of God is an eternal reality; it is a glory that never fades, and even when the grandeurs of antiquity became very dim the holiness of God could be reflected by his preachers and thereby give light to the faithful. Preachers had to be holy, as Gregory saw it. They had to be set apart to the Lord. They had to demonstrate what they said. When holy preachers proclaimed the Word of God to a holy Church, then God was glorified.

The first twelve of Gregory's sermons on Ezekiel constitute a treatise on the preaching of the Word of God. Gregory seems to have had a preference for the word "preaching," or *praedicatio* in Latin. For him preaching was a cardinal component of Christian worship. The word *praedicatio* as Gregory uses it has a dynamic quality; it means setting forth the Word of God. The Latin verb *praedicare* has a very positive sense to it; it means to declare publicly, to speak out, or to proclaim, and it can mean to praise or to commend. *Praedicare* is the perfect word to speak of that part of the service of worship where the Church praises God by proclaiming his mighty acts for our salvation. By this time *praedicare* had not yet become a technical term for a specific liturgical act. In his *Regula pastoralis* Gregory gives much attention to the place of preaching in the pastoral ministry, but in actual fact what he says in these twelve sermons is considerably more interesting than what he says in that work. It is in these sermons that Gregory becomes the classic theologian of the proclamation of the Word. This is the case not only for preaching considered in relation to a total theology of the Word of God, but also for preaching considered in relation to the service of worship.

C. Theology of the Word

We might organize Gregory's thoughts on the theology of the Word of God around three main themes: the authority of the Word of God, the graciousness of the Word of God, and the inspiration of the Word of God.

1. The Authority of the Word of God

Gregory makes a major point of the fact that it was God who called Ezekiel and gave him a very specific word for a very specific time and place. The prophet had authority because God had sent him, and even more because the word he had been given to preach was God's Word. It is quite obvious that for Gregory the significant point is that it is above all God's Word which has authority and that it has authority, to be exact, because it is God's Word. Commenting on Ezekiel 2:4, "'I send you to them; and you shall say to them, "Thus says the Lord God,"'" Gregory says:

> But notice that authority is conferred on the person of the prophet when he adds: "And you shall say to them, 'Thus says the Lord God'"; quite obviously what is being said is, that because you of yourself would be despised it is necessary that you speak with my voice, and lest you be condemned, you who have been sent, hold forth my Word thereby showing who it was who sent you.[82]

To be sure, the person of the preacher has authority so that the work can be done, but that authority is granted for the sake of the Word to be preached. This is made very clear a bit further on in the same sermon where he comments on verse 6: "'And you Son of man be not afraid of them, nor afraid of their words, though briars and thorns be with you and you sit upon scorpions. . . .'" It is "lest the prophet fear" that he is given the authority of preaching. And yet all of us who live in God are instruments of the truth. As Gregory sees it, the ministry of the Word is a ministry of the whole Christian community. Often through others the truth is given to us and often for others the truth is spoken by us, for so it ought to be since the authority of a good word is inherent in that word. It is important, however, that when the truth is spoken, it be spoken with humility.[83] That the authority of the word is inherent in that word is a fundamental principle of the Christian doctrine of revelation. An important turn in Gregory's thought at this point shows the depth of his

---

82. "Sed ecce auctoritas personae tribuitur, cum subditur: *Et dices ad eos: Haec dicit Dominus Deus.* Ac si aperte diceretur: Quia ex te despicieris, ex mea uoce necesse est ut loquaris. Ne contemnaris ipse qui mitteris; uerba mea proferens, ostende qui misit." Gregory, *In Hiezechihelem* 9.7.

83. "*Tu ergo, fili hominis, ne timeas eos, neque sermones eorum metuas, quoniam increduli et subuersores sunt tecum, et cum scorpionibus habitas.* . . . *Ne timeas,* prophetae datur auctoritas praedicationis. Et quia omnes qui in Deo uiuimus organa ueritatis sumus, ut saepe per alium mihi, saepe uero aliis loquatur per me, sic nobis boni uerbi inesse auctoritas debet, ut et is qui praeest dicat recta libere, et is qui subest inferre bona humiliter non reject. Bonum enim quod maiori a minore dicitur tunc uere bonum est, si humiliter dicatur." Gregory, *In Hiezechihelem* 9.12.

understanding of the whole question of authority. It is when the preacher witnesses to the authority in humility that the preacher witnesses most clearly to the divine authority of the message.[84]

Gregory understood that Ezekiel was called by God to preach a very specific word, a Word which God himself gave Ezekiel. For Gregory this was a clear indication of the authority of that Word. All this Gregory read quite simply from the opening chapters of Ezekiel, but Gregory finds something else in these opening chapters which speaks to him about the authority of the Word. This enigmatic vision which Ezekiel saw with its four living creatures darting to and fro, with its wheels turning in every direction all filled with eyes, its sparks and flashes of lightning, is a vision of the preaching of the Word. It is first of all a vision of Christ and yet at the same time a vision of the four Evangelists, and again a vision of the preachers of the Word, and finally a vision of all the elect as they hold forth the Word of God by living according to that Word. While all the elect may not speak forth the Word, they do hold it forth. That the four living creatures are the four Evangelists was for Gregory and those to whom he preached the most obvious sense of the vision of Ezekiel. This was a tradition of interpretation which was well established by that time.[85]

In the second sermon of the series Gregory develops this traditional interpretation by suggesting that these four Evangelists are the prototypes of all preachers of the gospel. In the fourth sermon Gregory takes another step in his interpretation of the vision by suggesting that Christ is the prototype of the four Evangelists on one hand and, on the other, that all the elect are signified by the vision because in living the gospel they hold it forth, they witness to it. All the elect participate in the ministry of the Word. As Gregory understands it then, this vision speaks of four distinct aspects of the proclamation of the Word. First it speaks of Christ, who is the Word who was in the beginning with God, who indeed is God. Second it represents the Evangelists, that is, the original writers of Scripture. Third it tells of preachers, and fourth it has to do with the faithful to whom the Word is preached and who live that Word.[86] All together are involved in the service of the Word.

This Word has authority because this is what Christ was all about. He is the Word of God, the Truth in and of himself. He is the Word, the

---

84. Gregory, *In Hiezechihelem* 9.12.
85. Gregory, *In Hiezechihelem* 2.15.
86. Gregory, *In Hiezechihelem* 4.1.

revelation of the redemptive love of God. It is about him that the Evangelists wrote and preachers ever since have preached. It is this Word which the believers have believed and in this believing have glorified God. This Word has authority because ultimately this Word is the Son of God, God of God, Light of Light, Very God of Very God. Ezekiel's vision of the Word made it clear, at least as Gregory understood it, that behind the preaching of the Word was the authority of Christ himself.

Further, the preaching of the Word has authority because the preachers move as they are directed by the Holy Spirit. What this means is that true preaching is the work of the Spirit. The preachers have been breathed into by the Holy Breath. That breath is the breath of life, according to Ezekiel, the breath which gives life to the valley of dry bones. This valley of the dry bones is one of the central images found in the prophecies of Ezekiel and is elaborated in its full form in the thirty-seventh chapter. It is one of the classic passages from which the doctrine of the Holy Spirit has developed. One might even go so far as to say that Ezekiel is the prophet of the Holy Spirit, so clearly is the doctrine of the Holy Spirit central to his message. Gregory understands this and makes it equally important in the doctrine of the Word of God. As Gregory puts it in the second sermon:

> It is not the prophet but the Holy Spirit who speaks through the prophet. Truly the prophets speak for the Holy Spirit, because it is through the prophets that the Holy Spirit makes the discourse. The prophets speak concerning him and for him because by the inspiration of the Holy Spirit they speak.[87]

That the prophets, the Evangelists, or the preachers of the Gospel are filled with the Holy Spirit and speak at the bidding of the Holy Spirit is clear at a number of points in this series.[88] The preaching of the gospel has authority because it is the work of the Holy Spirit in and through the Church.

---

87. "Sed sciendum est quia hi qui prophetiae spiritu replentur, per hoc quod aperte nonnumquam loquuntur de se, et nonnumquam sic de se uerba tamquam de aliis proferunt, indicant quia non propheta, sed Spiritus sanctus loquitur per prophetam. Pro eo enim quod per ipsos sermo fit, ipsi loquuntur de se, et pro eo quod aspirante sancto Spiritu loquuntur, idem Spiritus sanctus per ipsos loquitur de ipsis, Veritate attestante quae dicit: *Non enim uos estis qui loquimini, sed Spiritus Patris uestri qui loquitur in uobis.*" Gregory, *In Hiezechihelem* 2.8.

88. Gregory, *In Hiezechihelem* 1.16, 3.19, 5.2, and 10.25-26.

2. *The Graciousness of the Word of God*

Let us turn now to another dimension of Gregory's theology of the Word. The preaching of the Word of God is an act of grace. It is a miracle divinely wrought, a wondrous work of God. We could formulate Gregory's perception in a number of different ways, but the heart of it is this strong bond between grace and revelation. Revelation is gracious from beginning to end. The Word is a saving grace, and it is through his Word that God brings about our salvation. This is perhaps the most prominent dimension of Gregory's theology of the Word of God: The Word of God is an act of grace. Let us look at several passages where this idea comes out with particular clarity.

In the third sermon there is a striking passage in which Gregory tells us that the word of preaching is seed in the heart of the hearer. And a good hearer bears from that seed a great harvest of knowledge, although he received it at first as the small seed of the tongue. To illustrate this point Gregory recalls the story of the miracle performed by the prophet Elisha. A certain widow, lest her two sons be claimed by her creditor, obeyed the word of the prophet and from her small supply of oil filled all the empty jars she could find, filling them up even to the last one. Selling this oil, she was able to satisfy the debt she owed to her creditor.[89] Gregory asks his congregation, Who might be signified by this woman other than the Church? It is she who is mother of two people, the Jews and the Gentiles. She first through perversion accepted something from the creditor, and she feared that the two sons born of faith would have to be sent away. But obeying the words of the prophet, that is, the precepts of Holy Scripture, from the little oil that she had she filled the empty jars, because while it is just a little which comes from the mouth of the teacher, what was heard concerning the love of God was heard by the empty minds of many. Gregory's point is very simple. Grace is abundant to overflowing! By the anointing of divine love all the jars and pots were filled up, even to the last one. And now the hearts of many, which at first were but empty jars, are filled by the anointing of the Spirit. It was only from a little bit of oil that they are seen to have been infused. And this anointing is given to others and still to yet others that faith be received by the hearers. And

---

89. Apparently Gregory has confused the story of Elijah and the widow of Zarephath (Sareptana in the Latin text) with the story of Elisha and the woman whose two sons were claimed by her creditor. Cf. I Kings 17:9-16 and II Kings 4:1-7. Gregory, *In Hiezechihelem* 3.6.

so it is that now the woman, obviously the Church, is not obligated to her creditors.[90] As much as we may smile at this allegorical interpretation, it certainly shows us how Gregory understood the preaching of the Word to be miraculous and therefore gracious. In fact, this passage makes abundantly clear that in Scripture the miraculous has a way of being a sign of the gracious. Miracles seem to point to the overflowing generosity of God.

Another extraordinary passage on the miraculous nature of revelation is found in Sermon 7. Right from the beginning there is no question but that Gregory finds Scripture to have a miraculous ability to open itself up to those who are seeking the truth. The passage at first seems to speak of everything else but grace; nevertheless, as we read along the passage opens up and it becomes clear that it is grace about which Gregory is speaking. Commenting on 1:19, "And when the living creatures went, the wheels went beside them; and when the living creatures rose from the earth, the wheels rose," Gregory tells us that the living creatures move forward when consecrated men learn from the sacred Scriptures how they are to live in a moral manner. The living creatures are lifted up from the earth when these consecrated men are enwrapped in contemplation. And it is with any one of these consecrated men that however much he makes use of Holy Scripture, so much Holy Scripture opens up to him. That is what the text means by saying, "And when the living creatures went, the wheels went beside them; and when the living creatures rose from the earth, the wheels rose," for the Holy Word grows or increases with reading. For as much as one understands the divine revelation, so much does the revelation

---

90. "Verbum quippe praedicationis semen in corde audientis est. Et auditor bonus inde profert postmodum magnam messem scientiae, unde paruum prius acceperit semen linguae. Cui rei bene concinit facturm in uidua ab Helisaeo propheta prophetae dictis oboediuit, et ex eo quod parum olei habebat, per uasa uacua effudit, quae cuncta post usque ad summum repleta sunt, et ex eorum repletione mulier a creditoris sui debito est soluta. Quae uidelicet mulier quam aliam nisi sanctam Ecclesiam signat, duorum populorum, id est Iudaici et gentilis, quasi duorum filiorum matrem? Quae prius ex peruerso opere per callidi spiritus persuasionem quasi quemdam peccati nummum a creditore acceperat, et duos quos in fide genuit amittere filios timebat. Sed prophetae uerbis, id es Scripturae sacrae praeceptis, obediens, ex paruo quod habebat olei uasa uacua infundit, quia dum ab unius ore doctoris parum quid de amore Diuinitatis multorum uacuae mentes audiunt, exuberante gratia, unguento diuini amoris usque ad summum replentur. Et iam nunc multorum corda, quae prius fuerant uacua uascula, unguento spiritus plena sunt, quae ex paucitate olei solummodo infusa uidebantur. Quod dum aliis atque aliis datur et ab auditoribus fides accipitur, Sareptana [!] mulier, uidelicet sancta Ecclesia, sub creditoris sui iam debito non tenetur." Gregory, *In Hiezechihelem* 3.6.

increase. When anyone reading the Word of sacred Scripture finds the sense of the divine Word tepid, his mind is not excited, and in his thinking on these things his understanding is not enlightened; the wheels are idle. The point Gregory is trying to make is that the usefulness of Scripture increases with use. The living creature goes forward by seeking the ways of living well and discovers through the advances of the heart how one takes the steps toward a good life. He goes forward as do the wheels, for one advances in the sacred Word as much as one benefits from it. If indeed the winged living creatures spread themselves out in contemplation, the wheels are lifted up immediately. And so it comes about that one senses that the words of Holy Scripture are heavenly, if one is illumined through the grace of contemplation and the ineffable virtue of the sacred Word is recognized when the soul is penetrated by eternal love through its reading. This is what is meant by the text "And when the living creatures rose from the earth the wheels rose."[91]

Clearly, for Gregory at least, one does not read Scripture the way one reads any other book, and clearly one does not understand Scripture the way one understands any other book. Scripture is God's self-revelation; by the means of the same Scripture God both opens himself up and veils himself. And yet, as Jesus put it, those who seek find and to those who

---

91. "*Cumque ambularent animalia, ambulabant pariter et rotae iuxta ea; et cum eleuarentur animalia de terra, eleuabantur simul et rotae.* Ambulant animalia cum sancti uiri in Scriptura sacra intellegunt quemadmodum moraliter uiuant. Eleuantur uero a terra animalia cum sancti uiri se in contemplatione suspendunt. Et quia unusquisque Sanctorum quanto ipse in Scriptura sacra profecerit, tanto haec eadem Scriptura sacra proficit apud ipsum, recte dicitur: *Cum ambularent animalia, ambulabant pariter et rotae; et cum eleuarentur animalia de terra, eleuabantur simul et rotae,* quia diuina eloquia cum legente crescunt, nam tanto illa quisque altius intellegit, quanto in eis altius intendit. Vnde nec eleuantur rotae, si non eleuantur animalia, quia nisi legentium mentes ad alta profecerint, diuina dicta, uelut in imis, non intellecta iacent. Cum enim legenti cuilibet sermo Scripturae sacrae (se tepidus uidetur sensus diuini eloquii) eius mentem non excitat, et in cogitatione sua nullo intellectus lumine emicat, rota et otiosa et in terra est, quia animal non eleuatur a terra. At uero si animal ambulet, id est bene uiuendi ordines quaerat, et per gressum cordis inueniat quemadmodum gressum boni operis ponat, ambulant pariter et rotae, quia tantum in sacro eloquio prouectum inuenis, quantum apud illud ipse profeceris. Si uero pennatum animal sese in contemplatione tetenderit, rotae protinus a terra subleuantur, quia terrena non esse intellegis, quae prius in sacro eloquio iuxta terrenum morem dicta credidisti. Fitque ut Scripturae sacrae uerba esse caelestia sentias, si accensus per contemplationis gratiam temetipsum ad caelestia suspendas. Et mira atque ineffabilis sacri eloquii uirtus agnoscitur, cum superno amore legentis animus penetratur. Quia ergo animal ad alta se subleuat, rota uolat." Gregory, *In Hiezechihelem* 7.8.

knock it shall be opened (Matt. 7:7). Gregory puts it all quite vividly, and yet this belongs to the commonsense wisdom of the Church. How often we have heard it said that the Bible is so simple that the simplest child can understand it and so profound that the greatest scholar is constantly delighted by it. Behind this is the recognition that God works through Scripture, that it is a means of grace. The sacred writings, unlike any other writings, reach out to those who read them. That is both their miraculous and their gracious quality.

Developing this in a most interesting way, Gregory continues with the next verse, "Wherever the spirit would go, they went, and the wheels rose with them." Gregory comments:

> To what then the spirit of the reader turns, the sacred Word turns as well, because if in them one seeks anything high either in regard to the way one lives or how one is to understand things, this same sacred Word grows with the seeker, and with him they ascend to the heights. It is well said then: "They follow the spirit." The spirit of the reader, if he seeks to know either the moral teaching or the historical teaching, the sense of the moral or historical follows. If he wants to understand that which has a typological sense, soon he recognizes the figures. If he wants something for contemplation, at once the wheels take wings and one mounts into the air, because in the sacred Word the intelligence of heavenly things is opened. "Wherever the spirit would go, they went and the wheels rose with them." The wheels then follow the spirit, because the sacred Word, as has often now been said, grows in proportion to the understanding of the reader.[92]

Here we have what may be regarded as a rather extreme example of the idea that God accommodates the revelation to the capacity of those who are to receive it. Gregory goes on to say that in regard to interpreting

---

92. "*Quocumque ibat spiritus, illuc eunte spiritu et rotae pariter leuabantur, sequentes eum.* Quo enim spiritus legentis tendit, illuc et diuina eloquia leuantur, quia si in eis altum quid uidendo et sentiendo quaesieris, haec eadem sacra eloquia tecum crescunt, tecum in altiora ascendunt. Bene autem de eisdem rotis dicitur: *Sequentes eum.* Legentis enim spiritus, si quid in eis scire morale aut historicum quaerit, sensus hunc moralis historiae sequitur. Si quid typicum, mox figurata locutio agnoscitur. Si quid contemplatiuum, statim rotae quasi pennas accipiunt et in aere suspenduntur, quia in uerbis sacri eloquii intellegentia caelestis aperitur. *Quocumque ergo ibat spiritus, illuc eunte spiritu et rotae pariter leuabantur, sequentes eum.* Rotae enim spiritum sequuntur, quia uerba sacri eloquii, ut saepe iam dictum est, iuxta sensum legentium per intellectum crescunt." Gregory, *In Hiezechihelem* 7.9.

Scripture either in a literal sense or a spiritual sense, it does not make too much difference because the Word responds to the needs and capacities of those who seek the truth by studying that Word.[93] Some of us might have a hard time conceiving of God being all that accommodating, and yet, as one reads over the sermons that have been most treasured by Christians over the centuries, one senses that there is something that is true here. Strangely enough those who simply read the historical sense of the text are nourished thereby, just as those who contemplate the spiritual sense of the same text are likewise fed on the Word of God. This is what Gregory is apparently saying. And it seems incredulous to the modern biblical scholar, no doubt, but Gregory does seem to have a point. One reads these sermons and marvels at the wisdom Gregory seems to impart, and yet one shakes one's head at how he pulls it out of the text. God is gracious, those who seek find, and to those who knock it is opened.

Surely there is something very true here, but something else must also be said. God has a way of challenging us to leave inadequate ways and obscure understandings behind us and to enter into better ways and better understandings. It is one thing for God to speak to someone at the beginning of the Dark Ages in terms of fantastic allegories, and quite another for him to speak to us that way. Those who go to the trouble of learning the original languages and studying the historical and cultural situations out of which it all came stand to receive an even greater blessing. Particularly in our day, to neglect all the means available to enter into a more precise understanding of Scripture and simply to rely on the sort of contemplation on which Gregory relied would constitute a sort of spiritual pride, a sort of religious reverse snobbery which would risk God's anger rather than his blessing. God is not likely to pour out the grace of illumination on either the lazy or the intransigent.

But Gregory has more to say on the graciousness of revelation. Ezekiel supplies him with a new thought which makes it possible for him to show even more clearly this grace. Ezekiel now tells us that this spirit which was in the wheels is the Spirit of life, or, at least, that is the way Gregory reads the text. It is not the human spirit but the Holy Spirit.

> In the wheels is the Spirit of life, because through the sacred Word we are made alive by the gift of the Spirit so that we cast out from us that which works death in us. One is able to understand that the Spirit is

93. Gregory, *In Hiezechihelem* 7.10.

moving when God touches the soul of the reader in different ways and manners when one person through the Word of sacred Scripture is stirred up with zeal for higher things, or to another patience is given or another instructed in preaching or still another brought to the remorse of repentance. But let us run briefly through this same Word about which we have been talking and we will see in what manner the wheels follow the Spirit.[94]

Elaborating on some examples he had mentioned, he comes to how the Holy Spirit moves some to be preachers:

If the Spirit of life excites the soul of the reader to devote himself to preaching, at once the wheels follow. For in the sacred Word Moses is discovered, all in God's directives, preaching words of freedom to the king of Egypt. For Stephen taught the faithless Jews, "You always resist the Holy Spirit," and even among the stones they threw at him he was without fear. Or there is the case of Peter who was beaten by rods lest he speak in the name of Jesus. With great liberty he responded, "It is fitting to obey God rather than men." Finally there is the case of Paul who was bound in prison with chains, even though the Word of God is never bound.[95]

One wonders whether Gregory's notaries have given us the full text as their bishop preached it here, because with meditation the four terse examples suggest considerably more than has actually been reported. In all four cases the Word was preached under the most difficult circumstances. That under

94. "*Spiritus enim uitae erat in rotis.* In rotis enim spiritus uitae est, quia per sacra eloquia dono spiritus uiuificamur ut mortifera a nobis opera repellamus. Potest enim intellegi quia spiritus uadit, cum legentis animum diuersis modis et ordinibus tangit Deus, quando hunc per uerba sacri eloquii modo in zelo excitans ad ultionem erigit, modo ad patientiam mitigat, modo in praedicationem instruit, modo ad paenitentiae lamenta compungit. Sed curramus breuiter per haec eadem uerba quae diximus, et uideamus quodomo sequuntur rotae spiritum, qui uitae spiritus dicitur, et rotis inesse perhibetur." Gregory, *In Hiezechihelem* 7.11.

95. "Si uitae spiritus legentis animum ad studium praedicationis excitat, statim sequuntur et rotae, quia in sacris eloquiis inuenit Moyses, iubente Domino, contra Aegypti regem in quantis se praedicationis liberae uerbis erexit. Quod Stephanus Iudaeis perfidiantibus diceret: *Vos semper Spiritui sancto restitistis,* nec inter lapides timuit. Quod Petrus, fustibus caesus, ne in nomine Iesu loquatur, cum magna libertate respondit: *Oboedire oportet Deo magis quam hominibus.* Quod Paulus catenarum uinculis stringitur sed tamen uerbum Dei non est alligatum." Gregory, *In Hiezechihelem* 7.13.

such circumstances the Word could actually be gotten through was highly unlikely, at least when considered from a merely human point of view, and yet by the grace of God and the moving of the Holy Spirit the message was delivered and bore its fruit. In each case the powers of this world were deployed to ensure that the Word would not be preached and would not bear its fruit. When one contemplates these examples, as Gregory so often tells us to contemplate the Scriptures, it is clear that all four tell us of the power the revelation bears within itself to get through all kinds of opposition and to bring about what God will have it bring about.

Gregory has yet another insight on the power of the Word of God. Further on in this same sermon he tells us:

> By these words of Scripture God makes us alive because through them he demonstrates to us the spiritual life and even pours it into our minds by the inspiration of the Spirit, because daily through the gift of grace it has its effect in the minds of the elect. Truly it is said, "The Spirit of life was in the wheels."[96]

In our first volume, particularly in our section on the First Epistle of Peter, we spoke of how the earliest Christians found a vitality in the Word of God. We spoke of how in the New Testament Church the preaching of the gospel was understood to be "a word of life." Gregory uses this imagery of God pouring spiritual life into his people when they daily read the Scriptures to make the point that the Word of God has life within itself which kindles spiritual life in those who read that Word.

> The Scriptures become for us a light to lighten the way in the present darkness. This indeed Peter said, "You will do well to pay attention to this as to a lamp shining in a dark place" (II Peter 1:19). This the psalmist said, "Thy Word is a lamp to my feet and a light to my path" (Psalm 119:105). Nevertheless, we know that our own light is dim for us, unless the truth illumines this in our minds. Again the psalmist says, "Yea, thou dost light my lamp; the LORD my God lightens my darkness" (Psalm 18:28). What is a burning lamp, unless it is a light, but created light does not shine in us unless it is illuminated by an uncreated light.

---

96. "In eis itaque nos uiuificat, quia per haec nobis spiritalem uitam demonstrat eamque per afflatum spiritus nostris mentibus infundit. Quod quia cotidie per donum gratiae in electorum mentibus agitur, recte dicitur: *Spiritus uitae erat in rotis.*" Gregory, *In Hiezechihelem* 7.16.

Because, therefore, Almighty God both gave us the holy Scriptures for our salvation and opened up those same Scriptures for us so that they are effective for our salvation, we understand then that the Spirit of life is in the wheels.[97]

This is a paradox greatly loved in the patristic period. It points up the continuity between the incarnate Word who is Christ and the Word which gives understanding. Gregory was not one to drive a hard distinction between the Word of God who is Christ and the Word of God which is Scripture.

3. The Inspiration of the Word of God

Let us turn to another dimension of Gregory's theology of the Word, namely, the doctrine of inspiration. His affirmations on this subject are both strong and explicit. This becomes clear in the first sermon in the series, which Gregory devotes to the subject of the prophetic ministry. Characteristic of Gregory's doctrine of inspiration is that he speaks not only of the inspiration of the prophet, or biblical writer, but also of the preacher who interprets the Scriptures, and even of the one who hears the Word preached or for that matter reads the Word and meditates upon it. One might say that Gregory sees the doctrine of inspiration in three phases. First is the inspiration of the biblical writers, second the inspiration of the preacher, and third the inspiration of the hearer.

In recent times there has been much discussion of the inspiration of the biblical writers but not much of the inspiration of the preacher. Gregory, in contrast, tells us of the inspiration of the scholar who contemplates the Scriptures in preparation for the delivery of the sermon. In fact, the opening lines of the first sermon tell us that Gregory understands preachers of the Word to be inspired:

---

97. "Haec nobis Scriptura in tenebris uitae praesentis facta est lumen itineris. Hinc etenim Petrus ait: *Cui benefacitis intendentes, quasi lucernae lucenti in caliginoso loco.* Hinc psalmista dicit: *Lucerna pedibus meis uerbum tuum, Domine, et lumen semitis meis.* Scimus tamen quia et ipsa nobis nostra lucerna obscura est, nisi hanc nostris mentibus ueritas illustret. Vnde iterum psalmista ait: *Quoniam tu illuminas lucernam meam, Domine, Deus meus, illumina tenebras meas.* Qui enim lucerna ardens, nisi lumen est? Sed lumen creatum nobis non lucet, nisi illuminetur a lumine non creato. Quia ergo omnipotens Deus ad salutem nostram sanctorum Testamentorum dicta et ipse creauit, et ipse aperuit, spiritus uitae erat in rotis." Gregory, *In Hiezechihelem* 7.17.

> God Almighty granting to me the inspiration to speak of the prophet
> Ezekiel, I ought first to open both the matter of times and the manner
> of speaking which belongs to prophetic speech, that his perception might
> be better shown, his virtue better recognized.[98]

In his preaching Gregory prayed that he might be divinely inspired.

As Gregory understands it, there is something unique about the
writings of the Scriptures which sets them apart from other literature, and
that is this spiritual gift of prophecy. The Prophets, the Gospels, the Psalms,
the Epistles, and the Historical Books all share this spirit of prophecy. The
essence of prophecy is not that it is the gift of foresight but rather the gift
of seeing what is hidden. The real issue is not prophecy so much as it is
revelation, that is, being enabled to view that which ordinarily is hidden
from human eyes. Gregory cites three examples from Scripture in which
the gift of prophecy is shown to speak of different times. First there is the
famous prophecy of the virgin birth of Christ in Isaiah 7:14. This clearly
concerns the future. Here prophecy has its customary meaning, but then
Gregory quotes the first verse of Genesis concerning the beginning of the
world. This is obviously about the past, but since it happened before any
human being was around it is a statement about something to which
human knowledge does not have access; that is, it depends on revelation.
The spirit of prophecy often has to do with present time as well, as we
find in I Corinthians 14:24-25 where prophecy reveals the secrets of the
hearts of those who are present. The secrets of our hearts are hidden, but
when the gift of prophecy reveals them there is revelation.[99] The point
Gregory wants to make here is quite different from the sort of thing that
theologians tried to say during the Age of the Enlightenment. For the
Enlightenment revelation was as much a problem as was prophecy.

As Gregory understands it, the gift of prophecy is different from
clairvoyance. The prophet does not have some strange ability that others
do not, but can only see those hidden things which God reveals. When
Jesus approached John the Baptist at the Jordan River, John was able to
say, "Behold the lamb of God who takes away the sin of the world," but
later when he was in prison he was in doubt as to whether the Lamb of

---

98. "Dei omnipotentis aspiratione de Hiezechihele propheta locuturus, prius debeo
tempora et modos aperire prophetiae, ut dum accessus eius ostenditur, uirtus melius
cognoscatur." Gregory, *In Hiezechihelem* 1.1.

99. Gregory, *In Hiezechihelem* 1.1.

God was the awaited Messiah.[100] In his old age Isaac was not able to distinguish between Esau, whom he had sent out hunting that he might be given the blessing, and Jacob, who stealthily entered in and received the blessing intended for his brother. Yet in giving that blessing Isaac uttered a prophetic oracle which revealed the plans of God for centuries.[101] In the same way the apostle Paul made it clear that the mystery of the gospel was given to him by revelation (Gal. 1:11-12 and Eph. 3:3), and yet when he was on his way to Jerusalem he did not know what was in store for him.[102] Gregory offers a number of other biblical illustrations that give us a sense of the expanse of his doctrine of inspiration, but one thing is always clear: Inspiration is not a matter of human genius. It is a matter of God showing the prophets, the Evangelists, and the apostles in many and various ways the truth God wants to reveal.

Turning to the inspiration of the preacher on one hand and the listening congregation on the other, we find Gregory most helpful. He gives us two similes. The first is: Preaching is like a spark which spreads the blaze of eternal love from God to us.[103] The words of the preacher are too inadequate to communicate the eternal mysteries, and yet when the preacher enters into communion with God he begins to glow with this holy fire and his words become sparks of that same eternal love. When he glows with desire to enter into the eternal reality his listeners catch sight of his passion, and soon they too have been ignited with the same devotion.[104] The second simile is: The preaching of the Word of God is like lightning.[105] The preachers of the gospel flash through the heavens when they contemplate eternal realities. On the one· hand they are anchored to the clouds by their love of the heavenly homeland, but because of the weight of human concerns they fall upon the earth. And yet they are able to contemplate heavenly things at least in a flash of intuition. They are able to intimate to their brethren by their bursts of ardor something of the deep experience of divine love which can only be seen in those sudden flashes of speech which somehow inflame the hearts of those who listen.[106] Those who listen are inspired, just as those who preach are. What

100. Gregory, *In Hiezechihelem* 1.5.
101. Gregory, *In Hiezechihelem* 1.6.
102. Gregory, *In Hiezechihelem* 1.9.
103. Gregory, *In Hiezechihelem* 3.5.
104. Gregory, *In Hiezechihelem* 3.5.
105. Gregory, *In Hiezechihelem* 5.13.
106. Gregory, *In Hiezechihelem* 5.13.

is interesting in these two figures is the way they give attention to the personal nature of the witness. Gregory recognized that something transpires between the preacher and the listener which is more than an objective communication of information. There is that, of course, yet it is more. It is a divinely given inspiration.

D. The Word as Worship

As we have seen, one of the characteristics of Gregory's theology of the Word is the way he sees the writing of the prophets and apostles, the proclamation of the Christian preacher, and the hearing of the congregation as a whole. Each is a different moment in divine revelation. Because of this characteristic it is much easier for Gregory to speak to us about the Word as worship. It is in regard to the last of these three moments, namely, the hearing of the congregation, that we find the thoughts of Gregory particularly interesting.

As an introduction to the fifth sermon we find the following figure for the relation between Scripture lesson and sermon. To hear a sermon is to enter into a cool forest on a hot day. There we are refreshed from the summer heat of the cares of this world. In the reading of the Scripture lesson the tender greens and most succulent fruits are gathered, and then in the sermon they are prepared into a tasty meal and served to be enjoyed by God's people. We get the impression that for Gregory a service of worship with Scripture readings and no sermon would be somewhat disappointing, something like dinner in a fast-food joint.

Meditation on the Word, or contemplation, as he often calls it, is a cardinal dimension of the ministry of the Word. Contemplation is essential to the preparation of a sermon, but it is also in terms of contemplation that Gregory thinks of the actual sermon itself. Contemplation and meditation are synonyms for Gregory and do not yet mean the sort of thing the medieval mystics meant by them. Meditation means to think about the meaning of a passage of Scripture, to chew the thoughts over, to ponder its application. When God's people meditate on the Word, God's Word resonates in them. This meditation is part of the divine service whether it is done by the preacher in preparation for the sermon or by the congregation in listening to the sermon.

This meditation on the Scripture lesson Gregory finds as the necessary preparation for the preaching of the Scriptures. It is not, however, the same thing as the systematic exegetical study of a passage of Scripture which today we find so important for the preparation of a sermon. Meditation is not the same thing as analysis, nor is it research into the meaning of the text. However, it certainly included some of the things we think of when we talk about exegetical studies, one of which was surely the searching out of parallel passages. Occasionally one gets a hint that Gregory has studied the commentaries of others on the passage before him. He often speaks of "the saints" and how they understood Scripture, by which he no doubt means Christians of an earlier age. By Gregory's time there was a sizeable library of Christian literature and much of it was in the form of commentaries. In one place he specifically mentions the opinion of Jerome on a particular passage. Jerome had written an extended commentary on Ezekiel which he started in 411, a year after the sacking of Rome, and continued working on while trying to help refugees from that disastrous event. Jerome's commentary must have been very interesting reading for the bishop of Rome almost two hundred years later when history was once more repeating itself.[107] Jerome had made extensive use of the commentary of Origen as well as both Jewish and Christian commentaries which were around then, but Gregory had, apparently, never busied himself with learning Greek, let alone Hebrew. He may have had secretaries who could report to him on Greek commentaries; that sort of thing would have been standard procedure for a man of his position in that day. Be all that as it may, certain traditional lines of interpretation of the prophet Ezekiel had already developed both in the synagogue and the Church by that time, and Gregory informed himself of these traditions. All this would have certainly been included in the spiritual service of meditating on God's Word.

That meditation on the Word of God is worship goes far back in the biblical tradition. One of the most significant witnesses to this is the first psalm, which serves as a preface to the whole collection of 150 psalms. There we learn that for the godly it is a delight to meditate on the Law of the Lord day and night. The canonical book of Psalms is our oldest collection of liturgical texts, and it was no doubt collected to serve this purpose. Meditating on these texts was understood as worship. Benedictine monasticism, which so strongly influenced Gregory, has always understood

---

107. J. N. D. Kelly, *Jerome, His Life, Writings, and Controversies* (London: Gerald Duckworth & Co., 1957), pp. 305ff.

meditation on the Word of God as being at the center of worship. That was what the daily office was all about.

Something else needs to be said about how Gregory understood the ministry of the Word as being worship. Here we are concerned with conversion, that is, with the converting power of the Word. Gregory gives us a perfect example of what we have elsewhere described as a kerygmatic doxology, but he also exemplifies what we have described as a prophetic doxology; both these approaches to the theology of worship are magnificently combined. Gregory's theology of worship is kerygmatic because for him the reading and preaching of the Scriptures proclaims the glory of God. In fact, the ministry of the Word proclaims the glory of God as nothing else does, because it has the power to convert all manner of men and women to a godly life. When this happens the glory of God is reflected in the life of his creatures. Gregory's theology of worship is prophetic because righteousness and holiness are understood as of the essence of the divine glory and God's people reflect, even magnify, God's glory when they are righteous and holy before him.

Gregory has put it about as powerfully as anyone has:

> What is this that the prophet hears, the sound of wings as the sound of many waters, unless it is from the holiness of Almighty God. Those wings are virtue, which at first gives out but a small sound, issuing only from the saints but when as it is now, it is diffused over all by the ministry of preaching; it resonates through the conversion of many peoples.[108]

There are two words to notice here: "resonate" and "conversion." Worship is a sort of resonating of the glory of God; that is, it is a reflection of the glory of God. When God's people contemplate the Word of God, when they ruminate, or chew it over, then the Word resonates. Resonating occurs when we as God's people sound forth in harmony with the glory of God; the people of God become the sounding board, as it were, of the glory of God. When we hear the Word and live by the Word, we amplify God's glory. A holy people amplifies the holy word of a holy God. The word "conversion" at this point is most significant. The glory of God which

---

108. "Quid est ergo quod propheta alarum sonum audit quasi sonum aquarum multarum, nisi quod ex omnipotentis Dei pietate illae alae uirtutum, quae in paucis prius Sanctis sonabant, etiam nunc praedicatione diffusa, in multorum populorum conuersatione resonant?" Gregory, *In Hiezechihelem* 8.1.

sounds forth in the preaching of the Gospel is a converting glory. It is a glory that is effective, a glory that transforms the creature into the image of God:

> At the time of the incarnation, the passion, the resurrection of the Lord, there were not many of these winged living beings our text speaks about, . . . but after the Gospel of his divinity had been diffused about the world, who knows how many little ones, how many serious old men, how many strong youths, how many weak, simple people, how many converted sinners, how many elderly virgins have through faith, hope, and love taken flight toward heavenly realms. Behold the sound of the wings, which first came from but a few creatures, now resonates among many peoples; now many desiring a heavenly life take to flight. . . . It is well said, "And I heard the sound of wings as the sound of many waters."[109]

Worship is both the quiet meditation of the scholar and the attentive listening of the congregation. The devout listening of the congregation is a chorus of faith which echoes the sacred Word. It is the harmonious chorus of a great throng of worshipers all buzzing about the honey of God's Word. This sound of many wings, like the sound of many waters, whether in Ezekiel or in Revelation, glorifies God.

---

109. "Incarnato enim, passo, ac resurgente Domino, pauca pennata animalia fuerunt, quia rari ualde exstiterunt, qui caelestia desiderarent, et uirtutum pennis se in alta suspenderent. Sed postquam diuinitatis eius praedicatio in mundo diffusa est, quanti iam paruuli, quanti grauiores, quanti fortes iuuenes, quanti imbecilles, quantae conuersae peccatrices, quantae anus uirgines per fidem, per spem, per amorem ad caelestia euolant, quis dicere, quis aestimare sufficiat. Ecce alarum sonitus, qui prius in paucis animalibus fuit, iam nunc in populis resonat, iam nunc mundi multitudinem ad caeleste desiderium pennae uirtutum leuant. Bene ergo dicitur: *Et audiebam sonum alarum, quasi sonum aquarum multarum.*" Gregory, *In Hiezechihelem* 8.1.

Bibliography

Sources for Chapter I

Bardy, Gustave. "Cyrille de Jerusalem." *Dictionnaire d'histoire et géographie ecclésiastique,* 13:1181-85.

Basil of Caesarea. *Homélies sur l'Hexaéméron.* Greek text, introduction, and French translation by S. Giet. Sources chrétiennes, vol. 26. Paris: Les Éditions du Cerf, 1968.

————. *Saint Basil: Exegetical Homilies.* English translation by Sister Agnes Clare Way, C.D.P. Washington, D.C.: Catholic University of America Press, 1963.

Benoît, André. *La baptême chrétien au second siècle.* Paris: Presses Universitaires de France, 1953.

Bernardi, Jean. *La Prédication des Pères Cappodociens.* Paris: Presses Universitaires de France, 1968.

Botte, Bernard. *Les origines de la Noël et de l'Épiphanie, Études historiques.* Louvain: Abbaye du Mont César, 1932.

Brevarium Syriacum of 411. Edited by B. Mariani. Rome, 1956.

Campbell, James M. *The Influence of the Second Sophistic on the Style of the Sermons of St. Basil the Great.* Patristic Studies, vol. 2. Washington, D.C.: Catholic University of America, 1922.

Campenhausen, Hans Freiherr von. *Griechische Kirchenväter.* 3rd ed. Stuttgart: W. Kohlhammer Verlag, 1961.

Casel, Odo. *Das Christliche Kultmysterium.* 4th ed. Regensburg: Fr. Pustet, 1960.

Courtonne, Yves. *Saint Basile et l'hellénisme. Études sur la rencontre de la pensée chrétienne avec la sagesse antique dans l'Hexaéméron de Basile le Grand.* Paris: Firmin-Didot, 1934.

Cullmann, Oscar. *Noël dans l'Église ancienne.* Neuchâtel: Delachaux & Niestlé, 1949.

Cyril of Alexandria. *Commentary on the Gospel of St. Luke.* Translated by R. Payne Smith. N.p.: Studion Publishers, 1983.

Cyril of Jerusalem. *Catechetical Lectures.* Edited by E. H. Gifford. Nicene and Post-Nicene Fathers, 2nd ser., vol. 7. Grand Rapids: Wm. B. Eerdmans Publishing Co., 1975.

—————. *Catéchèses mystagogiques.* Edited by Auguste Piédagnel. Sources chrétiennes, vol. 126. Paris: Les Éditions du Cerf, 1966.

Daniélou, Jean. "Le mystère du cult dans les sermons de saint Grégoire de Nysse." In *Vom christlichen Mysterium.* Festschrift O. Casel. Düsseldorf: Patmos Verlag, 1951, pp. 76-93.

—————. *Platonisme et Theologie mystique.* Paris: Éditions Montaigne, 1954.

Engberding, Hieronymus. "Der 25. Dezember als Tag der Feier der Geburt des Herrn." *Archiv für Liturgiewissenschaft,* II (1952).

Etheria. *Journal de Voyage.* Latin text, introduction, and translation by Hélène Pétré. Sources chrétiennes, vol. 21. Paris: Les Éditions du Cerf, 1948.

Fox, M. M. *The Life and Times of St. Basil the Great as Revealed in His Works.* Patristic Studies, vol. 57. Washington, 1937.

Frank, Hieronymus. "Frühgeschichte und Ursprung des römischen Weihnachtsfestes im Lichte neuerer Forschung." *Archiv für Liturgiewissenschaft,* II (1952).

Gallay, Paul. *La vie de S. Grégoire de Nazianze.* Lyon and Paris: E. Vitte, 1943.

Godet, P. *Dictionnaire de Théologie Catholique,* 6:1847-52.

Gregory of Nazianzus. *Discours 27-31 (Discours théologiques).* Introduction, critical text, French translation, and notes by Paul Gallay. Sources chrétiennes, vol. 250. Paris: Les Éditions du Cerf, 1978.

—————. *Discours 38-41.* Introduction, critical text, and notes by Claudio Mareschini. Translated by Paul Gallay. Sources chrétiennes, vol. 358. Paris: Les Éditions du Cerf, 1990.

—————. *Theological Discourses.* Translated by Charles Gordon Browne and James Edward Swallow. Nicene and Post-Nicene Fathers, 2nd ser., vol. 7. Grand Rapids: Wm. B. Eerdmans Publishing Co., 1975.

Gregory of Nyssa. *The Lord's Prayer, the Beatitudes.* Translated by H. C. Graef. Ancient Christian Writers, vol. 18, pp. 85-175. Westminster, Md.: Newman Press, 1954.

Hesychius of Jerusalem. *Les homélies festales.* Greek text with French translation by Michel Aubineau. 2 vols. Brussels: Société des Bollandistes, 1978-80.

—————. *Homélies sur Job.* Armenian text with French translation. Edited by Charles Renoux. Patrologia Orientalis, vol. 42. Turnhout, Belgium: Brepols, 1983.

Jacks, Leo V. "Saint Basil and Greek Literature." *Catholic University of America Patristic Studies* I (1922).

Jounel, P. "Le temps de Noël." In *L'Église en Prière*, edited by A. G. Martimort. Tournai: Desclée & Cie, 1961.

Kennedy, George A. *Classical Rhetoric and Its Christian and Secular Tradition from Ancient to Modern Times.* Chapel Hill: University of North Carolina Press, 1980.

Kerrigan, Alexander. *St. Cyril of Alexandria: Interpreter of the Old Testament.* Rome: Pontificio Istituto Biblico, 1951.

Leclercq, Henri. "Grégoire de Nazianze." *Dictionnaire d'archaeologie chrétienne et de liturgie,* 15 vols. Paris: Letouzey et Ane, 1907-53. 6/2:1667-1711.

Leclercq, Jean. "Aux origines du cycle de Nöel." *Ephemerides Liturgicae* 73 (1959).

Lefherz, Friedhelm. *Studien zu Gregor von Nazianz.* Bonn: Rheinische Friedrich Wilhelms-Universität, 1958.

Lietzmann, Hans. *A History of the Early Church.* Translated by Bertram Lee Woolf. 4 vols. Cleveland: World Publishing Co., 1961.

Lossky, Vladimir. *Vision de Dieu.* Neuchâtel: Éditions Delachaux et Niestlé, 1962.

Mazza, Enrico. *Mystagogy: A Theology of Liturgy in the Patristic Age.* Translated by Matthew J. O'Connell. New York: Pueblo Publishing Co., 1989.

Migne, J.-P. *Patrologia Graeca.* Paris: Migne, 1857-66.

Mohrmann, Christine. "Epiphania." In *Études sur le latin des Chrétiens.* Rome, 1958.

Owen, E. C. E. "St. Gregory of Nyssa: Grammar, Vocabulary, and Style." *Journal of Theological Studies* 26 (1925): 64-71.

Paulin, A. *Saint Cyrille de Jérusalem catéchète.* Lex Orandi, vol. 29. Paris: Les Éditions du Cerf, 1959.

Pelikan, Jaroslav. *The Christian Tradition: A History of the Development of Doctrine.* 5 vols. Chicago: University of Chicago Press, 1971-89.

Plagnieux, Jean. *Saint Grégoire de Nazianze Theologien.* Paris: Éditions franciscaines, 1952.

Quasten, Johannes. *Patrology.* 4 vols. Utrecht and Antwerp: Spectrum Publishers; Westminster, Md.: Christian Classics, 1966-94.

Renoux, Athanase. *Le codex arménien Jérusalem 121.* 2 vols. Patrologia orientalis, vols. 35 and 36. Turnholt: Brepols, 1969-71.

Renoux, Charles. "L'Épiphanie à Jérusalem au IVe et Ve siècle." In *Noël Épiphanie, retour du Christ,* edited by B. Botte et al. Paris: Les Éditions du Cerf, 1967.

Ruether, Rosemary Radford. *Gregory of Nazianzus: Rhetor and Philosopher.* Oxford: Clarendon Press, 1969.

Schnackenburg, Rudolf. *Baptism in the Thought of St. Paul.* Translated by G. R. Beasley-Murray. Oxford: Blackwell, 1964.

Tarchnischvili, M. *Le Grand Lectionnaire de l'Église de Jérusalem: (Ve-VIIIe Siècle).* Corpus scriptorum christianorum orientalium, vols. 188, 189, 204, and 205. Louvain: Secretariat du Corpus SCO, 1959-60.

461

Telfer, W., trans. *Cyril of Jerusalem and Nemesius of Emesa.* Library of Christian Classics, vol. 4. Philadelphia: Westminster Press, 1955.

Thyen, Hartwig. *Der Stil der jüdisch-hellenistische Homilie.* Göttingen: Vandenhoeck & Ruprecht, 1955.

Venables, E. "Basilius of Caesarea." In *Dictionary of Christian Biography,* 1(1877): 282-97.

Völker, W. "Zur Gotteslehre Gregors von Nyssa." *Vigiliae Christianae* 9 (1955): 103-28.

Wagner, Gunter. *Das religionsgeschichtliche Problem von Römer 6,1-11.* Zurich: Zwingli Verlag, 1962.

Wilken, Robert L. *Judaism and the Early Christian Mind: A Study of Cyril of Alexandria's Exegesis and Theology.* New Haven and London: Yale University Press, 1971.

Zerfass, Rolf. *Die Schriftlesung im Kathedraloffizium Jerusalems.* Münster im Westphalia: Aschendorff, 1968.

Sources for Chapter II

Baumstark, Anton. *Liturgie comparée.* English ed. Westminster, Md.: Newman Press, 1958.

————. *Nocturna laus: Typen frühchristlicher Virgilienfeier und ihr Fortleben vor allem im römischen und monastischen Ritus.* Münster im Westphalia: Aschendorff, 1967.

Fischer, B. "Le lectionnaire arménien le plus ancien." *Consilium* 102 (1975): 39-45.

Hesychius of Jerusalem. *Les homélies festales.* Greek text with French translation. Edited by Michel Aubineau. 2 vols. Brussels: Société des Bollandistes, 1978.

Jounel, Pierre. "Le temps de Noël." In *L'Église en Prière,* edited by A. G. Martimort. Tournai: Desclée & Cie., 1961.

Jüssen, Klaudius. *Die dogmatischen Anschauungen des Hesychius von Jerusalem.* 2 vols. Münster im Westphalia: Aschendorff, 1931-34.

Kniazeff, Alexis. "La lecture de l'Ancien et du Nouveau Testament dans le rite byzantin." In *Le Prière des Heurs,* edited by Mgr. Cassien and Dom Bernard Botte, pp. 201-51. Paris: Les Éditions du Cerf, 1963.

Kretschmar, G. "Die frühe Geschichte der Jerusalemer Liturgie." *Jahrbuch für Liturgie und Hymnologie* 2 (1956): 22-46.

Leclercq, Jean. "Aux origines du cycle de Nöel." *Ephemerides Liturgicae* 73 (1959).

Martin, Ch. "Aux sources de l'hagiographie et de l'homilétique byzantum." *Byzantion* 12 (1937): 347-62.

Mohrmann, Christine. "Epiphania." In *Études sur le latin des Chrétiens.* Rome: Edizioni di storia e letteratura, 1958.

Renoux, Athanase. "Liturgie de Jérusalem et Lectionnaire Arménien." In *Le Prière des Heurs,* edited by Mgr. Cassien and Dom Bernard Botte, pp. 167-99. Paris: Les Éditions du Cerf, 1963.

Renoux, Charles. "L'Épiphanie à Jérusalem au IVe et Ve siècle." In *Noël Épiphanie, retour du Christ,* edited by B. Botte et al. Paris: Les Éditions du Cerf, 1967.

Tarchnischvili, M. *Le Grand Lectionnaire de l'Église de Jérusalem: (Ve-VIIIe Siècle).* Corpus scriptorum christianorum orientalium, vols. 188, 189, 204, and 205. Louvain: Secretariat du Corpus SCO, 1959-60.

Zerfass, Rolf. *Die Schriftlesung im Kathedraloffizium Jerusalems.* Münster im Westphalia: Aschendorff, 1968.

Sources for Chapter III

Amann, E. "Théodore de Mopsueste." *Dictionnaire de Théologie Catholique,* 15:235-79.

Bardy, Gustave. "Interpretation chez les pères." *Dictionnaire Biblique,* Supplement 4 (Paris, 1949): 569-91.

Baur, Chrysostomus. *John Chrysostom and His Time.* English translation by M. Gonzaga. 2 vols. Westminster, Md.: Newman Press, 1959-60.

Bonsdorf, Max von. *Zur Predigtätigkeit des Johannes Chrysostomus. Biographisch-Chronologische Studien über seine Homilienserien zu neutestamentlichen Büchern.* Helsinki: Mercators tryckeri aktiebolog, 1922.

Burns, Mary Albania. *St. John Chrysostom's Homilies on the Statues: A Study of Their Rhetorical Qualities and Form.* Washington, D.C.: Catholic University of America Press, 1930.

Campenhausen, Hans Freiherr von. *Griechische Kirchenväter.* Stuttgart: W. Kohlhammer Verlag, 1955.

Ceresa-Gastaldo, Aldo. *Giovanni Crisostomo: Le catechesi battesimali.* Rome, 1982.

Chase, Frederic Henry. *Chrysostom: A Study in the History of Biblical Interpretation.* Cambridge: Deighton, Bell; London: George Bell, 1887.

John Chrysostom. *Baptismal Instructions.* Translated by Paul Harkins. Westminster, Md.: Newman Press, 1933.

————. *Homilies on Colossians.* Translated by J. Ashworth. Nicene and Post-Nicene Fathers, 1st ser., vol. 13. Grand Rapids: Wm. B. Eerdmans Publishing Co., 1956.

————. *Homilies on Genesis.* Translated by Robert C. Hill. 3 vols. Washington, D.C.: Catholic University Press, 1985-92.

————. *Huit catéchèse baptismales inédites.* French translation by Antoine Wenger. Paris: Les Éditions du Cerf, 1970.

————. *On the Priesthood.* Translated by W. R. W. Stephens. Nicene and Post-

Nicene Fathers, 1st ser., vol. 9. Grand Rapids: Wm. B. Eerdmans Publishing Co., 1956.

—. *Sur le sacerdoce (dialogue et homélie)*. Edited by A. M. Malingurey. Sources chrétiennes, vol. 272. Paris: Les Éditions du Cerf, 1980.

—. *Trois catéchèses baptismales*. Introduction, critical text, French translation, and notes by Auguste Piédagnel. Sources chrétiennes, vol. 366. Paris: Les Éditions du Cerf, 1990.

Daniélou, Jean. *From Shadow to Reality: Studies in the Biblical Typology of the Fathers*. Translated by W. Hibbard. Westminster, Md.: Newman Press, 1961.

—. *A History of Early Christian Doctrine before the Council of Nicea*. Translated by J. A. Baker. 3 vols. Philadelphia: Westminster Press, 1977. See especially vol. 1, *The Theology of Jewish Christianity*.

Devreesse, Robert. *Essai sur Théodore de Mopsueste*. Vatican City: Biblioteca Apostolica Vaticana, 1948.

Diepen, H. M., and Jean Daniélou. "Théodoret et le dogme d'Éphèse." *Recherches de Sciences Religieuses* 44 (1956): 243-48.

Downey, Glanville. *Antioch in the Age of Theodosius the Great*. Norman: University of Oklahoma Press, 1962.

—. *A History of Antioch in Syria from Seleucus to the Arab Conquests*. Princeton: Princeton University Press, 1961.

Dumortier, Jean. "La culture profane de S. Jean Chrysostome." *Mélange de science religieuse* 8 (1953): 53-62.

Flanagan, M. H. *St. John Chrysostom's Doctrine of Condescension and Accuracy in Scripture*. Napier, 1948.

Froehlich, Karlfried. *Biblical Interpretation in the Early Church*. Philadelphia: Fortress Press, 1984.

Greer, R. A. *Theodore of Mopsuestia: Exegete and Theologian*. Westminster, Md.: Faith Press, 1961.

Hanssens, J. M. *Institutiones liturgicae de ritibus Orientalibus*. Rome: Gregorian University, 1930.

Hay, C. "Antiochene Exegesis and Christology." *Australian Biblical Review* 12 (1969): 10-23.

Hill, Robert C. "Chrysostom's Terminology for the Inspired Word." *Estudios Biblicos* 41 (1983): 367-73.

—. *St. John Chrysostom's Teaching on Inspiration in His Old Testament Homilies*. Sydney, 1981.

Jones, A. H. M. "St. John Chrysostom's Parentage and Education." *Harvard Theological Review* 46: 171-73.

Kaczynski, Reiner. *Das Wort Gottes in Liturgie und Alltag der Gemeinden des Johannes Chrysostomus*. Freiburg, Basel, and Vienna: Herder, 1974.

Leroux, J. M. "Saint Jean Chrysostome, les Homélies sur les Statues." *Studia Patristica 3. Texte und Untersuchungen* 87 (Berlin, 1961): 233-39.

Mazza, Enrico. *Mystagogy: A Theology of Liturgy in the Patristic Age.* Translated by Matthew J. O'Connell. New York: Pueblo Publishing Co., 1989.

Nautin, Pierre. "La valeur des lemmes dans l'*Éranistes* de Théodoret." *Revue d'Histoire Ecclésiastique* 46 (1951): 681-83.

Paverd, Frans van de. *St. John Chrysostom, the Homilies on the Statues: An Introduction.* Rome: Pontifical Institute of Oriental Studies, 1991.

————. *Zur Geschichte der Messliturgie in Antiocheia und Konstantinopel gegen Ende des vierten Jahrhunderts: Analyse der Quellen bei Johannes Chrysostomos.* Orientalia Christiana Analecta, vol. 187. Rome, 1970.

Pelikan, Jaroslav. *The Preaching of Chrysostom: Homilies on the Sermon on the Mount.* Philadelphia: Fortress Press, 1967.

Piazzino, C. *S. Giovanni Crisostomo: Omelie sulla lettera de S. Paolo ai Colossei.* Turin, 1940.

Quasten, Johannes. "The Liturgical Mysticism of Theodore of Mopsuestia." *Texte und Untersuchungen* 15 (1954): 431-39.

————. *Patrology.* 4 vols. Utrecht and Antwerp: Spectrum Publishers; Westminster, Md.: Christian Classics, 1966-93.

Reine, Francis Joseph. *The Eucharistic Doctrine and Liturgy of the Mystagogical Catechisms of Theodore of Mopsuestia.* Washington, D.C.: Catholic University of America Press, 1942.

Richard, M. "Notes sur les florilèges dogmatiques de Ve et du VIe siècle." *Actes du Congrès d'Études Byzantines* (Paris, 1948): 307-18.

Salet, L. "Les sources de l'*Éranistes* de Théodoret." *Revue d'Histoire Ecclésiastique* 6 (1905): 289-303, 513-36, 741-54.

Sartore, D. "Il misterio del battesimo nelle catechesi di S. Giovanni Crisostomo." *Lateranum* 50 (1984).

Schulz, Hans-Joachim. *The Byzantine Liturgy: Symbolic Structure and Faith Expression.* Translated by Matthew J. O'Connell. New York: Pueblo Publishing Co., 1986.

Schweizer, Eduard. "Diodor von Tarsus als Exeget." *Zeitschrift für die neutestamentliche Wissenschaft und die Kunde der älteren Kirche* 40 (1941/42): 33-75.

Theodore of Mopsuestia. *Commentary of Theodore of Mopsuestia on the Lord's Prayer and on the Sacraments of Baptism and the Eucharist.* Edited and translated by Alphonse Mingana. Woodbrooke Studies. Cambridge: W. Heffer & Sons, Ltd., 1933.

————. *Commentary of Theodore of Mopsuestia on the Nicene Creed.* Syriac Text and English translation by Alphonse Mingana. Woodbrooke Studies. Cambridge: W. Heffer & Sons, Ltd., 1932.

————. *Les homélies catéchétiques de Théodore de Mopsueste.* Translated by Raymond Tonneau in collaboration with Robert Devreesse. Vatican City: Biblioteca Apostolica Vaticana, 1949.

Theodoret of Cyrus. *On Divine Providence.* Translated by Thomas Halton. New York and Mahwah, N.J.: Newman Press, 1988.

Vaccari, A. "La theoria nella scuola esegetica de Antiochia." *Biblica* 1 (1920): 3-36.

Vandenberghe, Bruno H. *John of the Golden Mouth.* Westminster, Md.: Newman Press, 1958.

Wallace-Hadrill, D. S. *Christian Antioch: A Study of Early Christian Thought in the East.* New York and Cambridge: Cambridge University Press, 1982.

Wilken, Robert L. *John Chrysostom and the Jews.* Berkeley, Los Angeles, and London: University of California Press, 1983.

Sources for Chapter IV

Baumstark, Anton. *Geschichte der syrischen Literatur.* Bonn: A. Marcus und E. Weber, 1922.

―――. *Nichtevangelische syrische Perikopenordnungen des ersten jahrtausends.* Münster im Westphalia: Aschendorff, 1921.

―――. *Nocturna laus: Typen frühchristlicher Virgilienfeier und ihr Fortleben vor allem im römischen und monastischen Ritus.* Münster im Westphalia: Aschendorff, 1957.

Brock, Sebastian. *The Luminous Eye: The Spiritual World Vision of St. Ephrem.* Rome: CIIS, 1985.

Burkitt, F. C. *The Early Syriac Lectionary System.* London, 1921-23.

de Halleux, André. *Philoxène de Mabboug, sa vie, ses éscrits, sa théologie.* Louvain: Imprimerie Orientaliste, 1963.

Ephrem of Nisibis. *Das heiligen Ephraem des Syrers Paschahymnen, De azymis, De crucifixione, De resurrectione.* Translated by Edmund Beck. Corpus scriptorum christianorum orientalium, vol. 249. Louvain: Secrétariat du Corpus SCO, 1964.

―――. *Hymns on Paradise.* Translated by Sebastian Brock. Crestwood, N.Y.: St. Vladimir's Seminary Press, 1990.

―――. *Hymnes sur le Paradis.* French translation by René Lavenant. Introduction and notes by François Graffin. Sources chrétiennes, vol. 137. Paris: Les Éditions du Cerf, 1968.

Leloir, L. *Commentaire de L'Évangile concordant ou Diatessaron.* Sources chrétiennes, vol. 121. Paris: Les Éditions du Cerf, 1966.

Maclean, Arthur J. *East Syrian Daily Offices.* London: Rivington, Percival & Co., 1894.

McLeod, Frederick, trans. *Narsai's Metrical Homilies on the Nativity, Epiphany,*

Passion, Resurrection, and Ascension. Patrologia orientalis, vol. 40. Turnhout: Brepols, 1979-81.

McVey, Kathleen. *Ephrem the Syrian: Hymns.* Translated and introduced by Kathleen McVey. New York and Mahwah, N.J.: Paulist Press, 1989.

Murray, Robert. *Symbols of Church and Kingdom: A Study in Early Syriac Tradition.* Cambridge: Cambridge University Press, 1975.

Philoxenus of Mabbug. *Homélies.* French translation by Eugène Lemoine. Sources chrétiennes, vol. 44. Paris: Les Éditions du Cerf, 1956.

Sunquist, Scott. "Narsai's Doctrine of Creation and Redemption." Ph.D. diss., Princeton Theological Seminary, 1989.

Vööbus, Arthur. *Handschriftliche Überlieferung der Memre-Dichtung des Ja'qob von Serug.* Corpus scriptorum christianorum orientalium, vols. 184 and 197. Louvain: Secrétariat du Corpus SCO, 1973.

————. *History of Asceticism in the Syrian Orient.* Corpus scriptorum christianorum orientalium, vols. 184 and 197. Louvain: Secrétariat du CSCO, 1958-60. (This work gives considerable attention to the literary activity of the monasteries.)

Sources for Chapter V

Ambrose of Milan. *De sacramentis, des mystères. Nouvelle édition revue et augmentée de l'Explication du Symbole.* Text established, French translation, and annotation by Dom Bernard Botte. 2nd ed. Sources chrétiennes, vol. 25. Paris: Les Éditions du Cerf, 1961.

————. *On the Mysteries and Treatise on the Sacraments.* Translated by T. Thompson. Reedited by J. H. Srawley. London: SPCK, 1950.

————. *On the Sacraments.* Translated by R. J. Deferrari. The Fathers of the Church, vol. 40. Washington, D.C.: Catholic University Press, 1963.

————. "Sermon against Auxentius." Translated by H. de Romerstein. Nicene and Post-Nicene Fathers, 2nd ser., vol. 10, pp. 430-36. Grand Rapids: Wm. B. Eerdmans Publishing Co., 1976.

————. *Traité sur l'Évangile de S. Luc.* Edited by Gabriel Tissot. Sources chrétiennes, vols. 45 and 52. Paris: Les Éditions du Cerf, 1956 and 1958.

Augustine. *De catechizandis rudibus.* Edited by Joseph B. Bauer. Corpus Christianorum, series Latina, vol. 46. Turnholt, Belgium: Brepols, 1969.

————. *Commentaire de la première épître de S. Jean.* Latin text and French translation with introduction and notes by Paul Agaësse. Sources chrétiennes, vol. 75. Paris: Éditions du Cerf, 1961.

————. *De Doctrina christiana.* Edited by J. Martin. Corpus Christianorum, series Latina, vol. 32. Turnholt, Belgium: Brepols, 1962.

————. *Enarrationes in Psalmos.* Edited by Eligius Dekkers and Iohannes

Fraipont. Corpus Christianorum, series Latina, vols. 38 and 39. Turnholt, Belgium: Brepols, 1978 and 1981.

―――. *First Catechetical Instruction.* Translated by Joseph Christopher. Ancient Christian Writers, vol. 2. Westminster, Md.: Newman Bookshop, 1966.

―――. *Homilies on the Gospel of John.* Translated by John Gibb and James Innes. Nicene and Post-Nicene Fathers, 1st ser., vol. 7. Grand Rapids: Wm. B. Eerdmans Publishing Co., 1974.

―――. *In Iohannes evangelium tractatus CXXIV.* Edited by Radbodus Willems. Corpus Christianorum, series Latina, vol. 36. Turnholt, Belgium: Brepols, 1954.

―――. *On Christian Doctrine.* Translated by Durant Waite Robertson. New York: Macmillan, 1958.

―――. *On the Catechising of the Uninstructed.* Translated by S. D. F. Salmond. Nicene and Post-Nicene Fathers, 1st ser., vol. 3. Grand Rapids: Wm. B. Eerdmans Publishing Co., 1976.

―――. *St. Augustine on the Psalms.* Translated and annotated by Dame Scholastica Hebyin and Dame Felicitas Corrigan. Ancient Christian Writers, vols. 29-30. Westminster, Md.: Newman Press; London: Longmans, Green and Co., 1960-61.

―――. *St. Augustine's On Christian Doctrine.* Translated by J. F. Shaw. Nicene and Post-Nicene Fathers, 1st ser., vol. 2. Grand Rapids: Wm. B. Eerdmans Publishing Co., 1979.

―――. *Sermons pour la Pâque.* Introduction, critical text, translation, and notes by Suzanne Poque. Sources chrétiennes, vol. 116. Paris: Les Éditions du Cerf, 1966.

―――. *Tractates on the First Epistle of John.* Translated by John W. Rettig. The Fathers of the Church, vol. 92. Washington, D.C.: Catholic University of America Press, 1995.

―――. *Tractates on the Gospel of John.* Translated by John W. Rettig. The Fathers of the Church, vol. 92. Washington, D.C.: Catholic University of America Press, 1995.

Bardenhewer, O. *Geschichte der altenkirchlichen Literatur.* 5 vols. Freiburg im Breisgau: Herder, 1913-32.

Bardy, Gustave. *Saint Augustin, L'homme et l'oeuvre.* 7th ed. Paris: Desclée & Brouwer, 1948.

Belche, J. P. "Die Bekehrung zum Christentum nach des Augustinus Büchlein 'De catechizandis rudibus.'" *Augustiniana* 27 (1977): 26-69, 333-63, and 28 (1978): 255-87.

Bonner, Gerald. *St. Augustine of Hippo: Life and Controversies.* Philadelphia: Westminster Press, 1963.

Brown, Peter. *Augustine of Hippo: A Biography.* Berkeley and Los Angeles: University of California Press, 1967.

Campenhausen, Hans Freiherr von. *Ambrosius von Miland als Kirchenpolitiker.* Berlin and Leipzig: W. de Gruyter, 1929.

————. *Lateinische Kirchenväter.* 2nd rev. ed. Stuttgart: W. Kohlhammer, 1965.

Cavallera, Ferdinand. *S. Jérôme: Sa vie et son Oeuvre.* Louvain: "Spicilegium Sacrum Lovaniense" Bureaux; Paris: E. Champion, 1922.

Comeau, Marie. *Saint Augustin, exégète du quatrième évangile.* Paris: Gabriel Beauchesne, 1930.

Conroy, Marietta Cashen. *Imagery in the Sermones of Maximus of Turin.* Washington, D.C.: Catholic University of America Press, 1965.

Cordelier, J. F. *La pédagogie de saint Augustin dans les "Ennarationes in Psalmos."* Dijon, 1971.

DeBruyne, D. "'Ennarationes in psalmos' prêchées à Carthage." In *Miscellanea Agostiniana,* 2:321-26. Rome: Typografia poliglota vaticana, 1931.

Deferrari, R. J. "St. Augustine's Method of Composing and Delivering Sermons." *American Journal of Philology* 43 (1922): 97-123 and 193-219.

Delmare, T. "Lorsque St. Augustin expliquait les Psaumes." *La Vie spirituelle* 82 (1950): 115-36.

Duchrow, U. "Zum Prolog von Augustins 'De Doctrina Christiana.'" *Vigiliae Christianae* 17 (1963): 165-72.

Dudden, Frederick Homes. *The Life and Times of St. Ambrose.* 2 vols. Oxford: Clarendon Press, 1935.

Engelbrecht, August. *Studien über den Lukaskommentar des Ambrosius.* Vienna, 1903.

Grasso, D. "Saint Augustin évangélisateur." *Parole et Mission* 6 (1963): 357-78.

Hagendahl, Harald. *Latin Fathers and the Classics.* Göteborg: Elanders Boktr. Aktiebolag, 1958.

Hardy, Richard P. *Actualité de la Révélation divine.* Paris: Beauchesne, 1974.

————. "The Incarnation and Revelation in Augustine's 'Tractatus in Johannes Evangelium.'" *Église et théologie* 3 (1972): 193-200.

Jerome. *The Homilies of Saint Jerome.* Edited and translated by Sister Marie Liguori Ewald. 2 vols. Washington, D.C.: Catholic University of America Press, 1964 and 1966.

————. *S. Hieronymi presbyteri opera, pars II, opera homiletica.* Edited by Gérard Morin. Corpus Christianorum, series Latina, vol. 78. Turnholt, Belgium: Brepols, 1958.

Jordan, M. D. "Words and Word, Incarnation and Signification in Augustine's 'De doctrina christiana.'" *Augustinian Studies* 11 (1980): 177-96.

Jungmann, Josef A. *Missarum Sollemnia.* 5th ed., 2 vols. Vienna, Freiburg, and Basel: Herder, 1962.

Kelly, J. N. D. *Jerome, His Life, Writings, and Controversies.* London: Gerald Duckworth and Co., 1975.

Kevane, E. "Augustine's 'De doctrina christiana,' a Treatise on Christian Education." *Recherches Augustiniennes* 4 (1966): 97-133.

Kunzelmann, Adalbero. "Augustines Predigttätigkeit." In *Festschrift der Görres-Gesellschaft*, pp. 155-68. Cologne: G. P. Bachem, 1930.

——. "Die Chronologie der Sermones des hl. Augustinus." In *Miscellanea Agostiniana*, 2:417-520. Rome: Typografia poliglota vaticana, 1931.

Le Landais, M. "Deux années de prédication de S. Augustin." *Études Augustiniennes*. Paris, 1953.

Lietzmann, Hans. *A History of the Early Church*. Translated by Bertram Lee Woolf. Vol. 4, *The Era of the Church Fathers*. New York: World Publishing Co., 1953.

Lundberg, Per. *La Typologie Baptismale*. Leipzig: A. Lorenta; Uppsala: Lundquista bokhandeln, 1942.

Mara, Maria Grazia. "Ambrose of Milan." In *Patrology*, vol. 4, edited by Angelo di Bernardino, English translation by Placid Solari. Westminster, Md.: Christian Classics, 1994.

Maximus of Turin. *Collectionem sermonum antiquam, nonnullus sermonibus extravagantibus adjectis.* Edited by Almut Mutzenbecher. Corpus Christianorum, series Latina. Turnholt, Belgium: Brepols, 1962.

Mazza, Enrico. *Mystagogy: A Theology of Liturgy in the Patristic Age*. Translated by M. J. O'Connell. New York: Pueblo Publishing Co., 1989.

Mutzenbecher, A. "Der Festinhalt von Weihnachten und Epiphanie in den echten Sermones des Maximus von Turin." *Studia Patristica* 5 (1962).

Oggioni, G. "Il 'De catechizandis rudibus' di S. Augustino, catechesi per i lontani." *La Scuola Cattolica* 91 (1963): 117-26.

Paredi, Angelo. *St. Ambrose*. Translated by J. Costello. Notre Dame, Ind.: University of Notre Dame Press, 1963.

Penna, Angelo. *Principi e carattere dell'esegesi di S. Gerolamo*. Rome: Pontificio Istituto Biblico, 1950.

Polman, A. D. R. *The Word of God according to St. Augustine*. London: Hodder and Stoughton, 1961.

Pontet, Maurice. *L'exégèse de S. Augustin prédicateur*. Paris: Aubier, 1944.

——. *Saint Augustin: Sermons sur Saint Jean*. Namur, 1958.

Poque, Suzanne. "Les lectures liturgiques de l'Octave pascale à Hippone d'après les Traites de saint Augustin sur la Première Épître de S. Jean." *Revue Bénédictine* 74 (1964): 217-41.

Press, G. A. "The Subject and Structure of Augustine's 'De Doctrina Christiana.'" *Augustinian Studies* 11 (1980): 99-124.

Przydatek, C. *L'annucio del Vangelo nello spirito del dialog. Studio storico theologico sulla predicazione missionaria secondo l'opuscolo di S. Augustino "De catechizandis rudibus."* Rome, 1971.

Ramos-Lisson, D. "La doctrina de la 'salus' en la 'Expositio Evangelii secundum Lucam' de s. Ambrosio." *Scripta Teologica* 5 (1973): 629-66.

Rollero, P. *La Expositio Evangelii secundum di Ambrogio come fonte dell'esegesi agostiniana.* Turin, 1958.

―――. "L'influsso dell'Exposito in Lucam di Ambrogio nell'esegesi agostiniana." *Augustinus Magister.* 2 vols. Paris: Études Augustiniennes, 1954.

Roy, O. "L'expérience de l'amour et l'intelligence de la foi trinitaire selon saint Augustin." *Recherches Augustiniennes* 2 (1962): 415-45.

Schritzler, F. *Zur Theologie der Verkündigung in den Predigten des hl. Augustinus.* Freiburg, Basel, and Vienna: Herder, 1968.

Wieland, Wolfgang. *Offenbarung bei Augustinus.* Mainz: Matthias Grünwald Verlag, 1978.

Wilmart, André. "Easter Sermons of St. Augustine." *Journal of Theological Studies* 28 (1926): 113-44.

Wright, D. F. "The Manuscripts of St. Augustine's 'Tractatus in Evangelium Iohannis.'" *Recherches Augustiennes* 8 (1972): 55-143.

Sources for Chapter VI

Bardenhewer, O. *Geschichte der altenkirchlichen Literatur.* 5 vols. Freiburg im Breisgau: Herder, 1913-32.

Batiffol, Pierre. *Saint Grégoire le Grand.* Paris: J. Gabalda, 1928. English translation: *St. Gregory the Great,* trans. John Stoddard. New York: Benziger, 1929.

Beissel, Stephan. *Entstehung der Perikopen des römischen Messbuches.* Rome: Herder, 1967.

Böhmer, Gottfried. *Peter Chrysologus, Erzbishof von Ravenna, als Prediger.* Paderborn: Ferdinand Schöningh, 1919.

Dudden, Frederick Homes. *Gregory the Great: His Place in History and in Thought.* 2 vols. London: Longmans, Green and Co., 1905.

Gregory the Great. *Forty Gospel Homilies.* Translated by Dom David Hurst. Kalamazoo, Mich.: Cistercian Publications, 1990.

―――. *XL Homiliarum in evangelia libri duo.* Jacques-Paul Migne. *Patrologia Latina,* vol. 76. Paris: Migne, 1844-77.

―――. *Homélies sur Ézéchiel.* 2 vols. Latin text with French translation, notes, and introduction by Charles Morel, S.J. Sources chrétiennes, vols. 327 and 360. Paris: Les Éditions du Cerf, 1986 and 1990.

―――. *Homiliae in Hiezechihelem prophetam.* Edited by Marcus Adriaen. Corpus Christianorum, series Latina, vol. 142. Turnholt, Belgium: Brepols, 1971.

Halliwell, William J. *The Style of Pope St. Leo the Great.* Washington, D.C.: Catholic University of America Press, 1939.

Jalland, Trevor. *The Life and Times of St. Leo the Great.* London: SPCK, 1941.

Lang, Arthur Paul. *Leo der Grosse und die Texte des Altgelasianums.* Steyer: Verlags-buchhandlung, 1957.

Leclercq, Jean. *L'amour des lettres et la désire de Dieu.* Paris, 1954.

Leo the Great. *Léon le Grand, Sermons.* 4 vols. Latin text, French translation, and notes by Dom René Dolle, with introduction by Dom Jean Leclercq. Sources chrétiennes, vols. 22, 49, 74, and 200. Paris: Les Éditions du Cerf, 1949-73.

————. *Tractatus septem et nonaginta.* Edited by Antoine Chavasse. Corpus Christianorum, series Latina, vols. 138 and 138A. Turnholt, Belgium, and Paris: Brepols, 1973.

Lietzmann, Hans. "Leo I." *Pauly-Wissowa-Kroll, Realencyklopädie der klassischen Altertumswissenschaft,* 12/2 (1925): 1962-73.

Lubac, Henri de. *Exégèse médievale. Les quatre sens de l'Écriture.* 4 vols. Paris, 1959-64.

Migne, J.-P. *Patrologia latina.* Paris: Migne, 1953-66.

Olivar, Alexander. *Los sermones de san Petro Crisólogo.* Monserat, 1962.

————. "La duración de la predicación antigua." *Liturgica* 3 (Monserat, 1966): 143-84.

Pelikan, Jaroslav. *The Emergence of the Catholic Tradition (100-600).* Chicago and London: University of Chicago Press, 1971.

Peter Chrysologus. *Sancti Petri Chrysologi, Collectio sermonum a Felice Episcopo parata sermonibus extravagantibus adjectis.* Edited by Alexander Olivar. Corpus Christianorum, series Latina, vol. 24. Turnholt, Belgium: Brepols, 1975.

————. *Selected Sermons.* Trans. George E. Ganss, S.J. The Fathers of the Church, vol. 17. New York: Fathers of the Church, 1953.

Quasten, Johannes. *Patrology,* vol. 4. Edited by Angelo di Bernardino. English translation by Placid Solari. Westminster, Md.: Christian Classics, 1994.

Rush, A. C. "Gregory I (The Great), Pope, St." *New Catholic Encyclopaedia* (1967), 6:766-70.

Soos, Marie Bernard de. *Le mystére liturgique d'après saint Léon le grand.* Münster im Westphalia: Aschendorff, 1958.

Sottocornola, Franco. *L'anno liturgico nei sermoni de Pietro Crisologo. Ricera storico-critica sulla liturgica de Ravenna antica.* Cesena: Centro studi e recerche sulla antica provincia ecclesiastica ravennate, 1973.

Spinelli, M. "L'eco delle invasioni babariche nelle omelie di Pier Crisologo." *Vetera christianorum* 16 (1979): 87-93.

Index

473

DATE DUE

Printed in the United States
1399300005B/118-132